THE GUINNESS WHO'S WHO OF

INDIE AND NEW WAVE MUSIC

General Editor: Colin Larkin

Introduction by Johnny Rogan

GUINNESS PUBLISHING

Dedicated to John Peel

First published in 1992 by
GUINNESS PUBLISHING LTD
33 London Road, Enfield, Middlesex EN2 6DJ, England

GUINNESS is a registered trademark of Guinness Publishing Ltd

British Library Cataloguing-in-Publication data
A catalogue record for this book is available from the British Library

ISBN 0-85112-579-4

Conceived, designed, edited and produced by
SQUARE ONE BOOKS LTD
Iron Bridge House, 3 Bridge Approach, Chalk Farm, London NW1 8BD
Editor and Designer: Colin Larkin
Picture Editor: Colin Larkin
Editorial and production assistants: Susan Pipe, John Eley, Aileen Tyler, Pat Perry,
Graham Lock, Jon Staines, Janice Newman, Johnny Rogan, Brian Hogg and Jane Ehrlich.
Special thanks to Donald McFarlan and David Roberts of Guinness Publishing
and to Tony Gale of Pictorial Press
Logo concept: Darren Perry. Page make up: Tim Beard
This book has been produced on Apple Macintosh computers
using Quark Xpress and Microsoft Word
Image set by L & S Communications Ltd

Printed and bound in Great Britain by the Bath Press

EDITORS NOTE

The Guinness Who's Who Of Indie And New Wave Music forms a part of the multi-volume *Guinness Encyclopedia Of Popular Music*. A further 16 specialist single volumes are planned in the near future.

Also available:
The Guinness Who's Who Of Heavy Metal
The Guinness Who's Who Of Sixties Music
The Guinness Who's Who Of Jazz

The contributors to this volume were Alex Ogg, John Eley, Johnny Rogan, Jon Staines, Colin Larkin, John Reed, Dave Wilson, Alan Rowett, Alan Clayson, Simon Williams, Dave Laing, Mark Hodkinson, Lionel Robinson, Ben Watson, Chris Spencer, Tom Collier and Jeff Tamarkin.

Virtually all the photographs for this work were supplied by Tony Gale of Pictorial Press who has an extensive archive of popular music photographs.

The remaining photographs not from Pictorial Press are thanks to: Food Records for Blur. Beggars Banquet for the Charlatans, Go-Betweens. Anxious Records for Curve. Dedicated Records for Family Cat. Brian Hogg and Jacki Morton for the Buzzcocks, Cramps, Richard Hell, Rain Parade, Rezillos, Television. Alex Ogg for Carter USM, Julian Cope, Del Amitri, Fatima Mansions, Green On Red, Mega City Four, Men They Couldn't Hang, Moose, Nine Below Zero, Nirvana, Senseless Things, Michelle Shocked, Sonic Youth, Martin Stephenson, UK Subs, World Party, Young Fresh Fellows. John Eley for Dolly Mixture, Squeeze, Triffids, We've Got A Fuzzbox. Go! Discs for Robyn Hitchcock. Jayne Houghton for Jazz Butcher. 4AD for Lush, Spirea X, Throwing Muses. Creation Records for My Bloody Valentine, Primal Scream, Ride, Slowdive, Swervedriver, Teenage Fanclub. Big Life Records for the Orb. Furtive Records for Ned's Atomic Dustbin.

I would like to thank, in addition to the contributors; John Eley and Susan Pipe for an extraordinary effort in putting it all together at the end, and to Paola Simoneschi, Sallie Collins and Sarah Silvé for their production work. Donald McFarlan takes credit for finding Tim Beard who took a great deal of the strain away from us. Finally to Laura, Ben, Tom, Dan, Carmen and Timmy the dog who were still my family at the very end.

Colin Larkin, August 1992

INTRODUCTION

Of all the volumes in this series, *The Who's Who Of Indie Music And New Wave* is the most difficult to pin down. History is easy to capture when the dust has settled on an era and there is time for reflection and perspective. Writing about the present is a precarious business for encyclopaedists, the more so when the subjects are not established stars but aspiring ones. New artists emerge literally week by week while others break up just as they appear to be on the brink of achievement. Cataloguing such volatility requires the sharp eye of a trend spotter coupled with the serene nerve of a Nostradamus. Reflections on the indie scene are largely the preserve of the weekly music press, which constantly reviews, champions and derides a vast array of acts, whose prospects may change overnight with a hit single, acclaimed gig or surprise personnel change. Capturing it all in a volume of this scope is a courageous and challenging task, the more so given copy date deadlines and the knowledge that even as we go to press further changes are afoot. Part of the attraction of this work will be reviewing future editions to see short capsule entries blossom into rivetting career studies. One also wonders how many of the artists included herein will survive to reappear in the next edition and how many new acts will emerge between now and then. The future is indeed foreign territory.

Independent labels have always been crucial in signalling developments in rock 'n' roll, particularly in America.

During the immediate post-war period, following disputes over music publishing, labels proliferated, offering a rich selection of country, jazz and blues. In the history of rock 'n' roll, the most famous of these was Sun Records, which captured the pure essence of rockabilly in the early recordings of Elvis Presley. Many other greats passed through the studio in its heyday, including Carl Perkins, Johnny Cash, Jerry Lee Lewis, Roy Orbison and Charlie Rich. Words like purity and unadulterated became synonymous with independent labels, and not without good reason. Unlike the major labels, the humble independents did not require mass sales to achieve success in the marketplace but usually aimed at a small but devoted audience. This meant that musical experimentation was positively encouraged, rather than tolerated.

The driving forces behind the independents

were love of music and love of money. Creative mavericks founded independent labels to fulfil their own artistic ideas while canny entrepreneurs saw them as a means of securing greater control and wresting money away from major labels. In the UK, independent labels met with varying amounts of success during the 50s and 60s. However, the stranglehold of the major record companies, EMI, Decca and Philips, ensured that long term survival was unlikely. Many entrepreneurs and leading managers gambled on the success of independent ventures, and often to their cost. At the end of the 50s, Larry Parnes launched Elempi Records as a haven for young talent, but the grand scheme produced nothing of note. During the 60s, a number of new labels appeared, usually backed by well-known managers or producers. Joe Meek launched Triumph; Chris Blackwell found fame with Island; Andrew Oldham invigorated mid-60s pop with Immediate; Kit Lambert offered Track; Phil Solomon had Major Minor; Larry Page introduced Page One; Chris Wright and Terry Ellis formed the progressive Chrysalis; Gordon Mills founded MAM. Inevitably, these ventures met with contrasting fortunes. Both Triumph and Immediate spiralled into liquidation amid arrogance and bad organization, while Island and Chrysalis prospered and expanded.

Following the lead of their managers, a new breed of wealthy rock stars decided to launch their own labels, usually with unimpressive results. Many saw themselves as patrons of the arts or A&R specialists who could unearth important talents bypassed by their more conservative counterparts. Unfortunately, most of these enterprises created labels which were either over-ambitious, insular or poorly organized. The Beatles' Apple label was seen, at least by Paul McCartney, as 'a kind of Western Communism'. Its lofty ideals were typical of the time, as McCartney's words indicate. 'We want to help people', he announced, 'but without doing it as a charity. We always had to go to the big men on our knees and touch our forelocks . . . We're in the happy

position of not needing any money, so for the first time the bosses aren't in it for profit.' Initially, the Beatles took considerable interest in their label and releases by Mary Hopkin, Billy Preston, James Taylor and others showed great promise. After the first flush of talent, however, Apple fell victim to diminishing returns. Its laid back philosophy could not disguise the inevitable onslaught of financial problems and the dream of Western Communism soon subsided. In spite of Apple's story of woe, other artists convinced themselves that they could do better. The Rolling Stones, Led Zeppelin and Elton John all formed their own labels but none could argue that they had created a success story. How many major artists emerged from Rolling Stones Records, Swan Song or Rocket? The problems that beset these labels was that they were either mere playthings of their benefactors or could not hope to rival the better organized majors. Moreover, when swallowed up by major label distribution or finance they swiftly ceased to have any identity at all.

An important turning point for the independent label as a form came in 1977 when UK punk was in the ascendant. Although the leading protagonists, the Sex Pistols, were initially signed to the country's leading major label, EMI, they served as banner leaders for the independent ideal. Thrown off EMI and subsequently A&M, they ended up on Virgin, a former hippie label that had thrived in the afterglow of Mike Oldfield's mega-selling *Tubular Bells*. The label was quick to jump on the punk bandwagon and, unlike EMI and A&M, was unfazed by the Pistols' negative publicity. One of the most important legacies of the Pistols' assault on Britain was the formation of a legion of independent labels. Robert Last, founder of the independent Fast Product, recalls the importance of Malcolm McLaren, the Sex Pistols' manager: 'McLaren was an inspiration because he showed how you could use the music business as a game to make other points. You could have a group that was about other things besides selling records and use commerce to do something which was a bit more interesting and exciting.' Clearly, the do-it-yourself ethos of punk was pervasive.

In the USA, the Sex Pistols failed to take off and the same fate befell the major anglo-punk protagonists of the era. Nevertheless, the US had continued to release many exciting records through its independent labels. Berserkley, whose roster included the enigmatic Jonathan Richman And The Modern Lovers, was a much loved precursor of punk and helped pave the way for many New Wave acts. America embraced New Wave, a catch all term to describe musicians with punkish attitudes and sympathies who nevertheless favoured musical finesse. It says much for the vagueness of the term New Wave that it could be applied to a range of artists from Blondie to Talking Heads, Tom Petty to Elvis Costello and Joe Jackson to Mink De Ville. By the 80s the term became increasingly oblique and finally passe.

The legacy of punk continued in the UK via a variety of record labels. During the early flickerings of punk both Chiswick and Stiff Records established themselves as independents with distinctive sounds. Chiswick took much of its inspiration from the 50s, even listing Vince Taylor's 'Brand New Cadillac' among its early releases. Other Chiswick notables included Motorhead, Johnny And The Self Abusers (who later became Simple Minds), the Count Bishops, the 101ers (featuring Joe Strummer) and the Radio Stars. Jake Riviera's Stiff enjoyed the first punk hit via the Damned's 'New Rose' and swiftly signed an impressive catalogue of acts including Costello, Ian Dury And The Blockheads, Nick Lowe, Lene Lovich, Kirsty MacColl, and many more.

Like the beat boom of the 60s, the punk/new wave influence could be heard in every major city. From Belfast, Northern Ireland, Good Vibrations exported Rudi, Outcast and Protex alongside their major discovery, the Undertones. In Edinburgh Robert Last's Fast Product brought together the Gang Of Four, the Dead Kennedys and the Human League. Meanwhile, Alan Horne's highly respected Postcard label had put Scottish pop on the map with Josef K and Orange Juice. Manchester had New Hormones, which shot to fame with the Buzzcocks, before struggling on with Ludus and others. Tosh Ryan's Rabid Records had some rough edges with Slaughter And The Dogs and John Cooper Clarke and then startled everybody with Jilton John's self-titled lament, which went on to become a Top 5 hit on EMI. In Liverpool, Zoo created its own brand of late 70s pop psychedelia with a rich roster of acts that included Echo And The Bunnymen and the Teardrop Explodes. Beggar's Banquet signed the Lurkers, Johnny G and Bauhaus, but secured chart-topping success with Gary Numan's Tubeway Army. And these were just several of many success stories. Cherry Red, Do It, Fiction, 4AD, Illegal, Raw, Safari, Situation 2, Small Wonder, Some Bizzare, Step Forward . . . all had their moments of fame.

Most of the new labels with commercial product were forced to secure distribution deals with major record companies simply in order to survive financially or retain their developing acts. Some Bizzare's supremo Stevo managed to retain the identity of his label as a home for the outsider despite licensing The The to CBS and Soft Cell to Phonogram. With artists like Psychic TV, Einsturzende Neubauten, Test Department and Foetus, it was clear that Stevo valued experimentation and musical confrontation as a matter of policy. As he pithily observed: 'Some Bizzare is either a mental hospital or a community. It's for artists who've got integrity or who feel that no one can relate to them. They know if they come to Some Bizzare, they'll be appreciated and understood.'

Unfortunately, many other labels lost their identities in the transition to wider distribution and ended up resembling major label subsidiaries. Many major labels only dealt with independents in order to secure their prime act and had little or no interest in releasing or distributing less commercial product. As a result, many promising independents ceased to exist or continued in name only, devoid of any developing A&R policy. Many became a redundant footnote next to a major label masthead.

Despite financial pressure a number of prominent independents zealously refused to surrender to the majors. Chief amongst these was Rough Trade, which boasted a tradition of fearless eclecticism and musical experimentation. Label founder Geoff Travis watched as the Sex Pistols and the Clash had signed to major labels but felt uncomfortable with that process. 'I felt Stiff's distribution with EMI, and the way Malcolm McLaren and Bernard Rhodes decided to get as much from the majors as they could was a fundamental mistake', he stresses. 'I took a very long term view and thought that what we needed in this country was a distribution system that was completely separate from the majors, so that the input of music and other cultural elements into that system was controlled by people other than the majors, because I felt they were killing music. That was a political as well as an entrepreneurial point that Rough Trade has pursued ever since.'

Rough Trade offered a formidable selection of acts including Subway Sect, the Raincoats, the Slits, the Blue Orchids, Cabaret Voltaire, the Fall and countless more. There was also chart success courtesy of Scritti Politti and Aztec Camera. Inevitably, perhaps, the label failed to hang on to these acts once they had climbed the ladder of fame, and this was to prove a costly exercise. Like so many independents, Rough Trade was always in danger of becoming a mere testing ground for arcane talent which would then be siphoned off by the majors. For all that, the label offered substantial financial rewards for those who could succeed without the promotional push provided by the big record companies. The profit sharing system in operation at the company offered artists a potentially lucrative profit sharing agreement whereby recording costs were split 50:50 instead of being set against royalties. This meant that the act could accrue substantial monies provided their recordings sold in substantial quantities. Obviously, this would prove difficult in view of Rough Trade's lack of market penetration and low recording budgets. One group that did thrive under this system was the Smiths, who stayed with Rough Trade from their conception until their demise. Revenue from Smiths product ensured that Rough Trade was able to plough money into new projects and continue its uncompromising A&R policy successfully. More importantly, the Smiths' chart success and status as one of the 80s' most important groups was a brilliant advertisement for the state of independent music and inspired many new acts to follow their lead. Although the relationship between the Smiths and Rough Trade was often strained, the union continued for five years. During their final year of existence the Smiths did sign to EMI but split before any product was recorded for the major label. That too took on symbolic importance, ensuring that the Smiths would always be remembered as an independent group.

The Smiths stay at Rough Trade was paralleled by that of New Order at Factory Records. Here was the perfect relationship between an independent label and a consistently successful artist. Factory was founded in 1978 with a roster that rivalled Rough Trade in terms of esoteria. A Certain Ratio, Orchestral Manoeuvres In The Dark, X-O-Dus, the Distractions, Durutti Column, Crawling Chaos, Section 25, John Dowie, the Names, Crispy Ambulance, Tunnel Vision and the Stockholm Monsters were among the signings, but one act towered above the rest. Joy Division received critical acclaim, infiltrated the student heartland and seemed set to become one of the most important and influential groups of the 80s. Sadly, their career was tragically cut short following the suicide of lead singer Ian Curtis on 18 May 1980.

When New Order emerged from the chaos of Joy Division few could have predicted that they would still be around a decade later. Fewer still would have guessed that they would evolve into dance specialists and issue the 'biggest selling 12-inch single of all time' with 'Blue Monday'. Throughout this period, the group forged stronger links with Factory acquiring a financial interest along the way. In doing so, they achieved a greater control over their product than virtually any other hit group of the 80s. As manager Rob Gretton noted: 'If Joy Division and New Order had been signed to a major we'd sell a lot more records but we'd lose a great deal of control and wouldn't be able to do many of the unusual things we do with sleeves and choice of singles. New Order look upon Factory as their own label, even though the deal is 50:50'. Like the Smiths' relationship with Rough Trade, New Order's success has helped Factory maintain its eclectic A&R policy, which has brought its own rewards, most notably with the Happy Mondays.

In common with Rough Trade, Factory faces an uphill struggle in the early 90s as the recession bites. The resilience of both companies over the past decade and a half deserves full commendation. Similar praise is commanded by Daniel Miller's Mute Records which, following such early signings as the Normal and Fad Gadget, found the perfect artist in Vince Clarke. The latter's involvement in Depeche Mode, Yazoo and Erasure has provided Mute with lucrative hit records and established an exemplary artist/record company relationship.

Rough Trade, Factory and Mute have each shown that it is possible to survive and thrive as an independent and that lesson has not been lost on its successors. One of the great success stories of the past decade in terms of artistry and latterly sales has been Creation Records. Founded by the enthusiastic Alan McGee, the label released some cracking singles during the early 80s from a roster that included the Jasmine Minks, the Pastels, the Loft (which evolved into the Weather Prophets) and McGee's own group Biff Bang Pow. The real critical and commercial breakthrough, however, came with the Jesus And Mary Chain, one of the most controversial acts of their era whose aural assaults and inventive use of feedback saw them touted as 'the Sex Pistols of the 80s'. McGee fell out with the group, but Creation continued to prosper artistically. The releases

of Slaughter Joe, Primal Scream and Felt were well received, even though sales were less than staggering. The arrival of the House Of Love seemed a turning point in Creation's history and McGee fervently compared their importance and longevity with that of New Order. However, the group subsequently moved to Phonogram and left McGee's orbit. Like all important independent labels, Creation's challenge was to stay ahead of trends and this was achieved via the post acid house boom of the late 80s. One of the most remarkable metamorphoses came thanks to Creation faithfuls Primal Scream who embraced the new dance culture with relish and were feted following the release of *Screamadelica*. Creation has not been without its problems. Another mainstay, My Bloody Valentine, spent so much money on an album that they could no longer stay at the label. Creation still prospered with Ride, the Telescopes, Momus, Swervedriver, the Boo Radleys, Silverfish, Slowdive, Blur, Curve, Teenage Fanclub and others. From guitar pop through dance Creation continues the great tradition of the independent label.

The importance of the independent scene has been emphasized over the past decade by the prominent use of its own chart. This too has brought its own problems, culminating in the quibble, 'what defines an indie record?' According to the chart compilers the key issue is independent distribution, untainted by the helping hand of the majors. However, with so many acts financed by publishing money supplied by majors or affiliated with big record companies in America, the distinction is becoming increasingly nebulous. Whether the indie chart will be replaced by an alternative chart along American lines, and again include selected major label records, is currently under debate. Irrespective of the outcome, the appeal of the independent sector, however defined, shows no signs of abating.

Johnny Rogan, August 1992

A Certain Ratio

No UK act has crystalized independent, punk-influenced funk more than Manchester's A Certain Ratio. After years of enjoying cult status at Factory Records, the band left for A&M Records in 1989. The original line-up comprised Jeremy Kerr (bass), Simon Topping (vocals/trumpet), Peter Terel (guitar), Martin Moscrop (guitar/trumpet), Martha Tilson (ex-Occult Chemistry, vocals; although she had left by 1982) and Donald Johnson (drums, replacing a drum machine) - signed to Factory in 1979, for the cassette-only release, *The Graveyard And The Ballroom*, one side recorded at Graveyard Studios, the other live, supporting Talking Heads at London's Electric Ballroom. After releasing 'All Night Party', in May 1979, there was a pause before 'Flight', a UK independent Top 10 chart hit over a year later. In the meantime, the band had teamed up with Factory's European sister, Benelux, for a cover of Banbarra's mid-70s funk classic, 'Shack Up', in July 1980. *To Each...*, the band's official debut album, attracted BBC disc jockey John Peel in 1981, a year that also yielded 'Do The Du' (officially intended for release in the USA) and in December, 'Waterline' also fared well. 1982 kicked off with a move from the independent to the national charts as *Sextet* further established ACR. Like *To Each...*, *Sextet* housed an intriguing, mostly instrumental collection hinged around funk rhythms. A 12-inch single for Benelux, 'Guess Who' surfaced in July, followed by the *Knife Slits Water* EP in October, coinciding with the release of *I'd Like To See You Again*. The band also issued an obscure 12-inch single on the Rock Steady label, 'Abracadabra', under the guise Sir Horatio, in September 1982. A year later, 'I Need Someone Tonight' was released, reaching the UK independent Top 10. Topping and Terel had departed, to be replaced by Andy Connell, and 'Brazilia' became the band's first project of 1985, preceding 'Wild Party' in July. Those in anticipation of a new ACR album had to wait until the end of 1986 for *Force*, although a compilation, *The Old And The New*, had provided some consolation earlier in the year. 'Mickey Way' promoted *Force* and continued ACR's run of independent hits. By 1987, the band had outgrown the confines of mere cult status and, looking to branch out, signed with A&M. To bridge the gap, the Dojo label issued *Live In America* in February, alongside 'Greetings Four', for the European label Materiali Sonari. It was not until the summer of 1989 that new ACR product arrived; and both 'The Big E'

and 'Backs To The Wall' revealed a shift towards a more accessible sound. But neither these, nor 'Your Blue Eyes' in October, the *Four For The Floor* EP in February 1990 nor 'Won't Stop Loving You' in May could provide that elusive hit. As such, September 1989's *Good Together* made little impact and ACR left A&M soon after. Their experimental work and love of collage material has ensured their status as one of the most uncompromisingly original acts working in the post-punk era.
Albums: *The Graveyard And The Ballroom* (1979, cassette only), *To Each...* (1981), *Sextet* (1982), *I'd Like To See You Again* (1982), *Force* (1986), *Live In America* (1987), *Good Together* (1989), *MCR* (1990). Compilation: *The Old And The New* (1986).

Act

After Propaganda disbanded, German vocalist Claudia Brucken joined hands with electronics veteran, composer and vocalist Thomas Leer to form Act. Staying at Trevor Horn's ZTT label, the pair's first single, 'Snobbery And Decay', revealed their continued experimentation in the studio, and they were featured on BBC television's science programme *Tomorrow's World* to discuss new music technology. 'Absolutely Immune' followed in August (plus a remix, 'Absolutely Immune II'). In February 1988, Act issued 'I Can't Escape From You', backed by a bizarre re-working of the Smiths' 'Heaven Knows I'm Miserable Now', before unleashing their only album, *Laughter, Tears And Rage*, in July. Like their singles, this combined an array of studio wizardry with superbly crafted songs.
Album: *Laughter, Tears And Rage* (1988).

Action Pact

This pop-punk band originating from Essex, England, helped to brighten the early 80s with infectious diatribes on the state of the nation. The line-up featured Kim Igoe (bass), Des 'Wild Planet' (guitar), Joe Fungus (drums) and George Cheex (b. 1966; vocals). John, later guitarist for Dead Man's Shadow, was the original singer when the band were known as Bad Samaritans. Joe was recruited from local punk band Savage Upsurge. When John left, female vocalist George was auditioned and recruited. Fresh Records, after releasing one DMS single, decided to release a joint single with both bands. Their debut release was titled 'Heathrow Touchdown', and was aired while two of the band members were still at school. Action Pact's two tracks, 'London Bouncers' and 'All Purpose Action Footwear' were given heavy airplay by BBC disc jockey John Peel. After completing their first session for his Radio 1 show, the anti-glue sniffing 'Suicide Bag' emerged on *Fall Out*. Fungus and Grimly Fiendish. Kim 'Dr Phibes' left the band after the sessions for the debut album were completed, although he continued to write lyrics for them. His temporary replacement was Phil Langham (ex-the Dark). Another BBC session was completed, this time for disc jockey David 'Kid' Jensen. 'Thistles' took over the bass position, and was in place in time for the band's performance at the Leeds *Futurama '83* festival. Two more enticing singles, 'A Question Of Choice' and 'Yet Another Dole Queue Song', prefaced the band's final album.

Albums: *Mercury Theatre On the Air Again* (1983) *Survival Of The Fattest* (1984).

Adam Ant

Adam And The Ants

Formed in April 1977, this initially punk outfit comprised Adam Ant (b. Stuart Leslie Goddard, 3 November 1954, London, England; vocals/guitar), backed by Lester Square (guitar), Andy Warren (vocals/bass) and Paul Flanagan (drums). Heavily influenced by the Sex Pistols, they incorporated bondage gear and sado-masochistic imagery into their live act and repertoire. The line-up was relatively *ad hoc* between 1977-79 with Mark Gaumont replacing Lester Square (who joined the Monochrome Set - as Andy Warren would later do) and colourful manager Jordan occasionally taking vocals. Adam appeared with Toyah in Derek Jarman's movie *Jubilee* where he seemed more convincing than onstage. Although the first generation Ants released one album *Dirk Wears White Sox*, their critical reputation among new wave

writers was poor. At the end of the decade, Ant sought the advice of Pistols manager Malcolm McLaren, who took on the role of image consultant for a £1,000 fee. His advice was a radical shift of musical policy and a daring new look combining Red Indian imagery and piratical garb. In January 1980, however, the Ants fell victim to McLaren's charisma and abandoned their leader to form the newsworthy Bow Wow Wow. At this point, most observers assumed that Ant's career was over. In fact, it was just beginning.

With an entirely fresh set of Ants consisting of Marco Pirroni (vocals/guitar), Kevin Mooney (vocals/bass) and two drummers, Terry Lee Miall and Merrick (Chris Hughes), Ant effectively reinvented himself. Out went the punk riffs and bondage to be replaced by a sound heavily influenced by the Burundi Black drummers. With his Red Indian warpaint and colourful costume, the new Ant enjoyed three UK hits in 1980 culminating in the number 2 'Ant Music', in which he boldly dismissed his rivals and proclaimed his sound to be of the moment. His prognosis was correct. 1981 was the year of Adam And The Ants whose pop prescience was captured in a series of excellently produced videos. With his striking ex-anorexic looks and clever use of costume, Adam was a natural pin-up. His portrayal of a highwayman ('Stand And Deliver') and pantomime hero ('Prince Charming') brought two UK number 1 hits and ushered in an era of 'New Pop', where fancy dressing-up and catchy melodic songs without a message became the norm. Having dominated his group since 1977, it came as little surprise when Adam announced that he was dissolving the unit in early 1982 to pursue a solo career as Adam Ant.

Albums: *Dirk Wears White Sox* (1979), *Kings Of The Wild Frontier* (1980), *Prince Charming* (1981).

Adamson, Barry

The original bass player for Magazine (bass), and also a member of Visage, Adamson has recently been working on instrumental music intended for films, all of which reveal his appreciation of past masters of the genre. He is at present signed to the Mute label.

Albums: *Moss-Side Story* (1989), *Delusion - Original Motion Picture Soundtrack* (1991).

Adicts

The Adicts can be singled from the host of other UK punk hopefuls of the early 80s largely by their image. The adoption of black bowler hats and face make-up shared more than a passing resemblance to those rather unruly characters in Stanley Kubrick's controversial film *A Clockwork Orange*, and reflected the Adicts' brand of new wave music. The group were originally based in Ipswich, Suffolk, England and comprised lead singer Monkey (b. Keith

Warren), who had grotesquely perfected droog Alex's grin, plus Kid Dee (b. Michael Davison; drums), Pete Davidson (guitar) and Mel Ellis (bass). Their debut EP, *Lunch With The Adicts*, was the first release for the Dining Out label in 1981. This was followed by *Songs Of Praise* on the DWED label in October. The band then moved to the punk label Fall Out for 'Viva La Revolution', before they again changed labels, settling at the appropriately-named Razor Records. There they managed to release two UK Independent Top 10 singles, 'Chinese Takeaway' (1982), 'Bad Boy' (1983) and, *Sound Of Music* (which managed to scrape into the lower reaches of the charts). All was then quiet for two years, until the Adicts popped up in 1985, back at Fall Out, with a new EP, *Bar Room Bop*. The compilation, *This Is Your Life*, covered the band's earliest recordings from 1978-80. Since then, there has been a trickle of albums, as the Adicts have been adopted by a new generation aping the original punk spirit.
Albums: *Songs Of Praise* (1981), *Sound Of Music* (1982), *Fifth Overture* (1987), *Live And Loud!* (1987), *Rockers In Rags (Live In Alabama)* (1990).
Compilation: *This Is Your Life (1978-80)* (1985).

Adult Net

This 60s revivalist pop band was fronted by Laura Elise (aka 'Brix') Smith, b. California, USA. Her duel role was also as a member of husband Mark E. Smith's band, the Fall. Adult Net was inaugurated in 1985 when Brix, who was brought up in Hollywood, took the phrase Adult Net from a line in 'Stephen's Song', from the Fall's *Wonderful And Frightening World Of*. She had previously worked in the Rage and Burden Of Proof. In contrast to the Fall, whom many noted she pushed in a more commercial direction, Adult Net chose vocal harmony and bubblegum pop which harked back to her Californian roots, and the Beach Boys in particular. Her accomplices at one time included three ex-members of the Smiths; Andy Rourke, Mike Joyce and Craig Gannon, the line-up that saw the band make their live debut. Hastily arranged in order to impress Geffen Records, the band nevertheless acquired a contract from Fontana. 'Incense And Peppermints' (Strawberry Alarm Clock) and 'Edie', a tribute to the Andy Warhol protege, attracted plenty of press but few record sales. A cover of the Grassroots' 'Where Were You' preceded *The Honey Tangle*, an album of seamless but occasionally sickly pop. The line-up had transformed to include Clem Burke (ex-Blondie) and James Eller (ex-The The), while Gannon was retained from the earlier formation. A previous album, recorded in 1987 for Beggars Banquet, titled *Spin This Web*, remained unreleased. As *Honey Tangle*, named after a racehorse, was released, the personal and professional split between Brix and Mark E. Smith became public. A

version of Donovan's 'Hurdy Gurdy Man', featuring current boyfriend Nigel Kennedy on violin, was shelved when Phonogram dropped the band in October 1990.
Album: *The Honey Tangle* (1989).

Adventures

Formed in early 1984, the Adventures' story can be traced back six years to the Belfast, Northern Ireland powerpop/punk group the Starjets, which featured vocalist Terry Sharpe and guitarist Pat Gribben. The duo eventually sought their fortune on the London pub circuit and put together the Adventures with Eddie Gribben's wife Eileen on vocals, aided by Gerard 'Spud' Murphy (guitar), Tony Ayre (bass) and Paul Crowder (drums). A deal with Chrysalis Records brought minimal chart success during 1984 and 1985 prompting the group to take a sabbatical in order to rethink their approach. A new deal with Elektra Records saw them achieve modest acclaim for *Sea Of Love*, while the single 'Broken Land' entered the UK Top 20. Although the group attempted to consolidate their position, 'Down In The Sea Of Love' failed to reach the Top 40 and their subsequent career proved less than eventful.
Albums: *The Adventures* (1984), *Sea Of Love* (1988).

Adverts

The Adverts first came to prominence in 1976 at the celebrated London punk venue, the Roxy Club. Fronted by vocalist Tim 'TV' Smith and Gaye Advert (vocals/bass), the line-up was completed with Howard Pickup (guitar) and Laurie Driver (drums). Damned guitarist Brian James was so impressed by their performance that he offered them a support slot, as well as introducing them to the hip new wave label, Stiff. On tour they were initially promoted with the witty poster: 'The Adverts can play one chord, the Damned can play three. Come and see all four at . . .' Their debut single, the self-effacingly titled 'One Chord Wonders' was well received, but it was their second outing that attracted controversy and chart fame. 'Gary Gilmore's Eyes', a song based on the death-row criminal who had requested permission to donate his eyes to science, was a macabre but euphoric slice of punk/pop which catapulted the Adverts into the UK Top 20. One of the first punk groups to enjoy commercial success, the quartet also boasted the first female punk star in Gaye Advert. Despite some tabloid newspaper publicity, the next single, 'Safety In Numbers' failed to chart, though its successor 'No Time To Be 21' reached number 34. The group barely had time to record their debut album, *Crossing The Red Sea With The Adverts* (1978) before Laurie Driver was ousted and replaced by former Chelsea/Generation X drummer John Towe, who himself left shortly

afterwards, succeeded by Rod Latter. Changing record labels, personnel problems and unsuitable production dogged their progress while *Cast Of Thousands* (1979) was largely ignored. On 27 October 1979, with a line-up comprising Smith, Dave Sinclair, (drums), Mel Weston (keyboards), Eric Russell (guitar) and former Doctors Of Madness bassist, Colin Stoner, the Adverts gave their last performance at Slough College of Art. The group spawned one notable offshoot: TV Smith's Explorers.
Albums: *Crossing The Red Sea With The Adverts* (1978), *Cast Of Thousands* (1979).

A Flock Of Seagulls

This new wave electro-pop group from Liverpool, England had remarkable success in the USA before finding a large following in Britain. The band comprised, Mike Score (keyboards/vocals), Ali Score (drum machine/vocals), Paul Reynolds (b. 4 August 1962; guitar) and Frank Maudsley (b. 10 November 1959; bass). Following an adventurous EP on Bill Nelson's Cocteau label the band made their album debut with *A Flock Of Seagulls*, a splendid example of futurist pop that contained a number of notable tracks including 'I Ran (So Far Away)', which made the US Top 10 in 1982. Ex-hairdresser Mike Score received numerous press jibes for his 'silly haircut'; he had cultivated his none-too-natural blond locks to hang irritatingly over his keyboards. Although *Listen* was another infectious collection of songs, they were unable to find any lasting popularity in their homeland, other than 'Wishing (I Had A Photograph Of You)' which made the UK Top 10. Their last two albums were way below par and, following the departure of Paul Reynolds, they disintegrated.
Albums: *A Flock Of Seagulls* (1982), *Listen* (1983), *The Story Of A Young Heart* (1984), *Dream Come True* (1986). Compilation: *Best Of* (1988).

Afraid Of Mice

Previously known variously as Beano, the Press and the Jones, Liverpool's Afraid Of Mice were formed in early 1979 by ex-Next member, Philip Franz Jones (guitar/vocals), who for six years struggled with a continuously fluctuating personnel to find a suitable, permanent line-up. With the emergence of bands like Echo And The Bunnymen, the Teardrop Explodes and Orchestral Manoeuvres In The Dark, there was a great deal of interest in the second 'Liverpool Scene'. Consequently, their appearance on a local compilation *A Trip To The Dentist*, initiated a deal with Charisma Records. Following two well-received singles 'I'm On Fire' and 'Intercontinental', 1982 saw the release of *Afraid Of Mice*, with one-time David Bowie producer Tony Visconti at the controls. Described as 'power-pop with an edge', its mixture of raunchy guitars, angry lyrics and simple classic pop

achieved considerable critical acclaim. Even so, commercial success was to prove much more elusive. After one last single 'At The Club' and a give-away flexi-disc, 'Transparents', they parted company with Charisma. Although they continued to play live under various names, including the Lumberjack Ballet, Afraid Of Mice's final vinyl appearances were the live *Official Bootleg* in 1983 and a solitary track 'Don't Take Your Love Away' on the *Jobs For The Boys* compilation in 1985. The Mice were finally laid to rest in 1986 when Phil Jones teamed up with Alex McKechnie (ex-Passage and Modern Eon) in Two's A Crowd, who eventually became Up And Running.
Albums: *Afraid Of Mice* (1982), *Afraid Of Mice - The Official Bootleg* (1983).

Age Of Chance

These heavy guitar-fuelled dance heroes came from Leeds, Yorkshire, England, and at one point looked likely to translate Gang Of Four's vision to a mass audience. 'We're part experimental, part bop and we look pretty good as well.' With a line-up boasting Steve E (vocals), Neil H (guitar), Geoff T (bass), and Jan P (percussion, stand-up drums) their first single was 'Motorcity', on their own label, which proved a big hit with UK disc jockey John Peel. Its follow-up 'Bible Of The Beats' pushed them further in the direction of caustic dance. Although their early live sets rarely extended beyond 20 minutes, they proved attractive to a media that could make photogenic capital out of their lavish costumes (such as designer cyclist garb). Their metallic treatment of Prince's 'Kiss' was a mutant dance mini-classic, while a reading of the Trammps' 'Disco Inferno' brought them to within sniffing distance of the UK Top 40. Signing to Virgin, a succession of anonymous dance singles failed to get them any closer. Only the Public Enemy remixed 'Take It' (featuring embryonic rapping) was of much interest, before their vocalist left amidst considerable acrimony. Despite drafting in a replacement the band were soon dropped by Virgin.
Albums: *1000.Years Of Trouble* (1987), *Crush Collision* (1987), *Don't Get Mad Get Even* (1988).

Aire, Jane, And The Belvederes

This group was one of several new wave acts discovered in Akron, Ohio, USA, by producer Liam Sternberg and introduced to Stiff Records. Jane Aire (b. Jane Ashley, 2 December 1956, Akron, Ohio, USA) recorded initially for the Akron Compilation LP in 1978 and became the first of the featured artists to release a single - 'Yankee Wheels'. Sternberg used a band called the Edge as both session musicians and tour band but renamed them the Belvederes (after a type of turret-like building). The Edge consisted of former Damned guitarist Lu Edmunds (later in

Athletico Spizz 80, the Mekons and PiL), respected session players Gavin Povey and Glyn Havard on keyboards and bass respectively, plus drummer Jon Moss (b. 11 September 1957) who played with numerous punk bands including London and the Damned before finding fame with Culture Club. As well as backing Jane Aire, the Edge also played on some of Kirsty MacColl's early recordings and released their own material. After the Stiff single, Aire was signed to Virgin to record an album that featured the above musicians plus Chris Payne (trombone), Ray Warleigh (saxophone), and backing singers Rachel Sweet and Kirsty MacColl. After marrying the Boomtown Rat's Pete Briquette in 1980 and assembling a new bunch of Belvederes in Paul Cutler (guitar), Ian Curnon (keyboards), Sam Hartley (bass), Dave Ashley (drums), and former Deaf School saxophonist Ian Ritchie, Jane returned to Stiff to make a further single - a version of Dusty Springfield's 'I Close My Eyes And Count To Ten' - in 1982.
Album: *Jane Aire And The Belvederes* (1979).

Airhead (Jefferson)

This engaging UK pop band consisting of lyricist Michael Wallis (vocals), Steve Marshall (keyboards), Ben Kesteven (bass), and Sam Kesteven (his brother; drums). Marshall and Willis grew up in a small town outside Maidstone, Kent, England, the wonderfully named Snodland. They had played together in a variety of bands from 1987 onwards, but achieved little until they joined with the Kesteven brothers. Initial demos produced much interest throughout the major labels, and they were originally signed to WEA/Korova as the Apples in September 1990. Their opening single, 'Congratulations', was released in February 1991, produced by Leigh Gorman (Soho, ex-Bow Wow Wow). He also produced the band's second single, 'Scrap Happy', by which time they had become Jefferson Airhead, inspired by Jefferson Airplane. After objections from representatives of the group's record label they became simply Airhead. Their debut *Boing* and its attendant single 'Funny How' surfaced soon after the name change.
Album: *Boing* (1991).

Alarm

Formed in Rhyl, Wales during 1981, this energetic pop group comprised Mike Peters (b. 25 February 1959; vocals/guitar), David Sharp (b. 28 January 1959; vocals/guitar), Eddie MacDonald (b. 1 November 1959; bass) and Nigel Twist (b. 18 July 1958; drums). Originally known as 17, they changed their name after recording a self-penned song titled 'Alarm Alarm'. Peters was anxious to steer the group in the direction of U2, whose commitment and dedication appealed to his sense of rock as an expression of passion. However, by the time of the Alarm's first UK hit '68 Guns', their style and imagery most closely recalled punk rockers the Clash. The declamatory verve continued on 'Where Were You Hiding When The Storm Broke' and the traditional rock influence was emphasized in their long spiked hair, skin tight leather trousers and ostentatious belts. Behind the high energy, however, there was a lighter touch which was eloquently evinced on their reading of Pete Seeger's 'The Bells Of Rhymney', which they performed in aid of the coal miners' strike in 1984. The original U2 comparisons began to make more sense on the fourth album *Electric Folklore Live*, which displayed the power of their in-concert performance. *Change* (produced by Tony Visconti) saw them investigating their Celtic origins with the assistance of the Welsh Philharmonic Orchestra. Although they have yet to emerge as major stadium artists, their career plan impresses and their following is both strong and dedicated.
Albums: *Declaration* (1984), *Strength* (1985), *Eye Of The Hurricane* (1987), *Electric Folklore Live* (1988), *Change* (1989), *Raw* (1991). Compilation: *Standards* (1990).

Alien Sex Fiend

Alien Sex Fiend

Essentially an alias for the eccentric Nick Wade, Alien Sex Fiend emerged as part of the early 80s gothic punk movement from the UK, centred around London's Batcave venue. Wade previously served time with obscure acts like the Earwigs and Mr. And Mrs. Demeanour before releasing two singles as Demon Preacher. This was shortened to the Demons for a third single, but like its predecessors it vanished without a trace. After various short-lived projects, Wade eventually stumbled upon his long-term guise, Alien Sex Fiend in 1982, aided by David James (guitar), partner Christine Wade (synthesizer) and Johnny 'Ha Ha' Freshwater (drums). On the strength of a nine-track demo tape, the band had played the Batcave at the end of the year. Live tracks were added

All About Eve

to the tape and released as the cassette-only *The Lewd, The Mad, The Ugly And Old Nik*, before signing with Cherry Red Records subsidiary Anagram. Wade, whose stage image with ghoulish thick white pancake make-up, revealed his strongest influence, Alice Cooper in 'Ignore The Machine' (1983). *Who's Been Sleeping In My Brain*, was followed by 'Lips Can't Go' and in 1984 by 'R.I.P.'/'New Christian Music', 'Dead And Buried' and 'E.S.T. (Trip To The Moon)' to coincide with *Acid Bath*. Such was the album's reception in Japan that the group embarked on a tour there. *Liquid Head In Tokyo* celebrated the event, but was the last output for Johnny Ha Ha. As a three-piece, the band came up with 'I'm Doin' Time In A Maximum Security Twilight Home' (1985), accompanied by *Maximum Security*. *IT - The Album*, in time for a tour supporting Alice Cooper. A cover of Red Crayola's late 60s classic, 'Hurricane Fighter Plane', surfaced in early 1987, followed by 'The Impossible Mission'. A retrospective, *All Our Yesterdays*, coincided with Yaxi Highriser's departure. Under the guise of the Dynamic Duo, Wade then issued 'Where Are Batman And Robin?' (on the Riddler label!). 'Bun Ho' was the next Alien Sex Fiend single, continuing a more open-minded musical policy. *Another Planet* confirmed this, while

'Haunted House' saw the adoption of out-and-out dance techniques. After a tour (with Rat Fink Junior and Doc Milton) was captured on the double album *Too Much Acid?*, the band returned with 'Now I'm Being Zombified' in September 1990. That same month, Alien Sex Fiend released the experimental *Curse*.
Albums: *Who's Been Sleeping In My Brain* (1983), *Acid Bath* (1984), *Liquid Head In Tokyo* (1985), *Maximum Security* (1985), *IT - The Album* (1986), *Here Cum Germs* (1987), *Too Much Acid?* (1989), *Curse* (1990). Compilation: *All Our Yesterdays* (1988).

All About Eve

Originally called the Swarm, All About Eve emerged on the late 80s UK 'Gothic' scene. The group's nucleus of erstwhile rock journalist and Gene Loves Jezebel bass player Julianne Regan (vocals), along with Tim Bricheno (guitar - ex-Aemotti Crii), provided much of the band's song material. After various early personnel changes, the rhythm section was stabilized with Andy Cousin (bass - also ex-Aemotti Crii) and Mark Price (drums). Given encouragement by rising stars the Mission (for whom Regan had in the past sung backing vocals), All About Eve developed a solid following and with a

backdrop of hippy mysticism and imagery, along with Regan's predilection for white-witchcraft and Tarot cards, provided a taste of the exotic with a mixture of goth-rock and 70s folk. Early singles 'Our Summer' and 'Flowers In Our Hair' achieved great success in the UK independent charts and after signing to Mercury Records, their modest showings in the national charts finally gave them a Top 10 hit in July 1988 with 'Martha's Harbour'. Both albums reached the UK Top 10, confirmed their aspirations to be among the front-runners in British rock in the late 80s. However, this ambition was dealt a blow in 1990 when a rift between the group and guitarist Bricheno resulted in his departure to join their early champions, the Mission. The recruitment of Church guitarist Marty Willson-Piper on a part-time basis revitalized the group's drive, although the subsequent album, *Touched By Jesus*, only managed a brief visit to the UK Top 20, and indications that the group had undergone a born-again transformation have yet to be vindicated. A stormy dispute with their distributor, Phonogram, over the company's alleged priority for chart single success saw All About Eve leave the label in late 1991 and shortly afterwards sign to MCA Records.
Albums: *All About Eve* (1987), *Scarlet And Other Stories* (1989), *Touched By Jesus* (1991).

Altered Images

Formed in 1979, this Glasgow pop ensemble featured Clare Grogan (vocals), Johnny McElhone (guitar), Tony McDaid (bass) and Michael 'Tich' Anderson (drums). Even before their recorded debut, Grogan found herself cast in a film, *Gregory's Girl*, by director Bill Forsyth. That same year, Altered Images toured with Siouxsie And The Banshees and subsequently employed the services of their bassist Steve Severin as producer. Another champion of their work was the influential UK disc jockey, John Peel. Their BBC radio sessions resulted in the offer of a major recording contract by CBS subsidiary Epic, and two unsuccessful singles followed, 'Dead Pop Stars' and 'A Day's Wait'. With the addition of guitarist Jim McKniven, the group completed their debut, *Happy Birthday* (1981). The infectious title track, produced by Martin Rushent, soared to number 2 in the UK charts, establishing the elfin Grogan as a punkish Shirley Temple. 'I Could Be Happy' and 'See Those Eyes' were also hits, but the group's second album *Pinky Blue* was not well received by the critics. With 1983's *Bite*, Grogan took on a more sophisticated, adult image, lost several personnel and found a new co-producer, Tony Visconti. The experiment brought another Top 10 hit, 'Don't Talk To Me About Love', but the group split soon afterwards. Grogan pursued an acting career, recorded a solo album *Love Bomb* and later reappeared fronting a new

group, Universal Love School. Meanwhile, Altered Images' guitarist Johnny McElhone moved on to Hipsway and Texas.
Albums: *Happy Birthday* (1981), *Pinky Blue* (1982), *Bite* (1983).

Alternative TV

Formed in 1977, ATV was the brainchild of Mark Perry, the editor of Britain's seminal punk fanzine, *Sniffin' Glue*. The original line-up featured Perry (vocals), Alex Fergusson (b. 16 December 1952, Glasgow, Scotland; guitar), Micky Smith (bass) and John Towe (ex-Generation X, drums), but this unstable group later underwent several changes. Although ATV completed several albums throughout their career, they are best remembered for a series of uncompromising singles, including their self-effacing debut, 'Love Lies Limp' (free with *Sniffin' Glue*) and the declamatory 'How Much Longer?'. A disillusioned Perry abandoned the group in 1979 in favour of the Good Missionaries and subsequent projects, namely the Door And The Window and the Reflections. He returned to recording under the ATV banner in 1981 and continued to do so sporadically throughout the 80s. Fergusson went on to join Psychic TV, up until 1986, subsequently turning his hand to producing for the Gaye Bykers On Acid and the Popguns.
Albums: *The Image Has Cracked* (1978), with Here And Now *What You See Is What You Are* (1978), *Vibing Up The Senile Man* (1979), *Live At The Rat Club '77* (1979), *Strange Kicks* (1981), *Peep Show* (1987), *Dragon Love* (1990). Compilations: *Action Time Vision* (1980), *Splitting In Two* (1989).

Altern 8

Hardcore house ravers from Stafford, England and leaders of the new techno dance movement. Altern 8 consist primarily of Mark Archer, Chris Peat and disc jockey Andy Stanley, and are an offshoot of Archer and Peat's Nexus 21 pure techno act. Former deckchair attendants (or so they claim), they made the UK Top 20 with 'Infiltrate 202'. Of the two, Archer is the house music aficionado, while Peat is a former music technology student, with his main interests lying in computers. They were aided in their chart success by the circulation of fictitious press stories concerning their alleged activities. These include; patronage of the decongestant Vicks Vapour Rub, which, it is claimed, can heighten the effects of imbibing the drug Ecstasy; making their own confectionery, and playing shows in a hot air balloon. Their live 'events' are also designed as eye catching, surreal performances where the band don RAF chemical warfare suits and dust masks: 'Dance music is there to be danced to, not to be looked at like rock music is. Unfortunately, dance acts have to perform

Altered Images; Claire Grogan

live on occasion, and, when we do, we want to provide something visual'. In this they are aided by their resident dancers Crez and John Parkes. Their vinyl outings so far, in addition to the hit, have consisted of the *Overload* EP (1990), 'Activ 8' (1991), 'E Vapor 8' (1991) and 'Frequency', 10,000 copies of which were on sale for a single day only. A projected album is to be called *Inner City*, though the protagonists maintain that this is a temporary diversion from their main project, Nexus 21.

Amazulu

This predominantly female ska band earned themselves a string of UK hit singles in the mid-80s. They comprised Annie Ruddock (b. Ann-Marie Teresa Antoinette Ruddock, 2 July 1961; lead vocals), Claire Kenny (bass), Lesley Beach (b. 30 September 1954; saxophone), Sharon Bailey (b. 22 November 1957; percussion) and Margo Sagov (guitar), plus the lone male of the group, Nardo Bailey (drums). They made their initial impact on the lower regions of the UK single charts with 'Cairo', but achieved greater success in July 1985 with 'Excitable', which reached the UK Top 20. This success was followed by other hits, including; 'Don't You Just Know It', 'Too Good To Be Forgotten' and 'Montego Bay'. Their album was released on Island Records in 1988. Claire Kenny later joined the initial line-up of Coming Up Roses and subsequently joined Shakespear's Sister.
Album: *Amazulu* (1988).

Amory Kane

b. c.1947 San Francisco, California, USA. Singer songwriter Kane moved to England in 1967, having previously toured Europe. He had failed an audition with Family Dogg, not through lack of ability, but because producer Steve Rowland felt he should carve a solo career. Unfortunately this course never reached the heights his introspective, yet lyrically strong, material deserved. His debut *Memories Of Time Unwound* found few takers other than interested critics.
Album: *Memories Of Time Unwound* (1968).

An Emotional Fish

This four-piece power pop band in the mould of U2 or INXS, was formed in Dublin, Eire with a line-up of Gerard Wheland (vocals), Enda Wyatt (bass), Dave Frew (guitar) and Martin Murphy (drums). They began with two Irish hits on U2's Mother label, the second of which, 'Celebrate', was given a UK release. BBC disc jockey Mark Goodier invited them to do a session, and Radio 1 was so impressed by the band that they sponsored their UK tour. However, this soon backfired as the press made them scapegoats for what they saw as 'odious and corrupt' practices on behalf of a public broadcasting service. This fuelled further invective when the band's debut album was unveiled, 'weighty, overblown and held back by windy rhetoric' being among the kinder reviews. 'Lace Virginia' and 'Blue', the follow-up singles, sank without trace as Radio 1 judiciously withdrew from the controversy, failing to give the band airplay in the process.
Album: *An Emotional Fish* (1990).

Anastasia Screamed

Formed in 1987 by Christopher Burdett (b. 8 March 1968, Boston, Massachusetts, USA; drums), Christopher Cugini (b. 23 November 1966, Malden, Massachusetts, USA; guitar), Andy Jagolinzer (b. 11 June 1969, Framingham, Massachusetts, USA; vocals) and Scott Lerner (b. 3 March 1966, Boston, Massachusets, USA), the last being the first of a litany of short-term bass players to pass through the band's ranks. Chick Graning (b. 28 October 1966, Vancouver, Canada) replaced Jagolinzer before the end of the year, and added an extra touch of hysteria to a flowing, sub-hardcore guitar sound which hardly needed to be destabilized any further. Following a brace of independent singles which garnered much appreciation from the US college radio circuit, in 1989 the band solved their bass playing problems by bringing in Charlie Bock (b. 26 January 1965, Nashville, Tennessee, USA) and also relocated from Boston to Nashville. A year later Anastasia Screamed signed to the British Fire label and started to earn applause from Europe, broadening their horizons with a topsy-turvy brand of rock 'n' roll and toured extensively with Throwing Muses.
Albums: *Laughing Down The Limehouse* (1990), *Moontime* (1991).

And All Because The Lady Loves

Formed in 1987, this Newcastle born female duo, Nicky Rushton (b. 1961; guitar/vocals) and Rachel Collins (b. 1965; bass/vocals) achieved critical acclaim on the UK club circuit with their sets of bitter-sweet love songs, combined with a sense of political consciousness. Accompanied by simple, but effective, guitar and bass, their songs are off-set with superb, strong - almost a cappella - vocal harmonies and punchy melodies. They toured with Microdisney and Michelle Shocked while promoting their 1988 EP *If You Risk Nothing* and this led to an album on the small independent label Paint It Red, which won widespread critical acclaim. In 1990 they released their second album on the duo's own Newcastle-based label, Roundabout. Their most recent work has seen them employing the use of backing musicians, live and in the studio.
Albums: *Anything But A Soft Centre* (1988), *Centred* (1991), *Sugar Baby Love* (1991).

Angelic Upstarts

This socially and politically aware, hard-line punk quartet formed in 1977, in South Shields, England. They were the brainchild of Mensi (vocals), and strongly influenced by the Clash, Damned and Sex Pistols. With Cowie, Warrington and Taylor completing the line-up, they signed to the independent Small Wonder label and released the underground classic 'Murder Of Liddle Towers' in 1979. The song condemned police brutality and identified strongly with the youth culture of the day. It led to a deal with Warner Brothers, which produced 'Teenage Warning' and 'We Gotta Get Out Of This Place' in 1979 and 1980 respectively. Both these albums were *bona fide* punk classics, featuring provocative lyrics which ridiculed the Thatcherite policies of the time. Characterized by Mensi's nasal snarl, the band suffered from regular outbreaks of violence at their live shows from National Front fascist supporters, who sought to counter the group's left-wing politics after initially misinterpreting their patriotic stance. As the 80s progressed, the band gradually saw their fan-base disappear. They had become entrenched in a musical style that was rapidly becoming outdated. The Angelic Upstarts continued to release material, but with ever-declining success. The band ground to a halt in 1986, but reformed for a brief period in 1988 and then once again in 1992, releasing *Bombed Out* on the Roadrunner label. In the 90s, Mensi has become a leading member of the Anti Fascist Action group.

Albums: *Teenage Warning* (1979), *We Gotta Get Out Of This Place* (1980), *Live* (1981), *2 Million Voices* (1981), *Still From The Heart* (1982), *Angel Dust* (1983), *Bootlegs And Rarities* (1985), *Last Tango In Moscow* (1985), *Live In Yugoslavia* (1985), *Blood On The Terraces* (1986), *Power Of The Press* (1986), *Bombed Out* (1992).

Angry Samoans

Formed in August 1978, Van Nuys, California, USA, the Angry Samoans were one of the original Los Angeles punk bands, along with Fear, Black Flag, Circle Jerks and X. After numerous personnel changes, the most solid line-up consisted of Mike Saunders (guitar/vocals), Todd Homer (bass/vocals), Gregg Turner (guitar/vocals), Steve Drojensky (guitar) and Bill Vockeroth (drums). Leaning toward the humorous side of punk, in the same way as the Ramones, some of the Samoans' songs featured titles such as 'I'm A Pig', 'My Old Man's A Fatso', 'Attack Of The Mushroom People' and 'They Saved Hitler's Cock'. The group signed to PVC Records and released three EPs and one album. In 1990 they signed to Triple X Records and issued a second full-length album.

Albums: *STP Not LSD* (1988), *Live At Rhino Records* (1990).

Anti-Nowhere League

Leading lights in the early 80s UK punk scene along with contempories, GBH and Exploited, this quartet from Tunbridge Wells, Kent, betrayed their talent in biker leather, chains and hardcore obscenity. Their catalogue of sexual outrage veered from the satirical to the appallingly offensive, with a string of four-letter words, rabid misogyny and the glorification of bestiality. Their most memorable moment was a thrashy re-run of Ralph McTell's 'Streets Of London' which replaced the song's folky sentimentality with the barbed, snarling rhetoric of the gutter. Thousands of copies of the single were seized and destroyed by the police as the b-side, 'So What' was deemed obscene. This incident however, did nothing to prevent the group reaching number 1 in the UK Independent single charts, a feat accomplished a further three times in 1982 with 'I Hate People', 'Woman' and 'For You'. As their punkish appeal receded, the group abbreviated their name to the League before disbanding.

Albums: *We Are ... The League* (1982), *Live In Yugoslavia* (1983), *Long Live The League* (1986), *The Perfect Crime* (1987).

Anti-Pasti

Hailing from Derbyshire, England, Anti-Pasti were part of the commercially successful but critically reviled second wave of punk. The group comprising of Will (bass), Dugi (guitar), Kev (drums) and Martin Roper (lead vocals) signed to the punk/heavy metal label Rondelet in 1980 and they debuted with the EP *Four Sore Points*, followed by another, *Let Them Free* in January 1981. Later that year, Anti-Pasti unleashed *The Last Call*, which reached the UK Top 40, while their third single 'Six Guns' appeared at end of the year and reached number 1 in the UK Independent chart, as did the successful joint venture with Oi! punk legends the Exploited on a 12-inch single EP, *Don't Let 'Em Grind You Down*. 'East To The West', released in 1982, preceded the last Anti-Pasti album and single, both named 'Caution To The Wind', although a self-titled singles retrospective surfaced a year later.

Albums: *The Last Call* (1981), *Caution To the Wind* (1982). Compilation: *Anti-Pasti* (1983).

Any Trouble

In 1980, *Melody Maker* labelled Any Trouble: 'the most exciting new rock 'n' roll group since the Pretenders.' Formed in Stoke, England, by songwriter Clive Gregson, they were part of a 'pub-rock' scene that also included Dr. Feelgood and Elvis Costello's Flip City. The line-up was completed with Chris

Parks (lead guitar), Mel Harley (drums) and Phil Barnes (bass). Stiff Records signed them and backed the single 'Yesterday's Love' with full page adverts in the music press. *Where Are All The Nice Girls* was an assured debut but the promotional-only live album (just 500 were pressed) was a better example of their tough, bluesy music. They toured Europe and the USA as part of 'The Stiff Tour' but the label began concentrating on the US market because in the UK, Gregson, with his black-rimmed glasses and cynical lyrics, was often dismissed as an Elvis Costello imitator. *Wheels In Motion* lacked brightness, and Mike Howlett was an odd choice as producer, having just worked with Orchestral Manoeuvres In The Dark. Stiff lost faith and after releasing Any Trouble from their contract, drummer Martin Hughes (who had replaced Mel Harley) and Chris Parks both quit. Any Trouble made a comeback in 1982, supporting John Martyn on a British tour and signing to EMI America. Only Gregson and Barnes remained from the first line-up with new members Steve Gurl on keyboards and Andy Ebsworth on drums. Any Trouble was over-produced and Gregson himself later referred to it as 'dull'. *Wrong End Of The Race*, a double album, was the band's swansong but it was not backed by EMI America and soon afterwards the group split. Their final performance was at London's Dingwalls venue at Christmas 1984. Gregson went on to work with Richard Thompson and record with the accomplished vocalist, Christine Collister as Gregson And Collister.

Albums: *Where Are All The Nice Girls* (1980), *Wheels In Motion* (1981), *Any Trouble* (1983), *Wrong End of the Race* (1984).

Apples

This four-piece band from Edinburgh, Scotland, were accused of attempting to cash in on the 'indie dance movement'. Their act is built around lyricist and vocalist Callum McNair, with a soundscape built on a pop rock beat punctuated by lots of samples (similar to EMF, and Jesus Jones). The similarity to the aforementioned has seen the critics overlook their competent but uninspired music. Signed to Epic, their debut album included the single 'Stay People Child'.

Album: *Here Is Tomorrow* (1991).

AR Kane

This act proved popular in the independent UK charts of the late 80s. The group comprised Alex and Rudi from the te a sleeve shot taken by celebrated New York photographer Robert Mapplethorpe. *Sleight Of Hand*, was Armatrading's first self-produced album, which she recorded in her own quaintly named Bumpkin studio, and which was remixed by Steve Lillywhite. This was her least successful album

in commercial terms since her debut, stalling outside the Top 30 of the UK chart and considerably lower in the USA, even despite the fact that this time the sleeve photographer was Lord Snowdon.

1988's *The Shouting Stage* was arguably her most impressive album in some time but failed to reach the height achieved by many of its predecessors despite featuring Mark Knopfler of Dire Straits and Mark Brzezicks of Big Country as guests. *Hearts And Flowers* again demonstrated that even though the quality of Armatrading's output was seldom less than exemplary, it rarely achieved its commercial desserts. 1991 brought a further compilation album, *The Very Best Of Joan Armatrading*, which largely updated the earlier *Track Record*, and included a remix (by Hugh Padgham) of 'Love And Affection' which was released as a single. Armatrading seems to have reached a plateau in her career which is slightly below the top echelon in commercial terms, but which will enable her to continue recording with reasonable success (especially in critical terms) for as long as she desires. She has also contributed her services to a number of charitable concerts, such as the Prince's Trust, the 1988 Nelson Mandela Concert and Amnesty International. She is equally at home reading through her considerable collection of comics. She is to be applauded for remaining unpretentious, and is also in the enviable position of being able to choose her own touring and recording timetable.

Albums: *Whatever's For Us* (1972), *Back To The Night* (1975), *Joan Armatrading* (1976), *Show Some Emotion* (1977), *To The Limit* (1978), *Steppin' Out* (1978), *Me Myself I* (1980), *Walk Under Ladders* (1981), *The Key* (1983), *Secret Secrets* (1985), *Sleight Of Hand* (1986), *Shouting Stage* (1988), *Hearts And Flowers* (1990). Compilations: *Track Record* (1983), *The Very Best Of Joan Armatrading* (1991).

Armoury Show

Formed in 1984 by Richard Jobson (b. 6 October 1960, Dunfermline, Fife, Scotland; vocals/guitar) and Russell Webb (bass/vocals), longstanding members of the Skids. The group was initially completed by John McGeoch (b. 28 May 1955, Greenock, Strathclyde, Scotland; guitar), formerly of Magazine and Siouxsie And The Banshees and John Doyle (drums). Although the quartet enjoyed two minor hit singles with 'Castles In Spain' (1984) and 'We Can Be Brave Again' (1985), the two latter musicians proved incompatible and left following the completion of the group's sole album. *Waiting For The Floods* was an uncomfortable mix of different styles, but a 1987 single, 'New York City', which featured Jobson, Webb and sundry session musicians, showed a greater sense of purpose. Although redolent of early Simple Minds, the release suggested a newfound confidence, but the group broke up in the wake of Jobson's burgeoning modelling and media-based career. Album: *Waiting For The Floods* (1985).

Artery

Latter-day interest in UK-based Artery tends to stem from the presence of Simon Hinkler, keyboardist with the Cure. However, the Sheffield band's sound was an interesting blend of post-punk and funk, and worthy of attention in its own right. Hinkler was accompanied by Mark Gouldthorpe (vocals/guitar), Michael Fidler (vocals/guitar), Neil Mackenzie (bass) and Gary Wilson (drums), the team first appearing on 'Mother Moon' via the Limited Edition label in 1979. A move to Aardvark Records spawned two singles, 'Unbalanced' (with a free live EP) and 'Afterwards', before Artery signed to Red Flame Records. August 1982's 'The Clown' hinted at the promise found on their debut mini-album, *Oceans* and a further single, 'The Slide'. It was then over a year before Artery offered their rendition of 'Alabama Song' (a co-release with Virgin), and they left Red Flame soon after, signing to Golden Dawn Records. After 'Big Machine' in May 1984 and 'Diamonds In The Mine Field' in October, the band issued their first full-length album, *Terminal - The Second Coming*, but there was little response. Only a live album followed in 1986, although some three years later, 'Afterwards' was issued as a cassette on the label, Pleasantly Surprised.
Albums: *Oceans* (1982), *Terminal - The Second Coming* (1985), *Live In Amsterdam* (1986).

Ash, Daniel

A founder member of Bauhaus, Tones On Tail, and Love And Rockets, Ash emerged in 1991 with his first solo album, *Coming Down*, on Beggars Banquet. It made number 109 in the US charts, on the back of Love And Rocket's US popularity. However, a single from it, 'This Love', though highly commercial, failed to chart.
Album: *Coming Down* (1991).

Ashes

Formed in Los Angeles, California, USA, this folk-rock attraction initially comprised Pat Taylor (vocals), John Merrill (guitar), Al Brackett (bass) and Spencer Dryden (drums), although Jim Voigt succeeded the last on his departure for Jefferson Airplane in 1966. The reshaped line-up completed two singles, including a version of Paul Simon's 'Homeward Bound', before Taylor was replaced by Sandi Robinson. Guitarist Lance Fent was also added to the group which, in late 1966, took the name the Peanut Butter Conspiracy. The Ashes' legacy was not altogether forgotten as several archive selections appeared on the compilation *West Coast Love-In* (1967). The discovery of further unreleased recordings led to the release of *The Ashes*.
Album: *The Ashes* (1968).

Associates

Vocalist Billy MacKenzie (b. 27 March 1957, Dundee, Scotland) and Alan Rankine had performed in a variety of local groups before finally forming the Associates in 1979. After a minor label recording of David Bowie's 'Boys Keep Swinging', they were signed to Fiction Records where they released the critically acclaimed *The Affectionate Punch*. After a spell on the Beggars Banquet subsidiary Situation 2, they formed their own Associates label, distributed by WEA. The extra push provided a Top 10 chart breakthrough courtesy of 'Party Fears Two', which boasted an engaging and distinctive keyboards arrangement. Two further Top 30 hits followed with 'Club Country' and '18 Carat Love Affair'/'Love Hangover'. Meanwhile, MacKenzie became involved in other projects, most notably a cameo appearance on BEF's extravagant *Songs Of Quality And Distinction*. It was not until 1984 that the Associates reconvened and this was followed by several very low chart entries and a relatively poor selling album, *Perhaps*. Not surprisingly, Rankine and MacKenzie reverted to solo work, leaving the Associates as something of an occasional group. It was not until 1990 that the group returned with a new album, *Wild And Lonely*, which was stylistically similar to their earlier work.
Albums: *The Affectionate Punch* (1980), *Sulk* (1982), *Perhaps* (1985), *Wild And Lonely* (1990). Compilation: *Fourth Drawer Down* (1984).

Astley, Virginia

Astley was a former member of the Ravishing Beauties along with Nicola Holland and Kate St. John. As classically trained musicians they attempted, with some degree of success, to cross over into the pop field, working with amongst others, Echo And The Bunnymen and the Teardrop Explodes. Astley broke away to pursue a solo career in 1982. Her first single, 'Love's A Lonely Place To Be' was a melancholy paeon to the feeling of isolation when a love affair breaks down and the song's choral, almost boy soprano feel, gave it an ephemeral quality. It reached number 7 in the UK Independent chart and fitted in well with the then-current fashion for 'quiet pop'. Her debut album in 1983 confirmed her love of all things English and pastoral. Largely an instrumental album, this dreamy atmospheric piece incorporated the sounds of the countryside on a summer's day. Complete with authentic bird songs and farm sounds, it gave the feel of a modern day piece by Delius. It took three years for her second album to be released and the Ryuichi Sakamoto produced *Hope In Darkened Heart* concentrated on

Astley's preoccupation with the loss of childhood's innocence and adulthood's uncertainty. This accomplished musician remains for the time being, on the periphery of the music scene and can occasionally be found guesting for other artists.

Albums: *From Gardens Where We Feel Secure* (1983), *Hope In Darkened Heart* (1986).

Attila The Stockbroker

After graduating from the University of Kent with a degree in French, this performance poet (b. John Baine, 21 October 1957) really was a stockbroker, or on the way to becoming one, before he set out on the live music circuit. Accompanied on occasion by his own mandolin backing, he regaled his audience with good-humoured invective on the state of the world. Viewed as one of the new 'Ranting Poets', a term he disliked, his influences were poets Roger McCoughlan and Brian Patton, alongside Monty Python and the energy of punk. After playing in forgotten punk bands English Disease and Brighton Riot Squad, he joined Brussels based punk band Contingent. His usual early environment, indeed, was supporting punk bands. He played frequently enough to earn himself a session for BBC disc jockey John Peel, which in turn led to a deal with Cherry Red Records and his debut *Ranting At The Nation* was a highly colourful selection of verse and spoken word highlighting the absurdity of British life. Nightmare visions of Soviets running the social security system and his affection for obscure European soccer clubs were among the targets: 'So go to your Job Centre - I'll bet you'll see, Albanian students get handouts for free, and drug-crazed punk rockers cavort and caress, in the interview booths of the D.H.S.S.'. Critics were not convinced, however, one citing the contents as 'an inarticulate mish-mash of bad humour and popular cliches'. The *Cocktails* EP, from October 1982, boasted some of his finest pieces to date, from the serious ('Contributory Negligence') to the absurd ('The Night I Slept With Seething Wells'). 1984's *Sawdust And Empire* saw a greater emphasis on music. Increasingly Attila was seeing himself as a folk artist, and in between releases was becoming a near permanent fixture at various festivals, working alongside John Otway and TV Smith (ex-the Adverts). He recently released a new album for Musidisc, and also the managed The Tender Trap. He was involved in the staging of *Cheryl The Rock Opera*, alongside Otway and Blyth Power, for whom he occasionally plucks a fiddle, and has contributed to the pages of the *Guardian* with his essays on social change in eastern Europe while on tour in the region. Attila's humorous ranting lyrics, complete with references to fish, Albanians and Russians has ensured a cult status, particularly on the UK college circuit.

Albums: *Ranting At The Nation* (1983), *Sawdust And Empire* (1984), *Libyan Students From Hell* (1987), *Scornflakes* (1988), *Live At The Rivioli* (1990), *Donkey's Years* (1991).

Attractions

Formed in May 1977 to back Elvis Costello, the Attractions provided sympathetic support to the singer's contrasting, and often demanding, compositions. Steve Nieve (b. Steven Nason; keyboards), Bruce Thomas (b. Stockton on Tees, Cleveland, England; bass) and Pete Thomas (b. 9 August 1954, Sheffield, Yorkshire, England; drums) were already experienced musicians - Bruce Thomas with the Sutherland Brothers and Quiver, Pete Thomas with Chilli Willi And The Red Hot Peppers and John Stewart - while Nieve's dexterity on keyboards added colour to many of the unit's exemplary releases. In 1980 the Attractions completed a low-key album, *Mad About The Wrong Boy*, but their position as Costello's natural backing group became increasingly unsure as their leader embarked on a plethora of guises. Nieve recorded a solo collection, *Playboy* (1987) and later led the houseband, along with Pete Thomas as Steve Nieve And The Playboys, on television's *Jonathan Ross Show*, while Bruce Thomas began a literary career with *The Big Wheel* (1990), an impressionistic autobiography.

Album: *Mad About The Wrong Boy* (1980).

Au Pairs

Lesley Woods (guitar/vocals), Paul Ford (guitar/Vocals), Jane Munro (bass), Pete Hammond (drums). Formed in Birmingham in 1979, the Au Pairs matched driving, guitar-led rock to lyrics (mostly by Woods) that dissected the politics of sexual relationships. Their first single, 'You', came out on their own 021 label in September 1979; their second, 'It's Obvious', which topped the Indie charts, was released by Human Records, who also issued their debut, *Playing With A Different Sex*, in May 1981. Meanwhile, the group had achieved fame of sorts when the BBC banned their song 'Come Again', after realizing it referred to orgasm. (Hardly licentious, the song was actually a satirical dig at the patronising sexual manners of the so-called 'new man'.) A third single, 'Inconvenience', added trumpet and brought out the soulful side of Wood's punk-Joplin vocals, but it did not achieve the breakthrough to chart success. A second album, *Sense And Sensuality*, also failed to impress. Late in 1982 the group added synthesizer player Tina Wawrzynowicz to the line-up, but the following year the unit disbanded. Woods went to live for a while in Amsterdam, Ford and Hammond returned to Birmingham to play in a jazz group. In retrospect, the Au Pairs' music and politics were probably a shade too aggressive to win them mass popularity in the UK; but if you caught them live, on a good night, you would have heard some of the most thrilling, incandescent music of the entire punk era.

Albums: *Playing With a Different Sex* (1981), *Sense And Sensuality* (1982), *Live In Berlin* (1983).

Avant Gardeners

Headed by Russell Murch (vocals/guitar) with Martin Saunders (guitar), Nigel Rae (bass) and Mike Kelly (drums), they released their debut EP in the summer of 1977 on the Virgin label. Their 60s influenced rock was obviously affected by the climate of the time, with strong overtones of punk, and consequently the new year saw two tracks from the EP, 'Gotta Turn Back' and 'Strange Girl In Clothes', included on Virgin's new wave showcase *Guillotine*. Whereas the album was a stepping stone with varying degrees of success for most of the other bands, Avant Gardener was ignored in the UK, although minor interest was shown abroad. With the addition of an 'S' to their name and a revised line-up of mainman Richard Murch (vocals/guitar), Rob Hill (bass) and Mike Roberts (guitar), they released *Dig It* on Appaloosa in 1980. Three tracks from the EP were included, as well as a cover version of Roky Erikson's 'Two Headed Dog', who also appeared on the *Guillotine* compilation. This was a good indication of the band's future direction away from their punk debut and throughout the early 80s, they continued to play live, releasing a single 'Deadwood Stage' in 1983, and the 'psychedelic' *The Church Of The Inner Cosmos* in 1984.

Albums: *Dig It* (1980), *The Church Of The Inner Cosmos* (1984).

Avengers

Formed in San Francisco, USA in 1977, the Avengers joined the Dils and Crime as one of the city's prime punk/hardcore attractions. The original line-up featured Penelope Housten (vocals), Greg Westermark (guitar), Johnathan Postal (bass) and Danny Furious (drums), but only Housten and Furious survived the unit's interminable changes. The group's debut release, 'Car Crash'/'We Are The One'/'I Believe In Me' (1977), captured their powerful sound, but a subsequent EP, *The American In Me* (aka *White Nigger*) (1979), produced by former Sex Pistols' guitarist Steve Jones, was also of merit. Both sets formed the basis of the Avengers' sole, and posthumous, album.

Album: *The Avengers 1977-1979* (1983).

A Witness

Hailing from Manchester, England, A Witness shared the distinctive sound adopted by the Ron Johnson label acts; fast, quirky songs with an obvious debt to both Captain Beefheart and Pere Ubu. The band comprised, K. Curtis (vocals), R. Aitken (guitar), V. Hunt (bass) and A. Brown (drums). An EP, *Loudhailer Songs* in 1985, attracted the *New Musical Express*, who included the band on their seminal *C86* sampler tape. An album, *I Am John Pancreas*, followed in 1986, full of manic, awkward guitar riffs and off-beat lyrics. After the release of another EP, *Raw Patch* (1988), the Ron Johnson label folded, prompting a short-lived period at Fundamental Records who issued A Witness's second album, *Sacred Cow Heart*. The Membranes' Vinyl Drip label was responsible for the band's next single and possibly their finest, 'I Love You Mr. Disposable Razors' (1990). Since then, Strange Fruit Records have combined A Witness's two 1988 sessions for BBC disc jockey John Peel on a mini-album. The band have also covered the Doors' 'Break On Through' on a tribute album to the music of 1967, *Through The Looking Glass*.

Albums: *I Am John Pancreas* (1985), *Sacred Cow Heart* (1988), *Double Peel Sessions* (1989).

Aztec Camera; Roddy Frame

Aztec Camera

This acclaimed UK pop outfit was formed in 1980 by Roddy Frame (b. 29 January 1964, East Kilbride, Scotland), as a vehicle for his songwriting talent. The other members, Campbell Owens (bass), and Dave Mulholland (drums), soon passed through, and a regular turnover in band members ensued while

Frame put together the songs that made up the exceptionally strong debut *High Land, Hard Rain*. Their three hits in the UK independent charts on the influential Postcard label had already made the band a critics' favourite, but this sparkling album of light acoustic songs with a mature influence of jazz and Latin rhythms was a memorable work. 'Oblivious' put them into the national bestsellers, while excellent songs like the uplifting 'Walk Out To Winter' and the expertly crafted 'We Could Send Letters' indicated a major talent in the ascendant. The Mark Knopfler-produced *Knife* broke no new ground, but now signed to the massive WEA Records, the band was pushed into a world tour to promote the album. Frame was happier writing songs on his acoustic guitar back home in Scotland and retreated there following the tour, until *Love* in 1987. This introverted yet over-produced album showed Frame's continuing development with Elvis Costello-influenced song structures. The comparative failure of this collection was rectified the following year with two further hit singles 'How Men Are' and the catchy 'Somewhere In My Heart'. This stimulated interest in *Love* and the album became a substantial success. After a further fallow period, allowing Frame to create more gems, the band returned in 1990 with the highly acclaimed *Stray*, leaving no doubt that their brand of intelligent gentle pop has a considerable following.

Albums: *High Land, Hard Rain* (1983), *Knife* (1984), *Aztec Camera* (1985, 10-inch album), *Love* (1987), *Stray* (1990).

B

Babes In Toyland

This hardcore trio spearheaded a new wave of US female bands at the turn of the 90s. Their origins can be traced back to 1987, when Kat Bjelland (b. Woodburn, Oregon, USA - adopted, though she did not know it until she was much older; vocals/guitar) moved to Minneapolis. Previously she had played in bands with Courtney Love (Hole) and Jennifer (L7) when she was stationed in San Francisco. The trio was completed by Michelle Leon (bass) and Lorie Barbero (drums/vocals). They first came to prominence via the legendary singles club at Sub Pop Records, then made a deep impression on a European support tour with Sonic Youth. A debut album produced by Jack Endino, was recorded live

with the vocals overdubbed. Soon after, WEA A&R representative Tim Carr saw the band live in Minneapolis and was impressed. After signing to the label, they recorded the 1991 mini-album *To Mother*. Bjelland, meanwhile, was busy defending the band from the suspicious minds of a media that wanted to latch on to the girl groups as an amorphous movement: 'Men and women play their instruments to a completely different beat. Women are a lot more rhythmic - naturally - than men. It doesn't even have anything to do with music, it all has to do with timing'. The band look set to continue their ascendence, aided principally by Bjelland's distinctive guitar style and anachronistic appearance.

Albums: *Spanking Machine* (1990), *To Mother* (1991).

Baby Animals

This Australian indie-metal quartet were formed in 1990 by vocalist Suzi Demarchi and guitarist Dave Leslie. Recruiting bassist Eddie Parise and drummer Frank Delenza, they signed to the Imago label and debuted with a self-titled album in February 1992. Influenced by Heart, the Pretenders, AC/DC, INXS and Siouxsie And The Banshees, their sound is characterized by Demarchi's provocative growl and the understated guitar work of Leslie. They made a considerable impact in the UK as support act to Bryan Adams on his 1991 tour.

Album: *Baby Animals* (1992).

Bad Manners

Formed in 1979 when the UK 2-Tone ska revival was at its peak, the group comprised Buster Bloodvessel (b. Douglas Trendle, 6 September 1958; lead vocals), Gus 'Hot Lips' Herman (trumpet), Chris Kane (saxophone), Andrew 'Marcus Absent' Marson (saxophone), Winston Bazoomies (harmonica), Brian 'Chew-it' Tuitti (drums), David Farren (bass), Martin Stewart (keyboards) and Louis 'Alphonzo' Cook (guitar). Fronted by the exuberant Bloodvessel, whose shaven head, rotund build, protruding tongue and often outrageous costume provided a strong comic appeal, the group enjoyed a brief run of UK hits in the early 80s. Released on the Magnet label, their string of UK hits commenced with the catchy 'Ne-Ne Na-Na Na-Na Nu-Nu' followed by 11 UK chart entries, including four Top 10 hits, 'Special Brew', 'Can Can', 'Walking In The Sunshine' and a remake of Millie's hit retitled 'My Girl Lollipop'. Although this musically tight unit is still very popular on the live circuit, the group's mass novelty appeal had worn thin by the middle of 1983 when the hits ceased.

Albums: *Ska 'N' B* (1980), *Loonee Tunes* (1981), *Gosh, It's Bad Manners* (1981), *Forging Ahead* (1982), *Return Of The Ugly* (1989). Compilation: *The Height Of Bad Manners* (1983).

Badowski, Henry

After serving his apprenticeship in UK bands Norman And The Baskervilles, Lick It Dry and the New Rockets, Badowski joined punk band Chelsea on bass, but in early 1978, after only a few months, he left to enlist as drummer for Stiff Records artist Wreckless Eric. During the summer of that year, he sang and played keyboards with the short-lived King, a punk/psychedelic group that included Dave Berk (drums), Kim Bradshaw (bass) and ex-Damned, Captain Sensible (guitar). Consequently when King folded, Badowski took-up the bass with the re-formed the Damned off-shoot, the Doomed. With the new year came the new position of drummer with the Good Missionaries, an experimental band created by Mark Perry from Alternative TV. This association led to the start of his solo career in the summer of 1979, with the release of 'Making Love With My Wife' on Perry's Deptford Fun City label. Recorded at Pathway Studios, the track was performed completely by Badowski and displayed a strong 60s influence, with airs of Syd Barrett and Kevin Ayers. The b-side 'Baby Sign Here With Me', was originally part of the King live set and utilized the talents of James Stevenson (bass/guitar) from Chelsea, Alex Kolkowski (violin) and Dave Berk (drums), both from the Johnny Moped Band. The single drew favourable reviews and within a month he had signed a contract with A&M Records, releasing a further two singles 'My Face' and 'Henry's In Love', closely followed by the album Life Is A Grand, a classic slice of psychedelia that was to signal the end of Badowski's solo career.
Album: Life Is A Grand (1981).

Bad Religion

This USA hardcore band were formed in 1980 from the suburbs of north Los Angeles. Their first incarnation comprised Greg Graffin (vocals), Brett Gurewitz (guitar), Jay Lishrout (drums) and Jay Bentley (bass), with the name originating from their mutual distaste for organized religion. Their debut release was the poorly produced EP Bad Religion on Epitaph records, itself formed by founder member Gurewitz. Following several appearances on local compilation albums, Pete Finestone took over as drummer in 1982. The milestone How Could Hell Be Any Worse was recorded in Hollywood, creating a fair degree of local and national interest. By the following year Paul Dedona and Davy Goldman had joined as the new bass guitarist and drummer respectively. The subsequent Into The Unknown proved a minor disaster, disillusioning hardcore fans with the emphasis shifted to slick adult rock. 1984 saw further internal strife as Graffin became the only surviving member from the previous year, with Greg Hetson and Tim Gallegos taking over guitar and bass, and Pete Finestone

returning on drums, while Gurewitz took time out to conquer his drink and drug problems. A comeback EP, Back To The Known, revealed a much more purposeful outfit. A long period of inactivity was ended in 1987 when Gurewitz rejoined for a show which Hetson (working with former band Circle Jerks once more) could not attend. New material was written, and Suffer was released in 1988 to almost universal critical acclaim.
Albums: How Could Hell Be Any Worse? (1981), Into The Unknown (1983), Suffer (1988) No Control (1989).

Balaam And The Angel

This UK rock band included both post-punk gothic and 60s elements in their output. They were originally made up of the three Morris brothers, Jim (b. 25 November 1960, Motherwell, Scotland; guitar/recorder/keyboards), Mark (b. 15 January 1963, Motherwell, Scotland; lead vocals/bass) and Des (b. 27 June 1964, Motherwell, Scotland; drums). They began their career playing working mens clubs as a childrens' cabaret act in their native Motherwell, encouraged by their father who had insisted they all watch television's Top Of The Pops as children. They eventually moved down to Cannock in Staffordshire, where they are still based. An early gig at the ICA in London, 1985, saw a completely different approach to that with which Balaam would become identified. Playing in bare feet and pyjamas, they procured numerous covers of 60s love paeans, and a recorder solo. Somewhat falsely categorized as a gothic group after supporting the Cult on three successive tours, they were, in fact, self-consciously colourful in both appearance and approach. Early in their career they founded Chapter 22 Records, along with manager Craig Jennings. Their debut came on the label when 'World Of Light' appeared in 1984, although 'Day And Night' was their most impressive release from this period. Their debut The Greatest Story Ever Told, was named after the headline under which their first interview in Melody Maker appeared. It was apparently intended to be reminiscent of the Doors, though it fell some way short of this. They moved on to Virgin Records and, in September 1988, the band's second album was released after they had returned from support slots with Kiss and Iggy Pop in the USA. A new guitarist, Ian McKean, entered because of the need for two guitar parts on Live Free Or Die. They were dropped by Virgin however, and their first tour for over four years took place in 1990. Press speculation that Mark would join the Cult as replacement bass player for Jamie Stewart collapsed as Ian Astbury decided that he was too much of a 'front man'. In 1991, they truncated their name to Balaam, and the first release was a mini-album, No More Innocence.
Albums: The Greatest Story Ever Told (1986), Live Free

Or Die (1988), *No More Innocence* (1991).

B.A.L.L

Formed in New York in 1987, B.A.L.L. comprised of Mark Kramer (guitar/vocals) and David Licht (drums) – both ex-Shockabilly – and two ex-members of Half Japanese: Don Fleming (guitar/vocals) and Jay Speigel (drums). The quartet's debut, *Period/Another American Lie*, established their sound, which meshed loud, distorted guitars to the two drummers' solid, uncompromising beat. Humour, however, was an integral part of the group and *Bird* came replete with a sleeve design which parodied the infamous Beatles' 'butcher cover'. Songs by T. Rex and Bob Dylan were mercilessly re-created while the second side was devoted to their tribute to the *Concert For Bangladesh*. *Trouble Doll* featured studio and live recordings, while *Four...Hardball*, recorded just prior to the group's break-up, contains a side devoted to unfinished instrumentals. Fleming subsequently pursued a career as performer and producer while Kramer continued to administrate his Shimmy Disc label and record prolifically with its many acts.

Albums: *Period/Another American Lie* (1987), *Bird* (1988), *Trouble Doll* (1989), *Four...Hardball* (1990).

Ball, Dave

b. 3 May 1959, Blackpool, Lancashire, England. Ball came to notice as the keyboard player in the duo Soft Cell with Marc Almond. His early interest in electronics crystallized at Leeds Polytechnic where he joined a band which utilized three vacuum cleaners. This led to his composing music to accompany Almond's theatrical shows and the formation of Soft Cell in October 1979. Although contributing much to their sound, Ball maintained a low profile. In June 1983, he scored the music for a revival of Tennessee Williams's play *Suddenly Last Summer*. Later that year Ball released the solo instrumental *In Strict Tempo*, before the break-up of Soft Cell in December. The following year he wrote the score for the German film *Decoder* and produced the Virgin Prunes. The soundtrack to Derek Jarman's *Imagining Oktober* followed in 1985, and in 1987 he produced Jack The Tab. By the end of 1988 Ball had produced a single for train-robber Ronnie Biggs in Brazil and had started working with Jack The Tab's acid-house singer Richard Norris. This evolved into psychedelic dance outfit the Grid, which quickly found acceptance in ambient/new age/dance clubs by exploring the interface between Kraftwerk, Brian Eno and Pink Floyd. Other current activities include composing music for television commercials (Shell, TSB etc), film soundtracks, re-mix/production work for Art Of Noise, Bhundu Boys and Marc Almond plus odd collaborations with LSD-guru Dr Timothy Leary and Rolf Harris.

Album: *In Strict Tempo* (1983).

Bambi Slam

An ambitious UK rock dance outfit, the Bambi Slam were formed in the mid-80s around would-be eccentric Roy Feldon (b. Ashton-under-Lyme, Lancashire, England). After a fairly inconsequential upbringing in the rosey suburb of Pickering, Toronto, Canada, the expatriate Feldon moved to California for a spell. Coming to Britain to seek his fame and fortune, he recruited Nick Maynard (drums) and Linda Mellor (cello), through an advert in the Royal Academy. Under the Bambi Slam banner they toured the country, sending demos to every copious record companies. The music resembled a rockier Public Image Limited. Product Inc., a subsidiary of Mute, picked up on them and released three singles, 'Bamp Bamp' through to the stirring 'Happy Birthday'. A tour supporting the Cult and a debut album were well under way and things were seemingly going to plan. However, Feldon suddenly underwent a period of artistic introspection resulting in the band going way over budget. This led to a split with Product Inc. and an unfinished album on which they owed a considerable amount of money. However, Rough Trade supremo Geoff Travis thought they had promise and signed them to Blanco Y Negro. There they released a flawed, eponymous debut, after which Feldon jettisoned the rest of the band.

Album: *The Bambi Slam* (1987).

Bananarama

Formed in London in 1980, this all-girl pop trio comprised Keren Woodward (b. Bristol), Sarah Dallin (b. Bristol) and Siobhan Fahey. After singing impromptu at various parties and pubs in London, the group were recorded by former Sex Pistols' guitarist Paul Cook on the Swahili Black Blood cover 'Ai A Mwana'. The single caught the attention of Fun Boy Three vocalist Terry Hall, who invited the girls to back his trio on their revival of 'It Ain't What You Do, It's The Way That You Do It'. In return, the Fun Boy Three backed Bananarama on their Velvelettes' cover 'Really Saying Something' which reached the UK Top 10 in 1982. From the outset, Bananarama had a strong visual image and an unselfconsciously amateur approach to choreography which was refreshing and appealing. Although they initially played down their talents, they retained considerable control over their careers, eschewing the usual overt sexism associated with the marketing of female troupes in pop. A tie-up with producers Tony Swain and Steve Jolley brought them Top 10 hits with 'Shy Boy', the Steam cover 'Na Na, Hey Hey, Kiss Him Goodbye' and 'Cruel Summer'. Their high-point during this phase was the clever and

appealing 'Robert De Niro's Waiting', which justly reached the Top 3 in the UK. In an attempt to tackle more serious subject matter, they next released 'Rough Justice', a protest song on the political situation in Northern Ireland. The title prophetically summed up the disc's chart fate. A lean period followed before the girls teamed up with the Stock, Aitken And Waterman production team for a remake of Shocking Blue's 'Venus', which brought them a number 1 in the USA. 'I Heard A Rumour' maintained the quality of their recent output, with some excellent harmonies and a strong arrangement. Their biggest UK hit followed with the exceptional 'Love In The First Degree', an intriguing lyric dramatizing a Kafkaesque nightmare in which Love itself is placed on trial. It proved to be their finest pop moment. In December 1987 Siobhan Fahey left the group, married the Eurythmics' David A. Stewart and subsequently formed Shakespear's Sister. Her replacement was Jacqui Sullivan, an old friend whose image fitted in reasonably well. During the 90s, the hits continued making Bananarama the most consistent and successful British female group in pop history. This effective formula underwent yet another change in 1991 when Sullivan departed for a solo career resulting in Sarah and Keren continuing for the first time as a duo.
Albums: *Deep Sea Skiving* (1983), *Bananarama* (1984), *True Confessions* (1986), *Wow!* (1987). Compilation: *The Greatest Hits Collection* (1988).

Band Of Susans

The membership of this articulate US guitar-based assembly was fluid but evolved around the songwriting partnership of Robert Poss (b. 20 November 1956, Buffalo, New York, USA; guitar/vocals) and Susan Stenger (b. 11 May 1955, Buffalo, New York, USA; bass/guitar/vocals). Poss had once been offered the guitarist's role in PiL when Keith Levene vacated that post. Both he and Stenger formerly worked with guitar composers Rhys Chatham, and eventually formed their own group. Their title was lifted from the fact that the original line-up contained no less than three Susans. Other members of the band have included Ron Spitzer (drums), later replaced by Joey Kaye, while Anne Husick has taken over from Karen Haglof as third guitarist. Bruce Gilbert from Wire also temporarily filled in for Haglof due to her aversion to touring. However, personnel changes have had little effect on the internal dynamics of the band because: 'When we audition new people we're not looking for an influx of new ideas, we like the way the band is . . . '. Two albums won them supporters on both sides of the Atlantic, after which they moved to Restless Records for 1991's *The Word And The Flesh*. The massed barrage of guitars on-stage remains a unique visual

and aural experience; the *New Musical Express* describing it as 'nothing less than pure, demonic euphoria'.
Albums: *Hope Against Hope* (1988), *Love Agenda* (1989), *The Word And The Flesh* (1991).

Bangles

Bangles

Formerly the Colours, the Bangs and finally the Bangles, this Los Angeles quartet playing melodic west coast guitar-based pop, hit the heights during the mid-80s. The band comprised: Susannah Hoffs (b. 17 January 1962, Newport Beach, California, USA; guitar/vocals), Debbi Peterson (b. 22 August 1961, Los Angeles, California, USA; drums/vocals), Vicki Peterson (b. 11 January 1958, Los Angeles, California, USA; guitar/vocals), and former Runaways member Michael Steele (b. 2 June 1954; bass/vocals) who replaced Annette Zilinkas. Their energetic harmonious style showed both a grasp and great affection for 60s' pop with their Beatles and Byrds-like sound. They emerged from the 'Paisley Underground' scene with bands like Rain Parade and Dream Syndicate. Their superb debut 'Hero Takes A Fall' failed to chart, as did their interpretation of the Soft Boys 'Going Down To Liverpool'. The idea of four glamorous middle-class American girls singing about trotting down to a labour exchange in Liverpool with their UB40 cards, was both bizarre and quaint. Again they failed to chart, although their sparkling debut *All Over The Place* scraped into the US chart. Following regular live work they built a strong following, although it was the hit single 'Manic Monday', written by Prince and the extraordinary success of *Different Light* earned them a wider audience. Both album and single narrowly missed the top of both US and UK charts, and throughout 1986 the Bangles could do no wrong. Their interpretation of Jules Sheer's 'If She Knew What She Wants' showed touches of mid-60s' Mamas And The Papas, while the unusual 'Walk Like An Egyptian' was pure 80s' gimmickry. Sadly they were unable to maintain their success and disbanded in 1989. Artistic integrity and personality clashes played a major role in their demise. The Bangles took on male-dominated west coast pop, and for brief time they fended off all opposition.

Albums: *Rainy Day* (1983), *All Over The Place* (1985), *Different Light* (1986), *Everything* (1988), Compilation: *The Bangles Greatest Hits* (1991).

Bates, Martyn

Former lead singer of UK group Eyeless In Gaza, Bates split to perform solo in the late 80s having previously released a solo set, *Letters Written* in 1982. Bates's songs were performed with no less a sense of intense, anguished passion as he did with his erstwhile partners, and although he maintained a minor cult following, national success eluded him. In 1990, with former Primitives guitarist Steve Dullaghan, he moved back to a group format with the formation of the five-piece Hungry I, releasing an EP *The Falling Orchard* in the summer of 1991.

Albums: *Letters Written* (1982), *Return Of The Quiet* (1987), *Love Smashed On A Rock* (1988), *Letters To A Scattered Family* (1990), *Stars Come Trembling* (1990).

Bauhaus; Peter Murphy

Bauhaus

Originally known as Bauhaus 1919, this Northamptonshire quartet comprised Peter Murphy (vocals), Daniel Ash (vocals/guitar), David Jay aka David J. (vocals/bass) and Kevin Haskins (drums).

Within months of their formation they made their recording debut in 1979 with the classic, brooding, nine-minute gothic anthem, 'Bela Lugosi's Dead'. Their career saw them move to various independent labels (Small Wonder, Axix, 4AD and Beggars Banquet) and along the way they cut some interesting singles, including 'Dark Entries', 'Terror Couple Kill Colonel' and a reworking of T. Rex's 'Telegram Sam'. Often insistent on spontaneity in the studio, they recorded four albums in as many years, of which *Mask* (1981) proved the most accessible. A cameo appearance in the movie *The Hunger*, starring David Bowie, showed them playing their memorable Bela Lugosi tribute. They later took advantage of the Bowie connection to record a carbon copy of 'Ziggy Stardust', which gave them their only UK Top 20 hit. Although there was further belated success with 'Lagartija Nick' and 'She's In Parties', the group disbanded in 1983. Vocalist Peter Murphy briefly joined Japan's Mick Karn in Dali's Car and the remaining three members soldiered on under the name Love And Rockets.

Albums: *In The Flat Field* (1980), *Mask* (1981), *The Sky's Gone Out* (1982), *Press The Eject And Give Me The Tape* (1982), *Burning From The Inside* (1983). Compilation: *1979-1983* (1985).

Beat (UK)

Founded in Birmingham, England in 1978, the original Beat comprised Dave Wakeling (b. 19 February 1956, Birmingham, England; vocals/guitar), Andy Cox (b. 25 January 1956, Birmingham, England; guitar), David Steele (b. 8 September 1960, Isle Of Wight, England; bass) and Everett Morton (b. 5 April 1951, St Kitts; drums). Local success on the pub circuit brought them to the attention of Jerry Dammers who duly signed them to his Coventry-based Two-Tone label. In the meantime, the Beat had expanded their ranks to include black punk rapper Ranking Roger (b. Roger Charlery, 21 February 1961, Birmingham, England) and a saxophonist simply named Saxa (b. Jamaica), who had the distinction of having played alongside that premier exponent of bluebeat Prince Buster. The new line-up proved perfect for the ska/pop fusion that exemplified the Beat at their best. Their debut single, a cover of Smokey Robinson's 'Tears Of A Clown', was a surprise Top 10 hit, but the best was yet to come. After forming their own label, Go Feet, they registered several hits during 1980 which ably displayed their talents as sharp-witted lyricists with the necessary strong danceability quotient. The uplifting yet acerbic 'Mirror In The Bathroom' and 'Best Friend' worked particularly well both as observations on personal relationships and more generalized putdowns of the 'Me' generation. This political awareness was more explicitly exposed on

'Stand Down Margaret', one of several anti-Thatcherite songs of the period. Donations to CND and benefit gigs for the unemployed linked the Beat with other radical Two-Tone outfits, such as the Specials. On record, the Beat sustained their verve and their debut album, *I Just Can't Stop It*, proved a solid collection, boosted by the inclusion of several hit singles. Within a year, however, their essentially pop-based style was replaced by a stronger reggae influence. *Wha'ppen* and *Special Beat Service* were generally well received, but the previously effortless run of chart hits had temporarily evaporated. By April 1982, Saxa had retired to be replaced by Wesley Magoogan. Although the Beat continued to tour extensively, their dissolution was imminent. Ironically, they ended their career as it had begun with an opportune cover of a 60's song, this time Andy Williams' 'Can't Get Used To Losing You', which gave the group their biggest UK hit. After the split, Ranking Roger and Dave Wakeling formed General Public while Andy Cox and David Steele recruited Roland Gift to launch the Fine Young Cannibals.
Albums: *I Just Can't Stop It* (1980), *Wha'ppen* (1981), *Special Beat Service* (1982). Compilation: *What Is Beat* (1983).

Beat (US)
Formed in San Francisco in 1979 the new wave/pop band the Beat were led by Paul Collins, who had previously played in the power pop band, the Nerves, with Peter Case, who later joined the Plimsouls, and songwriter Jack Lee (whose 'Hanging On The Telephone' was a hit for Blondie). The Beat signed with Bill Graham's management company and secured a recording deal with Columbia Records. Their debut, *The Beat*, was popular on college radio but never broke nationally. Their second album and a 1983 EP for Passport Records, recorded with a new line-up, failed to garner much interest and the group broke up.
Albums: *The Beat* (1979), *The Kids Are The Same* (1982), *To Beat Or Not To Beat* (1983, mini-album).

Beat Rodeo
Beat Rodeo was initially the name given to an EP recorded by Steve Almaas (b. Minneapolis, Minnesota, USA), a guitarist/vocalist formerly with the Minneapolis punk bands the Suicide Commandos and the Crackers. Almaas recorded the country-rock-oriented *Beat Rodeo* in 1981 with Richard Barone, formerly of the New York-New Jersey pop band the Bongos and record producer Mitch Easter, at the latter's North Carolina recording studio, the Drive-In. The EP was released on the independent Coyote Records, after which Almaas formed the group Beat Rodeo, in 1982, along with guitarist/vocalist Bill

Schunk (b. Riverhead, New York, USA). An early line-up of the group worked in clubs in the US north east and mid-west for two years before signing with I.R.S. Records. Their first version of their debut, *Staying Out Late*, was produced by Don Dixon at Easter's studio and released in Germany only in July 1984. That year, Almaas and Schunk replaced the original members with bassist Dan Prater and drummer Louis King. In early 1985 Almaas and Dixon returned to the Drive-In to remix the album and it was reissued, along with two new tracks added that year. *Home In The Heart Of The Beat* was recorded, with producer Scott Litt, in 1986. It failed to make a dent commercially and the band continued performing on the club circuit, but did not record.
Albums: *Staying Out Late* (1984), *Home In The Heart Of The Beat* (1986).

Beats International
This studio team of UK musicians was formed by Norman Cook (b. 31 July 1963; ex-Housemartins) on the advent of the break up of his former employers. Its basic composition was Norman Cook (bass), Lindy Layton (vocals), Lester Noel (ex-Grab Grab The Haddock, North Of Cornwallis; vocals), Andy Boucher (keyboards), and MC Wildski (rap). However, to these personnel can be added a gamut of occasional members ranging from Billy Bragg to Definition Of Sound to Captain Sensible. Following the Housemartins split Cook returned to Brighton and his old job as a disk jockey, and released 'Blame It On The Bassline' under his own name. Vocals on the a-side were provided by future Beats International member MC Wildski, while another future collaborator, Billy Bragg, wrote the b-side 'Won't Talk About It'. The follow-up single 'For Spacious Lies' garnered numerous rave reviews, and was much closer to traditional pop fare than subsequent releases. However, the group shot to prominence in the UK when 'Dub Be Good To Me' reached number 1 in the UK charts in 1990. Controversy followed it shortly afterwards, as the public, Paul Simonon amongst them, placed the bass line as a note for note lift from the Clash album track 'Guns Of Brixton'. In reality the song also borrowed heavily from the SOS Band's 'Just Be Good To Me'. This 'creative theft' may have diminished royalty cheques, but the interpretation of various styles and even passages of music proved quite a deliberate strategy in Beats Internationals' armoury. Although the subsequent 'Burundi Blues' single, a delicate mix of soul, jazz, and African musics failed to repeat the success of 'Dub Be Good To Me', Cook was heavily in demand as a remixer for a variety of projects, ranging from Aztec Camera to the Jungle Brothers. The impossibly diverse debut album charted at number 17, while the follow-up concentrated heavily on ska and reggae

rhthyms.

Albums: *Let Them Eat Bingo* (1990), *Excursion On The Version* (1991).

Beautiful South

This intriguing UK pop and rock combo were built out of the ashes of the commercially successful Housemartins. The line-up features both Paul Heaton (b. 9 May 1962, Birkenhead, Merseyside, England; vocals) and drummer David Hemmingway (also vocals) from Hull's self-proclaimed 'Fourth Best Band'. In reference to their previous dour Northern image Heaton sarcastically named his new band Beautiful South, recruiting Sean Welch (bass), Briana Corrigan (vocals, ex-Anthill Runaways), former Housemartins roadie David Stead (drums), and his new co-writer David Rotheray (guitar). Continuing an association with Go! Discs, their first single was the ballad 'Song For Whoever' which gave them instant chart success. After the rejection of the original sleeve concept for their debut album (a suicidal girl with gun in her mouth), *Welcome To The Beautiful South* emerged in October 1989 to an encouraging critical reception. The single 'A Little Time' became their first UK number 1 the following year. Built on a bitter duet between Corrigan and Hemmingway, it was aided by a memorable knife twisting domestic visual which won The Best Music Video award at the 1991 BRIT awards. Lyrically, Heaton had honed his songwriting to a more salubrious style which allowed the twists and ironies to develop more fully: 'I find it difficult to write straightforward optimistic love songs...I throw in a row, a fight, get a few knives out...'. Recent offerings such as 'Old Red Eyes Is Back', a picturesque but pathetic tale of the decline and death of a drinker, continue to reveal him as a lyricist able to deal with emotive subjects in an intelligent and considered manner.

Albums: *Welcome To The Beautiful South* (1989), *Choke* (1990), *0898* (1992).

BEF

The BEF (or British Electric Foundation) was a UK duo formed by ex-Human League members Martyn Ware (b. 19 May 1956) and Ian Craig Marsh (b. 11 November 1956). The first in the *Music Of Quality And Distinction* series arrived in 1982, featuring a series of guest artists covering songs of their own selection. Among them were Gary Glitter, Tina Turner, Billy McKenzie (ex-Associates) and Sandie Shaw. The concept was innovative and achieved minor commercial success, but the project was abandoned when Ware and Marsh reunited with vocalist Glenn Gregory in their other incarnation, Heaven 17. When that group ended a lucrative career in production ensued, notably with Terence Trent

D'Arby and Tina Turner. It was only in 1991 that they managed to burrow through the legal contracts binding the second volume's artists and repeat the formula. This time the album was more cohesive, consisting entirely of soul covers. It saw the return of Tina Turner, alongside Terence Trent D'Arby (his version of Bob Dylan's 'Its Alright Ma, I'm Only Bleeding' was approached as Otis Redding might have sung it), Chaka Khan, Billy Preston, and Mavis Staples, among others. Most surprising of all was the appearance of Billy McKenzie's version of Deniece Williams' 'Free'. Another unexpected facet of the recordings was the duo's use of traditional instruments and a backing band.

Albums: *Music Of Quality And Distinction Volume 1* (1982), *Music Of Quality And Distinction Volume 2* (1991).

Beggars Banquet Records

This independent UK record label was formed during the punk explosion of 1977. The label's first release was 'Shadow' by the Lurkers, Britain's three-chord answer to the Ramones. Signing the Doll, Johnny G., Jeff 'Duffo' Duff and Tubeway Army (Gary Numan) the same year, it was the latter's 'Are Friends Electric' that ensured Beggars Banquet's long-term future. This reached the number 1 spot in May 1979, during a 16-week residency in the UK singles charts. Tubeway Army, and lead vocalist Numan in particular, provided the main source of income for the label during the late 70s and early 80s. This allowed Beggars Banquet to sign a variety of mainly 'indie' bands and encourage their development. The label's roster subsequently included Goat, Bauhaus, the Fall, Icicle Works, Adult Net, Go-Betweens, Gene Loves Jezebel, Fields Of The Nephilim and Freeez.

Belle Stars

A splinter group from the Two-Tone influenced Bodysnatchers, this all-female septet from the UK comprised Sarah-Jane Owen (guitar), Miranda Joyce (saxophone), Judy Parsons (drums) and Jennie McKeown (bass). Signed by the independent Stiff Records in 1981, they charted the following year with remakes of the Dixie Cups' 'Iko Iko' and Shirley Ellis's 'The Clapping Song'. Unable to sustain a long term commercial appeal and subject to changing personnel, they nevertheless produced one memorable smash hit with 'Sign Of The Times', a catchy pop tune with a spoken word section reminiscent of the great, girl group sound of the mid-60s.

Album: *The Belle Stars* (1983).

Beloved

Initially known in 1983 as the Journey Through and

comprising Jon Marsh, Guy Gousden and Tim Havard, the Beloved fell into place a year later when Cambridge University student Steve Waddington joined on guitar. Tentative stabs at heavy psychedelia evolved into a more pop orientated formula by the mid-80s, with the Beloved's dark, danceable sounds often being compared to New Order and garnering much attention in Europe. It was not until 1988, however, that they started living up to their name: Waddington and Marsh, heavily infuenced by the nascent 'rave' scene in London at that time, split from Gousden and Havard and started forging their own path. Unshackled from the confines of a four-cornered set-up, the revitalized duo dived into the deep end of the exploding dance movement, subsequently breaking into commercial waters with the ambient textures of 'Sun Rising'. The *Happiness* album, backed by Marsh and Waddington's enthusiastic chatter concerning the virtues of floatation tanks and hallucinogenic substances, perfectly embodied the tripped-out mood of the times and sealed the Beloved's fashionable success in worldwide territories.

Albums: *Happiness* (1990), *Blissed Out* (remix of *Happiness* 1990).

Benny Profane

This late 80s Liverpool, England pop combo featured Dave Jackson (vocals), Joseph McKechnie (guitar/drums), Robin Surtees (guitar), and Becky Stringer (bass). The permanent drummer had been Frank Sparks (ex-Ex Post Facto) but when he left both Roger Sinek and Dave Brown helped out on the band's debut album. Jackson, Stringer and Peter Baker, who filled in as an additional member providing organ, had all previously played in the Room. In many ways they were effectively an update of that commercially overlooked group, though perhaps a little more parochial. The new member McKechnie was rescued from layout duties for the Merseyside health magazine *Who Cares?* They took their name from a character in Thomas Pynchon's book, *V*, and their first single, 'Where Is Pig', came from his dialogue in the novel. A succession of low-key gigs at Monroes pub in Liverpool gave them a high local profile. However, they never repeated the success of the other local group who made the venue their home, the La's.

Albums: *Trapdoor Swing* (1989), *Dunbluck Charm* (1990).

Berlin

This US band from Los Angeles was formed in the summer of 1979 as a new wave/electro pop group. The founding members were John Crawford (bass/synthesizer, ex-Videos) with Terri Nunn (vocals), Virginia McCalino (vocals), Jo Julian (synthesizer), Chris Velasco (guitar) and Dan Van Patten (drums, ex-Barbies). They signed to IRS in the USA, but managed only one single before they broke up in 1981. However, Crawford and Nunn formed a new band almost immediately with David Diamond (guitars), Rick Olsen (guitar), Matt Reid (keyboards) and Rod Learned (drums). Their first recording was the 1983 mini-album *Pleasure Victim* (not released in the UK) followed by the full long player *Love Life* the following year. They gained a US Top 30 hit in April 1984 with 'No More Words', before dropping down to a three piece of Crawford, Nunn and Rob Brill on drums the following year. By 1986 they had a number 1 hit on both sides of the Atlantic with a song they would become almost exclusively associated with, 'Take My Breath Away'. It was the theme song to the highly lucrative movie *Top Gun*, and had been produced and co-written by veteran producer Giorgio Moroder. Although follow-up singles fared less well, 'Breath...' has proved to be a perennial favourite re-entering the charts in 1988 and going to the UK Top 3 on re-issue in 1990 as a result of its use in television car commercials

Albums: *Love Life* (1984), *Count Three And Pray* (1987).

Berry, Heidi

An American singer and songwriter who has lived in London since childhood, Berry saw the first of her compositions released on Creation in 1987 with the mini-album *Firefly*. Numerous members of the Creation fold were used as backing musicians, notably Martin Duffy (Felt) on keyboards. Two years later the line-up also included her brother Christopher on acoustic guitar, and Rocky Holman on piano and synthesizer. However, after appearing on This Mortal Coil's *Blood*, singing a version of Rodney Crowell's 'Til I Gain Control Again', she switched to 4AD Records. The nucleus of Christopher Berry and Holman were retained for the subsequent *Love*, with additional contributions from Terry Bickers and Laurence O'Keefe (Levitation), Martin McCarrick (Siouxsie And The Banshees), Lol Coxhill and Ian Kearey (Blue Aeroplanes). The original compositions were augmented by a cover of Bob Mould's 'Up In The Air'.

Albums: *Firefly* (1987), *Below The Waves* (1989), *Love* (1991).

Beserkley Records

Independent record label founded in 1973 in Berkeley, California, USA, by Matthew King Kaufman, formerly of Baltimore, Maryland. Kaufman's initial goal was to revive the 45 rpm single in an era when the album had taken over as the primary format for record sales. His first signing was

Earthquake, a band from the East Bay area of the San Francisco region, whose first single was a cover of the Easybeats hit, 'Friday On My Mind'. The label continued to release only singles for three years. Kaufman signed a brief distribution deal with the short-lived Playboy Records in the US and Jonathan King's UK Records in England. Ultimately, Beserkley signed three other acts that comprised the bulk of its catalogue: the eccentric Jonathan Richman And The Modern Lovers, mainstream pop-rockers Greg Kihn and popsters the Rubinoos. Kihn became the label's largest seller, logging a number 2 US single with 'Jeopardy' in 1983, although the label and its artists were consistently more popular in Europe, where it featured a larger roster of talent, including the Smirks and the Tyla Gang (see Sean Tyla). By the mid-80s Earthquake had disbanded, the Rubinoos had sued Kaufman for mismanagement, and Kihn and Richman had signed to other labels, forcing Kaufman to fold the label. In 1990 he was considering reviving it but as yet no new releases have appeared.
Compilation: *Beserkeley Chartbusters Volume One* (1979).

Bethnal

Formed in London in 1972, Bethnal found themselves caught up in the 'new wave' of 1977 and were automatically re-defined as punk so as not to be ignored. They quickly severed their connection with the movement in 1978, when the press and media abandoned punk, describing it as 'dead'. Composed of George Csapo (vocals/keyboards/violin), Pete Dowling (drums), Nick Michaels (guitar) and Everton Williams (bass), they built up a large following through intense live gigging, and the end of 1977 saw them sign to Vertigo Records. Their debut came with 'The Fiddler', a live recording given away throughout their December UK tour. It was quickly followed by the release of 'We Gotta Get Out Of This Place', a cover of the classic Animals track. After a further single 'Don't Do It', they participated in the Reading Festival and continued a heavy gig schedule in preparation for the release of *Crash Landing*. It was recorded at Abbey Road Studios under the guidance of Pete Townshend as 'musical director'. Gaining much critical acclaim, the album marked a very creative period for Bethnal, displaying great originality and proficiency. Even so, the anticipated success did not arrive and in 1979 they left Vertigo and looked for a new contract. For almost a year they remained unsigned until tension within the band caused the final split in 1980.
Albums: *Dangerous Times* (1978), *Crash Landing* (1978).

Bevis Frond

Mistakenly believed to be a group, the Bevis Frond is

actually just one person - Nick Saloman. Influenced by Jimi Hendrix and Cream, Saloman formed the Bevis Frond Museum while still at school. The group disbanded and after a period playing acoustic sets in the Walthamstow area of London area he formed The Von Trap Family, later known as Room 13. In 1982, Saloman was seriously hurt in a motor-cycle accident. He used the money he received in compensation to record *Miasma* in his bedroom and it quickly became a collectors' item. *Pulsebeat* magazine referred to the tracks as 'like fireworks for inside your head.' Saloman released *Inner Marshland* and *Triptych* on his own Woronzow Records and his long psychedelic guitar workouts mapped out a style that was shamelessly archaic but appealing. London's Reckless Records re-released his first three albums and in 1988 released *Bevis Through The Looking Glass* and, a year later, *The Auntie Winnie Album*. Saloman's brand of raw, imaginative blues guitar drew many converts and *Any Gas Faster*, recorded in better-equipped studios, was widely lauded. *Rolling Stone* magazine said of it: 'With so much modern psychedelia cheapened by cliche or nostalgia, the Bevis Frond is the actual out-there item.' In 1991 Saloman released a double set, *New River Head*, on his own Woronzow Records, distributed in the USA by Reckless. As a tireless believer in the need for communication, he set up an underground magazine, *Ptolemaic Terrascope*, in the late 80s and like Saloman's music, it is a loyal correspondent of the UK psychedelic scene.
Albums: *Miasma* (1986), *Inner Marshland* (1987), *Triptych* (1988), *Bevis Through The Looking Glass* (1988), *The Aunty Winnie Album* (1989), *Any Gas Faster* (1990), *New River Head* (1991). Compilation: *A Gathering Of Fronds* (1992).

Beyond

Formed in Derby, England in 1988 the band consists of John Whitby (vocals), Andy Gatford (guitar), Jim Kersey (bass) and Neil Cooper (drums). Quickly gaining popularity on the live club circuit and obtaining a publishing contract with Island Music they attracted the attention of EMI Records thanks to some early demos. The band initially signed a year-long development arrangement with the label during which time they released two singles on the small independent Big Cat Records label. These were EP *Manic Sound Picnic* and the single 'No Excuse' both released in 1990 The following year the band released their first single, 'One Step Too Far', for EMI. This was quickly followed by the release of 'Empire' on the relaunched EMI subsidiary Harvest Records. The band's debut *Crawl* was also released on the same label in 1991. A cross between Janes Addiction, Voivod and Faith No More the album for some may be an amalgamation of too many musical styles but

was still well received by both the music press and the public. In support of the album they toured the UK and Europe with the American act Living Color and to coincide with the tour the Beyond released an EP *Raging*.
Album: *Crawl* (1991).

B-52's

B-52's

The quirky appearance, stage antics and lyrical content of the B-52's belie a formidable musical ability, as the band's rhythmically perfect pop songs show many influences, including 50s' rock 'n' roll, punk and funk. However, it was the late 70s' new-wave music fans that took them to their hearts. The group were formed in Athens, Georgia, USA in 1976 and took their name from the bouffant hairstyle worn by Kate Pierson (b. 27 April 1948, Weehawken, New Jersey, USA; organ/vocals) and Cindy Wilson (b. 28 February 1957, Athens, Georgia, USA; guitar/vocals). The line-up was completed by Cindy's brother Ricky (b. 19 March 1953, Athens, Georgia, USA; guitar), Fred Schneider (b. 1 July 1951, Newark, Georgia, USA; keyboards/vocals) and Keith Strickland (b. 26 October 1953, Athens, Georgia, USA; drums). The lyrically bizarre 'Rock Lobster' was originally a private pressing of 2,000 copies and came to the notice of the perceptive Chris Blackwell, who signed them to Island Records in the UK. The debut *B-52's* became a strong seller and established the band as a highly regarded unit with a particularly strong following on the American campus circuit during the early 80s. Their anthem 'Rock Lobster' became a belated US hit in 1980 and they received John Lennon's seal of approval that year as his favourite band. Their subsequent albums continued to make the group hard to categorize, and consequently they remained a popular cult band. Their music is: polyrhythmic Captain Beefheart meeting 50s' rock with punkish energy. Ricky Wilson died of cancer in 1986 and the band released no new work until their career reached a commercial peak in 1989 bringing with it a new generation of fans, with the powerful

hit single 'Love Shack' and its superb accompanying video. *Cosmic Thing* showed that the band had not lost their touch and they remain true originals by blending a number of non-original styles.
Albums: *B-52's* (1979), *Wild Planet* (1980), *Party Mix!* (1981 - remix of the first two albums), *Mesopotamia* (1982), *Whammy!* (1983), *Bouncing Off The Satellites* (1986), *Cosmic Thing* (1989), *Party Mix-Mesopotamia* (1991), *Good Stuff* (1992). Compilation: *Best Of the B-52's: Dance This Mess Around* (1990).

Bible

This Norwich, UK band's debut single 'Gracelands', was a classy pop song issued in 1986, as was the follow-up 'Mahalia' (a tribute to the gospel vocalist Mahalia Jackson). By the time Chrysalis had signed the Bible - Boo Hewerdine (vocals/guitar), Tony Shepherd (keyboards/percussion), Dave Larcombe (drums) and Leroy Lendor (bass) - the group already had an album's worth of well-crafted songs in *Walking The Ghost Back Home*. Chrysalis duly reissued 'Gracelands' in early 1987, but it eluded the charts, and the band spent the year recording a second album. Released in May 1988, *Eureka* shared the melodic quality of the Bible's debut, but neither single, 'Crystal Palace' in April and 'Honey Be Good' in September, made much impression. Desperate for the success they deserved, the band tried revamping 'Gracelands' and when that failed, reissued 'Honey Be Good'. A compilation release in late 1989, *The Best Of The Bible*, signalled the end of the band's association with their label.
Albums: *Walking The Ghost Back Home* (1986), *Eureka* (1988). Compilation: *The Best Of The Bible* (1989). Solo albums: Boo Hewerdine with Darden Smith *Evidence* (1989), *Ignorance* (1992).

Biff Bang Pow

Biff Bang Pow - a name derived from a song by 60s cult group the Creation - is an outlet for the musical aspirations of Alan McGee, the motivating force behind Creation Records, one of the UK's most innovative independent outlets. The group also featured business partner Dick Green (guitar) and despite its part-time nature, has completed several excellent releases, including the neo-psychedelic singles, '50 Year Of Fun' (1984) and 'Love's Going Out Of Fashion' (1986). *Pass The Paintbrush Honey* and *The Girl Who Runs The Beat Hotel* offered idiosyncratic, and often contrasting, views of pop, while *Love Is Forever* showed the influence of Neil Young, notably on 'Ice Cream Machine'. McGee's interest in contemporary styles in turn inspired *The Acid House Album*.
Albums: *Pass The Paintbrush Honey* (1985), *The Girl Who Lives At The Beat Hotel* (1987), *Love Is Forever* (1988), *The Acid House Album* (1989).

Big Audio Dynamite

After guitarist Mick Jones (b. 26 June 1955, Brixton, London, England) was fired from the Clash in 1984 he formed an ill-fated group with Topper Headon before linking up with ex-Roxy club disc jockey and film-maker Don Letts to form Big Audio Dynamite (or BAD, as they were commonly known). With Jones (guitar), Letts (keyboards and effects), they completed the line-up with Dan Donovan, son of famed photographer Terence Donovan (keyboards), Leo Williams (bass) and Greg Roberts (drums). *This Is Big Audio Dynamite* proved to be a natural progression from tracks like 'Inoculated City' on *Combat Rock*, the last Clash album that featured Jones, with cut-up funk spiced with sampled sounds (the first time this technique has been used). The follow-up album featured writing contributions from Joe Strummer, who happened to meet the band while they were recording in Soho, London. The group continued to record but hit their first crisis in 1988 when Jones came close to death from pneumonia, which caused a delay in the release of *Megatop Phoenix*. This in turn led to the break-up of the band and by 1990 and the *Kool-Aid*, Jones had assembled a completely new line-up (BAD II) featuring Nick Hawkins (guitar), Gary Stonedage (bass) and Chris Kavanagh (ex-Sigue Sigue Sputnik; drums). Disc jockey Zonka was also drafted in to provide live 'scratching' and mixing. Jones also contributed to the *Flashback* soundtrack and 'Good Morning Britain' single from Aztec Camera. Meanwhile he aroused disdain, not least from former colleagues, by insisting on putting a BAD track on the b-side to the posthumous Clash number 1 'Should I Stay Or Should I Go'. Donovan proved to be no stranger to controversy either, having married and separated from Eighth Wonder singer and actress Patsy Kensit. He went on to join the reformed Sigue Sigue Sputnik.
Albums: *This Is Big Audio Dynamite* (1985), *No. 10 Upping Street* (1986), *Tighten Up Vol. 88* (1988), *Megatop Phoenix* (1989), as B.A.D. *Kool-Aid* (1990), as BAD II *The Globe* (1991).

Big F

This Los Angeles, USA trio comprised Mark Christian (guitar), John Shreve (bass/vocals) and Rob Donin (drums). They unleashed a 'mind-blowing wall of noise', dominated by crashing drums and screeching feedback, while vocalist Shreve screamed incessantly. Psychedelia, Jimi Hendrix, the Stooges, the Cult and *avant garde* influences appear as reference points, but few bands will ever match the intensity and sheer energy generated by this outfit.
Album: *The Big F* (1990).

Big Flame

This Manchester trio featuring Alan Brown, David Brown and Gregory O'Keefe were perhaps the finest offering on the independent Ron Johnson label. Big Flame's uncompromising aural assault stemmed from a jagged, staccato guitar attack and offbeat feel, first heard on the EP *Sink* (on the Plaque label) in April 1984. Almost a year later, their first Ron Johnson EP *Rigour*, surfaced, followed in September by *Tough! Why Popstars Can't Dance*. The band were featured on the *New Musical Express C86* compilation of new talent, showcasing the brief 'New Way (Quick Wash And Brush Up With Liberation Theology)'. A retrospective 10-inch EP, *Two Can Guru* preceded a new EP, *Cubist Pop Manifesto*. The latter brought Big Flame critical, if not commercial support. But after a 12-inch maxi-EP, *XPQWRTZ* (a co-release with German label, Constrictor), the band broke up, with ex-members forming Great Leap Forwards.

Big In Japan

For a band that issued very little vinyl, Big In Japan received strong critical acclaim. The main reason for this interest was their line-up: Jayne Casey (vocals; later with Pink Industry/Military), Bill Drummond (guitar; later formed Lori And The Chameleons, ran the Zoo label, released a solo album and comprised half of the KLF), Dave Balfe (bass; worked with Drummond in Lori And The Chameleons, was later enrolled as keyboard player in the Teardrop Explodes and then founded the Food label), Budgie (drums; later briefly with the Slits and Siouxsie And The Banshees), Ian Broudie (guitar; who subsequently joined the Original Mirrors before carving out a successful career as producer, and later enjoyed a hit under the guise of the Lightning Seeds) and finally Holly on bass. After two country-styled singles, Holly joined Frankie Goes To Hollywood and is now the solo artist, Holly Johnson. On the b-side of their 1977 self-titled debut single was a track from the Chuddy Nuddies, who turned out to be the Yachts. After Big In Japan split, Drummond used four of their tracks for the first Zoo single, *From Y To Z And Never Again*, which stands as a delightfully quirky period piece. The remaining members of Big In Japan (vocalist Ken Ward and drummer Phil Allen) failed to emulate the success of their fellow travellers.

Birthday Party

One of the most creative and inspiring 'alternative' acts of the 80s, this Australian outfit had its roots in the new wave band Boys Next Door. After one album, the band relocated to London and switched names. In addition to featuring the embryonic genius of Nick Cave (vocals), their ranks were swelled by Roland S. Howard (ex-Obsessions, Young Charlatans; guitar), Mick Harvey (guitar, drums, organ, piano), Tracy Pew (bass) and Phil Calvert (drums). They chose the newly launched 4AD offshoot of Beggars Banquet as their new home, and made their debut with the impressive 'Fiend Catcher'. Music critics and BBC disc jockey John Peel became early and long-serving converts to the band's intense post-punk surges. Back in Australia, they recorded their first album, a transitional piece which nevertheless captured some fine aggressive rock statements. Their finest recording, however, was 'Release The Bats'. John Peel elected it the best record of 1981, though its subject matter unwittingly tied the band in with the emerging 'Gothic' subculture populated by Bauhaus and Sex Gang Children. As Pew was imprisoned for three months for drink-driving offences, Barry Adamson (ex-Magazine), Roland Howard's brother Harry and Chris Walsh helped out on the recording of the follow-up, and the band's increasingly torrid live shows. After collaborating with the Go-Betweens on the one-off single 'After The Fireworks' as the Tuf Monks, they shifted to Berlin to escape the constant exposure and expectations of them in the UK. Calvert was dropped (moving on to Psychedelic Furs), while the four remaining members moved on to collaborative projects with Lydia Lunch and Einsturzende Neubaten amongst others. They had already recorded a joint 12-inch, 'Drunk On The Pope's Blood', with Lunch, and Howard featured on much of her future output. When Harvey left in the summer of 1983, the band seemed set to fulfill their solo careers, even though he was temporarily replaced on drums by Des Heffner. However, after a final gig in Melbourne, Australia in June the band called it a day. Howard went on to join Crime And The City Solution alongside his brother and Harvey, who also continued in Cave's solo band the Bad Seeds.

Albums: *Prayers On Fire* (1981), *Junkyard* (1982), *The Bad Seed/Mutiny* (1989), *Hee-Haw* (1989).

Black Flag

Formed in 1977 in Los Angeles, California, Black Flag rose to become one of America's leading hardcore groups. The initial line-up - Keith Morris (vocals), Greg Ginn (guitar), Chuck Dukowski (bass) and Brian Migdol (drums) - completed the *Nervous Breakdown* EP in 1978, but the following year Morris left to form the Circle Jerks. Several members would join and leave before Henry Rollins (vocals), Dez Cadenza (guitar) and Robo (drums) joined Ginn and Dukowski for *Damaged*, the group's first full-length album. Originally scheduled for release by MCA, the company withdrew support, citing outrageous content, and the set appeared on the quintet's own label, SST. This prolific outlet has not only issued every subsequent Black Flag recording, but boasts a catalogue which includes Hüsker Dü, Sonic Youth, the Minutemen, the Meat Puppets and Dinosaur Jr. Administered by Ginn and Dukowski, the latter of whom left the group to concentrate his efforts more fully, the company has become one of America's leading, and most influential, independents. The former musician continued to lead Black Flag in tandem with Rollins, and although its rhythm section was still the subject of change, the music's power remained undiminished. Pivotal albums included *My War* and *In My Head* while their diversity was showcased on *Family Man*, which contrasted a side of Rollins'poetry with four excellent instrumentals. However, the group split up in 1986 following the release of a compulsive live set, *Who's Got The 10 1/2?*, following which Ginn switched his attentions to labelmates Gone.

Albums: *Damaged* (1981), *My War* (1984), *Family Man* (1984), *Slip It In* (1984), *Live '84* (1985), *Loose Nut* (1985), *In My Head* (1985), *Who's Got The 10 1/2?* (1986). Compilations: *Everything Went Black* (1983), *Wasted...Again* (1988), *The First Four Years* (1989).

Blake Babies

This US trio from Boston, Massachusetts, comprise Julianna Hatfield (bass/vocals), John Strohm (guitar/vocals) and Freda Love (drums). As part of a succession of groups to have emerged from a healthy rock scene in the Boston area in the late 80s/early 90s, Blake Babies have been able to mature slowly, showing signs of a major breakthrough in early 1992. Their debut *Nicely Nicely* was released on the group's own Chewbud label and the follow up, a mini-album, *Slow Learner* was released on Billy Bragg's re-activated Utility label. Signed to the North Carolina, Mammoth label *Earwig* and *Sunburn* consolidated the praise garnered from the music press, often drawing comparisons with fellow Bostonions, the Lemonheads and Buffalo Tom. The release of the EP *Rosy Jack World*, coupled with sell-out dates on a UK visit early in 1992 promises a bright future for the group.

Albums: *Nicely Nicely* (1988), *Slow Learner* (1989), *Earwig* (1990), *Sunburn* (1990).

Blancmange

This UK electro-pop duo featured Neil Arthur (b. 15 June 1958, Lancashire, England; vocals/guitar) and Steven Luscombe (b. 29 October 1954; keyboards). After debuting with an EP *Irene And Mavis*, they were invited by disc jockey/entrepreneur Stevo to appear on his influential 1981 Some Bizzare compilation. This led to a contract with London Records and a sythesizer-based album, *Happy Families*, which spawned two Top 10 singles, 'Living On The Ceiling' and 'Blind Vision'. Ambitiously eclectic at times, Blancmange employed orchestration and raga influences on their second album *Mange Tout* and enjoyed an unlikely hit with a cover of Abba's 'The Day Before You Came'. By 1985, the Blancmange experiment had effectively run its course and after a final album *Believe You Me*, Luscombe and Arthur went their separate ways.

Albums: *Happy Families* (1982), *Mange Tout* (1984), *Believe You Me* (1985).

Bleach

Brothers Neil (b. 14 September 1965, Ipswich, Suffolk, England; guitar) and Nick Singleton (b. 2 February 1968, Ipswich, Suffolk, England; bass) acted as catalysts for Bleach when, in July 1989, they were joined by Steve Scott (b. 29 November 1963, Norwich, Norfolk, England; drums) and the initially reluctant vocalist, Salli Carson (b. 6 October 1966, Yorkshire, England). Within a year they had stamped their mark on the UK Independent pop sector with the EP *Eclipse* - so called because it was actually recorded during an eclipse of the sun - on which their original twisted, spikey guitar sound garnered immediate praise from the national music press. The follow-up EP *Snag* boasted similarly tortured characteristics six months later, 'Dipping' emerging as one of the stand-out tracks. Exhaustive tours of Britain eventually warranted a compilation of the singles to continue the momentum.

Compilation: *Bleach* (1991).

Blegvad, Peter

b. 1951, New York City, New York, USA. Blegvad is a playful and witty songwriter and singer who has built up a cult following in the UK and the USA. Moving to England in the early 70s, he formed Slapp Happy with singer Dagmar Krause and keyboard player Anthony Moore. Described by one critic as a 'mutant cabaret group', they made two albums for Virgin and two more with *avant garde* band Henry Cow. When that group split in 1977, Blegvad worked briefly with the Art Bears before returning to New York. There he performed with John Zorn, the Ambitious Lovers and from 1985-87 Anton Fier's 'supergroup' the Golden Palaminos. Blegvad's solo recording career began in the mid-80s, when he made three albums for Virgin, with Andy Partridge of XTC producing *The Naked Shakespeare*. After making *Downtime* for *avant garde* label Recommended, Blegvad signed to Silvertone where Palaminos colleague Chris Blamey co-produced *King Strut*. Guest artists on the album included Syd Straw (vocals) and Danny Thompson (bass). Blegvad also began to contribute a weekly cartoon strip to the London newspaper *The Independent On Sunday*, entitled *Leviathan,* which displayed the same world-weary wit as his songwriting.

Albums: *The Naked Shakespeare* (1983), *Knights Like This* (1985), *Kew Rhone* (1986), *Downtime* (1988), *King Strut & Other Stories* (1991).

Blondie

Blondie was formed in New York City in 1974 when Debbie Harry (b. 1 July 1945, Miami, Florida, USA; vocals), Chris Stein (b. 5 January 1950, Brooklyn, New York, USA; guitar), Fred Smith (bass) and Bill O'Connor (drums) abandoned the revivalist Stilettos for an independent musical direction. Backing vocalists Julie and Jackie, then Tish and Snookie, augmented the new group's early line-up, but progress was undermined by the departure of Smith for Television and the loss of O'Connor. Newcomers James Destri (b. 13 April 1954; keyboards), Gary Valentine (bass) and Clement Burke (b. 24 November 1955, New York, USA; drums) joined Harry and Stein in a reshaped unit which secured a recording deal through the aegis of producer Richard Gottehrer. Originally released on the Private Stock label, *Blondie* was indebted to both contemporary punk and 60s' girl groups, adeptly combining melody with purpose. Although not a runaway commercial success, the album did engender interest, particularly in the UK, where the group became highly popular. Internal disputes resulted in the departure of Gary Valentine, but the arrival of Frank Infante (guitar) and Nigel Harrison (b. Princes Risborough, Buckinghamshire, England; bass) triggered the group's most consistent period. Having freed themselves from the restrictions of Private Stock and signed to Chrysalis Records, *Plastic Letters* contained two UK Top 10 hits in 'Denis' and '(I'm Always Touched By Your) Presence Dear' while *Parallel Lines*, produced by pop svengali Mike Chapman, included the chart-topping 'Heart Of Glass' and 'Sunday Girl' (both 1979). Although creatively uneven, *Eat To The Beat* signalled Blondie's dalliance with disco and the set spawned three highly-successful singles in 'Union City Blue', 'Atomic' and 'Call Me'. The last-named, culled from the soundtrack of *American Gigolo* and produced by Giorgio Moroder, reached number 1 in both the UK and US. *Autoamerican* provided two further US chart toppers in 'The Tide Is High' and 'Rapture' while the former song, originally recorded by reggae group the Paragons, reached the same position in Britain. However, despite this commercial ascendancy, Blondie was beset by internal difficulties as the media increasingly focused on their photogenic lead singer. The distinction between the group's name and Harry's persona became increasingly blurred, although a sense of distance between the two was created with the release of her solo album, *Koo Koo. The Hunter*, a generally disappointing set which Debbie completed under duress, became Blondie's final recording, their tenure ending when Stein's ill-health brought an attendant tour to a premature end.

The guitarist was suffering from the genetic disease pemphigus and between 1983-85, both he and Debbie Harry absented themselves from full-time performing. The latter then resumed her solo career, while former colleague Burke joined the Eurythmics. Albums: *Blondie* (1977), *Plastic Letters* (1978), *Parallel Lines* (1978), *Eat To The Beat* (1979), *Autoamerican* (1980), *The Hunter* (1982). Compilations: *The Best Of Blondie* (1981), *Once More Into The Bleach* (1988, contains remixes and rare cuts), *The Complete Picture - The Very Best Of Deborah Harry And Blondie* (1991).

Blood On The Saddle

This Los Angeles group was a leading light of the city's 'cowpunk' movement of the mid-80s, which blended elements of country, rockabilly and US hardcore. Greg Davis (guitar/vocals), Ron Botelho (bass) and Hermann Senac (drums/vocals) founded the unit in April 1983, but within months the line-up had been augmented by Annette Zilinskas (vocals), formerly of the Bangles. The acclaimed *Blood On The Saddle* was released the following year, but critical approbation was not matched by commercial success. A second set, *Poison Love*, was undermined by low-key distribution, but *Fresh Blood*, issued by the influential SST label, achieved a much higher profile. The album confirmed the group's energetic style, but persistent public indifference has undermined an early confidence.
Albums: *Blood On The Saddle* (1984), *Poison Love* (1986), *Fresh Blood* (1987).

Blow Monkeys

Led by the opinionated Dr. Robert (b. Bruce Robert Howard, 2 May 1961, Norfolk, England), the Blow Monkeys took their name from Australian slang for Aboriginal didgeriedoo players, something Robert picked up while living down under as a teenager. The nickname Doctor was pinned on him at boarding school because he was seen as a sympathetic listener. Before the Blow Monkeys began in the early 80s, he also had a spell at Norwich City Football Club, and dabbled in pop journalism. The other constituent elements of the band are Tony Kiley (b. 16 February 1962) and Mick Anger (b. 2 July 1957). They started recording for RCA in 1984 but singles such as 'Man From Russia', 'Atomic Lullaby' and 'Forbidden Fruit' made no headway in the charts. The band finally broke through in 1986 with the jazz tinged 'Digging Your Scene', one of the earliest songs about AIDS. The following January they had their biggest hit with 'It Doesn't Have To Be This Way'. Come May, this strongly socialist and vehemently anti-Thatcher band found their latest single, '(Celebrate) The Day After You', banned from the airwaves by the BBC until the General Election was over. The record also featured the voice of Curtis

Mayfield. Although reasonably successful, the band were sent a financial lifeline by contributing the track 'You Don't Own Me' to the hugely successful *Dirty Dancing* soundtrack. A series of minor hits followed, and 1989 opened with Doctor Robert recording a duet (under his own name) with soul singer Kym Mazelle. 'Wait' went into the UK Top 10, and the year ended with 'Slaves No More' back with the Monkeys, also featuring the vocal prowess of Sylvia Tella. Their most recent hit was 1990's 'Springtime For The World'.
Albums: *Limping For A Generation* (1984), *Animal Magic* (1986), *She Was Only A Grocer's Daughter* (1987), *Whoops There Goes The Neighbourhood* (1989), *Choices* (1989).

Blow Up

This UK Brighton-based group were fronted by former 14 Iced Bears member Nick Roughley (vocals), alongside Alan Stirner (guitar), Aziz Hashmix (bass) and Chris Window (drums), seemed ideal candidates for Creation Records. A blend of 60s influences and a strong melodic content dominated their debut for the label, 'Good For Me' (1987), backed on the 12-inch edition by two obscure psychedelic cover versions. The follow-up single, 'Pool Valley' (the name of Brighton's bus depot) trod a more mainstream brand of guitar rock, but Stirner soon left to join local peers Whirl, while Window also departed. By the time guitarist Justin Spear and drummer Paul Reeves were drafted in, relations with Creation had soured, so Blow Up moved to the short-lived Ediesta label for 'Forever Holiday', released in October 1988. When Ediesta folded, the band reissued the track on the veteran independent label, Cherry Red. In early 1990, the group finally delivered an album, *In Watermelon Sugar* (a reference to the novel by American west coast writer, Richard Brautigan), together with another single, 'One World Waiting'. Harder than previous efforts, the album matured with every listen. Blow Up maintained a low profile before returning a year later with 'World'. As a preview of the second album, *Amazon Eargasm* (issued that summer), the song perfectly illustrated their increasing confidence, both as songwriters and musicians.
Albums: *Rollercoaster* (1988), *In Watermelon Sugar* (1990), *Amazon Eargasm* (1991).

Blue Aeroplanes

The unlikely answer to the Velvet Underground, the Blue Aeroplanes formed in Bristol, England, have endured endless line-up changes since their inception in the early 80s. Their original aim, a desire to mix rock and poetry and to involve a large number of musicians in an almost communal manner, has remained. The nucleus of the band has always revolved around deadpan vocalist Gerard Langley, his brother John (drums/percussion), Nick Jacobs (guitar), Dave Chapman (multi-instrumentalist) and (aping the Velvets) dancer Wojtek Dmochowski. Along the way, individuals like Angelo Bruschini (guitar/bass/organ), John Stapleton (tapes), Ruth Coltrane (bass/mandolin), Ian Kearey (guitar/banjimer/harmonium), Rodney Allen (guitar), Simon Heathfield (bass) and Caroline Halcrow (guitar - who later left to pursue a solo career as Caroline Trettine) have all contributed to the Aeroplanes' melting pot. After a debut album for the Abstract label, *Bop Art*, in April 1984, the band signed with the fledgling Fire Records. Several well-received EPs followed - *Action Painting And Other Original Works* (1985), *Lover And Confidante And Other Stories Of Travel* and *Religion And Heartbreak* (March, 1986), followed by their second album *Tolerance* (October, 1986). The Aeroplanes' third album, *Spitting Out Miracles*, surfaced in 1987. All were characterized by Langley's monotone verse and a deluge of interesting instruments and sounds, albeit hinged around guitar. 'Veils Of Colour' (1988) coincided with *Night Tracks*, their February 1987 session for BBC Radio disc jockey, Janice Long. A double album, *Friendloverplane*, neatly concluded their time with Fire, compiling the Aeroplanes' progress to date. It was not until the start of the new decade that, following a stint supporting R.E.M. in the UK, the band re-emerged on the Ensign label with 'Jacket Hangs' in January 1990 and a new album, *Swagger*, the following month. Both suggested a more direct, straightforward approach, and this was confirmed with May's exploration into dance rock, *And Stones*. In 1991, an eight-strong line-up now comprising, Langley, Bruschini, Dmochowski, Allen, Paul Mulreany (drums - a former member of the Jazz Butcher), Andy McCreeth, Hazel Winter and Robin Key, released the roundly-acclaimed *Beatsongs*, co-produced by Elvis Costello and Larry Hirsch.

Albums: *Bop Art* (1984), *Tolerance* (1986), *Spitting Out Miracles* (1987), *Friendloverplane* (1988), *Swagger* (1990), *Beatsongs* (1991).

Bluebells

This Scottish quintet were formed in 1982, and originally comprised brothers David McCluskey (b. 13 January 1964; drums) and Ken McCluskey (b. 8 February 1962; vocals/harmonica), plus Robert 'Bobby Bluebell' Hodgens (b. 6 June 1959; vocals/guitar), Russell Irvine (guitar) and Lawrence Donegan (bass). The latter two were later replaced, respectively, by Craig Gannon (b. 30 July 1966) and Neal Baldwin. The group were fine exponents of the brand of 'jangly pop' emanating from Scotland in the early 80s alongside contemporaries, Orange Juice and Aztec Camera. Despite strong airplay on British radio, the inexplicable failure of 'Cath' to rise any further than number 62 in the UK chart in 1983 perplexed critics and fans, as did the similar fate that befell 'Sugar Bridge' that same year. The Bluebells did at last gain their deserved success in 1984 with the number 11 hit 'I'm Falling' and 'Young At Heart' which broached the Top 10, while their solitary album for the London label achieved Top 30 status. Riding on the wave of this success a re-issued 'Cath'/'She Will Always Be Waiting' belatedly broached the Top 40. After splitting, siblings Ken and David formed the McCluskey Brothers, releasing an album, *Aware Of All*, while Bobby formed Up and later worked with Paul Quinn out of Bourgie Bourgie. Craig Gannon stood-in, briefly, for the Smiths' bassist Andy Rourke who was having drug problems, then on Rouke's return, Gannon continued with the Smiths as second guitarist, subsequently joining the Adult Net.

Albums: *Sisters* (1984), *Second* (1992, early, previously unreleased recordings).

Blue Nile

A genuine oddity in a normal world, the Blue Nile formed in Glasgow, Scotland in 1981. Comprised of Paul Buchanan (b. Glasgow, Scotland; lead vocals/guitar/synthesizers), Robert Bell (b. Glasgow, Scotland; synthesizers) and Paul Joseph Moore (b. Glasgow, Scotland; piano/synthesizers), their debut single, 'I Love This Life' was recorded independently and subsequently picked up on by RSO Records, which promptly folded. Eventually, their demo-tapes found their way to hi-fi specialists Linn Products, so the company could test various types of music at their new cutting plant. In spite of their lack of experience in the record retail market, Linn immediately signed the band up to make 'A Walk Across The Rooftops', which came out in 1984 to vociferous praise. Suddenly, thanks to some gently emotive synthetics and an overall mood which seemed to revel in nocturnal atmospherics, the unsuspecting trio were thrust into the limelight. The term 'Paralysis through analysis' was coined as the Blue Nile pondered over the reasons for their success and, as a consequence, found themselves incapable of repeating the feat of the first album. Indeed, it was to be five years before the follow up, *Hats*, finally continued the shimmering legacy of its predecessor, whereupon the studio-bound collective took their first tentative steps into the live arena with enthusiastically-received shows in the USA and Britain before returning to the studio for another doubtlessly lengthy recording period.

Albums: *A Walk Across The Rooftops* (1984), *Hats* (1989).

Blue Orchids

This experimental pop combo were a spin-off from

their Manchester brethren the Fall. Una Baines (keyboards/vocals) and Martin Bramah (guitar/vocals) both found themselves outcasts from that band as the 80s dawned. They put together the Blue Orchids with Rick Goldstar (guitar), Steve Toyne (bass), and Joe Kin (drums), producing a sound that echoed the less esoteric moments of their former employer. Lyrics were usually spoken or half-sung, leaving a sinister and enticing set of songs which deserved a wider audience. These included their debut single 'The Flood', after which Ian Rogers became the first in a succession of drumming replacements. After the follow-up 'Work', the band embarked on a debut album. Toyne had left, leaving Bramah to fill in on bass, as their third drummer 'Toby' (ex-Ed Banger And The Nosebleeds) came into the line-up. *The Greatest Hit (Money Mountain)* was ambitious and slightly flawed. Mark Hellyer filled the vacant bass position, while Goldstraw departed, leaving Bramah to handle guitar duties on his own. 'Agents Of Chance' was the final Blue Orchids release for some time, before they returned with one 12-inch single, 'Sleepy Town', in 1985. Nick Marshall (drums) was the back-up to Baines and Bramah this time, on an effort produced by another ex-Fall man Tony Friel. Bramah moved on to Thirst, working, inevitably, with another Fall emigrate, Karl Burns. He would finally return to the Fall fold in 1989 to complete the cycle. However, the Blue Orchids reformed once more in 1991 with a single, 'Diamond Age', and the retrospective *A View From The City*. Contained among other forgotten period classics is 'Bad Education', better known for the cover treatment given it by Aztec Camera. The new line-up featured Bramah, Craig Gannon (ex-Bluebells and Smiths; guitar), Martin Hennin (bass), and Dick Harrison (drums). Baines, Bramah's now ex-wife, had departed. His new girlfriend was the Fall keyboard player Marcia Schofield who made a guest appearance on 'Diamond Age'. The Blue Orchids influence continues to be felt in the revival of the hammond organ sound, especially on the records of bands like the Inspiral Carpets (who once asked Bramah to join as singer).
Albums: *The Greatest Hit (Money Mountain)* (1982), *A View From The City* (1991).

Blue Zoo

Formed in 1980 and managed by Jazz Summers, Blue Zoo comprised Mike Ansell (b. 15 July 1960, Finchley, London, England; bass), Andy O (b. 21 March 1963, Braintree, Essex, England; vocals), Tim Parry (b. 21 June 1956, Reading, Berkshire, England; guitar/vocals), Micky Sparrow (b. 26 September 1960, Edmonton, London, England; drums). After a stint of looking New Romantic, being titled Modern Jazz and recording an *avant garde* single called 'I Shoot

Sheep', the boys became pop orientated and had a big UK hit with 'Cry Boy Cry' in 1982. Tim Pope (also the director for the Cure) made the video, which was considered unsuitable for children's viewing. After 1985's 'Somewhere In The World There's A Cowboy Smiling' failed to reach the charts, the group split.
Album: *Two By Two* (1983).

Blur

Formed in London via Colchester, Essex, while Damon Albarn (b. 23 March 1968, Whitechapel, London, England; vocals), Alex James (b. 21 November 1968, Dorset, England; bass), and Graham Coxon (b. 12 March 1969, West Germany; guitar) were studying at Goldsmith's College. Dave Rowntree (b. 8 April 1963, Colchester, Essex, England; drums) completed the line-up and the band - initially called Seymour - started on the lower rungs of the gig circuit. Within a year the quartet had signed to Food Records, changed their name to Blur and Albarn had garnered a somewhat notorious reputation with venue promoters thanks to a plethora of haphazardly implemented onstage stunts. Playing vibrant 90s-friendly pop with a sharp cutting edge, Blur's debut release 'She's So High', sneaked into the Top 50 of the UK chart. With the band displaying a justifiably breezy confidence in their abilities, there was little surprise when the infectious 'There's No Other Way' reached number 8 in the UK charts in the spring of 1991, despite its deployment of orthodox guitars in a market dominated by electronic technology. This success was subsequently validated when Blur's first album, *Leisure*, entered the UK charts at number 2 - a mere two years after the band had formed.
Album: *Leisure* (1991).

Blyth Power

The driving force behind this collection of post-punk train spotters (their name derives from the name of a steam engine) is drummer, lead singer and songwriter Josef Porta (b. 21 February 1962, Templecombe, Somerset, England). He had previously worked with a variety of bands; Valley Forge - while in Somerset in 1978 and on moving to London in 1979, Attitudes and the Entire Cosmos which was primarily made up from the road-crew of Here And Now. After brief stints joining and recording with Zounds, Null And Void and the Mob, Porta formed Blyth Power in 1983 with Curtis Youé. Porta's eloquent lyrics, coupled with a punk-influenced mixture of folk and rock drew analogies from England's history, such as Watt Tyler and Oliver Cromwell's army, to the state of present day politics, in particular a resistance to the 1979-92 Conservative government. His attacks on the ruination of the common man's right to English

Blur

heritage have endeared them to an audience of kindred spirits. The cohesive spirit within the band has ensured their survival while their contemporaries have fallen by the wayside

Albums: *A Little Touch Of Harry In The Middle Of The Night* (1984), *Wicked Women, Wicked Men And Wicket Keepers* (1986), *The Barman And Other Stories* (1988), *Alnwick And Tyne* (1990), *The Guns Of Castle Cary* (1991). Compilation: *Pont Au-Dessus De La Brue* (1988).

B-Movie

This post-punk keyboard and guitar combo originated from Mansfield, England. They were often falsely linked with the early 80s fad of New Romanticism. Graham Boffey (drums) and Paul Statham (guitar) were one-time members of punk band the Aborted, formed, like so many others, in the wake of the first Clash album. The duo invited Steve Hovington (vocals/bass) along to rehearsals, changing their name to Studio 10 before settling on B-Movie. Studio manager Andy Dransfield sent a demo tape of the band to Lincoln-based independent record label Dead Good. The result was two tracks on the compilation *East*. Soon after Rick Holliday joined as keyboard player. Their *Take Three* EP, was warmly received by critics, ensuring several local radio sessions and a six-track 12-inch single, headed by 'Nowhere Girl'. Eccentric entrepreneur Stevo noticed the band and became their manager. Moving to Deram Records, 'Remembrance Day' became the second single to attract strong support in the press. Unfortunately Stevo's connection saw the band categorized as part of the New Romantic movement, a perception which would act as a major constraint in their future. After 'Marilyn Dreams' only scraped the charts the band set out on a major European tour, during which they acquired the services of Luciano Codemo on bass, relieving Hovington to concentrate on his vocals. In turn he was replaced by Mike Pedham (ex-Everest The Hard Way, now the Chimes), and soon Boffey too departed, joining Soft As Ghosts. Martin Smedley and Andy Johnson were the new recruits, but they arrived just in time to see the departure of a frustrated Holliday. He joined Six Sed Red then MCX while the reduced B-Movie line-up signed with Sire. A highly commercial but disappointing single, 'A Letter From Afar', was remixed by Jellybean Benitez. An album eventually followed, but by this time the band had effectively fallen apart (Al Cash and Martin Winter were among the latter-day cast). Statham would go on to work with Pete Murphy and Then Jerico, Hovington formed One before returning to work with Holliday, and Boffey is currently a member of Slaughterhouse 5.

Albums: *Forever Running* (1985), *The Dead Good Tapes* (1988), *Remembrance Days* (1991), *Radio Days* (1991).

BMX Bandits

This group of independent mavericks from Glasgow, Scotland were built around the disputed genius of Douglas 'Bandit', who was formerly a member of the Pretty Flowers. Douglas is a talented writer who has never found his lack of musicianship a handicap. Sean Dickson was the Flowers' invisible member, supplying music for them. Together they formed the BMX Bandits with the original intention of playing one gig and retiring. However, Sean could not double up and play guitar and percussion live so the drum stool went to the band's former saxophonist. Dickson, however, left to form the more successful Soup Dragons. The rest of the band comprised Billy and James. Norman Blake of Teenage Fanclub played for the band frequently. Forever condemned as one of the 'shambling' or 'anorak' bands, Douglas did little to dispel their twee image by dispensing free sweets to audiences. However, calling their album *C86* was definitely a tongue in cheek move (named after the *New Musical Express* compilation which gave the much maligned movement a discernible identity). More recent outings have revealed a penchant for 'rocking out', leather trousers and all. *Star Wars* included a track 'Life Goes On' written by friends Captain America, while it is promised that further new material will be issued on Creation. Douglas was once a late-night television presenter, while legend has it that one original member left to become a Freemason. By no means the perfect pop band, they are not nearly as awful as their interesting history and reputation implies.

Albums: *C86* (1990), *Totally Groovy Live Experience* (c.1991), *Star Wars* (1992).

Bob

Formed in north London in 1986 by Richard Blackborow (b. 21 March 1966, Hackney, London, England), Simon Armstrong (b. 12 February 1966, Hull, Humberside, England), Jem Morris (b. Aberdare, South Wales; bass) and a drum machine, Bob seemed destined to become an archetypal 'indie' pop band. Their first release was on flexidisc only, laying the ground rules for a series of small-scale single releases and British tours to build a passionate following in the provinces. Gary Connors (b. London, England) replaced the drum machine in 1988, only to soon make way for Dean Leggett (b. 30 August 1963), who had previously drummed for Jamie Wednesday. With solid support from influential

BBC disc jockey John Peel and a healthy selection of earnest, old-fashioned guitar-based tunes such as 'Convenience', Bob ploughed an individualistic furrow around the outskirts of the music business, surviving another line-up alteration when Morris was replaced by the bassist from the Caretaker Race, Stephen Hersom (b. 28 April 1963, Plaistow, London, England). Perhaps fittingly after such a determined career, when Bob finally got round to making an album after five years the record's commercial potential was undermined by the collapse of the Rough Trade distribution system. Yet, far from being damaged by the experience, this disaster merely seemed to strengthen Bob's idiosyncratic resolve.

Album: *Leave The Straight Life Behind* (1991). Compilation: *Swag Sack* (1989).

Bodines

This UK rock/pop combo achieved a degree of critical success in the mid to late 80s, principally, and unjustly, via their connections with the fashionable Creation label. The band's line-up featured: lyricist Mike Ryan (vocals), Paul Brotherton (guitar), Tim Burtonwood (bass) and John Rowland (drums). Ryan and Rowland were schoolfriends from Glossop, while Brotherton grew up in Salford. The band was put together while its members were unemployed. Their first demo tape included raw versions of songs which would surface later, and Alan McGee at Creation decided he was interested. They became the youngest band to play the Factory Funhouse (at the Hacienda, Manchester), and two singles on Creation, 'God Bless' and 'Therese', produced by Ian Broudie (see Lightning Seeds), were impressive. However, they soon moved on when record sales failed to follow their good press. Subsequent singles 'Skankin' Queen' and 'Slip Slide' were undeservedly ignored, though their debut album was critically revered: 'Mick Ryan . . . is not going suddenly to sing songs about being happy; he's still stuck with betrayal, guilt and worry, but these feelings aren't smothered in some wet blanket, they're distilled into a crystal glass'. By this time they employed a brass section (Graham Lambyekski and Nelson Pandela), but when new label Magnet disappeared, so did the Bodines.

Album: *Played* (1986).

Bolshoi

Although much maligned for their perceived attachment to the dying embers of the mid-80s UK Gothic rock movement, the Bolshoi were nevertheless gifted songwriters. The band comprised Trevor Tanner (vocals/guitar), Nick Chown (bass) and Jan Kalicki (drums), with Paul Clark (keyboards) joining in time for the band's first album. However, it was 1985's mini-album *Giants* which gave first notice of their abilities, in particular the bittersweet growing pains described of 'Happy Boy'. Another epic single 'Books On The Bonfire' graced the follow-up *Friends*. However, the more manicured material gathered on *Lindy's Party* represented a difficult transition and one which marked the band's demise.

Albums: *Giants* (1985), *Friends* (1986), *Lindy's Party* (1987).

Bomb The Bass

This techno dance outfit were a collective front for Tim Simenon (b. c.1968, Brixton, London, England; of Malaysian and Scottish parents). After attending a course in studio engineering he shot to prominence in 1988 with 'Beat Dis', which reached the UK Top 50. Simenon then worked with Neneh Cherry (producing her hits 'Buffalo Stance' and 'Manchild'). After completing work on his new studio he took up production duties for an album by Prince sidekick Cat. Co-production on Adamski's 'Killer' and the Seal single 'Crazy' followed. However, feeling aggrieved at the lack of credit, and financial recompense he gained from these ventures, he returned to Bomb The Bass. His timing unfortunately was less than apt, as the 1991 Gulf War made continued use of the name indelicate. He reverted to his own name instead for the single 'Love So True', co-written with bass player Doug Wimbush (Sugarhill Gang and Tackhead) and vocalist Loretta Heywood. By this time he was also working extensively with guitarist Kenji Suzuki, in addition to a myriad of guest vocalists.

Albums: *Into The Dragon* (1988), *Unknown Territory* (1991).

Bongwater

Bongwater evolved in New York, USA in 1987 when (Mark) Kramer (guitar), formerly of Shockabilly and the Butthole Surfers, joined forces with vocalist/performance artist Ann Magnusson. The pair were already acquainted from the latter's previous group, Pulsallama, and the new act was one of the first to record for Kramer's Shimmy Disc label. The duo completed their debut EP, *Breaking No New Ground*, with the help of guitarist Fred Frith, and its content ranged from original material to a reconstructed interpretation of the Moody Blues' 'Ride My See-Saw'. The expansive *Double Bummer* introduced Dave Rick (guitar) and David Licht (drums) to a unit which would remain largely informal, although both contributed to subsequent releases. The new set included 'Dazed And Chinese', a version of Led Zeppelin's 'Dazed And Confused', sung in Chinese, as well as songs drawn from the Soft Machine, Monkees and Gary Glitter. Self-penned compositions embraced psychedelia, taped documentaries, pop culture and the *avant garde*, and if

derided as self-indulgent by some, the album confirmed the group's sense of adventure. *Too Much Sleep* was more conventional and while 'Splash 1' (the 13th Floor Elevators) and 'The Drum' (Slapp Happy) continued the duo's dalience with the obscure, their original material, notably the title song and 'He Loved The Weather', showed an unerring grasp of melody. Magnusson's semi-narrative intonation flourished freely on *The Power Of Pussy*, which encompassed sexuality in many contrasting forms. Layers of guitar lines and samples enhanced a genuinely highly-crafted collection, which confirmed the promise of earlier recordings. Bongwater have also undertaken several entertaining live appearances and enter the 90s as one of the independent circuit's most imaginative acts.

Albums: *Breaking No New Ground* (1987), *Double Bummer* (1988), *Too Much Sleep* (1990), *The Power Of Pussy* (1991), *The Big Sell Out* (1992). Compilation: *Double Bummer* (1989).

Boomtown Rats

One of the first new wave groups to emerge during the musical shake-ups of 1977, Boomtown Rats were also significant for spearheading an interest in young Irish rock. Originally formed in 1975, the group comprised Bob Geldof (b. Robert Frederick Zenon Geldof, 5 October 1954, Dun Laoghaire, Eire; vocals), Gerry Roberts (vocals/guitar), Johnny Fingers (keyboards), Pete Briquette (bass) and Simon Crowe (drums). Before moving to London, they signed to the recently established Ensign Records, which saw commercial possibilities in their high energy yet melodic work. Their self-titled debut album was a UK chart success and included two memorable singles, 'Looking After No. 1' and 'Mary Of The Fourth Form', which both reached the UK Top 20. The following summer, their *A Tonic For The Troops* was released to critical acclaim. Among its attendant hit singles were the biting 'She's So Modern' and quirky 'Like Clockwork'. By November 1978, a third hit from the album, the acerbic, urban protest 'Rat Trap', secured them their first UK number 1. In spite of their R&B leanings, the group were initially considered in some quarters as part of the punk upsurge and were banned in their home country. Unduly concerned they received considerable press thanks to the irrepressible loquaciousness of their lead singer. A third album, *The Fine Art Of Surfacing* coincided with their finest moment, 'I Don't Like Mondays', the harrowing true-life story of an American teenage girl who wounded eight children and killed her school janitor and headmaster. The weirdest aspect of the tale was her explanation on being confronted with the deed: 'I don't like Mondays, this livens up the day'. Geldof adapted those words to produce one of pop's most dramatic moments in years, with some startlingly effective piano-work from the appropriately named Johnny Fingers. A massive UK number 1, the single proved almost impossible to match, as the energetic but average follow-up 'Someone's Looking At You' proved. Nevertheless, the Rats were still hitting the Top 5 in the UK and even released an understated but effective comment on Northern Ireland in 'Banana Republic'. By 1982, however, the group had fallen from critical and commercial grace and their subsequent recordings seemed passe. For Geldof, more important work lay ahead with the founding of Band Aid and much-needed world publicity on the devastating famine in Ethiopia. The Rats performed at the Live Aid concert on 13 July 1985 before bowing out the following year at Dublin's Self Aid benefit.

Albums: *The Boomtown Rats* (1977), *A Tonic For The Troops* (1978), *The Fine Art Of Surfacing* (1979), *Modo Bongo* (1981), *V Deep* (1982), *In The Long Grass* (1984). Compilation: *Ratrospective* (1983).

Boo Radleys

This UK group was formed in 1988 in Liverpool by Sice (b. 18 June 1969, Wallasey, Merseyside, England; guitar/vocals), Martin Carr (b. 29 November 1968, Thurso, Highland Region, Scotland; guitar), Timothy Brown (b. 26 February 1969, Wallasey, Merseyside, England; bass) and Steve Drewitt (b. Northwich, England; drums). They took their name from a character in the novel *To Kill A Mockingbird*. After several years of sporadic activity they quietly released *Ichabod And I* on a small independent label which showcased the band's talent for guitar-blasted melodies, where timeless tunes were bolstered with up-to-date effects pedals. Unusually for a group with such a credible sound, the British music press was late to arrive on the scene, only paying attention after disc jockey John Peel had championed the quartet on BBC Radio 1 and introduced the band to thousands of new followers. In the summer of 1990 drummer Steve Drewitt left to join Breed and was replaced by Robert Geka (b. 4 August 1968, Birmingham, West Midlands, England), just as the Boo Radleys signed to Rough Trade Records. Within six months the band had started to fulfill their commercial potential by entering the Top 100 of the UK charts with the EP *Every Heaven*.

Album: *Ichabod And I* (1990).

Boothill Foot-Tappers

Formed in 1982 by Chris Thompson (b. 19 March 1957, Ashford, Middlesex, England; banjo/vocals) and Kevin Walsh (guitar/vocals), the Boothill's full line-up was completed by Wendy May (b. Wendy May Billingsley; vocals), Slim (b. Clive Pain; accordion/piano), Marnie Stephenson (washboard/vocals), Merrill Heatley (vocals) and her brother Danny (drums). As part of an emerging 'country cow-punk' movement in the UK duing the mid-80s (along with such acts as Helen And The Horns and Yip Yip Coyote), the Boothill Foot-Tappers proved to be the most adept at the genre and certainly one of the best live performers. They scored a minor UK hit on the Go! Discs/Chrysalis label with 'Get Your Feet Out Of My Shoes' in July 1984. Slim, who had been enjoying a parallel career as part of the Blubbery Hellbellies, left the group in 1983 before the recording of the Boothill's debut album and was replaced by Simon Edwards (melodeon) - although he occasionally re-joined the group for live performances. The group folded at the end of 1985 after touring to promote the album which failed to set the charts alight. After briefly working with B.J. Cole and Bob Loveday in the Rivals and later with the Devils In Disguise, Chris Thompson went on to form the Barely Works. Wendy May decided to concentrate on the running of the successful disco club 'Locomotion' at the Town And Country Club in Kentish Town, London.

Album: *Ain't That Far From Boothill* (1985).

Bow Wow Wow

Formed in London in 1980 by former Sex Pistols manager Malcolm McLaren, Bow Wow Wow consisted of three former members of Adam And The Ants: David Barbe (b. David Barbarossa, 1961, Mauritius; drums), Matthew Ashman (b. 1962, London, England) and Leigh Gorman (b. 1961; bass). This trio was called upon to back McLaren's latest protegee, a 14-year-old Burmese girl whom he had discovered singing in a dry cleaners in Kilburn, London. Annabella Lu Win (b. Myant Myant Aye, 1966, Rangoon, Burma) was McLaren's female equivalent of Frankie Lymon, a teenager with no previous musical experience who could be moulded to perfection. Bow Wow Wow debuted with 'C30, C60, C90, Go' a driving, Burundi Black-influenced paean to home taping composed by McLaren. Its follow-up the cassette-only *Your Cassette Pet* featured eight tracks in an EP format (including the bizarre 'Sexy Eiffel Towers'). In addition to the African Burundi-influence, the group combined a 50s sounding Gretsch guitar complete with echo and tremelo. Although innovative and exciting, the group received only limited chart rewards during their stay with EMI Records and like the Pistols before them soon sought a new record company. After signing with RCA, McLaren enlivened his promotion of the group with a series of publicity stunts, amid outrageous talk of paedophiliac pop. The jailbait Annabella had her head shaven into a Mohican style and began appearing in tribal clothes. Further controversy ensued when she was photographed

Boy George and Marilyn

semi-nude on an album sleeve pastiche of Manet's *Déjeuner sur l'Herbe*. A deserved UK Top 10 hit followed with 'Go Wild In The Country', a frenzied, almost animalistic display of sensuous exuberance. An average cover of the Strangeloves/Brian Poole And The Tremeloes' hit 'I Want Candy' also clipped the Top 10, but by then McLaren was losing control of his concept. A second lead singer was briefly recruited in the form of Lieutenant Lush, who threatened to steal the limelight from McLaren's *ingenue* and was subsequently ousted, only to reappear in Culture Club as Boy George. By 1983, amid uncertainty and disillusionment Bow Bow Wow folded. The backing group briefly soldiered on as the Chiefs Of Relief, while Annabella took a sabbatical, reappearing in 1985 for an unsuccessful solo career.

Albums: *See Jungle! See Jungle! Go Join Your Gang, Yeah, City All Over! Go Ape Crazy!* (1981), *I Want Candy* (1982), *When The Going Gets Tough, The Tough Get Going* (1983). Compilation: *The Best Of Bow Wow Wow* (1989).

Boy George

b. George O'Dowd, 14 June 1961, Eltham, Kent, England. During the early 80s, O'Dowd became a regular on the London New Romantic club scene. His appearances at clubs such as Billy's, Blitz, Heaven and Hell accompanied by Marilyn were regularly featured in the pages of the rock/art magazines *Blitz* and *The Face*. Dressing in a series of flamboyant cross-dressing styles he caught the attention of pop-svengali Malcolm McLaren who enroled George to appear alongside Bow Wow Wow's Annabella Lu Win, as Lieutenant Lush, at a concert at London's Rainbow Theatre. This partnership proved short-lived but useful as George's name was pushed further into the spotlight. A meeting with former disc jockey Mikey Craig (b. 15 February 1960, Hammersmith, London, England; bass) resulted in the forming of a band, In Praise Of Lemmings. After the addition of former Adam And The Ants/Damned drummer Jon Moss (b. 11 September 1957, Wandsworth, London, England; drums) plus Roy Hay (b. 12 August 1961, Southend-on-Sea, Essex, England; guitar/keyboards), the group was renamed Culture Club. Signed to Virgin Records, they became one of the most popular groups of the 80s. To the public Culture Club was to all intents and purposes, Boy George, and his appetite for publicity and clever manipulation of the media put many an old trouper to shame. His ambiguous sexuality, although no problem to his many fans, caused considerable comment in tabloid press. His most famous quote on sex - 'I'd much rather have a cup of tea' is legendary. Ultimately, it was not his homosexuality that was to cause his downfall, but rather his dalliance with drugs. A week after teasing journalists with the self-proclamation as 'your favourite junkie' at an anti-apartheid concert in London, the British national press had a field-day when it was revealed by George's brother that the star was indeed addicted to heroin. No sooner had this episode hit the headlines than another scandal broke. Visiting New York keyboard player, Michael Rudetski, died of a heroin overdose while staying at George's London home. Soon after, George was arrested on a charge of possession of cannabis resulting in successful treatment for his drug dependence. His public renouncement of drugs coincided with the dissolution of Culture Club and the launch of a solo career.

His first effort, a cover version of the Bread/Ken Boothe hit 'Everything I Own', in the spring of 1987 gave him his first UK number 1 hit since 'Karma Chameleon' in 1983. George's outspoken opposition to what was seen by some as the Conservative government's anti-homosexual bill, Clause 28, triggered off a series of releases damning the bill. He formed his own record label, More Protein in 1989 and fronted a new band, Jesus Loves You, which reflected his new-found spiritual awareness and continuing love of white soul.

Albums: *Sold* (1987), *Tense Nervous Headache* (1988). As Jesus Loves You; *The Martyr Mantras* (1991).

Boys

Emerging alongside the first wave of UK punk bands, the Boys were always more than three chord wonders. They were formed by factory worker and guitarist John Plain (b. Leeds, Yorkshire, England) who recruited fellow workers Duncan Reid and Jack Black on bass and drums respectively. 'Honest' John Plain was also acquainted with Matt Dangerfield (b. Leeds, Yorkshire, England) and recruited him as second guitarist. Dangerfield had played two rehearsal gigs with the infamous punk ensemble, London SS alongside Norwegian keyboards player Casino Steel. Steel, formerly of the Hollywood Brats, completed the line-up of the Boys in the summer of 1976. With Duncan 'Kid' Reid singing, and Steel/Dangerfield writing they made their name by touring with John Cale in April 1977. Signed to NEMS, 'I Don't Care' was their first single and although it did not fare well in the UK the Boys became successful on the continent particularly in Holland and Steel's native Norway. Further recordings followed for NEMS including the first of several Christmas singles recorded under the pseudonym the Yobs. In 1979 they signed with Safari where Dangerfield also acted as a producer for Toyah early in her career. Popular

with the press but unable to convert acclaim into sales the Boys eventually split. Plain teamed up with Peter Stride of the Lurkers as the New Guitars In Town for a short break in 1980, before the Boys final album was issued in 1981.

Albums: *The Boys* (1977), *Alternative Chartbusters* (1978), *To Hell With The Boys* (1979), *The Christmas Album* (1979), *Boys Only* (1981).

Billy Bragg

Bragg, Billy

b. Steven William Bragg, 20 December 1957, Barking, Essex, England. Popularly known as 'The Bard Of Barking' (or variations of), Bragg is generally regarded as one of the most committed left-wing political performers working in popular music. After forming the ill-fated punk group Riff Raff, Bragg briefly joined the British Army (Tank Corp), before buying his way out with what he later described as the most wisely spent £175 of his life. Between time working in a record store and absorbing his new found love of the blues and protest genre, he launched himself on a solo musical career. Armed with guitar, amplifier and voice, Bragg undertook a maverick tour of the concert halls of Britain, ready at a moment's notice to fill in as support for almost any act. He confounded the local youth with what would usually be a stark contrast to the music billed for that evening. Seeing himself as a 'one man Clash', his lyrics, full of passion, anger and wit, made him a truly original character on the UK music scene. During this time, managed by ex-Pink Floyd supremo Peter Jenner, his album *Life's A Riot With Spy Vs Spy*, formerly on Charisma, but now with the emergent independent label, Go-Discs/Utility, had begun to take a very firm hold on the UK independent charts, eventually peaking in the UK national charts at number 30. His follow-up, *Brewing Up With Billy Bragg* reached number 16 in the UK charts. As always, at Billy's insistence, and helped by the low production costs, the albums were kept at a below-average selling price. His credentials as a songwriter were given a boost in 1985 when Kirsty MacColl reached number 7 in the UK charts with his song 'New England'. Bragg became a fixture at political rallies, and benefits, particularly during the 1984 Miners Strike with his powerful pro-Union songs 'Which Side Are You On', 'There Is Power In The Union' and the EP title-track, 'Between The Wars'. He was instrumental in creating the socialist musicians collective 'Red Wedge', which included such pop luminaries as Paul Weller, Junior Giscombe and Jimmy Somerville. Despite the politicizing, Bragg was still able to pen classic love songs such as the much-acclaimed 'Levi Stubbs' Tears', which appeared on the UK Top 10 album *Talking To The Taxman About Poetry*. Bragg's political attentions soon spread to Russia and Central/South America. He often returned the host musician's hospitality by offering them places as support acts on his future UK tours.

In 1988 he reached the UK number 1 slot with a cover of the Beatles song, 'She's Leaving Home', on which he was accompanied by Cara Tivey on piano - this was part of a children's charity project of contemporary artists performing various Lennon And McCartney songs. Bragg shared this double a-side single release with Wet Wet Wet's version of 'With A Little Help From My Friends', which received the majority of radio play, effectively relegating Bragg's contribution to that of a b-side. In 1989 he re-activated the label Utility, for the purposes of encouraging young talent who had found difficulty in persuading the increasingly reticent major companies to take a gamble. These artists included Coming Up Roses, Jungr And Parker and Dead Famous People. In 1991, Bragg issued the critically acclaimed *Don't Try This At Home*, arguably his most commercial work to date. The album featured a shift towards personal politics, most noticeably on the liberating hit single, 'Sexuality'.

Albums: *Life's A Riot With Spy Vs Spy* (1983), *Brewing Up With Billy Bragg* (1984), *Talking With The Taxman About Poetry* (1986), *Workers Playtime* (1988), *Help Save The Youth Of America - Live And Dubious* (1988, a US/Canadian release), *The Internationale* (1990), *Don't Try This At Home* (1991), *The Peel Sessions Album* (1992, recordings from 1983-88).

Compilation: *Back To Basics* - a repackage of the first two albums (1987).

Further reading: *Midnight In Moscow*, Chris Salewicz.

Breeders

Restless with her role in Boston guitar band, the Pixies, bassist Kim Deal teamed up with Throwing Muses guitarist Tanya Donnelly and the Perfect Disaster's bass player Josephine Higgs in late 1989. The Breeders had been the name of Kim's pre-Pixies group, with her sister Kelly. Back in 1988, Deal and Donnelly had recorded together with the Muses' drummer David Narciso, but the sessions were abandoned. The catalyst of Big Black/Rapeman figure Steve Albini as producer proved the magical ingredient, and helped by Brit Walford of hardcore outfit Slint, the Breeders came up with *Pod*. The album shared the menacing dynamics of the Pixies with intricate guitar subtleties of the Throwing Muses, and was a commercial success. But despite rumours, this was not to be a full-time project. Kim returned to record a new Pixies album, although in late 1991, Donnelly quit Throwing Muses in order to work on a solo career and on possible future Breeders material. In 1992, Kim inaugurated Belly with former Muses' bassist Fred Abong and the Gorman brothers Chris (drums) and Thomas (lead guitar) releasing the EP *Slow Dust*.

Album: *Pod* (1990).

Brickell, Edie, And The New Bohemians

The US group, the New Bohemians - Kenny Withrow (guitar), John Bush (percussion), Brad Houser (bass), and Brando Aly (drums) already existed as a unit in their own right before Edie Brickell (guitar/vocals) jumped up on stage to sing with them. Following their contribution to the Island compilation *Deep Ellum*, Aly left and was replaced by Matt Chamberlain, with Wes Martin joining as additional guitarist. The new line-up signed to Geffen Records and recorded their debut *Shooting Rubberbands At The Stars* from whence came the UK hit single 'What I Am'. The work immediately established Brickell as one of the most interesting new songwriters of her era with a distinctive vocal style. The group subsequently toured with Bob Dylan. Their follow-up single 'Circle' also charted but only reached number 74 in the UK. *Ghost Of A Dog* included guest vocals by John Lydon on 'Strings Of Love' and displayed Brickell's characteristically oblique lyrics. In June 1992, Edie married Paul Simon.

Albums: *Shooting Rubberbands At The Stars* (1988), *Ghost Of A Dog* (1991).

Brigandage

This UK post punk (or 'positive punk') group were

notable for creating an almost audible 'buzz' in the London area before fizzling out just as rapidly. The focus of the band was Michelle (b. c.1960). Based in Camden, London, both she and boyfriend Richard North had been 'faces' at the beginning of punk. The two also ran their own stall, The Art Of Stealing, in Camden Market. Michelle was able to boast of being both the first in the queue for the 100 Club 'Punk Festival', and of being escorted to hospital in an ambulance by Mick Jones of the Clash. The original line-up featured Michelle (vocals), Mick (guitar), Ben (drums) and Scott (bass). However, their beliefs in 'positive punk' were savaged by critics, notably in the *New Musical Express*, and the band left Michelle with only the the name. Richard, the editor of *Kick* fanzine, (who also wrote for *Zig Zag* as Richard Kick and the *NME* as Richard North), was the first to be drafted in on bass. His assertion that he could not play was dismissed by Michelle, who added David Eaves (guitar) and Tim Nuttal (drums) before he had time to argue about it. Brigandage Mark 1 had collapsed, ironically, following Richard's almost infamous 'Positive Punk' piece in the *NME*. Unfortunatel /, they proved unable to capitalize on their live reputation and left little behind to testify to their talents.

Album: *Pretty Little Thing* (1986).

Bright, Bette

b. Anne Martin, Whitstable, Kent, England. A founder member of Liverpool cult-favourites Deaf School, vocalist Bright embarked on a solo career following the group's demise. Her early singles, 'My Boyfriend's Back' and 'Captain Of Your Ship', were remakes of well-known female-group classics by the Angels and Reparata And The Delrons respectively. The singer's sole UK Top 50 success was derived from a third release, 'Hello, I Am Your Heart'. Backed by the Illuminations which included Ian Broudie (guitar - later of Care and Lightning Seeds) and Clive Langer, Bette embarked on a tour of British clubs and colleges and completed a promising album which offered versions of Betty Wright's 'Shoorah Shoorah' and the Deaf School favourite 'Thunder And Lightning'. Unable to make a significant commercial breakthrough, she guested on several live appearances by Clive Langer And The Boxes, before reverting to a domestic life following her marriage to Madness' singer Graham 'Suggs' McPherson.

Album: *Rhythm Breaks The Ice* (1981).

Bright, Len, Combo

Eric Goulden (guitar/vocal), Russ Wilkins (bass) and Bruce Brand (drums) presided over a mid-80s rock scene in England's Medway towns that was as self-contained in its quieter way as Merseybeat.

Cultivating a comically seedy image and the artistic style of a backdated 60s beat group, the trio were popular on the college circuit with a set steered by Goulden's instinctive if indelicate audience control and monopolized by his compositions - some dating back to both his Captains Of Industry and an earlier incarnation as Wreckless Eric. By scorning a proper recording studio, the home-made passion of the Combo's debut album and its 'Someone Must've Nailed Us Together' single cost next to nothing to record on antiquated electronic paraphernalia assembled in Brand's Chatham attic. 1987's *Combo Time!* was a critical success but a commercial failure. Later that year, the trio was torn by dissent over future policy and Goulden's subsequent exit to resume his solo career.

Albums: *The Len Bright Combo Present...* (1986), *Combo Time!*

Brilliant

Brilliant, creatively fuelled by ex-Killing Joke bass player Youth (b. Martin Glover Youth, 27 December 1960, Africa), originally formed in England with Paul Ferguson (drums) and Paul Raven (bass). However, the latter pair soon defected back to Killing Joke. A second line-up featuring, among others, Tin Tin (b. France), Marcus (ex-Lemon Boys) and Stephan was equally short-lived. Brilliant, meanwhile, persevered with Youth on bass, Jimmy Cauty on guitar and June Lawrence on vocals. Though neither of the new members were experienced musically, Lawrence had studied fashion at art school and Jimmy had been a prominent comic artist. Much adored by the music press, their sole breakthrough came with a sumptuous cover of James Brown's 'It's A Man's Man's Man's World'.

Album: *Kiss The Lips Of Life* (1986).

Burnel, Jean Jacques

Out of the four original members of the Stranglers, bassist Jean Jacques Burnel (b. 1952, London, England) was probably the most forthright. Born of French parents he was staunchly pro-European. A keen biker, former skinhead, a black belt in karate and an Economics graduate from Bradford University. He was employed as a van driver in Guildford, Surrey when he first met Hugh Cornwell, through the American lead singer of the band Bobbysox whom Hugh was playing guitar with in the early 70s. Original plans to become a karate instructor were shelved (although he would return to this profession part-time), so he could play bass and sing in a band with Cornwell. As the Stranglers soared to success Burnel waged a personal battle with the press who dismissed the band as either being of higher intellect than their punk cohorts, or alternatively abject and brutal chauvinists. Several well-documented episodes led to violent resolution at Burnel's hands. Burnel was the first Strangler to work on a solo project, *Euroman Cometh*. As the title implied, this was a plea for the cause of European federalism, and somewhat ahead of its time. This was released early in 1979 with guests Brian James (guitar; ex-Damned), Lew Lewis (harmonica; ex-Eddie And The Hot Rods) with Carey Fortune (ex-Chelsea) and Pete Howells (ex-Drones) sharing drum duties. A short tour to promote the album was something of a disaster. The Euroband put together for the tour featured John Ellis (ex-Vibrators - who was also playing for the support band Rapid Eye Movement), Lewis, Howells, and Penny Tobin on keyboards. In 1980 'Girl From The Snow Country' was scheduled as a solo release but was withdrawn. Despite a later bootleg, the copies that slipped out are among the most collectable of new wave releases. The next musical project outside of the Stranglers was a collaboration with Dave Greenfield on a soundtrack for the Vincent Coudanne film *Ecoutez Vos Murs*. Ensuing years saw Burnel getting involved with a number of bands as either producer, guest musician or both. Typically the groups were largely non-English, including Taxi Girl (France), Ping Pong (Norway), the Revenge (Belgium) and ARB (Japan). The next major project was the formation in 1986 of a 60s cover outfit called the Purple Helmets. Consisting of Burnel, Ellis, Alex Gifford, and Laurent Sinclair the outfit was put together for a one-off gig at the *Trans Musicale Avant Festival* in France. So successful was the concert that the Helmets became an ongoing concern with Greenfield replacing Sinclair and Tears For Fears drummer Manny Elias joining. Burnel has since made one further solo album, *C'est Un Jour Parfait*, which was recorded almost entirely in French and released just about everywhere in Europe except Britain.

Albums: *Euroman Cometh* (1979), with Dave Greenfield *Fire And Water* (1983), *C'est Un Jour Parfait* (1989).

Butterfield 8

Butterfield 8 were the brainchild of former Higson's multi-instrumentalist Terry Edwards (b. Hornchurch, Essex, England) in collaboration with ex-Madness bassist Mark 'Bedders' Bedford (b. 24 August 1961, London, England). Edwards's long-time fascination with film and show scores fused with his other love of blues-tinged jazz in the Butterfield 8. The group provided a welcome outlet after the restriction of the funk-influenced Higsons. Named after the 1960 film starring Laurence Harvey and Elizabeth Taylor, the Butterfield 8's debut album included versions of Herbie Hancock's 'Watermelon Man'and the Viscounts 'Harlem Nocturne'. Among Edwards' other projects and collaborations, was the 70s glitter-

glam parody, the Eight Track Cartridge Family. He has also performed with, and produced, Yeah Jazz, worked with the Simon Lewis Partnership and in 1991 he released two EPs celebrating the music of the Jesus And Mary Chain and the Fall.
Album: *Blow* (1988).

Butthole Surfers

Butthole Surfers

Formerly known as the Ashtray Baby Heads, this maverick quartet from Austin, Texas, USA, made its recording debut in 1983 with their self-titled mini-album. Gibson 'Gibby' Haynes (vocals) Paul Leary Walthall aka Paul Sneef (guitar) and King Koffey (drums) were initially indebted to the punk/hardcore scene, as evinced by the startling 'The Shah Sleeps In Lee Harvey's Grave', but other selections were inspired by a variety of sources. Loping melodies, screaming guitar and heavy-metal riffs abound in a catalogue as zany as it is unclassifiable. Lyrically explicit, the group has polarized opinion between those who appreciate their boisterous humour and those deeming them prurient. Having endured a succession of bass players, including Kramer from Shockabilly and Bongwater, the Buttholes secured the permanent services of Jeff Pinker, alias Tooter, alias Pinkus, in 1985. The Surfers' strongest work appears on *Locust Abortion Technician* and *Hairway To Steven*, the former of which includes 'Sweet Loaf', a thinly disguised version of Black Sabbath's 'Sweet Leaf'. On the latter set, tracks are denoted by various simple drawings, including a defecating deer, rather than song titles, a practice which emphasized the group's controversial standing. In 1991 the release of *Digital Dump*, a house-music project undertaken by Haynes and Tooter under the Jack Officers epithet was released, followed closely by the Buttholes' ninth album, *Pioughd* which showed that their ability to enrage, bewilder and excite remained as sure as ever, and was marked by a curiously reverential version of Donovan's 'Hurdy Gurdy Man'. This set was closely followed by Paul Leary's excellent solo *The History Of Dogs*.

Buzzcocks

Albums: *Butthole Surfers* (1983), *PCP PEP* (1984), *Another Man's Sac* (1985), *Rembrandt Pussyhorse* (1986), *Locust Abortion Technician* (1987), *Stickmen With Rayguns* (1987), *Hairway To Steven* (1988), *Widowermaker* (1989), *Pioughd* (1991).

Buzzcocks

Originally formed in Manchester in January 1976, the group consisted of Pete Shelley (b. Peter McNeish, 17 April 1955; vocals/guitar), Howard Devoto (b. Howard Trafford; vocals), Steve Diggle (bass) and John Maher (drums). A support spot on the Sex Pistols' infamous 'Anarchy' tour prefaced their debut recording, the EP *Spiral Scratch*. The quartet's undeveloped promise was momentarily short-circuited when Devoto sensationally left in March 1977, only to resurface later that year with Magazine. A reshuffled Buzzcocks, with Shelley taking lead vocal and Garth Smith (later replaced by Steve Garvey) on bass, won a major deal with United Artists. During the next three years, they recorded some of the finest pop-punk singles of their era, including the Devoto/Shelley song 'Orgasm Addict' and, after the split, Shelley's 'What Do I Get?', 'Love You More', the classic 'Ever Fallen In Love (With Someone You Should't've)', 'Promises' (with Diggle), 'Everybody's Happy Nowadays' and Diggle's 'Harmony In My Head'. After three albums and nearly five years on the road, the group fell victim to disillusionment and Shelley quit for a solo career. Steve Diggle re-emerged with Flag Of Convenience, but neither party could reproduce the best of the Buzzcocks. With hindsight, the Buzzcocks' influence upon British 'indie-pop' of the late 80s is as incalculable as that of the Ramones or the Velvet Underground's. The group reformed in 1990 with former Smiths drummer Mike Joyce added to their ranks.

Albums: *Another Music In A Different Kitchen* (1978), *Love Bites* (1978), *A Different Kind Of Tension* (1979), *Lest We Forget* (1989, live recordings 1979-80), *The Peel Sessions Album* (1990), *Live At The Roxy, April '77* (1990), *Time's Up* (1991, rec. 1976), *Entertaining Friends (Live At The Hammersmith Odeon, March 1979)* (1992). Compilations: *Singles - Going Steady* (1981), *Product* (1989, 5 album/3 CD box set - contains previously unreleased recordings), *Operator's Manual - Buzzcocks Best* (1991).

Byrne, David

b. 14 May 1952, Dumbarton, Scotland, but raised in Baltimore, Ohio, USA. A graduate of the Rhode

Island School of Design, Byrne abandoned his training in visual and conceptual arts in favour of rock. He formed Talking Heads with two fellow students and this highly-respected unit evolved from its origins in the New York punk milieu into one of America's leading attractions. Much of its appeal was derived from Byrne's quirky, almost paranoid, diction and imaginative compositions, but the group rapidly proved too limiting for his widening artistic palate. *My Life In The Bush Of Ghosts*, a collaboration with Brian Eno, was widely praised by critics for its adventurous blend of sound collages, ethnic influences and vibrant percussion, which contrasted with Byrne's ensuing solo debut, *The Catherine Wheel*. The soundtrack to Twyla Tharp's modern ballet, this fascinating set was the prelude to an intensive period in the parent group's career, following which the artist began composing and scripting a feature film. Released in 1985, *True Stories*, which Byrne also directed and starred in, was the subject of an attendant Talking Heads' album. *The Knee Plays*, on which David worked with playwright Robert Wilson, confirmed interests emphasized in 1987 by his collaboration with Ryuichi Sakamoto and Cong Su on the soundtrack for Bertolucci's *The Last Emperor*. This highly-acclaimed film won nine Oscars, including one for Best Original Score. Byrne meanwhile continued recording commitments to his group, but by the end of the 80s intimated a reluctance to appear live with them. He instead assembled a 14-strong Latin-American ensemble which toured the USA, Canada, Europe and Japan to promote *Rei Momo*, while a 1991 statement established that Talking Heads were on 'indefinite furlough'. *The Forest* confirmed the artist's prodigious talent by invoking European orchestral music while his Luaka Bop label served as an outlet for a series of world music albums, including several devoted to Brazilian recordings.
Albums: with Brian Eno *My Life In The Bush Of Ghosts* (1981), *The Catherine Wheel* (1981), *Music For The Knee Plays* (1985), with Ryuichi Sakamoto and Cong Su *The Last Emperor* (1987, film soundtrack), *Rei Momo* (1989), *The Forest* (1991), *Uh-Oh* (1992).

C

Cabaret Voltaire

Formed in Sheffield, Yorkshire, England, in 1974, and named after the Dadaist collective, this experimental, innovative electronic-dance group consisted of Stephen Mallinder (bass/lead vocals), Richard H. Kirk (guitar/wind instruments) and Chris Watson (electronics and tapes). Influenced by Can and Brian Eno, the group strived to avoid the confines of traditional pop music and the trio's early appearances veered towards performance art. This attitude initially attracted the attention of Factory Records and the group contributed two tracks to the Manchester label's 1978 double EP, *A Factory Sample*. They eventually signed to Rough Trade Records that same year, producing the *Extended Play* EP which confirmed the band's experimental stance, although 'Nag, Nag, Nag', (1979), was a head-on rush of distorted guitar and a driving beat. The trio continued to break new ground, using sampled 'noise', cut-up techniques and tape loops. Often viewed as inaccessible, in the ensuing years Cabaret Voltaire released the UK Independent Top 10 singles 'Silent Command' (1979), 'Three Mantras' and 'Seconds Too Late' (both 1980). Their 1979 debut album, *Mix Up*, was followed by a more conventional offering, *The Voice Of America*. After *Live At The YMCA 27.10.79*, the group widened their horizons, with video and collaborative work, including work on the Belgian label, Les Disques du Crépescule and two Industrial label cassettes, *Cabaret Voltaire 1974-76* (their early recordings) and Kirk's solo *Disposable Half Truths*. In 1981, the group's prolific out-put was increased by the morbid but successful *Red Mecca* and by another cassette, *Live At The Lyceum*. Watson left in October 1981 to work in television and later resurfaced in the Hafler Trio. In 1982 Eric Random was recruited on guitar for a Solidarity benefit concert, performing under the name Pressure Company. The year also saw the release of *2 x 45*, 'Temperature Drop', plus the Japanese live album *Hai!* and a solo set from Mallinder, *Pow Wow*. Departing from Rough Trade in 1983, whilst also releasing 'Fools Game' on Les Disques du Crépescule and 'Yashar' on Factory, the group signed a joint deal with Some Bizzare/Virgin Records. The first fruits of this move, 'Just Fascination' and *The Crackdown* confirmed the Cabaret Voltaire's new approach and signalled a drastic shift towards rhythmic dance sounds (assisted by Soft Cell keyboard player, Dave Ball's presence). Yet another label entered the frame when Doublevision released the film soundtrack *Johnny Yesno*. Kirk's double set, *Time High Fiction*, came at the end of this productive year. Aside from a compilation video, *TV Wipeout*, 1984 was a quiet year, until 'Sensoria' (Some Bizzare) ripped the dance charts apart, setting the tone for much of Cabaret Voltaire's subsequent work, including 'James Brown', both featuring on *Micro-phonies*, and 'I Want You' (1985). In between, the pair concentrated on the video *Gasoline In Your Eye*, paralleled by the similarly-

Cabaret Voltaire

titled, double 12-inch 'Drinking Gasoline'. The critically acclaimed *The Covenant, The Sword And The Arm Of The Lord*, echoed the group's earlier work. Kirk's solo work continued apace in 1986 with *Black Jesus Voice*, and a mini-album, *Ugly Spirit*, plus a project with the Box's Peter Hope resulting in *Hoodoo Talk* in 1987. By July 1987, the duo had transferred to EMI/Parlophone, debuting with 'Don't Argue'. As with the follow-up releases, 'Here To Go' and 'Code', its dance sound had a purely commercial slant, lacking the pair's earlier, experimental approach. In 1988, Mallinder collaborated with Dave Ball and Mark Brydon, collectively known as Love Street, releasing 'Galaxy'. A new Cabaret Voltaire single 'Hypnotised' (1989), reflected their visit to the house music capital, Chicago. Kirk's 'Test One' (1990), issued under the guise of Sweet Exorcist, was pure acid-house. The group continued this style with the 'Keep On' and *Groovy, Laid Back And Nasty*. In the meantime, Mute Records methodically reissued the band's early back catalogue on CD, including many rare and previously unreleased recordings. Leaving EMI, Cabaret Voltaire returned to Les Disques du Crépescule for 'What Is Real' (1991), followed by the well-received *Body And Soul*. This only consolidated Cabaret Voltaire's pivotal role in hi-tech dance music, which they have helped develop over a decade-and-a-half.
Albums: *Mix Up* (1979), *The Voice Of America* (1980), *Live At The YMCA 27.10.79* (1980), *Red Mecca* (1981), *Live At The Lyceum* (1981), as Pressure Company *Live In Sheffield, 19 January 1982* (1982), *2 x 45* (1982), *Hai!* (1982), *Johnny Yesno* (1983, film soundtrack), *Micro-phonies* (1984), *The Covenant, The Sword And The Arm Of The Lord* (1985), *Code* (1987), *Groovy Laid Back And Nasty* (1990), *Body And Soul* (1991). Compilations: *Cabaret Voltaire 1974-76* (1981), *State Of Excitement* (1986), *The Golden Moments Of Cabaret Voltaire* (1987), *8 Crépescule Tracks* (1988), *Listen Up With Cabaret Voltaire* (1990), *The Living Legends* (1990), *Three Mantras* (1990). Solo

albums: Richard H. Kirk *Disposable Half Truths* (1981), *Time High Fiction* (1983), *Black Jesus Voice* (1986), *Ugly Spirit* (1986), with Peter Hope *Hoodoo Talk* (1987). Stephen Millinder *Pow Wow* (1982). As Sweet Exorcist *Clonk's Coming* (1990).

Camper Van Beethoven

This witty, often sarcastic garage rock band was formed in Redlands, California, USA in 1983 by schoolfriends, transferring to Santa Cruz when members attended college there. They were named by early member David McDaniels, although their line-ups were frequent and unstable. By 1987 the band solidified as David Lowery (vocals/guitar), Greg Lisher (guitar), Chris Pederson (guitar), Jonathan Segal (violin), Victor Krummenacher (bass) and Chris Molla (drums). Krummenacher was formerly a member of the jazz ensemble Wrestling Worms. Their debut *Telephone Free Landslide Victory* contained the amusing single 'Take The Skinheads Bowling'. It was typical of an armoury of songs which included 'The Day Lassie Went To The Moon', 'Joe Stalin's Cadillac', and 'ZZ Top Goes To Egypt'. They played their UK debut in March 1987, after which a second album emerged on their own Pitch A Tent label in the US. Meanwhile 'Take The Skinheads Bowling' had become a cult record in the UK, where the anagramatical *Vampire Can Mating Oven* wrapped up the last of their Rough Trade distributed tracks before a move to Virgin. A subsequent cover of Status Quo's 'Pictures Of Matchstick Men' amplified the band's discordant eclecticism, while they have also left a wake of occasionally inspired albums.
Albums: *Telephone Free Landslide Victory* (1986), *Camper Van Beethoven* (1986), *II & III* (1987), *Vampire Can Mating Oven* (1987), with Eugene Chadbourne *Camper Van Chadbourne* (1988), with Chadbourne *The Eddie Chatterbox Double Trio Love Album* (1988), *Our Beloved Revolutionary Sweetheart* (1988), *Key Lime Pie* (1990).

Captain Sensible

b. Raymond Burns, 24 April 1954, Balham, London, England. Having drifted from job to job after leaving school, Burns fell in with fellow reprobate Chris Miller, while working at the Croydon Fairfield Halls. Sharing common interests in drink, chaos and music, they eventually found themselves part of the burgeoning punk scene in west London in 1976. Together with Dave Vanian and Brian James, Miller (Rat Scabies) and Burns (Captain Sensible) formed what was to be one of the major punk bands of the period; the Damned. Initially enrolled as their bass player, he moved on to guitar following James's departure from the group. A riotous character with an unnerving sense of charm, Sensible frequently performed at gigs dressed in various guises, often in a tu-tu, a nurse's uniform or even nothing at all. Behind the comic-strip facade lurked a keen fan of 60s and 70s psychedelia; he was often quoted in later interviews as being influenced by Jimi Hendrix and the Soft Machine. This went against the punk ethos of the time. He was able to indulge in his esoteric taste in music by carving out a solo career by accident rather than design, owing to the frequent bouts of forced inactivity by the Damned. With ex-Chelsea bassist Henry Badowski, Sensible formed King, an outfit which lasted barely three months. That same year, he recorded 'Jet Boy Jet Girl', a lyrically improbable translation of Plastic Bertrand's 'Ca Plane Pour Moi' with the Softies and also performed on Johnny Moped's *Cycledelic*. A fervent campaigner for animal rights, and a CND supporter, he confirmed his anti-establishment credentials by recording an EP on the Crass label, *This Is Your Captain Speaking* in 1981.

With fellow Damned member Paul Gray, he produced the Dolly Mixture singles, 'Been Teen' and 'Everything And More'. Signed by A&M as a solo act, he recorded a cover version of Richard Rodgers/Oscar Hammerstein II's 'Happy Talk' which included Dolly Mixture on backing vocals. The single shot to the UK number 1 position in the summer of 1982. With his distinctive red beret and round shades, he become an instant media and family favourite, revealing an endearing fondness for rabbits, cricket and trains. He subsequently released two albums in close collaboration with lyricist Robyn Hitchcock, and had further hit singles with 'Wot' and 'Glad It's All Over'. Although he was keen not to let his solo success interfere with the Damned's activities, Sensible found himself gradually becoming isolated from the group due to internal politics and managerial disputes, resulting in his leaving the band in 1984, although he occasionally dropped in to guest on live performances.

One single in 1985 in partnership with girlfriend Rachel Bor of Dolly Mixture, billed as Captain Sensible & The Missus, 'Wot, No Meat?', emphasized his commitment to vegetarianism. He undertook one national tour in 1985, as well as studio work which culminated in the formation of his own Deltic label. His 1991 album *Revolution Now* received less favourable reviews. The double set did, however, show that his talent for catchy pop had not deserted him. He reunited with Paul Gray for some live performances in 1991.

Albums: *Women And Captains First* (1982), *The Power Of Love* (1983), *Revolution Now* (1989). Compilation: *Sensible Singles* (1984).

Caretaker Race

Formed by occasional rock journalist Andy Strickland (b. 16 August 1959, Newport, Isle Of Wight, England; guitar/lead vocals), Dave Mew (b. 11 May 1959, Epping, Essex, England), Henry Hersom (b. London, England; bass), Sally Ward (b. Preston, England; keyboards) and Andrew Deevey (b. 11 November 1964, Liverpool, England). The Caretaker Race came into existence in east London in 1986 after pivotal force Strickland left fellow London outfit the Loft, just as the independent circuit was held in the grip of the 'shambling' scene. While all around them feigned incompetence, however, the Caretaker Race chose a mature, melodic guitar path reminiscent of Australian group the Go-Betweens. This approach won them several friends and a stable sales figure. They started their own Roustabout Records in 1987 before switching to the Foundation label in 1989. Along the way they lost bassist Henry Hersom, who joined London outfit Bob, to be replaced by Jackie Carrera (b. 6 June 1964, London, England), and also Sally Ward, who left to take up teaching.
Album: *Hangover Square* (1990).

Carter The Unstoppable Sex Machine

When Jamie Wednesday folded in the face of public apathy, they left two singles, 'Vote For Love' and 'We Three Kings Of Orient Aren't', on the Pink label, in their wake. Before that, there had been several bands, namely the Ballpoints, the End, Dead Clergy and Peter Pan's Playground. Then the south London pair of Jimbob (b. James Morrison, 22 November 1960) and Fruitbat (b. Leslie Carter, 12 February 1958) acquired a drum machine and took their name from a newspaper cutting, sometime in 1988, to create Carter The Unstoppable Sex Machine. The single 'Sheltered Life', on the independent label Big Cat, revealed a dance formula that had more in common with those other irreverent samplers such as the KLF than the Pet Shop Boys or Erasure. The single made little impression, unlike Carter's next single, 'Sheriff Fatman' (1989), an exciting amalgam of a great riff, a great rhythm and great lyrics about a maverick landlord. The follow-up, *101 Damnations*, was an innovative melting pot of samples, ideas and tunes, all mixed with a punk-inspired ethos. Lyrically, the duo used a mix-and-match approach, pairing words and phrases in a manner that soon became a trademark. 'Rubbish' (1990) followed 'Fatman' into the UK indie charts, and attracted considerable attention, helped by a cover of the Pet Shop Boys' 'Rent' on the b-side. Carter moved to Rough Trade, by the end of the year releasing their fourth single, 'Anytime, Anyplace, Anywhere' (a play on the Who's mid-60s classic, 'Anyway, Anyhow, Anywhere'). After the export-only *Handbuilt For Perverts* and a special Christmas giveaway single, 'Christmas Shopper's Paradise', came the controversial 'Bloodsports For All' in 1991. This received very little airplay as it coincided with the

Carter USM

start of the Iraqi conflict, but *30 Something* topped the UK Independent chart and reached the national Top 10. Financial upheaval at Rough Trade and Carter's growing success led to a deal with Chrysalis, commencing with a chart-bound reissue of 'Sheriff Fatman' in June. In the meantime, the band visited the USA and toured Japan later in the year. Carter's Top 20 hit later in 1991, 'After The Watershed' motivated lawyers representing the Rolling Stones to demand substantial payment (allegedly 100% of all royalties) for an infringement of copyright in using a snippet of the Stones' 1967 hit, 'Ruby Tuesday'.

Carter's lighting engineer and MC, Jon 'Fat' Beast has ingratiated himself within the group's 'image', despite Carter and Beast amicably parting company in early 1992, and deserves a mention as one of the UK Independent scenes' prime concert promoters in London in mid-80s. One of his most successful ventures was running the 'Timebox' nights at north London's Bull And Gate venue.

Albums: *101 Damnations* (1990), *30 Something* (1991), *1992 - The Love Album* (1992).

Cassandra Complex

This electronic and guitar band was formed in Leeds, England in the mid-80s, with a line-up consisting of Rodney Orpheus (vocals), Paul Dillon (keyboards) and Andy Booth (guitar). Their first single 'March' came out in April 1985 on their own Complex RAP label. Lyrically, it concerned the perception of liberty: 'Everyone's got a concept of freedom. Some people think that freedom is having the right to work; to another way of thinking, having the right not to work is freedom'. Before this they had also constructed their own basement studio, and organized several 'events' which would take the form of live shows with visuals, run on an autonomous basis. They were originally housed on Rouska Records, a small independent based in Leeds, for which they released the singles 'Datakill' and 'Moscow Idaho', and the album *Grenade* in 1986. The latter contained some potent, though some argued egocentric, observations: 'When I grow up I'm gonna buy myself a bomb big enough to blow up the future'. Significantly, they were not averse to covering Throbbing Gristle's 'Something Came Over Me' live and on record. However, their real audience seemed to be Europe, where they are now based. Signing to Play It Again Sam, they released *Theomania* in the summer of 1988, followed by *Finland* two years later. One of the tracks on this album, 'Let's Go To Europe', was semi-autobiographical. Their most recent album took its title from a quote by Russian mystic Gurdjieff, and was typically cluttered with pseudo-intellectual baggage throughout. It is little surprise that their guitar/synthesizer hard pop remains more popular on the Continent than in their homeland.

Albums: *Grenade* (1986), *Hello America* (1987), *Feel The Width* (1987), *Theomania* (1988), *Satan, Bugs Bunny And Me* (1989), *Finland* (1990), *Cyberpunx* (1990), *The War Against Sleep* (1991).

Catherine Wheel

After spending time in various local bands Rob Dickinson (b. 23 July 1965, Norwich, Norfolk, England; vocals) and Brian Futter (b. 7 December 1965, London, England; guitar) instigated the Catherine Wheel in the spring of 1990 in the time honoured tradition of recording on an 8 track tape machine in a bedroom. Joined by the rhythm section of Neil Sims (b. 4 October 1965, Norwich, Norfolk, England; drums) and David Hawes (b. 10 November 1965, Great Yarmouth, Norfolk, England; bass) for live shows, the band had an immediate impact which took them by surprise. Armed with a guitar-propelled sound which was sufficiently fashionable to attract attention without sacrificing creative depth, they released a debut EP *She's My Friend* on the Wilde Club label at the start of 1991. This hinted at a potential which warranted certain members of the group forsaking lucrative jobs in the local oil industry and concentrating on playing full-time. British tours with such names as Blur and the Charlatans gave the Catherine Wheel an even higher profile, resulting in a major deal with Fontana Records during the summer of the same year. They never even needed to exploit the family ties between singer Rob Dickinson and cousin Bruce, frontman of heavy metal outfit, Iron Maiden.

Album: *Ferment* (1992).

Cave, Nick, And The Bad Seeds

After the Birthday Party split, the enigmatic Australian vocalist Nick Cave retained his association with Berlin by teaming up with ex-Einsturzende Neubauten member Blixa Bargeld (guitar), together with ex-Magazine personnel Barry Adamson (bass and other instruments) and multi-instrumentalist Mick Harvey. The debut album *From Here To Eternity* was joined by a startling rendition of the Elvis Presley classic 'In the Ghetto', showing Cave had lost none of his passion and the ability to inject tension in his music. *The First Born Is Dead* followed a year later, promoted by the excellent 'Tupelo', but the Bad Seeds made their mark with *Kicking Against The Pricks* in the summer of 1986, bolstered by the UK Independent number 1, 'The Singer'. Cave had always drawn from a variety of sources, from Captain Beefheart to delta blues, and the Bad Seeds' material betrayed a claustrophobic, swamp-like aura. Although purely cover versions, *Kicking Against The Pricks* (which included drummer Thomas Wylder) fully displayed Cave's ability as an original interpreter of

artist's material. However, *Your Funeral, My Trial* emphasized the power of his self-penned work. After a brief hiatus from recording, it was two years before Cave returned, but it was worth the wait. 'The Mercy Seat' was a taut, violent single, followed by the milder 'Oh Deanna'. Both elements were present on October 1988's *Tender Prey*. 'The Ship Song', released in February 1990, continued Cave's exploration of the more traditional ballad, and was followed by another strong album, *The Good Son*, in April. Cave's literary aspirations were given an outlet by Black Spring Press in 1989 by publishing his novel *And The Ass Saw The Angel*. His film appearances include Wim Wenders' *Wings Of Desire* (1987) and a powerful performance as a prison inmate in the Australian production, *Ghosts Of The Civil Dead* (1989).
Albums: *From Here To Eternity* (1984), *The First Born Is Dead* (1985), *Kicking Against The Pricks* (1986), *Your Funeral, My Trial* (1986), *Tender Prey* (1988), with Mick Harvey, Blixa Bargeld *Ghosts Of The Civil Dead* (1989, film soundtrack), *The Good Son* (1990), *Henry's Dream* (1992).
Futher reading: a collection of song lyrics and verse, *King Ink*, Nick Cave.

Chameleons

Formed in 1981 in Middleton, Manchester, this highly promising but ill-fated group comprised Mark Burgess (vocals/bass), Reg Smithies (guitar), Dave Fielding (guitar) and Brian Schofield (drums). After some successful BBC radio sessions, the unit were signed to the CBS subsidiary Epic and released 'In Shreds'. Its lack of success saw the group switch to the independent label Statik where they issued 'As High As You Can Go' and 'A Person Isn't Safe Anywhere These Days'. Their *Script Of The Bridge* and *What Does Anything Mean Basically?* revealed them as a promising guitar-based group with a strong melodic sense. Regular touring won them a contract with Geffen Records and their third album *Strange Times* was very well received by the critics. Just as a breakthrough beckoned, however, their manager Tony Fletcher died and amid the ensuing chaos the group folded. Two spin-off groups, the Sun And The Moon and the Reegs lacked the charm of their powerful but unrealized mother group.
Albums: *Script Of The Bridge* (1983), *What Does Anything Mean Basically?* (1985), *Fan And The Bellows* (1986), *Strange Times* (1987), *Tripping Dogs* (1990, early recordings), *Peel Sessions* (1990, early recordings).

Channel 3

This US based hardcore band, comprised Mike McGrann (vocals/guitar), Kimm Gardner (guitar), Larry Kelley (bass) and Mike Burton (the most permanent of their first four drummers). Hailing from the suburban community of Cerritos in south Los Angeles, they originally formed in 1980. Their first release was an EP on Californian label Posh Boy in 1981. One track from this, 'Manzanar', was played heavily by UK disc jockey John Peel, which resulted in Posh Boy's Robbie Fields licensing a three track EP to No Future Records. This was headed by the title track 'I've Got A Gun'. 'Manzanar' was again present, and concerned McGrann's mother (he is partially of Japanese origin) being sent to a work camp in World War II. Considering it was early in the band's career, the lyrics showed surprising maturity: 'Adolf really caught your eye, ain't it fun to knock the Warsaw zone, but you turned the other way, when we screwed some of our very own'. 1982 saw Jack Debaun become their next drummer, and *Fear Of Life* was re-titled *I've Got A Gun* in the UK with some differences in the track-listing. 1983's *After The Lights Go Out* was a superior and more consistent effort, although it failed to recapture the spark of interest which came with their first UK single. McGrann's summation of their brief existence was thus: 'Channel 3 was a band formed around friendships, if we weren't playing guitars together we'd probably be bowling or robbing Laundramats together.'
Albums: *Fear Of Life/I've Got A Gun* (1982), *After The Lights Go Out* (1983).

Chapterhouse

Formed in Reading in 1987 by Andrew Sherriff (b. 5 May 1969, Wokingham, England; guitar/vocals), Stephen Patman (b. 8 November 1968, Windsor, Berkshire, England; guitar), Simon Rowe (b. 23 June 1969, Reading, Berkshire, England; guitar), Jon Curtis (bass) and Ashley Bates (b. 2 November 1971, Reading, Berkshire, England; drums), Chapterhouse took the unusual step of rehearsing and gigging for well over a year before recording even a demotape. Initially lumped in with the British acid rock scene of the time, a mistake hardly rectified by the band's early performances supporting the rather laidback Spacemen 3. Chapterhouse eventually escaped from one genre only to find themselves thrust amongst the infamous 'shoegazer' groups of 1991 (with Lush, Moose and Slowdive), so called because of the bands' static live shows and insular music. Bassist Jon Curtis left early on to study, being replaced by Russell Barrett (b. 7 November 1968, Vermont, USA) who also fronted his own garage band, the Bikinis. Chapterhouse eventually signed to the newly-formed Dedicated label, releasing a series of lavishly-acclaimed singles, including 'Pearl', which reached the UK Top 75, and which revelled in distorted melodies and attracted a healthy indiginous following, while the autumn of 1991 saw the band aiming their

Charlatans

sights on the anticipatory American market.
Album: *Whirlpool* (1991).

Charlatans

Of all the 'Manchester' bands to emerge in 1989 and
1990, the Charlatans' rise was undoubtedly the
swiftest. Hinging around Tim Burgess (b. 30 May
1968, Salford, Manchester, England; lead vocals, ex-
Electric Crayons) and Martin Blunt (b. 1965; bass,
ex-Makin' Time), supported by Jon Baker (b. 1969;
guitar), Jon Brookes (b. 1969; drums) and Rob
Collins (b. 1967; keyboards), the band fused 60s
melodies, Hammond organ riffs and a generally loose
feel that was instantly adopted by those taken with
the Stone Roses and the Happy Mondays. The
group's stage presentation was boosted by the
recruitmant of veteran Californian lightsman 'Captain
Whizzo' who provided the psychedelic visuals. With
all the optimism that accompanies a new decade,
1990's 'Indian Rope', a 12-inch only debut on their
own Dead Dead Good label, sold well enough to
secure a contract with Beggars Banquet/Situation 2.
That was nothing compared to 'The Only One I
Know', a swirling, groovy pop song that borrowed
from the Byrds and Booker T. And The MGs. to
provide the perfect summer anthem. A UK Top 10
hit, the single catapulted the Charlatans into the big
league, and was consolidated by the follow-up
'Then', and the band's debut album later that year.
With the delightful sounds that made up the UK
chart-topping *Some Friendly*, the band ended the year
on a high note. 1991 proved far quieter on the
recording front, although a fourth single and a further
hit, 'Over Rising', steered away from the band's
organ-based approach.
Albums: *Some Friendly* (1990), *Between 10th And 11th*
(1992).

Chefs

The Chefs, from Brighton, East Sussex, only survived
three singles before splitting, and one of these was a
reissue! Along with other aspiring local talent in the
late 70s, the Chefs - Helen McCookerybook (b.
Helen McCallum; vocals/bass), James McCallum
(guitar), Russell Greenwood (drums), Carl Evans
(guitar) - were signed to the town's resident label
Attrix. The EP *Sweetie*, issued in September 1980,
was far from being sweet, dealing frankly with sex,
personal hygiene and other matters. But '24 Hours'
(1981) was nothing short of a great pop song and was
strong enough to warrant a reissue on the Midlands
label, Graduate. The band changed their name to

Skat for a guitar-based cover of the Velevet Underground's 'Femme Fatale'. Helen McCookerybook left to form Helen And The Horns, a bold brass dominated group with influences taken from the American west. 'Pioneer Town' and a remake of Doris Day's 'Secret Love' were both interesting excursions, although the band floundered due to Helen's increasing stage fright.

Chelsea

This London-based punk outfit was formed in 1977 by vocalist Gene October. Recruiting Brian James (guitar), Geoff Myles (bass) and Chris Bashford (drums), they were a band with a strong social conscience. Specializing in sub-three minute vitriolic outbursts on unemployment, inner city decay and the deconstruction of society under Thatcherite rule, their lyrics were always more interesting than their music. The songs were generally identikit-style uptempo numbers, marred by low-tech studio techniques. Their most noteworthy song is 'Right To Work', which became a working-class anthem during the late 70s. They have continued to record throughout the 80s, but with an ever-changing line-up and an image that is rather anachronistic.
Albums: *Chelsea* (1979), *Alternative Hits* (1980), *Evacuate* (1982), *Just For The Record* (1985), *Rocks Off* (1986), *Backtrax* (1988), *Unreleased Stuff* (1988), *Under Wraps* (1989), *Ultra Prophets* (1989).

Cherry, Neneh

b. 10 March 1964, Stockholm, Sweden. Cherry is the step-daughter of jazz trumpeter Don Cherry. She joined English post-punk band Rip, Rig And Panic in 1981 as a vocalist, later performing with several ex-members of that band as Float Up CP. In the mid-80s she also sang backing vocals for the Slits and The The ('Slow Train To Dawn', 1987). In 1989, Cherry recorded a series of dance hits for Circa. They included 'Buffalo Stance' (which was featured on the soundtrack of the film *Slaves Of New York*, 'Manchild' and 'Kisses On The Wind'. Her main co-writer was Cameron McVey, whom she married. Cherry contributed to the AIDS-charity collection, *Red Hot And Blue*, singing Cole Porter's 'I've Got You Under My Skin'. Neneh Cherry's half-sister Titiyo is also a singer. Born in Sweden in 1968, she had international success with 'Flowers' in 1990, a track from her first album, produced by Magnus Frykberg.
Album: *Raw Like Sushi* (1989).

Cherry Vanilla

This US punk outfit was fronted by the sexually provocative Cherry Vanilla (b. New York, USA). With the addition of Stuart Elliot (drums), Howie Finkel (bass), Louis Lepere (guitar) and Zecca Esquibel (keyboards), they specialized in commercial pop-rock anthems, rather than hard-line punk. Signing to RCA, they supported Johnny Thunders And The Heartbreakers on their UK tour in 1978. Following the release of the follow-up *Venus De Vinyl*, the group left RCA for an uncertain future.
Albums: *Bad Girl* (1978), *Venus De Vinyl* (1979).

Chesterfields

For a while, the Chesterfields' charming, jolly guitar pop, was very much in vogue. They were formed in Yeovil, Somerset, England in the summer of 1984, by David Goldsworthy (guitar/vocals), Simon Barber (bass/vocals) and Dominic Manns (drums). In 1985 they were joined by guitarist Brendan Holden. They contributed 'Nose Out Of Joint' alongside a track from Scotland's Shop Assistants, whom they joined at Bristol's Subway Organisation Records in time for the EP *A Guitar In Your Bath* (1986), four slices of frothy guitar pop. 'Completely And Utterly' continued the formula, but for the next single, 'Ask Johnny Dee' in 1987, the Chesterfields offered a less abrasive style. *Kettle* show-cased the band's songwriting talents admirably. Back in April, Brendan had left the band, temporarily replaced by Rodney Allen (later with the Blue Aeroplanes) and former Loft guitarist Andy Strickland (on loan from the Caretaker Race). A more permanent guitarist was later found in Simon's brother Mark. A compilation of the band's singles, *Westward Ho!*, coincided with the release of their session for BBC disc jockey, Janice Long. A month later, the band set up their own label, Household. In March 1988 they issued 'Goodbye Goodbye' a more melancholy offering than previous efforts. This was followed by 'Blame' and a new album, *Crocodile Tears*. The latter was not as warmly received as *Kettle* and both Dominic and David left soon after. The Chesterfields continued with Simon and Mark co-fronting the band, assisted by various drummers and guitarists, before splitting up in July 1989. Their last offering, 'Fool Is A Man' was perhaps their finest moment. Simon went on to front Yeovil-based Basinger, while Mark led the Bristol-based Grape.
Albums: *Kettle* (1987), *Crocodile Tears* (1988). Compilation: *Westward Ho!* (1987).

Chills

The ever-changing line-ups that have made up New Zealand guitar pop band the Chills are kept constant by founder member Martin Phillipps (b. 1963, Dunedin, New Zealand) whose musical apprenticeship began when he was asked to join punk band the Same as guitarist in 1978. Inspired by New Zealand's top punk acts the Enemy and the Clean, the Same churned out a standard set of 60s garage band covers without ever recording. When that band split Phillipps took his sister Rachel, and bassist Jane

Todd (later of the Verlaines) into the first incarnation of the Chills in 1980. Signed to the influential New Zealand independent label Flying Nun, the Chills began to release a number of seminal guitar-pop singles, mostly in New Zealand. Other members to pass through the band over the years included Fraser Batts (keyboards), Terry Moore (bass), Martin Kean (guitar), Peter Allison (keyboards), Alan Haig (drums), and Martyn Bull (drums) - the latter of whom died in 1983 of leukæmia. It was to him that Phillipps dedicated 'I Love My Leather Jacket', as the said apparel was Bull's parting gift. In 1985, already on their ninth line-up, Phillipps brought the Chills to London for some dates and Alan McGee released the *Kaleidoscope World* compilation on his Creation label. On returning to New Zealand the band dissolved again and Phillipps once more found new musicians including Justin Harwood (bass), Andrew Todd (keyboards), Caroline Easther (drums) and Jimmy Stephenson (drums). Despite the constant upheavals, and the relative lack of recorded material for a band with a 10-year career, the Chills have continued to produce good clean guitar driven pop.

Albums: *Kaleidoscope World* (1986), *Brave Words* (1987), *Submarine Bells* (1990).

China Crisis

This UK, Liverpool-based group was formed in 1979 around the core of Gary Daly (b. 5 May 1962, Kirkby, Merseyside, England; vocals) and Eddie Lundon (b. 9 June 1962, Kirkby, Merseyside, England; guitar). In 1982, their first single, 'African And White', initially on the independent Inevitable label, was picked up for distribution by Virgin Records and made a critical impact, despite only just breaking into the UK Top 50. The single's b-side was 'Red Sails', a perfect early example of China Crisis's pastoral electro-pop. Having now signed to the Virgin label, the duo formed a more permanent line-up with the recruitment of Gazza Johnson (bass) and Kevin Wilkinson (drums). The following single, 'Christian', taken from the debut album *Difficult Shapes And Passive Rhythms* was a UK number 12 hit. With the follow-up to their second album, they scored two further Top 50 hits with 'Tragedy And Mystery' and 'Working With Fire And Steel', the former featuring the trade-mark on the forthcoming album - the ethereal oboe accompaniment. 'Wishful Thinking' in 1984 gave the group a Top 10 hit, while the following year gave them two further Top 20 hits with 'Black Man Ray' and 'King In A Catholic Style (Wake Up)'. While *Flaunt The Imperfection*, produced by Walter Becker, reached the UK Top 10, the follow-up, the uneven *What Price Paradise?* (produced by Clive Langer and Alan Winstanley), saw a drop in China Crisis's fortunes, when the album peaked at number 63. A two-year hiatus saw a reunion with Becker which resulted in the critically acclaimed *Diary Of A Hollow Horse*, although this success was not reflected in sales. Since their split with Virgin and the release of a deserved reappraisal of the group's career with a compilation in 1990, activities within the China Crisis camp has been quiet.

Albums: *Difficult Shapes And Passive Rhythms* (1983), *Working With Fire And Steel - Possible Pop Songs Volume Two* (1983), *Flaunt The Imperfection* (1985), *What Price Paradise?* (1986), *Diary Of A Hollow Horse* (1989). Compilation: *The China Crisis Collection* (1990).

Chris And Cosey

Chris Carter and Cosey Fanni Tutti (b. Christine Newby) became partners while with late 70s 'industrial' sound pioneers Throbbing Gristle. When the latter split in 1981, the couple decided to operate both as Chris And Cosey and as CTI (Creative Technology Institute). The debut album *Heartbeat*, credited to CTI, drew from Throbbing Gristle's rhythmic undercurrents but the pair's next album, *Trance*, was soured by a disagreement with Rough Trade Records over its selling price. 1983 yielded two singles, the Japanese-only 'Nikki' (a collaboration with John Duncan) and the relatively mainstream 'October (Love Song)', followed in 1984 by *Songs Of Love And Lust*. Also in 1984, the duo issued *Elemental 7* in collaboration with John Lacey on Cabaret Voltaire's Doublevision label and further projects, as CTI, with Lustmord's Brian Williams and Glenn Wallis of Knostructivitis followed later that year as did *European Rendezvous*. CTI's *Mondo Beat* in 1985, was originally conceived by Chris as a 12-inch single. By this time, the pair's relationship with Rough Trade had become strained and they left after *Techno Primitiv* and 'Sweet Surprise', a project with the Eurythmics. They then joined Vancouver label Nettwerk Productions, while in Europe, they were handled by renowned Brussels label, Play It Again Sam (who have also reissued much of their product). Since then, Chris And Cosey have gradually steered towards the 'New Beat' dance sound, with singles like 'Obsession', 'Exotica' (both 1987) and 'Rise' (1989). Early 90s albums *Reflection* and *Pagan Tango*, confirmed their adoption of hi-tech dance music.

Albums: *Heartbeat* (1981), *Trance* (1982), *Songs Of Love And Lust* (1984), *Elemental 7* (1984), *European Rendezvous* (1984), *Mondo Beat* (1985), *Techno Primitiv* (1985), *Take Five* (1986), *Action* (1987), *Exotica* (1987), *Sweet Surprise* (1987), with various artists *Core* (1988), *Trust* (1989), *Reflection* (1990), *Pagan Tango* (1991). Compilations: *Best Of Chris And Cosey* (1989), *Collectiv 1, 2, 3, & 4* (1990).

Christian Death

This art-rock group were formed in Los Angeles, California in 1979 by singer Rozz Williams. The original line-up comprised Rikk Agnew (guitar), James McGearly (bass) and George Belanger (drums). In finding success in their homeland elusive, the group relocated to Europe in 1983, were they fitted in perfectly with the gothic rock fashion. Shunning the easy route to success, the band have since remained on the periphery of rock and Christian Death's independence from prevailing trends has secured for themselves a strong cult-following. Early releases were on the Au Suicide label and the group has since continued to release material on the Contemporary International label. In 1986 the group fell under the control of songwriter and singer Valor Kand (b. Australia) who made radical changes to the the line-up. Principal members now included Gitane Demone (vocals/keyboards) and David Glass (drums).Their often provocative material often made as its target the subject of war and organized religion, particularly that of Catholicism, siting corruption in the church and links with politicians. Recent album cover artwork, such as in the case of *Sex, Drugs And Jesus Christ*, which depicted a Christ-like figure injecting heroin caused a suitable amount of publicity and controversy.

Albums: *Only Theatre Of Pain* (1982), *Deathwish* (1983), *Catastrophe Ballet* (1984), *Ashes* (1985), *Wind Kissed Pictures* (1985), *The Decomposition Of Violets* (1986), *Anthology Of Live Bootlegs* (1986), *Atrocities* (1986), *Past And Present* (1987), *Scriptures* (1987), *Sex, Drugs And Jesus Christ* (1988), *The Heretics Alive* (1989), *All The Love* (1989), *All The Hate* (1989), *Insanus, Ultio, Proditio Misericordiaque* (1990), *Past, Present And Forever* (1991). Compilation: *Jesus Points The Bone At You* (1992, singles collection from 1986-1990).

Christians

This UK group was formed in Liverpool in 1984 and comprised former Yachts and It's Immaterial keyboard player Henry Priestman (b. 21 June 1955, Hull, Humberside, England) and the Christain brothers Roger (b. 1950, Merseyside, England), Garry (b. Garrison Christian, 1955, Merseyside, England) and Russell (b. 8 July 1956, Merseyside, England). Up until then, the brothers, who came from a family of 11, with a Jamaican immigrant father and Liverpudlian mother, had performed as a soul a cappella trio and had previously worked under a variety of names, most notably as Natural High when they made an appearence on ITV's *Opportunity Knocks* talent show in 1974. The Christian brothers met Priestman, who would become the group's main songwriter, at Pete Wylie's Liverpool studios, where Priestman would convince the trio to try recording

his compositions. The resulting demo session tapes would eventually lead to the Christians signing to Island Records. The group's combination of pop and soul earned the group a string of UK hits including, in 1987, 'Forgotten Town', 'Hooverville (They Promised Us The World)', 'When The Fingers Point' and 'Ideal World'. The media usually focused their attention on the striking appearance of the tall, shaven-headed Garry. This, and a reluctance to tour, led Roger quit the group in 1987. The Christians' self-titled album meanwhile, would become Island's best-selling debut. With the exception of the Top 30 hit 'Born Again' in the spring, 1988 was much quieter with the group touring and recording. The year was brought to a climax however with the Top 10 cover of the Isley Brothers hit, 'Harvest For The World'. The Hillsborough crowd disaster in April 1989, resulted in the being given joint credit on the charity single 'Ferry Cross The Mersey' with Paul McCartney, Gerry Marsden, Holly Johnson and Stock, Aitken And Waterman. In 1989, Roger Christian released a solo single 'Take It From Me' achieving a minor UK hit, plus an well-received album, *Roger Christian*. The Christians' only chart that year came with the the the Top 20 'Words'. The labours over recording the second album, *Colours*, was rewarded by it hitting the UK number 1 spot on its first week in the chart. Despite subsequent singles failing to break into the Top 50, the group have the luxury of an established mature fan-base.

Albums: *The Christians* (1987), *Colour* (1990).

Chumbawamba

This eight-piece anarchist/situationist group was formed in Leeds, England out of a collective household situated in the shadow of Armley jail, in a similar manner to Crass, who were an obvious early influence. Original members all originate from either Barnsley or Burnley, England. First playing live in 1983, the band alternate between instruments/theatricals on stage and record. Their line-up comprising Harry, Alice Nutter, Boffo, Mavis Dillan, Lou, Danbert Norbacon, Simon, Dunst, was subject to change according to the internal dynamics of the household, with ages ranging from teens to thirties at their inception. Their first single 'Revolution' was startling, opening with the sound of John Lennon's 'Imagine' before it is taken off the stereo and smashed. It was just as precise lyrically: 'The history books from every age, have the same words written on every page: always starting with revolution, always ending with capitulation. Always silenced by the truncheon, or bought out with concessions, always repetition . . .'. It was a powerful introduction, finishing at number 6 in BBC disc jockey John Peel's 1985 Festive Fifty radio poll. The follow-up, 'We Are The World', was banned from airplay, owing to its explicit support of direct action. *Pictures Of Starving Children Sell Records* used polemic and agit-prop to subvert a common theme in the music industry at that time, denouncing Band Aid. Other targets included multinationals (the band had published a booklet on immoral activities titled *Dirty Fingers In Dirty Pies*), apartheid and imperialism. Their discourse was made all the more articulate by the surprising virtuosity of music employed, from polka, to ballad, to thrash. Pouring red paint over the Clash on their comeback 'busking' tour in Leeds demonstrated their contempt for what they saw as false prophets, while the second album considered the role of government in oppression and the futility of the vote. *English Rebel Songs* acknowledged their place in the folk protest movement, and *Slap!* saw hope in the rebellious dance music which characterized the end of the 80s. Still active in various spheres, the band have produced a legacy of fine, politically active music which continued the thread of bands like Crass, Conflict and Flux Of Pink Indians, imbuing it with intelligence and realism.

Albums: *Pictures Of Starving Children Sell Records* (1986), *Never Mind The Ballots* (1987), *English Rebel Songs* (1989), *Slap!* (1990).

Church

Church

Formed in Canberra, Australia in 1980, the Church, led by Steve Kilbey (b. Australia; bass/vocals) comprised Peter Koppes (b. Australia; guitar/vocals), Marty Willson-Piper (b. Sweden; guitar/vocals) and Richard Ploog (b. Australia; drums). Their debut release in 1981, *Of Skins And Heart* gained some radio and television exposure and the European release *The Church*, which included the stand-out track 'The Unguarded Moment', gave indications of great promise. The Church's 60s/Byrds revivalist stance, coupled with a distinctive 12-stringed, 'jangly' guitar approach was exemplified on *The Blurred Crusade* by such songs as 'Almost With You', 'When You Were Mine' and 'Fields Of Mars'. *Starfish* saw the band gain college radio airplay in the USA, earning them a US

Top 30 hit with 'Under The Milky Way', and strengthened their audiences in parts of Europe although the group found themselves restricted to a loyal cult following. Much of the group's activities have been interrupted periodically due to internal problems and for solo projects and collaborations. Ploog's departure in 1991 saw the addition of former Patti Smith group drummer, Jay Dee Daugherty. Marty Willson-Piper (b. Sweden) released two solo albums and took on a part-time role as guitarist for All About Eve in 1991. Kilbey has recorded several as well as publishing a book of poems. In 1991 he teamed up Go-Betweens guitarist Grant McLennan to record under the name of Jack Frost. Peter Koppes completed a EP *When Reason Forbids* in 1987.

Albums: *Of Skins & Heart* aka *The Church* (1981), *Blurred Crusade* (1982), *The Seance* (1983), *Remote Luxury* (1985), *Heyday* (1986), *Starfish* (1988), *Gold Afternoon Fix* (1990), *Priest = Aura* (1992). Compilations: *Conception* (1988), *A Quick Smoke At Spots (Archives 1986-1990)* (1991). Solo albums: Marty Willson-Piper *In Reflection Chase* (1987), *Art Attack Survival* (1988); Steve Kilbey *Unearthed* (1987), *The Slow Crack* (1987), with Grant McLennan (as Jack Frost) *Jack Frost* (1991).

Ciccone Youth

A satirical offshoot from New York rock innovators Sonic Youth, Ciccone Youth comprise essentially the same personnel Thurston Moore (guitar/vocals), Kim Gordon (bass/vocals), Lee Renaldo (guitar) plus, various drummers and other collaborators. The band had long been fascinated by the impact Madonna was having on a generation. Moore had previously mounted a photo of the artist on the cover of his own fanzine *Killer*. The band's infatuation was also prefaced with the track 'Madonna, Sean And Me' on Sonic Youth's *E.V.O.L.* album. It was November 1986 when the name Ciccone Youth was first employed, however. The single 'Into The Groove(y)' was a direct parody of Madonna's original, with Moore's vocals overlaid in a manner which suggested a duet. Assistance on the recording came from Firehose and Mike Batt (ex-Minutemen). Further pastiche was served up with *The Whitey Album*. Despite rumours that it would be made up entirely of covers of the Beatles' similarly titled original, it proved to be the band's most eclectic release to date. 'We just wanted to steal blatantly from these records. We're not trying to hide anything. We took the bass drums of L.L. Cool J and Run DMC records. We took stuff off Jimi Hendrix records...' Notable was the deliberately lifeless rendering of Robert Palmer's 'Addicted To Love', and the cover of John Cage's 'Silence' pastiche. While not an unqualified success, the album served to rid the band of some of their excesses without committing them to the catalogue of

Sonic Youth.
Albums: *The Whitey Album* (1989).

Circle Jerks

Formed in Los Angeles, USA in 1980, this powerful
punk band was founded by vocalist Keith Morris (ex-
Black Flag) and guitarist Greg Hetson (ex-Redd
Kross). Roger (Dowding) Rogerson and Lucky
Lehrer completed the line-up featured on the
quartet's early albums, the second of which, *Wild In
The Streets*, was initially issued on Police manager
Miles Copeland's Step Forward/Faulty label.
Appearances on several influential 'new music'
compilations, including *Decline Of Western Civilisation*
and *Let Them Eat Jelly Beans* confirmed the Circle
Jerks' position at the vanguard of California's virulent
hardcore movement. Longstanding members Morris
and Hetson have remained at the helm of this
compulsive group which, by 1989, was completed by
Zander 'Snake' Scloss (bass) and Keith 'Adolph' Clark
(drums).
Albums: *Group Sex* (1981), *Wild In The Streets* (1982),
Golden Shower (1983), *V1* (1987), *Wonderful* (1989).

Clarke, John Cooper

b. 25 January 1949, Salford, Manchester, England.
With a 1965-style Bob Dylan suit and sunglasses and
a quickfire delivery, Clarke enjoyed a brief vogue as a
'punk poet'. He compositions which showed the
influence of the punning wordplay of Roger
McGough and also the tougher 'hip' approach of the
American beats. Clarke recited his poetry in local folk
clubs and working with Rick Goldstraw's group, the
Ferretts, he began to mix his poems with musical
backing. Goldstraw's involvement with the
independent record label, Rabid led, in 1977, to
Clarke recording the co-produced Martin Hannett
single 'Psycle Sluts' - '...those nubile nihilists of the
north circular the lean leonine leatherette lovelies of
the Leeds intersection luftwaffe angels locked in a
pagan paradise - no cash a passion for trash...' With
the onset of punk, Clarke found himself encountering
livelier audiences when he shared a bill with the
Buzzcocks. The popularity of his performances with
such audiences led to an increase in the phenomenon
of the 'punk poet', giving rise to the careers of such
artists as Attila The Stockbroker, Seething Wells and
Joolz. After touring with Be-Bop DeLuxe, he was
signed to Epic where Bill Nelson produced his debut
album. The single 'Gimmix' was a UK Top 40 hit in
1979. Produced by Martin Hannett and with backing
music by the Invisible Girls, it also appeared on *Snap
Crackle And Bop*, along with 'Beasley Street',
described by one reviewer as 'an English "Desolation
Row"'. Clarke went into semi-retirement later in the
80s, forming a domestic partnership with ex-Velvet
Underground singer Nico. Into the 90s, Clarke

remains active on the pub and club circuit and is
engaged in various film and book projects.
Albums: *Disguise In Love* (1978), *Snap Crackle And
Bop* (1979), *Qu'est Le Maison De Fromage* (1980), *Me
And My Big Mouth* (1981), *Zip Style Method* (1982).
Further reading: *Ten Years In An Open Necked Shirt*,
John Cooper Clarke.

Clash

Clash

The Clash at first tucked in snugly behind punk's
loudest noise, the Sex Pistols (whom they supported
on 'the Anarchy tour'), and later became a much
more consistent and intriguing force. Guitarist Mick
Jones (b. 26 June 1953, London, England) had
formed London SS in 1975, whose members at one
time included bassist Paul Simonon (b. 15 December
1956, London, England) and drummer Nicky
'Topper' Headon (b. 30 May 1955, Bromley, Kent,
England). Joe Strummer (b. John Graham Mellor, 21
August 1952, Ankara, Turkey) had spent the mid-70s
fronting a pub-rock group called the 101ers, playing
early rock 'n' roll style numbers like 'Keys To Your
Heart'. The early line-up of the Clash was completed
by guitarist Keith Levine but he left early in 1976
with another original member, drummer Terry
Chimes, whose services were called upon
intermittently during the following years. They
signed to CBS Records and during three weekends
they recorded *The Clash* in London with sound

engineer, Mickey Foote, taking on the producer's role. In 1977 *Rolling Stone* magazine called it the 'definitive punk album' and elsewhere it was recognized that they had brilliantly distilled the anger, depression and energy of mid-70s England. More importantly, they had infused the message and sloganeering with strong tunes and pop hooks, as on 'I'm So Bored With The USA' and 'Career Opportunities'. The album reached number 12 in the UK charts and garnered almost universal praise. CBS was keen to infiltrate the American market and Blue Oyster Cult's founder/lyricist Sandy Pearlman was brought in to produce *Give 'Em Enough Rope*. The label's manipulative approach failed and it had very poor sales in the USA but in the UK it reached number 2, despite pertinent claims that its more rounded edges amounted to a sell out of the band's earlier much flaunted punk ethics. They increasingly embraced reggae elements, seemingly a natural progression of their anti-racist stance, and had a minor UK hit with '(White Man) In Hammersmith Palais' in July 1978 and followed it up with the frothy punk-pop of 'Tommy Gun' - their first Top 20 hit. Their debut album was finally released in the USA as a double set including tracks from their singles and it sold healthily before *London Calling*, produced by the volatile Guy Stevens, marked a return to almost top form. They played to packed houses across the USA early in 1980 and were cover stars on many prestigious rock magazines. Typically, their next move was over-ambitious and the triple set *Sandinista!* was leaden and too sprawling after the acute concentration of earlier records. It scraped into the UK Top 20 and sales were disappointing despite CBS making it available at a special cut-price. The experienced rock producer, Glyn Johns, was brought in to instigate a tightening-up and *Combat Rock* was as snappy as anticipated. It was recorded with Terry Chimes on drums after Headon had abruptly left the group. Chimes was later replaced by Pete Howard. 'Rock The Casbah', a jaunty, humorous song written by Headon, became a Top 10 hit in the USA and reached number 30 in the UK, aided by a sardonic video. During 1982, they toured the USA supporting the Who at their stadium concerts. Many observers were critical of a band that had once ridiculed superstar status, for becoming part of the same legend. A simmering tension between Jones and Strummer eventually led to bitterness and Jones left in 1983 after Strummer accused him of becoming lazy and he told the press: 'He wasn't with us any more'. Strummer later apologised for lambasting Jones and admitted he was mainly to blame for the break-up of a successful songwriting partnership: 'I stabbed him in the back' was his own honest account of proceedings. The Clash struggled without Jones's input although the toothless *Cut The Crap* reached number 16 in the the

UK charts in 1985. Mick Jones formed Big Audio Dynamite with another product of the 70s London scene, Don Letts, and for several years became a relevant force merging dance with powerful, spikey pop choruses. Strummer finally disbanded the Clash in 1986 and after a brief tour with Latino Rockabilly War and a period playing rhythm guitar with the Pogues, he turned almost full time to acting and production. He supervised the soundtrack to the film, *Sid And Nancy*, about the former Sex Pistols bassist Sid Vicious and his girlfriend Nancy Spungen. In 1988, the Clash's most furious but tuneful songs were gathered together on the excellent compilation, *The Story Of The Clash*. They made a dramatic and unexpected return to the charts in 1991 when 'Should I Stay Or Should I Go?', originally a UK number 17 hit in October 1982, was re-released by CBS after the song appeared in a Levi's jeans advertisement. Incredibly, the song reached number 1, thereby prompting more reissues of Clash material and fuelling widespread rumours of a band reunion.
Albums: *The Clash* (1977), *Give 'Em Enough Rope* (1978), *London's Calling* (1979), *Sandinista!* (1980), *Combat Rock* (1982), *Cut The Crap* (1985). Compilations: *The Story Of The Clash* (1988), *The Singles Collection* (1991).

Classix Nouveaux

This 80s UK experimental quartet was fronted by the shaven-headed Sal Solo (b. 5 September 1954, Hatfield, Hertfordshire, England), whose uncompromising vocal style gelled uneasily with his musicians' synthesizer dance beat. Originally appearing on Stevo's Some Bizzare Records sample album, the group signed to Liberty Records in 1981 and recorded a series of albums, ranging from the gargantuan to the quirkily unmelodic. Four of their singles reached the UK Top 75 during 1981 and the following year they scored their biggest success with 'Is It A Dream' which climbed to number 11. Perpetually on the periphery, the group's limited chart success and affiliation with a major label did little to offset their determinedly *avant garde* approach. By the mid-80s, the unit folded with Sal going solo.
Albums: *Night People* (1981), *La Verité* (1982), *Secret* (1983). Solo: Sal Solo *Heart And Soul* (1985).

Clock DVA

One of a batch of groups forming the so-called 'industrial' scene of Sheffield in the early 80s, Clock DVA's first release was, appropriately, on Throbbing Gristle's Industrial label. The cassette-only (until its re-release in 1990) *White Souls In Black Suits* featured Adi Newton (ex-the Studs, the Future, Veer; vocals), Steven James Taylor (ex-Block Opposite; bass/vocals/guitar), Paul Widger (ex-They Must Be Russians; guitar), Roger Quail (drums) and Charlie

Collins (saxophone). However, there had already been three previous line-ups, including guitarist Dave Hammond, and synthesizer players Joseph Hurst and Simon Elliot-Kemp. 1981 saw the band's *Thirst*, available through independent label Fetish. With the ground for such 'difficult music' having been prepared by Throbbing Gristle, the press reaction was remarkably favourable. Nevertheless, the band disintegrated at the end of the year. Newton kept the name while the other three joined the Box. By 1983 replacements were found in John Valentine Carruthers (guitar), Paul Browse (saxophone), Dean Dennis (bass) and Nick Sanderson (drums). A brace of singles prefaced *Advantage*, their first album for Polydor. The following year Carruthers and Sanderson departed as Clock DVA continued as a trio. Though it would be five years before a follow-up, Newton was kept busy with his visual project the Anti Group (TAGC), and several singles. *Buried Dreams* finally arrived in 1989. By the time of 1991's *Transitional Voices*, Browse had been replaced by Robert Baker, a veteran of TAGC. Newton has long since described the process of making music as his research: 'We feel music is something that should change and not remain too rigid, evolve with ourselves as we grow, change our perception . . .' Although their recorded history is sparse, it represents a more thoughtful and reflective body of work than that which dominates their peer group. In particular, Newton's grasp of the philosophical connotations of technology have placed him apart from the majority of its practitioners.
Albums: *Thirst* (1981), *Advantage* (1983), *Buried Dreams* (1989), *White Souls In Black Suits* (1990), *Transitional Voices* (1991), *Man-Amplified* (1992).

Close Lobsters

Formed in 1985 by Andrew Burnett (b. 11 February 1965, Johnstone, Scotland; vocals), brother Robert (b. 11 September 1962, Johnstone, Scotland), Stewart McFadeyn (b. 26 September 1965, Paisley, Scotland), Graeme Wilmington (b. 22 August 1965, Johnstone, Scotland) and Thomas Donnelly (b. 29 August 1962, Johnstone, Scotland; guitar). Close Lobsters first crept into the limelight by featuring 'Firestation Towers' on the *C86* cassette organized by the *New Musical Express* and designed to bring together the best of the new independent bands appearing in 1986. Thanks to an intense mixture of agitated guitars and Andrew Burnett's peculiar - frequently unfathomable - lyrics, Close Lobsters manufactured a partisan following in Britain and garnered an enthusiastic response from US college radio stations. An invitation to the prestigious New York Music Seminar in 1989 led to an extensive Stateside tour as the band virtually emigrated to America in a bid to crack the record market. In spite of respectable sales the pressure was

too much for Donnelly, who departed at the close of the year. His ex-colleagues followed this example by taking a two-year break from the public eye before returning to the live circuit at the start of 1991.
Albums: *Foxheads Stalk This Land* (1987), *Headache Rhetoric* (1989).

Cockney Rejects

Cockney Rejects

Discovered by Jimmy Pursey of Sham 69, this east London-based skinhead group came to the fore in 1980 with an irreverent brand of proletariat rock. The group comprised of Jefferson Turner (vocals), Vince Riordan (bass/vocals), Micky Geggus (guitar/vocals) and Keith Warrington (drums). Daring anti-everything, they were virtually a parody of the 'kick over the traces' punk attitude, while also betraying a stubborn parochialism in keeping with their group title. The 'anarchic' contents of their albums were reflected in their garishly tasteless record sleeves. Yet, they had a certain subversive humour, titling their first album *Greatest Hits* when the sum of their UK Top 40 achievements rested with 'The Greatest Cockney Ripoff' at number 21 and the West Ham United football anthem 'I'm Forever Blowing Bubbles' at number 35. On their second album they included the chant 'Oi! Oi! Oi!', thereby giving birth to a musical sub-genre which came to define the brash inarticulacy of skinhead politics. By the time of 1982's *The Wild Ones* the group were veering away

Cocteau Twins

from their original punk influences towards heavy metal. Significantly, their new producer was UFO bassist Pete Way. Equally significantly, their career was well in the descendant by that point.

Albums: *Greatest Hits Volume 1* (1980), *Greatest Hits Volume 2* (1980), *Greatest Hits Volume 3 (Live And Loud)* (1981), *The Power And The Glory* (1981), *The Wild Ones* (1982), *Unheard Rejects* (1985, a collection of early unreleased recordings). Compilation: *We Are The Firm* (1986).

Cocteau Twins

Hailing from Grangemouth, Scotland, the Cocteau Twins are responsible for some of the most unique, and moving contemporary pop music to emerge since the early 80s. An enigmatic collection of musicians, centring on the duo of Elizabeth Fraser (b. 29 August 1958) and Robin Guthrie, they have very few peers in modern popular music. Arguably, the central point of interest in the Cocteau's music lies in the remarkable vocal style of Elizabeth Fraser. This petite figure is able to produce the most astonishing variety of vocal impressions and inflections, using words more for their sound than their meaning. Her vocal style has been viewed with a mixture of bemusement and amusement, yet has made her one of most

popular singers of the 80s and 90s. The musical back-drop to all this has been controlled by Fraser's partner Robin Guthrie. As composer (utilizing guitar, tape loops, echo boxes and drum machines) and studio producer, he has been a driving force and artistic controller. Guthrie formed the group in 1982 with his friend, bass player Will Heggie, and had recruited Fraser as a singer reputably after seeing her dancing in a Grangemouth discotheque. Subsequent demo tapes fell into the hands Ivo Watts-Russell, the owner of the 4AD label. His enthusiasm for the Cocteau's music prompted the band's move to London to record for the label. The first album generated enormous interest and airplay from BBC Radio 1 disc jockey, John Peel. Their debut album, *Garlands*, released in 1982, initially encouraged lazy comparisions to the style of Siouxsie And The Banshees, but this was soon erased as the Cocteau Twins began to carve their own niche in modern music. By spring 1983, Heggie had departed (to later re-emerge in Nightshift), leaving Fraser and Guthrie to record the second, transitional album, *Head Over Heels*. Having smoothed over the rougher edges of its predecessor with Guthrie adding layers of echo and phased drum effects the album and allowed Fraser's voice full rein to experiment. This resulted in a

Lloyd Cole And The Commotions

dreamlike quality that permeated the set. During this period the group were involved in the 4AD label project, This Mortal Coil, for which Fraser and Guthrie's version of the Tim Buckley song, 'Song To the Siren' has since been acknowledged as one of the finest independent label recordings of the 80s. Simon Raymonde had by now been enrolled as bass player, eventually becoming a valuable assest in composing, arranging and production. The release of two superb EP collections, *Sunburst And Snowblind* and *Pearly-Dewdrops' Drops* dominated the Independent charts, with the latter broaching the national Top 30. The Cocteau's reluctance to reveal much of their private lives or play the music business 'games' won them respect from most quarters and annoyance from others. They have strived to avoid the image imposed upon them by their fans as fey, mystical characters – an image contradicted, notably by Guthrie, in interviews as being earthy, cantankerous and most definitely of this world. One benefit of their refusal to place photos of the group on record sleeves was the superb cover art produced by the 23 Envelope art studio.

The arrival of *Treasure* in 1984 saw the group scaling new heights and remained for some time the Cocteau aficionados' favourite album. The next couple of years were marked by the release of several EPs, *Aikea-Guinea*, *Tiny Dynamite* and *Echoes In A Shallow Bay*, each displaying richer, more complex textures than previously heard. *Victorialand*, featured a lighter, almost acoustic sound, marked by the absence of Raymonde, but included a guesting role for Richard Thomas (saxophone/tablas) of 4AD stablemates Dif Juz. Raymonde returned for the subsequent EP set, *Love's Easy Tears* and a not altogether successful collaboration with Harold Budd in late 1986. A hiatus of almost two years ended with the release of *Blue Bell Knoll* showing that they had not lost their touch. The emotional impact of the birth of Fraser and Guthrie's child was reflected in the songs on the stunning *Heaven And Las Vegas*. The single 'Iceblink Luck' also saw a return to the UK Top 40 and combined with a renewed urgency to take the music onto the road, including the unlikely setting of Las Vegas. This burst of activity saw the Cocteau's desire to break away from the confines and protective enclaves of 4AD in March 1991. For much of that year Guthrie continued with studio production work, notably with the promising new 4AD group, Lush. The Cocteau Twins eventually signed a new deal with the Fontana label in March 1992.

Albums: *Garlands* (1982), *Head Over Heels* (1983),

Treasure (1984), *Victorialand* (1986), with Harold Budd *The Moon And The Melodies* (1986), *Blue Bell Knoll* (1988), *Heaven Or Las Vegas* (1990). Compilations: *The Pink Opaque* (1986 - US, CD only release), *The Singles Collection* (1991).

Cole, Lloyd, (And The Commotions)

b. 31 January 1961, Buxton, Derbyshire, England. Despite his birthplace, this literate singer-songwriter emerged from Glasgow's post-punk renaissance. Neil Clark (b. 3 July 1955; guitar), Blair Cowan (keyboards), Lawrence Donegan (b. 13 July 1961; bass) and Stephen Irvine (b. 16 December 1959; drums) completed the line-up responsible for *Rattlesnakes*, a critically lauded set which merged Byrds-like guitar figures to Cole's languid, Lou Reed inspired intonation. A representative selection fron the album, 'Perfect Skin', reached the UK Top 30 when issued as a single, while a follow-up album, *Easy Pieces*, spawned two Top 20 entries in 'Brand New Friend' and 'Lost Weekend'. However, the style which came so easily on these early outings seemed laboured on *Mainstream*, after which Cole disbanded his group. Retaining Cowan, he switched bases to New York, and emphasized the infatuation with Lou Reed's music by recruiting sidemen Robert Quine (guitar) and Fred Maher (drums), the latter of whom also acted as producer. *Lloyd Cole* showed signs of an artistic rejuvenation, but Cole has yet to stamp a wholly original personae, and capitalize on his undoubted talent.
Albums: with the Commotions *Rattlesnakes* (1984), *Easy Pieces* (1985), *Mainstream* (1987); solo *Lloyd Cole* (1989), *Don't Get Weird On Me, Babe* (1991). Compilation: *1984-1989* (1989).

Colenso Parade

This interesting pop/rock act was formed in October 1984 in Belfast, Northern Ireland. They released two singles, 'Standing Up' and 'Down By The Border' on their own Goliath label before an early appearance at the Futurama Festival saw Stiff Records put them in touch with manager Dave Bedford. Soon after, they moved to London where Bedford had set up Fire Records. From the original line-up Oscar (vocals), Linda Clandinning (keyboards) and Neil Lawson (bass) remained the nucleus of the band. Terry Bickers (later of House Of Love and Levitation) replaced the original guitarist Jackie Forgie after the first single, and was in turn dropped in favour of John Watt. Owen Howell (ex-Big Self) would also replace Robert Wakeman as drummer. Following 'Hallelujah Chorus' they scored heavy airplay with 'Fontana Eyes' in 1986, a classic 12-bar blues workout founded on captivating lyrical epigrams, 'I'm holding my breath, cos there's no-one to hold'. A split came soon after their only album when a deal with a major label

fell through. Further demos were recorded but nothing surfaced, although Oscar was invited to join Echo And The Bunnymen as singer following the departure of Ian McCulloch. He declined the invitation, and is now working in video.
Album: *Glentorran* (1987).

Colorblind James Experience

Hailing from Rochester, New York, USA, this four-piece group led by Colorblind James (guitar/vibraphone/vocals) with Phillip Marshall (lead guitar/vocals), Bernie Heveron (bass/vocals) and Jim McAvaney (drums) utilized the many forms of North American music, from country, cocktail-lounge jazz, folk, rockabilly, blues and good-time rock 'n' roll in order to express James' odd-ball view of the world. It was BBC disc jockey John Peel who first gave the group the exposure necessary to make them realize what they were doing was right. Their debut album was an eclectic work, notable for its engaging black humour. The high point of the album, the sprawling 'I'm Considering A Move To Memphis', was reminiscent of David Byrne. By the time of the release of their second album, *Why Should I Stand Up?*, the line-up had increased to a sextet with the addition of John Ebert (trombone/tuba/vocals), Ken Frank (bass/violin/vocals - replacing Heveron) and Dave McIntire (sax/clarinet/vocals). On occasions the group have put aside their electric instruments and stand revealed as Colorblind James And The Death Valley Boys indulging in the more basic side of country-blues, gospel and jug band music. The result of these sessions was *Strange Sounds From The Basement* which carried on Colorblind's general infatuation with the underside of contemporary American life.
Albums: *Colorblind James Experience* (1988), *Why Should I Stand Up?* (1989), as Colorblind James And The Death Valley Boys *Strange Sounds From The Basement* (1990).

Colour Field

After appearing with the Specials and the Fun Boy Three, Terry Hall (b. 19 March 1959, Coventry, West Midlands, England; guitar/vocals) formed the Colour Field with Karl Sharle (bass) and Toby Lyons (guitar/keyboards) in 1983. Having been involved in a band that was responsible for the ska/mod revival, (then a vocal based trio), Hall's third band of the 80's was a basic group of three musicians. He was aided by friends, and produced strong pop songs featuring his rather flat vocals. After the instant success of his two previous bands, Colour Field found the going hard. Although they had positive reviews from the music press, it took nearly 18 months for the band to break into the UK Top 20 with 'Thinking Of You' in 1985. Their debut album reached number 12 in the UK, but the failure of subsequent singles soon reduced them down to a duo of Hall and Lyons. They reappeared in 1987 with a weak cover version of Sly And The Family Stone's 'Running Away' and a second album which gave a poor showing on the UK chart, which resulted in the group dissolving. Hall later released a solo album with assistance from Blair Booth (keyboards/vocals) and Anouchka Grooe (guitar).

Albums: *Virgins And Philistines* (1985), *Deception* (1987). Solo album: Terry Hall *Ultra Modern Nursery Rhymes* (1989).

Coming Up Roses

This unit was formed in 1986 by the songwriting partnership of ex-Dolly Mixture members, Debsey Wykes (b. 21 December 1960, Hammersmith, London, England; guitar/vocals) and Hester Smith (b. 28 October 1960, West Africa; drums) along with Nicky Brodie (vocals/percussion), Patricia O'Flynn (saxophone, ex-Shillelagh Sisters), Leigh Luscious (guitar) and ex-Amazulu bassist Claire Kenny, later replaced by Sophie Cherry (bass). Their melodic pop dance style, described by the group as 'ballroom soul', mixed witty and caustic lyrics - in 'I Could Have Been Your Girlfriend (If You'd Asked Me To)' Debsey sang, 'She's so dumb, she's so sweet/I didn't think she'd last a week . . . She's so pretty she's so fine, she is such a waste of time/Well so she's cute, well I don't care, she's got stinking underwear!'. They signed to Billy Bragg's Utility Records label releasing one album in 1989. The group toured the UK as part of the pop-socialist collective Red Wedge troupe in 1987. After various personnel changes, but still retaining the nucleus of Wykes and Smith along with Brodie, the group in 1990 settled on a more stable line-up with Tony Watts (lead guitar), Midus (bass) and Jane Keay (saxophone). However, disillusion with the music business's preoccupation with current trends prompted the group's demise in March 1991, leaving behind a legacy of timeless pop songs.

Album: *I Said Ballroom* (1989).

Communards

After leaving Bronski Beat in the spring of 1985, vocalist Jimmy Somerville (b. 22 June 1961, Glasgow, Scotland) teamed up with the classically-trained pianist Richard Coles (b. 23 June 1962, Northampton, England) to form the Committee. When a rival group laid claim to that name, they became the Communards, a title borrowed from a 19th century group of French Republicans. Their debut single, the disco-styled 'You Are My World' reached the UK Top 30. The follow-up, 'Disenchanted', was another minor hit, after which the duo decided to augment the line-up with various backing musicians. Meanwhile, their self-titled debut

album climbed to number 2 in the UK. In September 1986, the group unexpectedly reached number 1 with a revival of Harold Melvin's 'Don't Leave Me This Way'. The song was most memorable for the vocal interplay between the falsetto of Somerville and the husky tones of guest singer Sarah Jane Morris. Her statuesque presence added much to the group's live appeal, especially when dancing alongside the diminutive Somerville. A further UK Top 10 hit followed with 'So Cold The Night'. After touring extensively, the group issued a second album, *Red*. produced by Stephen Hague. A series of singles were culled from the album, including 'Tomorrow', their comment on wife-beating, which reached number 23. The group returned to the Top 5 with a stirring revival of Gloria Gaynor's 'Never Can Say Goodbye'. During 1988, they registered two more minor UK hits with 'For A Friend' and 'There's More To Love'. With their fusion of disco-revival and falsetto pop, the Communards proved one of the more accomplished new acts of the mid-late 80s and seemed likely to enjoy further success in the new decade. As with Bronski Beat, however, Somerville showed a restlessness with the British music scene and wound down the group's activities, after which he went solo and scored hits with a cover of Sylvester's 'You Make Me Feel (Mighty Real)' and 'Read My Lips' before relocating to San Francisco.

Albums: *Communards* (1986), *Red* (1987). Compilation: *The Singles Collection, 1984-1990* (1990, includes recordings from Bronski Beat and the Communards). Solo album: Jimmy Somerville *Read My Lips* (1989).

Comsat Angels

Three major record deals, no hit singles, legal complications - and yet the Comsat Angels survived to make thoughtful, expressive guitar music for more than 10 years. Formed in Sheffield, England, at the end of the 70s, they initially merged the zest of punk with a mature songwriting approach, using keyboards quite strongly on their promising debut, *Waiting For A Miracle*. The line-up of Stephen Fellows (guitar/vocals), Mik Glaisher (drums), Kevin Bacon (bass) and Andy Peake (keyboards) was to remain constant throughout their career. In the USA they were forced to shorten their name to CS Angels after the communications giant, Comsat, threatened legal action. *Sleep No More* was their highest UK chart placing at number 51 but after *Fiction* only skimmed the lower reaches of the Top 100, Polydor Records lost patience and the band moved to the CBS subsidiary, Jive. *Land* spawned a near-hit with the catchy 'Independence Day' which had previously appeared on their first album. The single was released in various formats, including a double-single set, but did not provide the success the band required. Other groups with a similar driving guitar sound fared better and they were surpassed commercially by the likes of Simple Minds and U2. Another attempt to regenerate their career was made by Island in the late 80s but early in 1990 the band announced they were changing their name to Headhunters in the hope that it would bring about a change of fortune. The band invested heavily in their own recording studio in Sheffield and it has become a focus for the city's musical creativity.

Albums: *Waiting For A Miracle* (1980), *Sleep No More* (1981), *Fiction* (1982), *Land* (1983), *7-Day Weekend* (1985), *Chasing Shadows* (1987). Compilation: *Enz* (1984, Dutch release).

Conflict

This anarchist punk band were formed in south east London in 1979, previously existing under a variety of names such as Splattered Rock Stars. Having followed Crass around the country they were essentially motivated by similar concerns: pacifism, animal welfare, anarchism. 'We call ourselves anarchists. That doesn't mean we believe in chaos - our ideal society would be one of small self-governing communities, with people being able to run their own lives. But above all we're trying to say that we don't want to be used by the political left or right.' They played their first gig in their native Eltham in April 1981. The basic line-up featured Colin Jerwood (b. 6 May, 1962, London, England; vocals) Graham (guitar) Ken (drums) and John Clifford (bass), although their early line-ups were very fluid, with newcomers Steve and Paco taking over on guitar and drums soon after. Paul Fryday, meanwhile, became technician, visuals supervisor and general motivator. Their debut EP *The House That Man Built* came out on the Crass label, with Pauline Beck adding vocals. 'To A Nation Of Animal Lovers', on which Crass' Steve Ignorant guested, saw the band faced with incitement charges over the cover. Their policy of direct action in protest to many causes, in particular the Orkney seal hunters, led to many live appearances being broken up by police action. After this there were numerous line-up changes, the most significant of which was the two-year tenure of Ignorant as joint vocalist between 1987 and 1989. Jerwood, meanwhile, had been assaulted at a pub in Eltham, nearly losing the use of his eye in the process. Conflict set up their own Motorhate label, going on to release albums throughout the 80s for a loyal audience of social miscreants. The best of their efforts were the studio side of *Increase The Pressure* and *The Ungovernable Force*, in 1984 and 1985 respectively. The widescale rioting which occurred after the band's 1987 Brixton Academy gig was documented by *Turning Rebellion Into Money*. The group continue into the early 90s to perform and record whenever possible.

Albums: *It's Time To See Who's Who* (1983), *Increase The Pressure* (1984), *The Ungovernable Force* (1985), *Turning Rebellion Into Money* (1987), *Standard Issue* (1989), *The Final Conflict* (1989), *Against All Odds* (1989).

Contortions

Formed by James Siegfried in 1980, James Chance And The Contortions were a collision of punk and harmolodic jazz that, along with Bill Laswell's Material and James Blood Ulmer, constituted New York's No Wave scene. Siegfried went to school with Mark Johnson (Cassandra Wilson's drummer) and recruited guitarist Bern Nix from Ornette Coleman's Prime Time. This awareness of cutting-edge jazz - and a defiantly original saxophone style, an unholy combination of Captain Beefheart and Maceo Parker - injected punk with a brittle energy that was unmatched. A later version of the band, James White And The Blacks, fomented Defunkt as a separate entity, kick-starting the black rock movement that begat Living Color. Heroin problems prevented James Chance reaching a large audience, but his spiky, beautiful music remains to testify that jazz chops do not necessarily make for tedious rock music.

Albums: *Buy* (1979), *Live In New York* (1981), as James White And The Blacks *Off White* (1979), *Sax Maniac* (1982), *James White's Flaming Demonics* (1983), *Soul Exorcism* (1991, live 1980 recording in Amsterdam).

Cope, Julian

b. 21 October 1957, Deri, Mid Glamorgan, Wales. Cope first attracted attention as an integral part of Liverpool's post-punk renaissance, most notably as a member of the short-lived but seminal group, the Crucial Three which also included Ian McCulloch and Pete Wylie. In 1978 Cope began writing songs with Ian McCulloch in A Shallow Madness, but the pair quickly fell out over the direction of the group. While McCulloch formed Echo And The Bunnymen, Cope founded the Teardrop Explodes whose early releases enjoyed critical acclaim. The band scored several hit singles but an introspective second album, *Wilder*, was heavily criticized before dissension within the ranks led to their inevitable demise. In 1984 Cope embarked on a solo career with *World Shut Your Mouth* but misfortune dogged his progress. The singer intentionally gashed his stomach with a broken microphone stand during an appearance at London's Hammersmith Palais and his pronouncements on the benefits of mind-expanding substances exacerbated an already wayward, unconventional image. The sleeve of his second album, *Fried*, featured a naked Cope cowering under a turtle shell and commentators drew parallels with rock casualties Roky Erickson and Syd Barrett, both of whom Julian admired. Another of his heroes, Scott Walker, enjoyed a upsurge in interest in his recordings when Cope constantly gave the reclusive 60s singer name-checks in interviews. A third album, *Skellington*, was rejected by his label, which resulted in Cope switching to Island Records. Paradoxically he then enjoyed a UK Top 20 single with a newly-recorded version of 'World Shut Your Mouth'. *Saint Julian* then became the artist's best-selling album to date, but a tour to promote Cope's next collection, *My Nation Underground*, was abandoned when he became too ill to continue. Over subsequent months Julian maintained a low profile, but re-emerged in 1990 at London's anti-Poll Tax demonstration dressed in the costume of a space alien, Mr Sqwubbsy. However, this unconventional behaviour was tempered by a new realism and in 1991 he scored another major hit with 'Beautiful Love'. Commentators also noted a newfound maturity on the attendant double album *Peggy Suicide*, which garnered considerable praise.

Albums: *World Shut Your Mouth* (1984), *Fried* (1984), *Saint Julian* (1987), *My Nation Underground* (1988), *Skellington* and *Droolian* (1990, both fan club only releases), *Peggy Suicide* (1991).

Julian Cope

Cortinas

Originally an R&B band, the Cortinas were formed during July 1976 in Bristol, England by Jeremy Valentine (vocals), Nick Sheppard (guitar), Mike Fewins (guitar), Dexter Dalwood (bass) and Daniel Swan (drums). The advent of the late 70s 'new wave' brought a change to their usual live set of 60s cover versions, which were replaced with self-penned tracks like 'Television Families' and 'I Wanna Have It With You'. The remainder were given the 'punk treatment', which created an exciting live spectacle. In the beginning of June 1977, 'Fascist Dictator' was released on the Step Forward label, capturing perfectly the raw energy of the time, although it lacked any real originality. This new-found popularity brought with it problems, as many of their hometown gigs ended in trouble, prompting the band to cut their ties with punk. Consequently the live set saw a return to cover versions, where even 'Fascist Dictator' was excluded. *True Romances* was released on CBS in 1978 and contained a remake of Smokey Robinson's 'First I Look At The Purse', together with 12 originals. The album had lost the power and bite of previous offerings, the result being mediocre. One last single 'Heartache' was extracted before they split at the end of the year. Mike Fewins joined Essential Bop, whereas Nick Sheppard formed the Spics, two of the most prominent new wave bands to emerge from Bristol in 1979.

Album: *True Romances* (1978).

Costello, Elvis

b. Declan McManus, 25 August 1955, Paddington, London, England, but brought up in Liverpool. The son of singer and bandleader Ross McManus first came to prominence during the UK punk era of 1977. The former computer programmer toured A&R offices giving impromptu performances. While appealing to the new wave market, the sensitive issues he wrote about, combined with the structure of the way he composed them, indicated a major talent that would survive and outgrow this comparatively narrow field. Following a tenure in Flip City he was signed to Jake Riviera's pioneering Stiff Records, Costello failed to chart with his early releases, which included the anti-fascist 'Less Than Zero' and the sublime ballad of a broken relationship, 'Alison'. His Nick Lowe-produced debut *My Aim Is True* featured members of the west-coast cult band Clover, who in turn had Huey Lewis as their vocalist. The album is a classic of lyrical brilliance. Costello spat, shouted and crooned a cornucopia of radical issues and was hailed by the critics. His debut hit single 'Watching The Detectives' contained scathing verses about wife-beating over a beautifully simple reggae beat. His new band, the Attractions, gave Costello a solid and tight sound that put them into rock's first division. The

Elvis Costello

comparative failure. The following year with seven albums already behind him, the prolific Elvis released another outstanding collection, *Imperial Bedroom*, many of the songs are romantic excursions into mistrust and deceit, including 'Man Out Of Time', 'I'm Your Toy'. The fast paced 'Beyond Belief' is a perfect example of vintage Costello lyricism: 'History repeats the old conceits, the glib replies the same defeats, keep your finger on important issues with crocodile tears and a pocketful of tissues'. That year Robert Wyatt recorded the best-ever interpretation of an Elvis song. The superlative 'Shipbuilding' was a wickedly subtle indictment of the Falklands War. Wyatt's high strained voice gave true depth to the lines 'Is it worth it, a new winter coat and shoes for the wife, and a bicycle on the boy's birthday' while later on the listener is awakened to the reality of the irony with: 'diving for dear life, when we should be diving for pearls'. The next year Costello as the Imposter released 'Pills And Soap', a similar theme cleverly masking a bellicose attack on Thatcherism. Both *Punch The Clock* and *Goodbye Cruel World* maintained the high standards that Costello had already set and astonishingly he had found the time to produce albums by the Specials, Squeeze, the Bluebells and the Pogues (where he met his future wife Cait O'Riordan). During 1984 he played a retarded brother on BBC television in Alan Bleasdale's *Scully*. The following year he bravely took the stage at Live Aid and in front of millions, he poignantly and unselfishly sang Lennon's 'All You Need Is Love' accompanied by his solo guitar. His version of the Animals' 'Don't Let Me Be Misunderstood' was a minor hit in 1986 and during another punishing year he released two albums; the rock 'n' roll influenced *King Of America*, yet another success with notable production from T-Bone Burnett and guitar contributions from the legendary James Burton and, reunited with the Attractions and producer Nick Lowe, Costello stalled with the less than perfect *Blood And Chocolate*. Towards the end of the 80s he collaborated with Paul McCartney and co-wrote a number of songs for *Flowers In The Dirt*, and returned after a brief hiatus (by Costello standards) with the excellent *Spike* in 1989. During 1990 he wrote and sang with Roger McGuinn for his 1991 comeback *Back To Rio*. During that year a heavily bearded and long-haired Elvis co-wrote the soundtrack to the highly controversial television series *GBH*, (written by Bleasdale) and delivered another success, *Mighty Like A Rose*. With lyrics as sharp as any of his previous work, this introspective and reflective album had Costello denying he was ever cynical - merely realistic. Costello is without doubt one of the finest songwriters and lyricists Britain has ever produced, his left-of-centre political views have not clouded his horizon; he remains a critics'

combination of Bruce Thomas (b. Stockton-on-Tees, Cleveland, England; bass), ex-Chilli Willi And The Red Hot Peppers' Pete Thomas (b. 9 August 1954, Sheffield, Yorkshire, England; drums) and Steve Nieve (b. Steven Nason; keyboards), became an integral part of the Costello sound. The Attractions provided the backing for the strong *This Year's Model* and further magnificent singles ensued prior to the release of another landmark, *Armed Forces* in 1979. This vitriolic collection narrowly missed the coveted number 1 position in the UK and reached the Top 10 in the USA. Costello's standing in the USA was seriouly dented by his regrettably flippant dismissal of Ray Charles as 'an ignorant, blind nigger', an opinion which he later recanted. 'Oliver's Army', a major hit taken from the album, was a bitter attack on the mercenary soldier, sung in a happy-go-lucky fashion. By the end of the 70s Costello was firmly established as both performer and songwriter with Linda Ronstadt and Dave Edmunds having success with his compositions. During 1981 Elvis spent time in Nashville recording a country album *Almost Blue* with the legendary producer Billy Sherrill. An honest UK television documentary showed work in progress, with Sherrill unable to be totally complimentary to Costello. George Jones's 'Good Year For The Roses' became the album's major hit, although a superb reading of Patsy Cline's 'Sweet Dreams' was a favourite with his credibility as high as ever.

Albums: *My Aim Is True* (1977), *This Year's Model* (1978), *Armed Forces* (1979), *Get Happy* (1980), *Trust* (1981), *Almost Blue* (1981), *Imperial Bedroom* (1982), *Punch The Clock* (1983), *Goodbye Cruel World* (1984), *King Of America* (1986), *Blood And Chocolate* (1986), *Spike* (1989), *Mighty Like A Rose* (1991). Compilations: *Ten Bloody Marys And Ten Hows Your Fathers* (1984), *The Best Of Elvis Costello - The Man* (1985), *Girls Girls Girls* (1989), *Out Of Our Idiot* (1987).

Cowboy Junkies

Toronto-based musicians, Michael Timmins (b. 21 April 1959, Montreal, Canada; guitar) and Alan Anton (b. Alan Alizojvodic, 22 June 1959, Montreal, Canada; bass), formed a group called Hunger Project in 1979. It was not successful and, basing themselves in the UK, they formed an experimental instrumental group, Germinal. Returning to Toronto, they joined forces with Timmins' sister Margo (b. 27 June 1961, Montreal, Canada; vocal) and brother Peter (b. 29 October 1965, Montreal, Canada; drums). As the Cowboy Junkies (which was simply an attention-grabbing name), they recorded their first album, *Whites Off Earth Now!!*, in a private house. Their second album, *The Trinity Session*, was made with one microphone in the Church of Holy Trinity, Toronto for $250. The band's spartan, less-is-more sound captivated listeners and, with little publicity, the second album sold 250,000 copies in North America. The tracks included a curious reinterpretation of 'Blue Moon' called 'Blue Moon Revisited (Song For Elvis)' and the country standards, 'I'm So Lonesome I Could Cry' and 'Walking After Midnight'. Lou Reed praised their version of his song, 'Sweet Jane', and, in 1991, they contributed 'To Lay Me Down' in a tribute to the Grateful Dead, *Deadicated*. Their 1990 album, *The Caution Horses*, included several vintage country songs which, true to form, were performed in their whispered, five miles-per-hour style. The extent of the Cowboy Junkies' fast growing reputation was sufficiant for them to promote the 1992 album *Black-Eyed Man* at London's Royal Albert Hall.

Albums: *Whites Off Earth Now!!* (1986), *The Trinity Session* (1988), *The Caution Horses* (1990), *Black-Eyed Man* (1992).

Cramps

Formed in Ohio, USA in 1976, the original Cramps, Lux Interior (b. Erick Lee Purkhiser; vocals), 'Poison' Ivy Rorschach (b. Kirsty Marlana Wallace; guitar), Bryan Gregory (guitar) and his sister, Pam Balam (drums), later moved to New York, where they were embroiled in the emergent punk scene centred on the CBGBs rock venue. Miriam Linna briefly replaced

Cramps

Balam, before Nick Knox (b. Nick Stephanoff) became the group's permanent drummer. The Cramps' early work was recorded at the famed Sun studio under the aegis of producer Alex Chilton. Their early singles and debut album blended the frantic rush of rockabilly with a dose of 60s garage-band panache and an obvious love of ghoulish b-movies. Bryan Gregory's sudden departure followed the release of the compulsive 'Drug Train' single. Former Gun Club acolyte, Kid Congo (Powers) (b. Brian Tristan), appeared on *Psychedelic Jungle*, but he later rejoined his erstwhile colleagues and the Cramps have since employed several, often female, replacements, including Fur and Candy Del Mar. Despite the group's momentum being rudely interrupted by a protracted legal wrangle with the IRS label during the early 80s, the Cramps' horror-cum-trash style, supplemented with a healthy dose of humour and sex, has nonetheless remained intact throughout their career. Wary of outside manipulation, the Cramps now steer their own course to good effect in touring and recording, proving themselves the masters of the genre. In 1991 Interior and Rorschach re-emerged fronting a rejuvenated line-up of Slim Chance (bass) and Jim Sclavunos (drums).

Albums: *Songs The Lord Taught Us* (1980), *Psychedelic Jungle* (1981), *Smell Of Female* (1983), *A Date With Elvis* (1986), *Stay Sick* (1990), *Look Mom No Head!* (1991). Compilation: *Off The Bone* (1983).

Further reading: *The Wild, Wild World Of The Cramps*, Ian Johnston.

Cranberries. This highly touted Irish band hailed from Limerick and boasted the honeyed voice of Delores O'Riordan (b. circa 1971). From a rural Catholic background, she had sung since the age of four in schools and churches. The male personnel, songwriter Noel Hogan (guitar), his brother Mike (bass) and Ferg Lawler (drums), had been involved as a band, influenced by the Cure, R.E.M. and the

Smiths, for some time but never amounted to much, until they joined forces with O'Riordan. Resulting demo tapes sent a ripple of anticipation through record companies looking for a new Sundays. Their debut EP *Uncertain*, on the obscure Xeric label late in 1991, revealed their promise, and they were quickly snapped up by Island, for whom they are preparing new material.

Cranes

This Portsmouth, England-based band continued the musical metaphors of their obvious forebears the Cocteau Twins and My Bloody Valentine in the late 80s and early 90s. They are built around vocalist and lyricist Alison Shaw, who together with brother Jim (drums) comprises the main songwriting unit. The line-up is completed by Mark Francombe (guitar) and Matt Cope (bass). After five years of writing and perfecting songs for themselves, and contributions to a plethora of various artist compilations, the band picked up support from BBC disc jockey John Peel with the mini-album *Self-Non-Self*. They signed to the BMG/RCA subsidiary Dedicated in July 1990, attracting further plaudits for *Wings Of Joy*, described variously as 'foetal...minimalist...metallic and funereal'.

Albums: *Self-Non-Self* (1990), *Wings Of Joy* (1991).

Crass

Formed in 1978 by Steve Ignorant and Penny Rimbaud, Crass's music was a confrontational hybrid of buzzsaw, off-beat guitars, military drumming and shouted vocals but this was always secondary to their message. They believed in anarchy (which they defined as 'respect for yourself and others as human beings') in the UK and took their multi-media performances to hundreds of unlikely venues. Formed by the members of a commune based in Epping, Essex, England, Crass had a fluid line-up and its members wore black and adopted pseudonyms to save their message becoming diluted by personalities. *Feeding The 5,000* was raw and frantic, peppered with swear words but clearly authentic and heartfelt. *Stations Of The Crass*, a double album, was much of the same and challenged contemporary issues like the dissolution of the punk ethos ('White Punks On Hope') and British class divisions ('Time Out'). The group's most notorious offering was the post-Falklands war single, directed at the Prime Minister, Margaret Thatcher 'How Does It Feel (To Be The Mother Of A 1,000 Dead)' and topped the UK Independent chart. The line-up at the time was listed as: Ignorant (vocals), Rimbaud (drums), Eve Libertine (vocals), Joy De Vivre (vocals), Phil Free (guitar), N.A. Palmer (guitar), Pete Wright (bass) and G (backing vocals). Crass maintained a high degree of autonomy through their own Crass Records and

supported other like-minded groups. They issued two compilation albums of other people's music, *Bullshit Detectors 1* and *2* (a title borrowed from the Clash song, a group that Crass often accused of 'selling out') and released records by the Poison Girls, Flux Of Pink Indians, Captain Sensible, Rudimentary Peni, the Mob (which included Josef Porta, later of Blyth Power), Andy T and many others. On *Penis Envy* the female members took on lead vocals and the record was a sustained and tuneful attack on sexism in modern society. It marked the band's creative apex because by *Christ The Album* and *Yes Sir, I Will* - where poetry and experimental music were combined - the initial energy and inspiration was missing. The group split in 1984, as they often said they would, and to this day remain one of the few groups to loyally adhere to their original ideals. Steve Ignorant later joined Conflict in the latter part of 80s.

Albums: *The Feeding Of The 5,000* (1978), *Stations Of The Crass* (1980), *Penis Envy* (1981), *Yes Sir, I Will* (1982), *Christ The Album* (1983). Compilation: *Best Before* (1987, a singles collection).

Cravats

From the UK midlands town of Redditch, Worcestershire, the Cravats' weird brand of rock was first heard on the classic 'Gordon', a co-release with Small Wonder and their own label in October 1978. After joining Small Wonder, the band, consisting of Shend (b. Chris Harz; vocals/bass), Robin Dallaway (guitar/vocals), Dave Bennett (drums) and Richard London (saxophone), put out a series of entertaining singles, starting with the EP *Burning Bridges* in 1979. It was over a year before 'Precinct' appeared in 1980, alongside what proved to be their only album, *Cravats In Toytown*. After releasing 'You're Driving Me' and 'Off The Beach' in 1981, the band moved to Glass Records for 'Terminus' in 1982, but it was only a one-off single, 'Rub Me Out', on the Crass label that made any headway into the UK Independent chart. A retrospective EP, *The Cravats Sing Terminus And Other Hits*, surfaced before the band laid low. A solitary EP, *In The Land Of the Giants*, on the Reflex label some three years later was all the band could offer before mutating into the Very Things. Pursuing an acting career, Shend later made various minor role television appearences, in particular the BBC television series, *EastEnders*.

Album: *The Cravats In Toytown* (1980).

Crazyhead

This guitar band formed in Leicester, England in 1986, were signed to the fledgling Food label. Their first two releases saw quick independent chart success; '(What Gives You The Idea That) You're So Amazing Baby?' and 'Baby Turpentine' both reaching number 2. In common with Gaye Bikers On Acid,

Bomb Party and Pop Will Eat Itself, the group were linked with the media-fuelled 'biker' or 'grebo' rock genre. By the time of their third single 'Time Has Taken Its Toll On You' and debut album in 1988 their career was in decline, despite later minor national chart success in 1989 with the *Have Love, Will Travel* EP and 'Like Princes Do' on the Food label's Christmas EP. Enjoying ludicrous names like Vom, Superfast Blind Dick, Ian 'Anderson Pork Beast' (vocals) and stranger still, Kevin, they were dropped from Food in 1989. Their second album, produced by Pat Collier, saw them housed on Black records.

Albums: *Desert Orchid* (1988), *Some Kind Of Fever* (1990).

Creaming Jesus

This satirical UK hardcore/metal quintet were formed in 1987 by vocalist Andy and guitarists Richard and Mario. With the addition of drummer Roy and bassist Tally, they signed to the independent Jungle label. Chainsaw guitars collide with machine-gun drumming, whilst the lyrics deal with contemporary issues such as television evangelists, sexual perverts, childhood anxieties and warmongerers. The musical equivalent of a poke in the eye with a sharp stick!

Albums: *Too Fat To Run, Too Stupid To Hide* (1990), *Guilt By Association* (1992).

Creation Records

This independent record label was formed by music business entrepreneur Alan McGee, whose first venture was the dubious Laughing Apple. Brought up in East Kilbride, Scotland, childhood friends included what would become Creation's first big moneyspinner, the Jesus And Mary Chain. His first love was 60s music, particularly psychedelia, and he named his label after the UK cult band of the same name. With this he combined a fond regard for the energy and irreverence of punk, and after a tentative step into the world of fanzines with *Communication Blur*, he moved to London in 1982. There he established the Living Room, a venue of no fixed abode. The first release on Creation, however, did little to justify his already bold claims. ''77 In '83' was the work of The Legend!, a fanzine editor as eccentric by reputation as McGee. The next 20 singles cultivated a strong identity, if not fervent sales. They came in wraparound sleeve and plastic sleeve, with 1,000 pressings for each. The best of these saw the debut of the Pastels, which had charm to compensate for the nostalgic arrangements and impoverished production values it shared with its brethren. Other featured bands included the Revolving Paint Dream, Jasmine Minks and McGee's own Biff Bang Pow!. There were however, three

milestone records which really signposted the arrival of the label. The first was the Loft's 'Why Does The Rain?', similar in feel to many Creation singles but with a much more focused and emotive delivery. The second was the Jesus And Mary Chain's 'Upside Down'. The Mary Chain crystalized the meeting of 60s songwriting with punk's brash shock value, inspiring massive interest in the band, the label, and the numerous imitators that sprung up around them. Finally, Primal Scream's 'Velocity Girl', although not their first record, was the one that brought them to the public's attention. Although the Loft would be short lived, and the Jesus And Mary Chain would switch to the major distributor Blanco Y Negro, Creation had earned its spurs with the public. Primal Scream would prove pivotal, the lucrative jewel in the Creation crown. Although the glut of success dried up with the arrival of diverse acts such as Nikki Sudden, Clive Langer and Baby Amphetamine, the House Of Love revived fortunes in 1987. They were another band who later left for a larger record company, but new mainstays arrived with the music press favourites My Bloody Valentine and, more recently, Ride. The high recording costs incurred by the former led to yet another parting of the ways after 1991's *Loveless*. McGee, meanwhile, continues to be as uniquely provocative as ever: 'No praise is high enough for Creation. What we are doing is wonderful'. In truth, Creation can arguably lay claim to being the most genuinely innovative of the UK independents. As one critic noted: 'His willingness to give free reign to bands who seem impossible commercial ventures has resulted in occasionally great artistic, and ironically fiscal, success.'

Compilations: *Creation Soup (Volumes 1-5)* (1991).

Creatures.

This on-off collaboration between Siouxsie And The Banshees members Siouxsie Sioux and drummer/percussionist Budgie won them a string of UK hits starting with 'Mad Eyed Screamer' (1981) and 'Miss The Girl' (1983) - both achieving Top 30 status. Their greatest success came that same year with Herbie Mann and Carl Sigman's swing composition, 'Right Now' which reached number 14. Away from the more rock constraints of the parent group, the Creatures allowed Budgie to experiment with more exotic percussive instruments and give the sound a freer, more expressive feel. Conceived primarily as a studio-only set-up, the Creatures did not make their live debut until 1990.

Albums: *Feast* (1983), *Boomerang* (1989).

Crime

Formed in San Francsico, USA in 1976, this punk act originally comprised of Frankie Fix (guitar), Johnny Strike (guitar), Ron Greco (aka Ron the Ripper) (bass) and Brittley Black (drums). They made their debut on their own Crime label with 'Hot Wire My Heart'/'Baby You're So Repulsive' (1976), the a-side of which was covered by Sonic Youth on *Sister*. 'Murder By Guitar'/'Frustration' was issued the following year and taken together these singles confirmed the quartet as one of the Bay Area's leading new wave attractions. A projected album was, however, shelved and the quartet disbanded following the release of 'Maserati'/'Gangster Funk' (1980). Black subsequently surfaced, albeit briefly, in the Flamin' Groovies, a group Greco was once a member of, albeit under their early appellation, the Chosen Few.

Crispy Ambulance
Many bands tired to emulate the moody magnificence of Joy Division but few succeeded as well as fellow Mancunians Crispy Ambulance. So similar were they that vocalist Alan Hempsall stood in for Ian Curtis at a Joy Division gig when the singer was incapacitated by an epileptic attack. They were formed in Manchester in 1978 by Hempsall, Robert Davenport (guitar), Keith Darbyshire (bass) and Gary Madeley (drums) - a line-up which would remain constant throughout the band's existence. They began by playing Hawkwind and Magazine covers but by 1979 the influence of their famous peers had become evident. A debut single, 'From The Cradle to the Grave', was released on their own Aural Assault label, and was brought to the attention of Rob Gretton, manager of Joy Division and later New Order. He arranged for their next release - the 10-inch single 'Unsightly and Serene' - to come out on Factory Records, while future releases such as 1981's excellent 'Live On A Hot August Night' 12-inch single (produced by Martin Hannett) appeared on Factory Benelux. The band split in November 1981 but later reformed as Ram Ram Kino with some additional members. They would release one single on Genesis P. Orridge's Psychic Temple label late in 1985.
Album: *The Plateau Phase* (1982).

Crybabys
This bluesy rock 'n' roll quartet from the UK, were formed in 1991 by former Boys' guitarist 'Honest' John Plain. Recruiting Darrell Garth (guitar/vocals), Mark Duncan (bass) and Robbie Rushton (drums) they signed with Receiver Records the same year. Drawing inspiration from Mott The Hoople, Hanoi Rocks and the Georgia Satellites, the Crybabys successfully bridge the gap between punk and rock 'n' roll. Shambolic, chaotic and full of stamina, they debuted with *Where Have All The Good Girls Gone?* This compares favourably with the best that either the Dogs D'Amour or Quireboys have produced.

Album: *Where Have All The Good Girls Gone?* (1991).

Cuban Heels
This UK group was headed by John Malarky (vocals), previously a member of Johnny And The Self Abusers, the Scottish punk band that metamorphosed into Simple Minds. Cuban Heels' formation in Glasgow 1978 was completed with the addition of Laurie Cuffe (guitar), Paul Armour (bass) and Davie Duncan (drums). Initially an R&B band with the odd punk track, they soon found growing popularity with the mod revival crowd. Consequently their live set was balanced between originals like 'Modern Girl', 'Too Much, Too Loud', 'Samantha's World' and 'Young Pretender', plus covers such as Cat Stevens' 'Matthew And Son' and Cliff Richard's 'On The Beach'. The debut single released on the Housewives Choice label in March 1978, was a pop-punk reworking of Petula Clark's hit 'Downtown'. With the new year came a change in line-up, with Nick Clarke (bass) and Ali McKenzie (drums), replacing Armour and Duncan. Throughout 1979-80 they continued an exhausting live schedule and released two more independent singles, 'Little Girl' and 'Walk On Water'. Their lack of commercial success prompted the band to settle on a more comfortable pop sound, with image to match. A deal with Virgin Records saw *Walk Our Way To Heaven* and a string of singles, 'Sweet Charity', 'My Colours Fly' and a remake of 'Walk On Water', suffer the same fate as previous offerings. The band split during 1982.
Album: *Walk Our Way To Heaven* (1981).

Cud
Formed in Leeds in 1987 by Carl Puttnam (b. 1967, Ilford, Essex, England; vocals), Mike Dunphy (b. 1967, Northumberland, England; guitar), William Potter (b. 1968, Derby, England; bass) and Steve 'The Drummer From Cud' Goodwin (b. 1967, Croydon, Surrey, England; drums). The quartet sprung into existence when they discovered the remains of a deserted drum kit in a rubbish skip. They debuted on the Wedding Present's Reception label and spent two years building up a small but fanatical north England following with a comical hybrid of funk and the uglier elements of independent music. Threatened by a not entirely undeserved 'joker' tag - helped by Cud's desire to perform absurd versions of Hot Chocolate and Jethro Tull songs - 1990 brought 'a new sense of sanity and professionalism' to the band. Critical acclaim coincided with a more nationwide spread of supporters, and their newfound attitude reaped commercial dividends when the 'Robinson Crusoe' single reached number 86 in the UK charts, closely followed by 'Magic' peaking at number 80. With financial viability suddenly outweighing the band's odder idiosyncrasies, major labels tussled for

their signatures until Cud decided to go with A&M Records in 1991 for the simple reason that the label's logo 'had the trumpet'!

Albums: *When In Rome, Kill Me* (1989), *Elvis Belt* (1990), *Leggy Mambo* (1990).

Cuddly Toys

Emerging from the ashes of glam-punk outfit Raped, the Irish-based Cuddly Toys consisted of Sean Purcell (vocals), Tony Baggett (bass), Faebhean Kwest (guitar) and Billy Surgeoner (guitar) and Paddy Phield (drums). Both 1980 releases *Guillotine Theatre* and a cover of David Bowie's 'Madmen' were co-releases for Raped's old label Parole and Fresh. 'Astral Joe' came later that year, followed by 'Someone's Crying' in 1981, but the band seemed derivative and soon endured line-up changes. Terry Noakes joined on guitar and Robert Parker on drums. After 'It's A Shame' and a second album, *Trials And Crosses* in 1982, the band disappeared from view.

Albums: *Guillotine Theatre* (1981), *Trials And Crosses* (1982).

Cult

Formerly known as Southern Death Cult, the band were formed by lead singer Ian Astbury (b. Ian Lindsay, 14 May 1962, Heswell, Merseyside, England) in Bradford 1981. With the line-up eventually stabilized by Jamie Stewart (bass), Les Warner (b. 13 February 1961; drums) and ex-Theatre Of Hate guitarist Billy Duffy (b. 12 May 1959, Manchester, England), they were born out of the new wave/punk movement, and initially adopted a gothic-like image. Signing to Beggars Banquet Records, they debuted with *Dreamtime* in 1984. This featured material that was low-key, atmospheric and verged on the surreal. The legacy of the late 70s was being played out as the band dressed all in black, had pale complexions and wore love beads. The band's big break came with *Love* in 1985, which comprised more hard-rock song structures and pushed Duffy's raunchy guitar lines to the fore. It spawned two UK Top 20 hit singles in the epical 'She Sells Sanctuary' and 'Rain'. *Electric* saw the band's transition to heavy rock completed. The songs drew inspiration from Led Zeppelin, AC/DC and Bad Company. Produced by Rick Rubin, *Electric* was a bold and brash statement of intent, that oozed energy and pure rock 'n' roll from every note. It became a success on both sides of the Atlantic, peaking at number 4 and 38 in the UK and US charts respectively. Two years later, *Sonic Temple* emerged, which consolidated the band's success, reaching number 10 on the *Billboard* album chart and number 3 in the UK. The band were now down to a three-piece following the departure of Warner. Mickey Curry was hired to fill in on drums, and the album combined the atmospheric passion of

Love, with the unbridled energy of *Electric*. Bassist Stewart quit in 1990, with the core of the band reduced to just a duo comprising Astbury and Duffy. *Ceremony* was released in 1991, with the help of Charley Drayton (bass) and Curry. This was a retrogressive collection of songs, that had more in common with *Love*, than their previous two albums. Nevertheless, having already established an enormous fan-base, success was virtually guaranteed. The Cult remain one of the most revered acts working within their particular genre.

Albums: *Dreamtime* (1984), *Love* (1985), *Electric* (1987), *Sonic Temple* (1989), *Ceremony* (1991).

Culture Club

Harbingers of the so-called 'new pop' that swept through the UK charts in the early 80s, Culture Club comprized: Boy George (b. George O'Dowd, 14 June 1961, Eltham, Kent, England; vocals), Roy Hay (b. 12 August 1961, Southend-on-Sea, Essex, England; guitar/keyboards), Mikey Craig (b. 15 February 1960, Hammersmith, London, England; bass) and Jon Moss (b. 11 September 1957, Wandsworth, London, England; drums). The group came together in 1981 after George, a nightclub *habitué*, had briefly appeared with Bow Wow Wow (under the name Lieutentant Lush) and played alongside Craig in the Sex Gang Children. The elder drummer Moss had the most band experience having already appeared with London, the Damned and Adam Ant. After failing an audition with EMI, Culture Club were signed to Virgin Records in the spring of 1982, and released a couple of non-chart singles, 'White Boy' and 'I'm Afraid Of Me'. By autumn of that year, however, the group were firmly established as one of the most popular new acts in the country. The melodic and subtly arranged 'Do You Really Want To Hurt Me?' took them to number 1 in the UK and they deserved another chart-topper with the Top 3 follow-up, 'Time (Clock Of The Heart)'. Although their first album *Kissing To Be Clever* lacked the consistent excellence of their singles, it was still a fine pop record. By this time, George was already one of pop's major talking points with his dreadlocks, make-up and androgynous persona. Never short of a quote for the press, he would later stress such virtues as celibacy with the anti-sex quip, 'I'd rather have a cup of tea'. The launching of MTV in the USA ensured that many UK acts were infiltrating the American charts and the colourful persona of George, coupled with the irresistible charm of Culture Club's melodies, effectively broke them Stateside early in 1983. *Kissing To Be Clever* climbed into the Top 20 of the US album charts, while their two UK singles hits both reached number 2. Suddenly, Culture Club were one of the most popular groups in the world. Back at home, the

Cult; Ian Astbury

passionate 'Church Of The Poison Mind', with Helen Terry on counter vocals with George, gave them another number 2 hit. The group reached their commercial peak later that year with the release of the infectious 'Karma Chameleon', which topped the charts on both sides of the Atlantic and sold in excess of a million copies. The second album, *Colour By Numbers* was another UK number 1 and was only kept off the top in the US by Michael Jackson's mega-selling *Thriller*. The momentum was maintained through 1983-84 with strong singles such as 'Victims', 'It's A Miracle' and 'Miss You Blind', which charted in either the US or UK Top 10. Ironically, it was one their biggest UK hits which presaged Culture Club's fall from critical grace. In October 1984, 'The War Song' hit number 2 but was widely criticized for its simplistic politicizing. Thereafter, chart performances took an increasing backseat to the tabloid newspaper adventures of George. Indeed, 1986's 'Move Away' was to be their only other Top 10 hit. The media-conscious singer had signed a Faustian pact with Fleet Street which led to his downfall in 1986. Having confessed that he was a herion addict, he found himself persecuted by the press and was eventually arrested for possession of cannabis. Early in 1987, he appeared on the high-rating UK television show Wogan and declared that he was cured. The announcement coincided with the news that Culture Club no longer existed. However, George would continue to enjoy chart-topping success as a soloist.

Albums: *Kissing To Be Clever* (1982), *Colour By Numbers* (1983), *Waking Up To The House On Fire* (1984), *From Luxury To Heartache* (1986), *This Time* (1987).

Cure

Formed in 1976 as the Easy Cure, this UK group was based around the musicianship of Robert Smith (b. 21 April 1959, Crawley, Sussex, England; guitar/vocals), Michael Dempsey (bass) and Lol Tolhurst (drums). After struggling to find a niche during the first flashes of punk, the group issued the Albert Camus-inspired 'Killing An Arab' on the independent Small Wonder in mid-1978. It proved sufficient to draw them to the attention of producer and Fiction label manager Chris Parry, who reissued the single the following year. By May 1979, the group were attracting glowing reviews, particularly in the wake of 'Boys Don't Cry', whose style recalled mid-60s British beat, with the added attraction of Smith's deadpan vocal. The attendant album *Three Imaginary Boys* was also well-received and was followed by a support spot with Siouxsie And The Banshees, on which Smith joined the headliners onstage. Another strong single, 'Jumping Someone Else's Train' performed predictably well in the

independent charts but, in common with previous releases, narrowly missed the national chart. A pseudonymous single 'I'm A Cult Hero', under the name the Cult Heroes passed unnoticed and, soon after its release, Dempsey was replaced on bass by Simon Gallup. Amid the shake-up keyboards player Mathieu Hartley was added to the line-up. By the spring of 1980, the Cure were developing less as a pop group than a guitar-laden rock group. The atmospheric 12-inch single 'A Forest' gave them their first UK Top 40 hit, while the stronger second album, *17 Seconds* reached the Top 20. Thereafter, the Cure's cult following ensured that their work regularly appeared in the lower regions of the charts. After consolidating their position during 1981 with 'Primary', 'Charlotte Sometimes' and 'Faith', the group looked to the new year for a new direction. A major breakthrough with *Pornography* threatened to place them in the major league of new UK acts, but there were internal problems to overcome. The keyboards player, Hartley, had lasted only a few months and, early in 1982, the other 'new boy' Gallup was fired and replaced by Steve Goulding. Meanwhile, Smith briefly joined Siouxsie And The Banshees as a temporary replacement for John McGeogh. As well as contributing the excellent psychedelic-tinged guitar work to their hit 'Dear Prudence', Smith subsequently teamed up with Banshee Steve Severin and Jeanette Landray in the Glove. The Cure, meanwhile, continued to record and during the summer enjoyed their first UK Top 20 singles appearance with the electronics-tinged 'The Walk'. Four months later, they were in the Top 10 with the radically contrasting straightforward pop single, 'The Love Cats'. Further success followed with 'The Caterpillar', another unusual single, highlighted by Smith's eccentric violin playing. The charts confirmed that the Cure were now one of the most eclectic and eccentric ensembles working in British pop. Smith's heavy eye make-up, smudged, crimson lipstick and shock-spiked hair was quite striking and the group's videos, directed by Tim Pope, seemed increasingly enigmatic. In 1985, the group released their most commercially successful album yet, *The Head On The Door*. The following year, they re-recorded their second single, 'Boys Don't Cry', which this time became a minor UK hit. By now, the group was effectively Smith and Tolhurst, with members such as Gallup and others, flitting through the group's line-up from year to year. With the retrospective *Standing On A Beach* singles collection, the group underlined their longevity during an otherwise quiet year. During 1987, the Cure undertook a tour of South America and enjoyed several more minor UK hits with 'Why Can't I Be You?', 'Catch' and 'Just Like Heaven'. The latter also reached the US Top 40, as did their

Cure; Robert Smith

double album, *Kiss Me, Kiss Me, Kiss Me*. A two-year hiatus followed before the release of the follow-up, *Disintegration* which climbed into the UK Top 3. During the same period, the group had continued to register regular hits with such singles as 'Lullaby', 'Lovesong', 'Pictures Of You' and the fiery 'Never Enough'. Along the way, they continued their run of line-up changes, which culminated in the departure of Tolhurst (and later, Presence), leaving Smith as the sole original member. Although it was assumed that the Cure would attempt to consolidate their promising sales in the USA, Smith announced that he would not be undertaking any further tours of America. 1990 ended with the release of *Mixed Up*, a double album collecting together re-recordings and remixes of their 12-inch singles. By 1992, the Cure line-up comprised Smith, Gallup, Perry Bamonte (keyboards/guitar), Porl Thompson (guitar) and Boris Williams (drums), and with the critically acclaimed *Wish*, consolidated their position as one of the world's top groups.

Albums: *Three Imaginary Boys* (1979), *Boys Don't Cry* (1979), *17 Seconds* (1980), *Faith* (1981), *Pornography* (1982), *The Top* (1984), *Concert - The Cure Live* (1984), *Concert And Curiosity - Cure Anomalies 1977-1984* (1984), *Head On The Door* (1985), *Kiss Me, Kiss Me, Kiss Me* (1987), *Disintegration* (1989), *Entreat* (1991), *Wish* (1992). Compilations: *Japanese Whispers*

- *The Cure Singles Nov 1982-Nov 1983* (1983), *Standing On The Beach - The Singles* (1986), *Mixed Up* (1990).

Curiosity Killed The Cat

This late 80s UK pop group graced the covers of all the teen-pop magazines. The various group members all had showbusiness/theatrical backgrounds. The line-up comprized: Ben Volpeliere-Pierrot, (b. 19 May 1964, London, England), Julian Godfrey Brookhouse, (b. 13 May 1963, London, England), Nicholas Bernard Throp, (b. 25 October 1964, London, England) and Migi/Michael Drummond (b. Miguel John Drummond, 27 January 1964, Middlesex, England). Volpeliere-Pierrot's father was a celebrity photographer and his mother a model - Ben's surname was a double-barrelled convolution of their surnames. His childhood was dotted with visits from various Beatles, Rolling Stones and other faces of the 60s who held court at his parents' home. A pretty child, he was in a Kodak commercial in 1970 and by his teens was a regular model in teenage girls' magazines. He also appeared in videos for XTC and the Thompson Twins in the early 80s. Volpeliere-Pierrot first played alongside the other members in the punk-influenced Twilight Children. Drummond was the son of a film and video maker and also brushed with the stars when his father's company made videos for bands such as the Police. After discovering punk he took up drumming, and met Throp at art school before an invitation to join the Twilight Children. In mid-1984 Volpeliere-Pierrot was dating Drummond's sister and the boys invited him to sing in their band, kicking out the old vocalist in the process. Later that same year Toby Anderson also joined the group as keyboardist and songwriter. A demo of a song called 'Curiosity Killed the Cat' was heard by businessman Peter Rosengard who became their manager and they changed their name to that of the song. A debut gig was held at the Embassy Club in December 1984 at which point there were still numerous extra musicians and singers on stage. They shed the excess baggage although Anderson remained the 'fifth' Cat until late 1986. Signed to Phonogram in 1985, they started recording towards the end of the year. Their album was held up for almost a year after original producers Sly Dunbar and Robbie Shakespeare were dropped in favour of Stewart Levine. 'Misfit' followed in July but flopped. Another face from the 60s, Andy Warhol, met the band at a London art exhibition and he championed them, even appearing in a video for 'Misfit'. His involvement, though useful, was cut short when he died in 1987. Several television appearances helped to push the second single 'Down To Earth', which entered the charts in December 1986 reaching the Top 10 in the New Year. A series of further hits

Curve

followed, including a re-issued 'Misfit'. However, after 'Free' in September 1987 they underwent a quiet period but returned in 1989 with 'Name And Number' - now simply credited to Curiosity.

Albums: *Keep Your Distance* (1987), *Getahead* (1989).

Curry, Cherie

Former lead vocalist of the Runaways, Cherie Curry embarked on a solo career after quitting the all-girl group in 1977. Continuing in the same vein as her former band, she specialized in undistinguished three-minute pop-rock anthems. Employing a variety of talented session men, including Toto members Steve Lukather (guitar) and Mike Porcaro (bass), the songs were hindered by Curry's limited range and vocal dynamics. *Messin' With The Boys* featured sister Marie and pursued a more hard-rock direction, but once again had very little to recommend it. It appears that the initial accusations of Curry being a 'talentless bimbo', may have some foundation.

Albums: *Beauty's Only Skin Deep* (1978), *Messin' With The Boys* (1980).

Curve

This UK independent label act featured the distinctive and opinionated voice of Toni Halliday (b.

c.1965), one of three children born to a liberal Roman Catholic mother and single parent. Her major collaborator and songwriting partner was Dean Garcia (guitar). Halliday secured her first record deal at the age of 14, moving to London where she floundered with pop duo the Uncles. She later met David A. Stewart in Sunderland and they stayed friends, making the acquaintance of another member of Stewart's inner sanctum, Garcia, who had played on the Eurythmics' albums *Touch* and *Be Yourself Tonight*. They joined forces in the equally pallid State Of Play, who were signed to Virgin Records and released two singles and an album, *Balancing The Scales*. After their acrimonious split, Halliday released the solo *Hearts And Handshakes* in 1989, before reuniting with Garcia to sign to the Eurythmics Anxious label. Halliday had taken a tape of the song 'Ten Little Girls' to Stewart, who was immediately impressed. The results were three EPs that reached number 1 in the UK independent chart in 1991: *Blindfold*, *Frozen* and *Cherry*, all of which were well reviewed despite the media cynics citing Halliday as a stubborn careerist. Whatever Halliday's motives, Curves' blend of goth, dance and indie guitar rock had gelled perfectly for a willing audience. 1992's 'Fait Accompli' was yet another indie number 1, and

the accompanying album, *Doppelganger* likewise. The groundwork has been laid for a potentially rich recording career; they have created their own studio, and filled out the line-up to include Debbie Smith and Alex Mitchell (guitars) and Monti (drums).
Album: *Doppelganger* (1992).

Czukay, Holger

b. 24 March 1938, Danzig, Germany. Czukay was a founder member of the progressive electronic group Can whose solo work of the 80s used tape loops and *musique concrete* methods. He studied with *avant garde* composer Karlheinz Stockhausen before joining Can as bassist in 1968. The group pioneered the use of electronics in a rock context and made numerous albums and composed several film soundtracks before Czukay left in the late 70s. As Cluster, he worked with Brian Eno, recording two albums for RCA before creating the highly praised *Movies*. Its backing musicians included African percussionist Kwaku Baah and his former Can colleagues. Among Czukay's later collaborators were Jah Wobble (1982) and David Sylvian (1988-89). Czukay caused an outcry in 1986 when 'Blessed Easter' included a 'cut-up' extract of a Papal speech. In 1989 Czukay rejoined Can to make *Rite Time* on the Mercury label.
Albums: *Movies* (1979), with Jah Wobble *On The Way To The Peak Of Normal* (1982), *Der Osten Ist Rot* (1986), *Rome Remains Rome* (1986), with David Sylvian *Plight And Premonition* (1988), with Sylvian *Flux And Mutability* (1989), *Radio Wave Surfer* (1991).

D

DAF

This German band specialized in minimalist electro-dance music. The initials stood for Deutsch Amerikanische Freundschaft and the line-up comprised Robert Gorl (drums/synthesizer), W. Spelmans (guitar), C. Hass (saxophone/synthesizer/bass) and Gabi Delgado-Lopez (vocals). Their first UK album was released on the Mute label in 1980, the title, *Die Kleinen Und Die Bosen*, is translated as The Small And The Evil. Recorded in London, the album was uneven and was generally considered as unrepresentative, dominated by 'songs' whose heritage combined *Pink Flag* era Wire and Can influences. Afterwards Gorl and Delgado-Lopez continued as a duo. They recorded three albums for Virgin in an 18-month period.

These comprised a mixture of Teutonic fantasy, love songs, and social statements. Delgado-Lopez's refusal to sing in English, condemned them to a minority international market. Contrary to their dour image, there is much to admire in the exemplary pop of singles such as 'Verlieb Dich In Mich'.
Albums: *Die Kleinen Und Die Bosen* (1980), *Alles Ist Gut* (1982), *Gold Und Liebe* (1982), *Fur Immer* (1983).

Daisy Chainsaw

Contrived, but fun, pop-punk outfit whose sudden appearance brightened-up the UK independent scene of the early 90s. Led by fragile singer Katie Jane Garside, the band also comprised Richard Adams (bass), Vince Johnson (drums) and Crispin Grey (guitar). They debuted with the *LoveSickPleasure* EP, which spiralled into the UK Top 30, aided by the highly colourful video for the lead track 'Love Your Money'. BBC's Radio 1 had picked up on the song's frenetic pace, and the music press were impressed by Garside's similar stage performances, but most importantly it was her visual image as a bedraggled, barefoot waif, in dirty torn dresses and petticoats - occasionally sucking on a baby's bottle, that attracted the most attention. Garside's allusions and references in interviews of having a past of sexual abuse and psychological disorder backfired slightly on the group, but there is little doubt that the band's presentation is disturbingly resonant of the child as victim. The success of the EP encouraged them to sign with larger independent One Little Indian, despite tantalizing offers from the major record labels.

Dalek I Love You

From the ashes of Liverpool punk band Radio Blank, Alan Gill (guitar/vocals) and David Balfe (bass/vocals/synthesizer), formed Dalek I Love You in November 1977. Disagreement over the band's name - David wanted the Daleks, whereas Alan preferred Darling I Love You - resulted in a combination of them both, and with the addition of Dave Hughes (keyboards), Chris 'Teepee' Shaw (synthesizer), plus a drum machine, the first of many loose line-ups was complete. In July 1978 Balfe left to join Big In Japan. After a string of critically acclaimed synthesizer-pop singles, 1980 saw the release of *Compass Kum'pass* which came in the wake of groups like Orchestral Manoeuvres In The Dark and Tubeway Army. A worldwide deal with Korova produced the singles, 'Holiday In Disneyland', 'Ambition' and the album *Dalek I Love You*, which meshed layered synth and psychedelic fragments with starry-eyed vocals, augmented by excellent harmonies. Again, none achieved any real commercial success and Phil Jones decided to put the band 'on ice'. During this period he was busy writing and recording the soundtrack for the film *Letter To*

Brezhnev (1985) and formed the Bopadub label in Birkenhead, which put out a series of cassettes culminating in 1985 with *Naive*, recorded by the reformed Dalek I. In 1986, after eight years of tentative existence, Phil Jones was still optimistic about future releases and subsequently, *Compass Kum'pass* was re-released by Fontana in 1989, acknowledging the importance of this seminal electronic band.

Albums: *Compass Kum'pass* (1980), *Dalek I Love You* (1983), as Dalek I *Naive* (1985).

Dali's Car

This was a brief a partnership between Bauhaus frontman Peter Murphy and Japan's distinctive bassist Mick Karn. Dali's Car first surfaced on a compilation cassette, *Jobs Not Yobs*, in 1982, but it was over two years before they signed with Virgin Records subsidiary Paradox. 'The Judgment Is The Mirror', in 1984, accompanied an album, *Waking Hour,* the month after, but the project was not warmly received and the pair soon went their separate ways.

Album: *Waking Hour* (1984).

Damned

Formed in 1976, this UK punk group comprised Captain Sensible (b. Ray Burns, 23 April 1955, England; bass), Rat Scabies (b. Chris Miller, 30 July 1957, Surrey, England; drums), Brian James (b. Brian Robertson, England; guitar) and Dave Vanian (b. David Letts, England; vocals). Scabies and James had previously played in the unwieldy punk ensemble London SS and, joined by Sensible, they backed Nick Kent's Subterraneans. The Damned emerged in May 1976 and two months later they were supporting the Sex Pistols at the 100 Club. After appearing at the celebrated Mont de Marsan punk festival in August, they were signed to Stiff Records one month later. In October, they released what is generally regarded as the first UK punk single, 'New Rose', which was backed by a frantic version of the Beatles' 'Help!' Apart from being dismissed as support act during the Sex Pistols' ill-fated Anarchy tour, they released UK punk's first album *Damned Damned Damned*, produced by Nick Lowe. The work was typical of the period, full of short, sharp songs played extremely fast, with high energy compensating for competence. During April 1977, they became the first UK punk group to tour the USA. By the summer of that year, they recruited a second guitarist, Lu Edmunds; and soon after drummer Rat Scabies quit. A temporary replacement, Dave Berk, deputized until the recruitment of London percussionist Jon Moss. In November, their second album *Music For Pleasure*, produced by Pink Floyd's Nick Mason, was mauled by the critics and worse followed when they were dropped from Stiff's roster. Increasingly dismissed for

their lack of earnestness and love of pantomime, they lost heart and split in early 1978. The members went in various directions: Sensible joined the Softies, Moss and Edmunds formed the Edge, Vanian teamed-up with Doctors Of Madness and James founded Tanz Der Youth.

The second part of the Damned story reopened one year later when Sensible, Vanian and Scabies formed the Doomed. In November 1978, they were allowed to use the name Damned and opened this new phase of their career with their first Top 20 single, 'Love Song'. Some minor hits followed and the group was pleasantly surprised to find themselves a formidable concert attraction. When their recently recruited bassist Algy Ward (previously with the Saints) left to join Tank, he was replaced by Paul Gray, from Eddie And The Hot Rods. The group continued to reach the lower regions of the chart during the next year while Captain Sensible simultaneously signed a solo deal with A&M Records. Amazingly, he zoomed to number 1 with a novel revival of 'Happy Talk', which outsold every Damned release. Although he stuck with the group for two more years, he finally left in August 1984. A third phase in the group's career ushered in new members and a more determined pop direction. In 1986, they enjoyed their biggest ever hit with a cover of Barry Ryan's 'Eloise'. Another 60s pastiche, this time a rather pedestrian reading of Love's classic 'Alone Again Or', gave them a minor UK hit. Still gigging regularly, the Damned have lasted much longer than any critic could have dreamed back in 1976.

Albums: *Damned Damned Damned* (1977), *Music For Pleasure* (1977), *Machine Gun Etiquette* (1979), *The Black Album* (1980), *Strawberries* (1982), *Phantasmagoria* (1985), *Anything* (1986), *Final Damnation* (1989, live 1988 recording), *Not The Captain's Birthday Party* (1991, live 1977 recording). Compilations: *The Best Of The Damned* (1981), *Light At The End Of The Tunnel* (1987).

Daniels, Phil, And The Cross

Daniels, a graduate of London's Anna Scher Theatre School and member of the Royal Shakespeare Company, had flirted with pop as one of Renoir. He had starred in both the mod retrospective movie *Quadrophenia* and, with Hazel O' Connor, in *Breaking Glass* before briefly forsaking acting to be a singing guitarist. Backed by Peter Hugodaly (keyboards), Barry Neil (bass) and John McWilliams (drums), he performed selections from a sole RCA album during a concert itinerary centred on the metropolis. However, despite full-page advertisements in the music press and a charitable reaction from some critics, Phil Daniels And The Cross did not appeal to many record buyers, and its figurehead resumed a more promising career in drama.

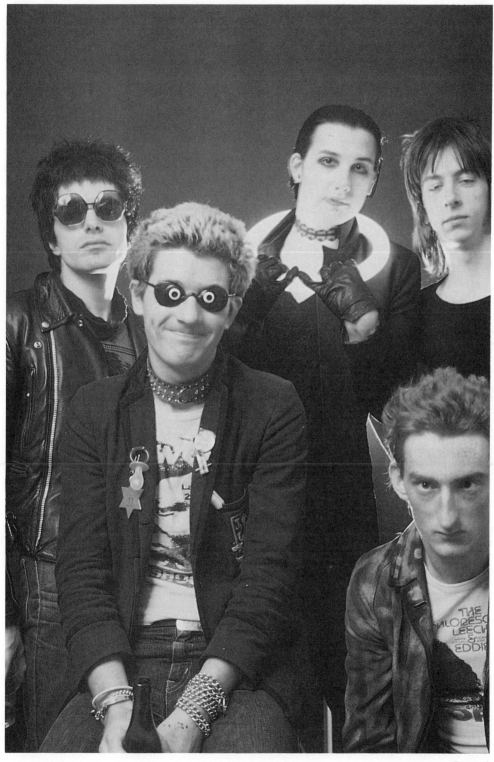

Damned

Album: *Phil Daniels And The Cross* (1980).

Danse Society

These UK gothic rock innovators evolved from Sheffield bands Y? and Lips-X. The two groups merged as Danse Crazy, establishing the line-up as Steve Rawlings (vocals) Paul Gilmartin (drums) Lyndon Scarfe (keyboards) and Paul Nash (guitar), as additional guitar and keyboard players were jettisoned. These included Paul Hampshire (aka Bee and Paul Hertz). They came to prominence first at the Futurama Festival 2 in Leeds which was filmed by the BBC. After a slight change of name to Danse Society, and the filling of the bass position with Tim Wright, they performed their first gig at the Marples in Sheffield. The self-produced 'Clock' single provided the band with some acclaim, despite its short run of 1,000 copies. Management duties were taken over by Marcus Featherby, who released their EP *No Shame In Death* on his own Pax label. However, they soon returned to their own Society Records. The mini-album *Seduction* garnered strong support in the media and the band embarked on a series of interviews and live dates. Following one more independent single they signed to Arista: 'We'd done the Society Records thing and taken it as far as we could independently, we were totally out of money.' The dramatic 'Wake Up' was their debut, its sense of mystery and dark charm pre-dating the 'gothic' scene by at least a year. *Heaven Is Waiting* provided their first full album's worth of material, and further airplay from BBC disc jockeys John Peel and Janice Long kept them in the ascendent. However, internal rifts saw the replacement of Scarfe with former Music For Pleasure member David Whitaker. Relations with their record company also deteriorated when Arista failed to back a US tour. Litigation delayed further activities until a compromise was reached in March 1985. When they returned with 'Say It Again' (produced by Stock, Aitken And Waterman), it was to a bemused audience who had not anticipated such a sudden shift in style. The more commercial nature of their subsequent work failed to impress, and Arista rejected their proposed second album *Heaven Again*. When they split in April 1986, Rawlings attempted to persevere with the funk-orientated Society, while the rest of the band continued briefly as Johnny In The Clouds
Albums: *Seduction* (1982), *Heaven Is Waiting* (1984).

Darling Buds

Formed in Wales in 1987 by Andrea Lewis (b. 25 March 1967, Newport, Wales), Harley Farr (b. 4 July 1964, Singapore), Bloss and Chris McDonagh (b. 6 March 1962, Newport, Wales), the early part of the Darling Buds' career was as much of a pure adrenalin rush as was their poppypunk music. Following in the tradition of classic pop records, the Buds produced a series of sparkling sub-three minute singles on the independent Native label, becoming embroiled in the superfluous 'Blond' scene of that time alongside the Primitives. With the added incentive of increasingly celebrational live performances, Epic Records swiftly signed the band in 1988 and earned moderate chart success for subsequent singles. Unfortunately, in the true spirit of bubblegum pop, the Darling Buds' balloon began to deflate. Drummer Bloss was replaced by Jimmy Hughes (b. Liverpool, England) and the band's second album, *Crawdaddy* witnessed a new sophisticated approach to recording which was at odds with their early material, creating few ripples in the musical pond.
Albums: *Pop Said* (1989), *Crawdaddy* (1990).

Dax, Danielle

b. Southend, Essex, England. Dax first came to prominence in 1980 with Karl Blake in the engaging Lemon Kittens. After *We Buy A Hammer For Daddy* and *The Big Dentist*, the group split in 1982. Dax next pursued a more straightforward pop route, mixed with forays into ethnic music and *avant garde*. Her first solo album, *Pop-Eyes* featured her playing 15 instruments, as well as composing and producing. She also displayed talents as a sleeve designer, contributing to Robert Fripp's *League Of Gentlemen* among others. After a brief detour into acting, during which she appeared in the film, *A Company Of Wolves*, she returned to the recording scene in 1984. *Jesus Egg That Wept* was a mini-album that preceded an extensive UK tour in which she was backed by Dave Knight, Steve Reeves, Ian Sturgess and Martin Watts. Her 1985 single 'Yummer Yummer Man' was well received and revealed her love of 60s psychedelia. *Inky Bloaters* was an exceptionally ecelectic work which maintained her reputation. After appearing at the new music seminar in Boston, she was signed by Seymour Stein to the fashionable Sire label. Her fourth album, produced by Stephen Street, included a revival of the Beatles' 'Tomorrow Never Knows'.
Albums: *Pop-Eyes* (1983), *Jesus Egg That Wept* (1984), *Inky Bloaters* (1987), *Blast The Human Flower* (1991).

dB's

Founder members of the US pop unit the dB's, Chris Stamey (guitars/vocals), Gene Holder (bass) and Will Rigby (drums) had made their name around North Carolina, USA, with the Sneakers, alongside Mitch Easter (guitar/vocals). After two EPs (in 1976 and 1978) on Alan Betrock's Car label, Easter departed (later surfacing with Let's Active), the remaining three teamed up with keyboardist Peter Holsapple (ex-H-Bombs), to create the dB's. Stamey and Holsapple had previously worked together in

Rittenhouse Square as early as 1972, while Stamey had indulged in a solo effort, 'Summer Sun' on Ork, in 1977. The dB's' debut single, 'I Thought (You Wanted To Know)', on the Car label, was issued towards the end of 1978, by which time the band had relocated to New York City. Signing with Shake, they then came up with 'Black And White', attracting attention in the UK, and sealing a contract with Albion. The dB's delivered two albums in as many years for Albion, both capturing an evocative blend of melodic, occasionally Beatles-styled songs and new wave sensibilities. 'Dynamite', 'Big Brown Eyes' and 'Judy' were drawn from *Stands For Decibels* (1981) while the following year's *Repercussions* spawned 'Amplifier', 'Neverland' and 'Living A Lie'. However, the dB's failed to make any significant commercial impact. Stamey was the first to leave and release a solo work, *In The Winter Of Love*, in 1984. An apathetic British reception meant that his second album, *It's Alright* on A&M Records, failed to secure a UK release. In the meantime, the dB's replaced Stamey with Jeff Beninato and reunited for *The Sound Of Music* on IRS, joined by guests Van Dyke Parks and Syd Straw. Since then, Peter Holsapple has been busy working in the wings with R.E.M.

Albums: *Stands For Decibels* (1981), *Repercussions* (1982), *Like This* (1985), *The Sound Of Music* (1987). Compilation: *Amplifier* (1986).

Dead Boys

One of the first wave punk bands in the USA, the Dead Boys formed in Cleveland in 1976 but relocated to New York the following year. They often played the infamous Bowery club CBGB's, the starting place for other bands such as the Ramones, Television, Blondie and Talking Heads. The band consisted of Stiv Bators (vocals), Jimmy Zero (rhythm guitar), Cheetah Chrome (b. Gene Connor; lead guitar), Jeff Magnum (bass) and Johnny Blitz (drums). The group took its cue from the Sex Pistols and the Damned by being as menacing, snarling and violently aggressive as possible. Signed to Sire Records in 1977, the group released two albums, the appropriately titled *Young, Loud And Snotty* and *We Have Come For Your Children*, the latter being produced by Felix Pappalardi. The band split in 1980, with Bators recording a pair of solo albums before forming Lords Of The New Church with former Damned and Sham 69 member Brian James. Bators was killed in an automobile accident in France in June 1990. The other original Dead Boys made no further impact after the group's dissolution.

Albums: *Young, Loud And Snotty* (1977), *We Have Come For Your Children* (1978), *Night Of The Living Dead Boys* (1981), *Younger, Louder And Snottier* (1989).

Dead Famous People

Hailing from New Zealand and signed to the independent Flying Nun label, the group comprised of Donna Savage (vocals), Biddy Leyland (keyboards), Wendy Kjestrup (guitar), Jenny Renals (bass) and Robin Tearle (drums). After achieving a modest degree of success on the New Zealand independent circuit the group transferred operations to the UK. Tearle, unable to travel, was replaced by Gill Moon, and later by Frances Gant. They were picked up by the label Utility, which was run by Billy Bragg, for whom Biddy Leyland had previously helped to organize a tour in New Zealand. The mini-album *Arriving Late In Torn And Filthy Jeans* included tracks originally recorded in New Zealand on the Flying Nun label and became Utility's biggest-selling release. The set featured highly lyrical and flowing, melodic songs such as 'Barlow's House' and 'Postcard From Paradise'. The sexual politics shown in 'Traitor To The Cause' won critical acclaim from many quarters. After a string of successful live appearances on the London club/bar circuit, the group looked set for higher things. However, by the middle of 1990 a rift within the group caused a split, leaving the main songwriters, Savage and Leyland, to work solo. An unexpected taste of success came later that year for Donna when she guested on St. Etienne's version of the Field Mice song, 'Let's Kiss And Make Up'. The following year saw the release of an album on the La-Di-Da label, *All Hail The Daffodil*, which consisted of material recorded in early 1990. The album vindicated much of the group's early promise.

Albums: *Arriving Late In Torn And Filthy Jeans* (1989), *All Hail The Daffodil* (1991).

Dead Kennedys

Although not the first of San Francisco's punk attractions, the Dead Kennedys, formed in 1977, became one of the genre's most successful exponents. Led by vocalist Jello Biafra, the group achieved instant notoriety for its pulsating debut single, 'California Über Alles' (1979), a vitriolic attack on state governor Jerry Brown. East Bay Ray (guitar), Klaus Flouride (bass) and Ted (drums) completed the line-up featured on *Fresh Fruit For Rotting Vegetables*, which included hardcore anthems in 'Kill The Poor', 'Holiday In Cambodia' and 'Nazi Punks, Fuck Off'. Although Biafra relied on a musically stereotyped punk style which often blighted the power of his lyrics, the group nonetheless proved influential, and their record label, Alternative Tentacles, released material by, among others, the Butthole Surfers. New drummer D.H. (Darren) Peligro was introduced on *Plastic Surgery Disasters*, but this second set was also marred by a sense of cliche. A refusal to compromise has resulted in recurrent clashes with authority - their 1981 single, 'Too Drunk To Fuck', incurred a radio ban, yet reached the UK Top 40 - while in America the group's albums have been the subject of seizure and prosecution, leading Biafra to join Frank Zappa in a campaign against censorship, notably by the PMRC, or 'Washington Wives' lobby. The singer was obliged to devote increasing energies to legal and political matters - he came fourth in a field of 10 during the 1979 San Francisco mayoral elections - and disbanded the Kennedys at the end of the 80s. He subsequently collaborated with DOA and Nomeansno and, in 1991, released a solo album *I Blow Minds For A Living*.

Albums: *Fresh Fruit For Rotting Vegetables* (1980), *Plastic Surgery Disasters* (1982), *Frankenchrist* (1985), *Bedtime For Democracy* (1986). Compilation: *Give Me Convenience Or Give Me Death* (1987). Solo albums: Jello Biafra *No More Cocoons* (1987), *High Priest Of Harmful Matter* (1989); Jello Biafra with Nomeansno *The Sky Is Falling And I Want My Mummy* (1991), *I Blow Minds For A Living* (1991).

Deep Freeze Mice

Alan Jenkins (b. 16 March 1959, Dudley, West Midlands, England; guitar/clarinet/vocals). Jenkins' one-man battle against the heads (and underlings) of the corporate music industry has seen him lead various bands since the late 70s. Along with the Chrysanthemums, Jody And The Creams and Ruth's Refrigerator, the majority of his output has been released under the Deep Freeze Mice monicker. Formed in 1979, the group's line-up has included Sherree Lawrence (b. 24 May 1959, Rushden, Northamptonshire, England; keyboards), Michael Bunnage (b. 21 December 1958, Romford, Essex, England; bass) and Graham Summers (b. 30 July 1958, Wellingborough, Northamptonshire, England; drums). Peter Gregory replaced Summers in 1983. The group's brand of English psychedelia, which drew upon such influences as Syd Barrett, Captain Beefheart, the Mothers Of Invention, Soft Machine, plus a soupçon of Velvet Underground, often made for uncomfortable listening, while also displaying a talent for the commercial pop song. Jenkins has privately published a booklet entitled, *How To Be In A Pop Group* (1990), an accurate, serious and funny account of the pitfalls to be endured along the road to possible fame and failure, naming names in the process. He continues to record on the periphery of the music business which he studiously despises for its lack of adventure.

Albums: *My Geraniums Are Bulletproof* (1979), *Teenage Head In My Refrigerator* (1981), *The Gates Of Lunch* (1982), *Ranch House* (1983), *I Love You Little Bobo With Your Delicate Golden Lions* (1984), *Hang On Constance Let Me Hear The News* (1985), *War, Famine, Death, Pestilence And Miss Timberlake* (1986), *Rain Is When The Earth Is Television* (1987), *Live In Switzerland* (1988), *The Tender Yellow Ponies Of Insomnia* (1989). As the Chrysanthemums *Is That A Fish On Your Shoulder, Or Are You Just Pleased To See Me?* (1987), *Little Flecks Of Foam Around Barking* (1988), *Odyssey And Oracle* (1989). As Jody And The Creams *A Big Dog* (1990).

Defunkt

This hard-funk act centred on trombonist Joseph Bowie who rose to prominence as a member of the Black Artists Group, an *avant garde* collective, based in St. Louis, and patterned after the Art Ensemble Of Chicago. Defunkt drew on this 'new wave' tradition but fused such radical jazz with the dancefloor punch of Parliament and Funkadelic to create an thrilling, invigorating style. Bowie, the brother of trumpeter Lester Bowie, was an inspired frontman and several propulsive albums, notably *Thermonuclear Sweat*, captured their exciting style. Defunkt undertook an enforced four-year sabbatical while its leader battled heroin addiction but emerged anew with *In America*. Bill Bickford, Ronnie Drayton (guitars), John Mulkerik (trumpet), Kim Annette Clarke (bass) and Kenny Martin (drums) joined Bowie for this compulsive set which, if shorn of melody, compensated with sheer excitement.

Albums: *Defunkt* (b.80s), *Thermonuclear Sweat* (1984), *In America* (1988). Compilation: *Avoid The Funk* (1988).

Del Amitri

A Glaswegian semi-acoustic rock band who emerged in the wake of the Postcard label scene when they were formed by 16-year-old singer, pianist and bassist Justin Currie (b. 11 December 1964) and his guitarist friend Iain Harvie (b. 19 May 1962). They were joined for their debut on the No Strings independent label, 'Sense Sickness', by Bryan Tolland (guitar) and Paul (drums). Numerous sessions for BBC disc jockey John Peel and tours with everyone from the Fall to the Smiths ensured a cult following and a growing reputation for Currie's wry lyrics. Having taken second guitarist David Cummings and drummer Brian McDermott aboard, they came to the attention of Chrysalis Records, who signed them to their own 'indie' label, Big Star. Del Amitri, meaning 'from the womb' in Greek, released their debut album in 1985 but fell foul of the label shortly afterwards. The band's career entered a restorative period during which they toured via a network of fans who organized and promoted events in individual regions. A tour of the US led to Del Amitri being signed to A&M in 1987 and resuming their recording career. They hit the UK singles chart with 'Kiss This Thing Goodbye', 'Nothing Ever Happens', and 'Spit In The Rain'. By now, Del Amitri had evolved an individual yet classic synthesis of rock, blues and country

Del Amitri

elements to counterpoint Currie's crisp lyrics. The reissue of 'Kiss' helped to break them in the US, while domestically the plaintive protest ballad 'Nothing Ever Happens' won many supporters: 'And computer terminals report some gains, On the values of copper and tin, While American businessmen snap up Van Goghs, For the price of a hospital wing'. Personnel changes soon afterwards brought in David Cummings (guitar) and Brian McDermott (drums) who played on 'Spit In The Rain' (1991) and 'Always The Last To Know', taken from the Gil Norton-produced 1992 album. Their recent growth in popularity is due to the reaction to the highly commercial *Change Everything* and at the time of writing Del Amitri can do no wrong. Of their transition from indie wordsmiths to stadium rockers, Currie, philosophically, prefers to think that 'Del Amitri fans only hold ironic lighters aloft'.
Albums: *Del Amitri* (1985), *Waking Hours* (1989), *Change Everything* (1992).

De La Soul

Garlanded with the dreadful label of 'Daisy Age Soul', New Yorkers Posdunos (b. Kelvin Mercer, 17 August 1969), Trugoy the Dove (b. David Jude Joliceur, 21 September 1958) and Pasemaster Mace (b. Vincent Lamont Mason Jnr, 24 March 1970) were contemporaries of Queen Latifah, Monie Love and A Tribe Called Quest. With the aforementioned they formed the Native Tongues collective who were at the forefront of the black renaissance of the early 90s. Less harsh than many of their contemporaries, De La Soul's pleasantly lilting rhythms helped them chart their debut album - one of the first such acts to cross into the album market. As well as hit singles such as 'Me Myself And I', and 'The Magic Number', they also charted in conjunction with Queen Latifah on 'Mama Gave Birth To The Soul Children' and guested on the Jungle Brothers' 'Doing Our Own Dang'. Some of De La Soul's more esoteric samples range from Curiosity Killed The Cat to Steely Dan, though their mellow approach belies difficult subject matter. *De La Soul Is Dead*, however, saw them return to tougher rhythms and a less whimsical melodic approach. With over 100 artists sampled, they sidestepped injunctions by gaining clearance from all concerned artists, though it delayed the album for over a year. Infectious songs like 'Ring Ring Ring (Ha Ha Hey)' have kept their profile high in the singles chart.
Albums: *3 Feet High And Rising* (1989), *De La Soul Is Dead* (1991).

Delta 5

Formed in Leeds, England, this new wave group had much in common with the Au Pairs, and more particularly, the Slits. The members comprised Juiz Sale (vocals), Alan Rigs (guitar), Roz Allen (bass), Bethan Peters (bass) and Kelvin Knight (drums). Inspired amateurs, they released several singles on Rough Trade, which highlighted insipid but endearing hook lines, particularly 'Mind Your Own Business'. The line-up featured Julie on vocals, Al (guitar), Kevin (drums) and two female bassists, Ros and Bethan. The latter were the only two remaining following a major transformation in personnel as they moved to the Pre label. They split up shortly after, though history would prove them to be a great influence on mid-80s 'indie' pop bands like the Shop Assistants and Talulah Gosh.

Album: *See The Whirl* (1981).

Dentists

Formed 1984 in Chatham, Kent, the group comprised Michael Murphy (b. 8 October 1963, Bexley, Kent, England; guitar/vocals), Robert Collins (b. 12 June 1965, Gillingham, Kent, England; lead guitar), Mark Matthew (b. 15 May 1965, Farnborough, Hampshire, England; bass) and drummer Ian Smith, subsequently replaced by Alun Gwynne Jones (b. 3 February 1966, Chatham, Kent, England) in 1986, and later by Robert Grigg (b. 28 July 1968, Canterbury, Kent, England) in 1991. The contemporaries of other Medway town bands such as the Milkshakes and the Prisoners, this hard-working band have been plying their brand of melodic, driving pop (reminiscent in parts of the Smiths), on the London club circuit into the 90s and have built up a sizable, loyal following. Their early EP, *Down And Out In Paris And Chatham* (1986) garnered critical acclaim as did *Writhing On The Shagpile* which made an appearance in the UK independent chart in 1987, but since then press attention has been diverted leaving the band to quietly go about their business, issuing several EPs on various labels. Their 1990 album, *Heads And How To Read Them*, their strongest collection to date, secured favourable press reviews, but probably not strong enough to push the group out of the lower divisions in the UK they have inhabited since their inception. However, during 1991-92 the Dentists would appear to have gained an appreciable audience on the US college circuit, indicating that, similar to the Jazz Butcher and Robyn Hitchcock, a more profitable future lay.

Albums: *You And Your Bloody Oranges* (1985), *Beer Bottle And Bannister Symphonie* (1988), *Heads And How To Read Them* (1990), *Dressed* (1992).

Department S

Taking their name from the spoof 60s television series, Department S evolved from the punk/ska combo Guns For Hire. Although it featured several members during its lifetime, Guns For Hire was essentially occasional *Face* writer Vaughan Toulouse (b. Vaughan Cotillard, 30 July 1959, St Helier, Jersey. d. 1991) on vocals, Mike Herbage on guitar, Tony Lordan on bass, and Mike Hasler on drums. Hasler, who drummed for Madness in their Invaders days and also managed the Nips, wrote Guns For Hire's only single - 'I'm Gonna Rough My Girlfriend's Boyfriend Up Tonight' - which came out on Korova. The group became Department S with the addition of Mark Taylor on keyboards, and drummer Stuart Mizan replaced Hasler. They made their live debut at the Rock Garden, London, in July 1980. Demon released their debut single, 'Is Vic There?' in 1981, but its success led to the better equipped RCA picking it up. Two further singles followed on Stiff but a planned album was aborted when neither single charted. Vaughan returned to work as a disc jockey, before re-emerging with Main T on Paul Weller's Respond label. When two further singles flopped it proved to be the end of his performing career, with the exception of contributions to Weller's Council Collective off-shoot on 'Soul Deep', a miners' strike benefit. He was also linked with the Style Council as one of the personalities behind the 'Cappacino Kid', whose writing graced the band's sleeves. Vaughan died in August 1991 after a long illness brought on by Aids. Of the remainder of the band, Lordan and Taylor were most recently accounted for as being a postman and cab driver respectively.

Depeche Mode

During the UK post-punk backlash at the turn of the 80s, when bands dispensed with guitars and drums, in favour of synthesizers and drum machines, Depeche Mode were formed, taking their name from a French style magazine. More than a decade later they are recognized as the most successful 'electro-synth' group ever. The band came together in Basildon, Essex, England and comprised: Vince Clarke (b. 3 July 1961; synthesizer), Andy Fletcher (b. 8 July 1961; synthesizer), Martin Gore (b. 23 July 1961; synthesizer), and Dave Gahan (b. 9 May 1962; vocals). Following a series of packed houses at the Bridge House Tavern in London's Canning Town they were spotted by Daniel Miller and issued one track on Stevo's *Some Bizzare* compilation in 1981. Shortly afterwards they were signed to the independent Mute label, where they remain. 'Dreaming Of Me' in 1981 started a remarkable run of hit singles which by 1990 had totalled 26. Main songwriter Vince Clarke left shortly after *Speak And Spell* to form Yazoo with Alison Moyet, and the writing reins were brilliantly taken over by Martin Gore, as Alan Wilder (b. 1 June 1963) settled into

Depeche Mode

Clarke's place. The hypnotic and gentle 'See You' was an early demonstration of Gore's sense of melody. The band is an enigma in the way that Pink Floyd were in the early 70s. Their success rests purely on the music, which is arresting yet easy on the ear, and is compulsively danceable. Their lyrics have strong sexual overtones, for example 'Master And Servant' tackles aspects of the sub-dom scene. All their albums have made the UK Top 10 and towards the end of the 80s they began to make massive inroads towards the French and American market, which were strangely late in discovering this very 'English' band. Depeche Mode have started the early 90s as huge concert stars in the USA, with *Music For The Masses* now having sold several million copies worldwide.

Albums: *Speak And Spell* (1981), *A Broken Frame* (1982), *Construction Time Again* (1983), *Some Great Reward* (1984), *The Singles 81-85* (1985), *Black Celebration* (1986), *Music For The Masses* (1987), *101* (1989).
Further reading: *Depeche Mode: The Photographs,* Anton Corbijn.

Desperate Bicycles

One of the first independent, do-it-yourself pop bands of the new wave era, the Desperate Bicycles hinged around vocalist Danny Wigley, the only member to survive an ever-changing line-up. At one stage, he was aided and abetted by Roger Stephens (bass), Dan Electro (guitar), Dave Papworth (drums) and Nick Stephens (keyboards), although Jeff Titley also served time behind the drum kit. In 1977 'Smokescreen'/'Handlebars' was released, featuring the two tracks on both sides; and was also released in mono on the band's own label, Refill. This set the pattern for all subsequent Desperate Bicycles releases. After several singles - 'The Medium Was Tedium', the *New Cross New Cross* EP, 'Occupied Territory' (all 1978) and 'Grief Is Very Private' (1979) - the group released an album, *Remorse Code*, and subsequently disbanded.
Album: *Remorse Code* (1979).

Devine And Statton

After laying low for several years after the demise of Weekend, and working with various local Cardiff bands while pursuing college studies, singer Alison Statton (b. March 1958, Cardiff, South Glamorgan, Wales) quietly re-emerged in 1989 with the album *The Prince Of Wales*, a set of songs written by former Ludus member Ian Devine (b. Ian Pincombe; guitar/vocals), which was released on the Belgian independent label, Les Disques Du Crepuscule. The album echoed the strong Celtic background of both members, blending folk styles with a polished, almost-MOR feel while the duo were backed admirably by Blaine I. Reininger (violin/mandolin/keyboards), Nicolas Fizman (bass) and Frank Michiels (percussion). Lyrically, the album professed a staunch sense of Welsh patriotism, most evident in the song, 'Turn The Aerials Away From England'. However, Alison's quiet English-sounding voice and light melodies belied this feeling. Their cover version of New Order's 'Bizarre Love Triangle' received favourable reviews and attracted the attention of New Order's Peter Hook, who expressed a desire to record with the duo on their next album. The duo also recruited guest guitarist, Marc Ribot, who in the past had recorded with Tom Waits. The defiantly titled *Cardiffians* continued where the debut left off and included a version of the Crystal Gayle hit, 'Don't It Make My Brown Eyes Blue'. The duo have yet to prove themselves on the live circuit, and Statton has publicly expressed a desire to contain her renewed musical career as a part-time venture.
Albums: *The Prince Of Wales* (1989), *Cardiffians* (1990).

Devo

Formed during 1972 in Ohio, USA, this band comprised, Jerry Casale (bass/vocal), Alan Myers (drums), Mark Mothersbaugh (vocal/keyboards/guitar), Bob Mothersbaugh (guitar/vocal), and Bob Casale (guitar/vocal). Devo made the unlikely step from novelty act to real chart contenders. Best described as a new wave version of Kiss, they are a band whose marketing and visual side is just as important as their music. Throughout the late 70s and early 80s the band built up a string of minor hits. Their biggest success in the UK was with an eccentric cover of the Rolling Stones' '(I Cant' Get No) Satisfaction'. Despite their quirkiness, Devo were applauded by many during their late 70s peak period, and inspired the title of Neil Young's major album *Rust Never Sleeps*. More success followed into the mid-80s, when they performed the theme to Dan Ackroyd's movie *Doctor Detroit*, and a single 'Whip It' gave them a million selling disc.

Albums: *Q:Are We Not Men? A: We Are Devo!* (1978), *Duty Now For The Future* (1979), *Freedom Of Choice* (1980), *New Traditionals* (1981), *Devo Live* (1981), *Oh No Its Devo* (1982), *Shout* (1985), *Greatest Hits* (1990), *Smooth Noodle Maps* (1990), *Hardcore Devo 74-77* (1991).

Devoto, Howard

b. Howard Trotter. After leaving the Buzzcocks just as they were becoming massive, Manchester student Howard Devoto formed the altogether more sober Magazine. After widespread critical acclaim, the band split in the early 80s, and Devoto, briefly embarked on a straightforward solo career with 1983's *Jerky Visions Of The Dream*. But despite two singles ('Rainy Season' and 'Cold Imagination'), the album failed to achieve the impact that Magazine had attained. Devoto approached later work using various disguises, such as Luxuria. Highly-influencial during the punk era, Devoto's role as a much-quoted spokesperson and innovator declined in the 80s. One writer perceptively dubbed the bespectacled new wave intellectual as 'the Orson Welles of punk'.

Album: *Jerky Visions Of The Dream* (1983).

Dexys Midnight Runners

Conceived by the uncompromising Kevin Rowland (b. 17 August 1953, Wolverhampton, England), Dexys proved one of the most original, eclectic and fascinating UK groups to achieve success in the early 80s. Vocalist Rowland and rhythm guitarist Al Archer were previously members of punk group, the Killjoys, before rehearsing the soul-inspired Dexys in July 1978. A further six members were added to the first line-up: Pete Williams (piano/organ), J.B. (tenor saxophone), Steve Spooner (alto saxophone), Pete Saunders (piano/organ), Big Jim Patterson (trombone) and Bobby Junior (drums). The unit took their name from the amphetamine dexedrine, a stimulant favoured by northern soul dancers. Their name notwithstanding, Dexys gained an almost puritanical reputation for their aversion to drink and drugs. Rowland brilliantly fashioned the group's image, using Robert De Niro's film *Mean Streets* as an inspiration for their New York Italian docker chic. The group's debut 'Dance Stance' was an extraordinary single, its simple title belieing what was a lyrically devastating attack on racism directed at the Irish community, with a superb background litany extolling the virtues of Ireland's finest literary figures. The single crept into the UK Top 40, but the follow-up 'Geno' (a tribute to 60's soul singer Geno Washington) climbed confidently to number 1 in May 1980. Two months later, *Searching For The Young Soul Rebels* was released to critical acclaim and commercial success. Many polls perhaps rightly suggested that it one of the finest debut albums ever issued; it showed Rowland's mastery of the pop-soul genre to spectacular effect. The epistolary 'There There My Dear', taken from the album, brought the group another UK Top 10 hit. The flip was a revival of Cliff Noble's instrumental 'The Horse', in keeping with Dexys' soul revivalism. The first signs of Rowland's artistic waywardness occurred with the release of the blatantly uncommercial 'Keep It Part Two (Inferiority Part One)', much against the group's wishes. Unquestionably his most intensely passionate work from the first Dexys phase, the song's almost unbearably agonized vocal line was double-tracked to create a bizarre but rivetting effect. The song precipitated the fragmentation of the original Dexys line-up.

With JB, Steve Spooner and Pete Williams defecting to the Bureau, Rowland and Patterson found a fresh line-up: former Secret Affair drummer Seb Shelton, Micky Billingham (keyboards), Paul Speare (tenor saxophone), Brian Maurice (alto saxophone), Steve Wynne (bass) and Billy Adams (guitar). After one more single for EMI, the excellent 'Plan B', Dexys switched to Phonogram. By 1981 they had abandoned soul revivalism in order to investigate different music and a new look. Out went the balaclavas to be replaced by a new uniform of red anoraks, boxing boots, tracksuit bottoms, hoods and pony tails. Their 'ascetic athlete' phase saw the release of the more commercial 'Show Me' produced by Tony Visconti. This was followed by the idiosyncratic 'Liars A To E'. A highly acclaimed live show, 'The Projected Passion Review' followed, including a performance at London's Old Vic. Early 1982 saw Dexys augmented by a fiddle section, the Emerald Express, featuring Helen O'Hara, Steve Brennan and Roger McDuff. Rowland's latest experiment was to fuse Northern soul with Irish traditional music. As before, the shift in musical style was reflected in the image as Rowland created his own brand of hoedown gypsy chic - neckerchiefs, earrings, stubble and leather jerkins. The first release from the new group, 'The Celtic Soul Brothers' was a vital work that failed to chart, but its successor

'Come On Eileen' restored them to number 1 in the summer of 1982. The second album, *Too-Rye-Ay*, was another startling work and a best seller, reaching number 2 in the UK album charts. The group subsequently undertook an extensive tour, which revealed Rowland's love of theatre in its self-conscious grandeur. Further line-up changes followed, with the departure of Kevin's right-hand man Jim Patterson and two other brass players. Continuing under the autocratic title 'Kevin Rowland And Dexys Midnight Runners', the group went on to reap considerable success in the USA where 'Come On Eileen' reached number 1 in 1983. Further hits followed with a snappy cover of Van Morrison's 'Jackie Wilson Said' and 'Let's Get This Straight From The Start' before Dexys underwent a long hibernation. They returned as a quartet comprising Rowland, Adams, O'Hara and Nicky Gatefield, and boasting a radically new image 'College Preppie' - chic shirts and ties and neatly-cut hair. *Don't Stand Me Down*, received very favourable reviews but sold poorly in spite of its qualities. An edited version of the brilliant 'This Is What She's Like' was issued as a single, but received little airplay. Although Dexys charted again with 'Because Of You' (later used as the theme for BBC television's, *Brush Strokes*), the commercial failure of the latest experiment forced Rowland to think again, and he finally dissolved the group in 1987. He returned the following year as a soloist with the light pop album, *The Wanderer*, which failed to produce a hit single. In 1990, Rowland, amid not unusual record company trouble, announced that he was resurrecting Dexys and bringing back his old colleague Jim Patterson. Dexys' career has been a series of broken contracts, group upheavals, total changes of image, diverse musical forays and an often bitter association with the music press. For all this, Rowland remains one of pop's most original, temperamental and singular characters, brutally uncompromising at times, yet capable of producing number 1 hits on both sides of the Atlantic.
Albums: *Searching For The Young Soul Rebels* (1980), *Too-Rye-Ay* (1982), *Don't Stand Me Down* (1985). Compilation: *Geno* (1983).

Dharma Bums

A garage band in the best traditions of the MC5 and early 80s college-rock bands like Rain Parade and R.E.M., Dharma Bums comprised Jeremy Wilson (b. c.1969; vocals), John Moen (drums, vocals), Eric Lovre (guitar, vocals) and Jim Talstra (bass). They originated from Portland, Oregon, USA and began their career in 1987. A first album, *Haywire*, was recorded quickly for the PopLlama label in 1989, which had been advised of the band by Young Fresh Fellows' Scott McCaughey. He repeated the favour

by playing their debut album to Frontier Records boss Lisa Fancher. 1990 saw the more polished *Bliss* emerge. Featuring greatly improved songwriting, it covered subjects from rape and adolescence to suicide, in a mature fashion built on ragged rock textures.
Albums: *Haywire* (1989), *Bliss* (1990).

Dickies

Formed in 1977 in Los Angeles, California, USA, the Dickies were a punk rock band which specialized in speedy renditions of humorous songs, many of which were cover versions of earlier rock hits. The group consisted of keyboardist Chuck Wagon, guitarist Stan Lee, bassist Billy Club, vocalist Leonard Graves Phillips and drummer Karlos Kaballero. Wearing fashionably ludicrous, often grotesque clothing, the Dickies quickly became one of the most popular of the original LA punk bands, and were signed to A&M Records in 1978. In addition to their self-penned songs, the Dickies' early recordings included such previously-bombastic numbers as the Moody Blues' 'Nights In White Satin' and Black Sabbath's 'Paranoid', played at a furious pace and often clocking in at under two minutes. During their career they would also cover the Monkees, Led Zeppelin and others. Their original material often took its cue from cult b-movies, similar in style and attitude to New York's Ramones. After a prolific recording schedule in the early 80s, the Dickies kept a low profile for the rest of the decade and were still recording new material in 1988, although they were no longer in the spotlight.
Albums: *The Incredible Shrinking Dickies* (1979), *Dawn Of The Dickies* (1979), *Stukas Over Disneyland* (1983), *We Aren't The World!* (1986), *Second Coming* (1988).

Dictators

Formed in 1974 in New York City, the Dictators pre-dated the punk rock of bands such as the Ramones and Sex Pistols by two years, yet they exhibited many of that genre's hallmarks from their inception. Purveying loud, three-chord rock without long solos and drawing their lyrical inspiration and visual image from such disparate facets of popular culture as fast food, professional wrestling, cult movies and late-night television, the Dictators built a devoted fandom in their hometown and selected hip pockets in the USA and Europe, but were unable to succeed commercially and are rarely acknowledged for their pioneering efforts in helping to establish the new rock 'n' roll of the 70s and 80s. The group originally consisted of guitarists Scott 'Top Ten' Kempner and Ross 'The Boss' Funichello, bassist Adny Shernoff and drummer Stu Boy King. Vocalist 'Handsome Dick Manitoba' (b. Richard Blum) guested on the group's debut album and subsequently joined. King left after the release of that album and was replaced by Richie Teeter, and bassist Mark 'The Animal' Mendoza also joined at that time (1975), allowing Shernoff to switch to keyboards. That first album, *The Dictators Go Girl Crazy*, featured original songs by Shernoff with titles such as 'Teengenerate' and '(I Live For) Cars And Girls' and a cover of Sonny And Cher's 'I Got You Babe' and was released on Epic Records, which then dropped the group when the album failed to catch on. After the personnel shuffle of 1975, the Dictators signed to Elektra Records in late 1976 and released *Manifest Destiny*, their only album to chart. Before they recorded their third and last album, *Bloodbrothers*, in 1978, Mendoza left to join heavy metal outfit Twisted Sister. When the third album failed, they were dropped by Elektra and disbanded. The Dictators have reunited several times for single concert dates, one of which was recorded and released as a cassette-only album in 1981, *Fuck 'Em If They Can't Take A Joke*. During the 80s Kempner went on to form the Del-Lords, another straight-ahead rock group popular in New York, which recorded a few albums. Manitoba and Shernoff formed the quasi-metal band Manitoba's Wild Kingdom. Ross The Boss Funichello joined the short-lived Shakin' Street.

Albums: *The Dictators Go Girl Crazy* (1975), *Manifest Destiny* (1977), *Bloodbrothers* (1978), *Fuck 'Em If They Can't Take A Joke* (1981).

Died Pretty

Consisting of musicians (Brett Myers, Ronald S Peno, Frank Brunetti), all longstanding veterans of the alternative music scene in Brisbane, the band formed in Sydney in 1984. Probably due to journalist Brunetti's involvement, they attracted immediate critical attention. Their swirling sound, reminiscent of the early Doors, combined with the unique vocals and demented stage presence of Peno, soon established them as inner-city favourites. Their early singles hinted at greatness, but it was the 1985 *Next To Nothing* mini-LP, produced by Radio Birdman's Rob Younger, that established the band as a worldwide possibility. Over the next few years, constant touring toughened the once erratic live performances and their follow-up recordings expanded their musical territories. In 1990, after the departure of organist Brunetti and Mark Lock, the band recorded their fourth album in America with producer Jeff Eyrich. The result was a much more focussed and accessible album containing some of the band's finest work, particularly the propulsive single 'Whitlam Square'. Their subsequent tour of Australia proved successful and their future is promising.

Albums: *Free Dirt* (1986), *Pre Diety* (1987), *Lost* (1988), *Every Brilliant Eye* (1990).

Difford And Tilbrook

The two principal songwriters of Squeeze met after Chris Difford (b. 4 November 1954, London, England) had placed an advert in a Blackheath, south London shop window in search of a guitarist to join a (non-existent) band with a (non-existent) record contract. In answering the advert, Glenn Tilbrook (b. 31 August 1957, London, England) found a compatable songwriting partner and together they led one of the most popular British groups of the late 70s/early 80s. After suffering from the strain of holding Squeeze together, the duo decided to reassess their situation in 1982. Prior to recording an album, the duo had worked on the fringe theatre production of *Labelled With Love* at the Albany Theatre in their home area of Deptford. The album received a mixed reception and the only single to make any impact upon the UK charts was 'Love's Crashing Waves', narrowly missing out on the Top 50. Assisted by Andy Duncan (drums), Keith Wilkinson (bass), Guy Fletcher (keyboards), with a production credit by Tony Visconti, the album was an improvement on the last Squeeze offering, *Sweets From A Stranger*. Tracks like 'You Can't Hurt The Girl', 'Hope Fell Down' and 'On My Mind Tonight' particularly stood out. Having given themselves a sufficient rest from the group set-up, the duo resurrected Squeeze in 1985 after a successful charity reunion pub-date which led to the recording the excellent *Cosi Fan Tutti Frutti* that same year.

Album: *Difford And Tilbrook* (1984).

Dif Juz

A four-piece instrumental outfit based in west London, Dif Juz appeared sporadically during 1980 supporting the Birthday Party, Mass and Jah Wobble. A chance meeting with 4AD led to two EPs in rapid succession, *Huremics* and *Vibrating Air,* in 1981. For 1983's mini-album *Who Says So*, recorded on the Red Flame label, the band comprised David Curtis (guitar/keyboards), brother Alan (guitar), Gary Bromley (bass) and Richard Thomas (drums/saxophone, also an occasional drummer for Jesus And Mary Chain). After a cassette-only release, *Time Clock Turn Back*, for the Scottish label Pleasantly Surprised, Dif Juz finally committed themselves to an album, *Extractions* (1985). This return to the 4AD label was benefited by the presence of Cocteau Twins' Liz Fraser, appearing as guest vocalist, and the production work of Robin Guthrie. Richard Thomas subsequently guested on saxophone and tablas for the Cocteau's *Victorialand*. A compilation, *Out Of The Trees*, was issued, coupling the two earlier EPs; although tracks from *Vibrating Air* were partly re-recorded and entirely remixed. This coincided with the arrival of ex-Dead Can Dance bassist Scott Roger for a European tour.

Albums: *Who Says So* (1983), *Time Clock Turn Back* (1985), *Extractions* (1985). Compilation: *Out Of The Trees* (1986).

Dils

Formed in San Diego, California, USA in 1977, the Dils' most stable line-up comprised of Chip Kinman (guitar/vocals), Tony 'Nineteen' Kinman (guitar/vocals) and Endre Alquover (drums), who had replaced Pat Garrett. The trio was an integral part of the Los Angeles punk movement, completing two powerful singles in 'I Hate The Rich' and 'Class War' (both 1977). Drummers Rand McNally and John Silvers later passed through the line-up, but the group's only other release was their *Made In Canada* EP (1980). The Dils then evolved into Rank And File, in which the Kinman brothers were joined by ex-Nuns' guitarist Alejandro Escovado. The new act revived 'Sound Of The Rain', a track from the Dils last collection, on their *Long Gone Dead* album. 'I Hate The Rich'/'You're Not Blank' was reissued on the Gift Of Life label in 1991.
Albums: *Live: Dils* (1987), *Long Dead Gone* (c.80s).

Dislocation Dance

Quirky jazz-pop was the speciality of Manchester outfit Dislocation Dance. Signed to the Buzzcocks' New Hormones label after forming in late 1978, the band consisted of Ian Runacres (vocals/guitar), Dick Harrison (drums), Paul Emmerson (bass) and Andy Diagram (trumpet/vocals). An EP, *It's So Difficult* (1980), was a co-release with the band's Delicate Issues label. The EP, *Slip That Disc* (1981) included an offbeat version of the Beatles' 'We Can Work It Out' and was followed by, what was for the group, a transitional album, *Music Music Music*. Having now been joined by Kath Way (vocals/saxophone), Dislocation Dance then issued the comparatively poppy 'Rosemary' (1982), but left New Hormones after the fashionably bossa-nova tinged 'You'll Never Never Know' (both 1982). In 1983 a one-off single, 'Violette' for the Music Label, passed the time, before the band signed to Rough Trade later that year, releasing 'Show Me'. A second album, *Midnight Shift*, also appeared, but they left the label soon after. A final 12-inch single 'What's Going On' on the Slipped Discs label, signalled the end of Dislocation Dance in late 1985. Andy Diagram, also fronted the Diagram Brothers and later appeared with the Pale Fountains.
Albums: *Music Music Music* (1981), *Midnight Shift* (1984).

Disorder

This punk band from Bristol, England blended breakneck thrash with tales of gargantuan cider consumption. The first incarnation dated from 1980 with Mick (bass), Steve (guitar), Virus (drums) and Dean (vocals). They produced a demonstration tape which was sent to Riot City Records. They were turned down but formed their own Disorder Records. After the release of 'Complete Disorder', Mick left and was replaced by Steve Robinson. Their EP *Distortion Till Deafness* was released, before bizarre developments followed. Robinson split with girlfriend Beki Bondage (of Vice Squad, the band who had vetoed Disorder joining Riot City) and took up glue sniffing as a hobby. Then the CID caught up with Virus concerning the ownership of his new drumkit. Dean left too, going on to salubrious employment as toilet cleaner in Taunton. He was replaced by Taff (ex-X-Certs Review). With Taff on bass, they persuaded Boobs, their roadie, to take over vocals. Luckily he was almost through his current sentence for fraudulently sabotaging his electricity meter. After the recording of 'Perdition', they set about a short stint with the Varukers. Their first foreign tour was sabotaged by a typical series of farcical miscalculations concerning European geography and train timetables. Virus felt enough was enough and was replaced by Glenn (ex-Dead Popstars), while the band moved into a shared squat with friends Amebix. Later releases were somewhat more restrained, daring to flirt with melody on occasion.
Albums: *The Singles Collection* (1984), *Under The Scalpel Blade* (1984), *Live In Oslo* (1985), *One Day Son, All This Will Be Yours* (1986), *Violent World* (1989).

Distractions

This Manchester, England new wave band was first formed in 1975 by college friends Mike Finney (vocals) and Steve Perrin-Brown (guitar), together with Lawrence Tickle (bass) and Tony Trap (drums). Restructured under the influence of the Buzzcocks towards the end of 1977, Finney and Brown stabilized the line-up with the addition of Pip Nicholls (bass), Adrian Wright (guitar) and Alec Sidebottom (drums), who had previously played with the Purple Gang in the 60s. Their live set composed of 'Waiting For The Rain', 'Doesn't Bother Me', 'Pillow Talk', 'Do The', 'Valerie' and 'Paracetomol', mixing the spirit of punk with a taste of the 60s. After supporting most of the main bands in the Manchester area, they made their debut in January 1979 with 'You're Not Going Out Dressed Like That'. This resulted in a deal with Tony Wilson's Factory label, and the release of 'Time Goes By So Slow'. Originally the b-side 'Pillow Fight' was to be the main track, but was flipped over at the last minute. Both good pop songs, they had the potential to climb the national charts, but failed through lack of radio play and promotion. At the end of September they

signed to Island Records and released a re-recorded version of 'It Doesn't Bother Me'. In 1980 *Nobody's Perfect* was issued, a mixture of new and old songs from their early live set, followed by the singles 'Boys Cry' - a remake of the old Eden Kane hit - 'Something For The Weekend', the EP *And Then There's*. All received favourable reviews, but commercial success remained elusive, causing the inevitable split in 1981.
Album: *Nobody's Perfect* (1980).

Divinyls; Christina Amphlett

Divinyls

Led by the provocative Chrissie Amphlett, whose songwriting with guitarist Mark McEntee is the basis of the band, the Divinyls have recorded some excellent work. Amphlett's sexy image complemented the mesmerizing urgency of the music, and the band was guaranteed the audience's undivided attention. They formed in Sydney in 1987, and their first mini-LP was written for the 1982 film *Monkey Grip*, and produced the Australian Top 10 single 'Boys In Town' as well as the excellent ballad, 'Only The Lonely'. Signing with the UK label Chrysalis, their first album *Desperate* was a hit in Australia. Several hit singles and extensive touring bridged the gap to *What A Life* (1985), which was greeted enthusiastically; but the sales did not match the reviews. Later material, with the exception of the next single 'Pleasure And Pain' did not compare well

with their earliest work. The band now is basically a duo, with musicians added whenever a tour is undertaken. It has undergone a revival with its controversial single 'I Touch Myself', a blatant peon to masturbation, released in 1991 and reaching the UK Top 10.
Albums: *Desperate* (1983), *What A Life* (1985), *Temperamental* (1988), *Divinyls* (1991).

Doctor And The Medics

This psychedelic pop-rock outfit came to prominence in 1986 with a cover of Norman Greenbaum's 'Spirit In The Sky'. The single hit number 1 in the UK, but they found it difficult to consolidate their success, with the subsequent 'Burn' and 'Waterloo' only achieving UK chart placings of 29 and 46 respectively. *Laughing At The Pieces* peaked at number 25 in the charts, primarily on the back of major single success. Since then, every release has sunk without trace and the band were dropped by their label.
Albums: *Laughing At The Pieces* (1986), *Keep Thinking It's Thursday* (1987).

Doctors Of Madness

When punk exploded on an unsuspecting UK music scene in 1976, several relatively established bands waiting in the wings were somehow dragged along with it. The Doctors Of Madness were one such group. Comprising the weird Richard 'Kid' Strange (vocals, guitar, keyboards, percussion), Stoner (bass, vocals, percussion), Peter (drums, percussion, vocals) and Urban (guitar, violin), the Doctors were already signed to Polydor Records and had already issued two rock albums verging on the theatrical by late 1976: *Late Night Movies, All Night Brainstorms* and *Figments Of Emancipation*. Much of their momentum was lost, however, when they issued only one single in 1977, 'Bulletin', and it was not until 1978 that *Sons Of Survival* appeared. By that time, the post-punk era had arrived, awash with new ideas, and the Doctors Of Madness seemed acutely out of date. They broke up soon after, their career later summarized on a compilation, *Revisionism*. Richard Strange, meanwhile, set about an erratic but fascinating solo career, which included such singles as 'International Language' (1980) on Cherry Red and the narcissistically-entitled album *The Phenomenal Rise Of Richard Strange* (1981) on Virgin Records.
Albums: *Late Night Movies, All Night Brainstorms* (1976), *Figments Of Emancipation* (1976), *Sons Of Survival* (1978). Compilation: *Revisionism (1975-78)* (1981).

Dolby, Thomas

b. Thomas Morgan Robertson, 14 October 1958, Cairo, Egypt. Dolby is a self-taught musician/vocalist/songwriter, and computer programmer. After studying meteorology and projectionism at college, he started building his own synthesizers at the age of 18. With his own hand-built PA system he acted as sound engineer on tours by the Members, Fall and the Passions. Afterwards, he co-founded Camera Cub with Bruce Wooley in January 1979, before joining the Lene Lovich backing group in September 1980, for whom he wrote 'New Toy'. His first solo output was the single 'Urges' on the Armageddon label in 1981, before he scored hits the following year with 'Europa' and 'The Pirate Twins'. For a series of 1982 concerts at the Marquee he recruited ex-Soft Boy Matthew Seligman and Kevin Armstrong of the Thompson Twins, while finding time to contribute to albums by M, Joan Armatrading and Foreigner. Other collaborations included Stevie Wonder, Herbie Hancock, Dusty Springfield, Howard Jones and Grace Jones. The most visual of such appearances came when he backed David Bowie at Live Aid. A strong 'mad scientist' image proliferated in his videos, which also featured famous British eccentric Magnus Pike. These earned him a strong media profile, but, surprisingly, his best known singles 'She Blinded Me With Science' and 'Hyperactive' only peaked at numbers 31 and 17 respectively. The latter did however, reach the Top 5 in the USA. As well as production for Prefab Sprout and Joni Mitchell, he has scored music for several films including *Howard: A New Breed Of Hero*. He is married to actress Kathleen Beller (Kirby Colby from *Dynasty*). Dolby commands high respect in the music business, as his back-room contributions have already been considerable.

Albums: *The Golden Age Of Wireless* (1982), *The Flat Earth* (1984), *Aliens Ate My Buick* (1988).

Doll

Formed in late 1977, this UK new wave group originally comprised Marion Valentine (b. 1952, Brighton, Sussex, England; vocals/guitar), Christos Yianni (b. 6 September 1954, London, England; bass), Adonis Yianni (b. 10 October 1957, London, England; keyboards) and Mario Watts (b. 1958, London, England; drums). After signing to Beggar's Banquet, the group issued 'Don't Tango My Heart', but it was their second single, infectious 'Desire Me' that propelled them into the UK charts in 1978. Inter-group politics, exacerbated by the inevitable promotion of their female singer and lyricist, caused several line-up changes. By the time they came to record their sole album, *Listen To The Silence*, Dennis Hayes (keyboard), Jamie West-Oram (guitar) and Paul Turner (drums) had joined. The group split soon after, and although it was expected that the feline Valentine (complete with leopard-skin guitar and jump-suit) would be launched as a solo, she concentrated instead on songwriting, eventually

retiring from the music business.
Album: *Listen To The Silence* (1979).

Dolly Mixture

Dolly Mixture

This UK pop female trio comprised Debsey Wykes (b. 21 December 1960, Hammersmith, London, England; bass/piano/vocals), Rachel Bor (b. 16 May 1963, Wales; guitar/cello/vocals) and Hester Smith (b. 28 October 1960, West Africa; drums). The group was formed by the three school-friends in Cambridge, with a musical style that echoed the Shangri-Las and the 70s Undertones. Championed by influential UK disc jockey, John Peel, the group released a cover of the Shirelles hit, 'Baby It's You' (1980), on the Chrysalis label - which at the time of issue the group disowned, protesting at the label's attempted manipulation of their image. They were one of the first bands to record for Paul Weller's Respond label, releasing, 'Been Teen' (1981) and 'Everything And More' (1982), both of which were produced by Captain Sensible and Paul Gray of the Damned. The UK record-buying public found difficulty coming to terms with the trio's idiosyncratic mode of dress and independent attitude; something that the record companies and some of the music press also had problems with. They proved their worth, however, in their exhilarating live performances. In 1982 they released a double album, on their own Dead Good Dolly Platters label, featuring demo tapes collected over the previous four years. The album has since achieved cult status among later 80s independent groups. Dolly Mixture eventually found national fame by acting as Sensible's backing vocalists on his UK number 1 single 'Happy Talk' in 1982. They also guested on his subsequent singles and albums, while Rachel and the Captain formed a romantic partnership. Meanwhile, their own career foundered, despite the critical plaudits. The trio dissolved as a working band in 1984, leaving as their swan song a mini-album, released on Cordelia Records, *The Fireside EP*, a set consisting mainly of 'pop/chamber' music, featuring their often ignored talents on piano and cello. In 1986, Debsey and Hester resurfaced with the group, Coming Up Roses. Album: *The Demonstration Tapes* (1982).

Do Ré Mi

One of the more respected post-punk bands, Do Ré Mi has achieved limited success both in Australia and overseas since its formation in Sydney in 1981. It had success with its second single 'Man Overboard' from its debut album in 1985, although previously releasing a rather obscure mini-album in 1982. Subsequent releases did not catch the mainstream listeners and thus its excellent album *Domestic Harmony*, while critically acclaimed did not sell well. Lead vocalist, Deborah Conway, is currently pursuing a solo career and her talent has attracted the attention of Pete Townshend.

Albums: *Domestic Harmony* (1985), *Happiest Place In Town* (1988).

Drive, She Said

Formed in 1986 by the former American Tears, Touch, and Michael Bolton keyboard player Mark Mangold, who was also a successful songwriter, co-writing Cher's hit 'I've Found Someone' along with Michael Bolton; and previously unknown vocalist/guitarist Al Fritsch. After signing to CBS in 1988 their self-titled debut album was released a year later in the USA and contained guest appearances by artists such as multi-instrumentalist Aldo Nova, Fiona Flanigan, and Bob Kulick of Balance, Kiss, and Meat Loaf fame. The collection of light-edged melodic rock songs, which included a reworking of the Touch classic 'Don't You Know What Love Is ?', was aimed directly at the American market, but failed to make any significant impact. The album, however, sold well on import in the UK, prompting the independent label Music For Nations to sign the band for the European market. The album was subsequently released in the UK in 1990 and was quickly followed by a club tour. *Drivin' Wheel*, a slightly harder-edged album, was released in 1991, preceded by the single 'Think About Love', both of which failed to achieve any significant success. Undetered by the lack of chart success, a UK tour is planned for 1992 with work on their third album to begin soon after.

Albums: *Drive, She Said* (1989), *Drivin' Wheel* (1991).

Drones

Very few punk bands actually stuck to their principles and shunned the lurid advances of the major record companies. Whether the Drones from Manchester, England were such a band or whether they were never given the opportunity is debatable. Either way, the band issued three singles and an ephemeral album that now seems to personify the new wave. Second

division punk they may have been, but they were exciting and vital nonetheless. The Drones' humble recording career began with an EP on the Ohm label, *Temptations Of A White Collar Worker*, in the spring of 1977. The release of 'Bone Idol' on their own Valer label later in the year was swiftly followed by a rough but enthusiastic album, entitled *Further Temptations*. The group ended the year with the inclusion on the Beggars Banquet sampler *Streets*. After that, M.J. Drone (lead vocals/rhythm guitar), Gus Callender (Gangrene to his friends; lead guitar/vocals), Pete Perfect (drums) and Steve 'Whisper' Cundall (bass) kept a low profile, turning up on the essential live punk document, *Short Circuit - Live At The Electric Circus*, in mid-1978. After a final single, 'Can't See' on the Fabulous label in 1980, the band struggled on, breaking-up finally in 1981.

Album: *Further Temptations* (1977).

Droogs

Formed in 1972, this Los Angeles-based group initially included Rich Albin (vocals), Roger Clay (guitar/vocals), Paul Motter (bass) and Kyle Raven (drums). Unashamedly inspired by 60s garage bands, the quartet founded their own label, Plug & Socket, on which they recorded cover versions of favourite songs and originals inspired by their heroes. Having completed a mere six singles in the space of 10 years, during which time the group's rhythm section underwent several changes, the Droogs found themselves avatars of the then in-vogue 'Paisley Underground' scene. *Stone Cold World* was sadly obscured in the flurry to praise Green On Red, the Long Ryders and Bangles, but Albin and Clay doggedly pursued their chosen direction when the fashion faded. *Want Something*, issued following a protracted absence, featured material by John Hiatt, the Kinks and Peter Holsapple (of the dB's), and continued the unit's dalliance with psychedelic guitar pop.

Albums: Stone Cold World (1984), *Kingdom Day* (1987), *Want Something* (1991).

Drummond, Bill

b. 29 April 1953, Butterworth, South Africa. After relocating to Scotland as a child, Drummond rose to fame in the music business during the late 70s rock renaissance in Liverpool. Drummond formed the Merseyside trio, Big In Japan, which lasted from 1977-78. Drummond subsequently founded the influential Zoo Record label and backed Lori Larty in Lori And The Chameleons. He then enjoyed considerable success as a manager overseeing the affairs of Echo And The Bunnymen and the Teardrop Explodes. When the Liverpool group scene saw artists moving south, Drummond left the city, and during the next decade was involved in a number of bizarre projects, which testified to his imagination and love of novelty. The controversial JAMMS (Justified Ancients Of Mu Mu), whose irreverent sampling was extremely innovative for the period, was a typical example of Drummond's pseudonymous mischief. The chart-topping Timelords was another spoof and, by the 90s, Drummond found himself at the heart of the creative sampling technology with the critically acclaimed and best-selling KLF. Along the way, the eccentric entrepreneur even managed to record a minor solo album, most notable for the track 'Julian Cope Is Dead', an answer song to the former Teardrop Explodes singer's witty 'Bill Drummond Said'.

Album: *The Man* (1987).

Drum Theatre

This cosmopolitan UK-based group comprised Kent B. (drums/keyboards), Gari Tarn (drums/vocals), Paul Snook (drums/bass guitar). Originally a very exciting visual act, they boasted six members, all of whom played the drums at some point. By the time the band were signed to a recording contract they had been slimmed down to a trio. They received attention when their first single of 1986, 'Living In The Past' made a small impact on the UK charts, while they were supporting the Human League on a European tour. The reissue of their 1985 single 'Eldorado', in 1987 received plenty of radio airplay and just missed the Top 40, and their debut album was released to mixed reaction and poor sales. The same fate met their subsequent singles.

Album: *Everyman* (1987).

Dugites

The Dugites emerged from Perth, Australia in 1978, at the tail-end of punk, and in the middle of a period heralding the arrival of several other other Australian bands which featured female lead singers, such as the Eurogliders, Divinyls and Do Ré Mi. While their early material was naive pop, their later work glistened with good production values and good playing, and deserved better recognition. Their first single, the plaintive 'In My Car' charted, but by the time the band gelled and matured for their last excellent album, their audience had lost interest.

Albums: *The Dugites* (1980), *West Of The World* (1981), *Cut The Talking* (1984).

Dukes Of Stratosphear

An alter ego of XTC, this group was a vehicle for Andy Partridge's psychedelic frustrations of being born a decade or two out of time. Both albums released so far contain brilliant pastiches of virtually every pop band during the mid-to late 60s. In many cases the Dukes' tongue-in-cheek parables are far superior to the songs to which they are gently

alluding. It was suggested that their albums actually outsold the XTC product available at the same time.

Albums: *25 O'Clock* (1985), *Psonic Psunspot* (1987).
Compilation: *Chips From The Chocolate Fireball* .

Durocs

Formed in 1979, this San Francisco-based act comprised of Ron Nagle (vocals/keyboards) and Scott Mathews (guitar/drums). Both musicians brought considerable experience to the project; Nagle, who founded the pioneering Mystery Trend, composed incidental music to several horror films, notably *The Exorcist* and co-wrote 'Don't Touch Me There', a best-seller for the Tubes. Mathews, meanwhile, was an ex-member of several groups, including the Elvin Bishop Band and the Hoodoo Rhythm Devils. The duo's songs were recorded by Michelle Phillips and Barbra Streisand, and having built a recording studio, the Pen, completed *The Durocs*, which took its name from a breed of pig noted for its large ears and genitals. The album was a strong effort but sold poorly, and the project was abandoned when Capitol Records refused to release a second set. Undeterred, the duo continued to compose and record together, and later released a single under a new name, the Profits. Their version of 'I'm A Hog For You Baby' continued the porcine metaphor, as did its Proud Pork Productions credit. Music notwithstanding, Nagle has since become one of the USA's leading exponents of ceramic art.

Album: *The Durocs* (1979).

Durutti Column

One of the more eclectic bands to emerge from Manchester's punk scene, Vini Reilly (b. Vincent Gerard Reilly, August 1953, Manchester, England) and his Durutti Column combined elements of jazz, electronic and even folk in their multitude of releases. However Vini's musical beginnings were as guitarist in more standard 1977 hopefuls Ed Banger And The Nosebleeds. Two other groups from 1977 - Fastbreeder and Flashback - had since merged into a new group, who were being managed by Manchester television presenter and Factory Records founder Anthony Wilson. Wilson invited Reilly to join guitarist Dave Rowbotham and drummer Chris Joyce in January 1978, and together they became the Durutti Column (after a political cartoon strip used by the SI in Strasbourg during the 60s). They were joined by vocalist Phil Rainford and bass player Tony Bowers and recorded for the famous 'A Factory Sampler EP' with the late Martin Hannett producing. These were the only recordings made by this line-up and the band broke up. Reilly carried on with the Durutti Column alone, while the others (except Rainford) formed the Moth Men. The debut *The Return Of The Durutti Column* appeared on Factory in

1980 and was largely recorded by Reilly, although Hannett, Pete Crooks (bass), and Toby (drums) also contributed. Durutti Column soon established a solid cult following, particularly abroad, where Reilly's moving instrument work was appreciated. Live appearances had been sporadic, however, as Reilly suffered from an eating disorder and was frequently too ill to play. The album was notable for its sandpaper sleeve, inspired by the anarchist movement Situationist Internatiside. Reilly and producer Hannett helped out on Pauline Murray's first solo album later in 1980. The Durutti Column's own recordings over the next few years were a mixed batch recorded by Reilly with assistance from drummers Donald Johnson, then Bruce Mitchell (ex-Alberto Y Lost Trios Paranoias), Maunagh Flemin and Simon Topping on horns, and much later further brass players Richard Henry, Tim Kellett, and Mervyn Fletcher plus violinist Blaine Reininger and celloist Caroline Lavelle. Dozens of other musicians have joined the nucleus of Reilly and Mitchell over the years and the band are still active today. A striking example of late period Durutti Column was captured on *Vini Reilly*, released in 1989. The guitarist cleverly incorporated the sampled voices of Joan Sutherland, Tracy Chapman, Otis Redding and Annie Lennox into a moving world of acoustic/electric ballads. Reilly has also lent some mesmerizing guitar to a host of recordings by artists such as Anne Clarke and Richard Jobson, and fellow Mancunian and friend Morrissey. On 8 November 1991, former Durutti guitarist Dave Rowbotham was discovered axed to death at his Manchester home. A murder hunt followed.

Albums: *The Return Of The Durutti Column* (1980), *Another Setting* (1983), *Live At The Venue London* (1983), *Amigos En Portugal* (1983), *Without Mercy* (1984), *Domo Arigato* (1985), *Valuable Passages* (1986), *Circuses And Bread* (1986), *The Guitar And Other Machines* (1987), *The Durutti Column-The First Four Albums* (1988), *Vini Reilly* (1989), *The Sporadic Recordings* (1989), *Obey The Time* (1990), *Lips That Would Kiss Form Prayers To Broken Stone* (1991), *Dry* (1991).

Dury, Ian

b. 12 May 1942, Billericay, Essex, England. The zenith of Dury's musical career, *New Boots And Panties*, came in 1977, when youth was being celebrated amid power chords and bondage trousers - he was 35 at the time. Stricken by polio at the age of seven, he initially decided on a career in art, and until his 28th birthday taught the subject at Canterbury School of Art. He began playing pubs and clubs in London with Kilburn And The High Roads, reinterpreting R&B numbers and later adding his own wry lyrics in a semi-spoken cockney slang. The

Ian Dury

group dissolved and the remainder became a new line-up called the Blockheads. In 1975 Stiff Records signed the group and considered Dury's aggressive but honest stance the perfect summary of the contemporary mood. The Blockheads' debut and finest moment, *New Boots And Panties*, received superlative reviews and spent more than a year in the UK albums chart. His dry wit, sensitivity and brilliant lyrical caricatures were evident in songs like 'Clever Trevor', 'Wake Up And Make Love To Me' and his tribute to Gene Vincent, 'Sweet Gene Vincent'. He lampooned the excesses of the music business on 'Sex And Drugs And Rock And Roll' and briefly crossed over from critical acclaim to commercial acceptance with the UK number 1 'Hit Me With Your Rhythm Stick' in December 1979. *Do It Yourself* and *Laughter* were similarly inspired although lacking the impact of his debut, and by his third album he had teamed up with Wilko Johnson (ex Dr. Feelgood) and lost the co-writing services of pianist Chaz Jankel. He continued to work towards a stronger dance context and employed the masterful rhythm section of Sly Dunbar and Robbie Shakespeare on *Lord Upminster* which also featured the celebrated jazz trumpeter Don Cherry. He continued to make thoughtful, polemic records in the 80s and audaciously suggested that his excellent song, 'Spasticus Autisticus', should be adopted as the musical emblem of the Year Of

The Disabled. Like many before him, he turned to acting and appeared in several television plays and films in the late 80s. In 1989 he wrote the musical *Apples* with another former member of the Blockheads, Mickey Gallagher. In the 90s Dury was seen hosting a late night UK television show *Metro*.

Albums: *Handsome* (1975), *Wot A Bunch* (1978), *Kilburn And The High Roads* (1982), *Upminster Kids* (1983), *New Boots And Panties* (1977), *Do It Yourself* (1979), *Laughter* (1980), *Lord Upminster* (1981), *Juke Box Dury* (1981), *Greatest Hits* (1981), *4,000 Weeks Holiday* (1984).

Easterhouse

Formed in Manchester, England by the Perry brothers, singer Andy and guitarist Ivor, during the mid-80s, Easterhouse first came to prominence after being championed by Morrissey of the Smiths. Taking their name from a working-class area of Glasgow, they signed to Rough Trade and were widely praised for early singles 'Inspiration' and 'Whistling In The Dark' which merged Andy's left wing political rhetoric with Ivor's echo-laden guitar patterns. *Contenders*, a confident but slightly blurred debut, also featured Peter Vanden (bass), Gary Rostock (drums) and Mike Murray (rhythm guitar). Arguments broke out soon after its release and Ivor Perry went on to form the short-lived Cradle. Andy Perry kept the name Easterhouse, but by the time of *Waiting For The Red Bird* he was the only remaining original band member. He was joined on the disappointing, over-ambitious record by David Verner (drums), Neil Taylor (lead guitar), Lance Sabin (rhythm guitar) and Steve Lovell (lead guitar). 'Come Out Fighting', with its anthemic, rock pretensions failed to make the singles chart and the new Easterhouse, with all songs written solely by Perry, was heavily criticized: the political content was still high with tracks like 'Stay With Me (Death On The Dole)' but the soul and subtle melodies were no longer present. Easterhouse's impact might have been minimal but along with other Manchester guitar groups, like the Chameleons, it laid the foundations for the later explosion boasting the Stone Roses, Happy Mondays, James and Inspiral Carpets, bands with a rare capacity to learn from others' mistakes.

Albums: *Contenders* (1986), *Waiting For The Red Bird* (1989).

Eater

This UK punk-rock band formed in 1976, while the band members were still at school. Comprising Andy Blade (vocals), Dee Generate (drums), Brian Chevette (guitar) and Ian Woodcock (bass), they made their vinyl debut with '15' (a bastardized version of Alice Cooper's 'Eighteen'), on *The Roxy, London W.C.2.* compilation, recorded during the spring of 1977. With equipment purchased from Woolworths, they were picked up by The Label, which released five singles including the debut 'Outside View' and 'Lock It Up', with the latter featuring a dire version of T. Rex's 'Jeepster' on the b- side. The album followed later the same year, but it only served to further highlight the band's obvious musical limitations.

Albums: *The Album* (1977), *The History Of Eater Vol.1* (1985).

Echo And The Bunnymen

The origins of this renowned 80s Liverpool group can be traced back to the spring of 1977 when vocalist Ian McCulloch (b. 5 May 1959, Liverpool, England) was a member of the Crucial Three with Julian Cope and Pete Wylie. While the last two later emerged in the Teardrop Explodes and Wah!, respectively, McCulloch put together his major group at the end of 1978. Initially a trio the group featured McCulloch, Will Sergeant (b. 12 April 1958, Liverpool, England; guitar); Les Patterson (b. 18 April 1958, Ormskirk, Merseyside, England; bass) and a drum machine which they christened 'Echo'. After making their first appearance at the famous Liverpool club, Eric's, they made their vinyl debut in March 1979 with 'Read It In Books', produced by whizz kid entrepreneurs Bill Drummond and Dave Balfe. The production was sparse but intriguing and helped the group to establish a sizeable cult following. McCulloch's brooding live performance and vocal inflexions were already drawing comparisons with the Doors' Jim Morrison. After signing to Korova Records (distributed by Warner Brothers) they replaced 'Echo' with a person: Pete De Freitas (b. 2 August 1961, Port Of Spain, Trinidad, West Indies, d. 1989). The second single, 'Rescue', was a considerable improvement on its predecessor, with a confident, driving sound that augured well for their forthcoming album. *Crocodiles* proved impressive with a wealth of strong arrangements and memorable guitar work. After the less melodic single, 'The Puppet', the group toured extensively and issued an EP *Shine So Hard*, which crept into the UK Top 40. The next album, *Heaven Up Here*, saw them regaled by the music press. Although a less accessible and melodic work than its predecessor, it sold well and topped various polls. *Porcupine* reinforced the group's appeal, while 'The Cutter' gave them their biggest hit so far. A gripping piece of work, the single was notable for its raga-like bagpipe drone. In 1984, they charted again with 'The Killing Moon', one of their finest moments. The epic quality of the piece was in keeping with the group's grandiloquent character and again showed a raga-tinged influence in their work. The 1984 album *Ocean Rain* sustained their appeal and brought them into the US Top 100 album charts. In February 1986, De Frietas left the group to be replaced by former Haircut 100 drummer Mark Fox, but he returned the following September. The group were treading water with *Echo And The Bunnymen*, but were still active during 1988 when they recorded a version of the Doors' 'People Are Strange'. The new recording was produced by Ray Manzarek who also played on the track, and it was used as a haunting theme for the cult film, *The Lost Boys* (1989.) In 1989, McCulloch made the shock announcement that he was henceforth pursuing a solo career. While he completed the well-received *Candleland*, the Bunnymen made the unexpected decision to carry on. Large numbers of audition tapes were listened to before they chose McCulloch's successor, Noel Burke, a Belfast boy who had previously recorded with St Vitus Dance. Just as they were beginning rehearsals, De Frietas was tragically killed in a road accident. The group bravely struggled on, recruiting new drummer Damien and adding road manager Jake Brockman on guitar/synthesizer. In 1990, they introduced the next phase of Bunnymen history with the promising *Reverberation*.

Albums: *Crocodiles* (1980), *Heaven Up Here* (1981), *Porcupine* (1983), *Ocean Rain* (1984), *Echo And The Bunnymen* (1987), *Reverberation* (1990). Compilation: *Songs To Learn And Sing* (1985). Solos: Will Sergeant *Themes For Grind* (1983), Ian McCulloch *Candleland* (1989).

Eddie And The Hot Rods

Formed in 1975, this quintet from Southend, Essex, England, originally comprised Barrie Masters (vocals), Lew Lewis (harmonica), Paul Gray (bass), Dave Higgs (guitar), Steve Nicol (drums) plus 'Eddie', a short-lived dummy that Masters pummelled on stage. After one classic single, 'Writing On The Wall', Lewis left, though he appeared on the high energy 'Horseplay', the flip-side of their cover of Sam The Sham And The Pharoahs' 'Wooly Bully'. Generally regarded as a younger, more energetic version of Dr Feelgood, the Rods pursued a tricky route between the conservatism of pub rock and the radicalism of punk. During the summer of 1976, the group broke house records at the Marquee Club with a scorching series of raucous, sweat-drenched performances. Their power was well captured on a live EP which included

a cover of ? And The Mysterians' '96 Tears' and a clever amalgamation of the Rolling Stones' 'Satisfaction' and Them's 'Gloria'.

The arrival of guitarist Graeme Douglas from the Kursaal Flyers gave the group a more commercial edge and a distinctive jingle-jangle sound. A guest appearance on former MC5 singer Robin Tyner's 'Till The Night Is Gone' was followed by the strident 'Do Anything You Want To Do', which provided a Top 10 hit in the UK. A fine second album, *Life On The Line* was striking enough to suggest a long term future, but the group fell victim to diminishing returns. Douglas left, followed by Gray, who joined the Damned. Masters disbanded the group for a spell but reformed the unit for pub gigs and small label appearances.

Albums: *Teenage Depression* (1976), *Life On The Line* (1977), *Thriller* (1979), *Fish 'n' Chips* (1980), *One Story Town* (1985), *The Curse Of The Rods* (1990).

Edge

This UK group was formed in 1978 by former Damned members Jon Moss (b. 11 September 1957, London, England; drums) and guitarist Lu Edmunds. They were joined by bassist Glyn Havard and pianist Gavin Povey. Although they gigged extensively and undertook studio work, backing Kirsty MacColl on the single 'They Don't Know' and touring as Jane Aire And The Belvederes, their own work was largely ignored. They issued three singles ('Macho Man', 'Downhill' and 'Watching You') during the late 70s, and issued the album *Square 1* in 1980 before disbanding. Moss went on to join Culture Club, while Edmunds teamed-up with Athletico Spizz 80 and later the Mekons. The remaining members returned to session work.

Album: *Square 1* (1980). Compilation: *The Moonlight Tapes* (1980).

Eighth Wonder

A vehicle for 'sex-kitten' singer Patsy Kensit (b. 4 March 1968, Waterloo, London, England), a former child actress at one time known for her role in a UK television advertisement. She pursued a parallel career as an actress, including a role in the Royal Shakespeare Company production of *Silas Marner* in 1984, and as a pop singer in Eighth Wonder, which comprised Geoff Beauchamp (guitar), Alex Godson (keyboards) and Jamie Kensit (guitar). The group gained a minor UK hit with 'Stay With Me' in 1985. Kensit later landed the role of Crêpe Suzette in Julien Temple's 1986 film of Colin McInnes's novel, *Absolute Beginners*. Surrounded by an intense media hype, the film, which also featured David Bowie, Sade Adu and Ray Davies of the Kinks, was a critical and commercial flop. Kensit and Eighth Wonder found greater success in 1988 with the UK Top 10

single, 'I'm Not Scared'. Two more chart singles followed that same year including the Top 20 hit, 'Cross My Heart' and a Top 50 album, *Fearless*. Kensit later restored her credibility as an actress in the 1991 Don Boyd film, *Twenty-One*, although the subsequent *Blame It On The Bellboy* drew less favourable reviews. Her marriage in January 1992 to Simple Minds singer Jim Kerr caused considerable interest in the British tabloid press.
Album: *Fearless* (1988).

808 State

This Manchester, England dance combo comprised Martin Price (b. 26 March 1955, owner of the influential Eastern Bloc record shop), Graham Massey (b. 4 August, 1960 ex-Biting Tongues) and Darren Partington and Andy Barker, a disc jockey double act. Massey had previously worked in a café opposite Price's shop, while Partington and Barker had been regular visitors to the premises, proffering a variety of tapes in the hope of getting a deal with Price's Creed label. Together with Gerald Simpson, they began recording as a loose Electro house collective, and rose to prominence at the end of 1989 when their single 'Pacific State' became a massive underground hit, topping both the Street Sales and soul charts in *Black Echoes* magazine. It proved to be a mixed blessing for the band as they were lumped in with the pervading Manchester independent dance boom (a term they despised). *Newbuild* and *Quadrastate* helped to establish them as premier exponents of techno dance, leading to a lucrative deal with ZTT Records. However, Simpson had left to form his own A Guy Called Gerald outfit, and launched a series of attacks on the band in the press concerning unpaid royalties. Their album, *Ex:El*, featured the vocals of New Order's Bernard Sumner on 'Spanish Heart', and the Sugarcubes' Bjork Gudmundsdottir on 'Oops' and 'Qmart'. They have also worked with Mancunian rapper MC Tunes on *North At Its Heights* and several singles, billed as 808 State Versus MC Tunes. In October 1991 Price declined to tour the USA with the band, electing to work on solo projects instead.
Albums: *Newbuild* (1988), *Quadrastate* (1989), *90* (1989), *North At Its Heights* (1990; jointly credited to MC Tunes), *Ex:El* (1991).

Einsturzende Neubaten

Formed out of the Berlin Arts Conglomerate Geniale Dilletanten, Einsturzende Neubaten made their live debut in April 1980. The line-up comprised Blixa Bargeld, N.U. Unruh, Beate Bartel and Gudrun Gut. Alexander Van Borsig, an occasional contributor, joined in time for the band's first single, 'Fur Den Untergang'. When Bartel and Gut departed to form Mania D and Matador they were replaced by F.M. (Mufti) and Einheit (ex-Abwarts). Einheit and Unruh formed the band's rhythmic backbone, experimenting with a variety of percussive effects, while Bargeld provided vocals and guitar. Their first official album (there were previously many tapes available) was *Kollaps*, a collage of sounds created by unusual rhythmic instruments ranging from steel girders to pipes and cannisters. Their 1982 12-inch single 'Durstiges Tier' involved contributions from the Birthday Party's Rowland S. Howard and Lydia Lunch, at which point Van Borsig had joined the band permanently as sound technician alongside new bass player Marc Chung (also ex-Abwarts). A British tour with the Birthday Party introduced them to Some Bizzare Records which released *Die Zeichnungen Das Patienten O.T.* 1984's *Strategien Gegen Architekturen* was compiled with Jim Thirwell (Foetus), while the band performed live at the ICA in London. Joined by Genesis P. Orridge (Psychic TV), Frank Tovey (Fad Gadget) and Stevo (Some Bizzare), the gig ended violently and attracted heated debate in the press. Bargeld spent the rest of the year touring as bass player for Nick Cave, going on to record several studio albums as Bad Seed. In 1987 Einsturzende Neubaten performed the soundtrack for *Andi*, a play at the Hamburg Schauspielhaus, and also released *Funf Auf Der Nach Oben Offenen Richterskala*. This was intended as a farewell album, but they, nevertheless, continued after its release. Bargeld's part-time career with the Bad Seeds continued, and in 1988 he featured alongside them in Wim Wenders' film *Angels Über Berlin*. Von Borsig, ironically, was now contributing to the work of Crime And The City Solution, featuring Cave's old Birthday Party colleagues. The band reunited, however, in time for 1989's *Haus Der Luge*.
Albums: *Kollaps* (1982), *Die Zeichnungen Des Patienten O.T.* (1983), *Strategien Gegen Architekturen* (1984), *Half Mensch* (1985), *Funf Auf Nach Oben Offenen Richterskala* (1987), *Haus Der Luge* (1989).

Einsturzende Neubauten

Electro Hippies

This eccentric grindcore outfit formed in 1988. Specializing in low-technological studio techniques, they have issued four albums to date. In each case, a distorted, bass-laden barrage is over-ridden by stomach-churning vocals that lack both finesse and cohesion. Chaotic and extreme, Electro Hippies criticize the whole recording industry.

Albums: *The Only Good Punk Is A Dead One* (1988), *Electro Hippies Live* (1989), *The Peaceville Recordings* (1989), *Play Loud Or Die* (1989).

Electronic

This powerful UK duo comprises Johnny Marr (b. John Maher 31 October 1963) and Bernard Sumner (b. 4 January 1956), both formerly key members of very successful Manchester-based bands, the Smiths and New Order respectively. Although they first worked together in 1983, Electronic was not formed until 1989. A somewhat unlikely pairing, Q magazine commented, 'It was a marriage made not in heaven,' because of their previous mutual mistrust. After a brief period as guitarist for Matt Johnson's The The and work with various well-known artists, such as David Byrne and the Pretenders, Electronic marked Marr's move into more commercial territory. His instinct for infectious, melodic pop guitar and Sumner's songwriting and programming ability proved to be an effective combination. Their first single, 'Getting Away With It' was released in 1989 on Manchester's highly respected Factory Records and featured the Pet Shop Boys' Neil Tennant as guest vocalist. This inspired move helped the record to number 12 in the UK chart. The individual track records of the three musicians immediately gave the band a high profile, arousing the interest of both the press and the public. This attention was intensified by the excitement surrounding the 'baggy' dance scene emerging from Manchester and the city's explosion of new musical talent, sparked by bands such as Happy Mondays and the Stone Roses. Electronic capitalized on the new crediblity that dance music had acquired and were influenced by the fusions that were taking place, using 'electronic' dance rhythms and indie guitar pop. In July 1991, a self-titled debut album followed two more UK Top 20 singles, 'Get The Message' and 'Feel Every Beat'. The singles were witty and distinctive and were praised by the critics. Not surprisingly, the album was also very well-received, entering the UK chart at number 4 and the independent chart at number 1. Intelligent, original and fashionably marrying the sounds of the guitar and the computer, the duo can expect a bright future.

Albums: *Electronic* (1991).

Eleventh Dream Day

This US group was formed in Chicago in the mid-80s and comprised Rick Rizzo (guitar/vocals), Janet Beveridge Bean (drums), Douglas McCombs (bass) and Baird Figi (guitar/vocals). Its brand of college-rock, in the mould of the Pixies and Dream Syndicate, drew on music from the 60s and 70s, with the guitar histrionics of Television, Neil Young and Crazy Horse combined with a whiff of psychedelia. Signed to the Atlantic label, Eleventh Dream Day seemed set to break away from their cult-status in the 90s. This impetus was struck a blow early in 1991 when Figi quit and was replaced by Wink O'Bannon. *Lived To Tell* was recorded in a studio-converted Kentucky barn in an attempt to obtain the feeling of a live recording.

Albums: *Eleventh Dream Day* (1987), *Prairie School Freakout* (1989), *Beet* (1990), *Lived To Tell* (1991).

Emotionals

This charming but derivative pop group much in the mould of Blondie, emerged from London, England in the late 80s. Featuring Emma Vine (vocals), Pete Maher (guitar/vocals), Roz Laney (bass) and Kieron James (drums/percussion), the Emotionals was originally formed in Brixton in 1988. Vine and Maher had met at school, but were more interested in following Richard Hell And The Voidoids than attending lessons. They moved to London and, from the summer of that year, they began an exhaustive promotional campaign which has barely ceased since its inception. Winning early support from US disc jockey Rodney Bingenheimer and Blondie's Nigel Harrison, they signed to Native Records from whence their two rather average albums have emerged.

Albums: *Personal Pleasure* (1990), *In Response* (1991).

Erasure

Keyboard player and arranger Vince Clarke had already enjoyed success as a member of Depeche Mode, Yazoo, and the Assembly when he decided to undertake a new project in 1985. The plan was to record an album with 10 different singers, but after auditioning vocalist Andy Bell, the duo Erasure was formed. After struggling with their first four singles, the group finally broke into the UK Top 20 in 1987 with 'It Doesn't Have To Be Me'. The following month their second album, *Circus,* reached the UK Top 10 and since then their popularity has rapidly grown. Hits such as 'Sometimes', 'Victim Of Love', 'The Circus', 'Ship Of Fools', 'A Little Respect', *Crackers International* (EP) and 'Drama!' have established them as serious rivals to the Pet Shop Boys as a vocal/synthesizer duo. Erasure's appeal lies in the unlikely pairing of the flamboyant Bell and the low-profile keyboards wizard and songwriter Clarke.

Although their image is not particularly strong, their album sales continue to increase with successive releases and *The Innocents, Wild!* and *Chorus* have all reached number 1 in the UK. It is also worth stressing that they have achieved their many successes working through an indepedent label, Mute Records. Albums: *Wonderland* (1986), *The Circus* (1987), *The Two Ring Circus* (1987), *The Innocents* (1988), *Wild!* (1989), *Chorus* (1991).

Essential Logic

Formed by Lora Logic, X Ray Spex's original saxophonist, in 1978, Essential Logic's first single was 'Aerosol Burns', a punk masterpiece of brash guitar and hiccoughing rhythms. The group delighted in odd, jangling harmonies and eccentric song shapes: Lora Logic's loopy punk vocals (a strong influence on more successful girl groups of the 80s such as Throwing Muses and Fuzzbox) and gorgeously primitive saxophone made *Beat Rhythm News* (1979) special. Her solo album, *Pedigree Charm*, had a smoother sound, but her work with Red Crayola had a new harshness and power. Lora Logic later joined the Hare Krishna cult and has now left music altogether.
Albums: *Beat Rhythm News* (1979), *Pedigree Charm* (1982).

Everything But The Girl

The duo of Tracey Thorn (b. 26 September 1962, Hertfordshire, England) and Ben Watt (b. 6 December 1962, England), first came together when they were students at Hull University, their name coming from a local furniture shop. Thorn was also a member of the Marine Girls who issued two albums, the second on the pioneering Cherry Red label. They performed together in 1982 and released a gentle and simply produced version of Cole Porter's 'Night And Day'. Thorn made the solo acoustic mini-album in 1982 *A Distant Shore* which was a strong seller in the UK independent charts, and Watt released the critically acclaimed *North Marine Drive* the following year. They left Cherry Red and signed to the Blanco y Negro label. In 1984 they made the national chart with 'Each And Everyone', which preceded their superb *Eden*. This jazz-flavoured pop collection contained some excellent material, and showed a great leap from the comparative naivete of their previous offerings. Their biggest single to date was a version of Danny Whitten's 'I Don't Want To Talk About It', which reached the UK Top 3 in 1988. Their subsequent albums have shown a gradual growth as they progress as songwriters and musicians. In particular Thorn's voice has become stronger and more confident. *The Language Of Life* stands as their best album to date; the jazz influence was stronger with crisper production, and it found critical acclaim.

One track, 'The Road', featured Stan Getz on saxophone. Followers of their career are left with the strong belief that the best is still to come as they fine-tune their already excellent blend of music. However, a more pop-orientated follow-up *World-wide* was released to mediocre reviews in 1991.
Albums: *Eden* (1984), *Love Not Money* (1985), *Baby The Stars Shine Bright* (1986), *Idlewild* (1988), *The Language Of Life* (1990), *World-wide* (1991). EP: with Robert Wyatt *Summer Into Winter* (1982).

Exploding White Mice

This hard-hitting guitar band was formed in Adelaide, Australia in early 1985 featuring Jeff Stephens (lead guitar), Paul Gilchrist (vocals) and Giles Barrow (rhythm guitar). Their style drew influences from the tough Detroit sound of the early Stooges with just a hint of Ramones-style 'dumb fun'. In fact they took their name from the laboratory rodents that featured in the Ramones' movie *Rock 'N' Roll High School*. Their debut recording featured three originals and three covers including 'Pipeline' and a burning version of Bo Diddley's 'Let The Kids Dance', and indicated a young band with considerable talent. Exploding White Mice quickly developed a huge live reputation and their 1987 double a-sided single, John Kongos' 'He's Gonna Step On You Again', should have broken them to a wider audience. However, another version by the seasoned cover band Party Boys, received more attention. Their first full-length album proved them to be one of the finest trash pop bands in the country. On their most recent album, the band have developed their pop sensibilities to the point where commercial acceptance is becoming a distinct possibility.
Albums: *Brute Force & Ignorance* (1988), *Exploding White Mice* (1990).

Exploited

This abrasive Scottish punk quartet was formed in 1980 by vocalist Wattie and guitarist Big John. Recruiting drummer Dru Stix and bassist Gary, they signed to the Secret label the following year. Specializing in two-minute blasts of high-speed blue vitriol, they released their first album, *Punk's Not Dead* in 1981. Lyrically they covered themes such as war, corruption, unemployment, police brutality and politics, amid a chaotic melee of crashing drums and flailing guitar chords. The band have become entrenched in their own musical and philosophical ideology, and have failed to progress since their inception. Continuing to release material on a regular basis, they have retained a small, but ever-declining cult following. The diminutive lead singer, with a multi-coloured mohican haircut, strikes an odd figure today. They were challenging, arrogant and provocative in 1981, but today they appear a musical curio from a previous era.

Albums: *Punk's Not Dead* (1981), *On Stage* (1981), *Troops Of Tomorrow* (1982), *Let's Start A War* (1983), *The Massacre* (1983), *Death Before Dishonour* (1984), *Inner City Decay* (1984), *Live, Lewd, Lust* (1985), *Horror Epics* (1986), *Totally Exploited* (1987), *Live And Loud* (1987), *Live On The Apocalypse Now Tour '81* (1987).

Eyeless In Gaza

Taking their name from Aldous Huxley's famous novel, this UK group was the brainchild of vocalists/musicians Martyn Bates and Peter Becker. Known for their tortured vocals and impressive arranging skills, the group established a reasonable following on the independent circuit with their 1981 debut, *Photographs As Memories*. Several more albums for the Cherry Red label saw them alternate between a melodramatic and meandering style that increasingly veered towards improvisation. Martyn subsequently teamed up with former Primitives bassist in Hate.

Albums: *Photographs As Memories* (1981), *Caught In Flux* (1981), *Pale Hands I Loved So Well* (1982), *Drumming The Beating Heart* (1983).

Fabulous

This UK post-punk band was formed in the wake of the media success of the Manic Street Preachers. Fabulous comprised *New Musical Express* Simon Dudfield (vocals), plus Martin Goodacre (guitar), 'Hodge' (drums), Russel Underwood (second guitar) and Ronnie Fabulous (bass). They were managed by former *NME* assistant editor James Brown. Dudfield was a contributer and both Goodacre and Underwood were photographers on the same paper. Live they were characterized by Dudfield's studied Iggy Pop impersonations, while musically and ideologically they borrowed from the situationist tack of the Sex Pistols. Their first single 'Destined To Be Free' was just a small part of their stated agenda to reinvent 1977 and rid the UK music scene of the 'Ecstasy' mentality. They also made a point of exhibiting a stolen carpet from EMI's offices. As more than one journalist has noted, the Sex Pistols had taken that record company for £50,000, which puts Fabulous' achievements in some sort of perspective.

Factory Records

Cambridge graduate Tony Wilson (b. 1950, Salford, Lancashire, England) was a regional television reporter working in Manchester when he started the Factory label in 1978. He was also responsible for the *So It Goes* and *What's On* television programmes, which in themselves had acted as an invaluable platform for the emerging new wave scene. Previously he had edited his university's *Shilling Paper*. From there he joined television news company ITN as a trainee reporter, writing bulletins for current events programmes. It was on regional news programmes based in Manchester that he first encountered his future collaborators in the Factory operation; Alan Erasmus, Peter Saville, Rob Gretton (manager of Joy Division) and producer Martin Hannett. Erasmus and Wilson began their operation by jointly managing the fledgling Durutti Column, opening the Factory Club venue soon after. The label's first catalogue number, FAC 1, was allocated to the poster promoting its opening event. This typified Wilson's approach to the whole Factory operation, the most famous assignation of which was FAC 51, the Hacienda nightclub. However, it was their records, and the impersonal, nondescriptive packaging that accompanied them, which saw the label make its mark. Among the first releases were OMD's 'Electricity' (later a hit on Dindisc), and A Certain Ratio's 'All Night Party'. But it was Joy Division, harnessing the anxieties of Manchester youth to a discordant, sombre musical landscape, that established the label in terms of public perception and financial security. With Curtis gone, New Order continued as the backbone of the Factory operation throughout the 80s, establishing themselves in the mainstream with the biggest selling 12-inch up until that time, 'Blue Monday'. Other mainstays included Section 25 and Stockholm Monsters, who steered a path too close to that of New Order, and the resourceful Durutti Column. It took the brief arrival of James to restore a pop sensibility (their subsequent departure would be a huge body blow), while New Order, somewhat astonishingly, took the England Football Squad to number 1 in the UK Charts with 'World In Motion'. The latter-day success of Electronic, the most successful of various New Order offshoots, and the Happy Mondays, a shambolic post-punk dance conglomerate, has diffused accusations of Factory being too reliant on a single band. Reported cashflow problems in 1991, although vehemently denied by Wilson, will most likely be eased by a bumper crop of albums on the horizon, including new material by New Order and the Happy Mondays. Additionally the four-album compilation, *Palatine*, showcased the label's achievements, of which Wilson has never been reticent: 'In my opinion (popular art) is as valid as any other art form . . . a lot

of the tracks on *Palatine* are phenomenal art. We're 35 years into pop now, and great records do not lose their power. The deference with which we treat this stuff is deserved.'
Album: *Palatine* (1991).

Fad Gadget

Effectively a monicker for UK-born vocalist and synthesizer player Frank Tovey, Fad Gadget enjoyed cult success with a series of bizarre releases on the Mute label during the early 80s. Tovey's background lay in his study of performance art at Leeds Art College. After moving to London, he transferred this interest into an unpredictable, often self-mutilating stage show. The first artist to sign with Daniel Miller's Mute label, Fad Gadget's 'Back To Nature' was released in 1979. 'Ricky's Hand' further combined Tovey's lyrical skill (observing the darker aspects of life) with an innovative use of electronics. Both these traits were evident on 'Fireside Favourites', a single and also the title of Fad Gadget's debut album. For the latter, Tovey was joined by Eric Radcliffe (guitar/bass), Nick Cash (drums), John Fryer (noises), Daniel Miller (drum machine/synthesizer) and Phil Wauquaire (bass synthesizer/guitar). After 'Make Room', (1981), came *Incontinent*, which was more violent, unnerving and disturbing than before. Tovey had also recruited new staff, working with Peter Balmer (bass/rhythm guitar), David Simmons (piano/synthesizer), singers B.J. Frost and Anne Clift, John Fryer (percussion), plus drummer Robert Gotobed of Wire. In 1982 'Saturday Night Special' and 'King Of Flies' preceded a third album, *Under The Flag*. Dealing with the twin themes of the Falklands conflict and Tovey's new-born child, the album featured Alison Moyet on saxophone and backing vocals. The following year saw new extremes as Tovey returned from a European tour with his legs in plaster, having broken them during a show. On the recording front, the year was fairly quiet apart from 'For Whom The Bell Tolls' and 'I Discover Love'. 'Collapsing New People' continued an impressive run of singles at the start of 1984, and was followed by Fad Gadget's final album, *Gag*. By this time, the band had swelled and supported Siouxsie And The Banshees at London's Royal Albert Hall. But Tovey opted to use his real identity from this point on. In November, he teamed up with American Boyd Rice for *Easy Listening For The Hard Of Hearing*. Since then, Tovey has issued four solo works, each of them as highly distinct and uncompromising as Fad Gadget's material.
Albums: *Fireside Favourites* (1980), *Incontinent* (1981), *Under The Flag* (1982), *Gag* (1984). Compilation: *The Fad Gadget Singles* (1986). As Frank Tovey: with Boyd Rice *Easy Listening For The Hard Of Hearing* (1984), *Snakes And Ladders* (1985), *Civilian* (1988), *Tyranny And The Hired Hand* (1989), with the Pyros *Grand Union* (1991).

Fairground Attraction

This jazz-tinged Anglo/Scottish pop band comprised Eddi Reader (b. 28 August 1959, Glasgow, Scotland; vocals), Mark Nevin (guitar), Simon Edwards (guitaron, a Mexican acoustic guitar shaped bass) and Roy Dodds (drums). After art school Reader made her first musical forays as backing singer for the Gang Of Four. She moved to London in 1983 where session and live work with the Eurythmics and Alison Moyet kept her gainfully employed. She first hooked up with Nevin for the Compact Organisation sampler album *The Compact Composers*, singing on two of his songs. Nevin and Reader began their first collaborations in 1985, after Nevin had graduated by playing in one of the numerous line-ups of Jane Aire And The Belvederes. He was also closely involved with Sandie Shaw's mid-80s comeback. Around his songs they built Fairground Attraction, adding Edwards and Dodds, a jazz drummer of over 20 years' standing who had spent time with Working Week and Terence Trent D'Arby. They signed to RCA and quickly set about recording a debut album, as the gentle skiffle of 'Perfect' topped the UK singles charts in May 1988. They subsequently won both Best Single and Best Album categories at the Brit awards. A slight hiatus in their career followed when Reader became pregnant. They followed their natural inclinations by filming the video for their 1989 single 'Clare' in Nashville, and were supplemented on tour by Graham Henderson (accordion) and Roger Beaujolais (vibes). The group's promise was then cut short when the band split, and Reader went on to acting (appearing in a BBC drama about the Scottish country and western scene) and a solo career.
Album: *First Of A Million Kisses* (1988), *Ay Fond Kiss* (1990). Solo album: Eddi Reader *Mir Mama* (1992).

Faith No More

Formed in San Fransisco in 1983, Faith No More were among the first outfits to experiment with the fusion of funk, thrash and hardcore styles into a new musical sub-genre. The band initially comprised Jim Martin (guitar), Roddy Bottum (keyboards), Bill Gould (bass), Mike Bordin (drums) and Chuck Mosely (vocals). This line-up recorded a low-budget, self-titled debut on the independent Mordam label, followed by the ground breaking *Introduce Yourself* on Slash, a subsidiary of London Records. It encompassed a variety of styles but exuded a rare warmth and energy, mainly through Mosley's 'over the top' vocals and was well received by the critics. Internal disputes led to the firing of Mosely on the eve of widespread press coverage and favourable live reviews. Against the odds, Mosely's replacement

Mike Patton was even more flamboyant and actually more accomplished as a singer. *The Real Thing* that followed was a runaway success, with the single 'Epic' denting the UK Top 20 singles chart. Their style was now both offbeat and unpredictable, yet retained enough melody to remain a commercial proposition. *Live At The Brixton Academy* was released as a stop-gap album, while the band toured on the back of the worldwide success of their last studio album.

Albums: *Faith No More* (1984), *Introduce Yourself* (1987), *The Real Thing* (1989), *Live At The Brixton Academy* (1990), *Angel Dust* (1992).

Faith Over Reason

This English group emerged on the independent scene in the early 90s. Their version of Nick Drake's 'Northern Sky' pigeon-holed the group as one firmly planted within the pastoral sound of British folk/rock era of the 70s, although conversely, the group's sound has often been compared with that of the Sundays and Smiths. Formed in Croydon, south London, the group consists of Moira Lambert (b. 13 October 1970, Chicester, West Sussex, England; lead vocals/acoustic guitar), William Lloyd (b. 17 March 1971, London, England; bass/keyboards), Simon Roots (b. 1 September 1970; guitar) and Mark Wilsher (b. 1 May 1970, Croydon, Surrey, England; drums). The release of two EPs in 1990, *Believing In Me* ('Evangeline'/'Believing In Me'/'Northern Sky') and *Billy Blue* ('High In The Sun'/'Ice Queen'/'Billy Blue'/'Move Closer') on the Big Cat label, drew well-earned praise from the music press. Moira in the meantime contributed vocals to St. Etienne's 'Only Love Can Break Your Heart', an indie-dance hit of 1990. The group's momentum was disrupted in late 1991 by the departure of Roots.

Album: *Eyes Wide Smile* (1992).

Fall

Formed in Manchester, England in 1977, the Fall was the brainchild of the mercurial Mark E. Smith (b. Mark Edward Smith, 5 March 1957, Salford, Manchester, England). Over the years, Smith ruthlessly went through a battalion of musicians while taking the group through a personal odyssey of his wayward musical and lyrical excursions. The first line-up featuring Una Baines, Martin Bramah, Karl Burns and Tony Friel made their debut on 'Bingo Master's Breakout', a typical example of Smith's surreal vision. Initially signed to the small independent label Step Forward the group recorded three singles, including the strange 'Fiery Jack' plus *Live At The Witch Trials*. In 1980, the unit signed to Rough Trade and went on to release the critically acclaimed but often wilfully bizarre singles 'How I Wrote Elastic Man' and 'Totally Wired'. Meanwhile,

a whole series of line-up changes saw the arrival and subsequent departures of Marc Riley, Mike Leigh, Martin Bramah, Yvonne Pawlett and Craig Scanlon. The Fall's convoluted career continued to produce a series of discordant, yet frequently fascinating albums from the early menace of *Dragnet* to the chaotic *Hex Enduction Hour*. An apparent change in the group's image and philosophy occured during 1983 with the arrival of Mark's wife Brix (Laura Elise Smith). As well as appearing with the Fall singer/guitarist, Brix simultaneously continued recording with her own group, the hard pop-orientated Adult Net. She first appeared on the Fall's *Perverted By Language* and her presence was felt more strongly when the group unexpectedly emerged as a potential chart act, successfully covering R. Dean Taylor's 'There's A Ghost In My House' and later the Kinks' 'Victoria'. The fusion of Brix's Rickenbacker guitar sound with Smith's deadpan vocals and distinctive phrasing and accentuation proved intriguing beyond expectations. On later albums such as *This Nation's Saving Grace* and *The Frenz Experiment*, they lost none of their baffling wordplay or nagging, insistent rhythms, but the work seemed more focused and accessible. The line-up changes had slowed, although more changes were afoot with the arrival of drummer Simon Wolthenscroft and Marcia Schofield. Proof of Smith's growing stature among the popular art cognescenti was the staging of his papal play *Hey! Luciani* and the involvement of dancer Michael Clark in the production of *I Am Kurious Oranj*. Any suggestions that the Fall might be slowly heading for a degree of commercial acceptance underestimated Smith's restless spirit. By 1990, Brix had left the singer and the group, and Schofield followed soon after. Unpredictable and unique, the Fall under Smith's guidance remain one of the most uncompromising yet finest groups in British rock history.

Albums: *Live At The Witch Trials* (1979), *Dragnet* (1979), *Totale's Turns (It's Now Or Never) (Live)* (1980), *Grotesque (After The Gramme)* (1980), *Slates* (1981), *Hex Enduction Hour* (1982), *Room To Live* (1982), *Perverted By Language* (1983), *The Wonderful And Frightening World Of . . .* (1984), *This Nation's Saving Grace* (1985), *Bend Sinister* (1986), *The Frenz Experiment* (1988), *I Am Kurious Oranj* (1988), *Seminal Live* (1989), *Extricate* (1990), *Shiftwork* (1991), *Code Selfish* (1992). Compilations: *458489* (1990), *458489-B Sides* (1990).

Further reading: *Paintwork: A Portrait Of The Fall*, Brian Edge.

Family Cat

Originally from Yeovil, Somerset, the Family Cat were formed in 1988 and comprise Paul 'Fred' Frederick (lead vocals/guitar), Stephen Jelbert (guitar), Tim McVey (guitar), John (bass) and Kevin (drums). Based in south London, the group drew their influences from a variety of styles and drew critical praise for the live appearances. A mini-album *Tell 'Em We're Surfin'* followed on from the unexpected success of their debut single 'Tom Verlaine' (1989) on the Bad Girl label. Despite the accolades from the British music press the group found it difficult to break out of the 'independent' mould. The Family Cat's persistence has paid off with well-received singles in 'Remember What It Is That You Love' and 'A Place With No Name' (both 1990), and 'Colour Me Grey' (1991, with backing vocals from the then future indie star, PJ (Polly) Harvey) has maintained the group's profile. A new album in 1992 on the Dedicated label, *Furthest From The Sun*, surprised many with a effective display of power and confidence, generating some of their best reviews yet.

Albums: *Tell 'Em We're Surfin'* (1989), *Furthest From The Sun* (1992).

Family Cat

Family Fodder

This independent band comprised Dominique Pearce (vocals), Alig Levillian (guitars/keyboards/saxophone, vocals), Felix Friedorowicz (keyboards/bassoon/violin), Mick Hobbs (bass/organ), Martin Frederick (bass/vocals), Rick WIlson (drums/vocals), Charles Bullen (drums, guitar/viola/vocals), Buzz Smith (drums) Mark Doffman (drums), Ian Hill (vocals/percussion), Judy Carter and Jan Beetlestone (backing vocals). Their best remembered contribution to modern music was the tribute single 'Debbie Harry', though other efforts such as 'Playing Golf', 'Warm', 'Savoire Faire' and 'Film Music' were entertaining for their idiosyncratic experimentalism. However, despite a reasonable line in songwriting craft from Pearce, it would have required greater commercial skill to sustain the legions of personnel. A greatest hits album was an ironic artefact in retrospect.

Album: *Monkey Banana Kitchen* (1985). Compilation: *Greatest Hits* (1986).

Farm

Farm

If perseverance warrants its own unique award, the Farm would not be going too far above themselves to expect the equivalent of the Nobel prize for their incessant efforts. Formed in 1983 by Peter Hooton (b. 28 September 1962, Liverpool, England; vocals), Steve Grimes (b. 4 June 1962, Liverpool, England; guitar), Phillip Strongman (bass) and Andy McVann (drums), the Farm were to become synonymous with so many cultural 'scenes' over the ensuing seven years that their music was rendered almost irrelevant. For much of the 80s the band flirted with politics, tagged 'The Soul Of Socialism', the 'Scally' fashions of their Liverpool hometown, and maintained strong soccer interests - primarily through singer Peter Hooton's own fanzine, *The End*. By 1984, John Melvin, George Maher, Steve Levy and Anthony Evans had joined, bringing with them a brass section and adding a northern soul influence to the Farm's unfashionable pop sound. Two years on, the line-up changed had changed again as McVann was killed in a police car chase. He was replaced by Roy Boulter (b. 2 July 1964, Liverpool, England) and the line-up was bolstered by Keith Mullen (b. Bootle, England; guitar) and new bassist Carl Hunter (b. 14 April 1965, Bootle, England). The horn section departed and Ben Leach (b. 2 May 1969, Liverpool, England; keyboards) completed a new six-piece collective which was destined to change the Farm's fortunes. After the synthpop flop of their fourth independent release, 'Body And Soul', the Farm started their own Produce label and had a fortuitous meeting with in vogue dance producer Terry Farley. Consequently, a cover version of the Monkees' 'Stepping Stone' was augmented with fashionable club beats and samples and, come 1990, the Farm suddenly found themselves being caught up in the Happy Mondays' 'Baggy' boom. The anthemic 'Groovy Train' and 'All Together Now' (the latter incorporating the sampling of the 17th century composer Johann Pachelbel's 'Canon And Gigue'), swept the band into the Top 10 of the UK charts, to be followed in 1991 by their debut album, *Spartacus*, going straight into the UK charts at number 1. If these placings were not proof enough of the Farm's new-found fame, the next achievement certainly was: the band's football connection was sealed when toy manufacturers Subbuteo designed a unique teamkit, just for the band!

Signed to the Sire label in the USA, the Farm signed a £1 million world-wide deal with Sony in 1992.

Album: *Spartacus* (1991).

Farmers Boys

Along with the Higsons, the Farmers Boys emerged from Norwich, Norfolk, England, in the early 80s with an amusing brand of wacky guitar pop. The excellent 'I Think I Need Help', issued in April 1982, was Baz, Frog, Mark and Stan's first offering (they never used surnames), followed by the equally impressive 'Whatever Is He Like' in the summer. For December's 'More Than A Dream', the band veered towards country and western, a formula successful enough to warrant its reissue as the Farmers Boys' first single for EMI. 'Muck It Out', issued in April 1983, played on the band's rural name in the search for a novelty hit, but chart success was something that would always elude them. After the catchy 'For You' in July, the group's only album appeared in the autumn, but despite a certain charm and melodic strength, *Get Out And Walk* could not sustain the impact of their singles over two sides. 'Apparently', issued in the late spring of 1984, benefited from the band's horn section of Andrew Hamilton (saxophone), Noel Harris (trumpet) and John Beecham (trombone), while a cover of Cliff Richard's 'In The Country' became the closest thing to a Farmers Boys hit in August. But after two further singles, 'Phew Wow' in October and 'I Built The World' early in 1985, the formula had started to wear thin and the band split up soon after.

Album: *Get Out And Walk* (1983).

Fashion

This outfit from Birmingham, England blended offbeat funk with an independent spirit that seemed destined to ensure them commercial success. Originally a trio, comprising John Mulligan (bass), Dix (drums) and Luke (guitar), Fashion issued three diverse singles on their own label, spurred on by the D.I.Y. attitudes in the wake of punk. After November 1978's 'Steady Eddie Steady' came 'Citinite' in June and then *Perfect Product*, an impressive debut album. 'Silver Blades' followed in March 1980, ensuring a deal with Arista. Now swelled to a six-piece with Martin Stoker (ex-Dance and the Bureau) on drums, ex-Neon Hearts vocalist Tony and main songwriter De Harriss, many

predicted that their resultant 45s would break the band on the back of the futurist scene of the early 80s. 'Street Player - Mechanik', in March 1982, 'Love Shadow' in August and later, 'Eye Talk' in January 1984, all scraped the lower reaches of the chart, but failed to establish the band in the public eye.

Despite this, Fashion enjoyed a strong undercurrent of support, reflected in a UK Top 10 album *Fabrique*, in June 1982. But interest gradually waned, the band moved to Epic, and *Twilight Of The Idols*, issued exactly two years on, was not as warmly received, despite two singles, 'Dreaming' in April 1984 and 'You In The Night' in June.

Albums: *Perfect Product* (1979), *Fabrique* (1982), *Twilight Of The Idols* (1984), *The Height Of Fashion* (1990).

Fatima Mansions

Fatima Mansions

This pop group which defies categorization was formed in August 1989 by Cork singer Cathal Coughlan, fresh from his stint with the more restrained Microdisney. The inspiration for the moniker came from a decrepit Dublin housing estate of the same name. *Against Nature* was released in September 1989 to almost universal critical acclaim and a large degree of astonishment; 'staggering in its weight of ideas . . . never loses its capacity to suddenly stun you' stated the *New Musical Express*. Its abrasive lyrics might have been anticipated with Coughlan's pedigree, but the directness of the musical attack certainly was not. Andreas O'Gruama's guitar, as ever, contributed richly to the final results. It was followed by 'Blues For Ceausescu', a fire and brimstone political tirade which held prophetic warnings of East European tragedy. Its operatic tilt enabled it to be at once hysterical, comic and sinister. Coughlan was now established in the press as a delicious anti-hero and mischief maker. *Bugs Fucking Funny* was dropped as the title of the second album, in favour of the comparatively non-descript *Viva Dead Ponies*. This time Coughlan's lyrics were totally submerged in vitriol and hysterical observations on the absurdities of living in the UK. The title-track, for instance, considered the case of Jesus being reincarnated as a Jewish shopkeeper. A particular vehemence, as ever, was reserved for British imperialism. It prompted the *Guardian* newspaper to number Coughlan as 'the most under-rated lyricist in pop today'. Further paranoia, bile and doses of his rich Irish voice were poured in to the mini-album *Bertie's Brochures* in 1991. Notable amongst its eight tracks is the massacre of R.E.M.'s 'Shiny Happy People'. The title track refers to an Irish artist wrongly imprisoned for terrorism, coinciding with highly topical, real-life events. Like Morrissey before him, Coughlan looks set to become the sort of left field maverick genius who makes the broad church of pop music infinitely more entertaining.

Albums: *Against Nature* (1989), *Viva Dead Ponies* (1990), *Bertie's Brochures* (1991).

Feelies

Formed in New Jersey, USA in 1977, the Feelies originally consisted of Glenn Mercer (b. Haledon, New Jersey, USA; lead guitar/vocals), Bill Million (b. William Clayton, Haledon, New Jersey, USA; rhythm guitar/vocals), Keith DeNunzio aka Keith Clayton (b. 27 April 1958, Reading, Pennsylvania, USA; bass) and Dave Weckerman (drums). Weckerman departed from the line-up and was replaced by Vinny DeNuzio (b. 15 August 1956) prior to the group's debut album, *Crazy Rhythms* which featured Anton 'Andy' Fier. This exceptional release brought to mind the jerky paranoia of an early Talking Heads and the compulsion of the Velvet Underground, while at the same time established the Feelies' polyrhythmic pulsebeats and Mercer's scratchy, but effective guitarwork. Despite criticial acclaim, *Crazy Rhythms* was a commercial failure and the group broke up. Fier subsequently formed the Golden Palaminos, an *ad hoc* unit featuring contributions from various, often contrasting, musicians including Jack Bruce and Syd Straw. Mercer and Million then embarked on several diverse projects which included work with three different groups; the Trypes, the Willies and Yung Wu. The latter unit also featured Weckerman and their lone album, *Sore Leave*, led directly to a Feelies' reformation. Stanley Demeski (drums) and Brenda Sauter (bass) joined the group and with Weckerman switching to percussion, the reformation was complete. The Feelies' second album, *The Good Earth*, was produced by R.E.M. guitarist Peter Buck, a long-time fan of *Crazy Rhythms*. Despite the gap between the releases, the new quintet showed much of the same fire and purpose, a factor confirmed by a third collection, *Only Life*. The group remains one of America's most inventive post-punk ensembles.

Albums: *Crazy Rhythms* (1980), *The Good Earth* (1986), *Only Life* (1989).

Fiat Lux

This three-piece synthesizer outfit took their name from the Latin for 'Let There Be Light'. Fiat Lux came together in Wakefield, Yorkshire around 1982. Vocalist Steve Wright and keyboard player David P. Crickmore had been at drama college together and Wright went on to join the well known Yorkshire Actors group. One of that company's patrons was the local guitarist and synthesizer wizard Bill Nelson (ex-Be Bop Deluxe and Red Noise) who on occasion provided music for their productions. Wright and Crickmore were writing material together and Wright decided to use his contact with Bill Nelson and send him a demo tape. Bill was impressed and decided to release the song 'Feels Like Winter Again' on his own Cocteau label. The first recordings were made using local session musicians but in April 1982 Bill's brother Ian, a saxophonist and keyboards player, was enrolled into Fiat Lux. Polydor picked up on the band and they recorded their first album in Liverpool. Tours with Blancmange and Howard Jones followed and their second and third Polydor singles - 'Secrets' and 'Blue Emotion' - both made the charts. 1985's 'Solitary Lovers' was not a success, however, and as synthesizer pop fell out of favour the band fell by the wayside, although Ian Nelson would go on to work occasionally with his brother.

Album: *Hired History* (1984).

Field Mice

Formed in Surrey, England in 1987 by principal songwriter Robert Wratten (b. 5 August 1966, Carshalton, Surrey, England; guitar/vocals) and Mark Dobson (b. 27 April 1965, Hartlepool, England; drums), the Field Mice linked up with Bristol-based Sarah Records for a series of records which unwittingly pigeon-holed both band and label as exponents of whimsical, sensitive pop songs. With the label's initial Independent idealism - which manifested itself in seven inch-only releases in the era of 12-inch singles and compact disc singles - merely adding fire to cynics' vitriol. The Field Mice helped found a small yet fanatical following which spread as far as Japan by virtue of gently struck acoustic guitars and lyrics of the decidedly lovelorn variety. The line-up was expanded by the arrival of label-mate Harvey Williams (b. 31 December 1965, Cornwall, England; guitar), who had previously worked under the name Another Sunny Day. It was unfortunate that the prejudice of the music business ensured that the Field Mice remained condemned to the alternative peripheries even though the band were furthering their eclectic tastes by developing a penchant for danceable electronics ('Triangle') and experimental

Fields Of The Nephilim

noise ('Humblebee'). And this was in spite of contemporary dance outfit St. Etienne taking the Field Mice into the nation's clubs by covering the band's 'Let's Kiss And Make Up' single. In 1990 the trio became a quintet with the arrival of Michael Hiscock (b. 24 February 1966, Carshalton, Surrey, England; bass) and Annemari Davies (b. 9 February 1971, Oxfordshire, England; guitar/keyboards). Having previously only issued material on 7-inch and mini-albums (including the 10-inch *Snowball*), it was not until 1991 that the group released their first full albums. The first, *Coastal* was a retrospective and *For Keeps*, a mature collection that promised much in the future. However, after the release of the acclaimed 'Missing The Moon', the Field Mice's frustrating reluctance to project a potentially rewarding higher profile, and a growing estrangement with their label, eventually led to the group dissolving in November 1991.

Albums: *Snowball* (1989), *Skywriting* (1990), *For Keeps* (1991). Compilation: *Coastal* (1991).

Fields Of The Nephilim

This British rock group were formed in Stevenage, Hertfordshire in 1983. Comprising Carl McCoy (vocals), Tony Pettitt (bass), Peter Yates (guitar) and the Wright brothers, Nod (b. Alexander; drums) and Paul (guitar). Their image, was that of a neo-western/desperado borrowed from such films as *Once Upon A Time In America* and *The Long Ryders*. They also had the bizarre habit of smothering their, predominantly black, clothes in flour/talc. Their version of Goth-rock, tempered with transatlantic overtones found favour with those already immersed in the sounds of the Sisters Of Mercy and the Mission. Signed to the Situation Two label, the Fields Of The Nephilim scored three major UK Independent hit singles with 'Preacher Man', the *Burning The Field* EP and 'Blue Water', while their first album, *Dawn Razor* gave a modest showing in the UK album chart. The second album, *The Nephilim*, reached number 14, announcing the group's arrival as one of the main rock acts of the day. Their devoted following also ensured a showing on the national singles chart, giving them minor hits with 'Moonchild' (1988 - also an independent chart number 1), 'Psychonaut' (1989) and 'Summerland (Dreamed)' (1990). In October 1991, McCoy left the group taking the 'Fields Of The Nephilim' name with him. The remaining members have since vowed to carry on. With the recruitment of a new vocalist, Alan Delaney, they have yet to name themselves, and

McCoy has to date yet to unveil his version of the Nephilim.

Albums: *Dawn Razor* (1987), *The Nephilim* (1988), *Elyzium* (1990), *Earth Inferno* (1991).

Fine Young Cannibals

This sophisticated English pop trio from the Midlands appeared after the demise of the Beat in 1983. Former members Andy Cox (b. 25 January 1960, Birmingham, England; guitar) and David Steele (b. 8 September 1960, Isle of Wight, England; bass/keyboards) invited Roland Gift (b. 28 April 1961, Birmingham, England; ex-Acrylic Victims and actor for the Hull Community Theatre; vocals) to relinquish his tenure in a London blues combo to join them. Taking their name from the Robert Wagner movie of similar name (relinquishing the 'All The' prefix), the group were quickly picked up by London Records after a video screening on the UK music television show *The Tube*. 'Johnny Come Home' was soon released on single, with the band joined on percussion by Martin Parry and on trumpet by Graeme Hamilton. Dominated by Gift's sparse and yearning vocal, it reached the UK Top 10 and defined the band's sound for years to come. The follow-up 'Blue' set out an early political agenda for the band, attacking Conservative Government policy and its effects. After the band's debut album rose to UK number 11, the first of a series of distinctive cover versions emerged with 'Suspicious Minds'. Backing vocals were handled by Jimmy Somerville. It was followed by a surprise, and radical, rendition of 'Ever Fallen In Love', which the Buzzcocks' Steve Diggle claimed he preferred to his band's original. Meanwhile Gift's parallel acting career got underway with the parochial *Sammy And Rosie Get Laid*, after all three members of the band had appeared in the previous year's *Tin Men*. While Gift's commitments continued Cox and Steele became involved in the release of an opportunistic house cut, 'I'm Tired Of Being Pushed Around', under the title Two Men, A Drum Machine And A Trumpet. On the back of regular club airings it became a surprise Top 20 hit in February 1988. More importantly, it attracted the interest of several dance acts who would seek out the duo for remixes, including Wee Papa Girl Rappers and Pop Will Eat Itself. Before the unveiling of Gift's latest film, *Scandal*, the band scored their biggest hit to date with the rock/dance fusion of 'She Drives Me Crazy'. The second album duly followed, featuring cultivated soul ballads to complement further material of a politically direct nature. It would top the charts on both sides of the Atlantic. Of the five singles taken from the album 'Good Thing' was the most successful, claiming a second US number 1. In 1990 they won both Best British Group and Best Album categories at the BRIT Awards, but felt compelled to return them because: '. . . it is wrong and inappropriate for us to be associated with what amounts to a photo opportunity for Margaret Thatcher and the Conservative Party'. It led to a predictable backlash in the right wing tabloid press. In 1990 Gift's appeared in Hull Truck's *Romeo And Juliet* stage performance, and left Cox and Steele to work on a remixed version of *The Raw And The Cooked*.

Albums: *Fine Young Cannibals* (1985), *The Raw And The Cooked* (1989).

Fingerprintz

This quirky Scottish new wave band was led by Jimmy O'Neil. They also included drummer Dogdan Wiczling, and acted as Lene Lovich's backing band for a time (O'Neil wrote her hit single 'Say When'). Their own releases included the 1981 single 'Shadowed', and their second album was produced by Nick Garvey of the Motors. O'Neil and Wiczling went on to play on Jaquie Brooke's album *Sob Stories*. Wiczling also toured and recorded with Adam Ant.

Albums: *The Very Dab* (1979), *Distinguishing Marks* (1980), *Beat Noire* (1981).

Finn, Tim

b. 25 June 1952, Te Awamutu, New Zealand. As lead singer of the New Zealand band Split Enz, Finn was recognized as a major songwriter and vocalist with a very distinctive singing voice. Even before the dissolution of the band in 1985, he had recorded his first solo album, *Escapade* on A&M, which became the Top Album of 1983 in Australia, featuring the singles, 'Fraction Too Much Friction', 'Made My Day' and 'Staring At The Embers', all excellent melodic pop tunes. The set also made a minor impact on the US charts. However, despite a high budget and more emphasis on production, his follow-up albums were not successful although they did provide one charting single. Moving from A&M to Virgin in 1985, he released *Big Canoe*, but the high budgets and strong emphasis on production buried his songs under layers of sound and the melodies were lost. A move to Capitol Records resulted the critically acclaimed self-titled album, but commercial success eluded him. The move to Capitol made it easy for Finn in 1991 to join stablemates Crowded House - the group formed by his brother Neil after the break up of Split Enz six years earlier. After achieving international success with Crowded House, and after the release of *Woodface*, Finn elected to return to a solo career in 1992.

Albums: *Escapade* (1983), *Big Canoe* (1986), *Tim Finn* (1989).

Fire Engines

Alongside UK Postcard label bands such as Orange Juice, Josef K and the Associates, the Fire Engines

were part of a burgeoning Scottish music scene in the early 80s. Formed in 1979 by David Henderson (vocals/guitar), Murray Slade (guitar), Russell Burn (drums/percussion) and Graham Main (bass), the band's debut surfaced on the independent label Codex Communications in late 1980. 'Get Up And Use Me' was a manic burst of estranged, frenetically delivered guitar broken by sharp, vocal outbursts. It also cut through the surrounding tendency for dense, synthesized sounds or second rate punk. The group received considerable promotion in the music press and were strongly tipped for success by the influential *New Musical Express. Lubricate Your Living Room (Background Music For Action People!)*, a mini-album's worth of near-instrumentals on the Accessory label, contained a similar barrage of awkward, angular funk guitar riffs. By spring 1981, the band had signed with aspiring Scottish label Pop: Aural releasing the excellent 'Candy Skin'. More overtly pop (Henderson's nasal tones were to the forefront for the first time), the single was backed by 'Meat Whiplash', a superb slab of nasty, breakneck guitar work conflicting with an aggressive drum rhythm. By comparison, 'Big Gold Dream' (1981) was relatively melodic, perhaps in an attempt to reach a wider audience. It failed, although all the Fire Engines' product fared well in Independent terms, and it was to be the band's last release. Ideologically, the Fire Engines tapped a similar aesthetic to Josef K, fuelled by a vehement hatred of 'rock' in the general sense and the realization that punk's spirit of innovation had to be continued. Both bands were true to that ethic, imploding rather than growing stale. Henderson, went on to form Win, managed by Postcard founder Alan Horne.
Album: *Lubricate Your Living Room (Background Music For Action People!)* (1981).

Firehose

This propulsive US hardcore trio was formed by two ex-members of the Minutemen, Mike Watt (bass) and George Hurley (drums), following the death of the latter group's founding guitarist D. Boon. Ed Crawford, aka eD fROMOHIO, completed the new venture's line-up which made its debut in 1987 with the impressive *Ragin', Full-On*. Although undeniably powerful, the material Firehose offered was less explicit than that of its predecessor, and showed a greater emphasis on melody. Successive releases, *If'n* and *fROMOHIO*, reveal a group which, although bedevilled by inconsistency, is nonetheless capable of inventive, exciting music. In 1991 the trio signed to the Columbia label.
Albums: *Ragin', Full-On* (1987), *If'n* (1988), *fROMOHIO* (1989), *Flyin' The Flannel* (1991).

Fisher, Morgan

Beginning his apprenticeship with Mott The Hoople as a pianist in 1973, initially only for live appearances, Fisher went on to form the abbreviated Mott in May 1975 with Dale Griffin and Overend Watts. They were completed by new members Ray Major and Nigel Benjamin, becoming the British Lions in May 1977 with John Fidler (ex-Medicine Head) replacing Benjamin. After two albums they split in the late 70s, and Fisher produced two albums for Cherry Red as Hybrid Kids (*A Collection Of Classic Mutants* and *Claws*). The first of these was supposedly filled by unknown new wave acts doing cover versions, but was actually Fisher and a few cronies. The tracks included Jah Wurzel's (Jah Wobble meets the Wurzels) 'Wuthering Heights', British Standard Unit's 'Do Ya Think I'm Sexy', the Burton's 'MacArthur Park', and a new version of 'All The Young Dudes'. Another 'concept' album, *Miniatures*, came out on Fisher's own Pipe label, and featured various artists doing songs less than a minute long. Included among the 51 tracks are Dave Vanian (Damned), John Otway, Andy Partridge (XTC), Robert Wyatt, George Melly, the Residents and David Cunningham. The album was later reissued on micro-cassette, presumably suitable solely for playing on dictaphones. Fisher has continued to record for Cherry Red throughout the 80s.
Albums: *A Collection Of Classic Mutants* (1980), *Miniatures* (1980), *Claws* (1982), *Seasons* (1983), *Look At Life* (1984), *Ivories* (1987).

Fischer Z

Basically a vehicle for the talents of musician/songwriter John Watts, Fischer Z was a bridge between new wave pop and the synthesizer wave of the early 80s. Watts and three other musicians performed on their first two albums, but by the time of the third Watts had taken over the keyboards and was co-producing as well. The first two singles, 'Wax Dolls' and 'Remember Russia', were both well received. The latter even boasted a Ralph Steadman cartoon sleeve. However, it was 'The Worker' in 1979 that gave them their sole single success. In 1982 Watt started recording under his own name. However, singles like 'I Smelt Roses In The Underground' and 'Mayday Mayday' attracted little interest.
Albums: *Word Salad* (1979), *Going Deaf For A Living* (1980), *Red Skies Over Paradise* (1981). John Watt solo *One More Twist* (1982), *The Iceberg Model* (1983).

Fist (Canada)

This Canadian heavy rock quartet were formed in 1978 by vocalist/guitarist Ron Chenier. After several false starts and numerous line-up changes the band stabilized with Chenier, plus Laurie Curry (keyboards), Bob Moffat (bass) and Bob Patterson (drums). Influenced by Triumph, Rush and Led Zeppelin, they released six albums of generally average hard rock between 1979-85, with *In The Red* from 1983, being undoubtedly the strongest. This featured the highly talented Dave McDonald on lead vocals instead of Chenier, who lacked both range and power. In order to prevent confusion with the British band Fist, their albums were released under the name Myofist in Europe.

Albums: *Round One* (1979), *Hot Spikes* (1980), *Fleet Street* (1981), *Thunder In Rock* (1982), *In The Red* (1982), *Danger Zone* (1985).

Fist (UK)

Formed In Newcastle-upon-Tyne, England in 1978 the band's original line-up consisted of Keith Satchfield (vocals/guitar), Dave Irwin (guitar), John Wylie (bass) and Harry Hill (drums). The band released a couple of mediocre singles via Neat Records in 1979. However, seeing potential, MCA Records signed the band and released their debut album *Turn The Hell On* in 1980. The album was a lacklustre affair of standard hard rock and was largely overlooked by both press and the public. Owing to this the band were subsequently dropped by MCA, and Satchfield left the band in 1981. Determined to carry on, the band replaced the departed vocalist/guitarist with Glenn Coates (vocals) and John Roach (guitar). The band then re-signed to Neat Records and released their second album *Back With A Vengeance* in 1982. Even though it was an improvemnet on their previous release, it still failed to attract any real interest.

Albums: *Turn The Hell On* (1980), *Back With A Vengeance* (1982).

Five Thirty

This north London based trio consisted óf Tara Milton (vocals/bass), Paul Bassett (vocals/guitar) and Phil Hooper (drums). The name was taken as a reaction against the grind of 9 to 5 employment: 'It's the time when everyone goes home and gets ready to go out'. A previous incarnation featuring Milton and Bassett had recorded the single 'Catcher In The Rye' shortly after they had left school. After three further singles with the new line-up, and a series of well received, energetic live outings, they recorded their album debut, *Bed*, on East West Records. Motivated by the Jam, in spirit if not style, they were one of a number of similar sounding bands to break through in 1991, and achieve approval from the rock press for their energetic live performances.

Album: *Bed* (1991).

Flatmates

The Flatmates were formed in Bristol, England by Subway Organization label boss and guitarist Martin Whitehead in the summer of 1985, while he was promoting gigs. Whitehead recruited Rocker (drums), soon joined by Deb Haynes (vocals) and Kath Beach (bass), spurred on by the sounds of the Velvet Underground, Blondie, the Stooges and the Ramones. After Kath was replaced by Sarah Fletcher in 1986, the Flatmates issued the frothy 'I Could Be In Heaven' on Subway. 'Happy All The Time' continued the power pop vein the following year, which also saw Joel O'Bierne drafted in as the new drummer. The Flatmates' third single, 'You're Gonna Cry' (1987) was followed by 'Shimmer' (1988), the latter featuring guitarist Tim Rippington's debut. Like its predecessors, this fared well in the Independent charts and justified the release of the band's BBC radio session for disc jockey Janice Long. Fletcher's departure was followed by the release of 'Heaven Knows', although this proved to be the band's last single. Rippington left in October 1988 after an on-stage fight with Whitehead, and the Flatmates eventually split the following April. A retrospective singles compilation, *Love And Death*, rounded it all off, by which time ex-members were busy with other projects. Martin and Joel formed the Sweet Young Things, later member Jackie Carrera (bass) had joined the Caretaker Race and Rocker teamed up with the Rosehips. After Subway folded in the spring of 1990, Whitehead started up a new label and fanzine, *Blaster!* As a final aside, the Flatmates' road manager Paul Roberts has since enjoyed a higher commercial profile than the band ever did with his outfit K-Class.

Compilation: *Love And Death* (1989).

Flesh For Lulu

Flesh For Lulu

This UK rock band were the creation of singer/guitarist Nick Marsh and drummer James Mitchell and took their name from an American cult movie. They were joined by Rocco Barker (ex-Wasted Youth) on guitar and Glen Bishop, replaced by Kevin Mills (ex-Specimen) on bass after the single

'Restless'. Derek Greening (keyboards/guitar) became the fifth member shortly afterwards. Previously their debut single had been 'Roman Candle' prefacing a first album which they would 'rather forget about'. *Blue Sisters Swing*, on the tiny Hybrid label, followed as a stop gap. The sleeve illustration of two nuns kissing resulted in bans in the USA and Europe. The release of *Big Fun City* was the first to do the band justice, even though it was hampered by artwork problems at Polydor Records, and featured everything from country ballads to basic rock 'n' roll. Their succession of labels grew longer as they moved on to Beggars Banquet in 1986. *Long Live The New Flesh* followed a year later, recorded at Abbey Road Studios and produced by Mike Hedges. Their approach to the sophistication of their new surroundings was typical: 'Forget the cerebral approach - just turn up them guitars!' Their most pop orientated album to date, *Plastic Fantastic*, was recorded in Australia by Mark Opitz, several titles from which were later employed for film soundtracks (*Uncle Buck* and *Flashback*). By this time, original members Marsh, Barking and Greening had been joined by Hans Perrson (drums) and Mike Steed (bass). Despite stronger songwriting than had been evident on previous recordings, the album failed and Beggars did not renew their option.
Albums: *Flesh For Lulu* (1984), *Blue Sisters Swing* (1985), *Big Fun City* (1985), *Long Live The New Flesh* (1987), *Plastic Fantastic* (1990).

Fleshtones

Formed in 1976 in the Queens district of New York City, the Fleshtones were first heard on British shores as part of a 'package' tour around 1980 with the dB's, the Raybeats and the Bush Tetras. Each band was different, drawing energy from punk and ideas from long ago. In the Fleshtones' case, Keith Strong (guitar), Peter Zaremba (vocals/keyboards), Jan Marek Pukulski (bass) and Bill Milhizer (drums, ex-Harry Toledo Band and Action Combo), fused the new wave with R&B and rockabilly. The group caught the attention of Miles Copeland's IRS label via 'American Beat', their debut single from 1979 on the Red Star label. The 12-inch EP *Up-Front* duly surfaced in 1980 in America, although it was not until 1981 that its strongest track, 'The Girl From Baltimore', secured a British release. It was followed by 'The World Has Changed' (though only in the US), and 'Shadow-Line' in early 1982. This coincided not only with the band's first official long player, *Roman Gods* but also *Blast Off!*, a cassette of their unreleased 1978 studio album on Reach Out International Records. All was comparatively quiet for over a year until the Fleshtones' unleashed *Hexbreaker*, promoted by two singles, 'Right Side Of A Good Thing' and the evocative 'Screaming Skull'

(both 1983). The material shared the hard rock 'n' roll sound of *Roman Gods*, but the band soon curtailed their activities, apart from the strange *Fleshtones Vs Reality* set in 1987.
Albums: *Roman Gods* (1982), *Blast Off!* (1982), *Hexbreaker* (1983), *Fleshtones Vs Reality* (1987).

Flipper

San Francisco punk band, Flipper, formed in 1979 with original members Will Shatter (vocals), Steve DePace (drums) both former members of Negative Trend, Bruce Lose (bass/vocals) and Ted Falconi (guitar). and also of Negative Trend, on drums. Following the single 'Love Canal'/'Ha Ha' on Subterranean, the group released its debut, and best-known album, *Generic Flipper*, in 1982. Sporting topical lyrics and both hardcore punk and noisy dirges, the album is recognized as a classic of west coast punk. Other albums followed on Subterranean in 1984 and 1986, but the following year Shatter died of an accidental heroin overdose.
Albums: *Generic Flipper* (1982), *Gone Fishin'* (1984), *Public Flipper Ltd.* (1986).

Flux Of Pink Indians

This UK Punk band was formed from the ashes of the Epileptics (who later changed their name to Epi-X due to letters of complaint from The British Epilepsy Association). Two surviving members were Colin (vocals) and Derek Birkett (b. 18 February 1961, London, England; bass), who would go on to form Flux Of Pink Indians, with guitarist Andy and drummer Sid. Their debut EP *Neu Smell* emerged on Crass Records. Alongside standard rejections of society, war, and the eating of flesh lay the joyful 'Tube Disasters', the sort of humour which was in short order in the grim world of anarcho punk. Sid (later Rubella Ballet) was soon replaced by Bambi, formerly of Discharge, while Andy was replaced by Simon. However, both departed quickly for their original band, the Insane, and were replaced by old Epileptics guitarist Kevin Hunter and drummer Martin Wilson. Their debut album *Strive To Survive Causing Least Suffering Possible* confirmed the promise of the single, and premiered the band's own Spiderleg label. Alongside standard thrash numbers were highly perceptive attacks on consumer society. The anti-religious 'Is Anybody There' was a particularly effective example, using simple but jarring lyrics to emphasize its point. The follow-up, *The Fucking Cunts Treat Us Like Pricks* was unsurprisingly banned by the retailers HMV, and copies were seized by Greater Manchester police from Eastern Bloc record shop, which was charged with displaying 'Obscene Articles For Publication For Gain'. The album, ironically, concerned violence between men and women, based on the experiences of a band member who had been sexually assaulted. The music contained within, was little short of a directionless cacophony, however. *Uncarved Block* was the most unexpected of the band's three studio albums, delivering more polemic allied to dance and funk rhythms which left their previous audience totally non-plussed. It was a brave effort, and one which, alongside their debut, stands up to repeated listening. Birkett, making use of his experiences with Spiderleg, has gone on to set up the highly successful One Little Indian label, and still uses the Flux title for occasional projects: 'Flux is just me and whoever I happen to be recording with'.

Albums: *Strive To Survive Causing Least Suffering Possible* (1982), *The Fucking Cunts Treat Us Like Pricks* (1984), *Uncarved Block* (1985), *Treat* (1986).

Flys

This UK Coventry-based group enjoyed a minor league role in the new wave, but owed more to power pop and astute songwriting than punk. Singer and guitarist Neil O'Connor (brother of Hazel O'Connor) met school kids David Freeman (guitar/vocals) and Joe Hughes (bass/vocals) in the mid-70s, and formed Midnight Circus, eventually recruiting Pete King on drums. A name change to the Flys coincided with the discovery of punk's first tremors and after a demo in April 1977 brought an apathetic response from the usual channels. The band issued *Bunch Of Five*, an energetic EP on their own Zama label in time for Christmas. Quick as a flash, EMI snapped them up, rushing out one of the EP tracks (and perhaps their finest ever moment), 'Love And A Molotov Cocktail', as a single. After a tour with the Buzzcocks and John Otway And Wild Willy Barrett came 'Fun City', recorded at Pathway Studios. *Waikiki Beach Refugees* (also the title of their next single) emerged in October 1978 to an enthusiastic response, while the band toured Europe. 1979 saw a flurry of singles - 'Beverley' in February, 'Name Dropping' in April and 'We Are The Lucky Ones' - but internal quarrels led to the recruitment of a riotous new drummer Graham Deakin (ex-Frankie Miller and John Entwistle's Ox). *Flys Own*, rawer than their debut, coincided with a tour with the Ruts in autumn 1979. The EP *Four From The Square* was released in February as the band were transferred to Parlophone Records, this was followed by 'What Will Mother Say' in May 1980. Internal pressures began to erupt and the Flys split up. O'Connor joined Hazel for two years and two albums before becoming a musical arranger, and then producer and engineer. Freeman issued a cover of the Supremes' 'Stop! In The Name Of Love', took a degree, published his poetry, sung on Alison Moyet's *Raindancing* and later formed the Lover Speaks with Hughes (after his spell with ex-Specials Roddy

Radiation And His Tearjerkers). Pete King, meanwhile, joined After The Fire, but sadly died aged 26. See For Miles records recently compiled an excellent self-titled retrospective of the band.

Albums: *Waikiki Beach Refugees* (1978), *Flys Own* (1979). Compilation: *The Flys* (1991).

Foetus

You've Got Foetus On Your Breath, Scraping Foetus Off The Wheel, Foetus Uber Alles, Foetus Inc. . . . all these titles are actually the pseudonym of one person: Australian emigre, Jim Thirlwell, alias Jim Foetus, Clint Ruin. After founding his own record company, Self Immolation in 1980, he set about 'recording works of aggression, insight and inspiration'. Backed with evocatively descriptive musical slogans such as 'positive negativism' and 'bleed now pay later', Foetus released a series of albums, several of which appeared through Stevo's Some Bizarre label. With stark one-word titles such as *Deaf*, *Ache*, *Hole* and *Nail*, Thirlwell presented a harrowing aural netherworld of death, lust, disease and spiritual decay. In November 1983, Foetus undertook a rare tour, performing with Marc Almond, Nick Cave and Lydia Lunch in the short-lived Immaculate Consumptive. Apart from these soul-mates, Foetus has also played live with the Swans' Rolli Mossiman in Wiseblood, Lydia Lunch in Stinkfist, and appeared on albums by several artist including The The, Einsturzende Neubauten, Nurse With Wound and Anne Hogan.

Albums: *Deaf* (1981), *Ache* (1981), *Hole* (1981), *Nail* (1985), *Bedrock* (1987), *Thaw* (1988), *Sink* (1990).

4AD

Few independent record labels can boast as distinctive a roster as 4AD, both aesthetically and musically. The label was formed in early 1980 by Ivo Watts-Russell and Peter Kent (who were both then working at Beggars Banquet) reputedly after hearing a demo from new act Modern English. At first, the label was called Axis for the initial clutch of singles by the Fast Set, the Bearz, Shox and most importantly Bauhaus, but this was changed to avoid confusion with a similar-named company and 4AD was born. A loan of £2,000 from Beggars Banquet ensured that 4AD got off the ground, signing Modern English, In Camera, Mass, Dance Chapter and Rema Rema, among others. Kent soon left to set up Situation 2, working heavily with Bauhaus who shortly graduated to Beggars Banquet. 4AD, however, steered away from their parent company, witnessing a one-off single for the then-unknown The The (and later, Matt Johnson's solo album), plus several uncompromising recordings from Australian outfit the Birthday Party, and providing a home for ex-Wire personnel Bruce Gilbert, Graham Lewis/Cupol and Colin Newman.

1981-82 brought new acts as eclectic as Sort Col, the Past Seven Days, My Captains, Dif Juz and the Happy Family, alongside solo works from ex-Bauhaus individuals David Jay and Daniel Ash/Tones On Tail and a collaboration between Lydia Lunch and the Birthday Party's Rowland S. Howard. More significanttly, Ivo stumbled upon the Cocteau Twins, who were to prove the act that aside from emerging as the label's major artists, crystalized the ethereal nature often associated with 4AD product, aided later by the oblique yet attractive sleeve designs from Vaughn Oliver's 23 Envelope art studio. There was also Colourbox, another 4AD mainstay who embodied the label's experimental approach to recording and the studio, as well as goth-band X-Mal Deutschland. Ivo soon teamed with the Cocteaus among others, for his own project in 1983, This Mortal Coil, which enjoyed both critical and commercial support.

Apart from Dead Can Dance, Xymox, Richenel and the Wolfgang Press, the mid-80s saw few signings as 4AD concentrated on their existing roster. The late 80s, on the other hand, signalled a slight reappraisal, with the departure of Colourbox and the signing of new American acts Throwing Muses, Boston exports the Pixies and New York's Ultra Vivid Scene. The influential but often-ignored A.R. Kane also arrived for a brief time, which spawned a one-off project with some of Colourbox, M.A.R.R.S's 'Pump Up The Volume'. A UK number 1 hit, this pivotal single was perhaps the first successful mesh of white rock and dance backgrounds, paving the way for a commercial and artistic revolution in both British dance and independent music. Then came the two-pronged attack of guitar bands Lush and the Pale Saints to see in the new decade, as the Pixies made serious commercial headway. In their wake came the Breeders, a project between involving Pixies, Throwing Muses and others. Treading a tightrope between financial well-being and artistic purity, 4AD has spotlighted an impressive yet diverse roster not only throughout the 80s but during the 90s as well.

Compilation: *Lonely Is An Eyesore* (1987).

400 Blows

Coming together in 1981 in Croydon, London, England, this versatile ensemble combined funk, reggae, African music and disco. Their obvious influences, in addition to various ethnic styles, included 23 Skidoo and Throbbing Gristle. The debut release was 'Beat The Devil', much in the vein of Cabaret Voltaire, which attracted the attention of Illuminated Records. The band was basically the creation of Edward Beer, who dismissed original collaborator Scott Fraser after the single. The two Anthonys, Thorpe and Lea, were recruited, but Beer

continued to maintain artistic control. Early controversy surrounded the title of their debut album *If I Kissed Her, I'd Have To Kill Her First*, which begged the question of whether or not they liked women; 'Oh,. . . maybe sexually I like them, but I don't like having them around that much. They just get on my nerves', was Beer's dubious reply. A minor hit came with 'Movin'', an update of the old Brass Construction number, at which point Beer had been joined by female vocalist Lee. By the late 80s and early 90s they were turning to the disco beat of acid house, releasing singles including 'Champion Sound' on Warrior Records.

Albums: *If I Kissed Her, I'd Have To Kill Her First* (1985), *The Good Clean English Fist* (1985), *Look* (1986).

4 Skins

As their name suggests, this UK band comprised four skinheads, who specialized in vitriolic three-chord 'yob-rock'. Taking their musical brief from outfits such as Sham 69, the Angelic Upstarts and the Cockney Rejects, they were a third generation punk band associated with the Oi movement. With a blatantly patriotic image, the band attracted National Front supporters to their live shows, which often erupted into full-scale riots. Lyrically they expounded on racism, police brutality, corrupt governments and the capitalist system in general. However, musically they were not so adventurous, being rigidly formularized and unable to develop from their simplistic origins. From a creative standpoint, the band had ground to a halt by 1983. Their fan-base continued to contract and they soon faded into oblivion.

Albums: *The Good, The Bad And The 4 Skins* (1981), *Wonderful World Of The 4 Skins* (1981), *Live And Loud* (1982), *A Fistful Of 4 Skins* (1983), *From Chaos To 1984* (1984), *Few 4 Skins More Vol. 1* (1985), *Few 4 Skins More Vol. 2* (1985).

14 Iced Bears

Few bands epitomized the mid-80s 'shambling' pop music scene in Britain more succinctly than Brighton's 14 Iced Bears. Formed in 1985 by Rob Sekula (b. 12 December 1963, Camberwell, Surrey, England), Alan White and Nick Emery, the band quickly became embroiled in an alternative network peppered with anoraks, cheap fanzines and guitar-based songs for which the word 'amateur' was probably invented. With more line-up changes than record releases, 14 Iced Bears' history is almost as shambolic as their music. Alan White soon departed to form Pleasure Splinters, to be replaced by Dominic Minques and guitarist Kevin Canham (b. 10 October 1964, Aldershot, Hampshire, England). Nick Roughley (b. West Riding, Yorkshire, England)

joined for the band's second single in 1987 before leaving to form Blow Up. Steve Ormsby and Bill Cox briefly replaced Minques and Emery before 1988 when 14 Iced Bears - then consisting of Sekula, Kevin Canham, Will Taylor (b. 23 August 1968, Brighton, Sussex, England; bass) and Graham Durrant (b. 10 October 1963, Camberwell, Surrey, England; drums) - finally got around to making an album. After suffering from the curse of 'shambling', *14 Iced Bears* demonstrated an admirable progression towards heavier, more psychedelic territories and benifitted from a scattering of warmly surprised responses from the UK music press. Fittingly, this line-up remained stable until 1991 when Tim White (b. 30 March 1967, Essex, England) replaced Taylor, who had moved over to Blow Up, and 14 Iced Bears recorded their second 60s-tinged album, *Wonder*. Soon after, an extra chapter was added to the Bears' story when White made way for Rob Colley (b. 27 June 1963, Brighton, Sussex, England) formerly in Whirl.
Albums: *14 Iced Bears* (1988), *Wonder* (1991). Compilation: *Precision* (1990).

Foxton, Bruce

b. 1 September 1955, Woking, Surrey, England. Following the break-up of the Jam, guitarist Foxton set out on a predictably difficult solo career. During the summer of 1983, he enjoyed UK Top 30 success with 'Freak'. His strong, straightforward pop, with often distinct Jam overtones, was generally well-produced, with Steve Littlewhite's 'This Is The Way', proving particularly effective. In 1984, Foxton released *Touch Sensitive*, which featured all-original compositions and another solid production. While deserving chart success, Foxton's work has, not surprisingly, been compared unfavourably with that of the Jam and, consequently, his solo career has suffered.
Album: *Touch Sensitive* (1984).

Foxx, John

b. Dennis Leigh Chorley, Lancashire, England. Foxx moved to London in 1974 and was a key instigator of 70s electro-pop. He was the founder member of Ultravox with whom he wrote, sang and dabbled in synthetic noises, before handing over to Midge Ure. Gary Numan cited him as his main influence, which was some consolation for the fact that Numan was having hits when Ultravox were dropped by Island Records. Foxx went solo in 1979 and formed his own label MetalBeat, distributed by Virgin. The infectious 'Underpass' began a short string of minor Top 40 UK hits which included 'No-One Driving', 'Burning Car' and 'Europe After The Rain'. Foxx's appearances on the singles and album charts ended in the mid-80s.
Albums: *Metamatic* (1980), *The Garden* (1981), *The*

Golden Section (1983), *In Mysterious Ways* (1985).

Frank Chickens

Formed by Kazuko Hohki (b. 1952, Tokyo, Japan; vocals) and Kazumi Taguchi (later replaced by Atsuko Kamura). The duo met in London in 1978 working with the Japanese-American Toy Theatre. The JATT would perform extracts from classic fiction using, for example toy figurines and mechanical robots and 'Godzilla' models as the central characters to the play. This bizarre concept was given publicity by BBC Radio 1 producer John Walters' *Walters' Week*. The Frank Chickens achieved something of a cult hit with 'Blue Canary' in 1985 which received airplay from disc jockey John Peel (whose producer was Walters). As well as depicting a socio-comic view of the modern Japanese woman in western society, the Frank Chickens also tackled the subject of the western male's perception of Japanese women in general, as in 'Yellow Toast'. Kazuko was, to some degree, also instrumental in popularizing the phenomenon of Karaoke to English culture by way of the Channel Four television programme, *The Karaoke Klub*. The Frank Chickens have continued to perform on the London fringe theatre and cabaret club circuit into the 90s.
Albums: *We Are Frank Chickens* (1984), *Get Chickenised* (1987), *Club Monkey* (1988), *Do The Karaoke* (1989). Compilation: *The Best Of Frank Chickens* (1987).

Frankie Goes To Hollywood

Formed in the summer of 1980, this Liverpool group comprised former Big In Japan vocalist Holly Johnson (b. William Johnson, 19 February 1960, Khartoum, Sudan) backed by Paul Rutherford (b. 8 December 1959, Liverpool, England; vocals), Nasher Nash (b. Brian Nash, 20 May 1963; guitar), Mark O'Toole (b. 6 January 1964, Liverpool, England; bass) and Peter Gill (b. 8 March 1964, Liverpool, England; drums). It was a further two years before the group started to make any real headway with television appearances and a record deal with Trevor Horn's label ZTT. Their debut single, 'Relax', produced by Horn, was a pyrotechnic production and superb dance track with a suitably suggestive lyric that led to a BBC radio and television ban in Britain. Paradoxically, the censorship produced even greater public interest in the single which topped the UK charts for five weeks, selling close to two million copies in the process. The promotion behind Frankie, engineered by former music journalist Paul Morley, was both clever and inventive, utilizing marketing techniques such as single word slogans and the production of best selling T-shirts that offered the enigmatic message 'Frankie Says...' The group's peculiar image of Liverpool laddishness coupled with the unashamed homosexuality of vocalists Johnson and Rutherford merely added to their curiosity value and sensationalism, while also providing them with a distinctive identity that their detractors seriously underestimated.

The follow up to 'Relax' was the even more astonishing 'Two Tribes'. An awesome production built round a throbbing, infectiously original riff, it showed off Johnson's distinctive vocal style to striking effect. Like all Frankie's singles, the record was available in various 7-inch and 12-inch remixed formats with superb packaging and artwork. The power of the single lay not merely in its appropriately epic production but the topicality of its lyric which dealt with the escalation of nuclear arms and the prospect of global annihilation. In order to reinforce the harrowing theme, the group included a chilling voice over from actor Patrick Allen taken from government papers on the dissemination of information to the public in the event of nuclear war. Allen's Orwellian instructions on how to avoid fall out while disposing of dogs, grandparents and other loved ones gave the disc a frightening authenticity that perfectly captured the mood of the time. Johnson's closing lines of the song, borrowed from an unnamed literary source, provided a neat rhetorical conclusion: 'Are we living in a land where sex and horror are the new gods?' The six-minute plus version of 'Two Tribes' was played in its entirety on UK lunch time radio shows and duly entered the chart at number 1, remaining in the premier position for an incredible nine weeks while the revitalized 'Relax' nestled alongside its successor at number 2. A Godley And Creme promotional film of 'Two Tribes' which featured caricatures of US President Reagan and Soviet leader Mr. Chernenko wrestling was rightly acclaimed as one of the best videos of the period and contributed strongly to the Frankie package.

Having dominated the upper echelons of the chart like no other artist since the Beatles, the pressure to produce an album for the Christmas market was immense. Welcome To The Pleasure Dome finally emerged as a double with a number of cover versions including interesting readings of Bruce Springsteen's 'Born To Run', Dionne Warwick's 'Do You Know The Way To San Jose?' and Gerry And The Pacemakers' 'Ferry Cross The Mersey'. Like all Frankie recordings, the sound was epic and glorious and the reviews proclaimed the album an undoubted hit, though some commentators felt its irresistible charm might prove ephemeral. 1984 ended with a necessary change of style as Frankie enjoyed their third number 1 hit with the moving festive ballad 'The Power Of Love'. Thus they joined Gerry And The Pacemakers as only the second act in UK pop history to see their first three singles reach the top.

History repeated itself the following year when, like Gerry, Frankie saw their fourth single ('Welcome To The Pleasure Dome') stall at number 2. Thereafter, they were never again to attain the ascendancy that they had enjoyed during the golden year of 1984.

A sabbatical spent in Eire for tax purposes meant that their comeback in 1986 had to be emphatic. Having failed to conquer America during the same period, merely increased the pressure. Critics had long been claiming that the group were little more than puppets in the hands of a talented producer despite the fact that they sang, played and even wrote their own material. The grand return with 'Rage Hard' (the title borrowed from Dylan Thomas) won them a number 4 UK hit, but that seemed decidedly anti-climactic. The second album, Liverpool, cost a small fortune but lacked the charm and vibrancy of its predecessor. Within a year Frankie split having crammed a decade of sales, creativity and controversy into less than 24 months. In many ways their fate was the perfect pop parable of the 80s. For a group that was so symptomatic of their age, it was appropriate that the Frankie saga should end not in the recording studio, but in the High Court. In a battle royal between Johnson and his former record company ZTT in early 1988, the artist not only won his artistic freedom but substantial damages which were to have vast implications for the British music business as a whole.

Albums: Welcome To The Pleasure Dome (1984), Liverpool (1986).

Frazier Chorus

Originally a four-piece band from Brighton, England, who - under the name Plop! - set out to be the antithesis of Wham!. However, singer and keyboardist Tim Freeman's songs were circulated on a demo and he and the rest of the band (Michéle Allardyce (percussion), Kate Holmes (flute) and Chris Taplin (clarinet) were signed to 4AD under the name of Frazier Chorus, a title taken from the back of a 50s US baseball jacket. With their unusual instrumental line-up which lent an almost synth-pop/pastoral feel, the 4AD debut, 'Sloppy Heart' (1987), did not fit easily with the harder edge the label were moving towards in the mid-80s. The band soon switched to Virgin. In 1989 they released their debut Sue which featured orchestral arrangements from David Bedford and contributions from Tim Sanders (tenor saxophone), Roddy Lorimer (trumpet/flugelhorn) and Simon Clarke (piccolo/saxophones). Freeman's lyrics, sung in an almost whispered singing style, eloquently chronicled a mundane exsistence with keen, ironic observations of an 'everyday' life and sexual relations. Minor UK hits with 'Dream Kitchen' and 'Typical' promised much, but their single releases all failed to break any higher than 51. A

reissue of 'Sloppy Heart' featured a laid-back version of the Sex Pistols' 'Anarchy In The UK' on its b-side. Allardyce left acrimoniously during the recording of the second album (with the Lightning Seeds' Ian Broudie on production) leaving the band as a trio. Allardyce, whose orientation was geared more to dance music, would continue to work as a journalist for disc jockey magazine *Jocks*. Further minor hits included the Paul Oakenfold re-mixes of 'Cloud 8' and 'Nothing', and 1991's 'Walking On Air' confirmed that Frazier Chorus's cult appeal had apparently peaked. Freeman also collaborated on the 4AD house project This Mortal Coil.
Albums: *Sue* (1989), *Ray* (1991).

Freshies

The seeds of this UK pop group were sown in 1971 when Chris Sievey and his brother hitched a lift to London and staged a sit-in at the Beatles' Apple Records headquarters - eventually going on to do a session. Subsequently Sievey recorded numerous demos which were sent to record companies, resulting in an avalanche of rejection slips he later published as a small book. Another book was dedicated to Virgin Records rejections alone. His own label Razz was formed in 1974, releasing a variety of singles, videos and over 60 cassettes. In the meantime, Sievey attempted to form his own band under the title the Freshies. Among a stream of musicians who collaborated were Martin Jackson (later Magazine and Swing Out Sister) and Billy Duffy (later the Cult). The most consistent line-up however, was Barry Spencer (guitar), Rick Sarko (bass, ex-Ed Banger And The Nosebleeds) and Mike Doherty (drums, ex-Smirks), the line-up operating between 1980-82. After several small pressings on Razz, Sievey finally hit the charts with 'I'm In Love With The Girl On The Manchester Virgin Megastore Checkout Desk', when it was re-released by MCA in 1981. Two other curious but enduring singles were also released on the major, the ambiguous anti-war ode 'Wrap Up The Rockets', and the paean to record collecting, 'I Can't Get (Boing Boing) Bouncing Babies By The Teardrop Explodes'. However, after a solitary single on Stiff the band split. Sievey, ever the optimist, went on to a similarly bizarre solo career alongside appearances with his alter-ego Frank Sidebottom. Incredibly, for a band with literally hundreds of songs behind them, the Freshies never released an album.

Fun Boy Three

When the Specials topped the UK charts in June 1981 with 'Ghost Town' few would have guessed that three of their members would depart immediately to form an offshoot group. By October, Terry Hall (vocals), Neville Staples (vocals/drums) and Lynval Golding (guitar) had launched the Fun Boy Three. Their UK Top 20 debut single was the extraordinary 'The Lunatics Have Taken Over The Asylum', a haunting protest against political conservatism, made all the more effective by Hall's deadpan, languid vocal. The single effectively established the trio as both original and innovative commentators, whose work compared favourably with that of their mother group, the Specials. For their follow-up, the Fun Boy Three teamed-up with the then unknown Bananarama for a hit revival of bandleader Jimmie Lunceford's 'It Ain't What You Do It's The Way That You Do It'. The Bananarama connection continued when the Fun Boy Three appeared on their hit 'Really Saying Something'. The girl trio also sang on several tracks of their mentors' self-titled debut album. By 1982, the Fun Boy Three were proving themselves adept at writing political songs and reviving classic songs which they moulded into their own distinctive style. Hall's lazy vocal on George Gershwin's 'Summertime' was a typical example of this and provided another Top 20 hit. The wonderfully cynical comment on teenage love and pregnancy, 'Tunnel Of Love' proved the trio's last major statement. Following a second album, they split during 1983, with Hall going on to form the Colour Field.
Albums: *Fun Boy Three* (1982), *Waiting* (1983).

Furniture

Formed by life-long friends James Irvin (b. 20 July 1959, London, England; lead vocals) and Timothy Whelan (b. 15 September 1958, London, England) with Hamilton Lee (b. 7 September 1958, London, England) in 1981. Having released a single on their own The Guy From Paraguay label, the trio were joined by Sally Still (b. 5 February 1964, London, England; bass) and Maya Gilder (b. 25 April 1964, Poonak, India; keyboards) in 1982 as the band forged a sound peppered with jazzy touches and fuelled by a cinematically-orientated 'bedsit angst'. Basically, Furniture created moody music. Unfortunately, a series of legal disasters undermined any commercial potential: having finally broken through into the mainstream in 1986 with the 'Brilliant Mind' single, Furniture saw the record reach number 21 in the UK chart before their new label, Stiff Records, collapsed and thus halted the rise. The album, *The Wrong People* - a delight for critics and fans alike by virtue of its stark emotions, sweeping pop sensibilities and gentle eccentricities - found itself part of a rescue package from ZTT Records, who eventually fulfilled the 30,000 advance orders and promptly deleted the album. Two years of legal wrangles later, Furniture were able to sign to the Arista label, but a radical restructuring of company personnel saw the band's new album, *Food Sex And Paranoia*, overlooked in all the upheaval. Mutual distrust saw the group depart for pastures new, but when another promised deal fell through Furniture went their separate ways, playing a farewell performance at the Reading Festival in 1990. James Irvin and Sally Still both became journalists on *Melody Maker*, Maya Gilder gained employment at the BBC, while Timothy Whelan worked on a new musical venture named the Transmittors.

Albums: *When The Boom Was On* (1983), *The Wrong People* (1986), *Food Sex And Paranoia* (1990). Compilations: *The Lovemongers* (1986), *She Gets Out The Scrapbook* (1991).

Fuzztones

Obsessed with the psychedelic punk sound of the late 60s, the Fuzztones emerged from New York in the mid-80s. The group consisted of the enigmatic Rudi Protrudi (vocals/guitar, ex-Tina Peel and Devil Dogs), Deb O'Nair (organ, also ex-Tina Peel), Elan Portnoy (guitar), Michael Jay (bass) and Michael Phillips (drums, ex-Polyrock). They had formed during 1980 after the break-up of Tina Peel, and spent their formative years gigging around the east coast of the USA. The Fuzztones' first UK release was a live album, *Leave Your Mind At Home*, on the Midnight Music label in 1984, which combined brash garage guitar riffs with a definite nod to the Cramps. 1985's *Lysergic Emanations* on the independent ABC label was less forthright and delved further into acid rock, although the singles, 'She's Wicked' (1985) and 'Bad News Travels Fast' (1986), were all-out slabs of loud, raunchy guitar rock. All was quiet in their wake as the Fuzztones returned to the States for a while, finally resurfacing in 1988 with 'Nine Months Later' on Music Maniac. However, the label folded after *Creatures That Time Forgot* early in 1989 and the band transferred to Situation 2. 'Hurt On Hold' accompanied the band's second album of that year, *In Heat*. 'Action Speaks Louder Than Words' continued the staple diet of garage trash in 1990 but, by then the Fuzztones' formula seemed to be wearing thin and they have since kept a low profile.

Albums: *Leave Your Mind At Home - Live* (1984), *Lysergic Emanations* (1985), *Creatures That Time Forgot* (1989), *In Heat* (1989).

G

Galactic Cowboys

This US metallic art-rock quartet was formed in 1990 by vocalist Ben Huggins and guitarist Dane Sonnier. With the addition of bassist Monty Colvin and drummer Alan Doss, they specialized in complex and densely melodic song structures that typically exceed the six-minute mark. They combined elements of Kings X, Metallica and Neil Young, with state-of-the-art technology to produce one of 1991's most impressive debut albums. Defying simple categorization, they surprise the listener, with what initially seems the *ad hoc* juxtaposition of incompatible styles. Somehow, the strange fusion works; manic thrashing gives way to harmonica solos, which in turn are followed by four-part vocal harmonies. The Galactic Cowboys are true innovators and are at the forefront of experimental hard-rock.

Albums: *Galactic Cowboys* (1991).

Galas, Diamanda

A confrontational writer whose glass shattering, pristine vocals are derived from the Schrei (shriek) opera of German expressionism where 'sounds become corporal and movements aural'. On stage this is achieved with the aid of four microphones and a system of delays and echoes. Galas is a classically trained Greek American who signed to Y Records in 1982, for which she recorded her debut, before moving on to Mute Records. Her self-titled 1984 album is typical, comprising; two 'endless plays of pain'. 'Panoptikon' deals with Jeremy Bentham's harrowing prison regime, while 'Song From The Blood Of Those Murdered' is dedicated to the Greek women killed by the Junta between 1967 and 1974. Galas went on to produce a series of albums dominated by her banshee-like delivery, rooted more in performance art than any notions of popular music.

Albums: *Litanies Of Satan* (1982), *Diamanda Galas* (1984), *The Divine Punishment* (1986), *Saint Of The Pit* (1987), *You Must Be Certain Of The Devil* (1987), *Plague Mass* (1991).

Galaxie 500

The foundations for Galaxie 500 were laid at a remarkably early stage, when Michael Dean Wareham (b. 1 August 1963, Wellington, New Zealand; guitar/vocals), Naomi Yang (b. 15 September 1964, New York City, New York, USA; bass) and Damon Krukowski (b. 6 September 1963, New York City, New York, USA; drums) met at a New York High School in their mid-teens. It was not until college however that the trio made Galaxie 500 a going concern, manufacturing a fragile, world-weary guitar sound which contrasted sharply with the heavier ambitions of their contemporaries in the American underground scene. Their debut album, *Today*, was a limited affair, appearing on the small local Aurora label in the autumn of 1988. News of this delicate band filtered through to Europe, particularly Britain, within six months, resulting in an international deal with Rough Trade Records and enormous acclaim from the British music press. This swift upward rise continued through two years, two more albums and - on a more bizarre note - a place on a tribute album for legendary Beatles spoof band the Rutles. Then, in the spring of 1991 singer Dean Wareham quit unexpectedly after a lengthy tour of the USA, just as Galaxie 500 were preparing to visit Japan. The band immediately dissolved, leaving Naomi Yang and Damon Krukowski to complete an off-shoot project under the name of Pierre Etoile, which followed Galaxie 500's tortured tradition, before embarking on a new venture with fellow musicians in the Boston, Massachusetts area. Wareham meanwhile guested with 'arty' New York outfit Mercury Rev in between working on solo material.

Albums: *Today* (1988), *On Fire* (1989), *This Is Our Music* (1990).

Gallon Drunk

This high energy UK rock 'n' roll band emerged in the early 90s. The band's line-up comprised James Johnston (vocals/guitar/organ), Mike Delanian (bass), both of whom were at school together, Max Decharne (drummer, also keyboard player with the Earls Of Suave), and Joe Byfield (maraccas), who spent a brief spell with My Bloody Valentine. Formed early in 1990 and based in London, original drummer Nick Combe was soon jettisoned. They quickly garnered plaudits from the music press, the *New Musical Express* describing them as: '. . . a synthesis of quite disparate elements, from Memphis soul slew to primal rockabilly'. Others noted a similarity to the more raucous Birthday Party/Nick Cave recordings. After releasing singles on their manager's own Massive label, they moved on to Clawfist where 1992 saw the release of their debut album.

Album: *Gallon Drunk* (1992).

Game Theory

Based in Sacremento, California, USA, rockband Game Theory comprised: Scott Miller (guitar/vocals/synthesizer), Nancy Becker (keyboards), Fred Juhos (bass) and Michael Irwin (drums) and made its recording debut in 1982. Although loosely associated with the Los Angeles' 'Paisley Underground' movement; (Miller was a previously a member of Alternative Learning with Joe Becker of True West and Thin White Rope), the quartet's progress was determined by their guitarist's infatuation with classic USA pop and melody, rather then temporary fashion. His creation has thus survived several personnel changes, including the leader's own temporary defection, without losing its sense of direction. Miller's fusion of 60s and 80s styles

is expertly captured on *Lolita Nations*, a fruitful partnership with R.E.M./dBs producer Mitch Easter, and *Two Steps From The Middle Ages*, which placed his group on a pop/rock pantheon with the equally accomplished, and under-rated, Shoes.

Albums: *Blaze Of Glory* (1982), *Pointed Accounts Of People You Know* (1983), *Distortion* (1984), *Dead Centre* (1984), *Real Night Time* (1985), *Lolita Nations* (1988), *Two Steps From The Middle Ages* (1988).

Gang Green

This Boston, Massachusetts, USA quartet specializing in a fusion of hardcore and thrash was put together by guitarist/vocalist Chris Doherty. Although formed originally in 1982, it was the 1985 re-incarnation that inked a deal with Taang Records. After numerous line-up changes, a degree of stability was achieved with Doherty, plus Brian Bertzger (drums), Fritz (guitar), and Joe Gittleman (bass), the latter eventually replaced by ex-DRI member Josh Papp. Extolling the virtues of alcohol and ridiculing the PMRC at every given moment, their music is fast, aggressive and occasionally abusive. The highlight of their career is the mini-album *I81B4U*, which has an irreverent sense of fun and puts 'two fingers up' at Van Halen's *OU812*. Unable to progress on the songwriting front, they quickly became stuck in a musical rut. Roadrunner Records lost faith, dropping them from their roster in 1990.

Albums: *Another Wasted Night* (1986), *You Got It* (1987), *I81B4U* (1988), *Older, Budweiser* (1989).

Gang Of Four

Formed in Leeds, Yorkshire, England in 1977, Gang Of Four - Jon King (vocals/melodica), Andy Gill (guitar), Dave Allen (drums) and Hugo Burnham (drums) - made their debut the following year with *Damaged Goods*. This uncompromising three-track EP introduced the group's strident approach, wherein Burham's pounding, compulsive drumming and Gill's staccato, stuttering guitarwork, reminiscent of Wilko Johnson from Dr. Feelgood, framed their overtly political lyrics. The quartet maintained this direction on *Entertainment*, while introducing the interest in dance music which marked future recordings. Its most impressive track, 'At Home He's A Tourist', was issued as a single, but encountered censorship problems over its pre-AIDS reference to prophylactics ('rubbers'). Internal strife resulted in Allen's departure, later to join Shriekback, in July 1981. He was replaced by Sara Lee, formerly of Jane Aire And The Belvederes, as the group pursued a fuller, more expansive sound. *Song Of The Free* featured the tongue-in-cheek single, 'I Love A Man In Uniform', which seemed destined for chart success until disappearing from radio playlists in the wake of the Falklands 'conflict'. Burnham was fired in 1983 and a three-piece line-up completed *Hard* with sundry session musicians. This disappointing release made little difference to a group unable to satisfy now divergent audiences and they split up the following year. However, following several rather inconclusive projects, King and Gill exhumed the Gang Of Four name in 1990.

Albums: *Entertainment* (1978), *Solid Gold* (1981), *Song Of The Free* (1982), *Hard* (1983), *At The Palace* (1984). Compilation: *A Brief History Of The Twentieth Century* (1990).

Gaye Bykers On Acid

This UK rock group employed an image which combined traditional biker attire with elements of psychedelia and hippie camp. They were led by the colourful figure of Mary Millington (male; vocals), alongside Kevin (drums), Robber (bass) and Tony (guitar). They were later complemented by disc jockey William Samuel Ronald Monroe ('Rocket Ronnie'). Mary, who had once come second in Leicester's Alternative Miss Universe competition, was often to be seen in platform shoes and dresses, which fuelled the critics' confusion with regard to the band's name and gender orientation. After leaving Virgin they set up their own label Naked Brain, quite conceivably because nobody else would have them. Subsequent to the band's demise, which may or may not prove permanent, Kevin instigated a new band G.R.O.W.T.H. with Jeff (ex-Janitors). Tony has joined Brad Bradbury in Camp Collision, and Mary has joined ex-members of Killing Joke, Ministry and PiL in the multi-member outfit Pigface.

Albums: *Drill Your Own Hole* (1987), *Stewed To The Gills* (1989), *GrooveDiveSoapDish* (1989), *Cancer Planet Mission* (1990).

G.B.H

Formerly known as Charged G.B.H., the band originated as the initial impetus of the punk movement was petering out in 1980. Comprising Cal (vocals), Jock (guitar), Ross (bass) and Wilf (drums), they had a violent and aggressive image, sporting multi-coloured mohican haircuts and dressed in studded and chained leathers. Musically, they combined influences such as the Ramones and Venom into a hardcore metallic barrage of angst-ridden frustration. With smash-the-system slogan-like lyrics, they were an uncompromising and extreme musical outfit during the early 80s. They had a profound influence on the thrash and hardcore movements that followed. However, their success has been limited due to an inability to progress musically. Kai replaced Wilf on drums in 1989, and the band veered away from regimented hardcore towards speed metal. This trend has continued with the arrival of new bassist Anthony Morgan. Even the mohicans had

disappeared on their 1991 tour to promote *Massacre Divine*.

Albums: *Why* (1980), *Never Again* (1981), *Hear Nothing, See Nothing, Say Nothing* (1981), *City Baby Attacked By Rats* (1982), *Live At City Garden* (1982), *City Babies Revenge* (1983), *Leather, Bristles, Studs And Acne* (1984), *The Clay Years* (1986), *Grave New World* (1986), *Midnight Madness And Beyond* (1986), *The Nightmare Continues* (1987), *A Fridge Too Far* (1989), *No Need To Panic* (1989), *Massacre Divine* (1991).

Gene Loves Jezebel

Identical twins Jay (John) and Mike Aston, ostensibly Gene Loves Jezebel, enjoyed cult appeal, largely within the UK gothic rock community, but like Love And Rockets achieved greater success in America. The pair grew up in the South Wales town of Porthcawl, together with guitarist Ian Hudson. After obtaining a drum machine, the trio became Slav Arian for a while, before changing their name to Gene Loves Jezebel and moving to London. A debut gig at the end of 1981 supporting the Higsons attracted the record label Situation 2, resulting in 'Shavin' My Neck' (a collection of demos) the following May. The dense, experimental sound was matched by live performances, featuring bassist Julianne Regan and drummer Dick Hawkins, where they mixed almost tribal rhythms with furious guitar work. After Jay's girlfriend Kim Chambers swelled the ranks for a BBC Radio 1 session, Hawkins was replaced by a succession of drummers, including John Murphy (ex-Associates and SPK) and Steve Goulding, while Regan left to front All About Eve. Her space was filled by Hudson, allowing Albio De Luca (later of Furyo) to work the guitar, in time for the tragic 'Screaming (For Emmalene)' in 1983. But with Luca's and Goulding's departure, Hudson reverted to guitar and Hawkins/Murphy offered a two-pronged drum attack, touring with X-Mal Deutschland. Murphy then left before a third single, the strong, commercial sound of 'Bruises' (1983). Hot on its heels came the Jezebels' powerful debut album, *Promise*, promoted by a John Peel BBC radio session. A trip to the USA in 1984 to work with John Cale ensued, before returning for two quick-fire singles 'Influenza (Relapse)' and 'Shame (Whole Heart Howl)'. Marshall then left, Mike Aston briefly switching from rhythm guitar to play bass, before Peter Rizzo was recruited. After an abandoned session with Steve Harley (and his younger brother on keyboards), ex-Spear Of Destiny drummer Chris Bell arrived in place of Hawkins, but it was a year before 'The Cow' hit the UK independent charts, preceding the in-demand album *Immigrant* in June 1985. Bell's space was then filled briefly by ex-Klaxon 5 drummer Marcus Gilvear for a short tour. After 'Desire' in November, the band left for a massive north American tour, a traumatic time that led to Hudson's departure, ex-Gen X guitarist James Stevenson taking his place. Gene Loves Jezebel's growing stature justified promotion to parent label Beggars Banquet, and they instantly skirted the Top 75 with 'Sweetest Thing' in March 1986. July's *Discover* (with a free live album) also flirted with the charts via a more refined sound, alongside 'Heartache', which hinted at a passing interest in dance. After that came a revitalized 'Desire' in October. By now, the band had made substantial inroads across in the USA where they subsequently concentrated their efforts. It was almost a year before 'The Motion Of Love', revealing a new subtlety in their music. This was more fully explored on the disappointing *House Of Dolls* in October, housing a more lightweight, club-oriented feel than previously. From it came 'Gorgeous' a month later. All was not well in the Jezebels camp, and the future of the band has seemed uncertain since Mike left the group in mid-1989. Despite rumours that they will continue, no recorded product has surfaced.

Albums: *Promise* (1983), *Immigrant* (1985), *Discover* (1986), *House Of Dolls* (1987).

Generation X

UK group Generation X emerged during the punk explosion of 1976. Billy Idol (b. William Broad, 30 November 1955, Stanmore, Middlesex, England; vocals) had previously worked with Tony James (bass/vocals) in the short-lived Chelsea. With Bob Andrews (guitar/vocals) and John Towe (drums), Generation X made their performing debut in London during December 1976. By the following May, Towe was replaced on drums by Mark Laff, while record companies sought their hand. Eventually they signed with Chrysalis Records. The group soon arrived in the lower regions of the UK chart with 'Your Generation' and 'Ready Steady Go'. The latter, strange for a punk group, was an affectionate tribute to the 60s, full of references to Bob Dylan, the Beatles, the Rolling Stones and Cathy McGowan (the legendary presenter of the UK music programme *Ready Steady Go!*). The group lasted until 1981, but were soon regarded as a rock band in punk garb. Their biggest commercial success was with the 1979 single 'King Rocker', which reached number 11 in the UK. Idol later went on to solo stardom, departing drummer John Towe reappeared in the Adverts, while Tony James reinvented himself in Sigue Sigue Sputnik.

Albums: *Generation X* (1979), *Valley Of The Dolls* (1979), as Gen X *Kiss Me Deadly* (1981). Compilation: *Best Of Generation X* (1985).

Germs

Los Angeles punk band the Germs was formed in April 1977 and quickly became one of the most popular and influential in that area of music. The original members were Darby Crash (vocals), Pat Smear (guitar), Lorna Doom (bass) and Belinda Carlisle (drums), later of the Go-Gos. She soon left and was replaced by a succession of drummers, including future X drummer D.J. Bonebrake. The group's first single, 'Forming', was issued on What? Records in 1977 and is considered by some to be the first example of the post-punk 'hardcore' genre, later popularized by bands such as Black Flag. Their next single was issued on Slash Records, which in 1979 released the group's only album, *GI*. The group disbanded in early 1980 but reformed later that year. A week after their first reunion concert, however, singer Crash died of a heroin overdose.

Album: *GI* (1979), *Germicide* (1983).

Ghost Dance

If ever a supergroup were created to fulfil the demands of the enormous 'goth' fraternity in Britain during the mid-80s then, on paper at least, Ghost Dance fitted the bill. Formed in 1985 by Gary Marx (guitar) from Sisters Of Mercy and Anne Marie (vocals), previously with Skeletal Family, the duo recruited Etch (bass) from the Citron Girls and added 'Pandora' the drum machine. Throughout 1986, Ghost Dance attracted a ready-made audience with their brand of brooding rock, utilizing extra guitarists Steve Smith and Paul Southern from Red Lorry Yellow Lorry and swiftly releasing three independent singles that became highly collectable items. At the close of the year Richard Steel joined on guitar and John Grant replaced the drum machine. Their commercial position fortified by 'A Word To The Wise' entering the Top 100 of the UK chart and a sell out nationwide tour, Ghost Dance signed to Chrysalis Records and struggled to lose the 'gothic' tag. Unfortunately, while recording their debut album, various band members started to drift apart, and the 'Celebrate' single, a further attempt to broaden the band's musical horizons, merely served to alienate Ghost Dance's diehard fans. Perplexed by their proteges' evolution, the label dropped the band halfway through an ironically successful European tour with the Ramones, encouraging the personal ructions to come to the fore and subsequently causing Ghost Dance to split at the beginning of 1990. Anne Marie embarked upon a solo career, Etch played guitar with the Mission and Loud, while Gary Marx concentrated on collaborating with local musicians.

Album: *Stop The World* (1989). Compilation: *Gathering Dust* (1988).

Giant Sand

Formed by singer/songwriter Howe Gelb (vocals/guitar, bass/keyboards) in his hometown of

Tucson, Arizona, USA, in 1980 with Rainer Ptacek (guitar) and Billy Sed (drums). The line-up recorded a four track EP as Giant Sandworms on a local label before departing for New York, where Sed's drug escapades forced a return to Arizona. They were joined by Dave Seger (bass) for a further EP, before he left to join Naked Prey. His replacement was Scott Gerber. Shortly afterwards the band's name was switched to Giant Sand (the original name had unintentional connotations with the wildlife in the science fiction novel *Dune*), with Gelb firing all personnel except Gerber in the process. Ptacek, though, reappeared in Gelb's countrified *alter ego* group, the Band Of Blacky Ranchette. Tom Larkins, who played concurrently with Naked Prey, joined as drummer, and together they recorded *Valley Of Rain* with guest pianist Chris Cavacas from Green On Red. Gelb's girlfriend Paula Brown (ex-Go Gos) joined on bass and guitar, and together they had their first child. After recording *Ballad Of A Thin Line Man* Gerber left to join the Sidewinders, eventually moving on to Los Cruzos with former Sandworm drummer Sed. A variety of personnel have populated more recent recordings, including Neil Harry (pedal steel guitar), John Convertino (drums) and Mark Walton (ex-Dream Syndicate; bass). It is this line-up which was most recently seen on tour. The band's early stark sound (often described as 'desert rock') has evolved into a crisp mix of swing, country, rock, and beatnik lyricism. It remains tempered, as ever, by Gelb's evocative, arid imagery.

Albums: *Valley Of Rain* (1985), as the Band Of Blacky Ranchette *The Band Of Blacky Ranchette* (1985), *Ballad Of A Thin Line Man* (1986), as the Band Of Blacky Ranchette *Heartland* (1986), *Storm* (1988), *The Love Songs LP* (1988), *Giant Songs* (1989), *Long Stem Rant* (1990), as the Band Of Blacky Ranchette *Sage Advice* (1990), *Ramp* (1991). Compilation: *Giant Sandwich* (1989).

Gilbert, Bruce

Bruce Gilbert forged a reputation as a purveyor of challenging music as guitarist/vocalist and composer with Wire. When this acclaimed art/punk quartet broke up in 1980, he joined group bassist Graham Lewis in Dome, a unit which continued its predecessor's *avant garde* inclinations. The duo also worked as P'o and Duet Emmo, the latter of which marked a collaboration with Mute label boss, Daniel Miller. Although Wire were reunited in 1984, Gilbert embarked on a concurrent solo career with *This Way*, the enthralling nature of which was maintained on the artist's second set, *The Shivering Man*. Both albums confirm his position as one of Britain's most innovative musicians.

Albums: *This Way* (1984), *The Shivering Man* (1989).

Glove

The Glove was essentially a one-off project for UK guitarist/vocalist Robert Smith of the Cure and bassist/multi-instrumentalist Steve Severin of Siouxsie And The Banshees, with singer/dancer Jeanette Landray. Heavily influenced by Sixties cult imagery and psychedelia, the Glove (the name taken from the film *Yellow Submarine*) recorded two singles, 'Like An Animal' (a minor hit) and 'Punish Me With Kisses', and a distinctive album, *Blue Sunshine,* issued on the Banshees' Wonderland label in August 1983. Although the material's multi-layered sound was endearing, the Glove was plainly a self-indulgent exercise for Severin and Smith (who was also a Banshee at that time) and rubbed off on both parties. The Banshees, especially, injected a strong late 60s feel into their music, not least with a cover of the Beatles' 'Dear Prudence'. The Glove, meanwhile, was destined to become history, although demand was strong enough to warrant a reissue of *Blue Sunshine* in 1990.

Albums: *Blue Sunshine* (1983).

Go-Betweens

Go-Betweens

Formed in Brisbane, Australia by Robert Forster (b. 29 June 1957, Brisbane, Queensland, Australia; guitar/vocals) and Grant McLennan (b. 12 February 1958, Rock Hampton, Queensland, Australia; bass/guitar/vocals). These two songwriters were influenced by Bob Dylan, the Velvet Underground, the Monkees and the then-burgeoning New York scene involving Television, Talking Heads and Patti Smith. Although sharing the same subject matter in trouble torn love songs, melancholy and desolation, Forster and McLennan's very different compositional styles fully complimented each other. The Go-Betweens first recorded as a trio on the Able label with drummer Dennis Cantwell. McLennan took on the bass-playing duties for 'Lee Remick'/'Karen' (1978) and 'People Say'/'Don't Let Him Come Back' (1979). By this time of the latter release the line-up had expanded to include Tim Mustafa (drums), Malcolm Kelly (organ), and Candice and Jacqueline on tambourine and vocals. The duo later reverted to the trio format on recruiting ex-Zero drummer, Lindy Morrison (b. 2 November 1951, Australia).

At the invitation of Postcard Records boss Alan Horne, the band came to Britain to record a single, 'I Need Two Heads'. After this brief visit the group returned to Australia and recorded *Send Me A Lullaby*, for the independent label, Missing Link. This roughly-hewn set, which when heard by Geoff Travis at Rough Trade Records in London, was picked up for distribution in the UK. Travis proposed that the Go-Betweens return to the UK, sign a recording deal and settle in London, which the group accepted. *Before Hollywood*, garnered favourable reviews prompting many to predict a rosy future for the group. The highlight of this set was McLennan's evocative, 'Cattle And Cane', one of the Go-Betweens' classic tracks. The problem of finding a permanent bass player was solved with the enrolment of Brisbane associate Robert Vickers (b. 25 November 1959; Australia) to the post, thus enabling McLennan to concentrate on guitar and giving the group a fuller sound. The move to a major label, Sire Records brought expectations of a 'big breakthrough' in terms of sales, but for all the critical acclaim heaped upon *Springhill Fair*, success still eluded them. The break with Sire left the group labelless and almost on the brink of returning to Australia. The intervention, and eventual signing to Beggars Banquet led them to a relationship which allowed the group to develop at their own pace. *Liberty Belle And The Black Diamond Express* presented what was by far their best album to date. The successful use of violins and oboes on *Liberty Belle . . .* led to the introduction of a fifth member, Amanda Brown (b. 17 November 1965, Australia; violin/oboe/guitar/keyboards), the addition contributing to an extra dimension and smoother texture to the band's sound. With *Tallulah* in 1987, the Go-Betweens made their best showing so far in the UK album chart, peaking at number 91. That same year, Robert Vickers left the group to reside in New York and was replaced by John Willsteed (b. 13 February 1957, Australia). Prior to the release of *16 Lovers Lane* in 1988 the single, 'Streets Of Your Town' a summery single with a dark undertone in tackling the subject of wife-battering, was given generous air-play. However, once again, the single failed to make any impact on the charts despite being lavished with praise from the UK music press. The album only managed to peak at number 81, a disappointing end for what was to be the definitive Go-Betweens album. After touring with the set, Forster and McLennan dissolved the group in December 1989. Remaining with Beggars Banquet, they both released solo albums, Forster's album, *Danger In The Past* was recorded with substantial assistance from Bad Seeds member, Mick Harvey. McLennan released an album with fellow Antipodean, Steve Kilbey from the Church, under the name of Jack Frost (for Arista Records), then crediting himself as G.W. McLennan. His full solo set, *Watershed*, proved that neither artist was lost without the other. Lindy Morrison and Amanda Brown meanwhile, had formed a group, Cleopatra Wong. Since McLennan joined Forster on-stage in 1991, rumours of a Go-Betweens reformation were strengthened by a Forster/McLennan support slot with Lloyd Cole in Toronto that same year. Whether Forster and McLennan can convince the mainstream public of their worth remains to be seen. As artists however, they remain two of the finest working musicians to emerge from the independent scene.
Albums: *Send Me A Lullaby* (1982), *Before Hollywood* (1983), *Springhill Fair* (1984), *Liberty Belle And The Black Diamond Express* (1986), *Tullulah* (1987), *16 Lover's Lane* (1988). Compilations: *Very Quick On The Eye* (1985), *Metal And Shells* (1985), *Go-Betweens 1978-1990* (1990). Solo: Robert Forster *Danger In The Past* (1990), Jack Frost (Grant McLennan and Steve Kilbey) *Jack Frost* (1990), Grant McLennan *Watershed* (1991).

Goddard, Vic, And The Subway Sect

Goddard, a native of the London suburb of Mortlake, put the band together during 1976, centring it on the friends with whom he used to attend Sex Pistols' gigs. Subway Sect made their live debut on 20 September 1976 at the 100 Club, featuring Goddard (vocals), Paul Myers (bass), Robert Miller (guitar), and Paul Smith (drums). They rehearsed in the Clash's studio. Their name came from brief flirtations with busking upon their inauguration. A series of short sets followed around the capital, featuring embryonic songwriting prowess to add to the abrasiveness they learnt at the hands of the Pistols. They opened for the Clash at Harlesdon and subsequently joined them for their *White Riot* tour. Mark Laff had replaced Smith, but he too was lured away (to Generation X) before they set out on their first European trek. Bob Ward was their new drummer when they released their

April 1978 debut 'Nobody's Scared'. However, a major split followed leaving Ward and Goddard to recruit John Britain (guitar), Colin Scott (bass) and Steve Atkinson (keyboards) in the summer of 1978. 'Ambition' was a trailblazing single, but afterwards the band fell into inactivity before reviving in 1980 with another new line-up with definite New Romantic leanings. This time the group featured Rob March (b. 13 October 1962, Bristol, England; guitar), Dave Collard (b. 17 January 1961, Bristol, England; keyboards), Chris Bostock (b. 23 November 1962, Bristol, England; bass) and Sean McLusky (b. 5 May 1961, Bristol, England; drums). *Songs For Sale* presented a collection of slick, swing-style songs with Goddard adopting a cocktail-lounge, crooner image. Supports with the Clash and Buzzcocks had transformed into guest spots on the Altered Images tour, and Goddard's new backing band would depart to find commercial success with JoBoxers. Disillusioned, Goddard has since retired from the music scene.

Albums: *What's The Matter Boy* (1980), *Songs For Sale* (1982), *Trouble* (1986). Compilation: *A Retrospective (1977-81)* (1985).

Godfathers

A tough R&B fired rock band, the Godfathers centred on brothers Peter and Chris Coyne (b. London, England). The groups beginnings were in the south London punk quartet Sid Presley Experience (the Coynes on vocals and bass, plus Del Bartle - guitar, and Kevin Murphy - drums) who released two singles in 1984 and toured with Billy Bragg on the 'Jobs For Youth' tour. They split in 1985 and Bartle and Murphy toured as the New Sid Presley Experience before recruiting Mad Dog Lucas and forming the Unholy Trinity. The Coyne brothers also retained the Sid Presley monicker for a while but having recruited Mike Gibson (b. London, England; guitar) and Kris Dollimore (b. Isle Of Sheppey, Kent, England; guitar) and George Mazur (b. Bradford, Yorkshire, England; drums), they became the Godfathers. 'Lonely Man' was released on their own Corporate Image label in 1985 and *Hit By Hit* came out the following year, collecting together their first three singles with other tracks. In 1986 came the first of their regular St Valentine's Day gigs in London which would take place at such venues as the London Dungeon as well as more conventional halls. With their reputation growing they were signed to the American end of the Epic organization who released their best known work - *Birth, School, Work, Death*. Kris Dollimore left in 1989 (he would later work with Stiv Bators) and was replaced in January 1990 by Chris Burrows. Burrows had previously worked with many bands including the Presidents Of Explosion which had also included former Sid Presley drummer Kevin Murphy. Constant touring, particularly in Europe, followed, and *Unreal World* came out in 1991.

Albums: *Hit By Hit* (1986), *Birth, School, Work, Death* (1988), *More Songs About Love And Hate* (1989), *Unreal World* (1991).

Go-Go's

This all-girl group, originally called the Misfits, were formed in California, USA, in 1978 by Belinda Carlisle (b. 16 August 1958, Hollywood, California, USA; lead vocals) and Jane Wiedlin (b. 20 May 1958, Oconomowoc, Wisconsin, USA; rhythm guitar/vocals). They were joined by Charlotte Caffey (b. 21 October 1953, Santa Monica, California, USA; lead guitar/keyboards), Elissa Bello (drums) and Margot Olaverra (bass). Inspired by the punk-inspired new wave scene, the Go-Go's performed bright, infectious harmony-pop songs and were initially signed to the UK independent label Stiff Records. After the one-off single, 'We Got The Beat', the Go-Go's were snapped up by Miles Copeland's IRS label, who released their debut album *Beauty And The Beat*. By the time of its release, Olaverra was replaced by ex-Textone Kathy Valentine and Bello by Gina Schock. Produced by Richard Gottehrer, who had earlier worked with a long line of girl singers in the 60s, *Beauty And The Beat* drew comparisons with Blondie, for whom Gottehrer had earlier worked with. The album, which stayed at the US number 1 spot for 6 weeks in 1981 included 'Our Lips Are Sealed' (US Top 20) which was co-written by Wiedlin with Terry Hall of the Fun Boy Three, and 'We Got The Beat' which gave the group a US number 2 hit the following year. The second album provided a further US Top 10 hit with the title track, but the group were by now showing signs of burn-out. Despite their 'safe' image, it later transpired that the Go-Go's were more than able to give the average all-male group a run for their money when it came to on-road excesses, which eventually took their toll. *Talk Show* reached the US Top 20, as was the most successful single culled from the set, 'Head Over Heels' (1984). With the break-up of the group in 1984, Belinda Carlisle subsequently pursued a successful solo career with assistance from Charlotte Caffey, who, for a time, appeared in her backing group. Caffey later formed the Graces with Meredith Brooks and Gia Campbell and recorded for A&M Records, releasing *Perfect View* in 1990. As well as recording as a solo artist, Wiedlin attempted to break into acting with a few minor film roles. Galvanized by Jane, the Go-Go's reformed briefly in 1990 for a benefit for the anti-fur trade organization PETA (People for the Ethical Treatment of Animals).

Album: *Beauty And The Beat* (1981), *Vacation* (1982), *Talk Show* (1984). Compilation: *Greatest* (1991).

Golden Palominos

This unorthodox rock group's profile has been much enhanced by the glittering array of celebrities who have contributed to their work. They are led by drummer Anton Fier, who gave birth to the group in 1981. Prior to this he had spent time in the ranks of experimental bands Lounge Lizards and Pere Ubu. The band's albums have seen guest appearances by John Lydon (Sex Pistols, PiL), Michael Stipe (R.E.M.), Daniel Ponce, T-Bone Burnett, Jack Bruce and Syd Straw amongst others. The other core members of the band are Bill Laswell (bass), Nicky Skopelitis (guitar) and Amanda Kramer (vocals). Their most recent outing; *Drunk With Passion*, features Stipe on 'Alive And Living Now', and former Hüsker Dü man Bob Mould on the excellent 'Dying From The Inside Out'. Richard Thompson also puts in an appearance. Whether the sum is greater or even equal to the parts, however, is open to conjecture.
Albums: *A Dead Horse* (1989), *Drunk With Passion* (1991).

Gorillas

Originally known as the Hammersmith Gorillas this English trio played their own brand of punk meets rhythm and blues meets heavy rock. Initially riding on the back of the punk movement they built up a loyal fan base and released a string of excellent singles during the mid to late 70s including 'You Really Got Me' (a cover of the Kinks classic), 'Gatecrasher', 'It's My Life' and 'She's My Gal'. Bandleader Jesse Hector (vocals/guitar), ably supported by Alan Butler (bass) and Gary Anderson (drums), was influenced by several dead 'stars'. The extravagantly side-burned singer was a noted self-publicist, whose passionate belief in the importance of the Gorillas' as the 'future of rock music' was taken all in, surprisingly, good humour by the UK music press. These included Elvis Presley, Eddie Cochran, Buddy Holly, Brian Jones, Marc Bolan and Jimi Hendrix. Indeed, several of the tracks on the Gorillas album were delivered in the musical style of his heroes, most notably a superb cover of Hendrix's 'Foxy Lady' and the Marc Bolan-influenced 'Going Fishing'. After a lenghty absence, Hector was to be found working the London live circuit in 1992 with his group, the Sound.
Album: *Message To The World* (1978).

Greedies

This UK-based trio featured Thin Lizzys' Phil Lynott (b. 20 August 1951, Dublin, Eire, d. 4 January 1986; vocals/bass) and the Sex Pistols' Steve Jones (b. 3 September 1955, London, England; guitar) and Paul Cook (b. 20 July 1956, London, England; drums). They amalgamated in December 1979 as the Greedies for the one-off UK hit, a frantic version of 'We Wish

You A Merry Christmas' titled 'A Merry Jingle', which peaked at number 28 in the first week of January 1980. Later on in the year Jones and Cook, recording as the Professionals, narrowly missed the UK Top 40 with '1-2-3'. Lynott died aged 34, from liver, kidney and heart failure and pneumonia following a drug overdose.

Green On Red

Green On Red

Formed as the Serfers in Tucson, Arizona, USA in 1981, the group featured Dan Stuart (guitar/vocals), Jack Waterson (bass) and Van Christian (drums). Christian was replaced by Alex MacNicol, and Chris Cacavas added on keyboards for the first EP *Two Bibles*, released under their new group name. The band attracted attention as part of the 60s-influenced 'paisley underground' alongside the Rain Parade and the Dream Syndicate. However, Green On Red's sound owed more to Neil Young and country/blues traditions, an influence that became more apparent when Chuck Prophet IV joined on lead guitar in 1984. Sophisticated arrangements on 1987's *The Killer Inside Me* saw the group pushing for mainstream recognition, but shortly afterwards Waterson and Cacavas left to pursue solo careers. The remaining duo, Prophet and Stuart, forged ahead, using session musicians for the excellent *Here Come The Snakes*. Both members have operated outside the confines of the group, most notably Stuart's involvement on

Danny And Dusty featuring Steve Wynn and members of the Long Ryders. In 1991 Green On Red re-emerged with *Scapegoats* recorded in Nashville with the help of Al Kooper on keyboards.

Albums: *Green On Red* (1982), *Gravity Talks* (1984), *Gas Food Lodging* (1985), *No Free Lunch* (1985), *The Killer Inside Me* (1987), *Here Come The Snakes* (1989), *Live At The Town And Country Club* (1989 - limited edition mini-album), *This Time Around* (1990), *Scapegoats* (1991). Solo albums: Chuck Prophet *Brother Aldo* (1990); Dan Stuart *Danny And Dusty - The Lost Weekend* (1985); Chris Cacavas *Junkyard Love* (1989); Jack Waterson *Whose Dog* (1988).

Gretton, Rob

Manchester, England-based entrepreneur Gretton first entered the music business as a fan during the heyday of British punk. In 1976 he struck up a friendship with Slaughter And The Dogs and began travelling with them to gigs, and even helped finance their first single. His enthusiasm persuaded him to promote several other punk groups, including Sioxsie And The Banshees, Johnny Thunders And The Heartbreakers and the Buzzcocks. He also worked as a disc jockey at Manchester clubs such as the Electric Circus and Rafters. It was during an evening at Rafters that he first saw Warsaw, whose lead singer Ian Curtis reminded him of Iggy Pop. Several months later, Gretton saw the group again and noted that they had changed their name to Joy Division. After watching their appearance at the a joint Stiff Records/Chiswick Records talent evening, he offered his services as manager. Joy Division went on to become one of the most respected and mysterious UK groups of their era, but their history ended on a tragic note with the suicide of Curtis on 18 May 1980. Gretton helped the group into their next phase as New Order. Uncompromisingly independent, both Gretton and New Order demonstrated that it was possible to maintain the autonomous values of punk, even in the harsh economic climate of the 80s. Much of the revenue that the group accrued from the sales of their recordings was used to assist such projects as the Haçienda club, in which Gretton had an interest. In more recent times, the manager has branched out again to form his own record label, Gretton.

Gribbin, Tom

b. 2 January 1949, Florida, USA. Gribbin trained as a lawyer but formed a band, the Saltwater Cowboys, for weekend work. They mixed country with rock and Caribbean influences. To add to their diversity, they recorded the Clash's song, 'Guns Of Brixton' but, following the Brixton riots in south London, England, the record was considered too sensitive for UK airplay. Gribbin and his band were surprisingly well-received at the Wembley Country Music Festival, which is usually a graveyard for the more radical acts. His first album, *Son Of Lightning*, was issued with two distinct covers, one for the shops and one for Wembley. For a short period, Gribbin looked as though he might be the first new wave country star to become established in the UK, but it did not happen. He returned to legal work and a weekend band.

Albums: *Son Of Lightning* (1981), *Useppa Island Rendezvous* (1984).

Grogan, Clare (see Altered Images)

Guana Batz

The late 70s UK rockabilly revival inspired the subsequent appearance of several new wave rockabilly - or psychobilly - acts such as the Guana Batz. Formed in Feltham, Middlesex, England the Guana Batz began gigging in 1983. The original line-up boasted Pip Hancox (vocals), Stuart Osbourne (guitar), Dave Turner (drums) and Mark White, though his electric bass was soon swapped for the stand-up double bass of Sam Sardi. With musical peers the Meteors and King Kurt spearheading the new high energy format ('We prefer to describe it as modern rockabilly'), the Guana Batz were soon signed to Big Beat records. An EP and single were released, but the breakthrough came when the band featured on the *Stompin' At The Klubfoot* compilation, the latter proving the premiere venue for psychobilly bands. ABC/ID records released their debut *Held Down To Vinyl . . . At Last* in 1985, gaining a high placing in the UK independent charts. Unfortunately on the tour Hancox broke a leg while attempting to hurdle two double basses on a BMX bike, and was forced to complete the tour in plaster. After a spirited assassination of Bruce Springsteen's 'I'm On Fire' their second album, *Loan Sharks*, entered the UK independent charts at number 2. The following year, *Live Over London* was only completed when Meteors drummer Ginger stepped in to replace temporarily the injured Turner. After the fourth album he left permanently, leaving the position vacant for Johnny Bowler (ex-Get Smart). Their most recent studio album is 1990's *Electra Glide In Blue*, after which Sardi was replaced on bass by Mark Pennington (ex-Caravans). The group continue to tour heavily, especially in Europe where they retain great popularity.

Albums: *Held Down To Vinyl . . . At Last* (1985), *Loan Sharks* (1986), *Rough Edges* (1988), *Electra Glide In Blue* (1990).

Gun Club

Briefly known as Creeping Ritual, the Gun Club was formed in Los Angeles, USA in 1980. Led by vocalist Jeffrey Lee Pierce, the group was initially completed by Kid Congo Powers (b. Brian Tristan; guitar), Rob Ritter (bass) and Terry Graham (drums). *Fire Of Love* established the unit's uncompromising style which drew from delta blues and psychobilly. The set included anarchic versions of Robert Johnson's 'Preaching The Blues' and Tommy Johnson's 'Cool Drink Of Water', but progress was undermined by Congo's defection to the Cramps. *Miami* was the first of several Gun Club recordings for Animal Records, owned by ex-Blondie guitarist Chris Stein. Although lacking the passion of its predecessor, the album established the group as one of America's leading 'alternative' acts, but further changes in personnel, including the return of the prodigal Congo, ultimately blunted Pierce's confidence which was unaided by a self-destructive alcohol problem. He disbanded the group for a solo career in 1985; *Two Sides Of The Beast* was then issued in commemoration, but the singer later reconstituted the Gun Club with Kid Congo, Nick Sanderson (drums) and Romi Mori (bass) which continues to provide a benchmark for impulsive, powerful music.

Albums: *Fire Of Love* (1981), *Miami* (1982), *Death Party* (1983), *Las Vegas Story* (1984), *The Birth, The Death, The Ghost* (1984), *Danse Kalinda Boom* (1985), *Two Sides Of The Beast* (1986), *Mother Juno* (1987), *Pastoral Hide And Seek* (1990), *Divinity* (1991).

GWAR

This theatrical shock-rock quintet emerged from Richmond, Virginia, USA. Assuming bizarre pseudonyms, they comprised Oderus Urungus (vocals), Balsac, The Jaws Of Death (guitar), Flattus Maximus (guitar), Beefcake The Mighty (bass) and Nippleus Erectus (drums). Renowned for an outrageous live show which involves the band adorned in hideous papier mâché masks and blood spattered torture implements, the music takes second place to the visuals. This is no more than amateurish thrash, complete with unintelligible vocals. Without the visual back-up, their albums are anti-climactic.

Albums: *Hell-O* (1988), *Scumdogs Of The Universe* (1990).

Gymslips

This all-girl pop punk UK trio achieved minor prominence during the early 80s with their classic tribute to alcoholic revelry, 'The Drinking Song'. They recorded a series of singles for the Abstract label, including a cover of Suzi Quatro's Chinn And Chapman hit '48 Crash'. They called themselves Renees, the moniker attributed to those who undertake an exclusive and excessive diet of alcohol and 'pie 'n' mash'. The band's line-up featured the talents of Suzanne Scott (bass/vocals), Karen Yarnell (drums/vocals), and Paula Richards (guitar/vocals). Kim Yarnell would go on to drum for the

appropriately titled Serious Drinking.

H

Hagen, Nina

b. 11 March 1955, Berlin, Germany. After her parents divorced in 1957, she was raised in a suburb in the eastern bloc by her actress mother and her stepfather, dissident poet and songwriter Wold Biermann. In 1964, she joined the Thalmann-Pioneers, a Communist youth organization and, four years later, the Freie Deutsche Jugend - from which she was excluded for her hand in a demonstration (instigated by Biermann) against the participation of East German militia in the Soviet invasion of Czechoslovakia. On failing a 1972 entrance test for a Berlin-Schönweide drama college, she sang a mixture of blues and soul with a Polish outfit for several months prior to enrolment at the Studio Für Unterhaltungsmusik (Studio For Popular Music) where she was an outstanding student. For a few years, she toured East Germany as featured vocalist with the Alfons Wonneberg Orchestra before fronting Automobil and then Fritzens Dampferband (Fred's Steamboat Band) but when Biermann was expelled from Soviet territory in 1976, she followed him to West Germany where her worth as an entertainer was sufficiently known for a recording contract to be offered. Her imagination captured by punk, she flew to London where she and Ari Up of the Slits collaborated on a number of songs. On returning to Germany, she formed the Nina Hagen Band with former members of Lok Kreuzberg - Bernhard Potschka (guitar) and Manfred Praeker (bass) - plus Herwig Mitteregger (drums). From the group's debut album, 1978's 'African Reggae' was enough of a 'turntable hit' to bring Hagen a cult following - particularly in Australia - which grew steadily during the 80s. Nevertheless, the saga of her rise to qualified fame remains more intriguing than her subsequent career.

Albums: *The Nina Hagen Band* (1978), *Unbehagen* (1979), *Nunsexmockrock* (1982), *Angstios* (1983), *Fearless* (1984).

Haig, Paul

b. 1960, Scotland. Haig was the former lead singer of the late 70s, Edinburgh post-punk 'art' band, Josef K. His work with the band led many to expect great things when he launched his solo career. Working

with the group project, Rhythm Of Life, his releases confirmed that Haig was still a man with promise, with the singles 'Big Blue World', 'Heaven Sent' and 'The Only Truth' displaying such. However, throughout the 80s the critical acclaim never moved Haig any further than a cult following, although his talents were appreciated in France and Belgium. The atmospheric *Cinematique...* displayed a maturity in style and adventurousness far removed from his humble beginnings in the 70s and yet it appears it will be in that latter capacity he will be remembered for.
Albums: *Rhythm Of Life* (1983), *Sense Of Fun* (1985), *European Sun* (1988), *R.O.L.* (1990), *Cinematique - Themes For Unknown Films, Volume One* (1991).

Haircut 100

Formed in Beckenham, Kent, England in 1980, the group began on a part-time basis with a line-up comprising Nick Heyward (b. 20 May 1961, Beckenham, Kent, England; vocals), Les Nemes (b. 5 December 1960, Croydon, Surrey, England; bass) and Graham Jones (b. 8 July 1961, Bridlington, North Yorkshire; guitar). Early the following year they were augmented by Memphis Blair Cunningham (b. 11 October 1957, Harlem, New York, USA; drums) , Phil Smith (b. 1 May 1959, Redbridge, Ilford, Essex; saxophone), and Mark Fox (b. 13 February 1958; percussion). Engineer/manager Karl Adams secured them a deal with Arista Records where they were placed in the hands of producer Bob Sargeant. Their teen appeal and smooth punk-pop sound was perfect for the time and it came as no surprise when their debut single 'Favourite Shirts (Boy Meets Girl)' climbed to number 4 in the UK charts. The follow-up, 'Love Plus One' did even better, firmly establishing the group as premier pop idols in 1982. Their career received a serious setback, however, when the engaging frontman Nick Heyward split for a solo career.
In January 1983 Haircut 100 were relaunched with replacement vocalist Mark Fox. Although the group hoped to succeed with a new audience,their singles sold poorly and following the release of their 1984 album *Paint On Paint*, they disbanded. Drummer Cunningham later reappeared in one of the many line-ups of the Pretenders.
Albums: *Pelican West* (1982), *Paint On Paint* (1984). Compilation: *Nick Heywood And Haircut 100; The Best Of* (1990).

Half Japanese

Formed by brothers Jad and David Fair in the punk aftermath of the late 70s, this cult US group has undergone numerous changes since its inception. Despite an erratic history, the unit remains an important outlet for the disparate talents of Jad Fair, who has also pursued a musically indistinguishable

solo career. Jad Fair aside, Half Japanese releases have included contributions from Kramer (Shockabilly and Bongwater), Don Fleming (B.A.L.L.) and Fred Frith (ex-Henry Cow), but are marked by the leader's idiosyncratic talent, which combines the naivety of Jonathan Richman with a love of classic 60s pop. Their best-known releases, including *The Band That Would Be King*, were issued on the 50 Skidillion Watts label, for which Maureen Tucker also recorded. In 1991 the former Velvet Underground drummer produced 'Everybody Knows' for Half Japanese.
Albums: *Half Gentlemen, Not Beasts* (1980), *Loud* (1981), *Horrible* (1983), *Our Solar System* (1984), *Sing No Evil* (1984), *Music To Strip By* (1987), *Charmed Life* (1988), *The Band That Would Be King* (1989).

Hannett, Martin

b. May 1948, Northside, Manchester, England, d. 9 April 1991. In his role as producer Hannett worked with practically all the bands from the Manchester area that came to prominence in the late 70s. He also intermittently produced the groups of the 80s that established Manchester's international reputation as a hot-bed of young musical talent. After completing further education, where he had spent all his time playing bass guitar in bands and promoting local concerts, he toured with Paul Young (of Mike And The Mechanics). He also managed a musicians' co-operative and worked as a soundman before being approached by the Buzzcocks to produce their *Spiral Scratch* EP in 1977. Following this he helped Joy Division fashion their sound in the studio, producing them, and encouraging their use of synthesizers. This resulted in the brutal and isolating feel of *Unknown Pleasures* on the one hand, and the mesmerizing beauty of *Closer* on the other, both now considered classic albums. The band worked with Hannett on 1981's *Movement*, their debut as New Order, but were disappointed with the results; this was to be their last collaboration. An integral part of the band's subsequent success, Hannett was made co-director of their label, Factory Records. This, however, did not interfere with his production schedule, working with U2, the Only Ones, OMD, Psychedelic Furs, Magazine and numerous other bands in the early 80s. As Manchester flourished for a second time, in the late '80s, again it was Hannett who helped shape the sound that had a profound influence on the UK music scene. He produced the Stone Roses' debut single 'So Young' and Happy Mondays' *Bummed* album which provided the blueprint for a host of young hopefuls as the 90s began. He was held in high regard throughout the UK music business, described by those who worked with him as a genius whose instincts behind the mixing desk almost always paid off. But away from the studio he had a reputation for

Happy Mondays

irresponsible behaviour and his drink-and-drugs lifestyle accelerated his declining health. He died from a heart attack on 9 April,1991.

Compilation album: *Martin* (1991 - contains selection of artists produced by Hannett).

Happy Mondays

Few debut records could lay claim to have had the impact (or length of title) as *Happy Mondays' Squirrel And G-Man Twenty Four Hour Party People Plastic Face Carnt Smile (White Out)*. The sextet's raw brand of urban folk with Shaun Ryder's accented, drawled vocals was almost universally acclaimed. John Cale, formerly of the Velvet Underground, produced and gave the record a fresh, live feel. The original line-up has remained unchanged (apart from the addition of backing singer, Rowetta) since the group formed in Manchester, England, early in the 80s. Joining singer Ryder is his brother, Paul Ryder (bass), Mark Day (guitar), Gary Whelan (drums), Paul Davis (keyboards) and Mark Berry (percussion). Nicknamed 'Bez', the percussionist was known for his manic onstage antics and gaunt appearance. Martin Hannett, famous chiefly for his work with Joy Division, produced *Bummed* and layered their music with diverse but strong dance rhythms. In 1990 they covered John Kongos' 'He's Gonna Step On You Again' (retitled 'Step On') and reached the Top 10 in the UK. *Pills 'N' Thrills And Bellyaches* went to number 1 in the UK and established the band as a major pop force. The album also coincided with support and repromotion of 60s singer Donovan, who appeared alongside them on the front covers of the music press. They even recorded a tribute song, *Donovan*, which paraphrased some lyrics of the singer's 60s hit 'Sunshine Superman'. Strong support from Factory Records and an unusually consistent output meant Happy Mondays fared better than many of the other Manchester groups who broke through at the same time but either became embroiled in legal disputes or ran out of material. However, the band's successes have been tempered with a fair share of unpleasant publicity which came to a head when Sean Ryder announced he was a heroin addict and was undergoing detoxication treatment. They are one of the most exciting prospects of the 90s in UK pop.

Albums: *Squirrel And G-Man Twenty Four Hour Party People Plastic Face Carnt Smile (White Out)* (1986), *Bummed* (1988), *Pills 'N' Thrills And Bellyaches* (1990), *Live* (1991).

Joey Ramone and Debbie Harry

Harper, Charlie

b. David Charles Perez, 25 April, 1944, London, England. Forming his first band at the age of 20, Charlie Harper's Free Press gave way to the Charlie Harper Band, although he made several appearances in another band called Bandana. By the advent of punk in 1976, Harper was playing with the Marauders, subsidized in part by his employment as a hairdresser. The Marauders would eventually transmute in to the Subs, and finally the UK Subs. With the UK Subs established, Harper was able to indulge himself a little in his favourite hobby, playing R&B and classic rock cover versions. Two singles, 'Barmy London Army' and 'Freaked' emerged in 1980 and 1981. The first was a tribute to Jimmy Pursey, the second notable for the oddly poignant b-side 'Jo'. These were followed a year later by *Stolen Property* on Flickknife Records. Notable covers included 'Pills', 'Louie Louie', 'Hey Joe', 'Light My Fire', 'Waiting For the Man', 'Femme Fatale' and 'Hoochie Coochie Man'. His other major project outside of the Subs has been the Urban Dogs, who released two albums in 1982 and 1985. They included various old members of the UK Subs, in addition to Knox (ex-Vibrators) and Simon Smith (ex-Merton Parkers). In 1986 Harper teamed up with old friends from Hanoi Rocks and Cherry Bombz in the Suicide Twins. Throughout the 80s and early 90s, he has continued to perform with the UK Subs, milking former glories as sustenance.
Album: *Stolen Property* (1981).

Harry, Debbie

b. 1 July 1946, Miami, Florida, USA. Raised in New Jersey, Harry was drawn to the alternative music emanating from New York's Greenwich Village in the mid-60s. Spells in a succession of *avant garde* groups, including the First National Unaphrenic Church And Bank, preceded her tenure in the Wind In The Willows, a baroque folk/rock act which completed an album for Capitol Records in 1968. For five years Harry abandoned music altogether, but resumed singing in 1973 as a member of the Stilettos, an exaggerated version of girl-group the Shangri-Las. The following year she formed Blondie with Fred Smith (bass), Billy O'Connor (drums) and longtime boyfriend Chris Stein (guitar). Having made its debut at the New York punk haven CBGBs, the group rose to become one of the leading pop attractions of the late 70s, scoring a succession of hits in the US and UK. Meanwhile, Harry established herself as the leading female rock sex-symbol of the time.

However, as the dividing line between the group and its photogenic lead singer became blurred, so inner tensions proved irreconcilable. In 1981 Harry released her solo debut *Koo Koo*, produced by Chic mainstays Nile Rodgers and Bernard Edwards. Despite the presence of Stein, the set failed to capture Blondie's sense of simple pop and the singer resumed her commitment to the parent act. Stein's recurrent ill-heath brought the group to an end and a further period of retirement ensued. Harry did pursue an acting career, including roles in *Union City Blue*, *Videodrome* and a memorable comic role in the 1987 John Water's film, *Hairspray*. In 1986 she released *Rockbird* which featured the UK Top 10 hit 'French Kissing In The USA'. It was not until three years later that Debbie made a return to the UK Top 20, this time with the Tom Bailey and Alannah Currie (aka the Thompson Twins) composition, 'I Want That Man'. The accompanying album, *Def, Dumb And Blonde*, credited to Deborah Harry, achieved a similar chart position, since which the singer has completed several tours, performing material drawn from Blondie and her subsequent work.
Albums: *Koo Koo* (1981), *Rockbird* (1986), *Def, Dumb And Blonde* (1989). Compilation: *Once More Into The Bleach* (1988 - credited to and includes, tracks from Debbie Harry's solo career and with Blondie).

Haza, Ofra
b. 1959, Israel. Despite being Israeli born, Haza was the daughter of Yemenite parents who fled from the Muslim regime in Yemen. At the age of 12 she joined the theatre group Hatvika, run by Bezalel Azoni. In her seven years with the group, Haza recorded with them and won a Grammy award for an outstanding performance. After serving two years national service in the Israeli army she recorded her first solo album and quickly rose to become one of Israel's top singers. She was voted second in the 1983 Eurovision Song Contest with 'Hi!' (translated: 'stay alive'). Haza's introduction to British house music came when her singing was sampled for the Eric B. And Rakim Top 20 hit, 'Paid In Full' (1987). Her unlikely success, in her own right, in the US dance charts in 1988 with 'Im Nin'alu' spread to the UK where it reached number 15. Her visual image with her colourful national dress and the exotic mixture of middle-eastern ballads and rhythms blended with western styles, helped to make her Israel's most well-known female solo singer in the UK. This success has seen Ofra feted by artists in various fields of music; from 'world music' and traditional folk, disco and house styles and, in an unlikely alliance in 1992, Haza recorded with the Sisters Of Mercy for the single 'Temple Of Love'. That same year also saw the release of Kirya, which involved the services of members of Was (Not Was) and Iggy Pop.

Selected albums: *Yemenite Songs* (1985), *A Place For Me* (1988, reisssue), *Chi* (1988, reissue), *Earth* (1988, reissue), *Ofra Haza* (1988, reissue), *Shaday* (1988), *Fifty Gates Of Wisdom* (1989, reissue), *Desert Wind* (1990), *Kirya* (1992).

Headboys
Formed in Edinburgh from the ashes of pop group Badger, the Headboys - Lou Lewis (guitar/vocals), Calum Malcolm (keyboards/vocals), George Boyter (bass/vocals) and Davy Ross (drums/vocals) - secured a lucrative deal with Robert Stigwood's RSO label on the strength of a set of superior demos recorded at Malcolm's own studio. They enjoyed a minor hit with 'The Shape Of Things To Come' (1979), but a faintly ludicrous schoolboy image undermined their grasp of power pop. *The Headboys* was not a commercial success and the group split up soon after its release. Malcolm later relocated his studio, *Castle Sound*, to a village on the outskirts of Edinburgh where it has since become one of the leading recording centres in Britain. Clients have included Simple Minds and the Blue Nile, for whom Malcolm has acted as an auxiliary member.
Album: *The Headboys* (1980).

Heart Throbs
Formed by Rose Carlotti (b. Rosemarie DeFreitas, 16 December 1963, Barbados, West Indies; guitar/vocals) and Stephen Ward (b. 19 April 1963, Chelmsford, Essex, England; guitar/vocals) from an idea conceived at college in Birmingham and developed in Reading in 1986, when Rose's sister Rachael (b. 25 May 1966, Oxfordshire, England; bass/vocals) and Mark Side (b. 24 June 1969, Oxfordshire, England; drums) completed the line-up. Within a year the Heart Throbs had made inroads towards infamy, supporting the Jesus And Mary Chain on tour and releasing 'Bang' in a controversial 'car crash' record sleeve. Further publicity followed at the close of the decade when the band started up their own Profumo label, named after the political sex scandal which rocked Britain in the early 60s, and which warranted tastefully 'saucy' pictures of singer Rose posing as the notorious Christine Keeler had done twenty years earlier, (added to which one of the main scandal protagonists shared the same name as guitarist Ward). In spite of these tactics and several waves of acclaim for their harshly bittersweet pop songs, commercial success remained out of reach. A deal with the One Little Indian label in the UK coincided with the band signing to Elektra in the USA. Now joined by guitarist Alan Barclay (b. 4 April 1968, Singapore), they achieved moderate success on both sides of the Atlantic with the long-awaited debut album *Cleopatra Grip* and embarked on a tense tour towards the end of 1990 which resulted

Heavenly

in the departure of both bassist Rachael Carlotti and drummer Mark Side, leaving the Heart Throbs to rebuild on some impressively solid foundations.
Album: *Cleopatra Grip* (1990).

Heartbreakers

Formed in New York in 1975 when Richard Hell, former bassist with Television, joined forces with Johnny Thunders (b. 15 July 1952, d. 23 April 1991; guitar/vocals) and Jerry Nolan (drums), disaffected members of the New York Dolls. The new act made one live appearance as a trio before adding Walter Lure (guitar/vocals) to the line-up. The original Heartbreakers enjoyed cult popularity, but by the following year the mercurial Hell left to found the Void-Oids. Drafting Billy Rath as his replacement, the quartet later moved to London, eager to embrace its nascent punk movement. They supported the Sex Pistols on the aborted *Anarchy* tour (December 1976) and were then signed to the ailing Track Records. 'Chinese Rocks', a paean to heroin co-written by Dee Dee Ramone of the Ramones, and the subsequent *L.A.M.F.*, gave an indication of the group's strength, but was marred by Speedy Keen's unfocused production. Nolan left the band in disgust, but returned to fulfil outstanding commitments. The Heartbreakers then severed connections with Track, but having broken up in November 1977, reformed the following year with new drummer Ty Styx. The name was subsequently dropped and resurrected on several occasions, notably in 1984, but such interludes vied with Thunders' other, equally temporary, outlets. This enigmatic artist was found dead in mysterious circumstances in April 1991.
Albums: *L.A.M.F.* (1977), *Live At Max's Kansas City* (1979), *D.T.K. Live At The Speakeasy* (1982), *Live At The Lyceum Ballroom 1984* (1984), *L.A.M.F. Revisited* (1985 - remixed version of debut album). Compilation: *D.T.K. - L.A.M.F.* (1984).

Heavenly

After the break-up of Talulah Gosh in 1988, Amelia Fletcher, Matthew Fletcher and Peter Momtchiloff re-formed, still in Oxford, in the summer of 1989 as Heavenly. The line-up was completed with the addition of the original 'Gosh bassist Robert Pursey (b. 27 May 1964, Chipping Sodbury, Avon, England). Whilst retaining the fun and, at times, some of the tweeness of the previous outfit, Heavenly displayed a tighter, mature sound, particularly in Amelia Fletcher's love-song lyrics and with Momtchiloff's guitar playing. Recording for Sarah Records, Heavenly's debut single in 1990 'I Fell In Love Last Night' was followed by 'Our Love Is

Heavenly'. The debut mini-album *Heavenly Vs Satan* was a perfect statement from the group, highlighted by 'Shallow' and 'Stop Before You Say It'. A perfect example of Amelia Fletcher's self-depreciating sense of humour was to found in the b-side 'Escort Crash On Marston Street (a re-working of the debut album's 'Wish Me Gone'). The group's line-up was enlarged in the summer of 1991 by the arrival of Cathy Rogers (b. 29 May 1968, Tatsfield, Surrey, England; keyboards/vocals) for the recording of the group's first full album, *Le Jardin de Heavenly*. With the break-up of the Field Mice in 1991, Heavenly can now claim to be the Sarah label's greatest asset. Amelia Fletcher also recorded a one-off solo EP *Can You Keep A Secret* for the Fierce label in 1988.
Albums: *Heavenly Vs Satan* (1991), *Le Jardin De Heavenly* (1992).

Helen And The Horns (see Chefs)

Richard Hell

Hell, Richard
b. Richard Myers, 2 October 1949, Lexington, Kentucky, USA. A seminal figure on New York's emergent punk scene, Hell was a founder member of the Neon Boys with guitarist Tom Verlaine. He first performed several of his best-known songs, including 'Love Comes In Spurts', while in this group. The Neon Boys subsequently mutated into Television, where Hell's torn clothing, the result of impoverishment, inspired Malcolm McLaren's ideas for the Sex Pistols. Personality clashes resulted in Hell's departure and he then formed the Heartbreakers with former New York Dolls' guitarist Johnny Thunders. He also left this group prematurely, but reappeared fronting his own unit, Richard Hell And The Voidoids, with Bob Quine and Ivan Julian (guitars) and Marc Bell (drums). Hell's debut EP was released in 1976 and its underground popularity secured a recording deal with Sire Records. The result was the artist's compulsive *Blank Generation*, the title track of which achieved anthem-like proportions. However the quartet's progress faltered when Bell left to join the Ramones, and although Hell retained the services of Quine, this excellent guitarist was eventually drawn into session work. Hell continued to work with variations of the Voidoids and remains an charismatic, if elusive, individual. His sporadic recordings have been punctuated by writing and film work, the most notable of which was a starring role in Susan Seidelman's *Smithereens*.
Albums: *Blank Generation* (1977), *Destiny Street* (1982), *R.I.P* (1985).

Heyward, Nick
b. 20 May 1961, Beckenham, Kent, England. The original lead vocalist in UK chart group Haircut 100, Heyward quit for a solo career in late 1982. Early the following year he returned with a couple of chart hits, 'Whistle Down The Wind' and 'Take That Situation', which showed off his talent as a blue-eyed soulful vocalist. His debut solo album, *North Of A Miracle*, which included the uptempo 'Blue Hat For A Blueday', was a solid effort which won critical approval and sold well. An uneasy move away from his teenage audience was completed with the funk-influenced 'Warning Sign' but like many former pin-up stars the transition has brought only limited commercial success. His considerable talent as a graphic artist has enabled him to pursue two careers.
Albums: *North Of A Miracle* (1983), *Postcards From Home* (1986).

High
Instigated in Manchester, England in October 1987 by Andy Couzens (b. 15 July 1965, Macclesfield, Cheshire, England; guitar), who had previously plied his trade in the yet-to-blossom Stone Roses. Joined by John Matthews (b. 23 September 1967, Torquay, Devon, England; vocals), Simon Davies (b. 24 January 1967, Manchester, England; bass) and Chris Goodwin (b. 10 August 1965, Oldham, Lancashire, England; drums), the High immediately eschewed the traditional paths open to small bands by avoiding the pitfalls of incessant touring. Instead, the quartet fabricated a set of unashamedly classic guitar/pop

songs and signed to London Records after just one high profile hometown show. Armed with such a simple musical formula, the High were able to work at an unusually brisk pace, releasing three singles in 1990, each of which gradually pushed the band further towards the brink of the public's consciousness. Eventually, at the turn of the year, a remixed version of their debut, 'Box Set Go' worked its way up to number 28 in the UK charts, allowing them to concentrate on creating new material throughout 1991.

Album: *Somewhere Soon* (1990).

Higsons

Formed at Norwich University, England in 1980 by Charlie 'Switch' Higson (lead vocals), Terry Edwards (guitar, saxophone, trumpet), Stuart McGeachin (guitar), Simon Charterton (drums), Colin Williams (bass) and Dave Cummings (guitar), who left the line-up early on. They originally appeared under a plethora of guises such as the Higson 5, the Higson Brothers, the Higson Experience and had settled for the Higsons by the time their first single 'I Don't Want To Live With Monkeys' (1981) on the independent label Romans In Britain was released. The song typified the Higsons' brand of quirky, tongue-in-cheek funk/pop and was treated to extensive airplay by the influential BBC radio disc jockey John Peel, achieving a number 2 position in the UK independent chart. A new label, Waap, brought with it a second single, 'The Lost And The Lonely' (1981), followed by 'Conspiracy' (1982). A contract with Chrysalis/2-Tone ensued for two singles, 'Tear The Whole Thing Down' (1982) and 'Run Me Down' (1983). They returned to Waap for 'Push Out The Boat' (1983) and yet another change of labels (Uptight) for a cover of Andy Williams' 'Music To Watch Girls By' (1984). The single failed to provide that elusive hit and was followed by the album, *The Curse Of The Higsons*, combining several single sides with new material. Another move, to EMI's R4 label, yielded 'Take It' in 1985, but although Cummings had rejoined for the single, the Higsons played their final gig in March 1986. A posthumous release by Waap, *Attack Of The Cannibal Zombie Businessmen*, married both sides of the first three 45s with six unreleased cuts, including a cover of the Buddy Miles track 'Them Changes'. By that time, Charlie Higson had turned his hand to writing for the UK television comedy series *Saturday Night Live* and most notably for comedian Harry Enfield. Charterton formed the short-lived Eat My Bed, and then Brazilian Nightmare with ex-Serious Drinking pair Pete Saunders (ex-Dexy's Midnight Runners) and Jem Moore. Terry Edwards later performed with, and produced Yeah Jazz, released a single as New York, New York ('Roger Wilson Said') and teamed

up with Madness's Mark 'Bedders' Bedford as the Butterfield 8. Dave Cummings, meanwhile, joined Lloyd Cole's Commotions in 1986 and later joined Del Amitri.

Albums: *Live At The Jacquard Club, Norwich* (1982), *The Curse Of The Higsons* (1984), *Attack Of The Cannibal Zombie Businessmen* (1987).

Hipsway

Hipsway emerged in the mid-80s onto a Scottish pop scene that had enjoyed a high profile, both commercially and critically, with acts like Orange Juice, the Associates, Simple Minds and Altered Images. It was ex-Altered Images' bassist Jon McElhone who teamed up with guitarist Pim Jones, drummer Harry Travers and vocalist Graham Skinner (previously in the White Savages) around 1984. As Hipsway, the band secured a deal with Mercury who were impressed enough to strongly promote both 'Broken Years' in June and the catchy 'Ask The Lord' later in 1985, though neither made much impact. However, the momentum led to a chart hit with their third single, 'Honey Thief' early in 1986, and in its wake came both Hipsway's self-titled album and a reissue of 'Ask The Lord' in April. Unfortunately, Graham Skinner's dramatic vocal style was the only distinctive feature aside from the previous promising singles. From it came 'Long White Car' in August but both fell quickly by the wayside after a modest chart run. It was three years before Hipsway would return but unfortunately they failed to manage what their second album, *Scratch The Surface,* suggested. 'Young Love' disappeared without trace, the album followed suit, and Hipsway broke up soon afterwards. McElhone would appear later as bassist for country rock-influenced Texas.

Albums: *Hipsway* (1986), *Scratch The Surface* (1989).

His Name Is Alive

Formed in 1987 and hailing from Michigan, USA, His Name Is Alive (an obscure reference to Abraham Lincoln) was formed by Warren Defever (b. 1969; guitar, bass, vocals, samples) with high school friends Angela Carozzo (vocals) and Karin Oliver (guitar, vocals). Their first single was the independently released cassette 'Riotousness And Postrophe' (1987) and was followed the idiosyncratic 'His Name Is Alive' (1987), 'I Had Sex With God' (1988) and 'Eutectic' (1988 - a commissioned piece for the Harbinger Dance Company in Detroit). The group slotted in perfectly in the set-up at 4AD, the label which, more than anyone else was capable of handling their brand of ethereal, dream-like elegance. After the release of *Livonia*, the group expanded to a sextet, despite the departure of Carozzo, to comprise Defever, Oliver, Denise James (vocals), Melissa Elliott (guitar), Jymn Auge (guitar) and Damian Lang (drums). Often compared to the Cocteau Twins and This Mortal Coil (among others, and all on 4AD), Defever's eclecticism took a pervese turn when a cover of Ritchie Blackmore's 'Man On The Silver Mountain', was included on the 1992 EP *Dirt Eaters*. Albums: *Livonia* (1990), *Home Is In Your Head* (1991).

Hitchcock, Robyn

The possessor of a lyrical vision of a latter-day Syd Barrett, Hitchcock made his early reputation with the post-punk psychedelic group, the Soft Boys, having previously appeared in various groups including the Beetles and Maureen And The Meat Packers. After the Soft Boys split in 1981 he spent some time writing for Captain Sensible, then formed his own group, the Egyptians, around erstwhile colleagues Andy Metcalfe (bass), Morris Windsor (drums) and Roger Jackson (keyboards). Hitchcock's live

Robyn Hitchcock

performances were punctuated by epic, surreal monologues of comic invention capable of baffling the uninitiated and delighting the converted. His sharp mind and predilection for the bizarre has revealed itself in many titles, such as 'Man With The Light Bulb Head' ('. . . I turn myself on in the dark'), 'My Wife And My Dead Wife' a tragi-comedy of a man coming to accept the intrusion into his life of deceased spouse, 'Trash' a well aimed diatribe against hopeless rock star hangers-on, 'Trams Of Old

London' a love and remembrance of a era long gone and a guide to bringing up children in the a cappella 'Uncorrected Personality Traits'. A move to A&M Records saw the release of *Globe Of Frogs*, which included the 'Ballroom Man', a favourite on US college radio which went some way to breaking new ground and earning Hitchcock a fresh audience. As a result, and despite his devoted cult following in the UK, the artist has in the early 90s concentrated more on recording and performing in the United States (occasionally guesting with R.E.M.). It remains to be seen whether the odd-ball workings of this endearing eccentric's mind will find a way into anything other than the US collegiate consciousness.

Albums: *Black Snake Diamond Role* (1981 - includes material recorded with the Soft Boys), *Groovy Decay* (1982), *I Often Dream Of Trains* (1984), *Fegmania!* (1985), *Gotta Let This Hen Out!* (1985), *Groovy Decoy* (1985), *Element Of Light* (1986), *Invisible Hitchcock* (1986), *Globe Of Frogs* (1988), *Queen Elvis* (1989), *Eye* (1990), *Perspex Island* (1991).

Hole

This exciting US hardcore guitar band fronted by the effervescent Courtney Love (vocals, guitar). An ex-actress, who had small roles in Alex Cox's *Sid And Nancy* and *Straight To Hell*, she was born to hippie parents and even attended the Woodstock Festival as a child. She spent the rest of her childhood years at boarding schools in England and New Zealand, where her parents had bought a sheep farm, before travelling around the world in her teens. Returning to Los Angeles, she appeared for a while as vocalist with Faith No More in an incarnation which only reached the rehearsal stage. There she formed Hole with Caroline (drums), Jill (Bass) and Eric (guitar), following the suggestion of Sonic Youth's Kim Gordon. The band quickly produced a trio of fine singles; 'Retard Girl', 'Dicknail', and 'Teenage Whore', which were pointed and unsettling dirges, set in a grimly sexual lyrical environment. Equally impressive was the debut album, produced by Don Fleming (Gumball), followed by massive exposure supporting Mudhoney throughout Europe. It was on this jaunt that Courtney achieved further notoriety by being the first woman musician to 'trash' her guitar on stage in the UK.

Album: *Pretty On The Inside* (1991).

Holly And The Italians

Holly Beth Vincent (b. Chicago, Illinois, USA) formed the band in Los Angeles in 1978 with herself on vocals and guitar, Mark Henry on bass, and New York born Steve Young on drums. Feeling more affinity with the UK music scene they flew to London shortly after their inauguration. There they met disc jockey Charlie Gillett and signed to his Oval

label, putting out 'Tell That Girl To Shut Up', which was later covered by Transvision Vamp. They played around the pub and club circuit before coming to prominence as support to Blondie. Signed to Virgin, they cut two fine new wave pop singles in 'Miles Away' and 'Youth Coup', with a debut album produced by Richard Gottehrer. However, soon after its release the group split, leaving behind just two further singles. Vincent moved on to pursue a solo career, with the confusingly titled album *Holly And The Italians*, which was credited solely to Holly Beth Vincent. She duetted with Joey Ramone on 'I Got You Babe', alongside further solo singles for Virgin. After a brief spell replacing Patty Donahue in the Waitresses, she appeared in an *ad hoc* combo called the Wild Things with Anthony Thistlethwaite of the Waterboys. They provided a track, 'Siberian Miles', for a fanzine *What A Nice Way To Turn 17*, with Vincent doing her best to sound like Peter Perrett (Only Ones).
Albums: *The Right To Be Italian* (1981), *Holly And The Italians* (1982).

Hollywood Brats

In 1973 a band came together in London and recorded an album that would later be cited as one of the most influential albums of the punk period even though it was not released in the UK until 1980. The group was led by Canadian vocalist Andrew Matheson but probably their strength was the Norwegian keyboard player Casino Steel. The rest of the band was Eunan Brady (guitar), Wayne Manor (bass) and Louis Sparks (drums). Hollywood Brats, with elements of Flamin' Groovies and New York Dolls, endeared it to European fans and some copies crept into the UK. However, by the time Cherry Red finally put out the 1979 single 'Then He Kissed Me' and the album the following year, the band had gone their separate ways. Matheson was still recording with Brady helping out in between spells with the Tools and Wreckless Eric's Last Orders. Steel joined the infamous London SS and did a couple of rehearsals before Mat Dangerfield dragged him off to help form the Boys in June 1976.
Album: *Hollywood Brats* (1980).

Honey Bane

b. Donna Tracy, England. Honey Bane was previously the young singer of the Fatal Microbes who released an EP *Violence Grows* and shared a 12-inch single release with the Poison Girls. She started her solo career in 1979 after escaping from a reform centre where she was admitted for alcohol abuse. 'You Can Be You' on the Crass label was recorded in a single day. Her backing band were the Kebabs, actually a pseudonym for the Crass, although the three 'anarcho-punk' songs still retained the spirit of Fatal Microbes. It was almost a year before the follow-up, 'Guilty' was released, on Honey's own label, and stirred up enough interest to secure a deal with EMI subsidiary, Zonophone. With the help of Peter Godwin from Metro and Jimmy Pursey from Sham 69, they tried to manufacture a pop star. In January 1981 'Turn Me On, Turn Me Off' peaked at number 37. Her provocative 'naughty girl' image had short-lived appeal and after one further glimpse at the charts with a cover version of the Supremes' 'Baby Love', her popularity made a rapid decline. Successive singles 'Jimmy . . . (Listen To Me)', 'Wish I Could Be Me' and 'Dizzy Dreamers', passed unnoticed, prompting Honey to concentrate on her acting career.

Honeyman-Scott, James

b. 1956, Hereford, England, d. 16 June 1982, London, England. This flaxen-headed guitarist who doubled on keyboards was a founder member of the Pretenders in 1978. If less prominent onstage than Chrissie Hynde, he was solidly at the music's heart: loud enough for vocal harmonies, but quietly ministering to overall effect instrumentally. Remembered principally as a guitarist, his riffs and solos were constructed to integrate with melodic and lyrical intent, rather than a flashier reaction to underlying chord sequences. This style was commensurate with a personality that permitted Hynde to take increasing control of the band's destiny after Pretenders II in 1981 - the year he married Peggy Sue Fender. Weakened by a detoxification course for drug addiction, his death in June 1982 occurred shortly after snorting cocaine at a London party. The group found a replacement in Robert McIntosh, a Honeyman-Scott soundalike.

Hothouse Flowers

This folk-inspired Irish rock group, who took their name from the title of a Wynton Marsalis album, are based around the nucleus of Liam O'Maonlai and Fiachna O'Broainain. O'Maonlai was formerly in a punk band called Congress which would later evolve into My Bloody Valentine. They started performing together as the Incomparable Benzini Brothers and busked in their native Dublin. In 1985 they won the Street Entertainers Of The Year Award. Recruiting Maria Doyle they became the Hothouse Flowers and landed a regular gig at the Magic Carpet Club just outside Dublin. Their notoriety spreading, they were highly praised in *Rolling Stone* magazine before they had even concluded a record deal. An appearance on RTE's Saturday night chat programme - *The Late Show* - led to the issue of a single on U2's Mother label. 'Love Don't Work That Way' came out in 1987 and though it wasn't a great success it brought them to the attention of PolyGram who signed them up. Their debut single for the major - 'Don't Go' - was a number 11 UK hit. Further hits followed, including a cover of Johnny Nash's 'I Can See Clearly Now', 'Give It Up', and 'Movies'. Their debut, *People*, reached number 2 in the UK charts. The band exist as part of a larger, looser 'Raggle Taggle' musical community, and members can be heard on material by the Indigo Girls, Adventures, Michelle Shocked and Maria McKee. They recently made their 'acting' debut in an episode of the UK television series *Lovejoy*.

Albums: *People* (1988), *Home* (1990).

House Of Love; Guy Chadwick

House Of Love

After a short spell with the ill-fated glam-rock inspired Kingdoms, UK-born vocalist/guitarist Guy Chadwick teamed up with drummer Pete Evans, guitarist Terry Bickers, bassist Chris Groothuizen and vocalist/guitarist Andrea Heukamp to form UK group, the House Of Love. Throughout 1986, the quintet played at small pubs and despatched a demo tape to Creation Records which, after constant play in the office, attracted the attention of label head, Alan McGee. He financed the recording of their debut single, the sparkling 'Shine On', which was released in May 1987. A follow-up 'Real Animal' was also issued but sold relatively poorly. After touring extensively under tough conditions, Andrea Heukamp decided to leave the group. Continuing as

a quartet, the House Of Love spent the spring of 1988 recording their debut album, which cost an astonishingly low £8,000 to complete. A pilot single, 'Christine', was rightly acclaimed as one of the best UK independent singles of the year. Its shimmering guitar work was exemplary and indicated the enormous potential of the ensemble.

The debut album did not disappoint and was included in many critics nominations for the best record of 1988. Already, the House Of Love were being tipped as the group most likely to succeed in 1989 and the release of the excellent 'Destroy The Heart' reinforced that view. Speculation was rife that they would sign to a major label and eventually PhonoGram secured their signatures. In keeping with their 60s/guitar-based image the group's releases were subsequently issued on the newly-revived Fonatana label. A torturous period followed. The first two singles for the label, 'Never' and 'I Don't Know Why I Love You' both stalled at number 41, while the album suffered interminable delays. By Christmas 1989, guitarist Terry Bickers had quit over what was euphemistically termed a personality clash. He was immediately replaced by Simon Walker, and early the following year the group's long-awaited £400,000 second album *Fontane* appeared to mixed reviews. As Chadwick later acknowledged: 'We'd stated everything on the first album'. Extensive touring followed, ending with the departure of Walker, tentatively replaced by original member Andrea Heukamp, who returned from Germany. Thereafter, Chadwick suffered a long period of writer's block while the departing Bickers enjoyed acclaim in Levitation. Although the House Of Love lost ground to newly-revered guitar groups such as the Stone Roses, they re-emerged in October 1991 with an acclaimed EP featuring the excellent 'The Girl With The Loneliest Eyes'. In 1992, the group's long awaited new album, *Babe Rainbow*, was released to critical acclaim.

Albums: *House Of Love* (1988), *Fontane* (1989), *Babe Rainbow* (1992). Compilation: *A Spy In The House Of Love* (1990).

Housemartins

Formed in 1984, this UK pop group comprised Paul Heaton (b. 9 May 1962, Hull, Humberside, England; vocals/guitar), Stan Collimore (b. 6 April 1962, Hull, Humberside, England; bass), Ted Key (guitar) and Hugh Whitaker (drums). After signing to Go! Discs the group humorously promoted themselves as 'the fourth best band from Hull'. Their modesty and distinctly plain image disguised a genuine songwriting talent, which soon emerged. During late 1985, Key departed and was replaced by Norman Cook (b. 31 July 1963, Brighton, Sussex, England). By 1986, the group achieved their first UK hit with their third release, the infectious 'Happy Hour', which climbed to number 3. Their UK Top 10 debut album *Hull 4, London 0* displayed a wit, freshness and verve that rapidly established them as one of Britain's most promising groups. In December 1986, their excellent a cappella version of 'Caravan Of Love' gave them a deserved UK number 1 hit. Early in 1987 the Housemartins received a coveted BPI award as the Best Newcomers of the year. In the summer, they underwent a line-up change, with Dave Hemmingway replacing drummer Hugh Whitaker. Another acclaimed album *Five Get Over Excited* followed, after which the group displayed their left-wing political preferences by performing at the 'Red Wedge' concerts. After securing another Top 20 hit with the catchy 'Me And The Farmer', the group issued their final studio album, the self-mocking *The People Who Grinned Themselves To Death*. Although still at the peak of their powers, the group split in June 1988, announcing that they had only intended the Housemartins to last for three years. The power of the original line-up was indicated by the subsequent successes of offshoot groups such as the Beautiful South and Beats International.

Albums: *London 0, Hull 4* (1986), *The People Who Grinned Themselves To Death* (1987). Compilation: *Now That's What I Call Quite Good!* (1988).

H2O

H2O was formed in Glasgow, Scotland during 1978 after lead singer, Ian Donaldson parted company with punk band Skroo and recruited Kenny Dorman (drums), Ross Alcock (keyboards), Colin Ferguson (bass), Colin Gavigan (saxophones) and Davie Wells (guitar), who was later replaced by Pete Keane. They built up a large local following, releasing their independent debut, 'Hollywood Dream' on Spock in 1981. It made little impression, but helped bring the band to the attention of RCA, who gave the sextet their breakthrough hit in the summer of 1983 with the moody and atmospheric 'I Dream To Sleep', reaching number 17 in the UK charts. With the follow-up 'Just Outside Of Heaven' peaking at number 38, their brief flirtation with the charts was over and the succession of singles and album that followed were unable to capture the inspiration or success of their only Top 20 hit.

Album: *Faith* (1984).

Hula

Based in Sheffield, England, Hula was one of the areas most prominent exponents of the independent music scene, churning out numerous albums and 12-inch singles of funky synthesized pop for Yorkshire's Red Rhino label. Hula hinged around Mark Albrow (keyboards/tapes), Alan Fish (drums/percussion, later replaced by Nort) and Ron Wright (vocals/guitar/tapes/clarinet), helped at first by Chakk's Mark Brydon (bass/percussion). Their debut EP, 1982's *Back Pop Workout*, was well-received but it was a year before *Cut From Inside*, was released. 1984 brought perhaps their best-known single, 'The Fever Car' in September, alongside a second album, *Murmur In November*. 'Get The Habit' and 'Walk On Stalks Of Shattered Glass' (for which Hula was joined by John Arery) were followed early in the new year by *One Thousand Years* and then *Freeze Out*, taken from sessions for BBC Radio 1 disc jockey John Peel. For *Shadowland*, Hula was aided by Adam Barnes and sleeve designer Simon Crump. This preceded 'Black Wall Blue' in November and 'Poison' in March 1987, produced by Daniel Miller. In May, Hula unleashed *Voice*, again enlisting outside help from Alan Fisch, Justin Bennett and Darrell D'Silva to add a wider instrumental range. 'Cut Me Loose' in August and *Threshold* in November meant that 1987 was Hula's busiest year; but strangely, it turned out to be their last. Red Rhino went bankrupt soon after and without the freedom the label had given them, Hula as a band disappeared, although members continue to work within Sheffield's active music scene.

Albums: *Cut From Inside* (1983), *Murmur* (1984), *One Thousand Hours* (1986), *Shadowland* (1986), *Voice* (1987), *Threshold* (1987).

Hunters And Collectors

Formed in Melbourne, Australia in 1981, Hunters And Collectors experimented with a punk/funk style, drawing comparisons in some quarters to the Talking Heads, something which earned them a strong following on the Australian alternative music scene. The core members of the group have over the years comprised Mark Seymour (guitar/lead vocals), Jeremy Smith (keyboards/saxophone), Doug Falconer (drums), John Archer (bass), Martin Lubran (guitar), Geoff Crosbie (keyboards), Greg Perano (percussion), and trombonists Michael Waters and Jack Howard (trombone). The band recorded a single, two EPs and an album in 1982. Their debut album incorporated harsh brass instruments and their second album extended this further, but their experimentation failed to impress the public. Then the band focused on lead singer, Mark Seymour's lyrics and songwriting, about troubled relationships, and his anguished voice propelled the band to new heights. The music took on a more solid, rock sound with dynamic arrangements, shifting the emphasis from horns to bass and drums. With each album honing and refining this sound, the band's audience expanded as it toured widely, eventually going to the USA and Europe. Given the high musicianship of the band, it is perhaps surprising that the emphasis in latter albums has been on Seymour's lyrics and the band's macho image.

Albums: *Hunters And Collectors* (1982), *Fireman's Curse* (1983), *Jaws Of Life* (1984), *Live* (1985), *Way To Go Out* (1985), *Human Frailty* (1986), *What's A Few Men* (1987), *Fate* (1988), *Ghost Nation* (1990).

Hurrah!

Originally known as the Green-Eyed Children, consisting of Paul Handyside (b. 28 September 1960, Newcastle-upon-Tyne, Tyne And Wear, England; guitar/vocals), David 'Taffy' Hughes (b. 16 March 1961, Southmoor, Northumberland, England; guitar/vocals), David Porterhouse (b. 17 August 1961, Gateshead, Tyne And Wear, England; bass) and Mark Sim (drums). Switching to the moniker of Hurrah!, the quartet signed to the new Kitchenware label in 1982. Mark Sim soon departed to be replaced by Damien Mahoney, whereupon a series of acclaimed singles such as 'The Sun Shines Here' and 'Hip Hip' earned the band great respect from the British Independent sector. Based upon the pivotal force of the singing/guitar-playing/songwriting partnership of Paul Handyside and David Hughes, Hurrah! mastered a jittery, urgent style rich in melodic content. By 1986, however, the band had pushed their sound towards a rockier terrain, replacing the initial charm with power and passion. Damien Mahoney left to join the police force in the spring of that year, allowing Steve Price to fill the vacant drum stool. Their debut *Tell God I'm Here*, saw the light of day in 1987, swiftly followed by a support date with U2 at London's Wembley and, on a more bizarre note, live shows in Iraq, Egypt and Jordan after accepting an invitation from the British Council. In spite of the band's determination, commercial success remained elusive. When *The Beautiful*, failed to have a significant impact on the marketplace Hurrah! parted company with the 'misunderstanding' Arista label and returned to the Independent sector. Adrian Evans (b. 6 March 1963, County Durham, England) became the band's fourth drummer when Steve Price emigrated to America.
Albums: *Tell God I'm Here* (1987), *The Beautiful* (1989). Compilation: *Boxed* (1985).

Hüsker Dü

Formed in Minneapolis, Minnesota, USA in 1979, Hüsker Dü was a punk trio consisting of guitarist/vocalist Bob Mould, bassist Greg Norton and drummer Grant Hart. Taking their name, which means 'Do you remember?', from a Swedish board game, they started out as an aggressive hardcore thrash band before challenging that genre's restrictions and expanding to other musical forms. Their first single, 'Statues', was released on the small Reflex label in 1981. The following year, their debut album, *Land Speed Record,* was released on New Alliance Records, followed by an EP, *In A Free Land,*

and *Everything Falls Apart*, in 1983 (back on Reflex). By the release of their second EP, *Metal Circus* (now on SST Records), Hüsker Dü had become a critics' favourite in the USA. *Zen Arcade*, in 1984, became their turning point - a two-record set, it followed a single storyline about a young boy leaving home and finding life even more difficult on his own. A 14-minute closing song, 'Reoccurring Dreams', in which it's revealed the boy's entire ordeal was a dream, broke all the rules of punk. A non-album cover of the Byrds' 'Eight Miles High' followed, and a 1985 album, *New Day Rising*, maintained the trio's reputation as a favourite of critics and college radio stations. After *Flip Your Wig*, the band signed with Warner Brothers Records, with which it issued *Candy Apple Grey* in 1986 and *Warehouse: Songs And Stories,* another double set, the following year. In 1988 Hart was dismissed from the group and it summarily disbanded. Mould and Hart have continued as solo artists.
Albums: *Land Speed Record* (1982), *Everything Falls Apart* (1983), *Zen Arcade* (1984), *New Day Rising* (1985), *Flip Your Wig* (1985), *Candy Apple Grey* (1986), *Warehouse: Songs And Stories* (1987).

Hypnotics (Thee)

Formed in High Wycombe, Buckinghamshire, England, this MC5 and Stooges-influenced group was the product of James Jones (vocals), Ray Hanson (guitar), Will Pepper (bass) and Mark Thompson (drums). On the strength of 'Love In A Different Vein' (1988), their debut single on the Hipsville label, the band signed to Beggars Banquet offshoot Situation 2 and enjoyed independent chart success early the following year with the eight-minute 'Justice In Freedom'. Awash with loud, distorted, wah-wah guitars and blues riffs, the single had to be re-pressed due to popular demand. The powerful 'Soul Trader' followed later that year; and after supports for Spacemen 3 and Gaye Bykers On Acid, the band commemorated their first national tour with a live mini-album, *Live'r Than God!*. A tour of the USA with the Cult won them praise across the Atlantic, before the band's first studio album surfaced early in 1990. *Come Down Heavy* was more refined and showed a definite nod towards early Santana, with guest appearances from Pretty Things Dick Taylor and Phil May. Two singles followed, 'Half Man Half Boy' and 'Floatin' In My Hoodoo Dream', and the band appeared at the 1990 Reading Festival.
Albums: *Live'r Than God!* (1989), *Come Down Heavy* (1990), *Soul, Glitter And Sin* (1991).

I

Icicle Works

Emerging from the profligate network of Liverpudlian bands that existed during the punk rock and new wave era, the Icicle Works were formed by Ian McNabb (b. 3 November 1962; vocals/guitar), Chris Layhe (bass) and Chris Sharrock (drums). McNabb was formerly in City Limits with the near legendary Edie Shit (Howie Mimms), and Sharrock played with the Cherry Boys (who also included Mimms at one point). Taking their name from a

Icicle Works

science fiction novel - *The Day The Icicle Works Closed Down* - they made their recording debut with a six-track cassette called *Ascending*, released on the local Probe emporium in 1981. The band then founded their own Troll Kitchen label on which they prepared 'Nirvana', their premier single. Gaining a lot of support from BBC disc jockey John Peel they came to the attention of Beggars Banquet Records, initially through their Situation 2 offshoot. Their second single, 'Birds Fly (Whisper To A Scream)', was an 'indie' hit but they had to wait for the next effort, 'Love Is A Wonderful Colour', to breach the UK Top 20. The subject matter was typically subverted by McNabb's irony and cynicism ('When love calls me, I shall be running swiftly, To find out, just what all the fuss is all about'). Teaming up with producer Ian Broudie (ex-Big In Japan, Care, and later Lightning Seeds) he helped them to a string of single successes over the years including 'Hollow Horse' and 'Understanding Jane', with their sound gradually shifting from subtle pop to harder rock territory. In 1986 they recruited Dave Green on keyboards, but the following year the group was turned upside down when both Sharrock and Layhe left within a short space of time. Sharrock joined the

La's and later drummed for World Party. Layhe's role was taken by former Black bassist Roy Corkhill, whilst the drummer's stool was claimed by Zak Starkey whose father Ringo Starr formerly drummed for another Liverpool band! This line-up prospered for a short while but in 1989 McNabb assembled a new band. Retaining only Corkhill he added Mark Revell on guitar, Dave Baldwin on keyboards, and Paul Burgess on drums. The band signed a new deal with Epic and released an album before McNabb split to go solo. 1992 saw him working on his debut album provisionally titled *Truth And Beauty*. One of England's most under-rated, natural lyricists, his cult status looks set to continue.

Albums: *The Icicle Works* (1984), *The Small Price Of A Bicycle* (1985), *7 Singles Deep* (1986), *If You Want To*

Billy Idol

Defeat Your Enemy Sing His Song (1987), *Blind* (1987), *Permanent Damage* (1990).

Idol, Billy

b. William Michael Albert Broad, 30 November 1955, Stanmore, Middlesex, England. While studying English Literature at Sussex University, Broad became involved with the 'Bromley contingent' followers of the Sex Pistols. Inspired by the energy of punk, he formed his own group, Chelsea, in 1976. The original outfit was short-lived and Billy Idol, as he was now known, next founded Generation X. The group lasted from 1976-81 after which Idol launched his solo career in New York and recorded *Don't Stop*, which featured a revival of Tommy James And The Shondells' UK number 1 'Mony Mony'. Through 1982-83, Idol's career blossomed and his acerbic vocal style and lively stage act brought a string of hits including 'Hot In The City', 'White Wedding', 'Rebel Yell' and 'Eyes Without A Face'. With his albums sales increasing each year, Idol actually became an idol and turned an old hit to advantage by taking 'Mony Mony' to number 1 in the US in 1987. Despite his legendary excessive lifestyle, Idol has appeared in several charity shows. In 1988, he took part in Neil Young's Bridge School Benefit concert and the following year guested in the charity performance of the Who's *Tommy* in London. After being slated for a part in the Oliver Stone film of the Doors, Idol almost emulated its central character by suffering an early death. A serious motorcycle crash seriously damaged his leg, but he recovered remarkably speedily. However, he soon found himself back in trouble, this time with the Los Angeles courts when, in 1992, he was put on probation for two years and fined $2,700 for an assault on a 'fan'. This all added fuel to the rebel image and, in many respects, he has become more successful than most of the punk founders with whom he rubbed shoulders back in 1977.

Albums: *Billy Idol* (1982), *Rebel Yell* (1984), *Whiplash Smile* (1986), *Charmed Life* (1990). Compilations: *Vital Idol* (1986), *Idol Sings - 11 Of The Best* (1988).

Iggy Pop

b. James Jewel Osterburg, 21 April 1947, Ypsilanti, Michigan, USA. The emaciated 'Godfather Of Punk' Iggy Pop was born just west of Detroit to an English father and raised in nearby Ann Arbor. He first joined bands while at high school, initially as a drummer, most notably with the Iguanas in 1964 where he picked up the nickname Iggy. The following year he joined the Denver blues-styled Prime Movers, but a year after that dropped out of the University Of Michigan to travel to Chicago and learn about the blues from former Howlin' Wolf and Paul Butterfield Blues Band drummer Sam Lay. On returning to Detroit as Iggy Stooge, and further inspired after seeing the Doors, he formed the Psychedelic Stooges with Ron Asheton of the Chosen Few. Iggy was vocalist and guitarist, Asheton initially played bass, and they later added Asheton's brother Scott on drums. Before the Chosen Few, Ron Asheton had also been in the Prime Movers with Iggy. The Psychedelic Stooges made their debut on Halloween night, 1967 in Ann Arbor. The same year Iggy also made his acting debut in a long forgotten Francoise De Monierre film that also featured Nico. Meanwhile Dave Alexander joined on bass and the word

Iggy Pop and Debbie Harry

'Psychedelic' was dropped from their name. Ron switched to guitar leaving Iggy free to concentrate on singing and showmanship. The Stooges were signed to Elektra in 1968 by A&R man Danny Fields (later manager of the Ramones). They recorded two albums (the first produced by John Cale) for the label which sold moderately at the time but later became regarded as classics, featuring such numbers as 'No Fun' and 'I Wanna Be Your Dog'. Steven MacKay joined on saxophone in 1970 in-between the first and second albums as did Bill Cheatham on second guitar. Cheatham and Alexander left in August 1970 with Zeke Zettner replacing Alexander and James Williamson replacing Cheatham but the Stooges split not long afterwards as Iggy fought a heroin problem. Stooge fan David Bowie tried to resurrect Iggy's career and helped him record *Raw Power* in London in the summer of 1972 (as Iggy and the Stooges, with Williamson on guitar, Scott Thurston on bass, and the Ashetons, who were flown in when suitable British musicians could not be found). The resultant album included the nihilistic anthem 'Search And Destroy'. Bowie's involvement continued (although his management company Mainman withdrew support because of constant drug allegations) as Iggy sailed through stormy seas (including self-admission to a mental hospital). The popular, but poor quality, live *Metallic KO* was released in France only at the

time. Iggy Pop live events had long been a legend in the music industry, and it is doubtful whether any other artist has sustained such a high level of abject self destruction on stage. It was his performance on *So It Goes*, for example, that ensured the programme would never air again. After *Raw Power* there were sessions for *Kill City*, although it was not released until 1978, credited then to Iggy Pop and James Williamson. It also featured Thurston, Hunt and Tony Sales, Brian Glascock (ex-Toe Fat and later in the Motels), and others. The Stooges had folded again in 1974 with Ron Asheton forming New Order and then Destroy All Monsters. Steve MacKay later died from a drugs overdose and Dave Alexander from alcohol abuse. Thurston also joined the Motels. Interest was stirred in Iggy with the arrival of punk, on which his influence was self evident (Television recorded the tribute 'Little Johnny Jewel'), and in 1977 Bowie produced two studio albums - *The Idiot* and *Lust For Life* - using Hunt and Tony Sales, with Bowie himself, unheralded, playing keyboards. Key tracks from these two seminal albums include 'Night Clubbin'', 'The Passenger', and 'China Girl' (co-written with and later recorded by Bowie). Iggy also returned one of the several favours he owed Bowie by guesting on backing vocals for *Low*. In the late 70s Iggy signed to Arista and released some rather average albums with occasional assistance from Glen Matlock (ex-Sex Pistols) and Ivan Karl. He went into (vinyl) exile after 1982's autobiography and the Chris-Stein produced *Zombie Birdhouse*. During his time out of the studio he cleaned up his drug problems and married. He started recording again in 1985 with Steve Jones (again ex-Sex Pistols) featuring on the next series of albums. He also developed his acting career (even taking lessons) appearing in *Sid And Nancy*, *The Color Of Money*, *Hardware*, and on television in *Miami Vice*. His big return came in 1986 with the Bowie-produced *Blah Blah Blah* and his first ever UK hit single 'Real Wild Child', a cover of Australian Johnny O'Keefe's 50s rocker. His most recent album featured Guns N' Roses guitarist Slash, who co-wrote four of the tracks, while his contribution to the *Red Hot And Blue* AIDS benefit was an endearing duet with Debbie Harry on 'Well Did You Evah?'. This was followed in 1991 by a duet with the B-52's Kate Pierson.
Albums: *The Stooges* (1969), *Fun House* (1970), *Raw Power* (1973), *Metallic KO* (1974), *The Idiot* (1977), *Lust For Life* (1977), *Kill City* (1978), *TV Eye Live* (1978), *New Values* (1979), *Soldier* (1980), *Party* (1981), *Zombie Birdhouse* (1982), *Blah Blah Blah* (1986), *Instinct* (1988), *Brick By Brick* (1990).
Further reading: *I Need More*, Iggy Pop.

Imposter (see Costello, Elvis)

Indigo Girls

This American duo comprised Amy Ray (vocals/guitar) and Emily Saliers (vocals/guitar). Saliers and Ray met while in school, in their home town of Decatur, Georgia, USA, and later started to perform together, initially as 'Saliers and Ray'. They changed their name to Indigo Girls while at university. The duo's early releases were on their own label, Indigo Records, and commenced with a single, 'Crazy Game' in 1985, followed by an EP the following year. The latter recording included 'Blood And Fire' and 'Land Of Canaan', both of which re-appeared on *Indigo Girls*. Ray and Saliers were signed to Epic in 1988, and the first release featured, among others, Michael Stipe of R.E.M., and the Irish group Hothouse Flowers. Indigo Girls toured heavily throughout the USA to promote the album, in addition to playing support to Neil Young and R.E.M. *Indigo Girls* went gold in September 1989, and the duo won a Grammy award as the 'Best Contemporary Folk Group' of 1989. *Strange Fire* was re-issued towards the end of 1989, but with an additional track, 'Get Together', made famous by the Youngbloods. In addition to playing an AIDS research benefit in Atlanta, Georgia, in 1989, the duo were also asked by Paul Simon to perform at a fundraising event, in 1990, for the Children's Health Fund, a New York based fund founded by the singer. *Nomads, Indians, Saints* included the excellent Saliers song 'Hammer And A Nail' which features Mary Chapin Carpenter on backing vocals.
Albums: *Strange Fire* (1987), *Indigo Girls* (1989), *Nomads, Indians, Saints* (1990).

Inspiral Carpets

During the late 80s, the Manchester area of England spawned a host of exciting new groups and Inspiral Carpets were among the leading pack with Happy Mondays, James, the Stone Roses and 808 State. The group was formed in Oldham by schoolfriends Graham Lambert (guitar) and Stephen Holt (vocals). They were joined by drummer Craig Gill and performed in their hometown of Oldham with various other members until they were joined by organist Clint Boon and bassist David Swift. Boon met the group when they began rehearsing at his studio in Ashton-under-Lyne. His Doors-influenced playing later became the group's trademark. Their debut EP, *Planecrash*, was released by the independent label, Playtime, and the group were asked to record a John Peel session for BBC Radio 1. In 1988 there was an acrimonious split between the band and label and also between the group members. Holt and Swift were replaced by Tom Hingley and Martin Walsh, formerly with local bands Too Much Texas and the Next Step respectively. The band formed their own label, Cow Records, and after a string of well-

Inspiral Carpets; Tim Hingley

received singles they signed a worldwide deal with Mute Records. 'This Is How It Feels' was a hit and *Life* was critically acclaimed for its mixture of sparkling pop and occasional experimental touches. Further singles had less impact and *The Beast Inside* received a mixed response, some critics claiming the band were becoming better known for their merchandise, like t-shirts and promotional milk bottles. The t-shirts, bearing the immortal words, 'Cool as Fuck!' inevitably aroused considerable controversy, particularly when a fan was arrested for causing offense by wearing such a garment! Albums: *Life* (1990), *The Beast Inside* (1991).

Into Paradise

This rock-pop outfit formed in Dublin, Eire, in 1986, as Backwards Into Paradise. By 1988 their line-up had stabilized as Dave Long (vocals, guitar), James Eadie (lead guitar, keyboards), Rachael Tighe (bass), and Ronan Clarke (drums). They gathered few second glances until the release *Under The Water*, early in 1990. A capricious and deceptive album, it secured many plaudits and a predictable response from the media. Being from Dublin, they were automatically compared to both U2 and the Hothouse Flowers. Other critics noted the proliferation of drink orientated songs, which placed them in a more definite Irish tradition. The follow-

up *Churchtown* on their new Ensign label was given an altogether more terse reception. However, providing Long's songwriting continues to mature, their future looks bright.

Albums: *Under The Water* (1990), *Churchtown* (1991).

In Tua Nua

This septet from Dublin, Eire combined traditional Irish instrumentation (pipes and whistles) with commercial instruments. Unlike the Pogues or the Saw Doctors, however, they used this musical platform to play more in the style of a rock act. Led by vocalist Leslie Dowdall other members included Brian O'Briaian, Martin Colncy, Vinnie Kilduf and Steve Wickham. 'Discovered' by Bono (U2) they were originally signed to Island but later moved to Virgin. Their singles included 'Comin' Thru', 'Take My Hand' (their Island debut in 1984), a version of Jefferson Airplane's 'Somebody To Love' (1985), 'Seven Into The Sea' (1986), 'Heaven Can Wait' (1987) and 'The Long Acre' (1988). Only 'All I Wanted' (1989) gave them a hit, and then it proved to be only a minor breakthrough. They gigged with Bob Dylan at the Irish Self Aid show, before Wickham left in 1986 to join the Waterboys. He was replaced on violin by Angela De Burca. *The Long Acre* was produced by Don Dixon of R.E.M. fame.

Albums: *Vaudeville* (1987), *The Long Acre* (1988).

Invisible Girls (see Murray, Pauline, And The Invisible Girls)

INXS

Formed in 1977 as the Farriss Brothers in Sydney, Australia, INXS comprised the three Farriss brothers Tim (b. 16 August 1957; guitar), Jon (b. 18 August 1961; drums) and Andrew (b. 27 March 1959; keyboards); Michael Hutchence (b. 22 January 1960, Lain Cove, Sydney, Australia; lead vocals), Kirk Pengilly (b. 4 July 1958; guitar/saxophone/vocals) and Garry Beers (b. 22 June 1957; bass/vocals). The group moved to Perth, Western Australia to develop their own distinctive rock sound which incorporated both black dance music and white soul influences. The band began its recording career in 1980 with a single, 'Simple Simon'/'We Are The Vegetables' on the independent Deluxe label. Over the next three years, half a dozen singles reached the lower Top 40 in Australia, but the second album, *Underneath The Colours* sold well, and the next *Shabooh Shoobah* reached the Top 5. It was with the 'Original Sin' single of early 1985 and its accompanying album, *The Swing*, that the band finally hit the top of the charts in Australia. The album and single generated interest in the band from the USA, Europe and South America, and the follow-up album, *Listen Like Thieves* consolidated their world-wide success, except in the

UK where critics savaged the band, but it would not be long before sales finally took off there as well. In 1986 Hutchence made his acting debut in the film, *Dogs In Space*. One song from the film, 'Rooms For The Memory' earned him a solo Australian Top 10 single. The band toured the States and Europe constantly, and MTV aired their videos, providing success with *Kick* receiving over 1 million sales on advance orders in the USA alone and finally a number one US hit with 'Need You Tonight' in January 1988. The band's success can be attributed to many factors including an unchanged line-up from the beginning, the sultry good looks of vocalist Michael Hutchence, unstinting touring schedules, a variety of songwriters in the band and consistently good and fresh production with the help of a new producer for each album. After *Kick* and before the release of *X*, all members had a 12-month break and got involved with other projects - Hutchence with Max Q; Andrew Farriss in production work with Jenny Morris; and Garry Beers joined the loose collection of friends for a tour and to record with Absent Friends. *Live Baby Live* is a document of the INXS Wembley Stadium concert in July 1991. Hutchence's much publicized romance with Kylie Minogue brought the group's name to the attention of whole new generation of potential fans.

Albums: *INXS* (1980), *Underneath The Colours* (1981), *Shabooh Shoobah* (1982), *The Swing* (1984), *Listen Like Thieves* (1985), *Kick* (1987), *X* (1990), *Live Baby Live* (1991). Solo albums: Max Q *Max Q* (1989); Absent Friends *Here's Looking Up Your Address* (1990).

IQ

A performance/art based assembly who formed in Southampton, England, in 1981, having previously existed as the Lens three years earlier. By the time of their debut album's release the line-up had stabilized with Pete Nicholls (vocals), Tim Esau (bass), Mike Holmes (guitar), Martin Orford (keyboards) and Mark Rideout (drums). Taking their influences from jazz, blues, rock and reggae, they also interspersed elements of theatre and drama similar to Bauhaus. Nicholls had some form of acting experience; the highlight of his early career being an appearance on children's television show *Cheggers Plays Pop*. Following the cassette-only *Seven Stories Into Eight*, his band's debut album received excellent reviews in the music press including the late *Sounds*, which ensured a healthy cult following. Moving away from their early gothic leanings, later recordings became further associated with the progressive rock movement and bands such as Twelfth Night. However, productive over the ensuing mid-80s, they rapidly acquiesced to the law of diminishing returns.

Albums: *Living Proof* (1986), *Nomzamo* (1987), *Tales From The Lush Attic* (1984), *The Wake* (1985).

J

Jackson, Joe

b. 11 August 1955, Burton-upon-Trent, Staffordshire, England. Having learnt violin and piano as a teenager, Jackson gained entrance to study piano at London's Royal College of Music. After two years of finding his way in the music business, first through being in Arms And Legs and then as musical director to Coffee And Cream, he was signed up by A&M Records in the summer of 1978. His accomplished debut 'Is She Really Going Out With Him?' was not an immediate hit; however, by the time *Look Sharp* was released that song had become one of his live shows' stand-out numbers and reached the UK charts, albeit some months after nudging the US Top 20. Jackson's first two albums demonstrated a confident writer of thoughtful lyrics, coupled with exciting new wave energy. 'Is She Really Going Out With Him?' has a classic opening line containing humour, irony and jealousy; 'Pretty women out walking with gorillas down my street'. While *Look Sharp* and *I'm The Man* were power pop, the following *Beat Crazy* (containing some reggae) started a trend of changing musical direction that Jackson began to relish. *Jumpin' Jive*, although superb, was a throwback to the music of the 40s; on this he covered classic songs by Cab Calloway and Louis Jordan. One of his most satisfying works came in 1982 with *Night And Day*. The album was recorded in New York, where Joe departed following his marriage break-up. The songs are introspective but positive. The hauntingly hummable 'Steppin' Out' with its mantric bass line and crisp piano is a superbly crafted pop song that won him many new admirers. The subsequent *Body And Soul* came close to repeating the success, and Jackson was critically acclaimed. *Big World*, minus the long-standing bass of Graham Maby, was a three-sided direct to two-track disc. The songs had less of an appeal and Jackson's commercial fortunes began to decline. The instrumental *Will Power*, although faultlessly recorded with a high standard of musicianship, put Jackson in a musical nether world. He had come so far musically, in such a short time, that his followers found it hard to keep up with him. The live album and the film soundtrack to *Tucker* both arrived in 1988 and despite the critical plaudits, following the commercial failure of *Blaze Of Glory* in 1989, his contract with A&M was not renewed. It was inconceivable that a talent as great as Jackson would be without a contract for long; by early 1991 he was signed to Virgin Records and released *Laughter And Lust* to little commercial success.

Albums: *Look Sharp!* (1979), *I'm The Man* (1979), *Beat Crazy* (1980), *Joe Jackson's Jumpin' Jive* (1981), *Night And Day* (1982), *Mike's Murder* (1983), *Body And Soul* (1984), *Big World* (1986), *Will Power* (1987), *Joe Jackson - Live* (1988), *Tucker; Original Soundtrack* (1988), *Blaze Of Glory* (1989), *Laughter And Lust* (1991). Compilation: *Steppin' Out - The Very Best Of Joe Jackson* (1990).

Jam

Jam

This highly successful late 70s group comprised Paul Weller (b. 25 May 1958, Woking, Surrey, England; vocals/bass), Bruce Foxton (b. 1 September 1955, England; guitar) and Rick Buckler (b. Paul Richard Buckler, 6 December 1955, Woking, Surrey, England; drums). After gigging consistently throughout 1976, the group were signed to Polydor Records early the following year. Although emerging at the peak of punk, the Jam seemed oddly divorced from the movement. Their leader, Paul Weller, professed to voting Conservative (although he would later switch dramatically to support the Labour Party), and the group's musical influences were firmly entrenched in the early Who-influenced mod style. Their debut, 'In The City' was a high energy outing, with Weller displaying his Rickenbacker guitar to the fore. With their next record, 'All Around The World' they infiltrated the UK Top 20 for the first time. For the next year, they registered only minor hits, including 'News Of The World' and a cover of the Kinks' 'David Watts'. A turning point in the group's critical fortunes occurred towards the end of 1978 with the release of 'Down In The Tube Station At Midnight'. This taut, dramatic anti-racist song saw them emerge as social commentators par excellence. *All Mod Cons* was widely acclaimed and thereafter the group rose to extraordinary heights. With *The Eton Rifles*, a quasi-concept album, Weller fused visions of British colonialism with urban decay and a satirical thrust at surburban life. The tone and execution of the work recalled the style of the Kinks' Ray Davies,

whose class-conscious vignettes of the 60s had clearly influenced the Jam. The title track of their album gave the Jam their first Top 10 single in late 1979. Early the following year, they secured their first UK number 1 with the harrowing 'Going Underground'. The fact that the song reached the top of the charts indicated the enormous strength of the group's fan base. By now, they were on their way to topping music paper polls with increasing regularity. Throughout 1982, the Jam were streets ahead of their nearest rivals but their parochial charm could not be translated into international success. While they continued to log number 1 hits with 'Start' and 'Town Called Malice', the USA market remained untapped. In late 1982, the group's recent run of UK chart-toppers was interrupted by 'The Bitterest Pill (I Ever Had To Swallow)' which peaked at number 2. Weller then announced that the group were to split, and that he intended to form a new outfit, the Style Council. It was a shock decision, as the group were still releasing some of the best music to come out of Britain and most certainly at their peak. Their final single, the exuberant, anthemic 'Beat Surrender' entered the UK chart at number 1, an extraordinary conclusion to a remarkable but brief career.

Albums: *In The City* (1977), *This Is The Modern World* (1977), *All Mod Cons* (1978), *The Eton Rifles* (1979), *Sound Affects* (1980), *The Gift* (1982), *Dig The New Breed* (1982). Compilation: *Snap!* (1983).

James

Championed initially by Morrissey of the Smiths, James signed with their hometown record label, Manchester's Factory Records in 1983. Their early singles, 'What's The World?' and 'Hymn From A Village', were acclaimed for their unusual mixture of folk and new-wave. The original line-up was Timothy Booth (vocals), James Glennie (bass), James Gott (guitar) and Gavan Whelan (drums). They signed to Sire Records in 1985 and began an unsettled three year relationship with the company. *Stutter* was a collection of strange but striking songs, followed two years later by *Strip Mine* which contained a stronger melodic edge. *One Man Clapping*, a live set recorded in Bath, England, marked a return to independent status with Rough Trade. Dave Baynton-Power replaced Whelan and soon afterwards the group was augmented by Saul Davies (guitar/violin), Mark Hunter (keyboards) and Andy Diagram (trumpet). Fontana Records, with its policy of signing England's leading independent bands, re-released 'Come Home' and 'Sit Down', the latter single reaching number 2 in the UK. *Gold Mother* was more accessible than previous albums; the band were writing in a more direct lyrical style. The title track was a paean to mothers and the extreme physical pain they underwent during childbirth.

James

Janes Addiction; Perry Farrell

Although their recording career stretched back further than their contemporaries, they became part of an upsurge in talent from Manchester during the late 80s and early 90s and the media attention on the city made it easier for them to move from independent to major-league status in their home country. The quality of *Seven* indicated that James were poised to become a major force in UK guitar-based pop.

Albums: *Stutter* (1986), *Strip Mine* (1988), *One Man Clapping* (1989), *Gold Mother* (1990), *Seven* (1992).

Jane's Addiction

This innovative, pseudo art-rock quartet was formed in Los Angeles, USA, in 1986, by vocalist Perry Farrell. With the addition of guitarist David Navarro, bassist Eric A. and drummer Stephen Perkins, they incorporate elements of thrash, punk, rock, folk and funk into their unique and unpredictable soundscape. They debuted with a live album on the independent Tripple X label, which received widespread critical acclaim. Drawing inspiration from the Doors, PiL, Velvet Underground and Faith No More, they delivered a hypnotic and thought-provoking blend of intoxicating rhythms, jagged and off-beat guitar lines and high-pitched vocals of mesmeric intensity. *Ritual De Lo Habitual* is a work of great depth and complexity, which requires repeated listening to

reveal its hidden melodies, subtle nuances and enigmatic qualities. Despite widespread media coverage, the band never made the breakthrough that their talents deserved. The group decided to go their separate ways after their 1991 US tour.

Albums: *Jane's Addiction* (1987), *Nothing's Shocking* (1988), *Ritual De Lo Habitual* (1991).

Japan

Formed in London in early 1974, this group comprised David Sylvian (b. David Batt, 23 February 1958, Lewisham, London, England; vocals), his brother Steve Jansen (b. Steven Batt, 1 December 1959, Lewisham, London, England; drums), Richard Barbieri (b. 30 November 1958; keyboards) and Mick Karn (b. Anthony Michaelides, 24 July 1958, London, England; saxophone). A second guitarist, Rob Dean, joined later and the group won a recording contract with the German record company Ariola-Hansa. During the same period, they signed to manager Simon Napier-Bell. The group's derivative pop style hampered their prospects during 1978, and they suffered a number of hostile reviews. Eminently unfashionable in the UK punk era, they first found success in Japan. After three albums with Ariola-Hansa, they switched to Virgin Records in 1980 and their fortunes improved a year later thanks to the surge of popularity in the new romantic movement.

Japan's androgynous image made them suddenly fashionable and they registered UK Top 20 hits with 'Quiet Life', 'Ghosts' and a cover of Smokey Robinson And The Miracles' 'I Second That Emotion'. Their album, *Tin Drum*, was also well received. Disagreements between Karn and Sylvian undermined the group's progress, just as they were achieving some long-overdue success and they split in late 1982. Sylvian and Karn went on to record solo with varying degrees of success.

Albums: *Adolescent Sex* (1978), *Obscure* (1978), *Quiet Life* (1980), *Gentlemen Take Polaroids* (1980), *Tin Drum* (1981), *Oil On Canvas* (1983). Compilations: *Assemblage* (1981), *Exorcising Ghosts* (1984).

Jazz Butcher

Jazz Butcher

The Jazz Butcher are a prime example of British rock eccentricity. Formed in 1982 and hailing from Northampton, the group served as a vehicle for the idiosyncratic, melodic songwriting talents of Pat Fish (b. Patrick Huntrods; guitar/vocals), otherwise known as the Jazz Butcher. Although early group line-ups were erratic - including Rolo McGinty and Alice Thompson, (both later to emerge in the Woodentops) and ex-Bauhaus bassist David J. - the one constant member during much of the early years was lead guitarist Max Eider, whose light jazz/blues feel gave an eloquence to even the most heavy-handed of tunes. In terms of style, there was a large

nod in the direction of Lou Reed and Jonathan Richman, while the songs' subject matter dealt with the diverse traumas of everyday life, taking in the joys and woes of small town living ('Living In A Village'), drink ('Soul Happy Hour'), fear and paranoia ('Death Dentist'), love ('Only A Rumour'/'Angels'), the virtues of public transport ('Groovin' In The Bus Lane'), film noir and Vladimir Ilyich Lenin. The classic Jazz Butcher line-up including Max Eider, Felix Ray (bass) and 'Mr' O.P. Jones (drums), underwent a major upheaval in 1987 with the departure of Eider, resulting in the unit disintegrating. By the time of *Fishcotheque*, Fish was working virtually alone, but for a new partner in guitarist Kizzy O'Callaghan. The Jazz Butcher (Conspiracy) was re-built to comprise Fish, O'Callaghan, Laurence O'Keefe (bass), Paul Mulreany (drums) and Alex Green (saxophone) and the group had undergone a change of label moving from Glass Records to Alan McGee's Creation Records. Subsequent albums saw an increasing use of cut-up film/television dialogue and continued to garner encouraging reviews. While the Jazz Butcher has found a large audience in Europe, and more recently in the USA, substantial success in his homeland continues to elude him.

Albums: *The Jazz Butcher In Bath Of Bacon* (1983), *A Scandal In Bohemia* (1984), *Sex And Travel* (1985), *The Jazz Butcher And The Sikkorskis From Hell - Hamburg - A Live Album* (1985), *Distressed Gentlefolk* (1986), *Fishcotheque* (1988), *Big Planet, Scary Planet* (1989), *Cult Of The Basement* (1990), *Condition Blue* (1991). Compilations: *The Gift Of Music* (1985), *Bloody Nonsense* (1986), *Big Questions - The Gift Of Music Vol 2* (1987), *Edward's Closet* (1991). Max Eider solo *The Best Kisser In The World* (1987).

Jellyfish

This US band from San Francisco broke into the 90s by brilliantly re-packaging the most gaudy elements of the 60s and 70s pop with irresistible kitsch appeal. The band's dress sense was particularly colourful, one critic observing that it could have been drawn from the wardrobes of colour blind charity shop consumers. The group are composed of Andy Sturmer (b. Pleasanton, San Fransisco, California, USA; drums/vocals), Jason (guitar), along with brothers Chris (b. Pleasanton, San Fransisco, California, USA; bass) and Roger (b. Pleasanton, San Fransisco, California, USA; keyboards). This hometown they describe as '*Twin Peaks* without the Tree'. Members of the band were previously in Beatnik Beach, a short-lived funk pop outfit on Atlantic. Their debut single, 'The King Is Half Undressed', was a classy slice of retro-pop. Allied to their childlike dress sense, the formula guaranteed immediate television exposure. An album followed shortly after, which was assured and close to outright

Beatles pastiche with strange overtones of Earth Opera. It was produced by Albhy Galuten, his first job since *Saturday Night Fever*. However, subsequent highly commercial singles; 'Baby's Coming Back', 'I Wanna Stay Home', and 'Now She Knows She's Wrong', failed to build on a strong chart platform. Jellyfish were more than happy to be able to play with at least two of their heroes, Ringo Starr and Brian Wilson, following introductions from Don Was from Was (Not Was). Their album remains one of the more exciting debuts of the 90s.

Album: *Bellybutton* (1991).

Jesus And Mary Chain

Jesus And Mary Chain

Formed in East Kilbride, Scotland, this quartet comprised William Reid (vocals/guitar), Jim Reid (vocals/guitar), Douglas Hart (bass) and Murray Dalglish (drums). In the summer of 1984, they moved to London and signed to Alan McGee's label Creation. Their debut, 'Upside Down' complete with trademark feedback, fared well in the independent charts and was backed with a versions of Syd Barrett's 'Vegetable Man'. In November 1984, Dalglish was replaced on drums by Primal Scream vocalist Bobby Gillespie. By the end of the year, the group were attracting considerable media attention due to the violence at their gigs and a series of bans followed. Early the following year, the group signed to the WEA/Rough Trade label Blanco Y Negro. The Reid brothers delighted in the charms of amphetamime sulphate, which gave their music a manic edge. Live performances usually lasted 20 minutes, which brought more controversy and truculence from traditional gig habitues, who felt short-changed. A cover of the Sex Pistols' 'Never Understand' underlined the comparisons with the anarchic school of 1977. For their next release, however, the group surprised many by issuing the more pop-orientated 'Just Like Honey'. By October 1985, Gillespie had grown tired of the Jesus And Mary Chain and returned to his former group, Primal Scream. One month later, the Reid Brothers issued

their highly-acclaimed debut *Psychocandy*. The album was full of multi-tracked guitar distortion, underscored with reasonably strong melodies. Many critics proclaimed it one of rock's most intriguing first albums. The following August the group reached the UK Top 20 with the melodic 'Some Candy Talking', which received curtailed radio play when it was alleged that the subject matter concerned heroin. During the same period, the group found a new drummer, John Moore, and parted from their manager Alan McGee. Further hits with 'April Skies' and 'Happy When It Rains' preceded their second album, *Darklands*. The album was again well received and was followed by a tempestuous tour of Canada and America, during which Reid was briefly arrested then acquitted on a charge of assaulting a fan. In the spring of 1988, a compilation of the group's various out-takes was issued. They consolidated their important position in the 90s with *Automatic* and *Honey's Dead*. The latter featured a major hit single 'Rverence' and is arguably their finest work to date. On this collection they had perfected and honed their wall of guitar sound with excellent compositions.

Albums: *Psychocandy* (1985), *Darklands* (1987), *Barbed Wire* (1988), *Automatic* (1990), *Honey's Dead* (1992).

Jesus Jones

Jesus Jones

Blending the driving force of the punk guitar with liberal use of samples and dance rhythms, Jesus Jones made an auaacious debut with the single 'Info Freako'. The song was voted into the Top 10 year-end charts of all the UK music papers. Singer/songwriter Mike Edwards (b. 22 June 1964, City of London, England) is supported by Gen (b. Simon Matthews, 23 April 1964, Devizes, Wiltshire, England; drums), Al Jaworski (b. 31 January 1966, Plymouth, Devon, England; bass), Jerry De Borg (b. 30 October 1963, Kentish Town, London, England; guitar) and Barry D (b. Iain Richard Foxwell Baker, 29 September 1965, Carshalton, Surrey, England; keyboards). The group was formed in London, England, early in 1988 and was signed soon afterwards by Food Records. *Liquidizer* was an energetic debut which provided more UK hits with 'Never Enough' and 'Bring It On Down'. In February 1990 they became one of the first British bands to play dates in Romania after the country's revolution. *Doubt*, produced mainly by Edwards, saw the band inject a stronger commercial element. After six weeks at the top of the US alternative chart it entered the *Billboard* chart and in the UK it reached number 1. In the summer of 1991 the band, which had always kept up a busy live schedule, became part of a nucleus of young UK bands scoring hits in the US. 'Right Here, Right Now' was a hit and along with EMF, they found their abrasive pop suddenly popular among the USA's generally conservative market.

Albums: *Liquidizer* (1989), *Doubt* (1991).

Jesus Lizard

Formed in 1989, the Jesus Lizard originally comprised of David Yow (vocals), David Wm. Sims (bass) – both formerly of the Austin, Texas act Scratch Acid – and Duane Denison (guitar). *Pure*, their mini-album debut, maintained the uncompromising style of the trio's predecessor with its ponderous bass lines, growled vocals and crashing guitar. The set was produced by Steve Albini (ex-Big Black), with whom Sims had worked in the controversally-named Rapeman. Albini engineered and co-produced *Head*, on which the Jesus Lizard was joined by drummer Mac McNeilly. The group's sound remained as powerful and compulsive as ever, although some critics have detected an artistic impasse.

Albums: *Pure* (1989), *Head* (1990).

Jett, Joan, And The Blackhearts

b. Joan Larkin, 22 September 1960, Philadelphia, Pennsylvania, USA. Jett was one of the most successful US female singers to emerge from the punk rock scene of the 70s. She spent most of her childhood in the Baltimore, Maryland area, where she learnt guitar as a child, playing along to favourite rock 'n' roll records. In 1972 her family relocated to Los Angeles, where she became enamoured with artist including David Bowie, Suzi Quatro, T. Rex and Gary Glitter. At the age of 15 she began infiltrating the Los Angeles rock scene and formed her first band. Producer Kim Fowley took the group under his wing and named it the Runaways, procuring a record deal with Mercury Records. The group recorded three punky hard-rock albums which were unsuccessful in the USA but hits in Japan, where they recorded a live album. Also successful in England, they recorded their swansong *And Now...The Runaways*, there in 1979. After the dissolution of the group, Jett moved to New York and teamed up with producer Kenny Laguna, who

became her manager. Laguna had previously been involved with a number of 60s bubblegum hits. Laguna produced Jett's first solo album which was released on the European Ariola label. When no US label would pick it up they issued it themselves and the album sold well, becoming one of the best-selling US independent records of that time. That led to a deal with Neil Bogart's Boardwalk Records, which reissued it as *Bad Reputation*, finally reaching number 51 in the USA. With her group the Blackhearts (guitarist Ricky Byrd, bassist Gary Ryan and drummer Lee Crystal), Jett recorded the album *I Love Rock 'N' Roll* in late 1981, produced by Laguna and Ritchie Cordell. The title track, originally an obscure b-side for UK group the Arrows, became a major hit, largely owing to the push by MTV, and spent seven weeks at number 1 in the USA in early 1982, one of the last outright raw rock songs to find such success. The follow-up single, a cover of Tommy James And The Shondells' 'Crimson And Clover', was itself a Top 10 hit, reaching number 7 in 1982. WIth Bogart's death, the group signed to MCA, which then distributed Blackheart Records. Subsequent releases on that label were nowhere near as successful as the Boardwalk releases, nor was 1990's *The Hit List*, with CBS now acting as distributor for Blackheart.

Albums: *Joan Jett* (1980), *Bad Reputation* (reissue of debut) (1981), *I Love Rock-n-Roll* (1981), *Album* (1983), *Glorious Results Of A Misspent Youth* (1984), *Good Music* (1986), *The Hit List* (1990).

Jilted John

Rabid Records, a new wave label based in Manchester, England, received a recording of 'Jilted John', composed and performed by a thespian named Graham Fellowes. Rabid released this semi-monologue concerning the woes of a young lover, and were soon so overwhelmed by demand that EMI had to take over its marketing in 1978. Fellowes slipped into his Jilted John character in media interviews - a few similarly gormless appearances on BBC television's *Top Of The Pops* pushed the record to number 4 in the UK chart - and necessitated the issue of an album and an 'answer' single by John's rival, Gordon The Moron. After this episode, however, Fellowes returned to his acting career which has since included roles in the Uk soap opera *Coronation Street* and a northern stage production of a play concerning John Lennon.

Album: *True Love Stories* (1978).

Jimmy The Hoover

Simon Barker (b. 22 July 1956, Malta; keyboards), Derek Dunbar (b. 31 August 1958, Aberdeen, Scotland; vocals), Carla Duplantier (b. Hollywood, Los Angeles California, USA; drums), Flinto (b. 11

March 1955, Zambia; bass) and Mark Rutherford (b. 14 April 1961, Hackney, London, England; guitar) formed the band in 1982. Malcolm McLaren gave them the name and a support tour with Bow Wow Wow. Cris Cole stepped in on bass guitar, and in 1983 they signed to CBS subsidiary Innervision. That year brought them their one hit 'Tantalise (Wo Wo Ee Yeh Yeh)' a good pop song with an African influence. Along with Innervision stablemates Wham! and Animal Nightlife, the group had 'legal' problems that interfered with the promotion of the second single 'Kill Me Quick', and tied them up for many months.

JoBoxers

This pop-soul group achieved minor fame in the early 80s with a sound built on fast beats and imagery from the film *On The Waterfront*. They comprised of Dig Wayne (b. 20 July 1958, USA; vocals), Rob Marche (b. 13 October 1962, Bristol, England; guitar), Dave Collard (b. 17 January 1961, Bristol, England; keyboards), Chris Bostock (b. 23 November 1962, Bristol, England; bass) and Sean McLusky (b. 5 May 1961, Bristol, England; drums). All except Wayne were former members of Vic Goddard And The Subway Sect (c.1981 onwards), the last incarnation of a punk band who ended their career by backing Goddard's affected crooning. He met the rest of the band at a street market where both had second-hand clothes stalls. As JoBoxers they first attracted attention after appearing on the BBC television's *Oxford Roadshow* in 1982. Signed to RCA, in February 1983 they released 'Boxer Beat', which was a Top 5 hit in the UK. The follow-up 'Just Got Lucky' also went into the Top 10 but subsequent singles such as 'Johnny Friendly' did less well. The band split early in 1986, with Wayne going on to a brief solo career (one album, *Square Business*, 1987) with a band that featured Dave Collard of JoBoxers and Mark Reilley (ex-Matt Bianco).
Albums: *Like Gangbusters* (1983), *Skin And Bone* (1985).

Jobson, Richard

b. October 6 1960, Dunfermline, Scotland. Brother of John, a striker for Meadowbank Thistle Football Club, for whom Richard was also on the books. After the Skids four year tenure (1977-81) Jobson moved on to join the Armoury Show, which failed to repeat the success of any of its illustrious personnel's former bands. With their demise Jobson toured the UK with Scottish acting company *Poines Plough*. Turning to poetry, he hit the road once more, falling between two stools in terms of critical reception. On one side rock critics viewed the move suspiciously, castigating him as pretentious, while the poetry critics reacted with venom to the vulgar intrusion of a rock singer. Placed in its proper context, Jobson was capable of writing good poetry, but was too much at the whim of his own indulgence. The worst example of this was his infamous live rendition of Sylvia Plath's 'Daddy'. He continued to release albums throughout the 80s, the best of which was *16 Years Of Alcohol*, also the title of a book he wrote, which related his alchohol problems. He also suffers from epilepsy. Meanwhile Jobson had chanced upon further careers in television and fashion. He appeared variously as the pop correspondent on BBC television's *The Garden Party*, as presenter for *01 For London*, and most recently in regional Arts programmes and opinion show *Biteback*. On top of this was his highly paid, and some might say unlikely stint as a fashion model. Most notable were a series of car adverts, for which he also composed the music. His most recent recording *Badman*, was released on Parlophone in 1988, produced by Ian Broudie. Though the imagery was typically grandiose, it did include a sprightly cover of Everything But The Girl's 'Angel'.
Albums: *Ten Thirty On A Summer Night* (1983), *The Ballad Of Etiquette* (1986), *The Other Man* (1986), *16 Years Of Alcohol* (1987), *Badman* (1988).

Johansen, David

b. 9 January 1950, Staten Island, New York, USA, Johansen gained recognition in the early 70s as lead singer of the New York Dolls. A R&B/rock group taking inspiration from the likes of the Rolling Stones, the Dolls' street attitude and outrageous sense of dress, thrust them into the glitter/glam scene, although their music had little in common with others of that nature. Prior to joining the Dolls, Johansen joined his first band, the Vagabond Missionaries, in high school. At the age of 17 he moved to Manhattan, New York, and briefly worked with a band called Fast Eddie And The Electric Japs. The Dolls came together in late 1971 and quickly built a devoted audience at New York clubs such as the Mercer Arts Center and Max's Kansas City. They recorded two albums for Mercury Records and held on until late 1976. After their demise they became an inspiration to numerous artists, from the newly forming punk bands such as the Sex Pistols to Kiss to the Smiths. Johansen launched a solo career in 1978, recording for Blue Sky Records. Less flamboyant than the Dolls' records, this was a solid rock effort that stressed Johansen's lyrical acumen. He released three other rock/R&B-oriented solo albums for Blue Sky and one for Passport Records before shifting career directions once again. In 1983 Johansen began booking small cabaret concert dates under the name Buster Poindexter, performing a slick, tightly-arranged set of vintage R&B numbers, show tunes, and jump blues. Dressing in a formal tuxedo and playing the lounge lizard, Poindexter built a following of his own, until Johansen the rocker literally ceased to exist; he completely gave up his rock act to pursue the new image full-time. He recorded two albums as Buster Poindexter, in 1987 and 1989, the first yielding a chart and club hit, a cover of Arrow's 1984 soca dance tune, 'Hot, Hot Hot'. He was still popular as Poindexter in the early 90s, touring with a 10-piece band and packing clubs, his repertoire now including Caribbean-flavoured music, torch songs, blues, as well as the early R&B. He also launched an acting career in the late 80s, appearing in films including *Scrooged* and *Married To The Mob*.

Albums: *David Johansen* (1978), *In Style* (1979), *Here Comes The Night* (1981), *Live It Up* (1982), *Sweet Revenge* (1984), as Buster Poindexter *Buster Poindexter* (1987), *Buster Goes Berserk* (1989).

Johnson, Matt

b. 1961, Essex, England. From an early age Johnson turned to music. Beginning with the school band Road Star, he went on to the electronic trio the Gadgets, who recorded three albums, the last of which was never released. His collaborators were Tom Johnson and Michael O'Shea, both of whom were ex-Plain Characters. While the band were still in progress, Johnson formed The The with Keith Laws (keyboards), Tom Johnston (bass) and Peter Ashworth (drums). Following two singles, one each for 4AD and Some Bizzare, the original formation disintegrated. Some backing tracks were salvaged however, and these formed the basis of Johnson's solo *Burning Blue Soul*, released in 1981. In cover design it parodied the Beatles *Rubber Soul* period psychedelia, but in execution it was a very personal affair: 'It is pretty close to the bone. It was one of the most innocent albums made, probably. And very pure, almost virginal in a way. But when I listen to it, its very honest'. Back under The The's monicker, Johnson recorded tracks for a proposed debut album *Pornography Of Despair*, which never appeared. Essentially a solo album, all of the tracks would eventually surface on subsequent The The albums or related releases.

Albums: *Burning Blue Soul* (1981).

Jo Jo Zep And The Falcons

This Australian R&B band was formed in Melbourne, Victoria in 1976 and based around talented frontman, Joe Camilleri, who shaped the band's musical direction and provided the focal point on stage. Initially the band recorded covers of well-known blues and R&B material, before eventually writing their own songs in the same vein. As a popular live act on the Melbourne circuit, their performances were exciting, their musicianship high

and the band were well regarded in the industry. Joe Camilleri gathered quality musicians around him, such as John Power (bass), songwriter Wayne Burt (guitar), Wilbur Wilde (saxophone) and Gary Young (drums). The band continued the tradition of hard work, playing the pubs and smaller venues along the Australian east coast. A contract with the Australian label Mushroom Records started an association with English producer Pete Solley, which led to five hit singles in Australia, and ensured that their records were released in the USA and the UK where the band also toured. The hits dried up and Camilleri shortened the name to Jo Jo Zep in 1982 for a new 11-piece band and a more modern sound. The band continued in a reduced format until the end of 1983, remaining a successful live act. In 1984 Camilleri's next project, the zydeco-influenced Black Sorrows was launched.

Albums: *Don't Waste It* (1976), *Whip It Out* (1977), *Let's Drip Awhile* (1979), *Screaming Targets* (1979), *Hats Off Step Lively* (1980), *Sounds Of* (1980).

Jones, Howard

b. John Howard Jones, 23 February 1955, Southampton, Hampshire, England. Coming to prominence as a synthezizer-pop maestro in the mid-80s, Jones had been trying to succeed as a musician for almost 15 years. His childhood saw him on the move from country to country but by the time he reached his teens he was settled in High Wycombe, England. He joined his first band in 1979 and over the next few years played in Warrior, the Bicycle Thieves, and Skin Tight. In 1974 he went to music college in Manchester and once graduated he began performing solo in his home town. He soon introduced dancer Jed Hoile to enliven his act by improvizing dance to his songs. Jones was offered a session by BBC disc jockey John Peel which led to tours with OMD and China Crisis. WEA signed him in the summer of 1983 and in September he charted with his first single 'New Song'. He won several Best New Artist awards and followed-up with hits like 'What Is Love', 'Hide And Seek', and 'Like To Get To Know You Well'. His debut *Human's Lib* topped the UK charts. Although he performed most of the music on his recordings in 1985 he formed a touring band with his brother Martin on bass, and Trevor Morais on drums. As the 80s drew to a close his singles charted lower and lower but he continues to record sporadically.

Albums: *Humans Lib* (1984), *The 12 Inch Album* (1984), *Dream Into Action* (1985), *One To One* (1986), *Cross That Line* (1989), *In The Running* (1992).

Josef K

This Edinburgh, Scotland-based band formed in the ashes of punk as TV Art and were influenced by

New York bands such as Television, Talking Heads and the Velvet Underground. The original trio of Paul Haig (vocals), Malcolm Ross (guitar) and Ron Torrance (drums) was joined briefly by Gary McCormack (later with the Exploited), before a more permanent bassist was found in David Weddell. After a name change inspired by Franz Kafka's 1925 novel, *The Trial*, Josef K recorded a 10-track demo before committing 'Chance Meeting' to release on Steven Daly's Absolute label, in late 1979. Daly, who was also the drummer for Orange Juice, was the co-founder of Postcard Records and so signed Josef K to the newly-formed label. 'Radio Drill Time' was more frantic than their debut, dominated by hectic, awkward chords and Haig's thin, nasal voice. After numerous support slots, 1980 ended with the more low-key, melodic sound of 'It's Kinda Funny'. The single fared well and Josef K were all set to release their debut *Sorry For Laughing*, during the early months of 1981. Unhappy with its production, the band scrapped it at the test pressing stage and moved to a Belgian studio, in conjunction with Les Disques du Crépescule label. The session yielded the re-recorded title track and their strongest single, 'Sorry For Laughing' (1981), which joined tracks from the unreleased album as a session for BBC radio disc jockey John Peel, while the band returned to Belgium to work on their album. Back at Postcard, they drafted Malcolm's brother Alistair to play trumpet on a new version of 'Chance Meeting', issued just two months later, coinciding with a full session for Peel. *The Only Fun In Town* emerged in July to a mixed reception. Its frantic, trebly live sound sounded unhurried, and betrayed the fact that it had been recorded in just six days. Josef K announced their demise soon after, prompted by the offer to Malcolm Ross to join Orange Juice. Crépescule issued Josef K's farewell single 'The Missionary' in 1982, while tracks surfaced on various compilations. After Ross had joined Orange Juice, Haig worked with Rhythm Of Life before embarking on a solo career. In 1987, Scottish label Supreme International Editions followed the excellent 'Heaven Sent' with *Young And Stupid*, a collection of Peel session material and tracks from the unreleased *Sorry For Laughing*. Then, in 1990, the entire recorded history of Josef K (plus tracks from their original demo) were compiled onto two definitive CDs by Les Temps Moderne.
Album: *The Only Fun In Town* (1981). Compilations: *Young And Stupid* (1989), *The Only Fun In Town/Sorry For Laughing* (1990).

Joy Division

Originally known as Warsaw, this Manchester post-punk outfit comprised of Ian Curtis (b. July 1956, Macclesfield, Cheshire, England, d. 18 May 1980; vocals), Bernard Dicken/Albrecht (b. 4 January 1956, Salford, Manchester, England; guitar/vocals), Peter Hook (b. 13 February 1956, Manchester, England; bass) and Steven Morris (b. 28 October 1957, Macclesfield, Cheshire, England; drums). Borrowing their name from the prostitution wing of a concentration camp, Joy Division emerged in 1978 as one of the most important groups of their era. After recording a regionally available EP, *An Ideal For Living*, they were signed to Manchester's recently formed Factory Records and placed in the hands of producer Martin Hannett. Their debut *Unknown Pleasures*, was a raw, intense affair, with Curtis at his most manically arresting in the insistent 'She's Lost Control'. With its stark, black cover, the album captured the group still coming to terms with the recording process, but displaying a vision that was piercing in its clinical evocation of an unsettling disorder. With Morris's drums employed as a lead instrument, backed by the leaden but compulsive bass lines of Hook, the sound of Joy Division was distinctive and disturbing. By the time of their single 'Transmission' the quartet had already established a strong cult following, which increased after each gig. Much of the attention centred on the charismatic Curtis, who was renowned for his neurotic choreography, like a demented marionette on wires. By the autumn of 1979, however, Curtis's performances were drawing attention for a more serious reason. On more than one occasion he suffered an epileptic seizure and blackouts onstage, the illness seemed to worsen with the group's increasingly demanding live schedule. On 18 May 1980, the eve of Joy Division's proposed visit to America, Ian Curtis was found hanged. The verdict was suicide. A note was allegedly found bearing the words: 'At this moment I wish I were dead. I just can't cope anymore'.
The full impact of the tragedy was underlined shortly afterwards, for it quickly became evident that Curtis had taken his life at the peak of his creativity. While it seemed inevitable that the group's posthumously released work would receive a sympathetic reaction, few could have anticipated the quality of the material that emerged in 1980. The single, 'Love Will Tear Us Apart' was probably the finest of the year, a haunting account of a fragmented relationship, sung by Curtis in a voice that few realized he possessed. The attendant album, *Closer*, was faultless, displaying the group at their creative peak. With spine-tingling cameos such as 'Isolation' and the extraordinary 'Twenty-Four Hours' the album eloquently articulated a sense of despair, yet simultaneously offered a therapeutic release. Instrumentally, the work showed maturity in every area and is deservedly regarded by many critics as the most brilliant rock album of the 80s. The following year, a double album, *Still* collected the remainder of the group's

material, most of it in primitive form. Within months of the Curtis tragedy, the remaining members sought a fresh start as New Order.

Albums: *Unknown Pleasures* (1979), *Closer* (1980), *Still* (1981), *The Peel Sessions* (1986).

June Brides

This mid-80s UK pop band were built around lyricist, guitarist and singer Phil Wilson. Operating in the independent sector, their sound was characterized by the unusual inclusion of a brass section; Jon Hunter (trumpet) and Frank (viola), alongside Simon Beesley (vocals/guitar), Ace (bass) and Dave (drums). Their first release was 'In The Rain', followed by 'Every Conversation', on which That Petrol Emotion's John O'Neill was brought in to help with production. Their only album, however, was disappointing in relation to singles such as 'No Place Called Home'. Frank guested on a number of Creation artefacts (Pete Astor, Meat Whiplash), and had another claim to fame in being beaten-up badly by skinheads while trying to protect a pregnant woman. Hunter also played with Marc Riley for one EP. Press darlings for a couple of months, June Brides nevertheless quickly departed from the scene because of 'frustration, lack of money, and some of us no longer enjoying being in the band'. Frank joined Brick Circus Hour and Wilson moved on to a solo career.

Album: *There Are Eight Million Stories* (1985).

Justified Ancients Of Mu Mu

Also known as the JAMS and comprised of Bill Drummond, Jimmy Cauty and some startlingly imaginative methods of undermining the pop ethos. Drummond had cut his teeth in the Liverpool scene of the early 80s and played a large part in setting up Zoo Records as well as being a veritable man about town. By 1987 he was working with Cauty and exploiting the techniques of sampling and computers inherent in the new technology. Their liberal use of other artists' material within the framework of their own songs resulted in a court case with Abba, following which all remaining copies of the JAMS' album *1987 (What The Fuck Is Going On?)* were legally bound to be destroyed. However, a handful of copies escaped annhialation and ended up on sale for £1000 each. The following year the duo switched guises to become the Timelords and have a worldwide hit with 'Doctorin' The Tardis', with Gary Glitter. A manual on how to have a number 1 single was written, to be succeeded by work on their own movie. By this time Drummond and Cauty were calling themselves the KLF and enjoying yet more global success with the Stadium House trilogy of singles, particularly within the confines of the rave scene which was sweeping Britain in 1989. In 1991

the JAMS monicker was reactivated for 'It's Grim Up North', a dance single which owed several musical moments to composer William Blake. Whereupon Drummond and Cauty promptly slipped back into KLF mode to record with country singer Tammy Wynette. As ever, we can expect the unexpected.

Albums: *1987 (What The Fuck Is Going On?)* (1987), *Who Killed The JAMS?* (1987).

K

Kane Gang

Martin Brammer (b. 13 May 1957, Easington, Co. Durham, England; songwriter/vocalist) and Dave Brewis (b. 3 June 1957, Sunderland, Tyne And Wear, England; songwriter/multi-instrumentalist) met at school in the northeast town of Seaham, Co. Durham, England. Teaming up with Paul Woods (b. 28 May 1956, Seaham, Co. Durham, England; vocals), the trio developed a liking for 60s/70s soul, funk and R&B which led them through several bands before forming the Kane Gang in late 1982. 'Brother Brother' was planned as their first single on Candle Records, a joint venture with friend Paddy McAloon of Prefab Sprout, but both bands were soon signed to new Newcastle label, Kitchenware. In 1984, the company licensed 'Brother Brother' to London Records, which signed the group, releasing their attack at the north-south divide, 'Smalltown Creed' (1984), produced by Pete Wingfield. In contrast, 'Closest Thing To Heaven' was a smooth ballad, and secured the Kane Gang a Top 20 chart hit. Further success followed that same year with a faithful cover of the Staple Singers' 'Respect Yourself', a song which featured soul veteran P.P. Arnold on backing vocals. *The Bad And Lowdown World Of The Kane Gang* in early 1985 effectively summarized the band's progress (and featured guest musicians included Sam Brown), alongside a single 'Gun Law', before a two-year pause. 'Motortown' (1987) brought another Top 40 hit, preceding a second album. Sporting a slicker, more sophisticated production, *Miracle* also spawned 'What Time Is It', and then a cover of Dennis Edwards' Don't Look Any Further' (1988), the latter reaching number 1 in the US dance chart. In 1991, vocalist Paul Woods departed to concentrate on a solo career.

Albums: *The Bad And Lowdown World Of The Kane Gang* (1985), *Miracle* (1987).

Karn, Mick

b. Anthony Michaelides, 24 July 1958, London, England. Karn first came to attention as the bassist in 80s UK hit group, Japan. Their demise in late 1982 coincided with the release of Karn's first solo work, *Titles*. The collection received mixed reviews and Karn subsequently teamed up with former Bauhaus' vocalist Peter Murphy in Dali's Car. The partnership proved relatively short-lived and Karn subsequently returned to solo work. In early 1987, he reached number 63 in the UK with 'Buoy', which was notable for the inclusion of his former Japan rival David Sylvian on guest vocals. Despite his uncompromising and occasionally evocative work, Karn has been unable to recapture the commercial appeal that graced his work with Japan.
Albums: *Titles* (1982), *Dreams Of Reason Produce Monsters* (1987).

Katrina And The Waves

This pop group had a big hit with 'Walking On Sunshine' in 1985, but were also well-known for their original version of 'Going Down To Liverpool' which was successfully covered by the Bangles. The band consisted of Katrina Leskanich (b. 1960, Topeka, Kansas, USA; vocals), Kimberley Rew (guitar), Vince De La Cruz (b. Texas, USA; bass) and Alex Cooper (drums). Leskanich and De La Cruz are Americans, but came to Britain during 1976 when their military fathers served in the UK. Based at Feltwell, Norfolk, where the airforce base was, Rew and Cooper were both graduates of Cambridge University. Rew was formerly in the Soft Boys and after leaving them released the solo *The Bible Of Pop*, in 1982. Many of the songs he wrote for his solo career were carried over into the Waves, where he became the chief songwriter. The band was formed in 1982, but the first two albums were only released in Canada. They followed up 'Walking On Sunshine' with 'Sun Street', which was their last hit, although they remain a poplar act on the college circuit.
Albums: *Walking On Sunshine* (1983), *Katrina And The Waves 2* (1984), *Katrina And The Waves* (1985), *Break Of Hearts* (1989).

Kilbey, Steve

b. Australia. As leader and main writer of the Church, Kilbey led the resurgence of interest in Australia for 60s music. His performances on the 12-string guitar evoked the sound of the Byrds and their ilk of the psychedelic era. The band enjoyed considerable success on the college radio network in the USA and on the European live circuit. This enabled Kilbey to have a prolific output outside the confines of the band with the publication of a book of poetry and the release of several solo albums on the small independent Red Eye label. This solo work is more

adventurous, and a little *avant garde* and risque compared to that of the Church. A 1991 collaboration with Grant McLennan of the Go-Betweens resulted in the album *Jack Frost*.
Albums: *Unearthed* (1987), *Earthed* (1987), *The Slow Crack* (1987), *Remindlessness* (1989), with Grant McLennan (as Jack Frost) *Jack Frost* (1991).

Killing Joke

Killing Joke

This immensely powerful early 80s UK post-punk band combined a furious rhythm section with near psychotic performances from Jaz Coleman (vocals/keyboards). The band came about when Coleman, of Egyptian descent, was introduced to Paul Ferguson, then drumming for the Matt Stagger Band. Coleman joined as a keyboard player, before they both quit to form their own group. This first incarnation added 'Geordie' (b. K. Walker, Newcastle-upon-Tyne, Tyne & Wear, England; guitar) and Youth (b. Martin Glover, 27 December 1960, Africa; bass), who had made his first public appearance at the Vortex in 1977 with forgotten punk band the Rage. After relocating to Notting Hill Gate, London, they paid for a rehearsal studio and borrowed money from Coleman's girlfriend to release the *Turn To Red* EP. Picked up by BBC disc jockey John Peel, the band provided a session which would become the most frequently requested of the many he has commissioned. Via Island Records the band were able to set up their own Malicious Damage label, on which they released 'Wardance' in February 1980. The single was notable for its remarkably savage b-side, 'Psyche': 'Look at the Controller, a Nazi with a Social Degree, a middle class hero, rapist with your eyes on me'. A succession of fine, aggressive singles followed, alongside live appearances with Joy Division. They were in a strong enough position to negotiate a three album deal with EG, which allowed them to keep the name Malicious Damage for their records. After the release of a typically harsh debut album, the band were banned from a Glasgow gig when council officials took exception to posters depicting Pope Pius XII giving his blessing to two columns of Hitler's Brown Shirts. It was typical of the black humour which pervaded the band, especially on their record sleeves and graphics.

After the recording of the third album was completed the band disintegrated when Coleman's fascination with the occult led him to the conclusion that apocalypse was imminent, and he fled to Iceland. He was followed later by Youth. When Youth returned it was to begin work with Ferguson on a new project, Brilliant. However, having second thought, Ferguson became the third Joker to flee to Iceland taking bass player Paul Raven (ex-Neon Hearts) with him. The Killing Joke output from then on lacks the menace which had made them so vital. However, *Night Time* combined commercial elements better than most, proffering the hit single 'Love Like Blood'. *Outside The Gate* was basically a Coleman solo album wrongly credited to the band. They returned with their best album for years with 1990's *Extremities, Dirt And Various Repressed Emotions*, which saw the drumming debut of Martin Atkins (ex-Public Image Limited). However, the band broke up once more with bitter acrimony flying across the pages of the press the same year. While his former co-conspirators have pronounced Killing Joke dead, Coleman has pledged to continue under the name.

Albums: *Killing Joke* (1980), *What's This For...!* (1981), *Revelations* (1982), *Ha! Killing Joke Live* (1982), *Fire Dances* (1983), *Night Time* (1983), *Brighter Than A Thousand Suns* (1986), *Outside The Gate* (1988), *Extremities, Dirt And Various Repressed Emotions* (1990).

King

This Coventry-based group was formed in 1983 after the break-up of the Reluctant Stereotypes of which Paul King (vocals) was a member. The remainder of King comprised Tony Wall (bass), Mick Roberts (keyboards), James Jackel Lantsbery (guitar) and ex-Members Adrian Lillywhite (drums). They made their debut supporting the Mighty Wah! and signed to CBS. Despite extensive touring and a sizeable following, their first three singles and *Steps In Time* sold poorly. The break came late in 1984 when they supported Culture Club and reached a whole new teen audience. 'Love And Pride' was released early next year, and made number 2 in the UK chart, while the album went to number 6. The hits continued throughout the year, most notably with the Top 10 hit, 'Alone Without You', and King abruptly disbanded in 1986. Paul King pursued a solo career, which at best gave him a minor hit with 'I Know' which reached number 59. The group will probably be remembered as much for their trademark spray-painted Dr. Martens boots and Paul King's

affable personality than for their engaging pop songs. Paul King later became a video jockey for MTV.
Albums: *Steps In Time* (1984), *Bitter Sweet* (1985).

Kitchens Of Distinction

Formed in London in 1986 by Patrick Fitzgerald (b. 7 April 1964, Basel, Switzerland), Julian Swales (b. 23 March 1964, Gwent, Wales) and Daniel Goodwin (b. 22 July 1964, Salamanca, Spain), Kitchens Of Distinction pursued a precarious path through the UK independent record minefield. A debut single in 1987 made minimal headway, but after signing to One Little Indian Records they hinted at an upturn in fortunes. Marrying a melodic sensibility with a stunning array of guitar effects, slight problems only appeared when the critical success of their first album, 'Love Is Hell', was not matched in commercial terms. The most popular theories for the band's slow rise centred upon their peculiar monicker and singer Patrick Fitzgerald's unwillingness to disguise or avoid the subject of his homosexuality, but whatever the reasons, the threesome struggled to break away from the threat of cult status. The battle seemed to pay dividends when the second album, *Strange Free World*, entered the UK charts at number 36, although the full-blown crossover their powerful, emotive songs so richly deserved, still, was not forthcoming. A nationwide tour with the Popinjays led to a friendship between the two groups, with the Kitchens often appearing under the pseudonym, the Toilets Of Destruction.
Albums: *Love Is Hell* (1989), *Strange Free World* (1991).

Klark Kent

Whether this Klark Kent is the same man who works as a reporter for the *Daily Planet* is unclear. His close friend Stewart Copeland (b. 16 July, 1952, Alexandria, Egypt), drummer with the Police tells us that Kent 'dabbles in politics, religion and anthropology'. He owns a huge multi-national company called the Kent Foundation, whose sinister influence is behind many world events. Kent is unable to tour because an unpleasant odour emitted from his body makes him intolerable to other musicians. . . The truth is, of course, that Kent and Copeland are one and the same. In 1978 when the Police were still waiting for their major breakthrough, Copeland was looking for some extra curricular activities, having previously been cited as a member of the unrealized group the Moors Murderers. Creating the *alter ego* of Kent, his first single 'Don't Care' was released on Kryptone in 1978 and later re-issued on A&M when it was a minor hit. The follow-up 'Too Kool To Kalypso' (back on the Krypton label) was pressed in lurid Kryptonite green, two more singles and a solitary mini-album followed, before Kent disappeared allowing Copeland to write film music and continue drumming with the Police. Album: *Klark Kent* (1980).

KLF

Since 1987, the KLF have operated under a series of guises, and have only recently revealed their true nature to the public at large. The band's principal spokesperson is Bill Drummond (b. William Butterworth, 29 April 1953, South Africa), who had already enjoyed a chequered music industry career. As co-founder of the influential Zoo label in the late 70s, he introduced and later managed Echo And The Bunnymen and the Teardrop Explodes. Later he joined forces with Jimmy Cauty (b. 1954), an artist of various persuasions and member of Brilliant in the mid-80s. Their first project was undertaken under the title JAMS (Justified Ancients Of Mu Mu, a title lifted from Robert Shea and Robert Anton Wilson's conspiracy novels dealing with the *Illuminati*). An early version of 'All You Need Is Love' caused little reaction compared to the provocatively titled album which followed - *1987 - What The Fuck Is Going On?* Released under the KLF moniker (standing for Kopyright Liberation Front), it liberally disposed of the works of the Beatles, Led Zeppelin *et al* with the careless abandon the duo had picked up from the heyday of punk. One of the disfigured groups, Abba, promptly took action to ensure the offending article was withdrawn. In the wake of the emerging house scene the next move was to compromise the theme tune to the much-loved British television show *Dr Who*, adding a strong disco-beat and Gary Glitter yelps to secure a UK number 1 with 'Doctorin' The Tardis' (1988). Working under the title Timelords, this one-off coup was achieved with such simplicity that its originators took the step of writing a book: *How To Have A Number One The Easy Way*. Returning as the KLF in 1990, they scored a big hit with the more legitimate cult dance hit 'What Time Is Love'. After the throwaway send-up of Australian pop 'Kylie Said To Jason', they hit big again with the more soulful dance of '3 A.M. Eternal'. There would be further releases from the myriad of names employed by the duo (JAMS: 'Down Town' and 'Its Grim Up North', Space: *Space*, Disco 2000: 'Uptight') while Cauty, alongside Alex Peterson, created the ambient production team the Orb. Of the band's most recent work, perhaps the most startling is their luxurious video for the KLF's 'Justified And Ancient', featuring Tammy Wynette. Urban guerrillas specializing in highly-original shock tactics, the KLF and their various disguises should continue, in one form or another, to be a feature of the 90s dance market.
Albums: as JAMS *1987 - What The Fuck Is Going On?* (1987), *Towards The Trance* (1988), as JAMS *Who Killed The JAMS?* (1988), *The What Time Is Love Story* (1989), as JAMS *Shag Times* (1988), *The White Room* (1989), *Chill Out* (1989).

Knack

Formed in Los Angeles in 1988, the Knack comprised Doug Fieger (vocals/guitar), Prescott Niles (bass), Berton Averre (guitar) and Bruce Gary (drums). Taking their name from a cult British movie of the 60s, they attempted to revive the spirit of the beat-boom with matching suits, and short songs boasting solid, easily memorable riffs. After garnering considerable media attention for their club appearances on the Californian coastline in early 1979, they became the fortuitous recipients of a record company bidding war, which ended in their signing to Capitol Records. The fact that this was the Beatles' US label was no coincidence, for the Knack consistently employed imagery borrowed from the 'Fab Four', both in their visual appearance and record sleeves. Their prospects were improved by the recruitment of renowned pop producer Mike Chapman, who had previously worked with Blondie. During the summer of 1979, the Knack's well-publicized debut single 'My Sharona' promptly topped the US charts for six weeks, as well as reaching the UK Top 10 and selling a million copies. The first album, *The Knack*, was a scintillating pop portfolio, full of clever hooks and driving rhythms and proved an instant hit, selling five million copies in its year of release. Implicit in the Knack's abrupt rise were the seeds of their imminent destruction. In adapting 60s pop to snappy 70s production, they had also spiced up the standard boy/girl love songs with slightly more risque lyrics for their modern audience. Critics, already suspicious of the powerful record company push and presumptuous Beatles comparisons, pilloried the group for their overt sexism in such songs as 'Good Girls Don't' as well as reacting harshly to Fieger's arrogance during interviews. At the height of the critical backlash, the Knack issued the apologetically-titled *But The Little Girls Understand*, a sentiment which was to prove over-optimistic. Both the sales and the songs were less impressive and by the time of their third album, *Round Trip*, their powerpop style seemed decidedly outmoded. By the end of 1981, they voluntarily disbanded with Fieger attempting unsuccessfully to rekindle recent fame with Taking Chances, while the others fared little better with the ill-fated Gama.
Albums: *The Knack* (1979), *But The Little Girls Understand* (1980), *Round Trip* (1981).

L

Lambrettas

This English, Brighton-based band comprised Jez Bird (vocals/guitar), Doug Saunders (guitar/vocals), Mark Ellis (bass/vocals) and Paul Wincer (drums). Together with Secret Affair, the Merton Parkas and the Chords, they were part of the UK's short-lived mod revival of 1979-80. After securing a deal with Elton John's Rocket Records, they had 'Go Steady' included on the label's compilation *499 2139*, alongside fellow mod hopefuls the Act, the Escalators, Les Elite and the Vye. A month later, in November 1979, the same version of 'Go Steady' was released as a single, with little success, but drew much attention from the growing mod audiences. Success arrived with 'Poison Ivy', a catchy remake of the Leiber And Stoller-penned classic, reaching number 7 in the UK charts during 1980, eight places higher than the Coasters' original version of 1959. Their popularity continued with follow-up singles entering the charts, 'D-a-a-ance' climbed to number 12, and 'Another Day (Another Girl)' just managed to scrape into the UK Top 50, reaching number 49. The latter was originally called 'Page Three', but threatened legal action by *The Sun* newspaper, persuaded the band to rethink the title. Their debut *Beat Boys In The Jet Age* peaked at number 28 and was also their last glimpse of the charts. Successive releases: 'Steppin' Out', 'Good Times', 'Anything You Want', 'Decent Town' and 'Somebody To Love', had little impact on either critics or record-buying public, and by the time they issued *Ambience* in 1981, the mod revival was dead and buried and the band quickly folded. In 1985, Razor Records unearthed the Lambrettas' back catalogue, releasing a compilation of their singles, entitled *Kick Start*.
Albums: *Beat Boys In The Jet Age* (1980), *Ambience* (1981). Compilation: *Kick Start* (1985).

La's

Formed in 1986 in Liverpool, the La's featured Lee Myers (b. 2 August 1962, Huyton, Liverpool, England; guitar/vocals), John Power (b. 14 September 1967; bass), Paul Hemmings (guitar) and John Timson (drums). Early demo tapes resulted in their signing with Go! Discs in 1987. After a well-received debut single, 'Way Out', the band took a year out before issuing the melodic 'There She Goes'. When this too eluded the charts, the La's, far from disillusioned, returned to the studio for two years to perfect tracks for their debut album. The line-up changed, too, with Lee's brother Neil (b. 8 July 1971,

Huyton, Liverpool, England) taking up drums, James Joyce (b. 23 September 1970) replaced Power and ex-Marshmellow Overcoats guitarist Cammy (b. Peter James Camell, 30 June 1967, Huyton, Liverpool, England) was added to the line-up. In the meantime, 'There She Goes' became a massive underground favourite, prompting a reissue two years on (after the tuneful 'Timeless Melody'). In October 1990, it reached its rightful place in the UK Top 20. *The La's* followed that same month, an all-embracing and truly musical collection of tunes. Any comparisons with the best of yesteryear stemmed from the band's obsession with real instruments, creating a rootsy, authentic air. After 'Feelin'' was drawn from the album, the La's set about recording tracks for a new work and spent much of 1991's summer touring America and Japan.
Album: *The La's* (1990).

Laugh

This UK, Manchester-based group first appeared via a flexidisc given free with the city's *Debris* magazine in 1986, with the punchy, guitar-dominated 'Take Your Time, Yeah!'. In November that same year, the track fronted their first vinyl single on the Remorse label, but although it was well-received, Laugh had to wait until August the following year before their second offering, a decidedly-poppy effort entitled 'Paul McCartney'. After 'Time To Lose' in 1988, which the UK independent chart Top 30, the band moved to the short-lived Sub Aqua label for *Sensation No. 1*, the title of both the album and a single. Neither made any significant impact and Martin Mittler, Spencer, Ian Bendelow and Martin Wright re-thought their strategy, later emerging as a dance outfit.
Album: *Sensation No.1* (1988).

Laughing Clowns

Based in Sydney, Australia, the Laughing Clowns were led by Ed Kuepper, who formed the band in 1979 after leaving the Saints. The group rehearsed for six months before gigging, and the music that emerged was complex. As the members: Louise Elliot (saxophone), Peter Doyle (trumpet), the Wallace-Crabbe brothers Ben and Dan (bass and keyboards respectively), Peter Walsh (bass) and Jeffrey Wegener (drums), come from different disciplines such as jazz many of Kuepper's fans had difficulty appreciating what the band was attempting. The media found difficulties in pigeon-holing the Laughing Clowns as easily as their contemporaries. Representative of their style, and an in-concert favourite was 'Eternally Yours' (1984). Despite this lack of acceptance the band recorded often on independent labels (mainly their own called Prince Melon). The band toured the UK and Europe from 1982 onwards, releasing several records there as well, but to no great success.

Undaunted, Kuepper continued solo, and formed a new oufit called the Yard Goes On Forever.

Albums: *Reign Of Terror* (1981), *Mr Uddich Schmuddich Goes To Town* (1981), *Law Of Nature* (1984), *Ghost Of Ideal Wife* (1985), *History Of Rock 'N' Roll, Volume 1* (1986, early 80s recordings).

Lauper, Cyndi

b. Cynthia Anne Stephanie Lauper, 22 June 1953, Queens, New York, USA. Starting her career as a singer in Manhattan's clubs, Lauper began writing her own material when she met pianist John Turi in 1977. They formed Blue Angel and released a self-titled album in 1980 which included raucous versions of rock classics as well as their own numbers. She split with Turi and in 1983 began working on what was to become her million-selling solo debut, *She's So Unusual*. It made number 4 in the USA and provided four hit singles - the exuberant 'Girls Just Want To Have Fun' which became a cult anthem for independent young women; 'Time After Time' (a US number 1 and later covered by Miles Davis on *You're Under Arrest*), 'She Bop' (which broached the unusual subject of female masturbation) and 'All Through The Night' (written by Jules Shear). The album also contained Prince's 'When You Were Mine'. At the end of 1984 *Billboard* magazine placed her first in the Top Female Album Artists and she was awarded a Grammy as Best New Artist. Her image was one that adapted, for the American market, something of a colourful 'punk' image that would not offend parents too much but at the same time still retain a sense of humour and rebelliousness that would appeal the youth. Pundits in the UK claimed to have seen through this straight away, yet they acknowledged Lauper's talent nonetheless. *True Colors* did not have the same commercial edge as its predecessor, yet the title track still provided her with an US number 1 and a Top 20 hit in the UK. In 1987, she took a role as a beautician in the poorly-received film, *Vibes*. She made a brief return to the charts in 1990 with the single 'I Drove All Night' from *A Night To Remember*. Another lacklustre film appearence in *Off And Running* was not seen in the UK until two years later. Seen in some quarters as little more than a visual and vocal oddity, Lauper has nevertheless written several magnificent pop tunes and, in 1985, boosted her credibility as a singer when she performed a stirring duet with Patti LaBelle at LaBelle's show at the Greek Theater in Los Angeles.

Albums: as Blue Angel *Blue Angel* (1980); solo *She's So Unusual* (1984), *True Colors* (1986), *A Night To Remember* (1989).

Leather Nun

This post-punk group was founded in Goreburg, Sweden. In the mid-70s disc jockey, fanzine editor, and Iggy Pop/Ramones enthusiast Jonas Almqvist made frequent trips to London to see bands and while there he formed a friendship with Genesis P. Orridge of Throbbing Gristle. Almqvist played him a demo of a song - 'Death Threat' - that he had written and Orridge agreed to issue it on his own Industrial Records. Returning to Sweden, Almqvist recruited Bengt Aronsson (guitar), Freddie (bass) and Gert Claesson (drums) from what was regarded as Sweden's finest punk band, Strait Jacket. This was the first line-up of Leather Nun and later in 1979 they released the EP *Slow Death* on Industrial Records. Their use of hardcore gay-pornographic films to illustrate their material provoked allegations of obscenity. This led to Freddie eventually leaving the band, though not before recording the seminal 'Prime Mover' in 1983. His replacement was Haken, a singer-songwriter rapidly trained to play the bass. The band also added Nils Wohlrabe as second guitarist. They recorded for five different labels by 1985 and enjoyed cult attention in the UK with their cover of Abba's 'Gimme Gimme Gimme (A Man After Midnight)'. Anders Olsen replaced Haken on bass soon after.

Albums: *Slow Death* (1984), *Alive* (1985), *Lust Games* (1986), *Steel Construction* (1987).

Legendary Pink Dots

This east London experimental group was formed in 1981, based around lyricist and singer Edward Ka-spel, and keyboard player Phillip Knight, who emerged as part of the burgeoning do-it-yourself scene of the late 70s. Performing what they described as 'psychedelic' - in an 'exploratory sense, rather than nostalgia' - they released their first album *Brighter Now* on the small, Birmingham, independent label Phaze, eventually running through two other homes before settling with Play It Again Sam. The band emigrated to the Netherlands in 1985, after Ka-spel had become disenchanted with his native country's reaction to *The Tower* (' . . . a really important album to me'). A series of recordings continued to fare better on the continent than in the UK, while Ka-spel recorded the latest of several solo albums with Steve Stapleton of Nurse With Wound. He has also branched out with a side project, the Maria Dimension, and worked with Skinny Puppy. The latest inauguration of Legendary Pink Dots, meanwhile, has added Nils Van Hoorne (saxophones/flute/bass/clarinet) and Bob Pisteer (guitars/bass/sitar).

Albums: *Brighter Now* (1982), *Curse* (1983), *Faces In The Fire* (1984), *The Tower* (1984), *The Lovers* (1985), *Asylum* (1985), *Island Of Jewels* (1986) *Stone Circles* (1988) *Any Day Now* (1988), *Greetings Nine* (1989), *The Golden Age* (1989), *Crushed Velvet Apocalypse* (1990). Solo albums: Edward Ka-spel *Laugh China Doll* (1984), *Eyes China Doll* (1985), *Chyekk China*

Doll (1986)

Lemonheads

From hardcore to melodic guitar rock, the Lemonheads, from Boston, Massachusetts, USA, progressed quickly in a short space of time. Comprising Even Dando (guitar/vocals), David Ryan (drums) and Jesse Peretz (bass), the band's early releases - 'Laughing All The Way', and two albums *Hate Your Friends* and *Creator* - attracted significant interest in hardcore circles. However, it was the band's version of Suzanne Vega's 'Luka' in 1989 that brought them across towards the mainstream. Obviously influenced, like their Massachusetts contemporaries Dinosaur Jr, by Neil Young's work with Crazy Horse, their mesh of melody and loud, dynamic guitar work on the single's parent album, *Lick*, was a mixture of the pleasant and the unruly, with an overriding languid feel. This mellowing continued with a cover of Michael Nesmith's 'Different Drum' in 1990, an independent hit that sealed a contract with Atlantic Records. The first fruits of this progression came with *Lovey* later that year and showcased a band with maturity and vitality, playing melodic guitar rock that was subdued at times and frenzied at others.
Albums: *Hate Your Friends* (1987), *Creator* (1988), *Lick* (1989), *Lovey* (1990).

Let's Active

Ostensibly the vehicle for veteran US all-rounder Mitch Easter, Let's Active issued three melodic albums during the mid-80s. Easter previously played alongside various members of the dB's in the Sneakers in the late 70s, and also worked with the H-Bombs and the Cosmopolitans. His first solo outing graced *Shake To Date*, a UK compilation of material from the US Shake label, in 1981. In between 'discovering' R.E.M. and then producing their early work, Easter eventually set up Let's Active. *Cypress* did not emerge until 1984, and featured Easter joined by Faye Hunter (bass) and Sam Romweber (drums). The songwriting skills were evident (and the debt to John Lennon and Paul McCartney was clear), but the album lacked bite. Almost two years later, Let's Active found that bite with *Big Plans For Everybody*, aided by drummers Eric Marshall and Rob Ladd and Angie Carlson (guitar/keyboards/vocals). Promoted by 'In Little Ways', the album seemed the perfect encapsulation of Easter's aims: superb production, an ingenious blend of instrumentation and, above all, strong songs. Easter's commitments elsewhere delayed the third Let's Active album for nearly three years, and as such *Every Dog Has His Day* (with John Heames now in the ranks) was slightly disappointing.
Albums: *Cypress* (1984), *Big Plans For Everybody* (1986), *Every Dog Has His Day* (1989).

Levellers

This five-piece unit from Brighton, Sussex, England combined folk instrumentation with rock and punk ethics: 'We draw on some Celtic influences because it's a powerful source, but we're a very English band - this country does have roots worth using'. They took their name, and much of their ideology from the Puritans active at the time of the English Civil War between 1647 and 1649, whose agenda advocated republicanism, a written constitution and abolition of the monarchy. Their original line-up featured Mark Chadwick (songwriter; lead vocals, guitar, banjo), Jon Sevink (fiddle), Alan Leveller (vocals, guitars, mandolin, harmonica), Jeremy Leveller (bass, bouzouki) and Charlie Heather (drums). Sevink's violin, like many of their instruments, was typically unconventional and ecologically pure, 'recycled' from three different broken violin bodies. Chadwick, meanwhile, used a guitar which had an old record player arm acting as pick-ups, as well as an amplifier acquired from the Revillos. The *Carry Me* EP was released on Brighton's Hag Records in May 1989, after label boss Phil Nelson had taken over their management. They signed to French label Musidisc in 1989, and Waterboys' producer Phil Tennant recorded their debut album. When their guitarist left during a tour of Belgium in April 1990, they recruited Simon instead, and set off on a typically extensive UK tour. After signing to China Records, they made a breakthrough into the national charts with minor UK hits in 1991 with 'One Way' and 'Far From Home'. Their popularity, particularly in live appearences during this period and into 1992, made them regulars in the music press, wherein they took to criticising the Men They Couldn't Hang and New Model Army who, paradoxically, appear to be their biggest influences! The Levellers' affinity with the neo-hippie/new age travellers looks likely to prevent them from ever achieving mass appeal, but in the meantime they have no worries about playing to a large and appreciative audience.
Albums: *A Weapon Called The Word* (1990), *Levelling The Land* (1991).

Levitation

This rock-pop combo featured several experienced UK musicians. Formed by Terry Bickers (vocals) and Dave Francollini (drums, ex-Something Pretty Beautiful) after an altercation between the former's ex-group leader Guy Chadwick of the House Of Love in 1989. Levitation's line-up was completed by Bic Hayes (guitar, ex-Cardiacs), Bob White (keyboards) and Laurence O'Keefe (bass, ex-Jazz Butcher). Their pedigree was enough to see them shoot to prominence in the UK press, but two EPs, *Coppelia* and *After Ever* revealed a band with no lack

of enthusiasm or ideas. They were ousted from an early Transvision Vamp support officially because there was not enough room on stage for their equipment. Another story suggests that singer Wendy James was concerned that the band's growing live reputation might overshadow her own group. Bickers has a reputation for being something of an eccentric, but would seem to have found a happier home for his obvious talents. Their new album *Coterie* features John McGeoch, from PiL, guesting on guitar.
Album: *Coterie* (1992).

Leyton Buzzards

This new wave/pop outfit was formed by Geoffrey Deanne (b. 10 December 1954, London, England; vocals) and David Jaymes (b. 28 December 1954, Woodford, Essex, England; bass). They recruited Kevin Steptoe (drums) and Dave Monk (guitar). From playing R&B covers on the pub circuit, they changed direction in 1976 after witnessing the new punk movement at the Roxy Club in London. By the following year they had secured a record deal with Small Wonder Records, releasing the single '19 & Mad', and changing surnames to the likes of Nick Nayme (Deanne) to reinforce their new image. After the single, Monk was replaced by Vernon Austin. After entering The Band Of Hope And Glory contest, jointly sponsored by the *Sun* newspaper and BBC Radio 1, they won the final at the London Palladium. Their prize was a recording contract with Chrysalis. The result was the band's best-remembered moment, as 'Saturday Night (Beneath The Plastic Palm Trees)' saw them appearing on *Top Of The Pops*, celebrating band members' former weekend drinking and fighting antics. Shortening their name to the Buzzards, they were unable to capitalize on their early success, though their last Chrysalis single 'We Make A Noise' featured a cover designed by Monty Python's Terry Gilliam. The contract-fulfilling *Jellied Eels To Record Deals* compiled early singles, demos, and radio session tracks. Their final recording was a one-off single for WEA titled 'Can't Get Used To Losing You', before Deane and Jaymes set up the more successful, salsa-flavoured Modern Romance.
Album: *Jellied Eels to Record Deals* (1979).

Lightning Seeds

Contrary to the multiples suggested by the moniker, Lightning Seeds was the brainchild of one man, Ian Broudie (b. 4 August 1958, Liverpool, England), who had gouged a significant niche in the Merseyside music scene throughout the 80s. Originally a member of Big In Japan - a forerunner of the likes of Echo And The Bunnymen and Teardrop Explodes, not to mention a breeding ground for future Frankie Goes To Hollywood singer Holly Johnson and drummer Budgie, who was later to join Siouxsie And The

Banshees. Broudie eventually ended up playing in the Original Mirrors and worked up an appetite for production work. His efforts on the first two Bunnymen albums acted as a springboard from whence Broudie was catapulted into the studio with numerous acts, including the Fall, Wah!, the Icicle Works and Frazier Chorus. On the creative front, Broudie collaborated with Wild Swans singer Paul Simpson under the name Care, releasing three immaculate singles and preparing the blueprint for his own pop-obsessed project come the end of the decade. Thus Lightning Seeds was born as an opportunity for Broudie to expand his own songwriting ideas. The project had an immediate impact when his first single, 'Pure', fuelled everyone's interest by virtue of being a deliberately low-key release and then went on to reach number 16 in the UK chart. *Cloudcuckooland* followed, encapsulating Broudie's notion of the perfect, sweet pop song, whereupon Broudie put his producer's hat back on to work with contemporary bands like Northside and the Primitives. He continued his work under the Lightning Seeds moniker in 1992 with *Sense*, another collection of perfect pop.
Albums: *Cloudcuckooland* (1990), *Sense* (1992).

Lilac Time

Turning his back on pop stardom as a solo performer, Stephen 'Tin Tin' Duffy dropped the 'Tin Tin' part of his name (after legal action by lawyers representing Hergé), and formed the Lilac Time with his brother, Nick (guitar), in 1987. Purposely low profile, the group's debut, *The Lilac Time*, was released by the tiny Birmingham label, Swordfish. The other group members were Michael Giri (bass) and Micky Harris (drums). The subtle blend of pop harmonies and folk instrumentation was well-received and Phonogram signed the band and re-released the debut. *Paradise Circus* was more commercial with pop gems like 'The Girl Who Waves At Trains'. *And Love For All*, produced jointly by Duffy, Andy Partridge of XTC and John Leckie, was more introspective and despite strong efforts by Phonogram the group failed to record a hit in the singles chart, mainly because of a general unwillingness to forget Duffy's rather twee past as a pop idol (he was also in the early line-up of Duran Duran). In 1991, the group signed with the leading independent label. Creation and released *Astronauts*. In the week of its release it was announced that the group had split and that Duffy would revert once again to solo status.
Albums: *The Lilac Time* (1987), *Paradise Circus* (1989), *And Love For All* (1990), *Astronauts* (1991).

Lillywhite, Steve

b. 1955, England. Lillywhite is a leading contemporary UK record producer, best known for his work with the Pogues and U2. He started out as a tape operator for Phonogram in 1972. After producing the demo tapes which won Ultravox a contract with Island Records, he joined the company as a staff producer. Lillywhite specialised in producing new wave bands such as Eddie And the Hot Rods, Siouxsie And the Banshees (the hit 'Hong Kong Garden'), the Members, Penetration, XTC and the Buzzards before he was approached to supervise Peter Gabriel's third solo album. By the early 80s, Lillywhite was widely recognised as one of the most accomplished of younger producers. Now a freelance, Island brought him in to work on U2's debut *Boy*. He also produced the group's next two albums. In addition he worked with artists as varied as singer-songwriter Joan Armatrading, stadium rockers Simple Minds, art-punks Psychedelic Furs and the Rolling Stones (*Dirty Work*, 1987). In 1987, Lillywhite produced contrasting albums by the Pogues and Talking Heads (*Naked*), continuing with the Pogues' follow-up *Peace And Love* (1988) and with David Byrne's solo effort *Rei Momo*. Among Lillywhite's other productions was *Kite* by Kirsty McColl whom he had married in 1984.

Liquid Jesus

This experimental, Los Angeles-based quintet were formed in 1990 by bassist Johnny Lonely and guitarist Scott Tracey. Adding Todd Rigione (guitar), Buck Murphy (vocals) and John Molo (drums), they gigged incessantly on the LA bar and club circuit. Fusing psychedelic, blues, jazz and metal influences to bizarre extremes, they debuted with an independently released live album. Tipped as the next possible Jane's Addiction, they were signed by Geffen Records in 1991 and delivered *Pour In The Sky*. This paid respect to Jimi Hendrix, Led Zeppelin, the Red Hot Chili Peppers and Queen, but carefully sidestepped accusations of plagiarism by virtue of their totally deranged and unpredictable delivery.
Albums: *Liquid Jesus Live* (1990), *Pour In The Sky* (1992).

Living In A Box

This Sheffield, UK-based pop group comprised Richard Darbyshire (b. 8 March 1960, Stockport, Cheshire, England; vocal/guitar), Marcus Vere (b. 29 January 1962; keyboard) and Anthony Critchlow (drums). Their first single, the self-referential, 'Living In A Box' was a UK Top 10 hit in the spring of 1987 and further successes followed over the next two years, most notably, 'Blow The House Down' and 'Room In Your Heart'. Meanwhile, vocalist Richard Darbyshire guested on Jellybean's *Jellybean Rocks The House*. Having enjoyed a hit album with their self-titled debut, the group consolidated their success with *Gatecrashing*.

Albums: *Living In A Box* (1987), *Gatecrashing* (1989).

Lloyd, Richard

Having established himself as a rhythm guitarist of standing in Television, Lloyd embarked on a solo career in 1979, releasing an album whose quality rivalled the efforts of his more illustrious ex-partners Tom Verlaine and Richard Hell. *Alchemy* should have projected Lloyd towards a bigger audience but its reviews were not matched by its sales and Richard failed to exploit the work due to an alarming slump into drug addiction. It was five years before a drug-free Lloyd returned with a new album, *Field Of Fire*, but since the mid-80s his output remained decidedly low. By 1991, he had joined Verlaine, Ficca and Smith in a reformed Television, spending much of the first part of 1992 rehearsing and recording.
Albums: *Alchemy* (1979), *Field Of Fire* (1985).

Lloyd, Robert

Inspired by T. Rex and the fact that girls tended to pin posters of pop stars on their walls and not the professional footballers that Robert Lloyd (b. 1959, Cannock, Staffordshire, England) aspired to emulate, the teenager switched his allegiance from the football field to concert hall. Between 1974 and 1976 he played in several bands that never escaped the rehearsal room. He left school at the age of 16 and in 1976 attended a concert by the Sex Pistols. He started to follow the Pistols around on the Anarchy Tour and at one of the gigs, he persuaded a promoter to offer him some gigs. The result was the hurriedly assembled Prefects in February 1977, consisting of Lloyd, Alan and Paul Appelby, and Joe Crow. After one performance at a private party and one at the famous Barbarella's club in Birmingham, the Prefects were offered the chance of standing in for the Slits at a Clash concert. When the Buzzcocks dropped out of the subsequent tour, the Prefects were offered a permanent place. Although the band recorded some John Peel BBC radio sessions, no records were released until after the band's split in 1979. Lloyd's next move was to form the Nightingales and his own Vindaloo label. When the Nightingales fell apart in the mid-80s he concentrated on the label and songwriting, the results of which surfaced in further Peel sessions (he holds the record for the most sessions for Peel in his various forms) under the name Robert Lloyd And The New Four Seasons. This led to a single with the In-Tape label and in 1989 he signed to Virgin. After a few false starts, the album emerged in 1990 and featured Steve Nieve and Pete Thomas (the Attractions), Andy Scott (the Sweet), and Craig Gannon (formerly of the Bluebells, Aztec Camera, the Colourfield and the Smiths) amongst others. However, when it came to promoting the album, Lloyd had to assemble a new band centred

around former Nightingale guitarist The Tank.
Album: *Me And My Mouth* (1990).

Loft

Formed in 1980 when Bill Prince (b. 19 July 1962, Devon, England) and Andy Strickland (b. 16 July 1959, Isle Of Wight, England; guitar/vocals) met with Peter Astor (b. 1959, Colchester, Essex, England), then singing in the group News Of Birds. Later joined by drummer Dave Morgan (drums), the band's first gig was under the name of the Living Room which, by sheer coincidence, was also the banner of a small but significant London venue set up by Scottish entrepreneur, Alan McGee. Fortunately, the freshly-named Loft linked up with McGee's nascent Creation Records label to release of the single 'Why Does The Rain?', which encapsulated their stylishly downbeat driving guitar sound. A year later, the follow-up, 'Up The Hill And Down The Slope', furthered the Loft's cause and strengthened their cult-status, bolstered by championing from BBC disc jockey, Janice Long. As their reputation grew, so did tensions within the band, causing them to split just as their career appeared to be in full motion. Both Strickland and Prince pursued journalistic vocations and started up the Caretaker Race and the Wishing Stones respectively. Peter Astor and Dave Morgan formed the marginally successful Weather Prophets until they disbanded at the end of the 80s, allowing Astor to concentrate upon a solo career whilst Morgan went on to join the country-flavoured Rockingbirds, who in 1992 looked on the verge of substantial success.
Compilation: *Once Around The Fair* (1989).

Logic, Lora

London art student Susan Whitby originally adopted the pseudonym Lora Logic during her stint as saxophonist in X-Ray Spex. After leaving that group following their debut single, she soon re-emerged in 1978 with her own outfit Essential Logic, who quickly recorded a couple of hard-edged EPs *Aerosol Burns* and *Wake Up*. One album was recorded, *Beat Rhythm News* (1979) before Lora commenced on a series of solo recordings in 1981. Her quirky, occasionally arresting, vocals were in evidence on her sole album, *Pedigree Charm* (1982) and she can be heard on a number of recordings by other artists including the Raincoats, Stranglers, Swell Maps and Red Crayola.
Album: *Pedigree Charm* (1982).

London

As punk sent an electric shock through a complacent late 70s UK music scene, major labels were to be found signing acts, regardless of ability. London, like many other second division new wavers, were

London

scooped up only to disappear after all the fuss had died down. Two releases in 1977, 'Everyone's A Winner' and 'No Time' were both of their time, punchy and urgent but ultimately lacking in substance. *Animal Games*, London's one and only album (and accompanying single) in 1978 followed suit, its power-pop feel lacking the true bite of punk's pioneers. Lead singer Riff Regan later had a stab at a solo career, while drummer Jon Moss joined the Edge before making his name in the early 80s with Culture Club.
Album: *Animal Games* (1978).

Lone Justice

Lone Justice

This group of US country-rockers were fronted by Maria McKee (b. 17 August 1964, Los Angeles, California, USA) who is the half-sister of Love's Bryan MacLean. When she was just three-years-old her brother would take her to the various clubs along Los Angeles' Sunset Strip and she was befriended by the likes of Frank Zappa and the Doors. When she grew up, she and MacLean formed a duo initially called the Maria McKee Band, but later changed to the Bryan MacLean Band to cash in on *his* slightly higher profile. Heavily immersed in country music, McKee formed the first incarnation of Lone Justice with Ryan Hedgecock (guitar), Don Heffington (drums), Marvin Etzioni (bass) and Benmont Tench (keyboards, ex-Tom Petty And The Heartbreakers). The group were signed to the Geffen label at the recommendation of Linda Ronstadt. McKee's talents were also admired by artists such as Bob Dylan, U2's Bono, who offered them a support slot on tour, and Tom Petty, who donated songs to the first album. One of these, 'Ways To Be Wicked', while not achieving any notable chart status, was responsible for bringing the group to the attention of the UK audience via an imaginative black-and-white, cut-up-and-scratched video. The band's more established line-up transmuted to that of ex-patriot Brit Shayne Fontayne (guitar), Bruce Brody (keyboards, ex-Patti Smith and John Cale), Greg Sutton (bass) and Rudy Richardson (drums). They were managed by the respected producer, Jimmy Iovine. In 1985, former Undertones singer Feargal Sharkey scored a UK number 1 hit with McKee's 'A Good Heart'. Lone Justice split suddenly in 1987 with McKee going on to record a solo album taking only Brody with her from the remnants of Lone Justice.

Albums: *Lone Justice* (1985), *Shelter* (1987).

Long Ryders

Long Ryders

Formed in November 1981, the Long Riders (as they were then known), initially included three ex-members of the Unclaimed - Sid Griffin (guitar/vocals), Barry Shank (bass/vocals) and Matt Roberts (drums). Steve Wynn completed this early line-up, but the guitarist was replaced by Stephen McCarthy on leaving to form the Dream Syndicate. Griffin and McCarthy remained at the helm throughout the group's turbulent history. As part of Los Angeles' 'paisley underground' movement, the Long Ryders' history is linked with, not only that of the Dream Syndicate, but also that of other guitar-oriented bands such as Rain Parade, (early) Bangles, Green On Red and Blood On The Saddle. A mini-album, *The Long Ryders*, was completed with Des Brewer (bass) and Greg Sowders (drums), although by

the time the quartet secured a permanent deal, Tom Stevens had joined in place of Brewer. *Native Sons*, an excellent set influenced by Buffalo Springfield and Gram Parsons, suggested a promising future, but the Long Ryders were unable to repeat its balance of melody and purpose. They withered on record company indecision and, unable to secure a release from their contract, the group broke up in 1987.

Albums: *The Long Ryders* (1983), *Native Sons* (1984), *State Of Our Union* (1985), *Two-Fisted Tales* (1987), *10-5-60* (1987). *Metallic B.O.* (1989, early recordings).

Loop

Along with the Spacemen 3, Loop, hailing from Croydon, south London, proved to be the UK's answer to the onslaught of harsh, guitar-wielding acts that dominated the late 80s independent scene. Whereas the Spacemen mellowed their sound towards the mesmerising sounds of Suicide, Loop gradually refined their fuzz-laden, pulsing guitar riffs, monotonous vocals and increasingly distinctive drum patterns. Loop's music was an uncompromising blend of late 60s Detroit rock (Stooges and MC5) and Germany's early 70s *avant garde* (Can and Faust), although the result was a dense, brooding mantra-like noise, not unlike early Hawkwind. Loop have always revolved around singer and guitarist Robert (Josh) Hampton, who formed the band with female drummer Bex and bassist Glen in 1986. After the garage-like feedback on '16 Dreams' kicked off 1987, Bex was replaced by John Wills, who introduced a stronger drum sound. This was further strengthened when James Endicott joined as second guitarist, after the reverberating psychedelia of 'Spinning' set the scene for Loop's impressive debut, *Heavens End*, in November. Alongside a cover of Suicide's 'Rocket USA' came a barrage of layered guitar noise awash with distortion and wah-wah. With a new bassist John McKay, Loop moved to Midlands label Chapter 22 for April 1988's dynamic 'Collision', backed by a cover of the Pop Group's 'Thief Of Fire'. After the departure of James Endicott and the Head label had compiled their singles on *The World In Your Eyes* in August, Loop were ready to skirt the national charts with *Fade Out* in November. Its sparser, more discordant sound saw the Can influence to the fore, indeed, a cover of Can's hypnotic magnum opus, 'Mother Sky', turned up on the b-side of 'Black Sun' the following month. After a quiet year, Loop ended 1989 with the powerful 'Arc-Lite', their first single for Situation Two and for new guitarist Scott. Chapter 22 signalled their departure with another collection of two 12-inch singles, but this time, Loop publicly denounced the set. *A Gilded Eternity*, in 1990, again fared well commercially, and moved further towards ethereal, guitar-dominated soundscapes and away from the aggression of *Fade Out*. Since then, Loop have coveted a decidedly low profile with rumours of a split, with only 1991's *Wolf Flow*, a double set of sessions for BBC disc jockey John Peel, to indicate otherwise.

Albums: *Heavens End* (1987), *Fade Out* (1988), *A Gilded Eternity* (1990). Compilations: *The World In Your Eyes* (1988), *Eternal* (1989), *Wolf Flow* (1991, rec. 1987-90).

Lords Of The New Church

Lords Of The New Church

This rock band was made up of several well-known personalities, often described as a punk 'supergroup'. Brian James (b. 18 February 1961; guitar, ex-Damned), Stiv Bators (b. 22 October 1956, Cleveland, Ohio, USA; vocals, ex-Dead Boys, Wanderers), Dave Treganna (b. 1954, Derby, England; bass, ex-Sham 69, Wanderers) and drummer Nicky Turner (b. 4 May 1959, ex-Barracudas). When Jimmy Pursey left Sham 69, the rest of the band had continued in the Wanderers, drafting in Stiv Bators. It was at this point that James contacted Bators with the view to setting up a group. Miles Copeland took on their management, their name coming from his original suggestion Lords Of Discipline. They made their live debut in Paris in 1981. Their debut vinyl 'New Church' helped to increase criticisms about the bands apparent blasphemy, hardly dispelled when the album appeared with lines like: 'Greed and murder is forgiven when in the name of the Church'. The self-titled debut premiered an authentic rock band with dark shades, flirting with apocalyptic and religious imagery. The single 'Dance With Me' from *Is Nothing Sacred* gained several MTV plays with a video directed by Derek Jarman. Unfortunately its success was scuppered after mistaken allegations about paedophilia saw it taken off air. Their final studio album *Method To Our Madness* revealed the band treading water with stifled heavy rock routines. They did not split officially until 1989, but before that Treganna had departed for Cherry Bombz, while Alistair Ward contributed some second guitar.

Albums: *Lords Of The New Church* (1983) *Is Nothing Sacred* (1983) *Method To Our Madness* (1984), *Killer Lords* (1985), *Live At The Spit* (1988, rec. 1982).

Lori And The Chameleons

Formed in 1979 in Liverpool, England, the group was a vehicle for the evocative teenage singer Lori Larty. With backing, production and songwriting provided by former Big In Japan alumni David Balfe and Bill Drummond, Lori emerged with an appealing, almost spoken-word tribute to Japan (the country), entitled 'Touch'. A sparkling arrangement, the disc entered the bottom of the UK charts and appeared to signal the emergence of a new talent. The concept of the group appeared to revolve vaguely around exotic, travelogue pop with each song title set in a specific geographical location: Japan, Peru, Russia and the Ganges River in India. The second single, 'The Lonely Spy', boasted another impressive, atmospheric vocal from Lori and an astonishing backing which emulated the bombastic scores associated with *James Bond* films. After four superb tracks, which represented some of the best UK pop of the period, the group ceased operating. The journeyman Troy Tate reappeared in the Teardrop Explodes, while Drummond turned to management and was later the brains behind a series of pseudonymous groups including the Justified Ancients Of Mu Mu (JAMS) and the Timelords who later emerged as the very successful KLF. Lori, meanwhile, spurned imminent pop success by returning to art college and effectively retiring from the music business. Her fleeting career provided as much mystery and instant appeal as the extraordinary discs on which she appeared.

Lotus Eaters

Rising from the ashes of the Wild Swans, Liverpool's Lotus Eaters enjoyed instant commercial success with a fragrant pop song 'The First Picture Of You', their debut single in June 1983. Revolving around Peter Coyle and Jeremy Kelly, the band never managed to repeat this Top 20 status again, despite four catchy follow-ups; 'You Don't Need Someone New' later that year, 'Set Me Apart' and 'Out On Your Own' (both 1984) and a final stab, 'It Hurts' (1985). Those who appreciate well-crafted, quality melodic pop should look no further than their only album, *No Sense Of Sin*, from 1984. Coyle and Kelly later reactivated the Wild Swans but were again unable to sustain significant interest.

Album: *No Sense Of Sin* (1984).

Love And Money

After the break-up of the Glasgow band, Friends Again in the mid-80s, guitarist James Grant formed the pop/funk influenced Love And Money, taking

with him erstwhile 'Friends', Paul McGeechan (keyboards) and Stuart Kerr (drums), plus Bobby Patterson (bass). The group were named after Grant's personal pledge as to what he wanted to achieve in the coming year. Since then, the group have achieved a string of minor hit singles in the UK starting with 'Candybar Express' (1986) released on the Mercury label, followed by the Fontana issued 'Love And Money' (1987), 'Hallelujah Man' (1988), 'Strange Kind Of Love', 'Jocelyn Square' (both 1989) and 'Winter' (1991). Stuart Kerr left the group in 1987 and subsequently joined the Glasgow-based, Texas. Love And Money recorded their second album as a trio. By the time of *Dogs In The Traffic* the line-up was bolstered by the addition of Douglas McIntyre (guitar/vocals) and Gordon Wilson (drums). Seemingly, forever on the fringes of success, Love And Money have yet to achieve that major breakthrough
Albums: *All You Need Is Love And Money* (1986), *A Strange Kind Of Love* (1988), *Dogs In The Traffic* (1991).

Love And Rockets

This *avant garde* UK rock band formed in Christmas 1985 from the ashes of Bauhaus. When David Jay (aka David J) had finished working with the Jazz Butcher on the *Sex And Travel* and *A Scandal In Bohemia* albums, he linked up once more with old colleague Daniel Ash, who had been working with Tones On Tail. Kevin Haskins also came with Ash, forming the band's nucleus of David Jay (vocals, bass, keyboards), Daniel Ash (vocals, guitar, keyboards) and Haskins (drums, keyboards). Early singles included 'Kundiluni Express', concerning Tuntric meditation, and a cover of the Temptations 'Ball Of Confusion'. The band's debut *Seventh Dream Of Teenage Heaven*, was a celebration of the rituals of youth, based loosely on their own experiences of going to rock concerts to see bands like Roxy Music. Like all of the post-Bauhaus projects, the band have failed to cultivate a UK audience to rival their previous standing. However, they scored a big hit single in the US with 'So Alive', where their work still sells moderately well.
Albums: *Seventh Dream Of Teenage Heaven* (1986), *Express* (1986), *Earth Sun Moon* (1987), *Love And Rockets* (1989).

Lovich, Lene

Vocalist Lovich was one of several acts launched by the Stiff label in 1978. The former horror-film soundtrack screamer joined new signings Mickey Jupp, Rachel Sweet and Jona Lewie on the *Be Stiff* national tour, of which this charismatic performer emerged as the undoubted star. Her arresting, gypsy-like appearance, and warbled intonation was matched by a sense of pop's dynamics, as evinced by her UK Top 3 hit, 'Lucky Number'. Shaven-head guitarist Les Chappell provided a visual and compositional foil to a singer who enjoyed further, albeit minor, hits with 'Say When', 'Bird Song' (both 1979) and 'New Toy' (1981). Lovich also entered the album charts with *Stateless*, which derived its title from the air of mystery the artist cultivated about her origins. Subsequent releases fared less well and her 1982 single, 'It's You Only You (Mein Schmerz)', provided Lovich with her final chart entry. Problems within Stiff undermined the progress of a singer who sadly failed to maintain early promise.
Albums: *Stateless* (1978), *Flex* (1979), *No Man's Land* (1982).

Lena Lovich

Ludus

Founded in 1978, this Manchester, England-based quartet was consistently fronted by the enigmatic lyricist/vocalist Linder (b. Linda Mulvey, 1954, Liverpool, England). The backing was provided by Arthur Cadmon (b. Peter Sadler, Stockport, England), formerly of Manicured Noise and originally the musical genius behind the group. The line-up was completed by bassist Willie Trotter (b. 1959, Manchester, England) and drummer Phil 'Toby' Tolman (ex-Ed Banger And The Nosebleeds). With their jazz-influenced forays and Linder's strong, sloganeering, elliptical feminist lyrics, the group were one of the most interesting of the Manchester New Wave of the late 70s. The departure of Cadmon and later Trotter, replaced by Ian Devine (Ian Pincombe), saw the group change direction, though the jazz influence remained. Linder, a former girlfriend of the Buzzcocks' Howard Devoto, later became a well-publicized confidante of Morrissey. In spite of some inspired moments with Ludus, the group almost wilfully avoided the mainstream. As manager Richard Boon concluded: 'Ludus were totally improvisational and their set list would read: bass, drums, voice, next number. There was something self-limiting about Linder. Any time she seemed on the brink of a breakthrough, even if that meant selling 50 extra records, she would retreat, just like the poet Stevie Smith'. Ian Devine teamed-up in 1989 with ex-Weekend singer, Alison Statton to form Devine And Statton.

Albums: *Pickpocket* (1981), *Let Me Go Where My Pictures Go* (1988).

Lunachicks

Legend has it that New York's Lunachicks were rescued from a life of streetgangs, drinking, idolatry and terrorism against humanity by being discovered by Sonic Youth, who recommended the all-girl band to Blast First Records so vociferously that the Lunachicks' debut *Babysitters On Acid* was barely recorded before it was let loose upon an unsuspecting public. The 'not-at-all-nice-girls' turned their rebellious behaviour into a stage act. Becky (drums), Squid Sid (bass), Gina (lead guitar) and Sindi (guitar) were the musicians with a taste for excessive volume. Theo was the singer with a predilection for blood-splattered wedding gowns. The Lunachicks can only be described as 'different'.

Album: *Babysitters On Acid* (1990).

Lunch, Lydia

The provocative Lydia Lunch was a pivotal figure in New York's 'no wave' scene of the late 70s and has worked with an array of talent since then. After spells with Teenage Jesus And The Jerks and Beirut Slump (the latter who were restricted to one US single, 'Try Me'), Rochester-born Lydia Lunch opted for the freedom of solo work with 1980's acclaimed *Queen Of Siam* on the Ze label. Her next project, Eight-Eyed Spy, toyed with funk and R&B while retaining her uncompromising vocal style and violent, experimental musical approach. Then came *13:13* on the Ruby label, which benefited from a harder, more co-ordinated feel. In 1982, she shared a 12-inch EP with the Birthday Party on 4AD, 'The Agony Is The Ecstacy', revealing her increasing fascination with the baser instincts of human nature. Members of the Birthday Party also backed Lydia on 'Some Velvet Morning', while Einsturzende Neubauten joined her

for 'Thirsty'. This marriage of the New York and Berlin undergrounds was further demonstrated on 'Der Karibische Western', on Zensor with Die Haut. Lunch continued this collaborative stance in 1983, working with Danish band Sort Sol. 1984's *In Limbo*, a mini-album for Cabaret Voltaire's Doublevision label, re-introduced her to solo work, and she soon founded Widowspeak Productions in 1985 as an outlet to document her work, starting appropriately with the *Uncensored Lydia Lunch* cassette. After a project with Michael Gira, entitled *Hard Rock* (a cassette on Ecstatic Peace), Lydia homed in on New York pranksters Sonic Youth for the 'Death Valley '69', a grungy, menacing start for Blast First Records. A sinister solo offering, *The Drowning Of Lady Hamilton*, was followed by a 10-inch EP with No Trend, entitled *Heart Of Darkness* (1985). The next release for Widowspeak was a limited edition box, *The Intimate Diaries Of The Sexually Insane*, containing a cassette of chronic case histories, a booklet and a book, 'Adulterers Anonymous', co-written by Lydia. 1987's remixed and remastered double album retrospective, *Hysterie*, summarized her work from 1976-86, before she paired with the man behind Foetus and Clint Ruin, Jim Thirlwell, for the awesome Stinkfist project, in 1989. That year also witnessed Harry Crews, an all-girl wall of guitar sound for which Lunch was joined by Sonic Youth bassist, Kim Gordon. Lunch, in conjunction with her soul-mate Thirlwell, has become known as an avid opponent of censorship. Her own work is uncomprisingly confrontational and base, and includes videos featuring her administering oral sex. The politics of outrage remain her gospel.

Albums: *Queen Of Siam* (1980), *13:13* (1982), *In Limbo* (1984), *Uncensored Lydia Lunch* (1985), *The Drowning Of Lady Hamilton* (1985), *The Intimate Diaries Of The Sexually Insane* (1986), *Honeymoon In Red* (1988), *Oral Fixation* (1989), with Rowland S. Howard *Shotgun Wedding* (1991). Compilation: *Hysterie* (1976-1986) (1989).

Lurkers

This second-generation UK punk quartet formed during 1977, in Uxbridge, London. Comprising Nigel Moore (bass), Howard Wall (lead vocals), Pete Stride (guitar) and Esso (drums), they were heralded as the British answer to the Ramones. They scored four minor UK hit singles between 1978-79, with 'Ain't Got A Clue' and 'I Don't Need To Tell Her' proving the most successful. They specialized in two-minute blasts of punky rock 'n' roll, delivered with almost naive charm. Their simple, yet effective style was instantly accessible and exuded warmth as well as energy. They never received the recognition their talents deserved, because of a lack of image and media support. Pete Stride teamed-up with John Plain in

Lush

1980, to record *New Guitar in Town*. The material on this album was very much in a Lurkers vein, but it met with limited success. The group reformed in the early 90s, appearing on punk nostalgia bills.
Albums: *Fulham Fallout* (1978), *God's Lonely Men* (1979), *King Of The Mountain* (1979), *Greatest Hit, Last Will And Testament* (1980), *This Dirty Town* (1980), *Wild Times Again* (1981).

Lush

Little was heard of London-based Lush's serene pop qualities and full-bodied guitar sound until their mini-album, *Scar*, was issued in October 1989 on 4AD Records. It was a critically acclaimed debut, and red-haired Miki Berenyi (vocals/guitar), Emma Anderson (guitar/backing vocals), Steve Rippon (bass guitar) and Christopher Acland (drums) found themselves topping the independent charts. Tours with the Darling Buds and Loop followed, plus an appearance on BBC2's *Snub TV* and a John Peel radio session. The EP *Mad Love*, issued in February 1990, was less raw but soared to new heights with the help of producer Robin Guthrie from the Cocteau Twins. Lush's consistent coverage in the music press, not least for their perpetual appearances at pre/post-gig parties, made them one of the leading UK independent groups of the year; one that was taken up with tours in the UK and Europe and an appearance at the Glastonbury Festival. Another EP, *Sweetness And Light* was a further move towards a commercial pop sound and only narrowly missed the national charts. The three EPs were compiled, originally for the US market, as *Gala*. Much of 1991 was spent recording the long-awaited full debut album, during which time the release of the EP, *Black Spring* (which included a cover of Dennis Wilson's 'Fallin' In Love') wetted appetites. When *Spooky* was finally released, many were disappointed, some citing Guthries' production work as swamping the group sound. Nevertheless, the album reached the national Top 20 and number 1 in the UK independent chart. During the winter of 1991/2 the group line-up changed when bassist Steve Rippon left amicably, to be replaced by *New Musical Express* picture researcher, Phil King.
Albums: *Scar* (1989, mini-album), *Spooky* (1992). Compilation: *Gala* (1990).

M

M was the brainchild of former art school student and folk singer Robin Scott. He started out as manager of the R&B band Roogalator and formed the Do It label to release an album by them. Do It later found critical success with the band Adam And The Ants. Scott moved to Paris in 1978, where he produced the Slits and several French bands. It was here that he got the idea for the band M, whose name was taken from the signs for the Paris Metro. Their debut single 'Moderne Man' was not successful and was released at the same time as a single by Comic Romance in which Scott also featured. However M's quirky and hook-laden second single 'Pop Musik' was a massive hit both in the UK and the USA as well as across Europe. As a gimmick, some copies of the single featured both a and b-sides on the one playing surface with the listener taking pot luck as to which groove the needle dropped on to. An album was released to capitalize on the hit and, as well as the singles, also featured a re-recording of the track 'Cowboys And Indians' - previously the b-side of the 'Comic Romance' single. The album was recorded using session musicians Wally Badarov (keyboards), Gary Barnacles (saxophone/flute), Philip Gould (drums), Julian Scott of Roogalator (bass), and Betty Vinchon (vocals). Among the musicians on the second album were Level 42's Mark King. After a couple of minor hit follow-ups, M's career slipped into rapid decline with subsequent singles (including a release on Stiff Records) failing to chart. Only a 1989 remix of 'Pop Musik' returned the name of M to the charts. Meanwhile, Scott worked with Ryûichi Sakamoto on two albums and put out his own solo album - *The Kiss Of Life* - in 1985.
Albums: *New York - London - Paris - Munich* (1979), *The Official Secrets Act* (1980).

McCarthy

Barking Abbey Comprehensive school, in Essex, England, acted as a meeting point for McCarthy in the early part of the 80s. Eventually, in 1984, Malcolm Eden (b. 1 September 1963, Ilford, Essex, England; vocals), Tim Gane (b. 12 July 1964, Barking, Essex, England; guitar), John Williamson (b. 28 December 1963, Ilford, Essex, England; bass) and Gary Baker (b. 8 September 1963, Barking, Essex, England; drums) formed the band and released a self-financed single, apparently limited to 485 copies. The quartet's profile was further raised with their inclusion (with 'Celestial City') on the *New Musical Express*'s influential 'C86' cassette, but while McCarthy certainly shared many contemporary bands' tastes for rough-edged guitars, they forced themselves away from the crowd by anointing their music with an extreme left wing political stance. Perhaps it was pure coincidence that the similarly-minded songwriter Billy Bragg attended the very same school, yet the 'Red Sleeping Beauty' single - a poetically-veiled commentary on the Thatcher government of the time - was just one of a series of sharply-toned releases where the message never suffocated McCarthy's melodic instinct. After a series of label changes and a highly successful last gasp evolution towards the more fashionable, upbeat sounds of 1990, McCarthy finally tired of battling against their apathetic surroundings and dissolved, playing their final gig at the London School of Economics at the start of the new decade. Gary Baker turned to radiography, Malcolm Eden concentrated on literary writing, while Tim Gane remained in music and started receiving numerous critical recommendations for his new band, Stereolab. Albums: *I Am A Wallet* (1987), *The Enraged Will Inherit The Earth* (1989), *Banking, Violence And The Inner Life Today* (1990). Compilations: *That's All Very Well But* (1991), *We'll Get You Soon You Creeps* (1991).

Kirsty MacColl

MacColl, Kirsty

b. 10 October 1959, England. The daughter of the celebrated folk singer Ewan MacColl, Kirsty enjoyed success in her own right as an accomplished songwriter and pop vocalist. Originally signed to Stiff Records as a 16-year-old, she was most unfortunate not to secure a massive hit with the earnest 'They Don't Know'. Many years later, the television comedienne Tracey Ullman took an inferior rendition of the song to number 2 in the UK charts. MacColl had to wait until 1981 for her first chart hit. A change of label to Polydor brought her deserved UK Top 20 success with the witty 'There's A Guy Works Down The Chip Shop Swears He's Elvis'. Her interest in country and pop influences was

discernible on her strong debut *Desperate Characters*. In 1984, MacColl married producer Steve Lillywhite, and during the same year she returned to the charts with a stirring version of Billy Bragg's 'A New England'. During the next couple of years, she gave birth to two children but still found herself in-demand as a backing singer. She guested on recordings by a number of prominent artists, including Simple Minds, the Smiths, the Rolling Stones, Talking Heads, Robert Plant, Van Morrison and Morrissey. In December 1987, she enjoyed her highest ever chart placing at number 2 when duetting with Shane McGowan on the Pogues' evocative vignette of Irish emigration, 'Fairytale Of New York'. In 1989, she returned to recording solo with the highly-accomplished *Kite*. The album included the brilliant, powerful 'Free World' and an exceptionally alluring version of the Kinks' 'Days', which brought her back to the UK Top 20. Smiths guitarist, Johnny Marr guested on several of the album's tracks and appeared on the excellent follow-up released in 1991. *Electric Landlady,* an amusing pun on the Jimi Hendrix Experience's *Electric Ladyland,* was another strong album which demonstrated MacColl's diversity and songwriting talent. The haunting, dance-influenced 'Walking Down Madison' gave her another Top 40 UK hit.

Albums: *Desperate Characters* (1981), *Kite* (1989), *Electric Landlady* (1991).

McGee, Alan

b. 1961, Glasgow, Scotland. After leaving school at the age of 17, McGee became an electrician, then relocated to London where he worked as a clerk for British Rail. In his spare time, he promoted gigs for his nomadic club, the Living Room, booking acts such as the Nightingales and the Television Personalities. To his surprise, he found that he was making a large amount of money, so elected to release records and formed the label Creation. During the early phase of the label's history, McGee issued singles by artists such as the Loft, the Pastels, Primal Scream, the Jasmine Minks and his own venture, Biff Bang Pow. After signing the Jesus And Mary Chain in 1984, McGee's credibility as a manager and label owner escalated dramatically. He stayed with the group for two, often stormy, years and along the way issued some fascinating product by Felt, the Bodines and the Weather Prophets. The ill-fated tie-up with Warner Brothers, Elevation Records, encouraged McGee to pursue the independent route with more vigour. During the latter half of the 80s, the Creation roster extended to include Nikki Sudden, Momus, Clive Langer and, most crucially, the House Of Love. After one album and two excellent singles, the latter signed to Phonogram. After 1988, McGee turned increasingly to the dance floor for inspiration. Initial releases by Love Corporation, Hynotone, JBC and DJ Danny Rampling were not commercial successes, but the new direction was sound. Ironically, it was former psychedelic outfit Primal Scream who embraced the dance culture most effectively, providing the label with hits such as 'Loaded'. Further success followed with the critically acclaimed and best-selling My Bloody Valentine and Ride as Creation entered its most productive phase yet. McGee's genuine love of music and thrust for innovation has made him one of the more influential music business entrepreneurs to emerge in the UK over the past decade.

Mackenzies

One of the more refreshing aspects of the *New Musical Express*/ICA Rock Week and accompanying *C86* cassette compilation was the Ron Johnson camp. This Manchester label threw up a handful of manic guitar acts whose shared sources appeared to be the Fall and Captain Beefheart. The Mackenzies were no exception. 'Big Jim (There's No Pubs In Heaven)' on *C86* started as a quirky thrash similar to the Fire Engines, then switched to militant jazz funk groove and back again. Similar ingredients were also found on 'New Breed' in April 1986 and the excellent 'Mealy Mouths' the following February. But the Mackenzies failed to capitalize on these, and nothing was heard from them, apart from a remix of 'Mealy Mouths' exactly a year later, in February 1988.

McLaren, Malcolm

b. 22 January 1946, London, England. After a tempestuous childhood, during which he was reared by his eccentric grandmother, McLaren spent the mid-late 60s at various art colleges. In 1969, he became romantically involved with fashion designer Vivienne Westwood and they subsequently had a son, Joseph. Malcolm was fascinated by the work of the Internationale Situationist, a Marxist/Dadaist group which espoused its doctrines through sharp political slogans such as 'be reasonable - demand the impossible'. Their use of 'situations' designed to enlighten the proletariat impressed McLaren and would later influence his entrepreneurial career. In 1971, he opened the shop Let It Rock in Chelsea's Kings Road, which catered for Teddy Boy fashions. Among the shop's many visitors were several members of the New York Dolls, whose management McLaren took over in late 1974. It was to prove an ill-fated venture, but McLaren did spend some time with them in New York and organized their 'Better Dead Than Red' tour. After returning to the UK, he decided to find a new, young group whose power, presence and rebelliousness equalled that of the Dolls. The result was the Sex Pistols, whose brief spell of public notoriety ushered in the era of punk. McLaren was at the peak of his powers during this period, riding the wave of self-inflicted chaos that the Pistols spewed forth. The highlights included McLaren taking sizeable cheques from both EMI and A&M Records, who signed then fired the group in quick succession. The creation of the tragic caricature Sid Vicious, the conflict with Johnny Rotten, the involvement with Great Train Robber Ronnie Biggs and, finally, a self-glorifying film *The Great Rock 'n' Roll Swindle*, were all part of the unbelievable saga. Following the Sex Pistols' demise, McLaren launched Bow Wow Wow, heavily promoting the 14-year-old singer Annabella Lu Win. Although their recordings were highly original for the period, the dividends proved unimpressive and the group split. In the meantime, McLaren had served as 'advisor' to and let slip through his hands 80s stars such as Adam Ant and Boy George (Culture Club). Eventually, McLaren decided to transform himself into a recording star, despite the fact that he could not sing. His singular ability to predict trends saw him assimilating various styles of music, from the Zulu tribes in Africa to the ethnic sounds of the Appalachian Mountains. The arduous sessions finally came to fruition with *Duck Rock*, which featured two UK Top 10 singles, 'Buffalo Girls' and 'Double Dutch'. The work pre-empted rock's interest in world music, as exemplified on the later massive-selling *Graceland* by Paul Simon. McLaren next persisted with the music of urban New York and was particularly interested in the 'scratching' sounds of street disc jockeys. *Would Ya Like More Scratchin'* again anticipated the strong dance culture that would envelop the UK pop scene in the late 80s. Ever restless, McLaren moved on to a strange fusion of pop and opera with Fans, which featured a startling version of 'Madam Butterfly' that became a UK Top 20 hit. Following his experimental forays in the music business, McLaren relocated to Hollywood for a relatively unsuccessful period in the film industry. Nothing substantial emerged from that sojourn, but McLaren remains as unpredictable and innovative as ever.

Albums: *Duck Rock* (1983), *Would Ya Like More Scratchin'* (1984), *Fans* (1984), *Waltz Darling* (1989).

Further reading: *Starmakers & Svengalis: The History Of British Pop Management*, Johnny Rogan, *The Wicked Ways Of Malcolm McLaren*, Craig Bromberg.

Madness

This highly-regarded UK ska/pop group evolved from the London-based Invaders to form the sextet Madness in the summer of 1979. Their line-up comprised Suggs McPherson (b. Graham McPherson, 13 January 1961, Hastings, Sussex, England; vocals), Mark Bedford (b. 24 August 1961, London, England; bass), Mike Barson (b. 21 April 1958, London,

Madness

best, Madness were the best commentators on London life since the Kinks in the late 60s. An ability to tease out a sense of melancholy beneath the fun permeated their more mature work, particularly on the 1982 album, *The Rise And Fall*. That same year Suggs married singer Bette Bright and the group finally topped the charts with their 12th chart entry, 'House Of Fun'. More UK Top hits followed, including 'Wings Of A Dove' and 'The Sun And The Rain', but in late 1983 the group suffered a serious setback when founding member Barson quit. The group continued to release some exceptional work in 1984 including 'Michael Caine' and 'One Better Day'. At the end of that year, they formed their own label, Zarjazz. The label's first release was Feargal Sharkey's 'Listen To Your Father' (written by the group), which reached the UK Top 30. Madness continued to enjoy relatively minor hits by previous standards with the contemplative 'Yesterday's Men', the exuberant 'Uncle Sam' and former Scritti Politti success, 'The Sweetest Girl'. In the autumn of 1986, the group announced that they were splitting. Seventeen months later, they reunited as a four-piece under the name the Madness, but failed to emulate previous successes.

Albums: *One Step Beyond* (1979), *Absolutely* (1980), *Madness 7* (1981), *The Rise And Fall* (1982), *Keep Moving* (1984), *Mad Not Mad* (1985). Compilations: *Complete Madness* (1982), *Utter Madness* (1986), *Divine Madness* (1992). As The Madness: *The Madness* (1988).

England; keyboards), Chris Foreman (8 August 1958, London, England; guitar), Lee Thompson (5 October 1957, London, England; saxophone), Chas Smash (Cathal Smythe, 14 January 1959; vocals/trumpet) and Dan Woodgate (19 October 1960, London, England; drums). After signing to Stiff Records they issued 'The Prince', a tribute to blue beat maestro Prince Buster (whose song 'Madness' had inspired the group's name). The song reached the UK Top 20 and the follow-up, 'One Step Beyond' (a Buster composition) did even better, peaking at number 7. An album of the same title revealed Madness' charm with its engaging mix of ska and exuberant pop, a fusion they humorously dubbed 'the nutty sound'. Over the next two years the group enjoyed an uninterrupted run of Top UK 10 hits, comprising 'My Girl', *Work Rest And Play* (EP), 'Baggy Trousers', 'Embarrassment', 'The Return Of The Los Palmas Seven', 'Grey Day', 'Shut Up' and 'It Must Be Love' (originally a hit for its composer, Labi Siffre). Finally, they topped the UK chart with their 12th chart entry 'House Of Fun'. Although Madness appealed mainly to a younger audience and were known as a zany, fun-loving group, their work occasionally took on a more serious note. Both 'Grey Day' and 'Our House' showed their ability to write about working-class family life in a fashion that was piercingly accurate, yet never patronizing. At their

Magazine

Magazine

The Buzzcocks vocalist Howard Devoto left that group in January 1977, although he continued to be involved on the fringe of their activities for some time. In April he met guitarist John McGeogh and together they started writing songs. They formed Magazine with Devoto on vocals, McGeogh on guitar, Barry Adamson on bass, Bob Dickinson on keyboards and Martin Jackson on drums. The group played their debut live gig at the closing night of the

Electric Circus, Manchester, in the autumn of 1977 as a last- minute addition to the bill. Their moody, cold keyboards and harsh rhythms were in sharp contrast to the mood of the day: 'Everybody was playing everything ultra fast, as fast as they could. I thought we could begin to play slow music again.' They were signed to Virgin but Dickinson left in November and, as a result, their debut 'Shot By Both Sides' was recorded by the four remaining members. Dave Formula was recruited in time to play on *Real Life*. Next to leave was Jackson who departed after their first tour. Paul Spencer came in temporarily before John Doyle was recruited in October 1978. This line-up remained for the next couple of years, although McGeogh was also playing with Siouxsie And The Banshees, and, along with Adamson and Formula, in Steve Strange's Visage. Their albums received universal acclaim but only their first single and 1980's 'Sweetheart Contract' dented the charts. As the latter was released McGeogh left to join Siouxsie full-time and Robin Simon (ex-Neo and Ultravox) was brought in on guitar. A tour of the USA and Australia - where a live album was recorded - led to Simon's departure and Bob Mandelson (ex-Amazorblades) came in for the band's last few months. The departure of Devoto in May 1981 signalled the unit's death knell. The body of work left behind, however, is surprisingly enduring given its angular and experimental slant.
Albums: *Real Life* (1978), *Secondhand Daylight* (1979), *The Correct Use Of Soap* (1980), *Play* (1980), *Magic, Murder And The Weather* (1981).

Manic Street Preachers

These UK punk revivalists had a love-hate relationship with the music press which provided a bizarre story in 1991. The catalyst was Richy Edwards, who cut the words '4 Real' into his forearm to the amazement of *New Musical Express* critic Steve Lamacq, when he dared to call into question the band's authenticity. The group hails from Blackwood, Gwent, Wales, and is comprised of James Dean Bradfield (b. 21 February 1969; vocals/guitar), Richey Edwards (b. 27 December 1969; rhythm guitar), Nicky Wire (bass) and Sean Moore (b. 30 July 1970; drums). Their calculated insults at a wide variety of targets, particularly their peers, had already won them infamy following the release of their debut 'Motown Junk'. Their personal manifesto was equally explicit: rock bands should cut down the previous generation, release one explosive album then disappear. Although the music press has pointed out the obvious contradictions and naivete of this credo, the band have polarized opinion to a degree which far outweighs their musical proficiency. The singles, 'Stay Beautiful' and 'Repeat' ('Repeat after me, fuck Queen and Country') have been inconclusive, but their injection of bile was perversely refreshing in a year of industry contraction and self-congratulation.
Album: *Generation Terrorists* (1992).

Marc And The Mambas

Formed by Marc Almond (b. Peter Marc Almond, 9 July 1956, Southport, Lancashire, England), Marc And The Mambas was a pseudonym that the singer employed for his more arcane and adventurous work. Weary of the restrictions that came with his pop star role in Soft Cell, the Mambas project enabled him to attempt more daring and original ideas without compromise. With the assistance of Annie Hogan, Almond completed *Untitled* in which he unveiled spirited revivals of material by artists such as Lou Reed and Jacques Brel. By 1983, Almond was plunging far deeper into the Marc And The Mambas project, despite the continued success of Soft Cell. This phase culminated in the release of a double album, *Torment And Toreros*. This was unquestionably Almond's most extreme and personal recording, full of melodrama with a burningly revealing glimpse into the singer's darker side. When the album received a poor review in one music paper, Almond was so despondent and incensed that he announced his retirement. What that comment actually meant was the imminent dissolution of Marc And The Mambas and a final return to Soft Cell. When they, too, collapsed at the end of 1983, Almond embarked on a solo career, although his first post-Soft Cell recording, *Vermin In Ermine* was credited to Marc And The Willing Sinners and featured several musicians who had joined in the Mambas experiment.
Albums: *Untitled* (1982), *Torment And Toreros* (1983).

March Violets

This rock band with definite 'gothic' leanings was formed in England during 1982. Hugh (bass) met Simon (vocals) in Leeds, and the latter recruited an old friend, Tom (guitar). Together with a hastily recruited female singer they entered the studios to record an EP which brought them subsequent exposure on BBC disc jockey John Peel's show. After further releases on the fashionable Merciful Release label, they acquired the services of Travis when he replaced the original drum machine in late 1984. Simon left owing to a 'mutual decision', while vocalist Cleo joined for their 'Snakedance' single in 1983. By this time the band behind her only retained Tom from the original line-up, with Loz the latest recruit on bass. In 1986, they signed to London Records, releasing 'Turn To The Sky', which just failed to scrape the charts. By this time they were trying to shake off the taint of the 'goth' tag, emphasizing that their influences were bands like Z.Z. Top, Led Zeppelin and the Pretenders. Critics used Cleo's blonde hair as justification for comparisons to Blondie, while musically they were somewhere between the two.

Album: *Natural History* (1984).

Marine Girls

This UK quartet was formed by four Hertfordshire school friends: Jane Fox (b. c.1963; bass/vocals), her sister Alice (b. c.1966; vocals/percussion), Tracey Thorn (b. 26 September 1962; guitar/vocals) and the soon-to-depart, Gina (percussion/vocals). The Marine Girls recorded their homemade *Beach Party* in a garden shed. Musically competent, within limitations, their lyrics showed remarkable strength and eloquence in dealing with the age-old problems of difficult boyfriends, new love and loneliness, often using the symbolic context of the sea and all its mysteries. With initial encouragement from the Television Personalities, the album was released by the Whaam! label and was later picked up Cherry Red Records, who signed the group for a second album. By this time, Tracey had left school to go to Hull University, where she struck up a romantic and artistic relationship with Cherry Red stable-mate Ben Watt. They recorded the Cole Porter song, 'Night And Day' under the name of Everything But The Girl. Thorn had also released a solo album in 1982, *A Distant Shore*, which was well-received by the critics and public. Pursuing a parallel career as a Marine Girl and as a duettist with Watt at first proved comfortable, but with the increasing popularity and media attention of Everything But The Girl, an amicable split with the Fox sisters came in late 1983, after the release of the successful *Lazy Ways*. Continuing their seaside/oceanic fixation, the sisters formed Grab Grab The Haddock, which produced two fine EPs on Cherry Red before folding in 1986. The line-up of Grab Grab The Haddock was notable for the inclusion of Lester Noel, who later joined former Housemartin Norman Cook in Beats International.

Albums: *Beach Party* (1981), *Lazy Ways* (1983).

Martha And the Muffins

The roots of this Canadian new wave band stem back to the mid-70s, when Martha Johnson was the organist with Oh Those Pants, a 10-piece 60s covers/send-up band which also included future members of the Cads. This was followed by a spell in another Toronto band the Doncasters, who specialized in revamping 60s garage band material. In 1977, Johnson joined up with Mark Gane (guitar), Carl Finkle (bass), Andy Haas (saxophone), and Tim Gane (drums) to form Martha and the Muffins. They were later joined by Martha Ladly, who initially played guitar but later moved to keyboards and trombone. They sent a tape to New York journalist

Glenn O'Brien, who referred them to the fledgling DinDisc label. This led to the release of their debut single 'Insect Love'. Success came in 1980 with 'Echo Beach" which was a big hit in the UK. Follow-ups, including 'Saigon' (with its double groove b-side - playable backwards and forwards) fared less well. In 1981, Ladly left to work with the Associates and formed the Scenery Club who released a single on DinDisc. The Muffins signed to RCA and session player Clara Hurst played keyboards temporarily but joined the Belle Stars in 1982, when Martha And The Muffins split up. Johnson and Mark Gane formed M+M, who had a hit with 'Black Stations White Stations'.

Albums: *Metro Music* (1980), *Trance And Dance* (1980), *This Is The Ice Age* (1981), *Danseparc* (1983).

Maximum Joy

Like other Y label acts Shriekback and Pigbag, Bristol-based Maximum Joy explored a refreshing brand of independent funk that was in vogue in the UK during the early 80s. Formed by ex-Pop Group members John Waddington (guitar/vocals) and Dan Katsis (bass), the band was swelled by Janine Rainforth (vocals/clarinet/violin), Tony Wrafter (saxophone/flute/trumpet) and Charles Llewellyn (drums/percussion). The group's first two singles 'Stretch' (1981), 'White And Green Place' (1982) featured in the UK Independent Top 20. Later in the year, 'In The Air' preceded what was to be Maximum Joy's sole album, by which time Katsis had been replaced by Kevin Evans. Produced by Adrian Sherwood, this encapsulated Maximum Joy's at times quirky blend of percussion and funky instrumental flair, characterized by distinctive horns. With the departure of Wrafter later in the year, Dan Katsis rejoined for saxophone duties. After a healthy rendition of Timmy Thomas' 70s soul classic, 'Why Can't We Live Together', Maximum Joy disbanded.

Album: *Station M.X.J.Y...* (1982).

Meat Puppets

Formed in Tempe, Arizona, USA, Curt Kirkwood (guitar/vocals), Cris Kirkwood (bass/vocals) and Derrick Bostrom (drums) released their debut on the influential hardcore label SST Records, *Meat Puppets I*, in 1983. Its blend of punk and country was captured to perfection on 'Tumblin' Tumbleweeds', a long-standing cowboy classic, but any seeming irreverence was denied by *Meat Puppets II,* which continued an undoubted affection for roots music. Two critically-acclaimed sets, *Up On The Sun* and *Mirage*, signalled a new direction as the trio flirted with pseudo-psychedelic melodies, whereas *Huevos* captured the no-frills punch of their in-concert appearances. These disparate elements were fused on the excellent *Monsters*, which combined memorable hook-lines with authoritative, hard rock riffs. The set was rightly lauded as one of 1989's leading independent releases, but it was not until 1991 that the trio re-emerged, signed to the London label.

Albums: *Meat Puppets I* (1983), *Meat Puppets II* (1984), *Up On The Sun* (1985), *Mirage* (1987), *Huevos* (1988), *Monsters* (1989), *Forbidden Places* (1991). Compilations: *No Strings Attached* (1990).

Mega City Four

Mega City Four

This UK thrash-pop outfit, influenced by Stiff Little Fingers and the Buzzcocks, utilized melodic, medium- paced punk. They started in 1982 as a band called Capricorn, which played a few gigs and recorded some demos. However, in 1986, the drummer Martin left. The replacement, Chris Jones, was recruited from local band Exit East. The rest of the unit comprised Wiz (b. Darren Brown; songwriter/vocals/guitar), brother Danny (b. Daniel Brown; rhythm guitar/backing vocals), and Gerry (b. Gerald Bryant; bass). Mega City Four had their first practice session on 1 January 1987, taking their name from the home base of *Judge Dredd*, the popular comic book enforcer. A self-financed single was recorded in the autumn and, although it took six months to surface, reviews were good and BBC disc jockey John Peel added his patronage. They also provided two tracks for the Link compilation *Underground Rockers*. Alongside their peers and friends

the Senseless Things, they began to make a national impact with a heavy touring schedule. Their rise to prominence coincided with a string of singles before a contract to Big Life Records was forthcoming.

Albums: *Tranzophobia* (1989), *Who Cares Wins* (1990), *Sebastapol Road* (1991).

Mekons

Although initially based in Leeds, England, the Mekons made their recording debut for the Edinburgh-based Fast Product label in 1978. 'Never Been In A Riot', the outlet's first release, was the subject of effusive music press praise, and its joyous amateurism set the standard for much of the group's subsequent work. Having completed a second single, 'Where Were You', the Mekons were signed to Virgin Records where a line-up of Andy Carrigan (vocals), Mark White (vocals), Kevin Lycett (guitar), Tom Greenhalgh (guitar), Ross Allen (bass) and Jon Langford (drums) completed *The Quality Of Mercy Is Not Strnen*. This unusual title was drawn from the axiom that, if you give a monkey a typewriter and an infinite amount of time, it would eventually produce the complete works of Shakespeare, inferring wry comment on the group's own musical ability. Nonetheless, the Mekons' enthusiasm, particularly in a live setting, was undoubtedly infectious and has contributed greatly to their long career. Despite numerous personnel changes, they have retained a sense of naive adventurousness, embracing world music, folk and roots material in their customarily ebullient manner.

Albums: *The Quality Of Mercy Is Not Strnen* (1979), *Mekons* (1980), *Mekons Story* (1982), *Original Sin* (1985), *The Edge Of The World* (1986), *Honky Tonkin'* (1987), *New York Mekons* (1988), *So Good It Hurts* (1988), *Fear And Whiskey* (1989), *Mekons Rock 'N' Roll* (1989), *F.U.N. 90* (1990), *The Curse Of The Mekons* (1991).

Members

One of the many UK bands inspired by punk, the Members came together in the summer of 1977, when former university student Nicky Tesco and French expatriate Jean-Marie Carroll, now a bank clerk in the UK, started working together. With Tesco on vocals and Carroll as guitarist and chief songwriter, they recruited Gary Baker on guitar, Adrian Lillywhite (brother of producer Steve Lillywhite) on drums, and a bass player. The bassist left after only a couple of months and was replaced by British Airways technician Chris Payne. They were based in Camberley, Surrey, England, where all the members (except Carroll) originated. The band's first recording - 'Fear On The Streets' - was for the Beggars Banquet punk compilation *Streets*. Despite this, it was Stiff Records that took the plunge and

Mekons

signed them. Their debut single, 'Solitary Confinement', was produced by Larry Wallis and earned them a contract with Virgin in November 1978, though by now Baker had departed and been replaced by Nigel Bennett. Their Virgin debut, 'Sound Of The Suburbs', was a hit in 1979, and was followed by the bloated but humorous reggae of 'Offshore Banking Business'. The b-side revisited 'Solitary Confinement', a song which the Newtown Neurotics would later update in the form of 'Living With Unemployment'. Their second album featured a guest appearance from Joe Jackson but it would be their last for Virgin, which they left in 1980. They were signed to Island briefly, but their third album came out on Albion Records, after which they disappeared. One other release of note is the Children Of 7's 'Solidarity' on Stiff, which featured both Carroll and Payne among the writing credits. More recently, 'Sound Of The Suburbs' featured as the title track to a nostalgic punk compilation which was advertised widely on UK television.

Albums: *At The Chelsea Nightclub* (1979), *1980 The Choice Is Yours* (1980), *Going West* (1983), *At the 1980 Chelsea Night Club, The Choice Is Yours* (1991).

Membranes

Formed in Preston, Lancashire in 1977, this UK punk group was based in the seaside town of Blackpool, later immortalized as 'Tatty Seaside Town'. Founder member John Robb (b. 4 May, 1961; bass) was initially joined by Mark Tilton (guitar), Martin Kelly (drums) and Martin Critchley (vocals), the latter soon departing as Critchley sidestepped from drums to keyboards, with 'Goofy Sid' Coulthart taking over behind the drumstool. Robb was to prove himself nothing if not a trier, organizing compilation appearances and inaugurating the near legendary, near indecipherable *Blackpool Rox* fanzine. Their first vinyl single was the 3-track 'Muscles' in 1981, gaining single of the week awards for its defiant, brash optimism and gaining ascendancy on the turntable of Radio 1's John Peel. It remains one of the most memorable DIY efforts of the early 80s. Steve Farmery joined on guitar after its release, with Martin Kelly leaving the keyboard position vacant. They joined Rondolet Records for 'Pin Stripe Hype', watching the label close down shortly after. This also saw off Farmery, leaving the band as a trio for much of the rest of their productive career. Missing out on the opportunity to be Creation Records first featured artists because of finance sent them down-market to

Criminal Damage. It, too, proved a less than satisfactory home, and ultimately saw the group relocate to Manchester in 1983 in typically eternal optimism. The single which should have broken them was the acclaimed 'Spike Milligan's Tape Recorder', which somewhat pre-dated the guitar barrage of Big Black and Sonic Youth. However, distribution problems killed off the enthusiasm reciprocated by the media. The same problems applied to the 'Death To Trad Rock', 12-inch, after which Tilton left to be replaced by bass player, Stan. Although they finally made their postponed mark on Creation with the disappointing *Gift Of Life*, the band's fortunes were now in decline. Stan was replaced by Wallas as the band concentrated on the European circuit. Nick Brown was added on second guitar in 1987, followed in short order by Keith Curtis. Meanwhile, Robb was becoming more active as a freelance journalist for *Sounds*, and eventually *Melody Maker* and a host of other magazines. Despite the production services of Steve Albini (Big Black) on 1988's *Kiss Ass Godhead*, Wallas was the next departure, to be replaced by Paul Morley (ex-Slum Turkeys). However, total disintegration was imminent as Robb concentrated on his writing career, and launched his new dance project Sensurround.

Albums: *Crack House* (1983), *Gift Of Life* (1985), *Songs Of Love And Fury* (1986), *Kiss Ass Godhead* (1988), *The Virgin Mary Versus Peter Sellers* (1988), *To Slay The Rock Pig* (1989).

Mental As Anything

Utilizing elements of rockabilly, rock and R&B combined with an energetic live act, Mental As Anything has proved a lasting, popular live and recording outfit. The group's debut album introduced Reg Mombasa (b. Chris O'Doherty, New Zealand; guitar/vocals), Wayne Delisle (b. Australia; drums) and the three songwriters: Martin Plaza (b. Martin Murphy, Australia; vocals/guitar), Greedy Smith (b. Andrew Smith, Australia; keyboards/harmonica/vocals) and Peter O'Doherty (b. New Zealand; bass). Despite their different writing styles, *Get Wet* achieved success, particularly with the enigmatically titled single 'The Nips Are Getting Better'. Their most fortuitous album, *Cats And Dogs*, saw the production smooth out the rough edges, and subsequent albums have maintained a high standard, with single releases constantly charting in Australia (two dozen to the end of 1990). Their single, 'Live It Up' gained considerable chart success in the UK in 1987, when it spent 13 weeks at number 3. Plaza has also released solo recordings which have enjoyed high sales in Australia.

Albums: *Get Wet* (1979), *Expresso Bongo* (1980), *Cats And Dogs* (1981), *Creatures Of Leisure* (1983),

Fundamental (1985), *Mouth To Mouth* (1987), *Cyclone Raymond* (1989).

Men They Couldn't Hang

Men They Couldn't Hang

In their seven-year span, the Men They Couldn't Hang combined folk, punk and roots music to create an essential live act alongside a wealth of recorded talent. The band emerged as the Pogues' sparring partners but, despite a blaze of early publicity and praise, they failed to follow them upwards, dogged as they were by numerous label changes. Busking in Shepherds Bush, Welsh singer Cush met up with bassist Shanne (who had been in the Nips with the Pogues' Shane McGowan), songwriter/guitarist Paul Simmonds, Scottish guitarist/singer Phil ('Swill') and his brother John on drums, in time for a ramshackle folk performance at London's alternative country music festival in Easter 1984. Labelled as part of some 'cowpunk' scene, the band were quickly signed by Elvis Costello to his Demon label, Imp. A cover of Eric Bogle's 'Green Fields Of France' in October 1984 became a runaway indie success, and a favourite on BBC disc jockey John Peel's show. While playing live, the Men matched their own incisive compositions with entertaining covers. June 1985's 'Iron Masters' was just as strong, if more manic, and was accompanied by an impressive and assured debut , *The Night Of A Thousand Candles*, both demonstrating the band's deep moral and political conscience.

Produced by Nick Lowe, 'Greenback Dollar' in November was less immediate, but its success swayed MCA to take the plunge, resulting in 'Gold Rush' in June 1986. The group's second album, *How Green Is The Valley*, coincided with 'Shirt Of Blue' in October, continuing their marriage of musical styles and a political sensibility drawn from an historical perspective. 'The Ghosts Of Cable Street', a single in April 1987, exemplified these ingredients, but MCA decided to drop the band. A move to Magnet Records catalyzed perhaps their finest work, not least with the commercial 'Island In The Rain' and the consistently listenable *Waiting For Bonaparte* in October. 'The Colours' in March 1988 was even more suited to Radio 1, but despite good airplay, it only skirted the charts, and when WEA took over Magnet, the band found itself out in the cold again after just one single, 'The Crest', in May. Fledgling label Silvertone's Andrew Lauder (who had worked with the group at Demon) soon came to the rescue, in time for 'Rain, Steam And Speed' in February 1989. Hot on its heels came *Silvertown*, tackling difficult themes against a diverse but occasionally weak musical backdrop. A comprehensive worldwide tour followed, while two singles kept the fires burning, 'A Place In The Sun' and 'A Map Of Morocco'.

1990 witnessed the final album, *The Domino Club*, switching from their usual producer, Mick Glossop, to ex-Vibrator Pat Collier, and adding full-time keyboard and accordion player Nick Muir. A planned Silvertone compilation, *Five Glorious Years,* was shelved, while a live album never materialised, and after 'Great Expectations' in July 1990, the Men They Couldn't Hang called it a day in the face of commercial apathy. A projected follow-up, 'The Lion And The Unicorn', was scrapped.

Albums: *Night Of A Thousand Candles* (1985), *How Green Is The Valley* (1986), *Waiting For Bonaparte* (1987, reissued 1988), *Silvertown* (1989), *The Domino Club* (1990), *Well Hung* (1991).

Men Without Hats

Formed in Montreal, Canada, in 1980, this act was the brainchild of siblings Ivan (vocals) and Jeremy (drums) Arrobas, who manufactured remaining accompaniment on their records with synthesizers. An independent EP, *Folk Of The 80s*, created overseas cult interest to the extent that it was re-issued on Britain's Stiff label, along with an edit of its 'Antarctica' track as a single. However, just after the release of 1981's 'Nationale Seven', Jeremy left to allow composer Ivan to front a Men Without Hats with the brothers Stefan (guitar/violin) and Colin Doroschuk (keyboards) plus Allan McCarthy (drums). Produced by manager Marc Durand, *Rhythm Of Youth* reached number 14 in the USA in the wake of 'Safety Dance', a global smash born of a truce between electro-pop and medieval jollity that carried an anti-nuclear message over into an arresting video. A sure sign of its impact was a parody by Al Yanovic. No more hits came the group's way, but their recordings still received a fair critical consideration.

Albums: *Rhythm Of Youth* (1982), *Folk Of the 80s Part III* (1984), *Pop Goes The Word* (1987).

Mercury Rev

This six-piece band from Buffalo, New York, USA, burst on to the music scene in 1991 to unanimous critical acclaim for their enterprising mix of Pink Floyd and Dinosaur Jnr. dynamics. However, the sounds produced by Jonathan Donahue (vocals/guitar), David Fridmann (bass), Jimmy Chambers (drums), Sean 'Grasshopper' Mackowiak (guitar), Suzanne Thorpe (flute) and David Baker (vocals/guitar) remain difficult to classify. Their album, *Yerself Is Steam*, although practically ignored in their native country, created a snowball of press acclaim in the UK which had not been accorded to a debut since the Jesus And Mary Chain's *Psychocandy*. The *Melody Maker*'s comment 'Universally acclaimed by UK critics as the draughtsmen behind the first, and so far only, great rock long player of 1991', was among the more conservative of the plaudits, and with only a handful of gigs under their belt Mercury Rev was to be seen filling support slots for My Bloody Valentine and Bob Dylan. BBC disc jockey John Peel summed up their appeal by stating that: 'Unlike many bands, you can't tell what's in their record collection'. The press undoubtedly saw them as the next step forward from the previous wave of influential US guitar bands like the Pixies, Sonic Youth and Dinosaur Jnr. However, whether they can capitalize on their flying start would seem to rest, rather precariously, on their ability to remain together as a collective unit. A variety of stories have filtered through concerning their self-destructive behaviour. The band has already been banned from one airline due to Donahue trying to remove Mackowiak's eye with a spoon. Another minor crisis concerned Fridmann's disposal of the band's entire advance for their 'Carwash Hair' single on a holiday for his mother in Bermuda, without telling anyone. The band's writing and recording is done in a similar, reckless manner: 'Basically, its whoever shouts loudest, or who has the biggest punch'.

Album: *Yerself Is Steam* (1991).

Merton Parkas

One of several late 70s mod revivalists to make the UK charts, the Merton Parkas began life as the Sneakers around 1975, playing old Motown classics. The line-up comprised brothers Mick (b. 11 September 1958; keyboards) and Danny Talbot (vocals), Neil Wurrell (bass) and Simon Smith (drums), and they chose their new name from Merton (the area of south London, they hailed from) and Parka (the ubiquitous item of mod attire). The Merton Parkas were great live favourites at the Bridgehouse in Canning Town, London but were unable to appear on the *Mods Mayday '79* live compilation because they were negotiating contracts with Beggars Banquet, after the label's first signing, the Lurkers, had recommended them. They were one of the first neo-mod bands to record, and their debut single, 'You Need Wheels' was a hit in August 1979.

Unfortunately, the rather trite lyrics had the Mertons branded as a novelty act, and they were often unfairly dismissed as bandwagon jumpers. Subsequent singles such as 'Plastic Smile', 'Give It To Me Now' (produced by Dennis Bovell of Matumbi), and 'Put Me In The Picture' failed to match the success of their debut. Mick Talbot was meanwhile making his name as an in-demand keyboard player on the Jam's *Setting Sons* and an album by the Chords. The Mertons soon disbanded and Talbot went on to join Dexy's Midnight Runners and the Bureau and appeared in the Style Council. Smith, meanwhile, joined the psychedelic revivalists Mood Six, and spent a while with the Times, before returning to the reformed Mood Six.

Album: *Face In The Crowd* (1979).

Meteors

The Meteors were the first UK group to combine punk's energy with raw 50s rockabilly and invent a new musical form — psychobilly. In the USA, the Cramps had discovered a similar formula, but theirs was less violent and more dramatic. Together, they influenced a whole movement and an accompanying youth culture during the 80s, that enabled the Meteors to record some 15 albums over 10 years. In the late 70s, P. Paul Fenech (singer/guitarist) and Nigel Lewis (double bass/vocals) were churning out rockabilly and rock 'n' roll standards in acts such as the Southern Boys and, as a duo, Rock Therapy. Around 1980, drummer Mark Robertson was recruited, coinciding with a name change to Raw Deal, and soon appeared on Alligator Records' *Home Grown Rockabilly* compilation. After a name change to the Meteors, the band issued a debut EP, *Meteor Madness*, for Ace Records in July 1981, which captured all the Meteors' ingredients across four tracks: raw rockabilly, with lyrics from graveyards to vampires, all performed in a crazed fashion. 'Radioactive Kid', followed suit, but although Island offered the band a deal, they chose instead to issue their debut, *In Heaven*, on their own Lost Souls label. Around the same time, the Meteors recorded an EP featuring a cover of the Electric Prunes' 'Get Me To The World On Time' under the guise of the Clapham South Escalators. Robertson left soon afterwards and was replaced by Woody, in time for a tour supporting Theatre Of Hate, but after releasing some demos, Lewis also departed to form the Tall Boys. Fenech was left to soldier on, bringing in electric bassist Mick White and Russell Jones for August 1982's 'Mutant Rock', an indie hit on the punk label WXYZ.

Another personnel change (Steve 'Ginger' Meadham joining on drums) preceded the Meteors second album, the infamously titled *Wreckin' Crew*, early in 1983, featuring the previous single, a wild cover of John Leyton's 'Johnny Remember Me'. That same year saw another departure, with White forming his own psychobilly act, the Guana Batz. His position was filled by Rick Ross for a national tour, captured on *Live*. Unfortunately, Ross left for the USA and in his place came Ian 'Spider' Cubitt, to record *Stampede*. This session also spawned two demented singles: 1984's 'I'm Just A Dog' and 1985's 'Fire, Fire'. Both were prime slices of the Meteors at their tightest and toughest and sold accordingly.

In addition to *The Curse Of The Mutants*, an unofficial collection of out-takes, *Monkey's Breath* featuring new bassist Neville Hunt surfaced in September 1985, alongside a cover of Creedence Clearwater Revival's 'Bad Moon Rising'. After two more unofficial offerings (*Live II* and the *Live And Loud*), the Meteors signed to Cherry Red's Anagram label, with Jan And Dean's 'Surf City' and *Sewertime Blues*, in late 1986. It failed to capture the excitement of earlier recordings, while *Don't Touch The Bang Bang Fruit* suffered no such problems, as heard on both resulting singles, the title track and a version of the Stranglers' 'Go Buddy Go'. By this time, Spider's place had been filled by Toby 'Jug' Griffin (ex-drummer with the Coffin Nails) and Austin H. Stones briefly deputized on bass. Lee Brown (ex-Pharaohs) took on a more permanent role on bass, in time for another punk cover in the Ramones' 'Somebody Put Something In My Drink', issued in February 1988. Hot on its heels came *Only The Meteors Are Pure Psychobilly*, featuring new recordings of old 'classics'. Newer material was included on *Mutant Monkey And The Surfers From Zorch* later that year, although 'Rawhide' proved to be another popular cover. Even more powerful was *Undead, Unfriendly And Unstoppable*, which benefitted from new drummer Mark Howe. The release of 'Please Don't Touch' proved that, despite waves of imitators, the Meteors were still the most vibrant psychobilly band around.

Albums: *In Heaven* (1981), *Wreckin' Crew* (1983), *Live* (1983), *Stampede* (1984), *The Curse Of The Mutants* (1984), *Monkey's Breath* (1985), *Live II* (1986), *Live And Loud* (1986), *Sewertime Blues* (1987), *Night Of The Werewolf* (1987), *Don't Touch The Bang Bang Fruit* (1987), *Only The Meteors Are Pure Psychobilly* (1988), *Mutant Monkey And The Surfers From Zorch* (1988), *Undead, Unfriendly And Unstoppable* (1989), *Live* (1989, reissue). Compilation: *Teenagers From Outer Space* (1986).

Microdisney

This incendiary pop/folk group were formed in Cork, Eire, in 1980. There was little cohesion in their early formations; 'We used to be much more frenzied in those days, a Fall-type mess, and our line-up was always changing. Originally Sean (O'Hagan) was going to play guitar and I (Cathal Coughlan) was

going to recite poetry, then one week it was guitar, bass, drums, then guitar keyboard and violin, then we had a drum machine. . .' After settling on the more traditional formation of drums, guitars, bass and keyboards, the band began releasing singles which eventually were collected together on *We Hate You White South African Bastards*. The title was typically inflammatory, and in direct opposition to that of their long-playing debut, *Everybody Is Fantastic*. An early clue to their subversive nature, on the surface Microdisney were purveyors of accessible and restrained pop music. This attracted Virgin Records, but the band had a dark edge in Coughlan's bitter lyricism. Their Virgin debut, 'Town To Town', dented the lower regions of the charts and was quickly followed by *Crooked Mile*. However, Microdisney elected to bite the hand that fed them with the near hit 'Singer's Hampstead Home', which thinly masked an attack on Virgin's fallen idol, Boy George. They bowed out with *39 Minutes,* by which time the vitriol was really flowing, counter-balanced as ever by O'Hagan's delicate country guitar. Despite critical acclaim, Microdisney's sales had remained disappointingly in the cult bracket. O'Hagan went on to release a solo album in 1990 (*High Llamas*), while Coughlan's Fatima Mansions has done much to spice up the late 80s and early 90s.
Albums: *Everybody Is Fantastic* (1984), *We Hate You White South African Bastards* (1984), *The Clock Comes Down The Stairs* (1985), *Crooked Mile* (1987), *39 Minutes* (1988), *Gale Force Wind* (1988).

Midnight Oil

Formed in Sydney, New South Wales, in 1975, and known as Farm, this strident band has pioneered its own course in Australian rock without relying on the established network of agencies and record companies. The original nucleus of the band comprised Martin Rotsey (guitar), Rob Hirst (drums) and Jim Moginie (guitar). They were later joined by law student Peter Garrett (lead vocals). The outfit became notorious for always insisting on total control over its recorded product and media releases, including photos, and when booking agencies denied the band gigs, the members organized their own venues and tours, taking advantage of the group's large following on the alternative rock scene. Joined by Dwayne 'Bones' Hillman (bass) in 1977 and changing their name to Midnight Oil, the group took a couple of album releases to refine its songwriting style, principally by Moginie and Hirst. As *Head Injuries* went gold in Australia, the imposing shaven-headed Garrett, who had by now received his law degree, began to make known his firm views on politics. Having signed a world-wide deal with CBS/Columbia, it was *10,9,8,7,6,5,4,3,2,1*, which saw the band gain mainstream radio airplay. Featuring

songs about the environment, anti-nuclear sentiments, anti-war songs and powerful anthems of anti-establishment; it also propelled the band into the international market place. The band performed at many charity concerts, promoting Koori (Australian aborigines) causes in Australia and the loquacious Garrett almost gained a seat in the Australian Parliament in 1984 while standing for the Nuclear Disarmament Party. The following album saw the band tour the USA and Europe, and *Rolling Stone* writers voted the album one of the best of 1989, despite a low profile there. While many regard *Red Sails In The Sunset* as their best work, the subsequent albums have been equally highly regarded. The group's peak album chart positions in the UK and USA were achieved with *Diesel And Dust* reaching the UK Top 20 and US number 21, while in the US the follow-up, *Blue Sky Mining* emulated that position. The group continued its antagonistic attitude towards major industrial companies in 1990, by organizing a protest concert outside the Manhattan offices of the Exxon oil company which was responsible for the Valdez oil slick in Alaska.
Albums: *Midnight Oil* (1978), *Head Injuries* (1979), *Place Without A Postcard* (1981), *10,9,8,7,6,5,4,3,2,1* (1982), *Red Sails In The Sunset* (1985), *Diesel And Dust* (1987), *Blue Sky Mining* (1990).
Further reading: *Strict Rules*, Andrew McMillan.

Mighty Lemon Drops

This UK independent label pop band broke through in 1985 with the highly-touted 'Like An Angel'. It featured Paul Marsh (vocals/guitar), David Newton (guitar), Tony Linehan (bass) and Keith Rowley (drums), who had all enjoyed chequered careers in numerous Wolverhampton outfits. Newton had previously played with Active Restraint in 1982, which also included Marsh and Linehan. They played regularly alongside Another Dream, and both bands featured on single releases by local label Watchdog Video And Records. Newton and Neal Cook of Another Dream put together the Wild Flowers, alongside Dave Atherton (also ex-Another Dream; guitar/keyboards), Pete Waldron (bass) and Dave Fisher (drums). After a further single and a support to Simple Minds, Newton moved on once more, forming the Mighty Lemon Drops with Marsh and Linehan. The temporary drummer was Martin Gilks (now with the Wonder Stuff), before Keith Rowley stepped in full-time. As part of the *New Musical Express*' 'C-86' generation, they were snapped up by Chrysalis subsidiary Blue Guitar. Despite the charm of several singles in an Echo And The Bunnymen vein, they failed to translate independent chart success into hits. Although they were dropped by Chrysalis after three albums, they remain favourites on the US college circuit.

Albums: *Happy Head* (1986), *World Without End* (1988), *Sound* (1991).

Mighty Mighty

Like many of the UK indie guitar pop favourites of the mid-80s, Birmingham, UK's Mighty Mighty owed more than a passing debt to Orange Juice and the Postcard label. Hugh (vocals/occasional harp), Mick Geoghegan (guitar/lyric writer), brother Peter (organ/guitar), D.J. Hennessy (drums) and Russell B. (bass/vocals) first appeared as part of the *New Musical Express*/ICA Rock Week and accompanied *C86* cassette compilation. This coincided nicely with Mighty Mighty's debut single, the catchy 'Everybody Knows The Monkey' in May 1986; like July's 'Is There Anyone Out There?' 12-inch, it was issued on the band's own Girlie label. However, aspiring local label Chapter 22 soon snapped them up, for a string of classy pop tunes that fared well on the independent sector. After December's 'Throwaway' (originally half of a fanzine flexidisc) came the raunchy 'Built Like A Car' in May 1987, 'One Way' in October and the attractive 'Born In A Maisonette' in the New Year. Unfortunately, Mighty Mighty failed to develop, and by the time *Sharks* was released in February 1988, their formula had worn thin. Apart from the excellent 'Blue And Green', Sharks had little to offer in the way of new ideas at a time when the independent scene was rapidly hardening up.
Album: *Sharks* (1988).

Milkshakes

This UK, Chatham, Kent-based group were originally conceived in the late 70s by Pop Rivit roadies Mickey Hampshire and Banana Bertie as Mickey And The Milkshakes. Often appearing on the same circuit as fellow Medway town bands, the Dentists and the Prisoners, the group performed as a 'psychobilly' outfit, supporting the Pop Rivits from time to time with Wreckless Eric covers. Pop Rivit leader Billy Childish then began writing with Hampshire and in 1980 formed a new version of Mickey And The Milkshakes. Eventually settling on a line-up of Childish and Hampshire (guitars/vocals), Russ Wilkins (bass) and Bruce Brand (drums), they started recording a string of albums featuring various R&B classics plus original material. After the first album they truncated their name. Later on, when John Agnew replaced Wilkins, they began to refer to themselves as Thee Milkshakes. In addition to their normal activities of gigging and recording, they also acted as the backing band to an all-girl vocal trio called the Del Monas. As prolific releasers of album material, The(e) Milkshakes were only modestly successful with singles, achieving two UK independent Top 20 hits with 'Brand New Cadillac' (1984) and 'Ambassadors Of Love' (1985). The group split in 1984 (although Milkshake material continued to be released long after), with Childish going on to form the equally productive Thee Mighty Caesars.
Albums: *Talkin' 'Bout Milkshakes* (1981), *Fourteen Rhythm And Blues Greats* (1982), *After School Session* (1983), *Milkshakes IV (The Men With The Golden Guitars)* (1983), *20 Rock And Roll Hits Of The 50s & 60s* (1984), *Nothing Can Stop These Men* (1984), *The Milkshakes In Germany* (1984), *Thee Knights Of Trash* (1984), *They Came, They Saw, They Conquered* (1985), *The Last Night Down At The Mic Club* (1986), *The 107 Tapes* (1986), *The Milkshakes Vs The Prisoners Live* (1987), *The Milkshakes Revenge* (1987), *Live From Chatham* (1987).

Mindfunk

This intense, American, thrash-funk quintet were formed in 1990 by vocalist Patrick R. Dubar and rhythm guitarist Jason Coppola. Adding John Monte (bass), Reed St. Mark (ex-Celtic Frost drummer) and Louis J. Suitek (guitar), they signed to Epic and debuted with a self-titled album the same year. Faith No More, Slayer, Red Hot Chili Peppers and Anthrax are obvious reference points, but the band perform with such aggression and conviction that these comparisons can become rather superfluous.
Album: *Mindfunk* (1991).

Mink Deville

The centre of the unit was Willy Deville (b. 27 August 1953, New York City, New York, USA), a guitarist and songwriter. He came to London in 1971 to form a band but, unable to find the right musicians, he performed as a solo artist before heading to San Francisco (via New York) and assembling the embryonic Mink Deville. The basic trio became Willy (vocals/guitar/harmonica), Ruben Siguenza (bass), and Thomas R. Allen (drums). The latter had played with various blues musicians. They relocated to New York and recruited several guitarists before chosing Lous X Erlanger. The band recorded three tracks for the *Live At CBGB's* album and put out their own debut in 1977. As well as a hit single with 'Spanish Stroll' the album, produced by Jack Nitzsche, included a version of the Patti And The Emblems' classic 'Mixed Up Shook Up'. *Return To Magenta* was publicized by releasing the single 'Soul Twist' in purple vinyl. By the time of the third album in 1980, the band comprised Willy and Erlanger plus Kenny Margolis (keyboards), Jerry Scheff (bass), Ron Tutt (drums), and Steve Douglas (saxophone). They continued recording throughout the 80s, and contributed three songs to the Al Pacino movie *Cruisin'*. In 1988, they gained a fresh slice of media attention with the well-received, Mark Knopler-produced *Miracle*.
Albums: *Mink Deville* (1977), *Return To Magenta*

(1978), *Le Chat Bleu* (1980), *Savoire Faire* (1981), *Where Angels Fear To Tread* (1983), *Sporting Life* (1986), *Cabretta* (1987), *Miracle* (1988).

Minutemen

Formed in 1980 in San Pedro, California, USA, and originally known as the Reactionaries. This influential hardcore trio initially comprised D. Boon (guitar/vocals), Mike Watt (bass) and Frank Tonche (drums), but the last named was replaced by George Hurley prior to recording. Although the trio donated tracks to several independent compilations, notably for the pivotal Radio Tokyo Tapes and the Posh Boy and New Alliance labels, their association with SST Records resulted in some of the genre's most impressive recordings. The unfettered rage of their early work was less apparent on *Buzz Or Howl Under The Influence Of Heat* and *Project: Mersh*, ('Mersh' is San Pedro slang for 'commercial'), but *Double Nickels On The Dime* and *3-Way Tie (For Last)* showed an undeterred passion and commitment. The Minutemen came to a premature end in 1986 following the death of D. Boon. Watt and Hurley decided to drop the group's name, and in its place formed fIREHOSE with guitarist Ed Crawford.
Albums: *The Punchline* (1980), *Bean Spill* (1982), *What Makes A Man Start Fires* (1983), *Buzz Or Howl Under The Influence Of Heat* (1983), *Politics Of Time* (1984), *Double Nickels On The Dime* (1984), *Project: Mersh* (1985), *3-Way Tie (For Last)* (1986), *Ballot Result* (1987). Compilations: *My First Bells* (1985), *Post-Mersh Volume 1* (1985), *Post-Mersh Volume 2* (1987), *Post-Mersh Volume 3* (1989).

Misfits

Like the 13th Floor Elevators in the 60s and the New York Dolls in the early 70s, this USA punk band was swiftly surrounded in a cloak of mythology and cult appeal. Long after their demise (they played their last live gig in 1983), their obscure US-only records were fetching large sums of money, in collecting circles, by those fascinated by the band's spine-chilling mix of horror-movie imagery and hardcore. The Misfits were formed in New York in 1977, by Gerry Only and Glenn Danzig and, like many aspiring new wave acts, played in venues like CBGBs. Later that year, 'Cough Cool' became their first single on their own Plan 9 label. A four-track single, 'Bullet' (in a sleeve showing J.F. Kennedy's assassination), was recorded before their debut, and followed by 'Horror Business'. A third single, 'Night Of The Living Dead', surfaced in 1979, the reference to the classic George A. Romero film revealing the Misfits' continued fascination with blood-and-guts horror. Then came an EP, *Three Hits From Hell*, recorded in 1980, but not issued until the following April, and a seasonal October single, 'Halloween'. Finally, the

Misfits rounded off 1981 by recording the seven-track EP *Evilive*, originally sold through the band's Fiend fan club, which secured a German 12-inch release. The band's only original UK release was a 12-inch EP *Beware*. Other Misfits releases included a 12-inch EP, *Wolf's Blood* and several albums: 1982's *Misfits Walk Among Us, Earth A.D.* and *Legacy Of Brutality*. Danzig issued a solo single in 1981, 'Who Killed Marilyn?', and was featured in heavy metal magazines in the late 80s. Hain issued a 12-inch, 'Unholy Passion' and two albums, *Initium* and *Coming Fire*.
Albums: *Misfits Walk Among Us* (1982), *Earth A.D.* (c.80s), *Legacy Of Brutality* (c.80s), *The Misfits* (c.80s).

Mission

This highly acclaimed UK rock band evolved from the Sisters Of Mercy, when Wayne Hussey (b. 26 May 1959, Bristol, England; ex-Walkie Talkies, Dead Or Alive) and Craig Adams split from Andrew Eldritch. They quickly recruited drummer Mick Brown (ex-Red Lorry, Yellow Lorry) and guitarist Simon Hinkler (ex-Artery). The original choice of title was the Sisterhood, which led to an undignified series of exchanges in the press between the band and Eldritch. In order to negate their use of the name, Eldritch put out a single under the name Sisterhood on his own Merciful Release label. Thus the title the Mission was selected instead. After two successful

Mission; Wayne Hussey

independent singles on the Chapter 22 label, they signed to Mercury in the autumn of 1986. Their major label debut, 'Stay With Me', entered the UK singles charts while the band worked on their debut album. *God's Own Medicine* was the outcome, revealing a tendency towards straightforward rock, and attracting criticism for its bombast. A heavy touring schedule ensued, with the band's off-stage antics attracting at least as much attention as their performances. A particularly indulgent tour of America saw Adams shipped home suffering from exhaustion. His temporary replacement on bass was Pete Turner. After headlining the Reading Festival, they began work on a new album under the auspices of Led Zeppelin bass player John Paul Jones as producer. *Children* was even more successful than its predecessor, reaching number 2 in the UK album charts, despite the customary critical disdain. 1990 brought 'Butterfly On A Wheel' as a single, providing further ammunition for accusations that the band were simply dredging up rock history. In February, the long-delayed third album, *Carved In Sand,* was released, revealing a more sophisticated approach to songwriting. During the world tour to promote the album, both Hinkler and Hussey became ill because of the excessive regime. Hinkler departed suddenly when they reached Toronto, leaving Dave Wolfenden to provide guitar for the rest of the tour. On their return, Paul Etchells took over the position on a more permanent basis. Hussey had meanwhile joined with the Wonder Stuff in proposing a fund-raising concert in London under the banner The Day Of Conscience, but the event self-destructed under a barrage of allegations about commercial intrusion. In a similar vein over the Christmas period, members of the band joined with Slade's Noddy Holder and Jim Lea to record 'Merry Xmas Everybody' for charity.
Albums: *God's Own Medicine* (1986), *Children* (1988), *Carved In Sand* (1990).

Mock Turtles

With their glorious UK hit single 'Can You Dig It?', the Mock Turtles followed a line of success stories that had emanated from Manchester, England, between 1989 and 1991. Like many of their contemporaries, the band had been playing the independent circuit for several years before realizing their potential. The band's lynch-pin was singer/guitarist/songwriter Martin Coogan, who had previously fronted Judge Happiness, won a Salford University talent contest and subsequently issued a single, 'Hey Judge', on the Mynah label in 1985. As the Mock Turtles, Coogan was joined by Steve Green (bass), Krzysztof Korab (keyboards) and Steve Cowen (drums), and their recordings surfaced on several of the Imaginary label's popular tribute compilations (covering Syd Barrett's 'No Good

Trying', Captain Beefheart's 'Big-Eyed Beans From Venus', the Kinks' 'Big Sky', the Byrds' 'Why' and the Velvet Underground's 'Pale Blue Eyes'), illustrating both good taste and individuality. Meanwhile, the band's first 12-inch EP *Pomona,* was issued in 1987, and although it owed an obvious debt to early David Bowie and veered towards the overblown, the confidence of musicians, string arrangements and songwriting was obvious. Guitarist Martin Glyn Murray joined the band in time for 'The Wicker Man' (from the film of the same name), followed by 'And Then She Smiles'. From pure folk to powerful songs verging on the pompous, the Mock Turtles conveyed a distinctive feel within their music. But it was their next single, 1990's 'Lay Me Down', which hinted at bigger things, sporting a sparse yet infectious shuffling backbeat. Hot on its heels came a well-received debut album, *Turtle Soup* in June, which fared well on the independent chart, as did the band's collaboration with one of Coogan's long-time influences, Bill Nelson, 'Take Your Time' (the b-side of their next single, 'Magic Boomerang'). This was enough to lure Siren Records, and for their first major label single, the band chose to rework the flip-side of 'Lay Me Down', 'Can You Dig It?'. The single was an instant hit with BBC television's *Top Of The Pops* appearances to match, and in its wake came another reissue of sorts, 'And Then She Smiles'. This failed to consolidate the success of 'Can You Dig It', and the Mock Turtles' highly commercial *Two Sides* suffered from a low profile, despite its abundance of musical muscle and carefully-crafted songs. In the meantime, Imaginary compiled most of their early single tracks on 1987-90, for those newcomers who had missed them first time around.
Albums: *Turtle Soup* (1990), *1987-90* (1991), *Two Sides* (1991).

Models

The Models were Australia's premier 'new wave' band to emerge from the punk period in the second half of 1978. Original member Sean Kelly (guitar/vocals) and James Freud (bass; who joined in 1982), provided much of the Models' song material. Both had played together previously in Melbourne punk band, the Teenage Radio Stars. The fluctuating line-up of the Models has in the past included notables Andrew Duffield (keyboards; replaced in 1983 by Roger Mason), drummers Janis 'Johnny Crash' Friedenfields and Barton Price, Mark Ferrie (bass/vocals) and James Valentine (keyboards). The band recorded often, and despite having substantial success on the Australian alternative charts, toured frequently and extensively to repay debts that would eventually lead to acrimony between the principal songwriters. Commercial success finally came in 1985 with the 'Out Of Sight Out Of Mind' single and album, and the 'Barbados' single. The band's material was either dense rock music or melodic pop, which alienated its long-standing fans. Since the band broke up in 1987, Freud has recorded a solo album, but despite its high production costs, it did not perform very well. Kelly, eased himself back into the limelight by co-forming a band called the Absent Friends with various other well-known Australian musicians, including INXS bassist, Garry Beers. Initially conceived as a part-time affair, the band developed into a more fully-fledged outfit which earned high respect around Sydney.

Albums: *Alphabetacharliedeltaechofoxtrot* (1980), *Local And/Or General* (1981), *Pleasure Of Your Company* (1983), *Out Of Sight Out Of Mind* (1985), *Media* (1986). Absent Friends *Here's Looking Up Your Address* (1990).

Modern English

Formed in Colchester, Essex, England, in 1979, their debut *Mesh And Lace* was released in suitably arty packaging by 4AD Records two years later. It drew heavily on the gloom already patented by bands like Joy Division, and had little originality or focus. *After The Snow*, recorded by the same line-up of Robbie Grey (vocals), Gary McDowell (guitar/vocals), Richard Brown (drums), Mick Conroy (bass /vocals) and Stephen Walker (keyboards), was a minor revelation, as they introduced warmth and strong guitar harmonies, rejecting the tinny bleakness of the debut. It was well-received in the USA, and the band re-located to New York to consolidate a popularity encouraged by college radio. *Richochet Days* had a crisper production but less creative experimentation. By *Stop Start*, released by Sire Records in 1986, Stephen Walker and Richard Brown had left, and Aaron Davidson (keyboards/guitar) had joined. The band had tried too hard for commercial approval and was left with an unspecific rock/pop sound which caused them to split soon afterwards. Robbie Gray returned to England to form a new group.

Albums: *Mesh And Lace* (1981), *After The Snow* (1982), *Richochet Days* (1984), *Stop Start* (1986).

Modern Lovers

Formed in Boston, Massachusetts, USA, the Modern Lovers revolved around the talents of uncompromising singer/songwriter Jonathan Richman (b. May 1951, Boston, Massachusetts, USA). The group, which included Jerry Harrison (b. 21 February 1949, Milwaukee, Wisconsin, USA; guitar - later of Talking Heads), Ernie Brooks (bass) and future Cars drummer David Robinson, offered an inspired amalgamation of 50s pop, garage bands, girl groups and the Velvet Underground, a style which both engendered a cult following and attracted the interest of ex-Velvet member John Cale, then a

staff producer at Warner Brothers. However, having completed a series of demos, a disillusioned Richman disbanded the line-up and retreated to Boston, although Cale marked their association by recording his protege's composition, 'Pablo Picasso', on *Helen Of Troy* (1975). In 1976, the unfinished tracks were purchased by the newly-founded Beserkley label, which remixed the masters, added two new performances and released the package as *The Modern Lovers*. The company also signed Richman, whose new album, *Jonathan Richman And The Modern Lovers*, was confusingly issued within months of the first selection. The second set revealed a less intensive talent, and his regression into almost child-like simplicity was confirmed on *Rock 'N' Roll With The Modern Lovers*. Richman's new group - Leroy Radcliffe (guitar), Greg 'Curly' Kerenen (bass) and D. Smart (drums) - was purely acoustic and featured a repertoire which, by including 'The Ice-Cream Man', 'Hey There Little Insect', 'The Wheels On The Bus' and 'I'm A Little Aeroplane', was deemed enchanting or irritating, according to taste. The Modern Lovers nonetheless enjoyed two surprise UK hits with 'Roadrunner' and 'Egyptian Reggae', which reached numbers 11 and 5, respectively, in 1977. However, as the unit was undeniably a vehicle for Richman's quirky vision, the Modern Lovers' name was dropped the following year when the singer embarked on a solo tour. He has nonetheless revived the title on occasions, notably on *It's Time For Jonathan Richman And The Modern Lovers* and *Modern Lovers 88*.

Albums: *The Modern Lovers* (1976), *Jonathan Richman And The Modern Lovers* (1976), *Rock 'N' Roll With The Modern Lovers* (1977), *The Modern Lovers Live* (1977), *It's Time For Jonathan Richman And The Modern Lovers* (1986), *Modern Lovers 88* (1988). Compilations: *The Original Modern Lovers* (1981, early recordings), *Jonathan Richman And The Modern Lovers - 23 Great Recordings* (1990).

Modern Romance

From the remnants of UK punk band, the (Leyton) Buzzards, crawled Geoff Deanne and David Jaymes. After becoming involved in the London club scene (alongside luminaries like Steve Strange), they formed a company called Business Art Productions with manager Brian O'Donoughue. Signed to WEA, they released 'Tonight'. This flopped, so in late 1980, Jaymes and Deanne formed a new line-up featuring Deanne (b. 10 December 1954; vocals), Jaymes (b. 28 November 1954; bass), brother Robbie Jaymes (b. 3 October 1962; keyboards), Paul Gendler (b. 11 August 1960; guitar) and Andy Kyriacou (b. 19 April 1958; drums, ex-Linx and Central Line). John Du Prez also featured on trumpet. Through their club connections they came across the Latin-American music salsa, which was set to be all the craze in the summer of 1981. They quickly recorded 'Everybody Salsa', which gave them their first hit. It was followed by other successful material in a similar vein; 'Ay Ay Ay Ay Moosey', 'Queen Of The Rapping Scene', and 'Cherry Pink And Apple Blossom White'. At this point Deanne left to release several solo singles and write for camp club act Divine. Former fireman Michael J. Mullins (b. 9 November 1956) was his replacement. Their hit run continued in 1983, with 'Best Years Of Our life', 'High Life' and 'Walking In The Rain'. A cover of Baltimora's 'Tarzan Boy' the following year fared less well. They disbanded shortly afterwards. David Jaymes released a solo single in 1988, while Deanne now writes comedy scripts. John Du Prez currently lives in Hollywood where he plays on film scores.

Albums: *Adventures In Clubland* (1981), *Trick Of The Light* (1983), *Party Tonight* (1983), *Move On* (1985).

Mo-Dettes

Despite the name, the timing of their appearance on the music scene, and the fact that they covered the Rolling Stones' 'Paint It Black', the Mo-Dettes were not modettes and disliked anyone who said they were. They were originally formed for a one-off gig at the Acklam Hall, supporting the Vincent Units. Their line-up was built around Kate Korus (b. Katherine Corris, New York, USA; guitar), who played with the Castrators before lasting just three gigs with the earliest line-up of the Slits. She left (to be replaced by Viv Albertine) and attempted to form several bands. Korus took a long time finding musicians with whom she was happy, but gradually she came across (on the set of *The Great Rock 'N' Roll Swindle* where both had non-acting jobs) drummer June Miles-Kingston (the sister of Bob Kingston of Tenpole Tudor) and bassist Jane Crockford. Crockford had previously played in the Banks Of Dresden with Richard Dudanski. Through a mutual friend they met Ramona Carlier, a singer from Switzerland whose experience to date had been backing vocals at a few sessions plus a one-off party gig with a band called the Bomberettes, and had been in England about a year. The first product of their labours was 'White Mice' - on their own Mode label through Rough Trade. Ramona left late in 1981 to start a solo career, and was replaced by Sue Slack. Soon after, Korus split to be replaced by Melissa Ritter. The final split came shortly after in 1982, owing to further internal friction. Miles-Kingston moved on to Fun Boy Three's backing band, before she produced a solo single for Go! Discs, joined the Communards and sang on various sessions. Kate Korus also released a single with Jenny of the Belle Stars.

Album: *The Story So Far* (1980).

Momus

b. Nicholas Currie, 1960, Paisley, Scotland. After living in Canada for a spell as a teenager, Currie returned to the UK and, during the mid-80s, began recording on the independent circuit. His primary influence was Jacques Brel, whose earthy sexuality soon infiltrated Momus's work. An EP, *Beast With No Backs*, on El Records garnered minor critical attention, as did the album *Circus Maximus*. Momus promised a follow-up, *The Poison Boyfriend*, but that title was abandoned after he signed with Alan McGee's Creation label. Finally, in 1988, Momus returned with *Tender Pervert*, a lacerating document of sexual and emotional psychoanalysis. His strength was his strong narrative line, particularly on songs such as 'Love On Ice' and 'Bishonen'. The following year, he issued *Don't Stop The Night*, which featured a more electronic, dance-orientated approach in keeping with current fashion. One song, 'Righthand Heart', was a less effective reworking of an essentially acoustic song on the previous album. Momus's lack of live experience has so far prevented any major excursion into performing. His 1991 album *Hippopotamomus* was less well received and was greeted with a zero out of 10 rating in the influential *New Musical Express* as a result of its moral perversity. The artist no doubt appreciated the irony.

Albums: *Circus Maximus* (1986), *Tender Pervert* (1988), *Don't Stop The Night* (1989), *Hippopotamomus* (1991), *Voyager* (1992), *The Ultracomformist* (1992). Compilation: *Monsters Of Love - Singles 1985-90* (1990).

Monochrome Set

Monochrome Set

Any all-encompassing classification of the Monochrome Set's music would be difficult. During a sporadic career that has spanned as many musical styles as it has record labels, they have been on the verge of breaking to a wider audience on a number of occasions, but there has always been an eccentric, art-school feel. Formed in the UK during late 1976, Andy Warren (bass), Lester Square (guitar) and Bid (guitar/vocals) were playing in the B-Sides with Adam Ant. When the B-Sides became the Adam And The Ants, Bid and Lester Square left. They formed the Monochrome Set in January 1978, later joined by Warren in 1979 after his role on the debut Ants album. With Jeremy Harrington (bass; ex-Gloria Mundi and Mean Street) and J.D. Haney (drums; ex-Art Attacks), the band issued singles during 1979-80 for Rough Trade including 'He's Frank', 'Eine Symphonie Des Graeuns', 'The Monochrome Set' and 'He's Frank (Slight Return)', each completely different in style and content.

For their debut, *The Strange Boutique*, the band joined Virgin's subsidiary Din Disc in 1980, and skirted the national charts. After the title track came further singles '405 Lines' and 'Apocalypso', and a second album later that year, *Love Zombies*. A one-off single for Charisma's Pre label ('Ten Don'ts For Honeymooners') ensued in 1981, before the band found themselves back with an indie label, Cherry Red, that shared their eclectic pop approach. Lex Crane briefly sat in on drums before ex-Soft Boys Morris Windsor joined for the release of 'The Mating Game' in July 1982, followed by 'Cast A Long Shadow' in October and the memorable *Eligible Bachelors*. By this time Carrie Booth had joined on keyboards while Nick Wesolowski took up the drums and Foz the guitar soon after. An ideal introduction to the Monochrome Set can be found on *Volume, Brilliance, Contrast,* compiling their Rough Trade recordings, which coincided with another indie hit, 'Jet Set Junta'. When Cherry Red's Mike Alway left to set up WEA's new Blanco Y Negro label, he took several acts with him, including the Monochrome Set. This resulted in their most commercial outing, 'Jacob's Ladder' which seemed a sure-fire hit for 1985. But like 'Wallflower' later that year and the charming, *The Lost Weekend*, all eluded the charts. Disheartened, the band split and it was left to Cherry Red's El subsidiary to issue a sympathetic retrospective, *Fin! Live*, a year later. Various collections filtered out over the next three years (*Colour Transmission* featured much of the Din Disc material, while *Westminster Affair* highlighted their earliest recordings). In December 1989, the band reformed, and Bid Lester and Warren were joined by Orson Presence on guitar and keyboards.
Albums: *The Strange Boutique* (1980), *Love Zombies* (1980), *Eligible Bachelors* (1982), *The Lost Weekend* (1985). Compilations: *Volume, Brilliance, Contrast* (1983), *Fin! Live* (1985), *Colour Transmission* (1987), *Westminster Affair* (1988).

Monroe, Michael

When Hanoi Rocks folded, following the death of drummer Razzle in 1984, Monroe took several years off before deciding to start again and build a solo career. In 1988, *Nights Are So Long* emerged on the independent Yahoo label, featuring a mixture of originals and covers of songs by the Heavy Metal Kids, Johnny Thunders, MC5 and the Flamin' Groovies. This low-key comeback was a soul-cleansing process for Monroe, before he signed to Mercury Records, and threw himself back into the spotlight with all guns blazing. Recruiting Phil Grande (guitar), Tommy Price (drums), Kenny Aaronson (bass) and Ed Roynesdal (keyboards), he recorded *Not Fakin' It*, a streetwise selection of sleazy rock 'n' roll numbers, delivered in Monroe's inimitable, gutter-cat style. The album was well received and the tour to support it was a triumph. It also suggested that Monroe had been the lynchpin in Hanoi Rocks, as all the other Hanoi spin-offs had met with little success.
Albums: *Nights Are So Long* (1988), *Not Fakin' It* (1989).

Monsoon

The nucleus of UK-based Monsoon were producer/writer/musician Steve Coe and his collaborator Martin Smith. Together they produced a hybrid of raga-pop, fusing Indian and Western influences. They were fronted by the schoolgirl vocalist Sheila Chandra (b. 14 March 1965, Waterloo, London, England), and augmented by session musicians, particularly on percussion instruments. Chandra had previously acted in the UK children's television programme *Grange Hill*. Monsoon's brief UK success arrived in 1982 with 'Ever So Lonely' and the follow up 'Shakti (The Meaning Of Within)'. However, when 'The Wings Of Dawn' failed Chandra elected to take a solo career, recording four albums with the assistance of Coe. After a five-year break she returned with *Roots And Wings* in 1990.
Album: *Third Eye* (1983).

Mood Six

Mood Six were central to the short-lived UK psychedelic revival that swept London's West End in the early 80s, and had evolved from various units with varying mod leanings. Drummer Simon Smith (ex-Merton Parkas), songwriter Tony Conway (ex-V.I.P.s), Andy Godfrey and Chris Connor debuted on WEA's 1982's new psychedelia compilation, *A Splash Of Colour*. The band contributed two tracks, the catchy 'Plastic Flowers' and the atmospheric 'Just Like A Dream', although both owed as much to late 60s pop as to psychedelia. The resulting publicity surrounding that scene led to an interview on BBC television's *Nationwide* and a deal with EMI. 'Plastic Flowers' became the band's first single but was commercially disappointing and the follow-up, 'She's Too Far', was scrapped as the band were dropped from the label.

Mood Six re-emerged early in 1985 on the psychedelic reissue label Psycho, with *The Difference Is...*, followed in May by a re-recording of 'Plastic Flowers'. The band then moved to the Cherry Red label for 1986's classy, 'What Have You Ever Done?', drawn from *A Matter Of!*. Unfortunately, although Mood Six were writing endearing pop music, the final sound was occasionally bland, lacking that spark of originality. After the release of 'I Saw The Light' in May 1987, the band broke up. Simon Smith recently turned up in Small Town Parade, another band with strong mod connections.

Albums: *The Difference Is...* (1985), *A Matter Of!* (1986).

Moose

Moose

This UK group comprised Russell Yates (vocals), Kevin McKillop (guitar), Damien Warburton (drums) and Lincoln Fong (bass). They inadvertently began the so-called 'shoegazing' movement, so dubbed because of the static nature of bands who focused on the floorboards instead of their audience, when Yates read lyrics taped to the floor. They rose to notoriety with supports to Lush, from whom they borrowed Chris Acland when Warburton failed to appear at gigs. Another temporary change arose when McKillop attended his child's birth, and Tim from Sterolab stepped in. Conversely Yates moonlights as a

Sterolab guitarist and McKillop has played with See See Rider. It is this sort of activity which fuelled 'The Scene That Celebrates Itself' tag, summoned by the *Melody Makers*' Steve Sutherland to describe the incestuous nature of a clutch of upcoming bands who were not indulging in traditional rivalries. Three EPs comprised the original batch of recordings, the last of which was the first to confirm that the band could offer more than the voguish My Bloody Valentine influences. The C&W-tinged 'This River Will Never Run Dry' was applauded from almost all corners. Yates also achieved prominence through the Lillies, the brainchild of Stuart Mutler, editor of football club Tottenham Hotspurs magazine *The Spur*. This included Miki Berenyi and Chris Acland from Lush, Yates and Kevin McKillop from Moose, and was masterminded by Simon Raymonde of the Cocteau Twins. Together they recorded a flexi-disc entitled: 'And David Seaman Will Be Very Disappointed About That'.

Moped, Johnny

b. Paul Halford, London, England. The bizarre Moped Bands, in their various incarnations, have produced a stream of influential musicians and personalities. The outfit gradually emerged in Croydon, starting off with the Black Witch Climax Blues Band, before switching names to Genetic Breakdown from 1971-75. Some of the key personnel included Ray Burns (later Captain Sensible), his brother Phil, the Berk brothers, and the mysterious Xerxes. It was not until 1974 that Moped joined, as the band became known first as Johnny Moped And The 5 Arrogant Superstars, then Johnny Moped's Assault And Buggery. However, it was the birth of punk which saw Moped finding an audience for his 'moronic rock 'n' roll'. Getting support slots with the Damned introduced new wave audiences to the strange phenomenon of J. Moped, the performer. After the Berk brothers' stint in the Unusuals (with Chrissie Hynde, soon to be of the Moors Murderers then the Pretenders on vocals), they rejoined the re-christened Captain Sensible in the third Johnny Moped line-up. Having found success with the Damned, the Captain only stayed for three months, his place taken by the hideously titled Slimey Toad. With several singles behind them, notably the charming 'No One'/'Incendiary Device', they recorded the legendary *Cycledelic*, an album acclaimed to this day by both R.E.M. and the Ramones. The band disappeared after its release, although Dave Berk did replace Rat Scabies in the Damned when the latter stormed off during their European tour. Scabies had previously performed one gig with the Moped band. Against all odds, the Johnny Moped Big Band reformed in 1991, playing live for the first time in 12 years and recording *The Search For Xerxes*. Live, they

were joined on stage by old colleagues Kirsty MaccColl and the Captain. As former band member Xerxes recently stated: 'It is odd, that such an untalented bunch of people are still held in such affection'.
Albums: *Cycledelic* (1978), *The Search For Xerxes* (1991).

Morells

Formed in Springfield, Missouri, USA in 1982, the Morells recorded only one album, *Shake And Push*, on Borrowed Records. Although it never charted, this roots-rock group built a devoted following on the USA alternative circuit. Consisting of bassist Lou Whitney (who had once performed with soul singer Arthur Conley), his wife, Maralie (keyboards), D. Clinton Thompson (guitar) and Ron Gremp (drums), the group started in the late 70s as the Skeletons and then the Original Symptoms before settling in as the Morells, combining within their sound rockabilly, soul, blues and jazz. The group disbanded in the mid-80s. Lou Whitney went on to produce the debut album by New York rockers the Del-Lords before re-forming the Skeletons in 1988, with Thompson.
Album: *Shake And Push* (1982).

Morrissey

b. Steven Patrick Morrissey, 22 May 1959, Davyhulme, Manchester, England. Morrissey began his career with the vague intention of succeeding as a music journalist. Unemployed in Manchester during the late 70s, he frequently wrote letters to the music press and was eventually taken on by *Record Mirror* as a freelance local reviewer. During this period, he also ran a New York Dolls' fan club and even wrote a booklet about them. Another small illustrated volume, *James Dean Is Not Dead*, briefly catalogued the career of another Morrissey obsession. Two other projects, on girl groups and minor film stars, failed to reach the printed page. In the meantime, Morrissey was attempting unsuccessfully to progress as a performer. He had played a couple of gigs with local group the Nosebleeds and failed a record company audition with a relaunched version of Slaughter And The Dogs. By the early 80s his chance of fame had apparently expired. In 1982, however, he was approached by Wythenshawe guitarist Johnny Maher (later Marr) with the idea of forming a songwriting team. They soon developed into the Smiths, one of the most important and critically-acclaimed UK groups of the 80s. Morrissey's arch lyrics, powerful persona and general newsworthiness made him a pop figure whose articulacy was unmatched by any of his contemporaries. By the late summer of 1987, the Smiths disbanded, leaving Morrissey to pursue a solo career. Early the following year, he issued his first post-Smiths single, 'Suedehead', with Vini Reilly

filling the guitarist's spot. The track was irresistibly commercial and reached the UK Top 5. The subsequent, *Viva Hate* hit the top soon after, indicating that the singer could look forward to a long and successful future with EMI.
A further UK Top 10 single with the John Betjemen-influenced 'Everyday Is Like Sunday' reiterated that point. In spite of his successes, Morrissey was initially keen on promoting a Smiths reunion but the closest this reached was the equivalent of a farewell concert in the unlikely setting of Wolverhampton Civic Hall. On 22 December 1988, Morrissey performed alongside former Smiths, Andy Rourke, Mike Joyce and Craig Gannon for a 1,700 capacity audience, many of whom had queued for days in order to gain admittance to the venue. The following year brought several problems for Morrissey. Although he continued to release strong singles such as 'The Last Of The Famous International Playboys' and 'Interesting Drug', both reviews and chart placings were slighter less successful than expected. By the time of 'Ouija Board, Ouija Board', Morrissey suffered the most disappointing reviews of his career and, despite its charm, the single only reached number 18. Financial wrangles and management changes, which had characterized the Smiths' career, were repeated by Morrissey the soloist.
A projected album *Bona Drag* was delayed and eventually cancelled, although the title served for a formidable hits and b-side compilation. In the meantime, Morrissey concentrated on the singles market, issuing some fascinating product, most notably the macabre 'November Spawned A Monster' and controversial 'Piccadilly Palare'. In March 1991, Morrissey issued his long-awaited *Kill Uncle*, a light yet not unappealing work, produced by Clive Langer and Alan Winstanley. By this time, Morrissey had not toured since the heyday of the Smiths, and there were some critics who wondered whether he would ever perform again. That question was answered in the summer and winter of 1991 when the singer embarked on a world tour, backed by a rockabilly group, whose raw energy and enthusiasm brought a new dimension to his recently understated studio work. The fruits of this collaboration were revealed on *Your Arsenal*, a neat fusion of 50s rockabilly influences and 70s glam rock. The presence of former David Bowie acolyte Mick Ronson as producer added to the effects. During 1992, Morrissey also hit the headlines when he issued a bitter attack on author Johnny Rogan. Prior to the publication of a book on the Smiths, which he had yet to read, Morrissey decreed: 'Personally, I hope Johnny Rogan ends his days very soon in an M3 pile-up'. The much publicized dispute merely served to focus attention on the book and heighten appreciation of his Smiths' work.

Albums: *Viva Hate* (1988), *Kill Uncle* (1991), *Your Arsenal* (1992). Compilation: *Bona Drag* (1990).
Further Reading: *Morrissey & Marr: The Severed Alliance*, Johnny Rogan.

Motello, Elton

Alan Ward had originally been the singer with punk hopefuls Bastard, which also included in its ranks future Damned guitarist Brian James. After the band split Ward assumed the pseudonym of Elton Motello, alternating between England and Belgium, where he had built up associations touring with Bastard. He made his debut appearance at the end of 1977 with 'Jet Boy, Jet Girl', first in Belgium on Pinball, followed a month later by the UK release on Lightning. The track achieved international success with the re-titled French version 'Ca Plane Pour Moi' by pop-punk Plastic Bertrand. Success for Motello's original was much more limited, even though it was released in many different countries. A few months later 'Jet Boy, Jet Girl' was re-recorded to greater notoriety by Captain Sensible And The Softies. Towards the end of 1978 Motello recorded his debut *Victim Of Time*, which was released in March 1979 by Attic Records, but only in Canada. He was backed by various players including Peter (guitar), Nobby (drums) and Willie Change (bass), with the help of Jet Staxx (guitar), Tony Boast (guitar) and former Pink Fairies and Pretty Things drummer John 'Twink' Alder. In addition to the single, the album included a remake of the Small Faces' 'Sha La La La Lee' and another 11 compositions that fluctuated between pop and punk. With the new decade came two further releases: '20th Century Fox' and the album *Pop Art*.
Albums: *Victim Of Time* (1979), *Pop Art* (1980).

Motels

Formed in Berkeley, California in the early 70s, the Motels comprised Martha Davis (vocals), Jeff Jourard (guitar), his brother Martin (keyboards/saxophone), former jazzer Michael Goodroe (bass) and UK session drummer Brian Glascock (ex-Toe Fat). Transferring to Los Angeles the group assembled for appearances at Hollywood's Whiskey club throughout July 1978. They attracted much music industry interest. In 1979, their stunning debut album was issued by Capitol. Like its remaining tracks, the hit ballad, 'Total Control', was produced by John Carter and composed by central figure Davis whose eclectic taste included blues, Broadway musicals and Stravinsky. Her onstage presence was 'exceptionally charismatic', wrote *The Los Angeles Times*, wrongly predicting that she 'could become one of the most influential female performers in rock'. Her boyfriend, Tim McGovern (ex-Captain Kopter And The Fabulous Twirlybirds), replaced Jeff Jourard during sessions for *Careful* with a

sleeve adorned with a print of a Dougie Fields' painting. Though its singles, 'Whose Problem' and 'Days Are OK', flitted into the US and UK charts, they fared well in regional charts in Australasia, a territory where the group made its strongest impact. At home, their albums and tie-in singles tended to hover around the lower half of the Top 40 after *All Four One* at number 16 marked the Motels' commercial zenith there, despite scoring two US Top 10 hits with 'Only The Lonely' (1982) and 'Suddenly Last Summer' (1983). The group folded in 1987.
Albums: *The Motels* (1979), *Careful* (1980), *All Four One* (1982), *Little Robbers* (1983), *Shock* (1985).

Mother Love Bone

This short-lived, Seattle based quintet comprised Andrew Wood (vocals), Greg Gilmore (drums), Bruce Fairweather (guitar), Stone Gossard (guitar) and Jeff Ament (bass). Drawing influences from the Doors, the Stooges, MC5 and the Velvet Underground they specialized in heavy-duty garage rock laced with psychotic overtones. Signing to Polydor, they debuted with *Apple* in 1990 to widespread critical acclaim. Their promising career was curtailed abruptly by the untimely death of vocalist Andrew Wood shortly after the album was released. Gossard and Ament went on to further success with Temple Of The Dog and later Pearl Jam.
Album: *Apple* (1990).

Motorcycle Boy

This UK 'indie' pop group were formed in 1987 by former Shop Assistants singer Alex Taylor (vocals) with ex-Meat Whiplash personnel Michael (guitar), Paul (drums), Eddie (bass) and outsider, Scottie (guitar). Their debut single for Rough Trade Records, 'Big Rock Candy Mountain'(formerly a title for Burl Ives), reached number 3 in the UK independent chart. Despite this promising start, and much music press attention, they failed, largely from disorganisation, to set the live circuit alight and subsequently broke up soon after the release of their lone album which was recorded for the major label Chrysalis Records. Alex Taylor was reportedly last spotted working as a shop assistant for a record store chain.
Album: *Scarlet* (1989).

Mould, Bob

The former guitarist, vocalist and composer of Hüsker Dü, Mould surprised many of that leading hardcore act's aficionados with his reflective solo debut, *Workbook*. Only one track, 'Whichever Way The Wind Blows', offered the maelstrom of guitars customary in the artist's work and instead the set was marked by a predominantly acoustic atmosphere. Cellist Jane Scarpantoni contributed to its air of melancholy, while Tony Maimone (bass) and Anton Fier (drums), two members of Pere Ubu, added sympathetic support, helping to emphasize the gift for melody always apparent in Mould's work. Maimone and Fier also provided notable support on *Black Sheets Of Rain* which marked a return to the uncompromising power of the guitarist's erstwhile unit. The set included the harrowing 'Hanging Tree' and apocalyptical 'Sacrifice Sacrifice/Let There Be Peace', but contrasted such doom-laden material with a brace of sprightly pop songs in 'It's Too Late' and 'Hear Me Calling', both of which echo R.E.M.. Mould's continued commitment to superior music bodes well for his future career.

Albums: *Workbook* (1989), *Black Sheets Of Rain* (1990).

Mudhoney

Miraculously forged from a host of hobbyist bands - among them Mr Epp, Limp Richard and Green River - in Seattle, USA, Mudhoney were to spearhead the Sub Pop label's assault on the ears of the world's adolescents. Taking their cue from early 70s hard rock and early 80s hardcore, Mark Arm, brother Steve Turner, Dan Peters and Matt Lukin created a monstrous guitar sound so distorted by effects pedals that they actually named their first album, *Superfuzz Big Muff*, after one of them. Backed up by equally heavy outfits such as Nirvana, Tad and Soundgarden, Mudhoney burst out of their homeland, and encouraged punters to turn stage-diving into an artform with shows that epitomised words like grunge and lurch. By 1991's *Every Good Boy Deserves Fudge*, this noise genre was starting to cross over into the traditionally conservative American mainstream in a mammoth way, suggesting that if Mudhoney could have as much level-headedness as they had fun, enormous major label riches were awaiting them.

Albums: *Superfuzz Big Muff* (1989), *Every Good Boy Deserves Fudge* (1991).

Murphy, Peter

The former Bauhaus vocalist set out on his solo career after a brief stint as half of Dali's Car, with former Japan member Mick Karn (one album: *The Waking Hour*). Murphy was already famous in his own right for appearing as the enigmatic figure in a Maxell Tapes television advertisement. His first solo output was a cover version of Magazine's 'The Light Pours Out Of Me', for the Beggars Banquet sampler *The State Of Things*. This was included on his debut album, which boasted a massive credit list including Daniel Ash, his old songwriting partner in Bauhaus, John McGeogh (who played on the original of 'The Light Pours Out Of Me') and Howard Hughes. The debut set a precedent for critical apathy (in the UK at least) which has accompanied all subsequent recordings. 1987's *Love Hysteria* included a cover of Iggy Pop's 'Fun Time', amongst other typically dramatic gestures. By the third album a regular band had been formed, consisting of Peter Bonas (guitar), Terl Bryant (drums), Eddie Branch (bass) and Paul Statham (keyboards/guitar). All four had played on the previous album, Branch and Bonas on the first as well. One of the better songs from *Deep*, 'Cuts You Deep', won the Top Modern Rock Track in the 1990 *Billboard* Year In Music Awards.

Albums: *Should The World Fail To Fall Apart* (1986), *Love Hysteria* (1987), *Deep* (1989), *Holy Smoke* (1992).

Murray, Pauline, And The Invisible Girls

Following the demise of Penetration, Murray (b. 8 March 1958, Durham, England) departed, with bass guitarist Robert Blamire, to form a new group. Producers Martin Hannett and Steve Hopkins were claimed to be the 'Invisible' members, while the actual line-up consisted of John Maher (ex-Buzzcocks), Dave Rowbotham and Dave Hassell. The Invisible Girls would also act as studio and road band for John Cooper Clarke, and include among its ranks Pete Shelley, Karl Burns (the Fall), Bill Nelson, Vini Reilly (Durutti Column) and numerous others. A self-titled album and single, 'Dream Sequence', announced the arrival of Pauline Murray And The Invisible Girls, gaining strong critical support. The album featured guest appearances from Wayne Hussey (ex-Dead Or Alive, Sisters Of Mercy, the Mission) in addition to the previously mentioned Invisible luminaries. Despite this fine collection, the band split after two subsequent single releases from it: 'Searching For Heaven' and 'Mr. X'. Blamire went into production work while Murray took two years away from the music industry. 'I just . . . retreated from music really, just backed right out and decided what I wanted to do. Which took about a year to two years . . . I think Penetration to the Invisible Girls was such a vast leap that it lost everyone. It lost us as well'. Blamire and Murray reunited in the similarly short-lived Pauline Murray And The Storm.

Album: *Pauline Murray And The Invisible Girls* (1981).

Mute Records

Daniel Miller's brainchild was originally set up for his single under the guise of the Normal. 'T.V.O.D.'/'Warm Leatherette' became the first Mute single in early 1978, a pioneering utilization of electronics that paved the way for Mute's alignment with synthesized and hi-tech sounds. Nearly 200 singles and a 100 albums later, Mute's singular artistic identity and experimental approach still cuts a distinctive chord through an apathetic music industry. Along with Factory and Rough Trade, Mute has demonstrated an ability to combine aesthetic

My Bloody Valentine

autonomy with survival. Among the label's early group roster were Fad Gadget, DAF and Depeche Mode. It was the success of the latter that convinced many that a post-punk independent label could succeed in producing a consistent chart act. Despite the offers made to the group from major labels, Depeche Mode resisted any temptation to move - a tribute to Miller's business acumen and his faith in Depeche Mode's artistic growth. The label has also been greatly assisted by ex-DM member Vince Clark's series of projects from Yazoo through to Erasure. Owing to Depeche Mode and Erasure's continuing international success, Mute has been able to finance less commercial acts such as Laibach, Crime And The City Solution, Diamanda Galas and Nitzer Ebb. The label's acquisition of the back catalogues of Cabaret Voltaire, Can and Throbbing Gristle has also ensured the continued availability of these artists' output.

Compilation: *International* (1991).

MX-80 Sound

Bruce Anderson (guitar), Rich Stim (guitar/keyboards/vocals/saxophone), Dave Sophiea (bass), Dave Mahoney (drums) and Jeff Armour, later replaced by Kevin Teare (drums). Hailing from Bloomington, Indiana, USA, MX-80 began as a trio of Anderson, Sophiea and Armour. In late 1975 they were joined by Stim and Mahoney. A single and EP on a local label were followed by their debut *Hard Attack* for Island Records. By this time they were based in San Francisco. *Hard Attack* achieved considerable attention; the avowed experimentation of the group (Captain Beefheart and Frank Zappa were often cited by critics) matched by a lyrical subject matter that fitted into the 'new wave' ethos of the period. The sound quality was also suitably murky. Signed to *Ralph*, the label run by the Residents, they produced two more albums and appeared on several compilations but their career tailed off in the early 80s. Stim entered law school and nothing further was heard except for Anderson's appearance in the Henry Kaiser Band. However, a clutch of tapes under a variety of names (Gizzards, Half-Life, O-Type) have appeared since 1987, apparently the work of Sophiea and Anderson, on the former's Quadruped label. These two, plus Stim and drummer Marc Weinstein, appear to constitute an MX for the 90s.

Albums: *Hard Attack* (1977), *Out Of The Tunnel* (1980), *Crowd Control* (1981).

My Bloody Valentine

It took several years for My Bloody Valentine to capture their ground-breaking hybrid of ethereal melodies and studio-oriented, discordant sounds which proved so influential on the independent scene of the late 80s. Their roots lay in Dublin, where singer/guitarist Kevin Shields joined drummer Colm O'Ciosoig in the short-lived Complex. Forming My Bloody Valentine in 1984, the pair moved to Berlin, joined by vocalist Dave Conway (vocals) and Tina (keyboards). A mini-album, *This Is Your Bloody Valentine*, on the obscure German Tycoon label in 1984, made little impression (although it was later reissued in the UK), so the band returned to London and recruited bassist Debbie Googe. The 12-inch EP, *Geek!* (and the accompanying, 'No Place To Go') emerged on Fever in mid-1986 which, like their debut, was strongly influenced by the Cramps and the Birthday Party. Later that year, the band signed with Joe Foster's fledgling Kaleidoscope Sound label for *The New Record By My Bloody Valentine* EP, which revealed a new influence, the Jesus And Mary Chain. A switch to the Primitives' label Lazy, produced 'Sunny Sundae Smile' (1987), which meshed bubblegum pop with buzzsaw guitars, a formula that dominated both the mini-album, *Ecstasy*, and 'Strawberry Wine' released later that year. The departure of Conway signalled a change in musical direction, reinforced by the arrival of vocalist Belinda Butcher. A further move to Creation Records allowed for a drastic reappraisal in recording techniques, first apparent on the formidable *You Made Me Realise* EP in 1988. Enticing melodic structures contrasted with the snarling, almost unworldly collage of noise, developed more fully that year on My Bloody Valentine's pivotal *Isn't Anything*, from which was drawn the barrage of guitars, 'Feed Me With Your Kiss'. At last, the group had unearthed a completely new sound. Since then, their status has mushroomed, despite a mere two EPs (and a flexi disc, 'Sugar', free with *The Catalogue* magazine). The release of EP *Glider* (1990), alongside a remix from the in-demand DJ Andy Weatherall, flirted with both dance music and the charts while 'Tremelo' (1991) must rank as arguably the most extreme piece of music to reach the Top 30. To quote the band, it 'sounded like it was being played through a transistor radio'. My Bloody Valentine's progressing maturity saw the meticulously-produced *Loveless* album reinforce their reputation as one of the prime influences on the late 80s' UK independent scene - one that such groups as Slowdive, Lush and Chapterhouse owe a great deal.
Albums: *This Is Your Bloody Valentine* (1984), *Ecstasy* (1987), *Isn't Anything* (1988), *Loveless* (1991).

N

Naked Prey

This US group was founded in 1981 in Tucson, Arizona by Van Christian (guitar/vocals), formerly of the Serfers. David Seger (guitar/vocals), Richard Badenious (bass) and Sam Blake (drums) completed the line-up featured on the unit's mini-album debut. The set was produced by ex-Serfer Dan Stuart, guitarist in Green On Red, but although comparisons were naturally drawn between the two, Naked Prey offered a louder, heavier sound. This was more clearly heard on *Under The Blue Marlin*, on which Blake had been replaced by Tom Larkins. *40 Miles From Nowhere*, which featured the Rolling Stones 'Silver Train' and Glen Campbell's 'Wichita Lineman', was regarded as a disappointment, and the group's musical momentum noticeably faltered. Van Christian nonetheless continues to front his creation, although it now seems doomed to cult status.
Albums: *Naked Prey* (1984), *Under The Blue Marlin* (1986), *40 Miles From Nowhere* (1987), *Kill The Messenger* (1989).

Napalm Death

This quartet from Birmingham, England, was formed in 1982. They combined punk and thrash metal influences in the new sub-genre of grindcore, the most extreme of all musical forms. Comprising Lee Dorrian (vocals), Bill Steer (guitar), Shane Embury (bass) and Mick Harris (drums), they specialized in sub-two minute blasts of metallic white noise, over-ridden by Dorrian's unintelligible vocal tirade. The lyrics deal with social and political injustices, but actually sound like somebody coughing up blood. They originally attracted a small but loyal cult following on the underground heavy metal scene. Since then, grindcore has developed considerably and found mass acceptance among the rank and file of the metal world. They remain, however, the antithesis of style, melody and taste and represent the punk concept taken to its ultimate extreme. The band members also have side projects; Bill Steer is a member of Carcass, Shane Embury plays with Unseen Terror and Mick Harris drums in Extreme Noise Terror.
Albums: *Scum* (1987), *From Enslavement To Obliteration* (1988), *The Peel Sessions* (1989), *Harmony Corruption* (1990), *Utopia Banished* (1992).

Native Hipsters

This London-based duo comprised William Wilding (b. 18 May 1953, Romford, Essex, England) and

Ned's Atomic Dustbin

Blatt (b. Nanette Greenblatt, 9 March 1952, Cape Town, South Africa). Prior to 1980 they had worked under names such as the Wildings, then later as the Patterns with Robert Cubitt and Tom Fawcett. In that guise, they released the challenging but largely incoherent 'The B'Shop Is In The Fridge'. They next emerged as (And The) Native Hipsters, again with Cubitt and Fawcett. It was as the latter that Wilding and Blatt achieved national recognition with their 1980 release 'There Goes Concorde Again'. Blatt's repetitive child-like enthusiasm at the sighting of the famed 'silverbird' captured the attention of UK Radio One disc jockey, John Peel, resulting in the single peaking at number 5 in the UK independent charts. Wilding turned down an offer from producer Tony Visconti to re-cut the single for national consumption, preferring total artistic control. Their next release in 1982, a four track EP, *Tenderly Hurt Me*, won them a respect from the music press who had previously condemned them as quirky odd-balls. The Hipsters' inventive and bizarre mixture of surreal poetry, diverse musical styles, original and sampled sounds, plus a vast array of musical instruments of whatever came to hand, managed to establish a cult following. Variously assisted by friends such as Lester Square (guitar, from the Monochrome Set), Annie

Whitehead (trombone), Chris Cornetto (cornet), Liduina Van Der Sman (saxophone) and Simon Davison (piano), Wilding and Blatt have over the years recorded countless sessions, live and in the studio, which were later compiled to form *Blatt On The Landscape*. During the early 90s Wilding performed on the London cabaret circuit as the iconoclastic Woody Bop Muddy, an act consisting of his passing a savage judgement on whatever and whoever's records passed through his hands, by way of smashing them with a hammer.

Albums: as the Wildings *Why Did I Buy Those Blue Pyjamas* (1979), as the Native Hipsters *Blatt On The Landscape* (1988 - cassette only edition).

Ned's Atomic Dustbin

Formed in the West Midlands in 1988 by local characters Jonn Penney (b. 17 September 1968; lead vocals), Rat (b. 8 November 1970; guitar), Matt Cheslin (b. 28 November 1970; bass), Alex Griffin (b. 29 August 1971; bass) and Dan Warton (b. 28 July 1972; drums). After dubious Gothic beginnings, Ned's Atomic Dustbin began to find their feet in 1989 when a series of tour supports, notably with regional contemporaries the Wonderstuff, attracted a strong following. Notable for having two bassists,

uniformly crimped hair and an unequivocally daft name (taken from the BBC radio's *The Goon Show*), the Ned's urgent, aggressive sub-hardcore sound still managed to offset any gimmicky connotations, turning a potential freak show into a challenging pop act. Armed with a plethora of original merchandising ideas - within three years the band produced 86 different t-shirt designs - their 'Kill Your Television' single entered the Top 50 of the UK chart and resulted in a major contract with Sony Music (formerly CBS). With the financial wherewithal to back their imagination, Ned's Atomic Dustbin soon translated their ideas into a phenomenal commercial success, peaking when *God Fodder* entered the UK charts at number four in 1991. The rest of the year was filled by hectic touring commitments, with America followed by Japan, a prestigious spot at the British Reading Festival, a UK number 21 hit with 'Trust', back to America (with Jesus Jones) and then a British tour which resulted in singer Jonn Penney collapsing from exhaustion on the last night.
Album: *God Fodder* (1991).

Nelson, Bill

b. William Nelson, 18 December 1948, Wakefield, West Yorkshire, England. Although noted chiefly for his innovative guitar work with Be-Bop Deluxe, his solo releases actually form more than four-fifths of his total output. *Smile* was a dreamy, acoustic debut after he had played throughout his home county with pre-progressive rock outfits like the Teenagers, Global Village and Gentle Revolution. He fronted Be-Bop Deluxe for most of the 70s before responding to punk and techno-rock forces by assembling Bill Nelson's Red Noise. *Sound-On-Sound*, released in 1979, was an agitated but confused debut from Red Noise and afterwards Nelson returned to solo work. The single 'Do You Dream In Colour?' provided his highest UK solo chart placing at number 52. It was released on his own label, Cocteau Records. Following a short-lived deal with Mercury Records he continued to release introspective, chiefly home-recorded albums. He was in demand as a producer and worked on sessions with many new-wave bands including the Skids and A Flock Of Seagulls. Surprisingly, after the demise of Be-Bop Deluxe he showed little inclination to use the guitar and preferred to experiment with keyboards and sampled sounds, composing thematic pieces which have been used in films and plays. He recorded backing music for the Yorkshire Actors Company's version of both *Das Kabinett* and *La Belle Et La Bette*, issued later as albums. Many of his releases throughout the 80s were of a whimsical, self-indulgent nature and missed the input of other musicians. Numerous albums were issued via his fan club and the quality was rarely

matched by the prolificacy, which twice ran to four-album boxed sets, *Trial By Intimacy* and *Demonstrations Of Affection*. In 1991 he moved markedly towards a stronger and more defined melodic style with *Luminous* on Manchester's independent label, Imaginary, and also spoke of returning to his first love, the guitar.
Albums: *Smile* (1971), *Sound On Sound* (1979), *Quit Dreaming And Get On The Beam* (1981), *Sounding The Ritual Echo* (1981), *Das Kabinett* (1981), *La Belle Et La Bette* (1982), *The Love That Whirls* (1982), *Chimera* (1983), *The Two Fold Aspect Of Everything* (1984), *Trial By Intimacy* (1984), *Map Of Dreams* (1984), *Aconography* (1986), *Chamber Of Dreams* (1986), *Summer Of God's Piano* (1986), *Chance Encounters In The Garden Of Light* (1988), *Optimism* (1988), *Pavillions Of The Heart And Soul* (1989), *Demonstrations Of Affection* (1989), *Duplex* (1989), *Luminous* (1991). Compilation: *Duplex: The Best Of Bill Nelson* (1990).

Newman, Colin

A founder member of Wire, guitarist/vocalist Newman began a solo career upon the group's demise in 1980. The promising *A-Z* continued the tenor of the artist's work on the preceding Wire album, *154*, and featured erstwhile colleagues Robert Gotobed (drums) and Mike Thorne (production). Two sets appeared the following year with the purely instrumental set *Provisionally Entitled The Singing Fish* offering an alternative insight to Newman's talents. *Not To*, issued a mere six months later, echoed the style of the artist's debut, but marked a temporary pause in his recording career. Newman initially withdrew from music; however, having obtained a grant, he journeyed to India to complete a series of recordings. His return in 1984 sparked the seeds for that year's Wire reunion; since then commitments to the group have been punctuated by further solo outings.
Albums: *A-Z* (1980), *Resurgence* (1981), *Provisionally Entitled The Singing Fish* (1981), *Not To* (1982), *Commercial Suicide* (1986), *It Seems* (1988).

New Model Army

With their roots embedded in the punk era, New Model Army were formed in Bradford, Yorkshire, in 1982, and immediately outlined their manifesto by naming themselves after the Sir Thomas Fairfax/Oliver Cromwell revolutionary army. References to this particular period of English history is not uncommon in post-punk rock, as can be seen in the lyrics of Blyth Power. Comprising Justin 'Slade The Leveller' Sullivan (b. 1956; guitar/vocals), Jason 'Moose' Harris (b. 1968; bass/guitar) and Robb Heaton (b. 1962; drums/guitar) their brand of punk folk/rock attracted a loyal cult following, much of

New Model Army

whom held a grievance towards the Tory government policies of the 80s as they came from towns and inner cities affected by unemployment. The groups championing of traditional working class ethics saw an unexpected boost for a dying art and trade; that of the clog. After releasing singles on Abstract, scoring a number 2 UK independent chart hit with 'The Price' (1984), they formed an unlikely alliance with the major company EMI, which saw the band acquire a higher profile and a significantly increased recording budget. They eventually broke through to a wider audience with 'No Rest' which peaked at number 28 on the UK Top 75 singles chart in 1985 - a position they were never to beat in an impressive run of 12 UK chart singles between 1985 and 1991. With often inflammatory lyrics, the band have never compromised their beliefs for commercial gain. They ran into trouble with the BBC *Top Of The Pops* chart show for donning T-shirts with the (albeit laudable) slogan, 'Only Stupid Bastards Use Heroin'. They continue to release quality albums, with considerable crossover potential, yet maintain credibility with their original fan-base. In December 1991, the group left EMI.
Albums: *Vengeance* (1984), *No Rest For The Wicked* (1985), *Ghost Of Cain* (1986), *Impurity* (1987), *Radio Sessions* (1988), *Thunder And Consolation* (1989), *Raw Melody Men* (1990). Compilation: *History* (1992).

New Musik

This UK pop group comprised Tony Mansfield (guitar/keyboards/vocals), Tony Hibbert (bass), Phil Towner (drums) and Clive Gates (keyboards). They came to prominence after a minor hit in 1979 with 'Straight Lines', during 1980 with three pop/synthesizer hits on the GTO label, 'Living By Numbers', 'The World Of Water' and 'Sanctuary'. Mansfield regarded their debut *From A To B* as rudimentary, but the succeeding *Anywhere* fared less well, despite its evident maturity. The change in style also took its toll on the band with the departure of Hibbert and Towner soon after its release. They were replaced by electronic percussionist Cliff Venner for the band's final and rather uninspired *Warp*. Full of empty electronic dance tracks it was notable for an daring attempt at the Beatles' *All You Need Is Love*. However, sales were very poor and they soon disbanded. Mansfield went on to produce hits for Captain Sensible, Mari Wilson, Naked Eyes and worked on A-Ha's debut album *Hunting High And Low*.
Albums: *From A To B* (1980), *Anywhere* (1981), *Warp* (1982).

New Order

New Order

When Joy Division's Ian Curtis committed suicide in May 1980 the three remaining members, Bernard Sumner (b. Bernard Dicken, 4 January 1956, Salford, Manchester, England; guitar/vocals), Peter Hook (b. 13 February 1956, Manchester, England; bass) and Stephen Morris (b. 28 October 1957, Macclesfield, Cheshire, England; drums) continued under the name New Order. Sumner took over vocal duties and the trio embarked upon a low-key tour of the USA, intent on continuing as an entity independent of the massive reputation Joy Division had achieved shortly before their demise. Later that same year they recruited Morris's girlfriend, Gillian Gilbert (b. 27 January 1961, Manchester, England; keyboards/guitar) and wrote and rehearsed their debut, *Movement*, which was released the following year. Their first single 'Ceremony', penned by Joy Division, was a UK Top 40 hit in the spring of 1981, and extended the legacy of their previous band. Hook's deep, resonant bassline and Morris's crisp, incessant drumming were both Joy Division trademarks. The vocals, however, were weak, Sumner clearly at this stage feeling uncomfortable as frontman. Much was made, in 1983, of the band's 'rising from the ashes' of Joy Division, in the music press, when *Power, Corruption And Lies* was released. Their experimentation with electronic gadgetry was fully realised and the album contained many surprises and memorable songs. The catchy bass riff and quirky lyrics of 'Age Of Consent' made it an instant classic, while the sign-off line, on the otherwise elegiac 'Your Silent Face', 'You've caught me at a bad time. So why don't you piss off', showed that Sumner no longer felt under any pressure to match the poetic, introspective lyricism of Ian Curtis. As well as redefining their sound they clearly now relished the role of 'most miserable sods in pop'.

'Blue Monday', released at this time in 12-inch format only, went on to become the biggest selling 12-inch single of all-time in the UK. In 1983 'disco' was a dirty word amongst the independent fraternity and 'Blue Monday', which combined an infectious dance beat with a calm, aloof vocal, was a brave step into uncharted territory. As well as influencing a legion of UK bands, it would be looked back upon as a crucial link between the disco of the 70s and the dance/house music wave at the end of the 80s. New Order had now clearly established themselves, and throughout the 80s and into the 90s they remained the top independent band in the UK, staying loyal to Manchester's Factory Records. Their subsequent collaboration with 'hot' New York hip-hop producer Arthur Baker spawned the anti-climactic 'Confusion' (1983) and 'Thieves Like Us' (1984). Both singles continued their preference for the 12-inch format, stretching in excess of six minutes, and stressing their lack of concern for the exposure gained by recording with mainstream radio in mind. *Low Life* appeared in 1985 and is perhaps their most consistently appealing album to date. While the 12-inch version of *Low Life*'s 'Perfect Kiss' was a magnificent single, showing the band at their most inspired and innovative, the collaboration with producer John Robie on the single version of 'Subculture' indicated that their tendency to experiment and 'play around' could also spell disaster.

Their next album, *Brotherhood* in 1986, although containing strong tracks such as 'Bizarre Love Triangle' offered nothing unexpected. It wasn't until the UK Top 5 single 'True Faith' in 1987, produced and co-written by Stephen Hague hot on the heels of his success with the Pet Shop Boys and accompanied by an award-winning Phillipe Decouffle video, that New Order found themselves satisfying long term fans and general public alike. The following year Quincy Jones' remix of 'Blue Monday' provided the group with another Top 5 hit. If the recycling of old songs and proposed 'personal' projects fuelled rumours of a split then 1989's *Technique* promptly dispelled them. The album, recorded in Ibiza, contained upbeat bass-and-drums-dominated tracks that characterized the best of their early output. Its most striking feature, however, was their flirtation with the popular Balearic style as in the hit single 'Fine Time', which contained lines like 'I've met a lot of cool chicks, But I've never met a girl with all her own teeth', delivered in a voice that parodied Barry White's notoriously sexist, gravelly vocals of the 70s. Meanwhile the band had changed significantly as a live act. Their reputation for inconsistency and apathy, as well as their staunch refusal to play encores, was by now replaced with confident, crowd-pleasing hour-long sets. In the summer of 1990 they reached the UK number 1 position with 'World In Motion', accompanied by the England World Cup Squad, with a song that earned the questionable accolade of best football record of all time, and caused a band member to observe that 'this is probably the last straw for Joy Division fans'. Rather than exploiting their recent successes with endless tours, the group unexpectedly branched out into various spin-off ventures. Hook formed the hard-rocking Revenge, Sumner joined former Smiths' guitarist Johnny Marr in Electronic and Morris/Gilbert recorded an album under the self-effacing title, *The Other Two*. The extra-curricular work prompted persistent rumours that New Order had irrevocably split, but no official announcement or press admission was forthcoming. In the summer of 1991 the group announced that they had reconvened for a new album, scheduled for release in 1992.

Albums: *Movement* (1981), *Power, Corruption And Lies* (1983), *Low Life* (1985), *Brotherhood* (1986), *Substance* (1987), *Technique* (1989). Compilations: *New Order 1981-2* (1982), *The Peel Sessions* (1990).

Newtown Neurotics

Formed in the English post-war 'new town' of Harlow, Essex, the Newtown Neurotics produced their finest blend of punk rock with a strong left-wing political slant. Coming together in the spring of 1978, the group comprised Steve Drewett (vocals/guitars), Colin Dredd (bass/vocals) and Tiggy Barber (drums). 'Hypocrite' (1979) and 'When The Oil Runs Out' (1980) appeared on their own No Wonder label, after which Barber was replaced by Simon Lomond. The Neurotics became increasingly involved in the agit-pop and ranting poetry scenes throughout the 80s, regularly playing at benefit concerts and festivals with the likes of Attila The

New York Dolls

Stockbroker. The strong socialist rhetoric was apparent on their third single on the short-lived but impressive CNT label, 'Kick Out The Tories' in May 1982, followed in December by an attack on Britain's 'Licensing Hours'. When CNT folded, the Newtown Neurotics moved to Razor Records for their debut. *Beggars Can Be Choosers* was an entertaining yet pertinent mix of scathing observation and new wave power and was promoted on single by a cover of the Ramones' 'Blitzkrieg Bop'. November 1984 saw the band move back to their No Wonder label for 'Suzie Is A Heartbreaker' (again hinting at Ramones' favourites), before the Neurotics dropped the 'Newtown' from their name, signing to Jungle Records in the process. The first fruits of this deal emerged as *Repercussions* in 1985, showcasing a group who'd lost none of their musical vigour or political evangelism. 'Living With Unemployment' followed in 1986 (with the help of ranting comedian Porky The Poet and the rumbustious Attila), preceding *Kickstarting A Backfiring Nation*. The Neurotics turned up occasionally during the late 80s (with 'Is Your Washroom Breeding Bolshovics?', for example) while the new decade was celebrated with *45 Revolutions Per Minute*, a singles compilation of the band's 'twelve blazing rock anthems' from 1979-84.

Albums: *Beggars Can Be Choosers* (1983), *Repercussions* (1985), *Kickstarting A Backfiring Nation* (1986), *Is Your Washroom Breeding Bolshovics?* (1988). Compilations: *45 Revolutions Per Minute* (1990).

New York Dolls

One of the most influential rock bands of the last 20 years, the New York Dolls pre-dated the punk and sleaze-metal movements which followed long after their own demise. Formed in 1972, the line-up stabilized with David Johansen (vocals), Johnny Thunders (guitar), Arthur Harold Kane (bass), Sylvain Sylvain (guitar/piano) and Jerry Nolan (drums), the last two having replaced Rick Rivets and Billy Murcia (who died in November 1972). The band sported an outrageous, glam-rock image: lipstick, high-heels and tacky leather outfits being the norm. Underneath, they were a first rate rock 'n' roll band, dragged up on the music of Stooges, Rolling Stones and MC5. Their self-titled debut, released in 1973, is a minor landmark in rock history, oozing attitude, vitality and controversy from every note. It was met with widespread critical acclaim, but this never transferred to commercial success. The follow-up, *Too Much Too Soon*, was an appropriate title and indicated that alcohol and drugs were beginning to take their toll. The album is a charismatic collection of punk/glam-rock anthems, delivered with a chaotic coolness, that has yet to be equalled. It received a unanimous thumbs down from the music press and the band began to implode shortly afterwards. Johansen embarked on a solo career and Thunders formed Heartbreakers. The Dolls continued for a short time with Blackie Lawless (now W.A.S.P.'s vocalist) on guitar, before eventually grinding to a halt in 1975. Jerry Nolan died as a result of a stroke on 14 January 1992 whilst undergoing treatment for pneumonia and meningitis. *Red Patent Leather* is a poor quality and posthumously-released live recording from May 1975.

Albums: *New York Dolls* (1973), *Too Much Too Soon* (1974), *Red Patent Leather* (1984). Compilation: *Lipstick Killers* (1983).

Nightingales

After a series of low-key UK school bands, Robert Lloyd (b. 1959, Cannock, Staffordshire, England) formed the Prefects - one of the earliest punk bands - who toured with the Clash. They split up in 1979 and Lloyd assembled the Nightingales using the best of the musicians who had passed through the ranks of the Prefects. The first of many subsequent Nightingales line-ups were Alan and Paul Apperley, Joe Crow, Eamonn Duffy and Lloyd himself. They were ably championed by BBC disc jockey John Peel, for whom Lloyd has recorded more sessions under various guises than any other artist. Peel himself said of them: '(their performances) will serve to confirm their excellence when we are far enough distanced from the 1980s to look at the period rationally, and other, infinitely better known bands stand revealed as charlatans'. The Nightingales' debut single, 'Idiot Strength', was released in 1981 on the band's own Vindaloo label in association with Rough Trade. Joe Crow then departed and his replacements, Nick Beales and Andy Lloyd, two of 15 personnel who would pass through the ranks, brought a totally different sound to the band. The Cherry Red label picked them up and the band's career began in earnest. Lloyd soon established himself as one of the more interesting lyricists of the independent chart. Most of his tirades were draped in humour: 'I'm too tired to do anything today, but tomorrow I'll start my diet, and answer some of my fan mail ('Elvis: The Last Ten Days'). Alternatively: 'I worked in a bakery . . . the jokes were handed down like diseases, I only worked there for the bread.' The lack of success of the subsequent releases led Lloyd and friends to the new Red Flame label started by Dave Kitson, the promoter of the Moonlight Club in London's Hampstead. Still unhappy with the way record companies were handling his band's career, Lloyd decided to reactivate the Vindaloo label. Ironically,

this led to the demise of the Nightingales as Lloyd needed to spend more time as songwriter, producer and label boss for his relatively successful roster of artists such as We've Got A Fuzzbox And We're Gonna Use It and Ted Chippington. When Fuzzbox toured America, taking the Nightingales' keyboard player with them, Lloyd dissolved the group and concentrated on a solo career.

Albums: *Pigs On Purpose* (1982), *Hysterics* (1983), *Just The Job* (1983), *In The Good Old Country Ways* (1986).

Nine Below Zero

Nine Below Zero

A British rhythm & blues band of the late 70s, the group took its name from a song by Sonny Boy Williamson II and was led by guitarist/singer Dennis Greaves and virtuoso harmonica player Mark Feltham. With Peter Clark (bass/vocals) and Kenny Bradley (drums), Feltham recorded the EP *Packed Fair And Square* (1979). This led to a recording deal with A&M and a live recording at London's Marquee Club where Nine Below Zero had a residency. The producer was Glyn Johns. With Stix Burkey replacing Bradley, the second album included some original songs while *Third Degree* was a minor UK hit. The band dissolved in the mid-80s as Feltham concentrated on session work and Greaves went on to a solo career and became a member of the Truth. However, Feltham revived Nine Below Zero at the end of the decade, signing a new recording contract with the China label.

Albums: *Live At The Marquee* (1980), *Don't Point Your Finger* (1981), *Third Degree* (1982), *Live At The Venue* (1990).

999

This London-based, UK punk band was formed in May 1977. Dispensing with earlier names such as the Dials, 48 Hours and the Fanatics, Nick Cash (b. Keith Lucas, 6 May 1950, Gosport, Hampshire, England; guitar/vocals) was a former Kilburn And The High Roads guitarist and studied at Canterbury College Of

Art under Ian Dury. Cash teamed up with Guy Days (guitar), Jon Watson (bass) and Pablo LaBrittain (drums) who set out to establish themselves on the thriving live scene in the capital. After releasing the fiery 'I'm Alive' on their own LaBrittain Records, United Artists signed them and quickly re-issued it. Two further singles, 'Nasty Nasty' and 'Emergency' were equally memorable for their energetic melodies, though 1978's debut album featured several weaker tracks. *Separates* was stronger, with compelling numbers like the single 'Homicide' resorting to muscular choruses instead of simple speed. However, LaBrittain was the subject of a motoring accident on the band's return from Scandinavia, and was replaced by friend Ed Case. With high sales of all their product in the USA, the band undertook a series of lucrative tours across the Atlantic, which earned them a degree of resentment from domestic supporters. Following the return of LaBrittain to the fold, the group signed a new contract with Radarscope Records, eventually transferring to Polydor. *The Biggest Prize In Sport* and *Concrete* represented their most accomplished work, although two follow-up cover version singles were evidence that inspiration was in short supply. This observation is certainly true of 1983's *13th Floor Madness*, though their last studio album *Face To Face* was more convincing. By the end of 1985 Watson had left and was replaced by Danny Palmer, with the band once more concentrating on touring in Europe and America. More recently, in the 90s, they have been the subject of a welter of compilations and live albums in the wake of renewed interest in punk nostalgia.

Albums: *999* (1978), *Separates* (1978), *The Biggest Prize In Sport* (1980), *Concrete* (1981), *13th Floor Madness* (1983), *Face to Face* (1985), *In Case Of Emergency* (1986). Compilations: *Greatest Hits* (1984), *Lust Power And Money* (1987), *The Early Stuff - The UA Years* (1992).

Nirvana

Nirvana

Formed in Aberdeen, Washington, USA in 1988,

Nirvana originally comprised Kurt Cobain, 20 February 1967; guitar/vocals), Chris Novoselic (b. 16 May 1965; bass) and Dave Grohl (b. 14 January 1969; drums). Grohl was 'something like our sixth drummer', explained Cobain, and had been recruited from east coast band Dave Brammage, having previously played with Scream, who recorded for Minor Threat's influential Dischord label. Their original drummer was Chad Channing; at one point Dinosaur Jr's J. Mascis had been touted as a permanent fixture, along with Dan Peters from Mudhoney. Having been signed by the Seattle-based Sub Pop label, the trio completed their debut single, 'Love Buzz'/'Big Cheese', the former a song written and first recorded by 60s Dutch group, Shocking Blue. Second guitarist Jason Everman was then added prior to *Bleach*, which cost a meagre $600 to record. The set confirmed Nirvana's ability to match heavy riffs with melody and it quickly attracted a cult following. However, Channing left the group following a European tour, and as a likely replacement proved hard to find, Dan Peters from labelmates Mudhoney stepped in on a temporary basis. He was featured on the single 'Sliver', Nirvana's sole 1990 release. Everman also dropped out of the line-up, but new drummer David Grohl reaffirmed a sense of stability. The revamped trio secured a prestigious deal with Geffen Records whose faith was rewarded with *Nevermind*, which broke them commercially. This was a startling collection of songs which transcended structural boundaries. It topped the US charts early in 1992, eclipsing much-vaunted competition from Michael Jackson and Dire Straits. and topped many polls for the Album of the Year. The opening track, 'Smells Like Teen Spirit', echoed the crossover appeal of the Pixies and by reaching the UK Top 10, the single confirmed that Nirvana now combined critical and popular acclaim. In early 1992 the romance of Cobain and Courtney Love of Hole was sealed when the couple married.

Albums: *Bleach* (1989), *Nevermind* (1991).

Nitzer Ebb

The driving forces behind this electronic-based band were Douglas McCarthy (b. 1 September 1966, Chelmsford, Essex, England; vocals) and Bon Harris (b. 12 August 1965, Chelmsford, Essex, England; percussion/vocals). Inspired by bands like DAF, Bauhaus and the Birthday Party, they began their first experiments with synthesizers and drum machines in 1983. They were joined in their amateur pursuits by school-mate David Gooday. They had summoned enough experience and confidence to release their first single the next year, 'Isn't It Funny How Your Body Works', on the Power Of Voice Communications label. They were nothing if not prolific, releasing a further five singles over the next

twelve months, which led to a deal with the premier UK electronic stable Mute, and Geffen in the USA. Their debut, *That Total Age*, (1987) was also the beginning of a long-term relationship with producer Flood, who would remix the single 'Join In The Chant'. On Gooday's departure Julian Beeston was enrolled. After a lengthy European tour with Depeche Mode, the band recorded *Belief*, and in 1989 followed up their own world tour with *Showtime*. Their third album revealed a swing in attitude, with music that was less confrontational and more consumer-friendly. This was particularly true in the USA, where the single 'Fun To Be Had' peaked at number 2 in the US dance charts. *Ebbhead* has confirmed their popularity with fans and a previously reluctant press. As McCarthy puts it: 'With the advent of *Ebbhead*, I think we've managed to twist listenability around to our way of thinking'.
Albums: *That Total Age* (1987), *Belief* (1988), *Showtime* (1989), *Ebbhead* (1991).

No Means No

This hardcore trio from Vancouver, Canada, have done much to expand the boundaries of the genre, fusing funk and fuzz pop with a continually questioning lyrical stance. The line-up features Andrew Kerr (guitar) and the brothers Rob Wright (bass) and John Wright (drums). Kerr joined shortly after their 1984 debut *Mama*. Recording for the Dead Kennedys' label Alternative Tentacles, they released an album backing Jello Biafra in 1991 which helped to introduce them to a larger audience in the UK. Taking their name from the phrase commonly used in connection with the rights of rape victims, their lyrics explore the middle ground between the individual and society, often in tones of self disgust: 'nobody knows you and nobody wants to' (from 'Body Bag'). Their abject rejection of the media, particularly the refusal to have press photos taken, has so far limited their accessibility. However, their extensive popularity in Europe is some compensation.
Albums: *Mama* (1984), *You Kill Me* (1985), *Sex Mad* (1987), *The Day Everything Became Nothing* (1988), *63* (1989), *Small Parts Isolated And Destroyed* (1989), *Wrong* (1989), with Jello Biafra *The Sky Is Falling And I Want My Mommy* (1991) *Live And Cuddly* (1991), *0 + 2 = 0* (1991).

Northside. This UK independent label dance music band was formed mid-1989 in Manchester by Warren 'Dermo' Dermody (vocals), Cliff Ogier (bass), Timmy Walsh (guitar) and Paul Walsh (drums). After signing to the premier Manchester independent Factory Records they released two singles in 1990, 'Shall We Take A Trip' and 'Rising Star', which benefited from the 'Madchester' explosion brought about by the success of label mates Happy Mondays.

Pilloried in the press as being an opportunistic 'baggy' band, their releases have so far done little to persuade critics of any real significance to their shambolic dance shuffles.
Album: *Chicken Rhythms* (1991).

Numan, Gary

b. Gary Anthony James Webb, 8 March 1958, Hammersmith, London, England. Originally appearing under the group name Tubeway Army, Numan enjoyed enormous success in the UK at the close of the 70s. His Kraftwerk/David Bowie-influenced electronic music saw Tubeway Army top the UK charts with 'Are Friends Electric?' By the end of 1979 Numan abandoned the group pseudonym for the follow-up single 'Cars' which also topped the UK charts and reached the US Top 10. At his peak, Numan was one of the best-selling artists in Britain and his albums *The Pleasure Principle* and *Telekon* both entered the charts at number 1. His science-fiction-orientated lyrics and synthesizer-based rhythms brought further Top 10 successes with 'We Are Glass', 'I Die: You Die', 'She's Got Claws' and 'We Take Mystery (To Bed)'. As the decade progressed his record sales steadily declined and his glum-robotic persona was replaced by that debonair man-about-town who also enjoyed aviation. In March 1982 he attempted to fly around the world in his light aircraft and was arrested in India on suspicion of spying. The charge was later dropped. While his reputation among music critics atrophied amid accusations of anachronism, his fan base remained solid and his recordings continue to reach the lower placings in the UK charts.
Albums: as Tubeway Army *Replicas* (1979), solo *The Pleasure Principle* (1979), *Telekon* (1980), *Living Ornaments 1979-80* (1981), *Dance* (1981), *I Assassin* (1982), *Warriors* (1983), *The Plan* (1984), *Berserker* (1984), *White Noise - Live* (1985), *The Fury* (1985), *Strange Charm* (1986), *Exhibition* (1987), *Metal Rhythm* (1988), *The Skin Mechanic* (1989), *Outland* (1991). Compilation: *New Man Numan - The Best Of Gary Numan* (1982).

Nuns

Formed in San Francisco, USA, in 1977, the Nuns were one of the city's leading punk/new wave attractions. Their insubstantial progress was made even worse by continual line-up problems, but such frustrations coalesced in their EP 'Savage'/'Suicide Child'. Their work appeared on several compilations, including *Rodney On The Roq* and *Experiments In Destiny*, but having split up in 1979, they reformed the following year to complete *The Nuns*, only to disband again. Ritchie Detrick (vocals), Jeff Olener (vocals), Alejandro Escovado (guitar), Jennifer Miro (keyboards), Mike Varney (bass) and Jeff Raphael

(drums) were among those passing through the Nuns' ranks, of whom Escavado subsequently joined Rank And File.
Album: *The Nuns* (1980).

O'Connor, Hazel
b. 16 May 1955, Coventry, England. After moving to London in the late 60s, the 16-year-old O'Connor journeyed to Marrakesh where she was raped. She briefly married a Polish cellist, worked as an erotic dancer and starred in the soft-core pornographic movie *Girls Come First*. At the close of the 70s, she signed to the Albion label and issued the single 'Ee-I-Adio', which failed to sell. Her profile increased when she appeared in the film *Breaking Glass*, a melodramatic portrayal of a fictional rock star. O'Connor's aggressive singing style and confrontational appearance was used to good effect on the Tony Visconti produced 'Eighth Day' (complete with 'robotic' intonation) which reached the UK Top 5. The following year, she registered two further Top 10 singles, 'D-Days' and the uncharacteristic ballad 'Will You'. Various disputes with her record company and management slowed down her career. Although she had frequently appeared in the tabloid press, her well-documented outrages seemed exhausted by the time of her final chart appearance in 1982. Two years later, she recorded *Smile* for RCA but the record sold poorly and the label declined to renew her option. O'Connor subsequently appeared in the musical *Girlfriends* in 1987.
Albums: *Breaking Glass* (1980), *Sons And Lovers* (1980), *Glass Houses* (1980), *Cover Plus* (1981), *Smile* (1984).

OMD
This UK synthesizer pop duo comprised Paul Humphreys (b. 27 February 1960, Liverpool, England) and Andy McCluskey (b. 24 June 1959, Liverpool, England). Originally combining in school band Equinox they moved on through VCL XI and Hitlerz Underpantz, and finally The Id. When that band split in 1978 McCluskey spent a short time with Dalek I Love You before he and Humphreys, together with Paul Collister, performed live in October 1978 under their full title Orchestral Manoeuvres In The Dark. Tony Wilson of Factory

Records became interested in the band, releasing their debut 'Electricity'. It was quickly re-released when Virgin subsidiary DinDisc signed them. Its success subsequently allowed the group the chance to build their own studio. They replaced their 4-track recorder ('Winston') with real personnel Malcom Holmes (ex-Equinox and the Id) and Dave Hughes (Dalek I Love You). 1980 saw 'Red Frame/White Light' released as a single to preface the band's first, self-titled album. Their breakthrough, however, came with the UK Top 10 'Enola Gay', and its laboured nuclear war sentiments. *Organisation* followed quickly, with Martin Cooper replacing Dave Hughes shortly afterwards. The more sophisticated *Architecture And Morality* showed a new romanticism particularly in the singles 'Joan Of Arc' and 'Maid Of Orleans'. 1983's *Dazzle Ships* was a flawed attempt at progression, highlighting dilemmas forced on them by popularity and DinDisc's collapse (the band transferred to Virgin). *Junk Culture* faced similar critical disdain, and did not boast the presence of a hit single, as 'Locomotion' had done for Dazzle Ships. *Crush* was a less orchestrated and more immediate affair, featuring the return of political commentary alongside the permanent insertion of Graham and Neil Weir into the line-up. *The Pacific Age* was premiered on another of the band's frequent worldwide touring endeavours, but it was obvious from its chart position that their domestic popularity was slipping. The six-piece line-up was proving too cumbersome and the Weir brothers departed shortly afterwards. The rift was compounded when Holmes and Cooper and, more importantly, Humphreys joined the list of departures. McCluskey retained the name and, after a long restorative period, resurfaced in 1991 with 'Sailing On The Seven Seas'. The resultant album harkened back to the era of *Architecture And Morality*, including the use of choral effects. Meanwhile, Humphreys formed a new band under the name the Listening Pool.
Albums: *Orchestral Manoeuvres In The Dark* (1980), *Organisation* (1980), *Architecture And Morality* (1981), *Dazzle Ships* (1983), *Junk Culture* (1984), *Crush* (1985), *The Pacific Age* (1986), *Sugar Tax* (1991).

One Little Indian Records
The roots of UK's One Little Indian record label lie in the anarcho-punk scene of the early 80s, and one of its pioneering factions, Flux Of Pink Indians. The precursor to One Little Indian was Spiderleg, which released records by the System, Subhumans, and Amebix in addition to Flux's own material. Both labels were spearheaded by Derek Birkett (b. 18 February 1961, London, England), Flux's bass player, alongside friends and colleagues from the 80s independent punk scene. This was reflected in early releases, which included Annie Anxiety, D&V and

the Very Things. Reflecting on lessons hard learnt, the label used expensive and tasteful cover art provided by Paul White's Me Company. When the Sugarcubes, a band Birkett previously knew when they were Kukl, broke through, financial security was assured, and this has allowed the label to prosper. While One Little Indian remains the 'ethical indie', or one of them, the operation is constructed on level-headed business practices: 'Our motives are artistic and business is reality'. Unlike many labels, the roster of bands does not reflect any sort of corporate identity. The bright and breezy pop of the Popinjays, Heart Throbs and Sugarcubes contrasts with the dance-orientated Shamen and Fini Tribe. The extremes include the delicate, crafted pop of Kitchens Of Distinction and the shattering volume of What? Noise. In addition, the label was also the temporary home for They Might Be Giants and released *Lincoln* and two singles. The recent success of the Shamen has consolidated the label's position in the UK charts as well as their familiar residency of the Independent hit parade. The label has released several 'Best Of' compilations which act as a good introduction to their wares.

Compilations: *Greatest Hits: One Little Indian* (1988), *One Little Indian Takes On The Cowboys* (1988).

101ers

Formed in London in May 1974, the 101ers made their performing debut four months later at the Telegraph pub in Brixton. Led by guitarist/vocalist Joe Strummer, the group established itself on a fading pub-rock circuit about to be undermined by the advent of punk. Support slots by the Sex Pistols confirmed Strummer's growing agitation and he left to join the Clash in June 1976. The 101ers then broke up with Clive Timperley (guitar) later joining the Passions. Dan Kelleher (bass) moved on to the Derelicts and Richard Dudanski (drums) went on to work with the Raincoats and Public Image Limited. The group was commemorated by 'Keys To Your Heart', issued on the independent Chiswick label the following month. In 1981 Strummer sanctioned the release of *Elgin Avenue Breakdown*, a collection of live recordings, BBC sessions and studio out-takes. The material ranged from traditional R&B - 'Too Much Monkey Business', 'Route 66' - to ebullient originals which showed the singer's abrasive delivery already in place.

Album: *Elgin Avenue Breakdown* (1981).

1,000 Violins

This late 80s UK independent label group were formed in Sheffield, Yorkshire, and comprised Darren Swindells (bass), Colin Gregory (guitar), Vincent Keenan (vocals), David Warmsley (keyboards/guitar) and Ian Addie (drums). Their brand of 60s, US-influenced pop gave them three UK independent chart hits, the biggest being 'Locked Out Of The Love-In' (1987), which reached number 16. Their lone album was released on the US run Immaculate Records.

Album: *Hey Man, That's Beautiful* (1988).

Only Ones

Formed in 1976 with a line-up comprising: Peter Perrett (vocals/guitar), John Perry (guitar), Alan Mair (bass) and Mike Killie (drums). Although touted as a new wave group, the unit included several old lags; Mair had previously worked with the Beatstalkers, while Killie had drummed with Spooky Tooth, Peter Frampton and Balls. After a promising independent single, 'Lovers Of Today', the group were signed by CBS Records and made their debut with the searing opus, 'Another Girl, Another Planet'. Front man Perrett, with his leopard-skin jacket and Lou Reed drawl, won considerable music press attention and the group's first album *The Only Ones* (1978) was very well-received. A second self-produced collection, *Even Serpents Shine* (1979) was also distinctive, but internal group friction and disagreements with their record company hampered their progress. Producer Colin Thurston took control of *Baby's Got A Gun* (1980) which included a guest appearance by Pauline Murray, but lacked the punch of their earlier work. With sales dwindling, CBS dropped the group from their roster and the Only Ones finally split in 1981. Since that time the group, and in particular, Perrett, had frequently been hailed as a much underrated, and influential group. After over-coming a period of drug addiction, Perrett made known his intentions for a come-back in 1991.

Albums: *The Only Ones* (1978), *Even Serpents Shine* (1979), *Baby's Got A Gun* (1980), *The Only Ones Live* (1989), *The Peel Sessions* (1989). Compilation: *The Immortal Story* (1992).

Orange Juice

Formed in Scotland at the end of the 70s, this engaging and, in some quarters, revered, pop group comprised Edwyn Collins (vocals/lead guitar), James Kirk (vocals/rhythm guitar), David McClymont (bass) and Steven Daly (drums). They began their career on the cult independent label Postcard where they issued some of the best pop records of the early 80s, including 'Blue Boy' and 'Falling And Laughing'. Collins' coy vocal and innocent romanticism gave them a charm which was, matched by strong musicianship. After signing to Polydor, they issued *You Can't Hide Your Love Forever*, a highly accomplished effort that augured well for the future. At that point, the group suffered an internal shake-up with Kirk and Daly replaced by Malcolm Ross and Zeke Manyika. *Rip It Up* was another strong work,

Orange Juice; Edwyn Collins

Orb

and the insistent title track reached the UK Top 10. Further musical differences saw the group reduced to Collins and Manyika and they completed a energetic mini-album, *Texas Fever*, and an eponymous third album, which included the wistful 'What Presence?' Collins subsequently recorded a couple of singles with Paul Quinn, after which he embarked on a solo career that has yet to fulfil its early promise. Ross joined the line-up of Roddy Frame's Aztec Camera. Manyika also spawned solo projects on Polydor and Parlophone.

Albums: *You Can't Hide Your Love Forever* (1982), *Rip It Up* (1982), *Texas Fever* (1984). Compilation: *In A Nutshell* (1985).

Orb

The Orb consists of one man, Dr Alex Paterson, whose specialist field is the creation of ambient house music. A former Killing Joke roadie and A&R man at EG Records, he formed the original Orb with Jimmy Cauty of Brilliant, KLF, and Justified Ancients Of Mu Mu fame. They later added Youth, formerly of Killing Joke and Brilliant. Cauty departed first to go and play his own brand of atmospheric music with the KLF (who won the race to record the first ambient house album with *Chill Out*), and Youth departed shortly afterwards. The latest recruit is Thrash, who joined in late 1991 from more of a punk/metal background. Their debut album (and the remix album of similar title) is based on a journey to dimensions beyond known levels of consciousness. It has led to a plunge of remixes for other artists (including Front 242 and Primal Scream). The album contains the ethereal, spaced out single 'Little Fluffy Clouds', and is fully in tune with the blissed out rave subculture of the early 90s, mingled with dashes of early 70s progressive rock. There is also an album's worth of recordings for disc jockey John Peel's radio show. This includes a 20-minute version of 'Huge Ever Growing Pulsating Brain' which prompted fellow disc jockey Andy Kershaw to ring the BBC to complain, mockingly, about the return of hippy indulgence on a gross scale polluting the nation's airwaves. 1992's *U.F.Orb* release was described as a 40 minute single.

Albums: *Adventures Beyond The Ultraworld* (1991), *Peel Sessions* (1991), *The Ultraworld Excursion (Aubrey Mixes)* (1991), *U.F.Orb* (1992).

Orchestral Manoeuvres In The Dark (See OMD)

Otway, John

b. 2 October, 1952, Aylesbury, Buckinghamshire, England. The enigmatic madcap John Otway first came to prominence in the early 70s with his guitar/fiddle-playing partner Wild Willie Barrett. Otway's animated performances and unusual vocal style caught the attention of Pete Townshend, who produced the duo's first two Track label singles, 'Murder Man' and 'Louisa On A Horse'. Extensive gigging, highlighted by crazed and highly entertaining stage antics, won Otway and Barrett a loyal collegiate following and finally a minor hit with 'Really Free' in 1977. Its b-side, 'Beware Of The Flowers ('Cause I'm Sure They're Going To Get You Yeh)' was equally appealing and eccentric and augured well for further hits. Although Otway (with and without Barrett) soldiered on with syllable-stretching versions of Tom Jones's 'Green Green Grass Of Home' and quirky novelty workouts such as 'Headbutts', he remains a 70s curio, still locked into the UK college/club circuit.

Albums: *John Otway And Wild Willie Barrett* (1977), *Deep And Meaningless* (1978), *Where Did I Go Right* (1979), *Way And Bar* (1980), *All Balls And No Willy* (1982), *The Wimp And The Wild* (1989). Compilations: *Gone With The Bin Or The Best Of Otway And Barre* (1981), *Greatest Hits* (1986).

Further reading: *Cor Baby That's Really Me*, John Otway.

Our Daughters Wedding

This New York, USA electronic trio comprised Keith Silva (vocal), Layne Rico (synthesizers/vocal) and Scott (keyboards). After extensive gigging, they relocated to the UK and signed to EMI. In the summer of 1981, they broached the UK Top 40 with the catchy 'Lawnchairs'. The follow-up EP *The Digital Cowboy* gained considerable press but proved less commercial. Despite a strong record company investment, the trio lost ground and their sole album was followed by their demise.

Album: *Moving Windows* (1982).

Outcasts

At one time the premier punk band stationed in Northern Ireland, their line-up revolved around the three Cowan brothers; Greg (b. c.1961; bass/vocals), Martin (b. c.1955; guitar) and Colin (b. c.1957; drums). This was the nucleus, though Gordon Blair had temporarily replaced Greg when he was injured in a car crash. The line-up was completed by Getty (b. c.1960; guitar) and Raymond (b. c.1965; additional drums). An impressive early single 'Magnum Force' earned them the support of BBC disc jockey John Peel. They went on to release a solid debut album, characterized by the heavy rhythms produced by the twin drummers. However, before the release of *Seven Deadly Sins*, Colin became the second of the brothers to be injured in a car crash, this time fatally.

Albums: *Blood And Thunder* (1983), *Seven Deadly Sins* (1984).

Ozric Tentacles

Predominantly an 80s UK festival band, Ozric Tentacles was originally a name conjured up by the band for a psychedelic breakfast cereal. Their original line-up featured Ed Wynne (guitar), his brother Roly (bass), Nick 'Tig' Van Gelder (drums), Gavin Griffiths (guitar) and Joie 'Ozrooniculator' Hinton (keyboards). They met at an open camp fire at Stonehenge in 1982. By the following year a second synthesizer player, Tom Brookes had joined. They started gigging in clubs such as the 'Crypt' in Deptford, south-east London. There they met their second percussionist Paul Hankin. They soon became regulars at another psychedelic 'head' venue, the Club Dog, at the George Robey pub in Finsbury Park, north London. The band's long existence has seen a number of shifts in personnel. In 1984 Griffiths left to from the Ullulators, and Brookes left a year later. Hinton remained but also played for the aforementioned Ullulators and also the Oroonies. The next major change arrived in 1987 when Merv Peopler replaced Van Gelder. More recently Steve Everett has replaced Brookes on synthesizers, while Marcus Carcus and John Egan have added extra percussion and flute. Considering their lengthy career it might appear that the band have had a relatively sporadic, and recent, recording output. However, much of their work from the mid-80s onwards was made available on six cassette-only albums.

Into the early 90s, with the British neo-hippy, new age travellers receiving a higher media profile and their role in organizing music festivals becoming increasingly important, bands such as the Ozric Tentacles and the Levellers benefited greatly and began to widen their audience.

Albums: *Pungent Effulgent* (1989), *Erp Land* (1990), *Strangeitude* (1991).

Pale Fountains

Pale Fountains

Formed in Liverpool in the early 80s by songwriter Michael Head (guitar/vocals) and Chris McCaffrey (bass) with Thomas Whelan (drums) and Andy Diagram, formerly of Dislocation Dance and the Diagram Brothers. Having been assimilated into the early 80s 'quiet pop/Bossa Nova' movement, Pale Fountains also drew upon such influences as the Beatles, the Mamas And The Papas and Love, but were probably better known for wearing short baggy trousers. Previously on the Operation Twilight label,

the group to break into the big-time when they signed to the Virgin label. Despite this lucrative move, this highly-touted group never broke out of their cult status. Their highest national chart position was the UK Top 50 'Thank You' in 1982.
Albums: *Pacific Street* (1984), *From Across The Kitchen Table* (1985).

Pale Saints

Formed in Leeds, Yorkshire, England in 1989 by Ian Masters (b. 4 January 1964, Potters Bar, Hertfordshire, England; bass), Chris Cooper (b. 17 November 1966, Portsmouth, England; drums) and Graeme Naysmith (b. 9 February 1967, Edinburgh, Scotland; guitar) from an advertisement in a music paper. Aided by occasional guitarist Ashley Horner, who eventually concentrated on his other band, Edsel Auctioneer, on a full time basis, the Pale Saints spent a year playing local venues and perfecting an idiosyncratic array of material which relied heavily on textures and effects rather than traditional arrangements or blatantly commercial choruses. That was not to say that they were unattractive: their first ever London gig in the spring of 1989 brought them a record deal with the 4AD label, and their debut album of six months later, *The Comforts Of Madness*, earned the band much critical appreciation and the number 40 spot in the UK charts. Meriel Barham (b. 15 October 1964, Yorkshire, England) joined as a permanent guitarist/vocalist soon after, as Pale Saints continued their decidedly obtuse - if not downright perverse - path into the new decade with tours of Europe and Japan and an elegant cover version of Nancy Sinatra's 'Kinky Love' which reached number 72 in the UK charts.
Albums: *The Comforts Of Madness* (1990), *Mrs Dolphin* (1991, Japanese release).

Parachute Men

Formed in Leeds, Yorkshire, England in 1985 by Fiona Gregg (b. 26 July 1963, Norwich, Norfolk, England; vocals), Stephen H. Gregg (b. 29 November 1960, Bishop Auckland, Co. Durham, England; guitar), Andrew Howes (bass) and Mark Boyce (drums), the Parachute Men proved to have a bat's ear for a tune, yet were persistently undersold by circumstance. Signing to Fire Records in 1987 was a promising move, particularly when 'The Innocents' was released to extremely warm approval, but soon after Andrew Howes and Mark Boyce departed acrimoniously, leaving Fiona and Stephen H. Gregg to tour as an acoustic set-up until Matthew Parkin (bass) and Paul Walker (b. 7 July 1966, West Yorkshire, England; drummer) filled the vacancies. The second album was released well over a year after it was recorded, costing the band valuable momentum and causing Matthew Parker to be

replaced by Colleen Browne (b. 25 August 1966, Kelowna, Canada), but the Parachute Men continue to create lovingly-textured guitar sounds.
Albums: *The Innocents* (1988), *Earth, Dogs And Eggshells* (1990).

Paris Angels

This UK pop band was formed in November 1989 and were subsequently signed to Virgin Records. The embryonic line-up of Scott Carey (bass/harmonica), Rikki Turner (vocals/wind instruments), Simon Worrall (drums) and Paul Wagstaff (guitar) were joined by Jayne Gill (vocals/percussion) and Mark Adge (rhythm guitar/percussion), formerly the group's sound engineer. They blossomed with the addition of the computer-literate Steven Tajti to help with programming and effects. After releasing a version of David Bowie's 'Stay' they signed to Sheer Joy for 'Perfume' in June 1990. The group's blend of rock/dance pigeon-holed them as late arrivals to the Manchester scene and the award of a 'single of the week' in the *New Musical Express* and 10 weeks in the UK independent chart justified Virgin's decision to move in after two more singles on the independent label. The last of these, 'Oh Yes' in early 1991, became *Sounds'* last ever single of the week, before the paper folded. Their debut album and a re-recorded 'Perfume' have yet to embrace the spirit of adventure that is promised.
Album: *Sundew* (1991).

Passions

Passions

This English post-punk group, with definite pop leanings, was formed in June 1978 and comprised Barbara Gogan (b. Dublin, Eire; vocals/guitar), Mitch Barker (vocals), Clive Timperley (guitar/vocals), Claire Bidwell (bass/vocals) and Richard Williams (drums). All save Timperley had featured in Rivers Of Passion, while all except Bidwell had spent time in the various incarnations of the Derelicts between 1974-76. During this time Timperley also played with Joe Strummer's 101er's. Gogan left her Dublin home at the age of 18 and settled in France within a Marxist commune. She came to London in 1972 and moved into a 'squat' near Ladbroke Grove, where she became involved with the Derelicts, a loose collection of like-minded left wingers. Evolving into the Passions they released their first single, 'Needles And Pins', on the tiny Soho label, also home of the Nips and the Inmates. They lost Barker in 1979 when a broken leg put paid to his musical activities. Continuing as a four-piece they signed to Fiction for their debut album, and one single, 'Hunted'. Bidwell left in July 1980 to form Schwarze Kapelle and then joined the Wall. David Agar, once a member of the fledgling Spandau Ballet, replaced her. Three days later they were dropped by Fiction but fell immediately on their feet with a contract to Polydor. They finally found success in 1981 with their second single for the label, 'I'm In Love With A German Film Star'. It would be their only hit, despite the eloquence and strength of later material. Timperley left to run a health shop in December 1981, while the recruitment of Kevin Armstrong (ex-Local Heroes SW9) on guitar and Jeff Smith (ex-Lene Lovich band) on keyboards. Armstrong himself left in August 1982 to be replaced by Steve Wright, but by this time the band was in its death throes.

Albums: *Michael And Miranda* (1980), *Thirty Thousand Feet Over China* (1981), *Sanctuary* (1982).

Pearl Harbor And The Explosions

Formed in San Francisco, California in 1979, this much-touted attraction was centred on vocalist Pearl Harbor (b. 1958, Germany, of a Filipino mother), who, as Pearl E. Gates, had previously been a dancer in the Tubes live show. She subsequently joined Jane Dornacker in Leila And The Snakes, before taking the group's rhythm section - Hilary Stench (bass) and John Stench (drums) - in this new act. Their act continued the theatricality of the Tubes, but Gates was more interested in conventional rock 'n' roll. To this end she recruited Peter Bilt (guitar) and formed Pearl Harbor And The Explosions in October 1978. They specialized in old fashioned rock 'n' roll/rockabilly spiced with 'new wave' energy. Their debut single 'Drivin'' (which was later covered by Jane Aire And The Belvederes) came out on the independent 415 Records label and became an cult hit. Its success encouraged Warner Brothers to sign the group. Their self-titled debut was a strong, promising work, but the group failed to complete a follow-up. They split in June 1980 leaving Pearl to continue with a solo album *Don't Follow Me I'm Lost* under her new name Pearl Harbor. The album was produced by Nicky Gallagher (former member of Ian Dury's Blockheads). The Stench brothers joined ex-Jefferson Airplane guitarist Jorma Kaukonen in Vital Parts, before embarking on an association with cult

avant garde act Chrome.

Albums: *Pearl Harbor And The Explosions* (1979), as Pearl Harbor *Don't Follow Me, I'm Lost* (1981).

Pearl Jam

This grunge-rock quintet were formed in Seattle, USA in the early 90s, and were put together by former Mother Love Bone members Jeff Ament (bass) and Stone Gossard (rhythm guitar). With former Temple Of The Dog guitarist Mike McCready, drummer Dave Krusen and vocalist Eddie Vedder completing the line-up, the band signed to Epic in 1991. Debuting the following year with *Ten*, they successfully incorporated elements of Soundgarden, Mother Love Bone, Nirvana and Temple Of The Dog with older influences such as the Doors, Velvet Underground, the Stooges and the MC5. Dynamic live performances and a subtle commercial edge to their material has catapulted them from total obscurity to virtual superstars in a very short time.

Album: *Ten* (1992).

Peel, John

b. John Robert Parker Ravenscroft, 30 August 1939, Heswall, Cheshire, England. Having moved to the USA during the early 60s to work in his father's cotton business, Peel's musical knowledge engendered several guest appearances on Dallas radio stations. By cultivating his near-Liverpool birthright, he became something of a local celebrity in the wake of Beatlemania which in turn led to a full-time job as a disc jockey on Oklahoma's KOMA station. By 1966 he was working at KMEN in San Bernadino, California, but the following year John returned to Britain where his knowledge of emergent US underground rock led to his joining the pirate radio ship Radio London. Now stripped of his 'Ravenscroft' surname in favour of a snappier appellation, Peel achieved almost instant fame for his late-night *Perfumed Garden* programme which introduced the then-mysterious delights of Country Joe And The Fish, the Velvet Underground and Captain Beefheart And His Magic Band to unsuspecting UK audiences. When the Marine Offences Bill effectively outlawed pirate radio, Peel moved to the BBC's new Radio 1 where he latterly took control of Sunday afternoon's *Top Gear*. Here, he continued to promote 'new' music, airing progressive acts from Britain and America and giving a plethora of groups, including Pink Floyd, Soft Machine, Jethro Tull, Moby Grape, Grateful Dead, Jefferson Airplane, Buffalo Springfield and Fleetwood Mac, their first substantive airings. Peel also established the ambitious Dandelion label, the roster of which included Medicine Head and Kevin Coyne, but his closest ties lay with Marc Bolan and

Tyrannosaurus Rex, whose later success was due, in part, to Peel's unswerving support during their early career. Rod Stewart and the Faces were also strong favourites although the Peel's influence lessened during the early 70s as their music became increasingly predictable. Peel nonetheless promoted such experimental acts as Matching Mole and Can, as well as reggae and soul, before finding renewed enthusiasm with the advent of punk. Saturation airplay of the first Ramones album alienated many entrenched listeners, but it excited a new, and generally younger, audience. Once again Peel, with the guidance of ever-present producer John Walters, was in the vanguard of an exciting musical upheaval as he broadcast material by Siouxsie And The Banshees, Joy Division, the Undertones and the Fall, the latter two of which were particular favourites. John Peel remains an important and influential figure. The sole survivor of Radio 1's initial intake, his weekend shows still gnaw at the barriers of popular music, be it rap, hardcore, reggae or ethnic music. The highly-successful *Peel Sessions* EP series on the Strange Fruit label, drawn from the extensive library of live performances recorded for his programmes, are a tribute to his intuition.

Compilations: various artist sessions recorded especially for Peel's programmes *Before The Fall - The Peel Sessions* (1991), *Winters Of Discontent - The Peel Sessions* (1991), *The New Breed - The Peel Sessions* (1991), *Too Pure - The Peel Sessions* (1992).

Pere Ubu

Formed in Cleveland, Ohio, USA in 1975, and taking their name from Alfred Jarry's surrealist play, Pere Ubu evolved from several of the region's experimental groups, including Rocket From The Tombs and Foggy And The Shrimps. Their initial line-up, comprising David Thomas (vocals), Peter Laughner (guitar), Tom Herman (guitar/bass/organ), Tim Wright (guitar/bass), Allen Ravenstine (synthesizer/saxophone) and Scott Krauss (drums) completed the compulsive '30 Seconds Over Tokyo', while a second single, 'Final Solution', was recorded following Ravenstine's departure. Wright and Laughner then left the fold, but new bassist Tony Maimone augmented the nucleus of Thomas, Herman and Krauss before the prodigal Ravenstine returned to complete the most innovative version of the group. Two more singles, 'Street Waves' and 'The Modern Dance', were released before the quintet secured an international recording deal. Their debut, *The Modern Dance*, was an exceptional collection, blending new-wave art-rock with early Roxy Music. Rhythmically, the group evoked Captain Beefheart's Magic Band while Thomas's vocal gymnastics were both distinctive and compelling. Two further releases, *Dub Housing* and

New Picnic Time, maintained this sense of adventure although the demonstrable power of that debut set was gradually becoming diffuse. Nonetheless, the three albums displayed a purpose and invention which deservedly received considerable critical approval.

In 1979 Tom Herman was replaced by former Red Crayola guitarist Mayo Thompson, who introduced a sculpted, measured approach to what had once seemed a propulsive, intuitive sound. *The Art Of Walking*, was deemed obtuse, and the group became pigeon-holed as both difficult and inconsequential. A dissatisfied Kraus left the line-up, and Anton Fier (ex-Feelies) joined Pere Ubu for the disappointing *Song Of The Bailing Man*. This lightweight selection appeared following the release of *The Sound Of The Sand*, David Thomas's first solo album, and reflected a general disinterest in the parent group's progress. Maimone then joined Krauss in Home And Garden, Herman surfaced with a new group, Tripod Jimmie, while Ravenstine and Thompson collaborated within a restructured Red Crayola. Thomas meanwhile enjoyed the highest profile with a further five albums. By 1985 both Maimone and Ravenstine were working with the singer's new group, the Wooden Birds. Scott Kraus set the seeds of a Pere Ubu reunion by appearing for an encore during a Cleveland concert. 'It walked like a duck, looked like a duck, quacked like a duck, so it was a duck,' Thomas later remarked and by the end of 1987, the Ubu name had been officially re-instated. Jim Jones (guitar) and Chris Cutler (drums) completed the new line-up for the exceptional *Tenement Year*, which coupled the charm of earlier work with a newfound accessibility. *Cloudland* emphasized this enchanting direction although the group's age-old instability still threatened their long-term ambitions. Both Cutler and Ravenstine left the line-up. The latter was replaced by Eric Drew Feldman, formerly of Captain Beefheart. Pere Ubu's ultimate fate depends on their ability to contain their disparate personalities and individual ambitions.

Albums: *The Modern Dance* (1977), *Dub Housing* (1978), *Datapanik In The Year Zero* (1979), *New Picnic Time* (1979), *The Art Of Walking* (1980), *390 Degrees Of Simulated Stereo - Ubu Live: Volume 1* (1981), *Song Of The Bailing Man* (1982), *The Tenement Year* (1988), *One Man Drives While The Other Man Screams - Live Volume 2: Pere Ubu On Tour* (1989), *Cloudland* (1989), *Worlds In Collision* (1991). Compilation: *Terminal Tower* (1985).

Perfect Disaster

Having tested the waters as Orange Disaster, then the Architects Of Disaster, these calamitously-inclined types finally settled on the Perfect Disaster in 1984 as the original rhythm section departed to form Fields

Of The Nephilim. The initial UK-based line-up consisted of Phil Parfitt, Allison Pates, John Saltwell and Malcolm Catto, although personnel changes were to plague the band's career. Ignored by the British music scene, the Perfect Disaster took their twisted, broody guitar sound to France for their self-titled debut album in 1985. There followed a couple of years of blank struggle on both sides of the English Channel before the band signed to Fire Records at home and released the critically-acclaimed *Asylum Road*. Prior to this, Saltwell and Pates both left, disillusioned, to be replaced by bassist Josephine Wiggs and long-term guitarist Dan Cross. 1989 suggested that better prospects lurked over the horizon: the *Up* album, which stretched splendidly from fiery two-chord blasts to near-suicidal ramblings, coincided with prestigious live shows with the likes of the Jesus And Mary Chain. And the band's initial inspiration, based upon singer Parfitt's spell working at a Victorian mental institution, looked set to reap some awards. The public, alas, didn't share the critics' enthusiasm for the band. Josephine Wiggs left in 1990 to spend more time on the Breeders, a side project which also involved Tanya Donelly from Throwing Muses and Kim Deal of the Pixies, allowing John Saltwell to return on bass. The *Heaven Scent* album continued the Perfect Disaster's foray into the darker side of alternative music, but rumours of the band's demise persisted throughout 1991.

Albums: *The Perfect Disaster* (1985), *Asylum Road* (1988), *Up* (1989), *Heaven Scent* (1991).

Perry, Mark

One of the first to spot the oncoming onslaught of UK punk, Mark Perry (b. c.1957, London, England) was a bank clerk who, inspired by the Ramones, started the *Sniffin' Glue (And Other Rock 'N' Roll Habits)* fanzine in mid-1976. After leaving his job and shortening his name to Mark P. Perry and South London pals like Danny Baker became the unofficial media messiahs of punk rock. *Sniffin' Glue* only lasted until August 1977 but by that time Perry was working on several labels and his new band, with Alex Ferguson; Alternative TV (Alternative *to* TV). He had previously played in a trio called the New Beatles with Steve Walsh and Tyrone Thomas. Perry soon adapted the new band's name to Alternative TV as everyone was either mispronouncing or misspelling it anyway. Their first release was a flexi on the Sniffin' Glue label. This was later reissued on Deptford Fun City, a label set up by Perry (in conjunction with Miles Copeland). ATV released several albums on DFC before becoming the Good Missionaries in 1979. After one album, *Fire From Heaven*, Perry left and recorded as the Reflection, the Door And The Window, and as a solo artist. There

were just two 1980 singles credited to him but he also cropped up on various compilations. ATV reformed in 1981 for *Strange Kicks* only to break up again. Perry's album *Snappy Turns* also appeared in that year. ATV reformed for a second time in 1984, initially for a gig at the Euston Tavern in Kings Cross and this reformation lasted about a year. They split up just long enough to give themselves time to reform again and stayed together until 1987. More recently Perry has been involved in a band called Baby Ice Dog.

Album: *Snappy Turns* (1981).

Peter And The Test Tube Babies

Punk rock can hardly stand as Brighton's major claim to fame, but the southern coastal town had its moments. In between the Piranhas' flirtations with the UK charts, Peter And The Test Tube Babies gained notoriety during the early 80s, with their brand of good-time Oi!-inspired punk. The group comprised of Chris Marchant, Nicholas Loizides, Peter Bywaters and Derek Greening. Locals may have remembered them from their contribution to resident label Attrix's *Vaultage* 1978 compilation, which featured the provocative 'Elvis Is Dead'. But it wasn't until 1982 that the Test Tube Babies' first single emerged on the No Future label. 'Banned From The Pubs' was followed by 'Run Like Hell' that same year, before the band set up their own label, Trapper. After the gruesome 'Zombie Creeping Flesh' and 'The Jinx' (both 1983), they at last emerged with an album's worth of indecent exposure, *The Mating Sounds Of South American Frogs*. The inelegantly titled *Pissed And Proud* followed one month later. The next two years saw the group release albums and single with various labels, including their own, Hairy Pie. The idiosyncratically entitled cassette-only release *Journey To The Centre Of Johnny Clarke's Head* was followed by the *Rotting In The Fart Sack* EP (1985) and *Another Noisy, Loud, Blaring Punk Rock LP*. The album *Soberphobia* saw the Test Tube Babies through to the end of 1986, but since then, all has been quiet, leaving it seems safe to assume that the band are no more.

Albums: *The Mating Sounds Of South American Frogs* (1983), *Pissed And Proud* (1983), *Journey To The Centre Of Johnny Clarke's Head* (1984, cassette only), *Another Noisy, Loud, Blaring Punk Rock LP* (1985), *3 X 45* (1985), *Soberphobia* (1986). Compilation: *The Best Of Peter And The Test Tube Babies* (1988).

Pet Shop Boys

Formed in 1981, this inventive UK pop duo featured Neil Tennant (b. 10 July 1954, North Shields, Northumberland, England; vocals) and Chris Lowe (b. 4 October 1959, Blackpool, Lancashire, England; keyboards). Lowe had previously played in a cabaret group, One Under The Eight, while Tennant was

Pet Shop Boys

well-received album, *Actually*, the group were featured in a film, *It Couldn't Happen Here*, which co-starred *Carry On* actress, Barbara Windsor. The film was given the cold shoulder by reviewers and was seen as mild hiccup in the duo's fortunes. A fourth UK number 1 with 'Heart' was followed by a production and songwriting credit on Eighth Wonder's 'I'm Not Scared'. *Introspective* (1988) spawned further hits in 'Domino Dancing', 'It's Alright' and 'Left To My Own Devices'. Having previously eschewed live tours (they had hitherto performed one-off concerts only), the Pet Shop Boys undertook their debut in Japan and the Far East, before finally reaching the UK. In typical manner, the show's concept took them as far away from the traditional pop concert as possible and incorporated the use of actors, dancers and film. A surprise collaboration with Liza Minnelli gave her a hit with 'Results'. The duo's own inventive wit was again in evidence on the laconic 'Being Boring' and an odd fusion of U2's 'Where The Streets Have No Name' and Andy Williams' 'Can't Take My Eyes Off You'. In 1991, the group issued one of the best compilation albums of the era with *Discography*.

Albums: *Please* (1986), *Disco* (1986), *Actually* (1987), *Introspective* (1988), *Behaviour* (1990). Compilation: *Discography* (1991).

Photos

employed as a journalist on the UK pop magazine *Smash Hits*. After writing and recording demos, they came under the wing of New York dance music producer Bobby 'O' Orlando. In the summer of 1984, they issued the Orlando-produced 'West End Girls', which passed unnoticed. After being dropped from Epic Records, they were picked up by EMI/Parlophone the following year. A second single 'Opportunities (Let's Make Lots Of Money)' also failed but a re-recording of 'West End Girls', produced by Stephen Hague, began selling in late 1985. In January 1986, this hypnotic single topped the charts in the UK and repeated the feat later in the USA. The group's debut *Please*, 'Love Comes Quickly', a re-mixed version of 'Opportunities (Let's Make Lots Of Money)' and 'Suburbia' consolidated their position in the UK during 1986. The following year, the duo returned to number 1 with the Cat Stevens' influenced 'It's A Sin'. By this time, they were critically feted as one of the more interesting groups of their time, with an engaging love of pop irony, camp imagery and arch wordplay. The quality of their melodies was also evident in the successful collaboration with Dusty Springfield, 'What Have I Done To Deserve This?' which reached number 2. By the end of the year the duo were back at the top in their home country with a cover of the Elvis Presley hit, 'Always On My Mind'. After another

Photos

Three-quarters of the Photos had previously been three quarters of DJM Records' token punk band Satans Rats, who released three singles in the late 70s. Hailing from Evesham, Worcestershire, this trio comprised Steve Eagles (b. 1958; guitar) and Ollie Harrison (drums), who were at college together, and Dave Sparrow (bass) who had been in the Ipswich-band Quorum. The boys were in a club when they came across the photogenic Wendy Wu (b. 29 November 1959, Winson Green, West Midlands, England) who had previously managed a small band and been a hotel receptionist. Recruiting Wendy as their vocalist they became the Photos and signed with

CBS in 1979. Their debut single was the stunningly accurate, if perhaps a little conceited, 'I'm So Attractive'. The four track EP released in 1980 included their own tribute to the Birmingham nightclub Barbarellas. None of their singles on CBS/Epic dented the charts despite Tony Visconti being called in as producer. Wendy left in 1981 and was briefly replaced by Che from the Orchids. By 1983 they had moved on to the Rialto label but soon split up. Wendy would later work with Steve Strange in the band Strange Cruise. Steve Eagles went on to join Blurt and more recently re-emerged in one the most promising new bands of 1992, Bang Bang Machine.
Album: *The Photos* (1980).

Phranc

b. 1958, Los Angeles, California, USA. Before her career as the self-styled 'Jewish-American lesbian folksinger' Phranc had served an appenticeship, of sorts, by appearing in LA 'hardcore' groups (Gender, Catholic Discipline and Castration Squad). On her return to acoustic playing in 1980, Phranc's sets consisted of autobiographical, part-comic songs, at times performed to similar hardcore audiences from her recent past. These appearences led to the gay coffee-house/folk circuit. Her warmly received *Folksinger* set a standard with titles such as 'Female Mudwrestling', 'Amazons' and 'One O'The Girls'. Her willingness to tackle such subjects as her sexuality, left-wing politics and her own family problems have so far prevented her from achieving anything beyond cult status. Phranc's third album was highlighted by her role as support act on Morrissey's first full British tour of 1991.
Albums: *Folksinger* (1986), *I Enjoy Being A Girl* (1989), *Positively Phranc* (1991).

Pigbag

Pigbag will be for ever linked with their debut single, and only hit, 'Papa's Got A Brand New Pigbag' (a play on words on the mid-60s James Brown classic, 'Papa's Got A Brand New Bag'). A quirky but nevertheless catchy funk/soul instrumental, the single was first released in May 1981, but took almost a year to reach the charts, peaking at number 3. Word had it that their label, Y, had deleted the single and then reactivated it when the demand was sufficient. The band had formed around the Gloucestershire and Avon region from the ashes of hardline militant funk act the Pop Group; Simon Underwood (bass) joined up with James Johnstone (guitar/keyboards), Ollie Moore (saxophone), Chip Carpenter (drums) and Roger Freeman (percussion). By the time of their hit, Pigbag already issued two further singles, 'Sunny Day' and 'Getting Up'. The debut album, *Dr Heckle And Mr Jive*, subsequently reached the UK Top 20. Despite shrewd promotion, Pigbag's heyday was short-lived. 'Big Bean' (1982) peaked at number 40 and 'Hit The "O" Deck' (1983), failed to make any impact. After a live album, the band broke up, although 'Papa's Got A Brand New Pigbag' was later re-recorded in 1987, to coincide with *The Best Of Pigbag*.
Albums: *Dr Heckle And Mr Jive* (1982), *Pigbag - Live* (1983). Compilation: *The Best Of Pigbag* (1987).

Pink Military/Pink Industry

This late 70s UK act were a central part of Liverpool's thriving post-punk scene. Distinctive vocalist Jayne Casey had fronted a now impressive-looking line-up in Big In Japan. But after their demise in the summer of 1978, she teamed up with John Highway (guitar), Wayne Wadden (bass), Paul Hornby (drums) and a certain Nicky (keyboards), to form Pink Military. An experimental 12-inch EP, *Blood And Lipstick*, appeared on local label Eric's (also the name of Liverpool's premier venue of the era), in 1979, and caused quite a stir. A deal with Virgin ensued, resulting in the more overtly commercial single, 'Did You See Her', in 1980. However, this belied the wealth and diversity of sounds to be found on the accompanying album, *Do Animals Believe In God?* By this time, Chris Joyce had been recruited on drums, while Wadden had been replaced by one Martin on bass. But the Virgin/Eric's collaboration soon fell apart, and their next EP, *Buddha Waking/Disney Sleeping*, came out on the label Last Trumpet. Pink Military soon split and gave way to Pink Industry, Casey collaborating with Ambrose Reynolds, later a member of an early Frankie Goes To Hollywood line-up. The first fruits were extremely promising and 'Is This The End?' (1982) stands as one of the year's most outstanding singles. *Low Technology* emerged just over a year later, exemplifying the band's off-beat, haunting qualities. *Who Told You You Were Naked* hinted at eastern influences, while further embracing new instrument and studio techniques. There was a two-year gap before *New Beginnings*, accompanied by a single, 'What I Wouldn't Give' (with a sleeve adorned by a photograph of Morrissey) in mid-1985. An increasingly reclusive existence since then has been broken only by a retrospective self-titled album on Cathexis, promoted by 'Don't Let Go' in 1987.
Albums: As Pink Military *Do Animals Believe In God?* (1980). As Pink Industry *Low Technology* (1983), *Who Told You You Were Naked* (1983). Compilation: *Pink Industry* (1988).

Pixies

This US group was formed in Boston, Massachusetts, by room-mates Charles Michael Kittridge Thompson IV aka Black Francis (b. Long Beach, California, USA; vocals, guitar) and Joey Santiago (guitar). A

Pixies; Black Francis

newspaper advertisement, requiring applicants for a 'Hüsker Dü/Peter, Paul And Mary band', solicited bassist Kim Deal (aka Mrs John Murphy) who in turn introduced drummer David Lovering. Originally known as Pixies In Panoply, the quartet secured a recording deal on the UK independent label 4AD on the strength of a series of superior demo tapes. Their debut release, *Come On Pilgrim*, introduced the band's abrasive, powerful sound and Francis' oblique lyrics. *Surfer Rosa*, produced by Big Black's Steve Albini, exaggerated the savage fury of its predecessor and the set was acclaimed Album Of The Year in much of the UK rock press. The superlative *Doolittle* emphasized the quartet's grasp of melody, yet retained their drive, and this thrilling collection scaled the national Top 10. The Pixies were now a highly popular attraction and their exciting live performances enhanced a growing reputation, establishing clear stage favourites in 'Debaser', 'Cactus', 'Wave Of Mutilation' and 'Bone Machine'. 1990's *Bossanova* showed an undiminished fire with a blend of pure pop with 'Allison' and sheer ferocity in 'Rock Music'. The band found themselves the darlings of the rock press and were once again widely regarded for recording one of the top albums of the year. Kim Deal later attracted glowing reviews for her offshoot project, the Breeders.
Albums: *Come On Pilgrim* (1987), *Surfer Rosa* (1988), *Dolittle* (1989), *Bossanova* (1990), *Trampe Le Monde* (1991).

PJ Harvey

Polly Harvey (b. c.1970, Corscombe, Dorset, England; lead vocals/guitar), from whose name the band's title is taken, completed an art foundation course before joining Bristol-based band Automatic Diamini for two and a half years. Bored with playing other people's material, she was taken under the wing of manager Mark Vernon. Moving to London, ostensibly to attend a course in sculpture (her other love), she was introduced to bass player Steven Vaughan and drummer and backing vocalist Rob Ellis. Together they played live for the first time in April 1991, using the name PJ Harvey. Independent record label Too Pure, home of Th' Faith Healers and Stereo Lab, were so convinced by these nebulous performances that they mortgaged their home to finance the debut single 'Dress'. Together with the most impressive 'Sheela-Na-Gig' and debut album *Dry*, it was enough to bring her to the attention not only of Island Records but also the mainstream press. Subverting the traditions of the female singer-songwriter with outbreaks of fire and brimstone guitar wailings, Polly possesses the sort of voice which, whilst not cultured in the traditional sense, is a highly emotive cudgel. Allied to lyrics which lay her own relationships and feelings naked, her revisionary attitude to feminism is best demonstrated by the *New Musical Express* cover on which she appeared topless, with her back to the photographer. An evocative and disturbing songwriter, she may leave too bitter an aftertaste for a mass audience.
Album: *Dry* (1992).

Plasmatics

Formed in 1979 in New York City, USA, the Plasmatics were a theatrical hardcore band which incorporated such violent acts as blowing up Cadillacs and chainsawing guitars in half into its performances. Assembled by and masterminded by former pornography entrepreneur Rod Swenson, the original personnel of the group included vocalist Wendy O. Williams, a former star of sex shows, who wore see-through lingerie, but for the most part, appeared topless with strategically-placed masking tape. The remainder of the band comprised Richie Stotts (guitar), who wore a blue mohawk haircut and a pink tutu on stage, Wes Beech (guitar), Stu Deutsch (drums) and Chosei Funahara (bass, later replaced by Jean Beauvoir). After releasing two EPs on the independent Vice Squad label in 1979, the Plasmatics signed with Stiff Records in the USA and the UK, releasing *New Hope For The Wretched* in 1980. It was largely panned by the critics but sold as a cult item due to the group's extensive press coverage, as did

such singles as 'Butcher Baby' and 'Monkey Suit'. A second album, *Beyond The Valley Of 1984*, was issued on Stiff in 1981, as was an EP, *Metal Princess*. In 1982 the Plasmatics signed to Capitol Records and released *Coup D'Etat*, but by then they had evolved into an outright heavy metal outfit and had lost most of their novelty appeal. Williams and Beauvoir recorded solo albums following the Plasmatics' mid-80s break-up.
Albums: *New Hope For The Wretched* (1980), *Beyond The Valley Of 1984* (1981), *Coup D'Etat* (1982). Solo albums: Wendy O. Williams *Deffest! And Baddest!* (1988); Jean Beauvoir *Drums Along The Mohawk* (1986), *Jacknifed* (1988).

Pogues

Pogues

The London punk scene of the late 70s inspired some unusual intermingling of styles and the Pogues (then known as Pogue Mahone) performed punky versions of traditional Irish folk songs in pubs throughout the capital. They were fronted by singer Shane MacGowan (b. 25 December 1957, Kent, England) and also included Peter 'Spider' Stacy (tin whistle), Jem Finer (banjo/mandolin), James Fearnley (guitar/piano accordion), Cait O'Riordan (bass) and Andrew Ranken (drums). MacGowan had spent his late teen years singing in a punk group called the Nipple Erectors ('the Nips') which also contained Fearney. After several complaints the band changed their name (Pogue Mahone is 'kiss my arse' in Gaelic) and soon attracted the attention of the Clash who asked them to be their opening act. Record companies were perturbed by the band's occasionally chaotic live act where they would sometimes fight onstage and Stacy kept time by banging his head with a beer tray. In 1984 Stiff Records signed them and recorded *Red Roses For Me,* containing several traditional tunes as well as excellent originals like 'Streams Of Whiskey' and 'Dark Streets Of London'. Elvis Costello produced *Rum, Sodomy And The Lash* on which Philip Chevron, formerly a guitarist with the Radiators From Space, replaced Finer who was on 'paternity leave'. The group was established as a

formidable and unique live act and the record entered the UK Top 20. There were further changes when the multi-instrumentalist Terry Woods (a co-founder of Steeleye Span) joined and Cait O'Riordan was replaced by Darryl Hunt. She later married Elvis Costello. The group developed a strong political stance and their video to accompany the single 'A Pair Of Brown Eyes' had to be re-edited because the group were filmed spitting on a poster of Prime Minister, Margaret Thatcher. 'We represent the people who don't get the breaks. People can look at us and say, "My God, if that bunch of tumbledown wrecks can do it, so can I"', explained Chevron in a press interview.
If I Should Fall From Grace With God was produced by Steve Lillywhite and embraced Middle Eastern and Spanish sounds. It sold more than 200,000 copies in the USA and 'Fairytale Of New York', a rumbustious but poignant duet by MacGowan and Lillywhite's wife Kirsty MacColl, was a Christmas number 2 hit in the UK in 1987. In the autumn of 1989 there were fears for the future of the group when MacGowan's heavy drinking led to him pulling out of several shows. He was due to join the band in the USA for a prestigious tour with Bob Dylan when he collapsed at London's Heathrow Airport. He missed all the support spots with Dylan and the band played without him. 'Other groups in a situation like that would've either said, "Let's get rid of the guy" or "Let's split up", but we're not the sort to do that. We're all part of each other's problems whether we like it or not', said Chevron. *Peace And Love* featured songs written by nearly every member of the group and its eclectic nature saw them picking up the hurdy-gurdy, the cittern and the mandola. Its erratic nature drew criticism from some quarters, mainly from original fans who had enjoyed the early folk-punk rants. While the rest of the group are clearly strong players it is widely accepted that MacGowan is the most talented songwriter. His output has always been highly sporadic but there are fears that the drinking that fuelled his earlier creativity may have slowed him to a standstill. In an interview in 1989 he said he had not been 'dead-straight sober' since he was 14 and that he drank in quantity because 'it opened his mind to paradise'. It was announced in September 1991 that MacGowan had left the band and had been replaced by the former Clash singer, Joe Strummer. This relationship lasted until June the following year when Strummer stepped down and the lead vocalist job went to Spider Stacy.
Albums: *Red Roses For Me* (1984), *Rum, Sodomy And The Lash* (1985), *If I Should Fall From Grace With God* (1988), *Peace And Love* (1989). Compilation: *The Best Of The Pogues* (1991), *The Rest Of The Best* (1992).

Poison Girls

The Poison Girls' political punk was first heard on a shared 12-inch EP, *Fatal Microbes Meet The Poison Girls*, a co-release for Small Wonder and the band's own label, Xntrix, in 1979. The band shared much of Crass's ideology (anarchism and communal living). Aided by the strangely named Bernhardt Rebours (bass), Lance D'Boyle (drums) and Richard Famous (guitar), middle-aged Vi Subversa (vocals) also injected a strong feminist stance into their music. For their second EP, *Hex* (1979), the band co-opted with Crass's label. But it was almost a year before they released 'Persons Unknown', another shared single, this time with Crass themselves. The Poison Girls' debut *Chappaquidick Bridge* originally contained a free flexi-disc, 'Statement'. Another free record, 'Pretty Polly', accompanied the fanzine *In The City* around this time. After 'All Systems Go' (1981), the group parted with Crass and a live album, *Total Exposure*, appeared later that year. *Where's The Pleasure* followed in 1982, before the band moved to a new label, Illuminated. But this proved short-lived, and after 'One Good Reason' and 'Are You Happy Now?' (both 1983), the Poison Girls returned to Xntrix for *Seven Year Scratch* in 1984. That same year, '(I'm Not A) Real Woman' continued the band's lyrical tack, but their next album was to be their last. After *Songs Of Praise*, and a one-off single for the Upright label ('The Price Of Grain'), the Poison Girls broke up.
Albums: *Chappaquidick Bridge* (1980), *Total Exposure* (1982), *Seven Year Scratch* (1984), *Songs Of Praise* (1985).

Poison Idea

These hardcore heavyweights' broad appearance gives little credence to the harsh, speedy rock path they pursue. Formed in Portland, Oregon, USA, in late 1980, their first incarnation featured Jerry A. (vocals), Pig Champion (guitar), Tense (bass) and Dean Johnson (drums). They debuted with the unwieldy EP *Pick Your King* which contained no less than 13 tracks, packaged in a sleeve featuring Elvis Presley on one side and Jesus Christ on the other. By the time of *Kings Of Punk* they were slightly more tuneful, but no less belligerent. However, Johnson and Tense were both fired and replaced by Steve 'Thee Slayer Hippy' Hanford (drums) and Tim Paul (ex-Final Warning, now Gruntruck; bass). The sound was also filled out with additional guitarist Vegetable (ex-Mayhem). However, Tim Paul only lasted one abortive gig (just one song) before being replaced by the returning Tense. His tenure, though slightly longer, lasted only until the release of *War All The Time*, after which Mondo (also ex-Mayhem) joined. The line-up wars continued after 'Getting The Fear' was released, with Vegetable sacked on New Years Eve, replaced by Kid Cocksman (ex-Gargoyle;

guitar), and Mondo quit after the appropriately titled 'Discontent'. Myrtle Tickner (ex-Oily Bloodmen) became the band's fourth and current bass player. Aldine Striknine (guitar, ex-Maimed For Life) stepped in for the next casualty Kid Cocksman (apparently kicked out for being too thin) to record *Feel The Darkness*, after which Mondo returned once more, this time on second guitar. At least two members of the band are obese, each therefore making celebrity stage-diving a precarious endeavour at their gigs. Despite the line-up confusions and obvious gimmickry, they have produced a body of work of some substance, characterized by a lyrical preference for matters alcoholic and sexual.
Albums: *Kings Of Punk* (1986), *War All The Time* (1987), *Record Collectors Are Pretentious Assholes* (1989), *Poison Idea* (1989), *Feel The Darkness* (1990), *Blank, Blackout, Vacant* (1992).

Police

The reggae-influenced minimalist pop sound of this highly talented UK trio was one of the musical high-points of the late 70s and early 80s. Their individual talent and egos ultimately got the better of them and they fragmented, although each of the strong-willed former members has never ruled out the possibility of a re-match. The group comprised Stewart Copeland (b. 16 July 1952, Alexandria, Egypt; drums/percussion/vocals), Andy Summers (b. Andrew Somers, 31 December 1942, Poulton Le Fylde, Lancashire, England; guitar) and Sting (b. Gordon Sumner, 2 October 1951, Wallsend, Tyne And Wear, England; bass/vocals). Masterminded by Miles Copeland, ex-Curved Air member Stewart and ex-Last Exit bassist Sting came together with the vastly experienced Summers, leaving the original member Henry Padovani no alternative but to leave. He had previously played on their independent chart hit 'Fall Out', released on Miles' Illegal label. Summers, a former session musician and ex-Zoot Money, Dantalians Chariot, Eric Burdon And The New Animals, Soft Machine and Kevin Ayers, blended instantly with Copeland's back-to-front reggae drum technique and Sting's unusual and remarkable voice. Summers added a sparse clean guitar utilizing a flanger with echo, a sound he arguably invented and most certainly popularized; he found many imitators during his career with the Police. The mixture of such unusual styles gave them a totally fresh sound which they honed and developed over five outstanding albums; each record was a step forward both in musical content and sales.
Astonishingly, their A&M debut 'Roxanne' failed to chart when first released, but this now-classic tale of a prostitute was a later success on the back of 'Can't Stand Losing You'. Their heavily reggae-influenced *Outlandos D'Amour* and *Regatta De Blanc* dominated

the UK charts for most of 1979 and contained such chart-toppers as 'Message In A Bottle' and 'Walking On The Moon'. Sting's simple but intelligently written lyrics were complete tales. By the time *Zenyatta Mondatta* was released their punk-styled bleached hair had black roots; they were never to be touched up, as the Police were on their way to becoming one of the world's leading bands. This album was their big breakthrough in America, Europe, Japan and indeed the rest of the world. The group's third number 1 'Don't Stand So Close To Me', a tale of the temptations of being a schoolteacher (which Sting had been previously), was closely followed by the lyrically rich yet simply titled 'De Do Do Do De Da Da Da'. The following year, having now conquered the world, they released the outstanding *Ghost In The Machine*, which contained Sting's most profound lyrics to date and was enriched by Hugh Padgham's fuller production. The major hit singles from this album were the thought-provoking 'Spirits In The Material World', 'Invisible Sun', a brooding atmospheric comment on Northern Ireland and the joyous Caribbean carnival sound of 'Every Little Thing She Does Is Magic' which provided their fourth UK number 1.

Following yet another multi-million seller, the band relaxed in 1982 to concentrate on solo projects. Stewart resurrected his Klark Kent *alter ego*, releasing *Klark Kent*, and wrote the music for the film *Rumblefish*. Andy had a book of photographs published to coincide with an exhibition of his camera work and also made an album with Robert Fripp. Sting appeared in the film adaptation of Dennis Potter's *Brimstone And Treacle* and had the UK gutter press speculate on his sexual preferences. The Police re-convened in 1983 and released the carefully crafted *Synchronicity*; almost as if they knew this would be their last album. The package was stunning, a superb album containing numerous potential hit singles and a series of expertly made accompanying videos. The magnificent 'Every Breath You Take', arguably their greatest song, stayed at number 1 in the UK for four weeks, and for twice as many weeks in the USA, while the album stayed at the top for an astonishing 17 weeks. The collection varies from gentle songs like 'Tea In The Sahara' and 'Wrapped Around Your Finger' to the mercurial energy of 'Synchronicity II'. To finish on such a high and to depart as undefeated champions must have satisfied the band. In retrospect, it is better to have produced five classic albums than a massive catalogue of indifferent collections. Like the Beatles, they never out-stayed their welcome, and thus are fondly remembered.

Albums: *Outlandos D'Amour* (1978), *Regatta De Blanc* (1979), *Zenyatta Mondatta* (1980), *Ghost In The Machine* (1981), *Synchronicity* (1983). Compilation: *Every Breath You Take - The Singles* (1986).

Poly Styrene

b. Marion Elliot. Hailing from Brixton, London, England singer and main writer of X-Ray Spex - Poly Styrene was writing songs by the age of nine and in 1976 a release on GTO Records, 'Silly Billy' by Mari Elliot, is believed to be her debut. Her subsequent work experiences on the sweet stall of Woolworths, and as a trainee clothes buyer, provided her with just as much songwriting stimulus. When punk reared its head Marion saw it as 'anti-racism, anti-nazism, and anti-sexism', and she quickly affirmed her identity with it. She assembled X-Ray Spex, wrote most of their material, and picked her new name from an advert. She was recognized as one of the leading lights of the punk movement in January 1978 when the BBC arts programme *Omnibus* broadcast the documentary *Who Is Poly Styrene?*. X-Ray Spex burnt out quickly and in 1980 Poly released her first solo single, 'Talk In Toytown', and the disappointing *Translucence* - especially moderate compared with the outstanding *Germ Free Adolescence* two years before. She then announced she was giving up pop music to devote herself to the Spiritual Life and Krishna Consciousness Movement, using the spiritual name Maharani Devi. She did, however, continue to play devotional music and to record at the temple's own studio (donated by George Harrison). At the bequest of her spiritual master she returned to pop music in 1986 with the Eastern-flavoured EP *Gods And Goddesses*. In 1991 she re-formed X-Ray Spex and announced that she was working on a 'counter culture street musical explosion' to be staged in 1992. She also appeared on Dream Academy's 1991 album *A Different Kind Of Weather* as vocalist on a version of John Lennon's 'Love'.

Album: *Translucence* (1980).

Pooh Sticks

Mix a slapstick parody of the archetypal UK independent guitar band, a wicked sense of humour and an uncanny knack of turning out catchy, astute pop tunes and that ably defines the Pooh Sticks. Formed in October 1987 in Wales when Hue Williams (b. 4 March 1968 - son of ex-Man and Dire Straits drummer, Terry Williams) and friend Paul teamed-up with three schoolgirls Trudi, Alison and Stephanie, the band released a single almost immediately on local label Fierce. 'On Tape' (1988) was a send-up of the independent scene at its most clichéd and attracted much interest, particularly as the band flew to New York for their first live appearance. A five-disc one-track single boxed set which included the legendary 'I Know Someone Who Knows Someone Who Knows Alan McGee Quite Well' (referring to the Creation Records head) followed in the summer, although these were transferred onto a

216

one-sided self-titled mini-album by the end of the year. 1989 saw two live albums, *Orgasm* on the Scottish 53rd & 3rd label and *Trademark Of Quality*, while the Poohs covered the Vaselines' 'Dying For It' in 1990. The lampoonery continued with the *The Great White Wonder* in 1991 when they tackled weightier icons from the 60s and 70s. In February of 1992 the Pooh Sticks signed a $1.2 million deal with the major BMG (formerly RCA) company in the USA.
Albums: *Pooh Sticks* (1988), *Orgasm* (1989), *Trademark Of Quality* (1989), *Formula One Generation* (1990), *Peel Sessions* (1991), *The Great White Wonder* (1991).

Pop Group

This seminal UK punk group operated from Bristol, Avon, in the late 70s, combining abstracted funk with chaos and expressionist vocals courtesy of Mark Stewart. The topics under consideration - starvation, war, exploitation - were similar to those expounded by anarcho-punks Crass, but the Pop Group's music was much more sophisticated. Their records are by turns inspirational and intolerable, some of the most extreme music to have been pressed onto vinyl. The masterpiece was *For How Much Longer Do We Tolerate Mass Murder*. No one is able to maintain such a pitch of intensity: bassist Simon Underwood went and formed Pigbag, a welcome relief from the drabness punk conformity had created, a riot of bright shirts, ethnic rhythms and James Brown references. Guitarist and saxophonist Gareth Sagar formed the irrepressible Rip Rig And Panic. Only singer Mark Stewart kept to his bleak viewpoint, forming the Maffia with the rhythm team from Sugarhill Records and working with producer Adrian Sherwood.
Albums: *Y* (1979), *For How Much Longer Must We Tolerate Mass Murder* (1980), *We Are Time* (1980).

Popguns

This UK Brighton-based group comprise Wendy Morgan (lead vocals), Simon Pickles (guitar), Greg Dixon (guitar), Pat Walkington (bass) and Shaun Charman (drums, ex-Wedding Present). The Popguns breezy power-pop and well-crafted songs accompanied by Wendy Morgan's lyrics of boyfriend trouble 'n' bliss and post-teen alienation. Despite a thin voice, Wendy more than adequately makes up for an loss of effect with an energetic delivery. The two EPs released in 1989, *Landslide* and *Waiting For The Winter* promised much and were later compiled along with 1990's *Someone You Love* on *Eugenie* on the Midnight Music label. The Popguns' first full album release in 1991 boasted an original production credit to Psychic TV's Genesis P. Orridge. The album achieved a healthy Independent Top 10 chart position and promised further success in the near future for this young band.

Album: *Snog* (1991). Compilation: *Eugenie* (1990).

Popinjays

Formed in London in 1988 by songwriters Wendy Robinson (b. 6 April 1964, Huddersfield, Yorkshire, England; vocals), Polly Hancock (b. 16 July 1964, Berkshire, England; guitar/vocals) and a drum machine. The Popinjays evolved out of the influential Timebox Club at the Bull & Gate pub in Kentish Town, north London (the duo later ran their own Pop Club at the same venue), by striving to perfect the ultimate pop formula. Dana Baldinger (b. 26 December 1963, California, USA; bass) joined in 1989 as the offer of a combination of sweets, comics and biscuits won the band a record deal with the One Little Indian label. Dana departed after one single, to be replaced by fellow countrywoman Anne Rogers (b. 17 October 1962, New York, USA) which in turn was followed by a plethora of critical recommendations for the debut *Bang Up To Date With The Popinjays*. Ever conscious of the importance of fun in music, their promo video for the 'Vote Elvis' single featured much Monkees-style running around with special guest Cathal Coughlan from Fatima Mansions. Drummer Seamus Feeney (b. 19 November 1964, Middlesex, England), caused the drum machine to be sacked at the close of 1990, just as the Popinjays were beginning to garner appreciative attention from America.
Albums: *Bang Up To Date With The Popinjays* (1990), *Flying Down To Mono Valley* (1992).

Pop Will Eat Itself

This UK group took its name from the heading of an article in the *New Musical Express*. Having previously rehearsed and gigged under the names From Eden and Wild And Wondering, the group emerged as Pop Will Eat Itself in 1986 with a line-up comprising Clint Mansell (vocals/guitar), Adam Mole (keyboards), Graham Crabb (drums, later vocals) and Richard Marsh (bass). Their first recording was the privately issued EP, *The Poppies Say Grr*, which was nominated as single of the week in the *NME*. BBC Radio sessions followed and the group appeared in the independent charts with the follow-up EPs *Poppiecock* and *The Covers*. Already known for their hard pop and vulgarisms, they ran into trouble with the release of 'Beaver Patrol', which was criticized for its puerile sexism. Their debut *Box Frenzy*, followed in late 1987 and displayed their odd mix of old pop and slices of modern sampling. The insistent 'There Is No Love Between Us Anymore' was their most impressive single to date and augured well for the future as did 'Def Con One' in 1988. During that year, they were invited to play in the USSR, and soon afterwards they signed to the major RCA. 'Can U Dig It' and 'Wise Up Sucker' were minor successes, as was their second album. A world tour sharpened their approach and during 1990, they achieved mainstream acclaim with 'Touched By The Hand Of Cicciolina', a paean addressed to the Italian porn star turned politician. Two further hit singles, 'X,Y & Zee' and '92 Degrees', followed in 1991. The group recruited a full-time (human) drummer in 1992 when Fuzz (b. Robert Townshend) joined.

Albums: *Box Frenzy* (1987), *Now For A Feast* (1989, early recordings), *This Is The Day, This Is The Hour, This Is This* (1989), *The Pop Will Eat Itself Cure For Sanity* (1990).

Postcard Records

After the impetus of punk's initial onslaught, like-minded individuals in every corner of Britain set about creating their own musical identity. If they could not play music, they went one better and founded their own label. Alan Horne set about realizing his ambition in late 70s Glasgow when he discovered local favourites Orange Juice. Here was a band that could be harnessed, and Horne set about creating Postcard Records with lead singer Edwyn Collins as the 'Sound Of Young Scotland'. Orange Juice's 'Falling And Laughing' was issued early in 1980, housed in distinctive foldaround, hand-coloured sleeves with a free flexi-disc. Much of the Postcard label's appeal would stem from the precious nature of its roster and the presentation of its releases as vital and desirable artefacts. To do this, Horne needed more than one band and after losing the Fire Engines, opted for manic Edinburgh act Josef K. Postcard's second release was also arguably their finest; Orange Juice's 'Blue Boy'. Their debut had caused a stir, certainly, but this formidable single, awash with frenetic guitar work and an unforgettably passionate melody, sent the critics reeling. Josef K's 'Radio Drill Time' was less accessible and more frenzied, but an aura had already surrounded the label.

Next came the Go-Betweens, an obscure Australian outfit whom Horne met while they were touring the UK. They promptly recorded 'I Need Two Heads', which became the fourth Postcard single, but this was to prove their only single for the label. Josef K's more relaxed 'It's Kinda Funny' and another Orange Juice classic, 'Simply Thrilled Honey' saw out 1980, and Horne took the end of year opportunity to redesign the label's image. The spartan brown labels (with a drum-beating pussycat) were replaced by a checked design to reflect the new sleeves, portraying a collage of Scottish national dress. In the meantime, Josef K hit a stumbling block. They were unhappy with the sound on their debut *Sorry For Laughing*, and eventually scrapped it before it reached the shops. Postcard instead relied on Orange Juice for 'Poor Old Soul', before introducing a new signing early in 1981,

Aztec Camera. Fronted by the 16-year-old Roddy Frame, their debut, 'Just Like Gold', was more traditional than other Postcard material, but nonetheless endearing. Josef K teamed up with Belgian label Les Disques du Crépuscule for 'Sorry For Laughing' (the title track to the abandoned album), and followed this with 'Chance Meeting', a re-recording of their first single. By this time, mid-1981, Postcard was basking in the critical sunshine and Orange Juice succumbed to a seductive offer from Polydor Records. Their next single, 'Wan Light', was abandoned and from this point on, Postcard fell apart. Josef K finally took the plunge with a re-recorded album, *The Only Fun In Town*, and Aztec Camera continued to ply their acoustic sensibilities with 'Mattress Of Wire', but Horne soon moved on to pastures new, leaving numerous projects on the shelf. In addition to the first long player from Aztec Camera (*Green Jacket Grey*), Horne had allocated numbers to singles from the Bluebells (later to enjoy commercial success at London), the Jazzateers (who joined Rough Trade) and Secret Goldfish (reputedly an Orange Juice pseudonym). Aztec Camera and the Go-Betweens also moved to Rough Trade, and Josef K split up, while Horne eventually re-surfaced managing the labels Win and Swamplands.

Prefab Sprout

Prefab Sprout

The intricate tales and thoughts in the lyrics of songwriter Paddy McAloon indicate a major songwriter. His Bob Dylan imagery and Elvis Costello bluntness have made Prefab Sprout one of the most refreshing pop bands of the late 80s and beyond. The band was formed in 1982 and comprised: Paddy McAloon (b. 7 June 1957, Durham, England; guitar/vocals), Martin McAloon (b. 4 January 1962, Durham, England; bass), Wendy Smith (b. 31 May 1963, Durham, England; vocals/guitar) and Neil Conti (b. 12 February 1959, London, England). Following a self-pressed single 'Lions In My Own Garden', Paddy attracted the attention of the independent label Kitchenware. They had further hits in the UK independent charts and their debut *Swoon* made the national chart. *Swoon* was a wordy album featuring songs with many chord changes that ultimately concentrated on lyrics rather than melody. Later that year the excellent 'When Love Breaks Down' failed to excite the single-buying public. A remixed version by Thomas Dolby was released the following year, but once again it failed. When *Steve McQueen* was issued in 1985 the band became media darlings, with Paddy McAloon coming near to over-exposure. The album was a critics' favourite and displayed hummable songs with fascinating lyrics, and it made a respectable showing in the charts. At the end of the year 'When Love Breaks Down' was issued for a third time and finally became a hit.

In the USA, *Steve McQueen* was forcibly retitled *Two Wheels Good*. A striking work, the album included a tribute to Faron Young and the arresting 'Goodbye Lucille # 1' (aka 'Johnny Johnny'). *From Langley Park To Memphis* in 1988 was a major success world-wide; Paddy had now refined his art to produce totally accessible yet inventive pop music. The album represented a courageous change of direction with MaAloon employing strings and composing melodies which recalled the great show musical writers of the pre-rock 'n' roll era. 'Nightingales' was very much in this vein, and the work ended with the strikingly melodramatic 'Nancy (Let Your Hair Down For Me)' and 'The Venus Of The Soup Kitchen'. Already the band had reached the stage of having superstar guests 'turning up on the album'. Both Stevie Wonder (harmonica solo on 'Nightingales') and Pete Townshend put in appearances. 'The King Of Rock 'N' Roll' became their biggest hit to date. *Protest Songs* was a collection scheduled to appear before their previous album and its success was muted by the continuing sales of both *Steve McQueen* and *From Langley Park To Memphis*. McAloon unleashed *Jordan: The Comeback* in 1990, and for many critics it was the album of the year. All McAloon's talents had combined to produce a concept album of magnificence. Over 64 minutes in length, the album boasted 19 tracks, full of striking melodies and fascinatingly oblique lyrics. The ghost of Elvis Presley haunted several of the songs, most notably the elegiac 'Moon Dog'. They are now established as one of Britain's major bands, and the media await their next move with interest.

Albums: *Swoon* (1984), *Steve McQueen* (1985), *From Langley Park To Memphis* (1988), *Protest Songs* (1989), *Jordan: The Comeback* (1990).

Pretenders

Chrissie Hynde (b. 17 September 1951, Akron, Ohio, USA), came to England to seek her fortune

Pretenders; Chrissie Hynde

aduring the early 70s. After meeting with *New Musical Express* writer Nick Kent she joined the paper and gained entrance into the world of rock. During her pre-Pretenders days she worked at Malcolm Maclaren's shop, SEX, played with Chris Spedding, joined Jack Rabbit, formed the Berk Brothers and made a tasteless, unreleased single as the Moors Murderers. By the time she assembled the band in 1978, Hynde had gained a great deal of experience. The classic Pretenders' line-up comprised: Pete Farndon (b. 2 June 1952, Hereford, England, d. 14 April 1983; bass), James Honeyman-Scott (b. 4 November 1956, Hereford, England d. 16 June 1982; guitar) and Martin Chambers (b. 4 September 1951, Hereford, England; drums). Their debut was a Nick Lowe produced version of the Kinks 'Stop Your Sobbing' in 1978. It scraped into the UK Top 40 the following year, having received critical praise and much interest. 'Kid' and the superb 'Brass In Pocket' followed. The latter was accompanied by a superb black and white video with Hynde portrayed as a waitress, and reached the number 1 position in the UK. It was their debut album that eventually put them on the road to becoming one of the decade's most important groups. *Pretenders* was a *tour-de-force* nd remains their finest work. In addition to their previous singles the album contained the reggae-styled 'Private Life' (later recorded by Grace Jones), the frenetic 'Precious', the Byrds-like 'Talk Of The Town' and the beautiful ballad 'Lovers Of Today'.

Throughout 1980 they became a major stadium attraction in the USA; it was in America that Chrissie met and fell in love with her musical idol, the Kinks' Ray Davies. Davies had already expressed an interest in Hynde during an interview in the rock magazine *Dark Star*. Their tempestuous relationship lasted four years, almost resulting in marriage. Davies stated that they had gone to a registry office by bus but spent so much time arguing that they changed their minds and came home. During their romance they brought each other onstage to play with their respective bands, much to the chagrin of the band members. *Pretenders II* came in 1982; it was another collection of melodious rock played with new-wave enthusiasm. Stand-out tracks were 'Message Of Love', the brilliantly confessional, 'The Adulteress' and another Davies' chestnut 'I Go To Sleep' first recorded by the Applejacks in 1964. During the turbulent month of June, Pete Farndon, whose drug abuse had been a problem for some time, was fired. Two days later Honeyman-Scott was found dead from a deadly concoction of heroin and cocaine. Nine months later Hynde gave birth to a daughter; the father was Ray Davies. Two months after this happy event, tragedy struck again. Pete Farndon was found dead in his bath from a drug overdose.

The new full-time Pretenders were Robbie McIntosh (ex-Average White Band on lead guitar, and bassist Malcolm Foster. They set about recording a third album and the band ended the year with another hit single, the Christmassy '2000 Miles'. *Learning To Crawl* was released at the beginning of another successful year. The album was erratic, but it did contain some gems, notably the epic 'Thin Line Between Love And Hate', the powerful 'Middle Of The Road' and the melodic, yet poignant tribute to Honeyman-Scott, 'Back On The Chain Gang'. The band embarked on another US tour, but Chrissie refused to be parted from her baby daughter who accompanied her, while Davies and his band were touring elsewhere. In May 1984, following a whirlwind affair, Hynde married Jim Kerr of Simple Minds. A solo Hynde appeared at Live Aid duetting with UB40 on the chart-topping reggae re-make of Sonny And Cher's 'I Got You Babe'. Following the birth of another daughter, (Jim Kerr is the father), Chrissie effectively dismantled the band. *Get Close* was released at the end of 1987 and was well received. Both 'Don't Get Me Wrong' and 'Hymn To Her' were substantial hits. In 1988 a solo Hynde performed with UB40 at the Nelson Mandela Concert and the subsequent duet 'Breakfast In Bed' was a Top 10 UK hit. Hynde has since spent much of her time campaigning for Animal Rights. Her marriage to Kerr collapsed and in 1990 she returned

with a new album *Packed*, still as the Pretenders. It was another critical and commercial success, demonstrating Hynde's natural gift for writing tight, melodic rock songs.

Albums: *Pretenders* (1980), *Pretenders II* (1981), *Learning To Crawl* (1984), *Get Close* (1986), *Packed* (1990). Compilation: *The Singles* (1987).

Price

This UK pop punk combo began in the mid-80s. Leigh was playing with the Others, whilst Mick partnered In The Dark. Both were locals from the Uxbridge area, and when the groups folded Mick volunteered his drumming skills for the proposed band Leigh was inaugurating. They found vocalist Malcolm through an advertisment in the weekly *Sounds* music paper and bass player Gary, a multi-instrumentalist, who was one of the Others original drummers. However, when he emigrated they drafted in another Gary, but he was as short-lived as his namesake. Huggy then stepped in as the permanent bass player. The final shift came in 1991 when Pete (also ex-Others) replaced Mick. Their first release came with a single jointly sponsored by *So What!* fanzine, 'The Price You Pay'. 1989 saw them joining the Released Emotions roster where they found Paul Fox (ex-Ruts) to produce their best recording, 'Between The Lies'. Their first album followed several months later.

Album: *Table Of Uncles* (1990).

Primal Scream

The line-up which achieved so much success in 1991 consisted of Bobby Gillespie (b. 22 June 1964), Andrew Innes, Robert Young, Henry Olsen, Tobay Toman, Martin Duffy and Denise Johnson, but Primal Scream had been a fluctuating affair since the middle of the 80s. Bobby Gillespie was the centrifugal force throughout, forming the band after a stint as stand-up drummer in the nascent Jesus And Mary Chain. Primal Scream achieved immediate popularity via *New Musical Express*'s alternative *C86* cassette compilation with 'Velocity Girl', an 80-second romp through the richer pastures of 60s guitar pop. After an album's worth of similarly melodic material for a brief liaison with the short-lived Elevation label, they veered towards rock territory near the end of the decade, revealing a penchant for leather trousers, wild guitars and idol-worshipping. The latter characteristic, at least, was to be a significant feature in their subsequent form, as Gillespie, encouraged by guitarist Andrew Innes, developed an interest in the burgeoning dance and drug scene. Come the start of the 90s, Primal Scream had been reinvented, with the aid of name remixers such as Andy Weatherall, into a groove machine. The 'Loaded' single was the first proof of the band's transformation, stealing from

Primal Scream

rock's heritage and cult biker movies yet invading Britain's dancefloors to become a Top 10 hit in the UK charts Their iconoclastic ideals persisted, no more so than on the road, where Primal Scream's hedonistic indulgences were well-publicized. 1991's *Screamadeliica* double album emphasized the band's cultural diversities and reaped rich critical acclaim, just before the band relocated to Tennessee to work on the follow up.

Albums: *Sonic Flower Groove* (1987), *Primal Scream* (1989), *Screamadelica* (1991).

Primitives

This highly-melodic group, from Coventry, England, formed in the summer of 1985, with a line-up featuring Kieron (vocals), Paul Court (b. 27 July 1965; vocals/guitar), Steve Dullaghan (b. 18 December 1966; bass) and Pete Tweedie (drums). Kieron was soon replaced by Tracy Tracy (b. 18 August 1967, Australia). The group set up their own label, Lazy Records, and achieved a modicum of success on the UK independent circuit with 'Thru The Flowers', 'Really Stupid' and 'Stop Killing Me'. Despite the label now having status as a subsidiary of the major RCA set-up, the Primitives maintained their roots in the 'indie' scene and were, for a time,

the pop press darlings. With echoes of Blondie and the Ramones, the Primitives' jangling guitar work brought them national fame in early 1988, when 'Crash', a classic piece of 'indie' pop, reached the UK Top 5. The accompanying album, *Lovely*, reached the UK Top 10, but any chance of consolidating this position was halted by personnel changes. The acrimonious ousting of Pete Tweedie saw the inclusion of Tig Williams, with further line-up changes in Andy Hobson replacing Dullaghan. Subsequent singles failed to emulate the success of 'Crash' and the follow-up *Pure* was only a partial success. The Primitives ended the 80s touring the USA and returned to UK to undergo extensive touring around Britain, hoping to regenerate those brief glory days.

Albums: *Lovely* (1988), *Pure* (1989), *Galore* (1992). Compilation: *Lazy 86-88* (1989).

Prisoners

This mod-influenced group hailed from the UK's Medway Valley in Kent. Chief songwriter Graham Day (guitar/vocals), Allan Crockford (bass), James 'Jamie' Taylor (Hammond organ) and Johnny Symons (drums) emerged in 1982 with a rough and raucous debut, *A Taste Of Pink*, on their Own Up

label. A deal with the Ace Records subsidiary, Big Beat, yielded *The Wisermiserdemelza* in 1983, a far more laid back, considered effort that ranged from powerful, 60s-influenced rock (the single, 'Hurricane') to tranquil ballads. The EP *Electric Fit* followed in 1984 and was notable for the excellent 'Melanie'. The band were featured on television's *The Tube* with other Big Beat acts, celebrated on the EP, *Four On Four: Trash On The Tube*, the Prisoners contributing the awesome 'Reaching My Head'. The group were unhappy with the sound on their second album and returned to Own Up for *The Last Fourfathers*, a less slick production, but a more mature offering. It was enough to secure a deal with Stiff/Countdown, but from the start the relations between band and label were poor. Although *In From The Cold* was an impressive album, it was far poppier and cleaner than the Prisoners had wished. Preceded by 'Whenever I'm Gone' (a re-recording from *The Last Fourfathers*), the album was badly promoted and the band, incredibly disillusioned with the proceedings, split soon after. Aside from two live albums shared with the Milkshakes, there has since been an album's worth of rarities, *Rare And Unissued*. As to the Prisoners themselves, James Taylor has since carved out a niche with his originally Booker T. Jones-influenced, and now rare groove-inspired, Quartet. Crockford joined him for a while before reuniting with Graham Day (after his spell with Milkshakes offshoot, Thee Mighty Caesars) in the Prime Movers. The Prisoners influenced many of the later Manchester bands, namely the Charlatans and the Inspiral Carpets.
Albums: *A Taste Of Pink* (1982), *The Wisermiserdemelza* (1983, reissued on CD with bonus tracks 1990), *The Last Fourfathers* (1985), with the Milkshakes *The Last Night At The MIC Club* (1986), *In From The Cold* (1986), *Milkshakes V Prisoners Live* (1987), *Rare And Unissued* (1991).

Proclaimers

This Scottish folk duo, who specialized in belligerent harmonies, consisted of identical twins Craig and Charlie Reid from Auchtermuchty. They had an early hit in 1987 with the Gerry Rafferty produced 'Letter From America'. Follow-ups included the typically boisterous 'Make My Heart Fly' and 'I'm Gonna Be'. Pete Wingfield was brought in to produce *Sunshine On Leith*, after which they took a two-year sabbatical. Writing for the third album was disrupted, however, when they spent much energy and money ensuring that their beloved, debt-ridden Hibernian Football Club did not close down. In common with many fans, they are now shareholders. They reappeared in 1990 with the *King Of The Road* EP. The title track, a cover of the old Roger Miller song, came from the film *The Crossing*. Other tracks

on the EP, which reached the UK Top 10, included the folk/country classic 'Long Black Veil'.
Albums: *This Is The Story* (1987), *Sunshine On Leith* (1988).

Professionals

This UK group was an offshoot from the notorious Sex Pistols and featured Paul Cook (drums/vocals) and Steve Jones (guitar/vocals) plus Ray McVeigh (guitar/vocals) and Paul Myers (bass, ex-Vic Goddard And The Subway Sect). The band received plenty of press attention thanks to the involvement of Cook and Jones but their debut album proved disappointing. A second album followed, plus a handful of singles, which still could not convince either the critics or the record-buying public that they had anything to offer.
Albums: *The Professionals* (1980), *I Didn't See It Coming* (1981).

Propaganda

Propaganda

This Euro pop/synthesizer band left their native Germany to arrive in England in 1983. Comprising Claudia Brücken (ex-Eggolinos; vocals), Michael Mertens (ex-Dusseldorf Symphony Orchestra; percussion), Susanne Freytag and Ralf Dorper (keyboards), they found an early advocate in Paul Morley of ZTT Records. Their first release, 'Dr. Mabuse', rallied well in the UK charts, reaching

number 27. However, due to the label, and Trevor Horn's commitment to Frankie Goes To Hollywood, the follow-up would not be released until over a year later. 'Duel'/'Jewel' was more successful still as Brücken moved permanently to England to wed Morley. The group's first live performance in June 1985 saw their line-up bolstered by Derek Forbes (ex-Simple Minds) on bass and Steve Jansen (ex-Japan, brother of David Sylvian) on drums. *A Secret Wish* and the single from it, 'P-Machinery', emerged a month later. Their European tour saw another line-up shuffle with Brian McGee (also ex-Simple Minds) taking over drums, and Kevin Armstrong on guitar, alongside Brücken, Mertens, Freytag and Forbes. Dorper had departed on the advent of the tour, and eventually only Mertens remained from the original line-up. They became involved in a huge legal battle with ZTT, and Brücken decided to stay with her husband's label. She formed Act with Thomas Leer in 1987. When the litigation had finished in 1988 the new Propaganda line-up featured Besti Miller, an American expatriate based in Germany on vocals. They released *1-2-3-4* in 1990, with contributions from old hands Freytag and Dorper, as well as Howard Jones and David Gilmour. Meanwhile, Brücken had embarked on a solo career.
Albums: *A Secret Wish* (1985), *1-2-3-4* (1990). Solo album: Claudia Brücken *Love; And A Million Other Things* (1991).

Psychedelic Furs

Psychedelic Furs
Until the recruitment of a drummer (Vince Ely) in 1979, Richard Butler (b. 5 June 1956, Kingston-upon-Thames, Surrey, England; vocals), Roger Morris (guitar), ex-Photon John Ashton (b. 30 November 1957; guitar), Duncan Kilburn (woodwinds) and Tim Butler (b. 7 December 1958; bass) had difficulties finding work. The group were also dogged by an unprepossessing sullenness in interview, an equally anachronistic group name - inspired by the 1966 Velvet Underground track, 'Venus In Furs' - and Richard Butler's grating one-

note style. It was not until a session on John Peel's BBC Radio 1 programme that they were invested with hip credibility - and a CBS recording contract. Under Steve Lillywhite's direction, their bleak debut album was followed by minor singles chart entries with 'Dumb Waiter' and 'Pretty In Pink', both selections from 1981's more tuneful *Talk Talk Talk*. Creeping even closer to the UK Top 40, 'Love My Way' was the chief single from *Forever Now*, produced in the USA by Todd Rundgren. On replacing Ely with Philip Calvert (ex-Birthday Party) in 1982, the outfit traded briefly as just 'the Furs' before *Mirror Moves* emitted a UK Top 30 hit with 'Heaven' (which was underpinned with a fashionable disco rhythm). Lucrative too were 'Ghost In You' and a re-recording of 'Pretty In Pink' for inclusion on 1986's *Midnight To Midnight* film soundtrack. That same year, they appeared at the mammoth Glastonbury Fayre festival - which, to many of their fans, remains the most abiding memory of the Psychedelic Furs as performers. By 1990, Ashton, the Butler brothers and hired hands were all that remained of a band that had become mostly a studio concern.
Albums: *Psychedelic Furs* (1980), *Talk Talk Talk* (1981), *Forever Now* (1982), *Mirror Moves* (1984), *Midnight To Midnight* (1987), *Book Of Days* (1989), *World Outside* (1991). Compilations: *All Of This And Nothing* (1988), *The Collection* (1991).

Psychic TV
This somewhat misunderstood UK rock group whose *avant garde*, aural experimentalism has been overshadowed by their connections with the literary underworld. They were formed by Genesis P. Orridge (b. c.1950; ex-Pork Dukes and Throbbing Gristle) and Peter Christopherson (ex-Throbbing Gristle). The line-up also included P. Orridge's long-term lover, Cosey Fanni Tutti and Geoff Rushton (former editor of *Stabmental* fanzine). However, Christopherson and Rushton soon left to form Coil. P. Orridge has been portrayed in much of the media as a deranged and dangerous madman. He had first come to the attention of the media and authorities as the organizer of the 'Prostitution' exhibition at London's ICA gallery in the late 70s. His shock tactics continued with his work in Throbbing Gristle and Psychic TV, and much use was made of fascinating/disturbing slide and film back projection at gigs. Alternatively, Genesis has repeatedly been revealed as a most personable and charming a character as the music industry has thrown up, albeit a little mischievous. P. Orridge takes his inspiration from the works of the Maquis De Sade, Charles Manson and particularly William Burroughs. Burroughs reciprocated the respect, and has stated of Psychic TV that they provide: 'the most important

work with communication that I know of in the popular medium'. This is central to the band, and the philosophical congregation which backs them, the Temple Ov Psychick Youth. Their use of guerrilla tactics in the information war follows on from Throbbing Gristle's work, and makes use of broad readings of situationist and deconstructionist thought. P. Orridge's respect for 60s stars Brian Wilson and Brian Jones were revealed with two minor UK chart singles in 1986. The surprisingly poppy 'Godstar' celebrated the former Rolling Stones' guitarist, while the tribute to Wilson was a cover of 'Good Vibrations'. In an ambitious project, from 1986, the group aimed to issue 23 live albums on the 23rd of each month (23 being a statistically, symbolic number), each from a different country from their world tour. After walking out of their deal with Some Bizarre (who released their debut single 'Just Driftin') the band no longer involve themselves with the business concerns of music, like promotion. The ranks of the band have been swelled by a variety of members, including John Gosling (ex-Zos Kia), Alex Ferguson (ex-Alternative TV), Daniel Black, Matthew Best, Dave Martin and many others. They have also branched out in to other media such as film and literature. (They made available recordings of Burroughs speeches for the first time.) Although the mainstream music press have continually painted a black picture of Psychic TV's music (and activities), it can at times be surprisingly bright and accessible. Conventional *society's* inability to come to terms with Psychic TV's message was demonstrated early in 1992 when police seized videos, books and magazines from Genesis P. Orridge's Brighton home after a performance art video was, it was claimed, shown out of context on a television programme about child abuse. The Orridges reportedly since fled the USA.

Albums: *Force The Hand Of Chance* (1982), *Dreams Less Sweet* (1983), *New York Scum Haters* (1984), *Themes* (1985), *Mouth Of The Night* (1985), *Live In Tokyo* (1986), *Pagan Day* (1987), *Live En Suisse* (1987), *Berlin Atonal, Vol. 1* (1987), *Live In Heaven* (1987), *Live In Reyjavik* (1987), *Live At Gottingen* (1987), *Temporary Temple* (1988), *Live At Mardi Gras* (1988), *Allegory And Self* (1988), *Live At Thee Circus* (1988), *Live In Glasgow* (1989), *Themes 3* (1989), *Live In Paris* (1989), *Live In Toronto* (1989), *Live At The Ritz* (1989), *Live At The Pyramid* (1989), *Kondole/Copycat* (1989), *Towards Thee Infinite Beat* (1990).

Public Image Limited

Public Image Ltd (PiL) was the 'company' formed by John Lydon (b. 31 January 1966, London, England) when he left behind both the Sex Pistols and previous monicker Johnny Rotten in January 1978. With Lydon on vocals, classically trained pianist and early

Public Image Limited; John Lydon

Clash guitarist Keith Levene on guitar, reggae influenced bass player Jah Wobble (b. John Wordle), and Canadian drummer Jim Walker (ex-Furies), the band were put together with the working title of the Carnivorous Buttock Flies. By the time the debut single - 'Public Image' was released in its newspaper sleeve in September, they had adopted the less ridiculous name. Their live debut followed in Paris on 14 December, and they played the UK for the first time on Christmas Day. In January 1979 ex-101ers and Raincoats' drummer Richard Dudanski replaced Walker, who went on to punk band the Straps. The *Metal Box* set came out later that year as a set of 12-inch records housed in tin 'film' cans (it was later re-issued as a normal album). One of the most radical and difficult albums of its era, its conception and execution was a remarkable blend of Lydon's antagonism and Levene's climatic guitar. The single 'Death Disco' also reached the UK charts. With Dudanski leaving, Fall drummer Karl Burns was enlisted until Martin Atkins (b. 3 August 1959, Coventry, England) from Mynd, joined in time to tour the USA in the spring of 1980. A live album, *Paris Au Printemps*, was recorded after which both Wobble and Atkins left. Wobble went on to record solo material and work for London Transport as a train guard while Atkins joined Brian Brain.

In May 1981 Lydon and Levene, augmented by hired

musicians, played from behind an onstage screen at the New York Ritz. The crowd failed to grasp the concept and 'bottled' the band. After *Flowers Of Romance* Pete Jones (b. 22 September 1957) became bass player, and Atkins returned on drums. Around this time subsidiary members Dave Crowe and Jeanette Lee, who had been with the band since the beginning in business roles, both departed and the group started a new era as Lydon decided to settle in Los Angeles. In 1983 Jones left as the hypnotic 'This Is Not A Love Song' became PiL's a Top 5 hit, and Levene also departed as it was climbing the chart. In a relatively quiet period when Lydon collaborated with Afrika Bambaataa on the Time Zone single 'World Destruction', PiL released only the 1984 album *This Is What You Want, This Is What You Get*, and another set of live recordings from foreign fields. Lydon also made his first feature film appearance in *Order Of Death*. They returned to the forefront with 1986's *Album*, from which came 'Single' aka 'Rise' featuring the drumming talent of Ginger Baker. The album included numerous guest/session musicians such as Steve Vai, Ryûichi Sakamoto and Tony Williams. The next year, Lydon assembled a permanent band once again, this time drawing on guitarists John McGeogh (ex-Magazine, Siouxsie And The Banshees, Armoury Show) and Lu Edmunds (ex-Damned, Mekons, 3 Mustaphas 3), bass player Allan Dias from America (formerly in nightclub backing bands and working with stars such as Tyrone Ashley and the *avant garde* Sun Ra), and drummer Bruce Smith (ex-Pop Group and various sessions). Lu Edmunds was forced to leave because he was suffering from tinnitus (Ted Chau was a temporary replacement) and Smith left as the band fell into inactivity again after 1988. The three remaining members came back to life in 1990 when Virgin Records put out a *Greatest Hits . . . So Far* compilation, confidently including the new single 'Don't Ask Me' - Lydon's nod to the environmental problems of the world. After several years and countless line-ups, Lydon has remained the *enfant terrible* of the music industry, a constant irritant and occasional source of brilliance: 'I've learnt to manipulate the music business. I have to deal with all kinds of stupid, sycophantic people. I've just learnt to understand my power. Everyone should learn that, otherwise they lose control'. PiL's new drummer is Mike Joyce (ex-Smiths, Buzzcocks).
Albums: *Public Image* (1978), *Metal Box* (1979), *Paris Au Printemps* (1980), *Flowers Of Romance* (1981), *Live In Tokyo* (1983), *This Is What You Want, This Is What You Get* (1984), *Album* (1986), *Happy?* (1987), *9* (1989), *That What Is Not* (1992). Compilation: *Greatest Hits . . . So Far* (1990).

Purple Hearts

This UK group was one of a wave of late 70s UK mod revivalists, hailing from Romford on the east London/Essex borders. Previously they had been Jack Plug And The Sockets, who were closer to punk than mod. By May 1978 however, they had changed their name to the Purple Hearts (after a drug much favoured by mods in the 60s). The line-up featured Robert Manton (vocals), Simon Stebbing (guitar), Jeff Shadbolt (bass) and Gary Sparks (drums). They signed to Fiction, the new label formed by Chris Parry. The group came to prominence on the *March Of The Mods* tour with Secret Affair and Back To Zero. Their debut single came in September 1979 with 'Millions Like Us', with 'Frustration' and 'Jimmy' following shortly afterwards. The first and last of the trio brushed the lower regions of the charts. By 1980 they had moved on to the Safari label and released 'My Life's A Jigsaw' and 'Plane Crash', after which they split up. They reformed in 1982 for a one-off single, 'Scooby Doo', on Roadrunner Records. They returned once more in 1986 to record their second album for Razor.
Albums: *Beat That* (1980), *Pop-Ish Frenzy* (1986).

Q Tips

Fronted by Paul Young (b. 17 January 1956, Luton, Bedfordshire, England), Q-Tips was one of the most renowned live bands on the UK club circuit in the early 80s, playing an estimated 800 gigs in under three years. The group was formed in 1979 by Young and other ex-members of Streetband, John Gifford (guitar/vocals) and Mick Pearl (bass/vocals). In place of their former band's rock sound, Q-Tips was organized as a classic soul group with an experienced brass section of Tony Hughes (trumpet),and saxophonists Steve Farr and Stewart Blandamer who had worked with Johnny Wakelin's Kinshasa Band, Jimmy James And the Vagabonds and the Flirtations. Other members were Barry Watts drums and Ian Kewley (keyboards) from Samson and latterly hard rock band Limey. With matching suits and arrangements out of the Tamla/Motown and Stax songbooks, Q-Tips were seen as part of a mod revival. After releasing a frantic version of Joe Tex's 'SYSLJFM (The Letter Song)' on the independent Shotgun label, the group signed to Chrysalis and covered the Miracles' 'Tracks Of My Tears'. By now

Clifford had been replaced by Garth Watt-Roy, whose career had included spells with Greatest Show On Earth, Fuzzy Duck, Marmalade and Limey. The debut album included Blandamer originals like 'A Man Can't Lose' as well as cover versions, but its lack of sales led to Chrysalis dropping the band. The group then signed to Rewind Records which chose a version of Boudleaux Bryant's 'Love Hurts' as a single. Although this failed to sell, it brought Young to the notice of CBS, which signed him as a solo artist at the start of 1982. This was the signal for the break-up of Q-Tips, and they disbanded after a farewell tour and the release of a live album. *Live At Last* included 'Broken Man', the first song co-written by Young and Kewley, who would continue their partnership during the first phase of the singer's triumphant solo career.

Albums: *Q-Tips* (1980), *Live At Last* (1982), *BBC Radio 1 Live In Concert* (1991).

Questions

Stephen Lennon (vocals/guitar), John Robertson (vocals/guitar), Paul Barry (vocals/bass) and Chris Kowalski (drums) were all pupils at a secondary school in Edinburgh, Scotland when their home-recorded demo tape secured a recording deal with Zoom, a local independent label. The group's two singles betrayed an obvious immaturity, but they also unveiled the germ of a songwriting talent. Voted 'Best Young Band' on television's *Saturday Banana* show, the Questions then came to the attention of Jam/Style Council leader Paul Weller who signed the quartet to his Respond label. When Lennon left the line-up, Paul Barry emerged as the group's principal songsmith and his melodic, soul-tinged direction was apparent on the unit's three minor hits, 'Price You Pay', 'Tear Soup' (both 1983) and 'Tuesday Sunshine' (1984). However, they were unable to secure a significant breakthrough and when Weller's own commercial fortunes declined, so did those of his several proteges, including the Questions.

Album: *Belief* (1984).

Quick

This UK studio-based duo featured Col Campsie (vocals/guitar), George McFarlane (synthesizers/bass/guitar). They not only worked on their own material but also wrote for Chaka Khan and produced Haywoode, Blue Zoo and Second Image. The Quick debuted in 1980 and instantly became club favourites with a string of singles aimed at the dancefloor. Only one single 'Rhythm Of The Jungle' managed to cross over to the singles chart, just missing the UK Top 40 position by one place. On the strength of the hit an album containing all the singles to date plus some of the b-sides was released to little success. By 1983 they had found club success in the USA, but the limited

following in the UK had dwindled so much that all future releases sank without trace. In 1988 the duo re-emerged as Giant Steps along with Gardner Cole (keyboards), Edie Lehmann (backgrounds), Bruce Gaitsch (guitar) and David Boruff (saxophone). The debut album and a single 'Another Lover' were both Top 20 hits in the USA.

Albums: *Fascinating Rhythm* (1982), *International Thing* (1984), *Wah Wah* (1986), as Giant Steps *The Book Of Pride* (1988).

R

Radical Dance Faction

Formed out of the ashes of UK anarcho reggae outfit Military Surplus, RDF, as they are commonly abbreviated, set out in 1987. Their line-ups have been erratic but are based around the one constant, lyricist and vocalist Chris Bowsher. Using beat poetry, with its imagery of modern decay and capitalism gone wrong, their chosen musical outlet is reggae. Bowsher was a veteran of the early punk explosion, and was particularly enamoured of bands like the Clash and Ruts who attempted to bridge the gap between rock and black music. Alongside the Levellers, they became prime movers in the media-christened 'crusty' movement (ie their following comprises largely the dispossessed and homeless, bonded by a political consciousness which has its roots in hippiedom, beatnik romanticism and early 80s anarcho-punk).

Albums: *Borderland Cases* (1989), *Wasteland* (1991).

Radio Stars

This UK group was formed in 1977 by Andy Ellison (vocals), Ian McLeod (guitar) and Martin Gordon (bass), all of whom were previously members of Jet. Drummer Steve Parry completed the line-up of a group engendering considerable interest through its association with John's Children (Ellison) and Sparks (Gordon). A series of tongue-in-cheek singles, including 'Dirty Pictures' and 'Nervous Wreck', captured the quartet's brand of quirky pop/punk, but although the latter reached the fringes of the Top 40, the group was unable to achieve consistent success. Trevor White, also ex-Sparks, was later added to the line-up but Gordon's departure in December 1978 undermined any lingering potential and Radio Stars disbanded the following year. Ellison and White subsequently undertook several low-key projects and

the singer later revived the group's name, but to little success.
Albums: *Songs For Swinging Lovers* (1977), *Radio Stars' Holiday Album* (1978).

Railway Children

Formed in 1985 by Gary Newby (b. 5 June 1966, Australia), Brian Bateman (b. 3 August 1966, Wigan, Lancashire, England), Stephen Hull (b. 7 July 1966, Wigan, Lancashire, England) and Guy Keegan (b. 16 June 1966, Wigan, Lancashire, England), the Railway Children started playing small gigs around the northwest of England. After a batch of demo tapes the four 19-year-olds found themselves being feted by numerous record companies, eventually settling on a contract-free deal with Factory Records. A brace of graceful singles which fused 60s harmonies with the early 80s pop sensibility of Liverpool paved the way for the fine *Reunion Wilderness* in 1987, and the Railway Children appeared set to follow guitar-based contemporaries the Smiths onto greater things. The band signed to Virgin Records that same year, and suddenly sounded a lot neater for it. The expensive production polish eradicated the quartet's rougher edges, and with pivotal creative force Gary Newby content to have his immense instinct smoothed by studio techniques, *Recurrence* appeared in 1988 to an uncertain audience confused by the band's Independent beginnings and the new, mellower sound. Although singles regularly entered the Top 75 of the UK charts and the Railway Children flirted with fashionable dance beats with particularly encouraging results in America, it was not until the start of 1991 that a re-released version of 'Every Beat Of The Heart' took the band into the upper echelons of the UK chart and thus validated their efforts of five years.
Albums: *Reunion Wilderness* (1987), *Recurrence* (1988), *Native Place* (1990).

Rain

This group originated in Liverpool, England in the late 80s and adopted the heritage of harmony pop in the vein of the Byrds. Rain were initially notable by dint of having three good harmony singers to back up their Rickenbacker guitar sound. They formed at the Merseyside Trade Union Community And Unemployed Resource Centre in Liverpool, set up with a £100,000 grant. The band's original locale was the severely depressed Huyton area, but eight months later they were signed to CBS and worked on album sessions with Nick Lowe. After a debut single, 'Lemonstone Desired', they courted controversy with the provocative nudity featured on the cover of 'Taste Of Rain'. Their debut album was honed by months of rehearsal with guest appearances by Green On Red and blues musician Joe Louis

Walker. The band comprise Ned Clark, Colin Murphy (singers, guitarists and songwriters), Martin Campbell and Tony McGuigan (bass and drums).
Album: *A Taste Of Rain* (1991).

Raincoats

This all-girl outfit epitomized the experimental approach that characterized much of punk's aftermath. Vicky Aspinall, Gina Birch, Ana Da Silva and Shirley O'Loughlin were originally joined by Palmolive before she left to concentrate on the Slits. This line-up was merely a nucleus for a flexible structure that involved numerous other musicians. The Raincoats' debut, 'Fairytale In The Supermarket', appeared on Rough Trade (a label that shared their ground-breaking stance) in 1979. A self-titled album that same year shared a similarly distinctive sound and both were revered by critics and a hardcore of admirers alike. *Odyshape* followed in 1981, but was less direct than their debut. Two further singles, a cover of Sly Stone's 'Running Away' (1982) and 'Animal Rhapsody' (1983) both hinted at unfulfilled potential. The Raincoats eventually delivered their swansong in 1984 with *Moving*. However, as fitting an epitaph as any can be found on *The Kitchen Tapes*, on the ROIR label originally released in 1983.
Albums: *The Raincoats* (1979), *Odyshape* (1981), *The Kitchen Tapes* (1983), *Moving* (1984).

Rain Parade

Rain Parade

Part of Los Angeles' rock renaissance of the early 80s, the Rain Parade drew from late 60s influences to forge a new brand of psychedelia-tinged rock. After a promising debut single, 'What She's Done To Your Mind' on their own Llama label, the band - David Roback (vocals, guitar, percussion), brother Steve (vocals, bass), Matthew Puicci (vocals, guitar, sitar), Will Glenn (keyboards, violin) and Eddie Kalwa (drums) - issued *Emergency Third Rail Power Trip* to critical acclaim in 1983, followed by the excellent 'You Are My Friend' in 1985. Such was their impetus that the Rain Parade signed with Island Records, despite the loss of key figure David Roback (who then formed Opal with partner and original Rain Parade bassist Kendra Smith). His replacement John Thoman arrived alongside new drummer Mark Marcum in time for *Beyond The Sunset*, drawn from live performances in Japan. A second studio set, *Crashing Dream*, emerged later in the year, but some of the original Rain Parade's other-worldly, evocative nature had been lost. It was not until 1988 that the band issued *Explosions In A Glass Palace* on Zippo. Whatever promise this album contained, it proved to be their last.

Albums: *Emergency Third Rail Power Trip* (1983), *Beyond The Sunset* (1985), *Crashing Dream* (1985), *Explosions In A Glass Palace* (1988).

Ramones

Ramones

The Ramones, comprising Johnny Ramone (b. John Cummings, 8 October 1951, Long Island, New York, USA; guitar), Dee Dee Ramone (b. Douglas Colvin, 18 September 1952, Vancouver, British Columbia, Canada; bass) and Joey Ramone (b. Jeffrey Hyman, 1952; drums) made their debut at New York's Performance Studio on 30 March 1974. Two months later manager Tommy Ramone (b. Tommy Erdelyi, 29 January 1952, Budapest, Hungary) replaced Joey on drums, who then switched to vocals. The quartet later secured a residency at the renowned

CBGB's club where they became one of the city's leading proponents of punk rock. The fever-paced *Ramones* was a startling first album. Its high-octane assault drew from 50s kitsch and 60s garage-bands, while leather jackets, ripped jeans and an affected dumbness enhanced their music's cartoon-like quality. The group's debut appearance in London in July 1976 influenced a generation of British punk musicians, while *The Ramones Leave Home*, which included 'Suzie Is A Headbanger' and 'Gimme Gimme Shock Treatment', confirmed the sonic attack of its predecessor. *Rocket To Russia* was marginally less frenetic as the group's novelty appeal waned, although 'Sheena Is A Punk Rocker' gave the group their first UK Top 30 hit, in 1977. In May 1978 Tommy Ramone left to pursue a career in production and former Richard Hell drummer Marc Bell, now Marky Ramone, replaced him for *Road To Ruin* as the band sought to expand their appealing, but limited, style. They took a starring role in the trivial *Rock 'N' Roll High School* film, a participation which led to their collaboration with producer Phil Spector. The resultant release, *End Of The Century*, was a curious hybrid, and while Johnny baulked at Spector's laborious recording technique, Joey, whose penchant for girl-group material gave the Ramones their sense of melody, was less noticeably critical. The album contained a sympathetic version of the Ronettes' 'Baby I Love You' which became the group's biggest UK hit single when it reached the Top 10.

The Ramones entered the 80s looking increasingly anachronistic, unable or unwilling to change. *Pleasant Dreams*, produced by Graham Gouldman, revealed a group now outshone by the emergent hard-core acts they had inspired. However, *Subterranean Jungle* showed a renewed purpose which was maintained sporadically on *Animal Boy* and *Halfway To Sanity*, the former containing 'Bonzo Goes To Bitburg', a hilarious riposte to Ronald Reagan's ill-advised visit to a cemetery containing graves of Nazi SS personnel. Although increasingly confined to pop's fringes, a revitalized line-up - Joey, Johnny, Marky and newcomer C.J. - undertook a successful 1990 US tour alongside fellow CBGB's graduate Deborah Harry and Talking Heads' offshoot Tom Tom Club.

Albums: *Ramones* (1976), *The Ramones Leave Home* (1977), *Rocket To Russia* (1977), *Road To Ruin* (1978), *It's Alive* (1979), *End Of The Century* (1980), *Pleasant Dreams* (1981), *Subterranean Jungle* (1983), *Too Tough To Die* (1984), *Animal Boy* (1986), *Halfway To Sanity* (1987), *Brain Drain* (1989), *Loco Live* (1991). Compilation: *Ramones Mania* (1988), *All The Stuff And More (Volume One)* (1990).

Rank And File

Formed in Los Angeles in 1981, Rank And File

228

comprised of former members of the Dils, Chip Kinman (guitar/vocals) and Tony Kinman (bass/vocals), and ex-Nuns' guitarist/vocalist Alejandro Escovedo. Drummer Slim Evans completed the line-up featured on *Sundown*, an exemplary blend of new wave and country. The album included 'Amanda Ruth', later recorded by the Everly Brothers. The Kinman brothers then took control of the group and, having moved to Austin, Texas, completed *Long Gone Dead* with session musicians, including Richard Greene (fiddle) and Stan Lynch, drummer with Tom Petty And The Heartbreakers. The new set emphasized the duo's love of pop melody, but the contents were still infused with C&W. A long hiatus ensued, but their third album proved a major disappointment, lacking the verve and charm of its predecessors. Rank And File was then disbanded with the Kinmans later founding Blackbird. Escovedo reappeared leading the acclaimed True Believers before embarking on a solo career.
Albums: *Sundown* (1982), *Long Gone Dead* (1984), *Rank And File* (1987).

Rapeman

This controversially-named US act was created when Steve Albini (ex-Big Black; guitar/vocals) joined forces with two former members of Scratch Acid, David Wm. Sims (bass) and Rey Washam (drums). The trio was short-lived and their output comprised of a single, 'Inkis' Butt Crack', released on the cult Sub Pop label, *Budd*, a 4-track set, and *Two Nuns And A Pack Mule*. The album maintained the loud, uncompromising sound the two previous groups had offered - tight, crashing drums, pounding bass and sheets of metallic guitarwork - and included a startling interpretation of Z.Z. Top's 'Just Got Paid'. However, the group was unable to shake off criticism of its repellent name which Albini took from a character in contemporary Japanese comics. Several distributors objected to handling the album and many venues were forced under pressure, particularly at colleges and universities, to cancel appearances, which in part explained the trio's demise. Sims subsequently resurfaced in the Jesus Lizard, which Albini produced.
Album: *Two Nuns And A Pack Mule* (1988).

Ratcat

Emerging in 1986 from Australia's thrash metal scene and based in Sydney, Ratcat relocated to the UK to promote their Ramones tinged pop rock. The trio comprises Simon Day (vocals, guitar), Amr Zaid (bass and occasional vocals) and Andrew Polin (drums). If UK audiences were surprised to see them occupy support slots for INXS, it was less of a shock in their homeland, where they regularly top the charts and

appear on the covers of teenage magazines. Despite the obvious commercial validity of the band, their music remains rooted in pure garage group aesthetics: 'We've always said that, at heart, we're basically scuzz rats. We're at our best when we're at our scuzziest'.
Albums: *Tingles* (1991), *Blind Love* (1991).

Razorcuts

Revolving around the songwriting talents of vocalist/guitarist Gregory Webster and bassist Tim Vass, the Razorcuts emerged at the tail end of the independent scene's melodic mid-80s phase. It was a time when bands wore their influences on their sleeves, from the Byrds to the Buzzcocks, and the Razorcuts were no exception. 'Big Pink Cake', issued on the Subway Organisation in 1986, had all the familiar trademarks of the period; a simple melody, a childlike theme sung in a childlike, out-of-tune voice, a hand-drawn sleeve and jangly guitars. The songs possessed a certain charm, particularly evident on November's 'Sorry To Embarrass You' EP. The presence of New Zealand drummer and music journalist David Smith led the band to antipodean label Flying Nun for their third single, 'I Heard You The First Time', released in June 1987. When the label ceased operations in the UK, the Razorcuts relocated, ending up at Creation, a label which sympathized with the band's 60s influences. And it was the Byrds' early sound which dominated *The Storyteller*. Issued in February 1988, it benefited from its musical intricacies, but did little to avoid accusations of plagiarism. A year later, *The World Keeps Turning* found a band struggling to develop their folk rock sound, despite the added clout of a second guitarist, Pete Momtchiloff, to beef up Webster's 12-string, a new drummer, Struan Robertson, backing vocals from Richard Mason and some attractive Hammond organ from producer John Rivers. When the Razorcuts split shortly afterwards, Vass formed Red Chair Fadeaway and combined folk elements with a laid-back psychedelic feel.
Albums: *The Storyteller* (1988), *The World Keeps Turning* (1989).

Real Kids

This American quartet gained recognition amid the punk-rock explosion in New York during the late 70s. Formed by vocalist/guitarist John Felice in 1975, they pre-dated the punk movement, but jumped on the bandwagon as soon as it started to roll. With bassist Allen 'Alpo' Paulino, Billy Borgioli (guitar) and Howard Ferguson (drums) completing the line-up, they were a talented outfit and competent musicians to boot. Delivering a varied and classy selection of predominantly high-energy rockers, they infused reggae, rock 'n' roll and pop influences into their songs, making them instantly memorable. Their self-titled debut, released in 1977, is one of the great unheralded classics of this genre. Borgioli and Ferguson departed to be replaced by Billy Cole and Robby 'Morocco' Morin before the recording of their second album. *Outta Place* was a disappointment, for Felice's new compositions lacked the infectious sparkle that made their debut so special. A shambolic live album, recorded in Paris, 1983 was their final offering, before disbanding.

Albums: *The Real Kids* (1977), *Outta Place* (1982), *All Kindsa Jerks Live* (1983).

Records

Will Birch (b. c.1950, Essex, England) started out on his drumming career in the 60s with local Southend band the Geezenstacks. He then moved on to the Tradewinds who performed two songs and appeared in a BBC television documentary about young people screened in June 1965. Next up came a stint in the Flowerpots with Wilko Johnson, before he played with Surly Bird, Glory, Cow Pie, the Hot Jets, and even a few gigs with Dr Feelgood. He later joined the Kursaal Fliers when they formed in October 1973. When the Kursaals split in November 1977 Birch formed a partnership with John Wicks who had been the Kursaals' lead singer for the last few months of their existence (and also played rhythm guitar). In February 1978 they recruited bassist Phil Brown (ex-the Janets) and guitarist Huw Gower, whom Birch spotted playing a one-off gig with Peter Perret's (Only Ones) old band, the Ratbites From Hell. This completed the Records, who made their live debut at Bristol Granary Club in March 1978. The debut single, 'Starry Eyes', was released in November, becoming a minor pop classic in the process. The band then used their connections to join the *Be Stiff* tour ostensibly to back Rachel Sweet, but they also opened the show (the only non Stiff act on board). They signed to Virgin and released further quality pop singles all co-written by Birch, mostly with Wicks as his partner. The best were gathered together on the debut *Shades In Bed* which included an old song dating from Kursaal days, 'Girls That Don't Exist', plus 'Starry Eyes', and 'Teenerama'. Initial copies of the album also included a free 12-inch single featuring Records' cover versions of various well known songs. Ian Gibbons was drafted in to play keyboards on the album. Birch also wrote 'Hearts In Her Eyes' for the Searchers' 1979 comeback album. Gower left just before the second album to be replaced by Judy Cole. He joined David Johannson's band before going solo. By the time of their final album in 1982 the line-up was Birch, Wicks and Brown plus Dave Whelan (guitar) and Chris Gent (vocals).

Albums: *Shades In Bed* (1979), *Crashes* (1980), *Music On Both Sides* (1982). Compilation: *Smashes, Crashes*

Records

& Near Misses (1988).

Red Guitars

This Hull based guitar pop band featured Jerry Kidd (vocals), Louise Barlow (bass), Hallam Lewis (lead guitar), John Rowley (rhythm guitar), and Matt Higgins (drums). Formed in 1982 by Lewis and Kidd, they released two superb singles 'Good Technology' and 'Fact' before scoring a number 1 on the independent charts with 'Marimba Jive'. The latter was included on *Slow To Fade* which emerged on Kidd's own Self Drive Records in November 1984. A highly polished and original pop album, with Kidd's analytical lyrics to the fore: 'I said that I love you, God knows I tried, You say you still love me, But you're always saying goodbye'. Fittingly, Kidd himself was to leave barely two months after the album's release. He issued a press statement to the effect that 'Technically we improved a lot during the last year but musically, from my point of view, we were standing still. New ideas and songs I had for the group no longer seemed to fit in. I still favour independence within the record industry and shall continue to look for success, both artistic and commercial, with releases on my own Self Drive Record label.' He was quickly replaced by Robert Holmes, who played his first gig with the band at the University of London Union on 24 May 1985. Lou Howard replaced Barlow on bass as *Tales Of The Expected* saw the band move to One Way Records, through Virgin. Although the lyrical focus of the band had changed, they were still capable of producing highly individual and moving music, notably on singles like 'National Avenue' and the yearning 'Be With Me'. Interestingly, both album sleeves featured quotes from poet Sean O'Brien. Hallam and Howard left to form the Planet Wilson in 1987, with drummer Jonah Oxburrow (ex-That Noble Porpoise), and released the album *Not Drowning But Waving*. Hallam now runs his own studio in Hull.

Albums: *Slow To Fade* (1984), *Tales Of The Expected* (1985).

Red Hot Chili Peppers

These engaging Hollywood ruffians mixed funk and punk in the mid-80s and encouraged a legion of bands to regurgitate the formula. Led by 'Antwan The Swan' (b. Anthony Kiedis; vocals), the band's original line-up also featured 'Flea' (b. Michael Balzary, Melbourne, Australia), Hillel Slovak (b. Israel; guitar) and Jack Irons (b. California, USA; drums). They began life as garage band Anthem before Balzary departed for seminal 80s punks Fear. When Irons and Slovak moved on to join the less notable What Is This?, the nails appeared to be firmly in place on the Anthem coffin. However, under their new name, the Red Hot Chili Peppers acquired a speculative recording deal with EMI America. Unfortunately, as Irons and Slovak were under contract with their new band, their debut album had to be recorded with Jack Sherman on guitar and Cliff Martinez (ex-Captain Beefheart, Weirdos) on drums. Production was handled, somewhat surprisingly, by the Gang Of Four's Andy Gill. The results were disappointing. Nevertheless the band set about building their considerable reputation as a live outfit,

Red Hot Chili Peppers

much of which was fuelled by their penchant for appearing semi-naked or worse. Slovak returned to guitar duties for the second album, this time produced by George Clinton. Also featured was a horn section comprising Maceo Parker and Fred Wesley, veterans of James Brown among others. Martinez returned shortly after to reinstate the original Anthem line-up, and their third album saw a shift back to rock from the soul infatuation of its predecessors. 1988 brought the release of their renowned *Abbey Road* EP, featuring a pastiche of the famous Beatles album pose on the cover (the band were totally naked save for socks covering their genitalia). However, the mood was darkened when Slovak took an accidental heroin overdose and died

in June. Deeply upset, Irons left, while the band recruited John Frusciante (guitar) and Chad Smith (drums). After the release of *Freaky Styley* the single 'Knock Me Down' was released as a tribute to Slovak. Of their most recent excursion, 1991's *Blood, Sex, Sugar, Magik*, they successfully diagnosed their motivation, and much of their attraction: 'Just recognizing that I was a freak, but knowing that was a cool place to be.' Producer Rick Rubin, usually associated with the harder end of the metal spectrum (Slayer, Danzig), nevertheless brought out the Peppers' first ballads. Such sensitivity has done little to deter the vanguard of critics who have long since raged at what they saw as the band's innate sexism.

Albums: *Uplift Mofo Party Plan* (1988), *Mother's Milk* (1989), *The Red Hot Chili Peppers* (1990), *Freaky Styley* (1990), *Blood, Sex, Sugar, Magik* (1991).

Red Letter Day

This Portsmouth, England-based pop punk band formed in 1983, with a line-up consisting of Ade (vocals, guitar), Ian Campbell (lead guitar), Pete White (bass) and Brian Lee (drums). However, nine months and two demos later, Ade was joined by Daryn Price (drums), Keith Metcalfe (bass) and Davie Egan (guitar) in the band's second incarnation. After the single 'Wherever You May Run' they found favour with BBC disc jockey John Peel who secured a session for them on his show. The 12-inch EP *Released Emotions* followed on Quiet Records (they would, confusingly, join a record company with the same title, so called because its boss was a fan of the band). Metcalfe was replaced by a temporary bass player before Steve (ex-Original Mirrors) took over on bass. The highlight of 1987 was one of the support slots at the Polderock Festival in Belgium alongside the Mission, Primitives and Sonic Youth. Now on the Released Emotions label, they recorded a joint album with the Sect, titled *Soft Lights And Loud Guitars*. This picked up a series of good reviews and they appeared on the Link Records sampler *Underground Rockers*, alongside other bands of a similar persuasion like Mega City Four and the Price. Egan left shortly afterwards, to be replaced by their present guitarist Ray. After a double a-sided single they completed work on their first full long player, *More Songs About Love And War*, in a rockier vein.

Albums: *Soft Lights And Loud Guitars* (with the Sect) (1988), *More Songs About Love And War* (1991).

Red Lorry Yellow Lorry

This post punk gothic band formed in Leeds, England, in 1982, and their first single was 'Take It All Away'. The line-up consisted of Chris Reed (vocals/rhythm guitar), Wolfie (lead guitar), Paul Southern (bass) and Mick (drums). The debut *Talk About The Weather*, included 'Hollow Eyes', which proved popular in Gothic circles following its regular airing on BBC disc jockey John Peel's BBC Radio 1 show. The album was an intoxicating mix of musical aggression and lyrical minimalism ('It was a strange dream/He stood and stared/Those shining faces/Those darkened eyes/And alone he ran/Alone he ran', comprised the entire scope of the track 'Strange Dream'). After seven singles on Red Rhino Records the band moved on to Situation 2. By this time their material had been revitalized by a broader approach to songwriting: 'People are surprised to find that we have a sense of humour. We do see the irony of things in life'. 1988's 'Only Dreaming' attested to this, becoming their first ballad. In early 1990 the band was forced to cancel four gigs when the current drummer Chil was hospitalized for a wrist operation. After eight years' service Wolfie was also absent, leaving Reed as the only surviving original member. His replacement was Gary Weight, alongside bassist Martin Scott. Whatever momentum they had in the 80s seems to have largely dissipated.

Albums: *Talk About The Weather* (1985), *Paint Your Wagon* (1986), *Nothing's Wrong* (1988), *Smashed Hits* (1988), *Blow* (1989), *Drop* (1989).

Redskins

Redskins

This politically-motivated English trio united the left-wing skinhead movement with a volatile mix of punk and northern soul, aggression and belligerence.

Originally formed in York as No Swastikas, they relocated to London where singer/guitarist and *New Musical Express* writer Chris Dean (b. c.1963) assumed the identity of X. Moore. The other original members were Martin Hewes (bass) and Nick King (drums). They were joined in the studio and on stage by a fluid brass section, the most permanent members of which were Lloyd Dwyer and Steve Nicol. After the strident debut 'Peasant Army' on Leeds based independent CNT in 1982, they secured a session for the John Peel BBC Radio 1 programme which would be repeated five times. The follow-up, 'Lean On Me' was voted Single Of The Year by *Sounds* journalist Gary Bushell. Given a high media profile by dint of their exclusively political lyrics (they were all members of the Socialist Workers Party), interest from major record companies soon followed, leading to a deal with London. After personal disagreements, King was replaced by Paul Hookham (ex-English Subtitles, Lemons, Woodentops) on the eve of the band's second major tour. By 1984 they had become vigorous supporters of the striking National Union of Miners, playing a host of benefits on their behalf, though 'Keep On Keeping On' and subsequent singles were no match for their earlier promise. The debut *Neither Washington Nor Moscow* was impressive, but critics still cited the band as under achievers, a fate they condemned themselves to when they broke up in 1986.

Album: *Neither Washington Nor Moscow* (1986).

Reegs

One of two splinter groups from the ashes of the underrated UK group the Chameleons, the Reegs was formed by guitarists Dave Fielding and Reg Smithies after they split in 1987. They were joined by vocalist Gary Lavery and a drum machine for their 1991 debut under their new title, *The Return Of The Sea Monkeys*. 'We didn't do anything for a while after the Chameleons split, I think we both needed to take some time out. . . there was never any question of us not working together again.' Fielding had kept busy with production work, the most successful of which was with the Inspiral Carpets. Following the enthusiasm shown by Imaginary Records, they made their first recording with 'See My Friend' for the Kinks' tribute album. The first of their own material came in the shape of two EPs, which formed the basis of the album.

Album: *The Return Of The Sea Monkeys* (1991).

R.E.M.

R.E.M. played their first concert in Athens, Georgia, USA on 19 April 1980. Their line-up, then as now, consisted of four drop-outs from the University of Georgia; Michael Stipe (vocals), Peter Buck (guitar), Mike Mills (bass) and Bill Berry (drums). Without the

R.E.M.

charisma of Stipe and his eccentric onstage behaviour, hurling himself about with abandon in between mumbling into the microphone, they could easily have been overlooked as just another bar band, relying on the harmonious guitar sound of the Byrds for their inspiration. Acquiring a healthy following among the college fraternity in their hometown, it wasn't long before they entered the studio to record their debut single 'Radio Free Europe', to be released independently on Hibtone Records. This was greeted with considerable praise by critics who conceded that the band amounted to more than the sum of their influences. Their country/folk sound was contradicted by a driving bassline and an urgency that put the listener more in mind of the Who in their early mod phase. Add to this the distinctive voice of Stipe and his, on the whole, inaudible, perhaps even non-existent, lyrics, and R.E.M. sounded quite unlike any other band in the USA, in the post-punk era of the early 80s. Gaining further favourable notices for the *Chronic Town* mini-LP, their debut full-length album was now eagerly anticipated; when it arrived in 1983 it surpassed all expectations, and was eventually made Album Of The Year by *Rolling Stone* magazine. As in the USA, the band earned a devoted cult following in Europe, largely comprised of college students, as a result of *Murmur*.

Reckoning appeared the following year and was permeated by a reckless spontaneity that had been missing from their earlier work. Recorded in only 12 days, the tracks varied in mood from frustration, as on 'So. Central Rain', to the tongue-in-cheek singalong '(Don't Go Back To) Rockville'. The songs were accessible enough but, as would be the case for most of the 80s, the singles culled from R.E.M.'s albums were generally deemed uncommercial by mainstream radio programmers. However, their cult reputation benefited from a series of flop singles on both sides of the Atlantic. Although received enthusiastically by critics, *Fables Of The Reconstruction* was a stark, morose album that mirrored a period of despondency within the band. Peter Buck summed it up in the 90s - 'If we were to record those songs again, they would be very different'. *Life's Rich Pageant*, in 1986, showed the first signs of a politicization within the band that would come to a head, and coincide with their commercial breakthrough, in the late 80s. Stipe's lyrics began to dwell increasingly on the prevailing amorality in the USA and question its inherited ethics, whilst still retaining their much vaunted obliqueness. Tracks like 'These Days' and 'Cuyahoga' were rallying cries to the young and disaffected; although the lyrics were reflective and almost bitter, the music was the most joyous and uplifting the band had recorded to date. This ironic approach to songwriting was typified by 'It's The End Of The World As We Know It (And I Feel Fine)', from the equally impressive *Document*. Released also as a single, it intentionally trivialized its subject matter with a witty and up-tempo infectiousness, more characteristic of the Housemartins.

Green arrived in 1988 and sold slowly but steadily in the USA, the attendant single 'Stand' reaching number 6 there, while 'Orange Crush' entered the UK Top 30. Apart from demonstrating their environmental awareness, particularly in 'You Are The Everything', the album laid more emphasis than previously on Stipe's vocals and lyrics. This, to the singer's dismay, led to his elevation as 'spokesman for a generation'. Already hero-worshipped by adoring long-term fans, Stipe insists 'Rock 'n' roll is a joke, people who take it seriously are the butt of the joke'. The world tour that coincided with the album's release saw R.E.M. making a smooth transition from medium-size venues to the stadium circuit, due as much to Stipe's individual choreography as to the elaborate, projected backdrops. After a break of two years the band re-emerged in 1991 with *Out Of Time*. Their previous use of horns and mandolins to embroider songs did not prepare their audience for the deployment of an entire string section, nor were the contributions from B-52s singer Kate Pierson and Boogie Down Productions' KRS-1 expected. Ostensibly all love songs, the album was unanimously hailed as a masterpiece and entered the UK Top 5 on its release, topping both US and UK album charts shortly afterwards. The accompanying single 'Losing My Religion' gave them their biggest hit in the UK, reaching number 19. R.E.M. are now delicately poised to become the major band of the 90s as they reluctantly face up to stardom.

Albums: *Chronic Town* (1982, mini-LP), *Murmur* (1983), *Reckoning* (1984), *Fables Of The Reconstruction* (1985), *Life's Rich Pageant* (1986), *Document* (1987), *Dead Letter Office* (1987, out-takes and b-sides), *Green* (1988), *Out Of Time* (1991). Compilation: *Eponymous* (1988).

Further reading: *It Crawled From The South; An R.E.M. Companion*, Marcus Gray.

Renees

This UK London-based pop group was loosely formed in 1987, in the aftermath of the break-up of the Gymslips a year earlier. Paula Richards (b. 1 August 1963, Kent, England; guitar/vocals), who had in the meantime been working with the ska/R&B outfits, the Deltones and Potato 5, re-united with Karen Yarnell (b. 2 April 1961; drums) using various friends to perform at gigs, often alongside contemporaries, Coming Up Roses. By 1989 the group had gone full-time with the recruitment of Katrina Slack (b. 14 July 1962; bass), Jacqui Callis (vocals, ex-Delta 5) and the lone male, Paul Seacroft (lead guitar, ex-Potato 5). The single 'He Called Me A Fat Pig (And Walked Out On Me)' suitably impressed the reviewers and the group signed to the French independent label Squale, releasing their only album, *Have You Got It!* in 1990. The album included an impressive version of 'Mama' Cass Elliot's 'California Earthquake' and the more English-flavoured 'Valerie'. However, with the dissolution of the label the following year, the group broke up, tired of battling against the growing tide of insularity within the capital's live club scene.

Album: *Have You Got It!* (1990).

Renegade Soundwave

The recordings of this London born and bred esoteric dance trio have been variously described as 'Dance-Noise-Terror' and 'Chas And Dave with a beatbox'. The group consisted of three multi-talented instrumentalists, Danny Briotett, Carl Bonnie and Gary Asquith. 'We're a by-product of punk. It forged the way we think, though the sound is nothing to do with it.' Their first single 'Kray Twins' emerged on Rhythm King Records, the sound of a television documentary set to a throbbing bass undertow. After the equally notorious 'Cocaine Sex' they switched to Mute because of the greater eclecticism of their catalogue. A series of dancefloor singles like 'Biting My Nails' and 'Probably A Robbery' prefaced a debut album which included an unlikely cover of

Andy Williams' 'Can't Get Used To Losing You' (also a hit for the Beat). Their aggressive dancefloor attack was continued the same year with *In Dub*, on which 'Holgertron' made use of the theme music to BBC television's *Doctor Who*. Bonnie has now gone on to work as a solo artist.

Albums: *Soundclash* (1990), *In Dub* (1990).

Replacements

This group was formed in Minneapolis, Minnesota, USA in 1979, with Paul Westerburg (b. 31 December 1960, Minneapolis, USA; guitar/vocals), Tommy Stinson (b. 6 October 1966, San Diego, California, USA; bass), Bob Stinson (b. 17 December 1959, Mound, Minnesota, USA; guitar) and Chris Mars (b. 26 April 1961, Minneapolis, USA; drums). Originally the Impediments, their early shambolic drunken gigs forced a name change to secure further work. Their debut album for the local Twintone label showcased their self-proclaimed power trash style, earning comparisons with hardcore legends Hüsker Dü. Subsequent albums saw the group diversifying to encompass influences from folk, country, and blues without straying far from their winning formula of rock 'n' roll married to the raw passion of punk rock. Beloved by critics on both sides of the Atlantic, the group appeared on the verge of mainstream success in America, with the release of *Pleased To Meet Me*. Bob Stimson was replaced by Slim Dunlap (keyboards) and Westerburg was at the height of his songwriting ability on the suicide anthem 'The Ledge' and the achingly melodic 'Skyway'. Greater success somehow eluded them and *All Shook Down* was a largely subdued affair, seeming to hint at an impending solo career for Westerburg.

Albums: *Sorry Ma, Forgot To Take Out The Trash* (1981), *Stink* (1982), *Hootenanny* (1983), *Let It Be* (1984), *The Shit Hits The Fans* (1985), *Tim* (1985), *Pleased To Meet Me* (1987), *Don't Tell A Soul* (1989), *All Shook Down* (1990).

Residents

Despite a recording career spanning two decades, the Residents have successfully - and deliberately - achieved an air of wilful obscurity. Mindful of the cult of personality, they studiously retain an anonymity and refuse to name personnel, thus ensuring total artistic freedom. Their origins are shrouded in mystery and mischief, although common currency agrees the group was founded in Shrieveport, Louisiana, USA. They later moved to San Mateo, California where a series of home-recorded tapes was undertaken. In 1971 the group collated several of these performances and sent the results to Hal Haverstadt of Warner Brothers, who had signed Captain Beefheart. No name had been included and thus the rejected package was returned marked 'for the attention of the residents', which the collective accepted as a sign of distinction. In 1972 the group was resettled in San Francisco where they launched Ralph Records as an outlet for their work. *Meet The Residents* established their unconventional style, matching bizarre reconstructions of 60s pop favourites with ambitious original material. Critics drew comparisons with the Mothers Of Invention, but any resemblance was purely superficial as the Residents drew reference from a wider variety of sources and showed a greater propensity to surprise. *Third Reich Rock 'N' Roll* contained two suites devoted to their twisted vision of contrasting cover versions, whereas *Not Available* comprised of material the group did not wish to release. It had been recorded under the Theory Of Obscurity, whereby a record should not be issued until its creators had forgotten its existence, but appeared as a stop-gap release during sessions for the ambitious *Eskimo*. *The Commercial Album* consisted of 40 tracks lasting exactly 1 minute and contrasted the Residents' next project, the *Mole Trilogy*, which comprised of *Mark Of The Mole*, *The Tunes Of Two Cities* and *The Big Bubble*. The group undertook extensive live appearances in the US and Europe to promote this expansive work, which in turn spawned several in-concert selections and an EP devoted to music played during the shows' intermission. Their subsequent American Composers Series has included *George And James*, a homage to George Gershwin and James Brown, *Stars And Hank Forever*, a celebration Hank Williams and John Phillip Sousa, and *The King And Eye*, an album of Elvis Presley hits. If this suggests a paucity of original material, it is worth recalling the Residents' strength lies in interpretation and use of cultural icons as templates for their idiosyncratic vision.

Albums: *Meet The Residents* (1974), *Blorp Esette* (1975), *Third Reich Rock 'N' Roll* (1976), *Fingerprince* (1976), *Not Available* (1978), *Duck Stab/Buster And Glen* (1978), *Subterranean Modern* (1979), *Eskimo* (1979), *The Commercial Album* (1980), *Mark Of The Mole* (1981), *Intermission* (1982), *The Tunes Of Two Cities* (1982), *The Big Bubble* (1983), *George And James* (1984), *Vileness Fats* (1984), *The Mole Show Live In Holland* (1983), *13th Anniversary Show Live In Holland* (1986), *13th Anniversary Show Live In Japan* (1986), *Stars And Hank Forever* (1986), *God In Three Persons* (1988), *The King And Eye* (1989), *Freakshow* (1991). Compilations: *Nibbles* (1979), *Ralph Before '84 Volume 1* (1984), *Ralph Before '84 Volume 2* (1985).

Revenge

Formed in Manchester in 1987, and now one of three offshoots featuring 'resting' members of New Order. Peter Hook (b. 13 February 1956, Salford, Manchester, England) was initially joined by David Hicks (ex-Southern Death Cult, Lavolta Lakota; guitar) and CJ (Hook's studio engineer, who had previously worked with the Chameleons and the Fall). The band was started because: 'Hooky likes playing gigs', and they performed their debut at London's Skin 2 Bondage Club in 1990. By this time they featured drummer Ashley Taylor and bassist David Potts, who had worked in Hook's Suite 16 studio. Unlike the more successful Electronic, the first releases by Revenge have garnered mediocre reviews at best. The album was prefaced by disappointing singles '7 Reasons' and 'Pineapple Face'. The third single, 'I'm Not Your Slave', came closest to familiar New Order territory and was the best of the bunch, with Hook's characteristic tugging bass. However, like its predecessors, it failed to make the UK charts. *One True Passion* garnered mixed reviews. Some critics pointed to song titles like 'Surf Nazi' and the recent 'Slave...' single as recalling the flirtation with fascist imagery which had dogged Joy Division and New Order. In spite of this, Hook has repeated his intention that Revenge should be an ongoing project.

Album: *One True Passion* (1990).

Revillos

Formed in March 1979 by Eugene Reynolds and Fay Fife, previously vocalists with the Rezillos. HiFi Harris (guitar), Rocky Rhythm (drums) and three backing singers - Jane White, Jane Brown and Tricia Bryce - completed the group's original line-up, but within months the latter trio had been replaced by Babs and Cherie Revette. The Revillos made their debut with 'Where's The Boy For Me' (1979), but although this exciting performance recalled the best of the previous group, it failed to emulate their success. Internal friction undermined the unit's undoubted potential - guitarists, bassists and singers were replaced with regularity as Reynolds, Fife and Rhythm pursued their uncompromising vision. An album, *Rev-Up*, captured the Revillos' enchanting mixture of girl-group, beat and science-fiction, but they were subsequently dropped by their record company. Undeterred the group inaugurated Superville for ensuing releases and embarked on two gruelling tours of the USA and Canada which they financed themselves. However an anticipated deal failed to materialize and this ebullient act later disintegrated.

Albums: *Rev Up* (1980), *Attack* (1983).

Revolver

This three piece UK 90s independent label pop group comprised Mat Flint (vocals, guitar), Nick Dewey (drums) and Hamish Brown (bass), all b. c.1969. Flint and Dewey were both from Winchester, had played in several bands for the previous three years, and met

Brown in London in September 1990. Influenced in their efforts by the Beach Boys, Beatles, Byrds, My Bloody Valentine, and the Jesus And Mary Chain, they played their first gig in December 1990. Soon after came the EP *Heaven Sent An Angel* after which the media, keen to establish some form of clearly defined trend, picked up on them and numerous other bands with a similar approach. They were clearly taken unawares by the glare of attention: 'We don't have a desire as individuals to be famous, but we want the band to be a famous name so we can grin down from bedroom walls and get to play in New York'. However, all three members of the band are still attempting to pursue a parallel academic career should they not succeed.

Revolving Paint Dream

The Revolving Paint Dream was not only the most mysterious act on Creation Records' original roster back in 1984, but also one of the most inventive. After a memorable psychedelia-tinged single, 'Flowers In The Sky'/'In The Afternoon', in February, the band disappeared for three years before a strange collection of what seemed like out-takes, *Off To Heaven*, reached the shelves in June 1987. 60s-influenced pop sat alongside weird, distorted soundscapes to create an album that lacked any overall identity but was stacked full with ideas. It transpired that the band comprised Primal Scream's second guitarist Andrew Innes, Nico-like vocalist Christine Wanless (also present on several Biff Bang Pow! recordings) and Luke Hayes, with probable involvement from label organizers Alan McGee and Richard Green. January 1989's *Mother Watch Me Burn* was even more experimental and the listener was hard pushed to believe that it was the same band performing the fragrant pop tune, 'Sun, Sea, Sand' (issued as a single) and the ferocious, almost unlistenable instrumentals.

Albums: *Off To Heaven* (1987), *Mother Watch Me Burn* (1989).

Rezillos

Formed in Edinburgh, Scotland in March 1976, the Rezillos were initially an informal aggregation consisting of Eugene Reynolds (b. Alan Forbes; vocals), Fay Fife (b. Sheila Hynde; vocals), Luke Warm aka Jo Callis (lead guitar), Hi Fi Harris (b. Mark Harris; guitar), Dr. D.K. Smythe (bass), Angel Patterson (b. Alan Patterson; drums) and Gale Warning (backing vocals). Their irreverent repertoire consisted of pre-beat favourites by Screaming Lord Sutch and the Piltdown Men, judicious material from the Dave Clark Five and glam-rock staples by the Sweet. Their image, part Marlon Brando, part Shangri-Las, allied them with the punk movement, although their love of pop heritage denied wholesale

Rezillos; Fay Fife

involvement. The Rezillos' debut single, 'I Can't Stand My Baby', encapsulated their crazed obsessions, but its success introduced a discipline at odds with their initial irreverence. Harris, Smythe and Warning left the line-up, while auxiliary member William Mysterious (b. William Donaldson; bass/saxophone) joined the group on a permanent basis. Now signed to a major label, Sire Records, the quintet undertook several tours and scored a UK Top 20 hit with the satirical 'Top Of The Pops' in August 1978. The group's debut *Can't Stand The Rezillos*, also charted, before internal pressures began pulling them apart. Mysterious was replaced by Simon Templar, but in December 1978 the Rezillos folded following a brief farewell tour. Fife and Reynolds formed the Revillos, while the rest of the band became known as Shake. Callis later found fame in the Human League.

Albums: *Can't Stand The Rezillos* (1978), *Mission Accomplished ... But The Beat Goes On* (1979).

Rhino Records

The Los Angeles-based record company was launched in 1978 by Richard Foos and Harold Bronson as an outgrowth of their Rhino Records retail store. At first the fledgling company specialized in novelty records, including an all-kazoo version of Led Zeppelin's 'Whole Lotta Love' by the Temple City Kazoo Orchestra and an album by one-time

Frank Zappa protege Wild Man Fischer. During the 80s the label took to reissuing out-of-print recordings from rock's 'golden era' including the catalogues of the Monkees and the Turtles and hits collections from a diverse list of artists including Jerry Lee Lewis, Nancy Sinatra and the Neville Brothers. Rhino also made an impact with its inventive various artists compilations, including two volumes of nothing but the song 'Louie, Louie' and collections of soul music, novelty records, early 70s AM radio hits, British Invasion, 'Frat Rock' and many others. By the mid-80s Rhino was recognized as the leading repackager in the USA.

Compilations: *Rhino Teen Magazine* (1984), *Rhino Brothers Greatest Flops* (1988).

Rhoda With The Special AKA

Rhoda Daker (a former member of UK group the Bodysnatchers) briefly teamed up with the Special AKA in 1981. The following year, they backed her in the above collaboration on 'The Boiler'. This extraordinary song about sexual attitudes towards women, chillingly evoked an attempted rape, ending with a blood-curdling scream. Because of its controversial subject matter and impassioned performance, moves were made to ban it, but it subsequently climbed into the UK Top 40.

Rich Kids

Formed in the UK during September 1977, the Rich Kids were the subject of exceptional initial interest. Centred on bassist Glen Matlock (b. 27 August 1956), a former member of the seminal Sex Pistols, his eminent role was emphasized by the inclusion of two 'unknown' musicians, Steve New (guitar/vocals) and Rusty Egan (drums). The group was later completed by Midge Ure, disillusioned frontman of struggling pop group, Slik, and this unusual mixture engendered criticism from unsympathetic quarters. The Rich Kids distanced themselves from punk, and their meagre releases were generally mainstream in execution. Indeed the group's ebullience recalled a 60s bonhomie, but this merely compounded criticism of their 'power pop' approach. The quartet was unable to transform their energy to record, while tension between Matlock and Ure increased to the extent that they were constantly squabbling. The group split up in November 1978, but denied the fact until free of contractual obligations. Egan and Ure later formed Visage, while their former colleagues pursued several low-key projects.

Album: *Ghosts Of Princes In Towers* (1978).

Richman, Jonathan

b. May 16 1951, Boston, Massachussetts, USA. Richman rose to prominence during the early 70s as leader of the Modern Lovers. Drawing inspiration from 50s pop and the Velvet Underground, the group initially offered a garage-band sound, as evinced on their UK hit 'Roadrunner' and the infectious instrumental 'Egyptian Reggae' in 1977. However, Richman increasingly distanced himself from electric music and latterly embraced an acoustic-based direction. He disbanded the group in 1978 to pursue an idiosyncratic solo career in which his naive style was deemed charming or irritating according to taste. His songs, including 'Ice Cream Man', 'My Love Is A Flower (Just Beginning To Bloom)', showed a child-like simplicity which seemed oblivious to changes in trends around him. Richman exhumed the Modern Lovers' name during the 80s without any alteration to his style and the artist continues to enjoy considerable cult popularity.

Albums: *Jonathan Richman And The Modern Lovers* (1977), *Back In Your Life* (1979), *The Jonathan Richman Songbook* (1980), *Jonathan Sings* (1984), *Its Time For Jonathan Richman And The Modern Lovers* (1986), *Jonathan Richman & Barence Whitfield* (1988), *Modern Lovers 88* (1988), *Jonathan Richman* (1989), *Jonathan Sings Country* (1990). Compilation: *23 Great Recordings* (1990).

Ride

Formed at Art School in Oxfordshire in 1988 by Mark Gardener, Andy Bell, Stephen Queralt and Laurence Colbert, Ride had a rapid impact on the alternative music scene. Initially described as 'The House Of Love with chainsaws', within a year the quartet's serrated guitar melodies were attracting unusual amounts of attention. At the start of 1990, their debut EP reached number 71 in the UK charts - the first time their label, Creation, had ever registered such a placing. By the end of the Spring, Ride had transcended their independent parameters and entered the Top 40 of the UK chart with the *Play* EP, helped by their youthful good looks and large-scale touring. The success continued with the *Nowhere* album reaching number 14 in the UK charts before the close of the year. Tours of Japan, Australia and America showed just how impressively swift the band's rise had been, especially when a third EP went straight into the Top 20 of the UK chart. Their success was sealed by a headlining appearance at 1991's Slough Music Festival in front of 8,000 fans. In 1992 Ride consolidated their position as one of the most interesting new bands with the excellent *Going Blank Again* and the hypnotic UK hit single 'Leave Them All Behind'.

Albums: *Nowhere* (1990), *Going Blank Again* (1992).

Ridgway, Stan

b. Stanard Ridgway, 1954, Los Angeles, California, USA. Ridgway was brought up as a Christian Scientist and his mother's tendency to bring Kirlian

Ride

photographs home for her son to look at may have contributed to his love of the more perverse elements of life. At school he was nicknamed Mr. Monster and formed the Monster Club. He also admits to being the 'man who cried when Bela Lugosi died!'. A sometime cab driver, Ridgway's first major musical venture was the soundtrack company - Acme - he formed with Marc Morehand. They became Wall Of Voodoo in 1977, the name taken with deference to Phil Spector's 'Wall Of Sound' recording techniques. In 1984 Ridgway collaborated with Stewart Copeland on the soundtrack for Francis Ford Coppolla's movie *Rumblefish*, but Ridgway enjoyed success in 1986 when his wacky 'death disc' 'Camouflage', became a surprise UK hit. The follow-up 'The Big Heat' was equally strong but failed to chart. An album of the same name- recorded with Chapter II, including wife Pietra on keyboards, was highly acclaimed. Ridgway's narrative songs such as 'Drive She Said' were particularly striking. Career problems were compounded when contractual disputes with Miles Copeland at IRS effectively put him out of action for two years. The resultant *Mosquitoes* featured 'Heat Takes A Walk', co-written with Beach Boys collaborator Van Dyke Parks, as well as 'Newspapers', which partially summed up his frustration with his career so far.
Albums: *Camouflage* (1986), *The Big Heat* (1986), *Mosquitoes* (1989).

Riley, Marc, And The Creepers

b. Manchester, England. Riley started playing in a band when he was aged 15, 'then I sort of wormed my way into the Fall when I was 16'. He left to form the Creepers, with Eddie Fenn (drums), Paul Fletcher (guitar) and Pete Keogh (bass). The last two were later replaced by Mark Tilton (guitar) and Phil Roberts (bass). The records that followed were full of hard-hitting humour and as opinionated as Riley's former boss Mark E. Smith (who apparently wrote the sarcastic 'Middle Mass' about Riley). Riley formed In Tape records with keyboardist Jim Khambatta, who also managed the Creepers. Starved of commercial success, and burdened by his heritage, Riley disbanded the Creepers in 1987 and formed the Lost Soul Crusaders.
Albums: *Gross Cut* (1984), *Cull* (1984), *Fancy Meeting God* (1985).

Rip Rig And Panic

Evolving out of Bristol's the Pop Group, Rip Rig And Panic was formed in 1981 as a conceptual musicians' collective, taking its name from an album by Roland Kirk. The group's prime movers were multi-instrumentalist and songwriter Gareth Sager, jazz trumpeter Don Cherry's stepdaughter Neneh Cherry (b. Stockholm, Sweden; vocals), Cherry's

partner and drummer Bruce Smith, Sean Oliver (bass) and Mark Springer (piano). Powerful and disturbing live, their playful, anarchic jazz-funk was well-captured on the irreverent 1981 debut album, *God*, which appeared as two 45rpm discs, but was too radical for daytime airplay or significant sales. They performed at the first WOMAD festival in 1982 shortly before Cherry returned to Sweden to have her first baby. Sean Oliver's sister Andrea temporarily took over vocals, and Louis Moholo joined on drums. The equally experimental second album, *I Am Cold*, appeared in 1982, followed by the more accessible *Attitude* in 1983. Unwilling to compromise further, but feeling the strain of constant innovation, they split in 1985, only to re-align as the smaller outfit, Float Up CP and, briefly, God Mother And Country, before Cherry went on to a successful solo career with Andrea Oliver contributing to some of her songs.
Albums: *God* (1981), *I Am Cold* (1982), *Attitude* (1983).

Robinson, Tom

b 1 July 1950, Cambridge, England. Robinson's wayward youth included the study of oboe, clarinet and bass guitar, and a spell in Finchden Manor, a readjustment centre in Kent, where he met guitarist Danny Kurstow with whom he formed his first group, Davanq, in 1971. However, two years later, as Cafe Society, he, Hereward Kaye and Ray Doyle were signed to the Kinks' Konk label. In 1974, *Cafe Society* was recorded with help from Ray Davies and Mick Avory. During the taping of an intended second album, administrative discord was manifested in what was now the Tom Robinson Band's on-stage mocking of Davies, and, later, the Kinks' reciprocal dig at Robinson in a 1977 b-side, 'Prince Of The Punks' - with whom Robinson's Band had been categorized (not entirely accurately) when contracted by EMI the previous year. Konk, nevertheless, retained publishing interests in 13 Robinson numbers. Some of these were selected for TRB's *Power In The Darkness* debut and attendant UK Top 40 singles - notably the catchy '2468 Motorway'. Backed by keyboardist Mark Ambler, drummer 'Dolphin' Taylor plus the faithful Kurstow, lead singer Robinson nurtured a homosexual image. His active support of many radical causes riddled his lyrical output but the gravity of 'Summer Of 79' and 'Up Against The Wall' was mitigated by grace-saving humour.
The quartet's *Rising Free* EP, for example, contained the singalong 'Glad To Be Gay' anthem - which was also a highlight of both TRB's 1978 benefit concert for the Northern Ireland Gay Rights and One Parent Families Association, and Robinson's solo set during a Lesbian and Gay Rights March in Washington in

1979, shortly after parting with his Band. This had followed a disappointed critical and market reaction to *TRB2* (supervised by Todd Rundgren) - on which the sloganeering was overdone and the musical performance tepid. While Kurstow joined ex-Sex Pistol Glen Matlock in the Spectres, Robinson led the short-lived Section 27 and began songwriting collaborations with Elton John and Peter Gabriel. By 1981, he had relocated to Berlin to record the solo *North By Northwest* and work in alternative cabaret and fringe theatre. Professionally, this period proved fruitful - with 1982's strident 'War Baby' and evocative 'Atmospherics' in the UK Top 40, and a revival of Steely Dan's 'Ricki Don't Lose That Number', from *Hope And Glory*, which fared as well as the original in the same chart. However, when *Still Loving You* produced no equivalent of even this modest triumph Robinson, now a contented father, regrouped his original band. Subsequent engagements were viewed by many as akin to a nostalgia revue - and certainly several old favourites were evident the Berlin concert set, *Last Tango*. However, Robinson's articulate and lyrical eloquence suggest that further solid work may lie ahead.
Albums: *Power In The Darkness* (1978), *TRB2* (1979), *Sector 27* (1980), *North By Northwest* (1982), *Hope And Glory* (1984), *Still Loving You* (1986), *Last Tango* (1989).

Rogue Male

Formed in London, England in 1984 the band's original line-up consisted of Jim Lyttle (vocals/guitar), John Fraser Binnie (guitar), Kevin Collier (bass) and Steve Kingsley (drums). Quickly signing to the Music For Nations Record label their debut *First Visit* was released in 1985. The album was full of fast, tough, punk-influenced metal. With live gigs showing mainman Jim Lyttle to be a charismatic bandleader they embarked on an ill-fated American tour. Blaming their American label Elecktra Records for a lack of promotion the band returned to England to begin work on their second album. At this point Steve Kingsley left the band to be replaced by session drummer Charlie Morgan who played on the album recordings, but he was replaced soon after by Danny Fury. *Animal Man* was released in 1986 but due to a lack of public interest the band dissolved soon after its release.
Albums: *First Visit* (1985), *Animal Man* (1986).

Room

An adventurous pop band formed in Liverpool, England, the Room quickly attracted strong support from the press with records variously acclaimed for their wit, irony, poise and intelligence. The line-up featured Dave Jackson (vocals), Paul Cavanagh (guitar), Becky Stringer (bass), and Alan Willis (drums). Early singles on Box records ('Bitter Reaction', 'Motion', 'In Sickness And In Health') revealed a talented band slipstreaming the innovations of Echo And The Bunnymen. More attractive still was their debut for Red Flame, 'Things Have Learnt To Walk That Should Only Crawl'. The band played several dates with Tom Verlaine in 1984, who went on to produce three tracks on *In Evil Hour*. Their first 'complete' album, it also featured John Porter (of Smiths fame) on production. Among the Verlaine slices was 'Jackpot Jack': 'You pulled the lever back/You hit the jackpot jack/And all the radios, are blaring new pop cack'. It was an ambitious statement of intent, and one not missed by critics of the day. However, the single 'New Dreams For Old', also included on the album, saw the band's best, and final, crack at the charts. By this time they had bolstered their line-up with the addition of Peter Baker (organ/synthesizer) and Phil Lucking (trombone/trumpet). However, the band 'just sort of fell out really. . .'. Jackson went on to front Benny Profane taking Stringer and Baker with him.
Albums: *Clear* (1983), *In Evil Hour* (1984), *Nemesis* (1986).

Rose Of Avalanche

This Yorkshire, England-based group came to the fore following heavy airplay from BBC disc jockey John Peel. The debut single 'LA Rain' finished high in his 1985 'Festive Fifty', although it was released before the band had performed. The follow-up 'Castles In the Sky' originated from hearing a man in a pub asking a girl if she wanted to 'See my castle in the sky?'. 'Velveteen', meanwhile, was a tribute to Nico. The bands principals were Phillip Morris (vocals) and Paul James Berry (guitar), while a host of supporting musicians passed through their ranks. These included: Mark Thompson and Andrew Parker (drums), Alan Davis, Nicol Mackay and Daren Horner (bass), and Glenn Shultz (guitar). Horner and Parker are the current encumbants of the rhythm section. After gaining early praise the band were stopped in their tracks for 18 months between 1987 and 1988, following disputes with their label, Fire. They responded by setting up their own Avalantic Records. Their two most recent collections, *String A Beads* and *I.C.E.* have brought about a transformation in the band's sound. Gone are the heavy rhythms and chiming guitar which saw them pigeon-holed as 'gothic', they have been replaced by material of a comparatively melodic and 'poppy' nature.
Albums: *Always There* (1986), *First Avalanche* (1987), *In Rock* (1988), *Never Another Sunset* (1989), *String A Beads* (1990), *I.C.E.* (1991).

Rough Trade Records

Initially based near west London's Portobello Road,

the Rough Trade retail shop opened in February 1976, just months prior to the rise of the punk rock phenomenon. Owned by Geoff Travis (b. 2 February 1952, Stoke Newington, London, England), it was an important outlet for punk and independent releases from the UK and USA. Travis's empathy for this musical revolution helped build the shop's reputation as a leading source for import material, British independent releases, complimentary reggae releases and as a selling point for the proliferation of music fanzines. The demand for outlets generated by bands inspired the formation of a distribution network and label, and the Rough Trade record label was launched two years later with the release of 'Paris Maquis' by Metal Urbain, which anticipated the 'Industrial' style flourishing later in the decade. Subsequent releases by reggae artist Augustus Pablo and *avant garde* act Cabaret Voltaire confirmed Rough Trade's reputation as an outlet for diverse talent. Stiff Little Fingers, Young Marble Giants, Aztec Camera, the Raincoats, the Go-Betweens, the Fall, Scritti Politti and the Pop Group maintained the company' reputation as purveyors of challenging music, while ı succession of excellent recordings by the Smiths combined perception with popular acclaim, making the group the company's biggest asset for much of its history. The label also became the natural outlet for several US acts, ranging from the guitar-orientated Feelies, Dream Syndicate, the idiosyncratic Jonathan Richman and Camper Van Beethoven, to the experimental styles of Pere Ubu and the offbeat country/folk of Souled American. Many defections to major labels most notably Aztec Camera and Scritti Politti undermined the pitfalls bedevilling independent outlets and in 1984, under the aegis of the giant Warner Brothers corporation, Travis established Blanco Y Negro on which acts who preferred the security of a major company could nonetheless enjoy the intimacy of an independent. Jesus And Mary Chain, Everything But The Girl and Dinosaur Jnr have been among the label's signings, confirming Travis as one of Britain's most astute executives. Rough Trade Records continued to serve as the natural outlet for independently-minded acts throughout the 80s, but defection to EMI by the aforementioned Smiths was a significant loss. Hopes were then pinned on the Sundays, but the collapse of the Rough Trade distribution network in 1991 put the label's fate in jeopardy. However, a trimming down of staff and operations found the company steadying its position and subsequent recordings by artists such as Robert Wyatt suggest that its long-term future as a haven for adventurism is still assured.

Album: *Wanna Buy A Bridge?* (1980).

Rubella Ballet

Formed in the summer of 1979, the first stable line-up of this UK punk band comprised Zillah Minx (b. 31 March 1961, Birkenhead, Merseyside, England; vocals), Sid Attion (b. 18 April 1960, Sutton Coalfield, England; drums), Pete Fender (ex-Honey Bane, Fatal Microbes; guitar), and several bass players. Other early members included Annie Anxiety, Womble, Colin (Flux Of Pink Indians) and the strangely named 'It'. Anxiety was to be the singer, but when she dropped out drummer Sid, who would also work with Flux Of Pink Indians, suggested his girlfriend Zillah fill the position (at extremely short notice). Their first release was the cassette-only 'Ballet Bag', followed by a series of snappy punk pop singles. Gemma (also ex-Fatal Microbes, and brother of Fender) took over the bass position, although still a schoolgirl. The two, incidentally, are the children of the Poison Girls' Vi Subversa. The line-up would continue to be fluid however, with several guitarists passing through the ranks once Fender departed. He would go on to build his own studio, and record the solo single '4 Formulas'. After spells with Xcentrix and Jungle records, they formed their own Ubiquitous label with enterprising singles 'Money Talks' and 'Artic Flowers', and eventually three albums. In 1983, they launched a major tour with Death Cult, and were joined by Rachel Minx (b. 12 November 1964, Birkenhead, Merseyside, England; Zillah's sister) on bass. Zillah and Sid also recorded a techno dance track for the compilation *Beyond The Threshold*, under the name Xenophobia.

Albums: *Ballet Bag* (1986), *If* (1986), *Cocktail Mix* (1987) *Birthday Box* (1988), *At The End Of The Rainbow* (1990).

Runaways

Formed in 1975, the Runaways were initially the product of producer/svengali Kim Fowley and teenage lyricist Kari Krome. Together they pieced together an adolescent girl-group following several auditions in the Los Angeles area. The original line-up consisted of Joan Jett (b. 22 September 1958, Philadelphia, Pennsylvania, USA; guitar/vocals), Micki Steele (bass - later of the Bangles) and Sandy West (drums), but was quickly bolstered by the addition of Lita Ford (b. 23 September 1959, London, England; guitar/vocals) and Cherie Currie (vocals). The departure of Steele prompted several replacements, the last of which was Jackie Fox who had failed her original audition. Although originally viewed as a vehicle for compositions by Fowley and associate Mars Bonfire (b. Dennis Edmonton), material by Jett and Krome helped assert the quintet's independence. *The Runaways* showed a group indebted to the 'glam-rock' of the Sweet and punchy pop of Suzie Quatro, and included the salutary 'Cherry Bomb'. *Queens Of Noise* repeated the pattern, but the strain of touring - the quintet were highly popular in Japan - took its toll of Jackie Fox, who left the line-up and abandoned music altogether. Personality clashes resulted in the departure of Cherie Currie, whose solo career stalled following the failure of her debut, *Beauty's Only Skin Deep*. Guitarist/vocalist Vicki Blue and bassist Laurie McAllister completed a revitalized Runaways, but the latter was quickly dropped. Subsequent releases lacked the appeal of the group's early work which, although tarred by both novelty and sexual implications, nonetheless showed a sense of purpose. The Runaways split in 1980 but both Jett and Ford later enjoyed solo careers, the former of which engendered considerable commercial success during the 80s. In 1985 the mischievous Fowley resurrected the old group's name with an all-new personnel. This opportunistic concoction split up on completing *Young And Fast*.

Albums: *The Runaways* (1976), *Queens Of Noise* (1977), *Live In Japan* (1977), *Waitin' For The Night* (1977), *And Now...The Runaways* (1979), *Flamin' Schoolgirls* (1982), *Young And Fast* (1987).

Runrig

The phenomenon of Runrig is an extraordinary example of 'regional taste'. This premier Scottish group has emerged from the traditional folk background to a higher profile in the pop/rock field and is arguably the most popular band north of Carlisle. The group first played as a three piece, featuring Rory MacDonald (b. 27 July 1949, Dornoch, Sutherland, Scotland; guitar/bass/vocals), Calum MacDonald (b. 12 November 1953, Lochmaddy, North Uist, Scotland; drums/ percussion), and Blair Douglas (accordion), in the Kelvin Hall, Glasgow, in 1973. Donnie Munro (b. 2 August 1953, Uig, Isle Of Skye, Scotland; guitar/vocals), joined the following year. Eventually Douglas left the group, and was replaced by Robert MacDonald (accordion). Sadly, Robert died of cancer in 1986. Their first recording, *Play Gaelic*, appeared on the Scottish Lismor Records label. At this time they were still not performing in a full-time capacity. However, with the higher profile, and the extra credibility of an album behind them, Runrig took the step of setting up their own label, Ridge Records, and started to perform on a full-time basis. After the release of *Highland Connection*, the group then added Iain Bayne (b. 22 January 1960, St. Andrews, Fife, Scotland; drums/percussion/piano) to the line-up. By the release of *Recovery*, it was clear that the band were more than just another folk/rock act. The music still retained it's Gaelic feel and traditions, with many of the songs being sung in Gaelic, but the group's sound took them outside the narrow boundaries of the folk arena. Eventually, English keyboard player Richard Cherns joined the group although he left in 1986,

and was replaced by former Big Country member Peter Wishart (b. 9 March 1962, Dunfermline, Scotland; keyboards).

After numerous changes of line-up, the current group of Donnie Munro, Rory and Calum MacDonald, Peter Wishart, Iain Bayne and Malcolm Jones (b. 12 July 1959, Inverness, Scotland; guitar/mandolin/ accordion), performed successful concerts in Canada and East Berlin in 1987, and played support to U2 at Murrayfield Stadium, Edinburgh, Scotland. After the release of *The Cutter And The Clan*, the group signed to Chrysalis the following year, who immediately re-released the album. Chart success followed, in 1989, with *Searchlight* almost making the Top 10 in the UK charts. Much touring followed, and in 1990, their EP *Capture The Heart*, entered the Top 50 in the UK singles chart. A television broadcast of a live performance elicited huge response from viewers, to the extent that five concerts at Glasgow's Royal Concert Hall sold out, and their subsequent video, *City Of Lights* sold well, reaching the Top 10-selling videos nationally. The highly-acclaimed *The Big Wheel* reached number 4 in the UK charts and the open air concert at Loch Lomond, was attended by 45,000 people. The single 'Hearthammer' broached the UK Top 30 in 1991, followed by successful tours of Europe, England and Scotland. The acceptance of Runrig outside Scotland now seems certain and with their national pride and political stance having been made, they are poised to awaken the world to Scottish popular and traditional music, without compromise.

Albums: *Play Gaelic* (1978), *Highland Connection* (1979), *Recovery* (1981), *Heartland* (1985), *The Cutter And The Clan* (1987), *Once In A Lifetime* (1988), *Searchlight* (1989), *The Big Wheel* (1991).
Further reading: *Going Home: The Runrig Story*, Tom Morton.

Ruts

This punk/reggae-influenced group comprised Malcolm Owen (vocals), Paul Fox (guitar/vocals), Dave Ruffy (drums) and John 'Segs' Jennings (bass). They first came to the fore in 1979 with the UK Top 10 single 'Babylon's Burning'. Their style resembled that of the Clash and Owen was occasionally compared to Joe Strummer. The strident 'Something That I Said' gave them another hit and their debut album *The Crack* was well received. The excellent 'Staring At The Rude Boys' neatly displayed their rock/dub talents but their progress was arrested by Owen's drug-related death on 14 July 1980. The remaining members were joined by Gary Barnacle and elected to continue as Ruts DC. They recorded two further albums under that name, moving towards funk-influenced reggae. Without Owen, however, the spirit of the group was not the same and they

faded from prominence .
Albums: *The Crack* (1979), *Grin And Bear It* (1980). As Ruts DC *Animal Now* (1981), *Rhythm Collision Vol 1* (1982).

S

Sad Lovers And Giants

This UK post-punk group, based in Watford, Hertfordshire, featured a line-up comprising Garce Allard (vocals), Tristan Garel Funk (guitar), David Wood (keyboards), Cliff Silver (bass) and Nigel Pollard (drums). After the release of early singles 'Colourless Dream' and 'Lost In A Moment', it was the release of 'Man Of Straw' and the accompanying *Feeding The Flame* which really established the group as masters of the double-edged lyric and sweeping, emotional textures of guitar and keyboard: 'Like confession whispered slowly, Hate's a word that's spoken softly, Standing lonely trusting no one, In disarray with collar undone'. The band had already fallen apart by the time the *Total Sound* mini-album, recorded live for broadcast on Dutch radio in 1983, was released. Another posthumous release, *In the Breeze*, consisting of demos, live tracks and alternative versions recorded for BBC disc jockey John Peel, pre-dated its release. The group was briefly reactivated in 1987, releasing the disappointing 'White Russians'.
Albums: *Epic Garden Music* (1982), *Feeding The Flame* (1983), *In The Breeze* ,(1984) *Total Sound* (1986).

St. Etienne

Pete Wiggs and music journalist Bob Stanley grew up together in Croydon, Surrey. In the early 80s, the pair began to experiment with party tapes, but did not make any serious inroads until forming St. Etienne around 1988, taking their name from the renowned French football team. Relocating to Camden in North London, the pair recruited Moira Lambert of Faith Over Reason for dance/reggae cover of Neil Young's 'Only Love Can Break Your Heart'. Issued in May 1990 on the aspiring Heavenly label, the single fared well in the nightclubs and surfaced on a magazine flexidisc remixed by labelmates Flowered Up (who appeared on the b-side) in July. Another cover, indie guitar band the Field Mice's 'Kiss And Make Up', was given a similar dance pop overhaul for St. Etienne's second single, fronted this time by New Zealand vocalist Donna

Savage of Dead Famous People. Then came the infectious Northern Soul-tinged 'Nothing Can Stop Us' in May 1991. Its strongly European feel reflected both their name, which helped attract strong support in France, and their logo (based on the European flag). It also benefitted from Sarah Cracknell's dreamy vocals, which would dominate St. Etienne's debut *Fox Base Alpha*, in the autumn. 'Only Love Can Break Your Heart' was reissued alongside the album, and provided them with a minor chart hit.
Album: *Fox Base Alpha* (1991).

Saints

Formed in Brisbane, Australia in 1975, the Saints were the first Australian punk band to be recognized as being relevant by the UK media. The band comprised Chris Bailey (vocals/guitar), Kym Bradshaw (bass, replaced by Alisdair Ward in 1977), Ed Kuepper (guitar) and Ivor Hay (drums). They were plucked from obscurity via their single 'I'm Stranded' being reviewed as single of the week by the now defunct UK weekly music paper, *Sounds*. Following this, and encouraging sales for their debut album, the band based itself in the UK. Although labelled a punk band, the Saints did not strictly conform to the English perception of punk, as their roots were more R&B-based. A refusal to imitate the punk fashion was certainly instrumental in their rapid fall from favour, although they have since attained considerable cult status. Co-founder Kuepper left the group in 1978 to form the Laughing Clowns. The band stayed together long enough, with various personnel, to record two more albums, disbanding in 1979. Chris Bailey performed with a variety of musicians during the 80s, using the Saints' name, as well as touring solo, playing acoustic guitar. He reformed the original line-up of the Saints in 1984 (minus Kuepper) and has recorded constantly over the ensuing decade. As a retaliation to Bailey's continued usage of Kuepper's songs in the latter-day Saints line-up, Kuepper formed the Aints in 1990.
Albums: *I'm Stranded* (1977), *Eternally Yours* (1978), *Prehistoric Sounds* (1978), *Monkey Puzzle* (1981), *Casablanca* (1982), *A Little Madness To Be Free* (1984), *Live In A Mud Hut* (1985), *All Fool's Day* (1986), *Prodigal Son* (1989). Compilation: *Songs Of Salvation 1976-1988* (1991).

Sarah Records

This fiercely independent UK Bristol-based label was formed in 1987 by Matt Haynes with Clare Wadd. Hayne's involvement with the UK independent music scene began with publishing the fanzine, *Are You Scared To Get Happy?* which supported the 'back-to-the-roots' idealism of the *New Musical Express*'s C86 compilation. He and Wadd cultivated a label determined to resist the growing fashion for CDs, maxi-singles and 12-inch singles by blatantly promoting the 7-inch single and the anti-hi tech flexi-single. Despite the later deviation from this ideology, the label have continued to promote this format, ignoring the industry claims for the death of vinyl and the single format. The musical content, quintessentially English pop, is aptly summed up in the sleeve notes for *Shadow Factory*: the songs are '. . . full of wrong notes and wrong chords, but crammed with right Everything Elses. . .'. Often derided by their contemporaries for being too soft and twee, the average Sarah group's lyrical content has tended not to stray very far from the timeless subject of boyfriends and girlfriends. Sarah's biggest asset, and the finest exponents of the 'Sarah sound', were, until their break-up in late 1991, the Field Mice. Amongst the other groups who have recorded for the label are the Sea Urchins, (who were responsible for the first Sarah release, the EP *Pristine Christine*), the Orchids, the Springfields, Another Sunny Day, St. Christopher, 14 Iced Bears, the Wake, Heavenly and, from Australia, Even As We Speak. Periodically, Sarah issue compilations, containing previously released singles, with the album titles and sleeve artwork reflecting the label's fondness for the Bristol area. The Sarah Records label, while not breaking down any barriers and creating a revolution, quietly go about their (necessary) business, ensuring an outlet for their type of music, treating it with love and respect - and continue to annoy the unbelievers.

Compilations: *Shadow Factory* (1988), *Temple Cloud* (1990), *Air Balloon Road* (1991, CD only release), *Glass Arcade* (1991).

Scarlet Party

Scarlet Party

The short-lived Beatlesque quartet were formed in 1981 by brothers Graham Dye (b. 2 August 1961, Barking, Essex, England; vocals/guitar), Steven Dye (b. 17 September 1963, Barking, Essex, England; bass/vocals/keyboards) and were joined by Sean Heaphy (drums) and Mark Gilmour (guitar), younger brother of Pink Floyd's David Gilmour. Their strong

composing ability led them to recording an album at the legendary Abbey Road studios, and performing live at the studio's 50th anniversary party. Much media attention was given to their debut '101 Damn-nations', which was released on the re-activated Parlophone, label 20 years after the Beatles' debut. Graham Dye's John Lennon-influenced vocals was another talking point and the band seemed set for stardom. This immaculate record surprisingly only reached the lower regions of the UK Top 50, and even more disappointing was that their strong follow-up 'Eyes Of Ice' failed to chart. Although they toured, supporting Steve Hackett, Huey Lewis and Sad Cafe, the band disintegrated through lack of commercial success. Graham returned in 1985 singing lead vocal on the Alan Parsons Project track 'Light Of The World', from *Stereotomy*, and again in 1990 with 'Little Hans' from Parsons' *Freudiana*. In 1992, the brothers were working on new material to submit to the record company that failed to capitalize on their remarkably fresh talent a decade earlier.

Scars

The Scars formed in Scotland - Bobby King (vocals), Paul Research (guitar), John Mackie (bass) and Calumn Mackay (drums) - evolved out of Edinburgh's late 70s punk milieu. Early live appearances were enthusiastic rather than accomplished, revealing the group's youthfulness, but they gradually asserted a competence and individuality. 'Adultery', released on the city's Fast Product label, showed an undoubted grasp of melody, and in 1981 the Scars were signed to Charisma's short-lived Pre subsidiary. *Author! Author!* was an excellent art/punk selection, but this highly promising set was the group's final recording, as they split up soon after its release.

Album: *Author! Author!* (1981).

Scratch Acid

Formed in Austin, Texas, USA in 1982, Scratch Acid originally comprised of Steve Anderson (vocals), David Wm. Sims (guitar), Brett Bradford (guitar), David Yow (bass) and Rey Washam (drums), although Anderson was quickly ousted. The reshaped quartet made their live debut as an instrumental act, supporting the Butthole Surfers, following which Yow switched to vocals with Sims taking up bass. Scratch Acid established a reputation as one of the state's leading post-hardcore noise exponents, creating a sound inspired by Killdozer and Big Black. They issued *Scratch Acid* in 1984, but it was two years before the group began recording a full-length album. Although *Just Keep Eating* lacked the arresting power of its predecessor, it confirmed the group's ambition and originality. *Berserker*, completed later the same year, reaffirmed their influential status and is chiefly recalled for its opening track, 'Mary Had A Little Drug Problem'. Scratch Acid then undertook extended tours of the Europe and the USA, but relations within the group had become strained and they split up in May 1987 following a live date at Austin's Cave Club. Sims and Washam then joined Steve Albini (ex-Big Black) in Rapeman, following which Sims was reunited with Yow in the Jesus Lizard.

Albums: *Scratch Acid* (1984), *Just Keep Eating* (1986), *Berseker* (1986). Compilation: *The Greatest Gift* (1991).

Screaming Blues Messiahs

Rising from the ashes of Motor Boys Motor, the Screaming Blue Messiahs were essentially a vehicle for shaven-headed American singer/songwriter and guitarist Bill Carter. Supported by Kenny Harris (drums) and Chris Thompson (bass), Carter churned out a tight, venomous rock formula drawn from R&B and new wave, first heard on the well-received mini-album, *Good And Gone*. Originally issued on Ace's Big Beat label in July 1984, it made sufficient noise to attract WEA, who duly re-promoted it a year later. 'Twin Cadillac Valentine' (1985), was a razor-sharp slab of dynamic guitar rock and paved the way for the Screaming Blue Messiahs' most impressive album, *Gun Shy*, the following year. A session previously recorded for BBC disc jockey John Peel in 1984 saw the light of day nearly three years later on the Strange Fruit 'Peel Sessions' series. This preceded the the Screaming Blue Messiahs' relatively low key *Bikini Red* in September 1986. The spawned the closest thing to a hit single the Messiahs ever achieved with the eccentric 'I Wanna Be A Flintstone', which broached the Top 30 in February 1988. It was two years before a new Screaming Blue Messiahs set and when *Totally Religious* (on WEA's Atlantic label) was released in October 1989, it failed to ignite an apathetic public. Although Carter's bite was still evident, the album failed to add to past achievements and little has been heard of the band since.

Albums: *Good And Gone* (1984), *Gun Shy* (1986), *Bikini Red* (1987), *Totally Religious* (1989).

Scritti Politti

The group was founded by Leeds art students in 1978. By the time of its first single, 'Skank Bloc Bologna', the nucleus of the band was Green Gartside (b. Green Strohmeyer-Gartside, 22 June 1956, Cardiff, Wales; vocals), Matthew Kay (keyboards/manager) and Tom Morley (drums/programming) and Nial Jinks (bass, departed 1980). At this stage, the group was explicitly political (Green had been a Young Communist), encouraging listeners to create their own music in the face of the record industry. Gartside also gained a reputation for convoluted word-play within his lyrics. This early *avant garde* phase gave way to a smooth sound which brought together elements of pop, jazz, soul and reggae on songs like 'The Sweetest Girl' (with Robert Wyatt on piano) and 'Asylums In Jerusalem'/'Jacques Derrida', which appeared on the debut album for Rough Trade, produced by Adam Kidron. Morley quit the group in November 1982, by which time Gartside *was* Scritti Politti. *Songs To Remember* became Rough Trade's most successful chart album; number 1 in the UK independent and, in the national chart, peaking at number 12 (beating Stiff Little Fingers' previous effort at number 14). After moving on to Virgin Records, Green linked up with New York musicians David Gamson (guitar) and Fred Maher (drums), who formed the basis of the group that made a series of UK hits in the years 1984-88. Produced by Arif Mardin, these included 'Wood Beez (Pray Like Aretha Franklin)' (number 10), 'Absolute' (number 17) and 'The Word Girl' (number 6). A three-year silence was broken by 'Oh Patti (Don't Feel Sorry For Loverboy)', lifted from *Provision*, and boasted a trumpet solo by Miles Davis. Gartside again maintained a low-profile for two years after 'First Boy In This Town (Love Sick)', failed to break into the UK Top 60 in late 1988. He returned in 1991 with a revival of the Beatles' 'She's A Woman', featuring leading reggae star Shabba Ranks while another Jamaican star, Sweetie Irie guested on a version of the Gladys Knight And The Pips 1967 hit 'Take Me In Your Arms And Love Me'.

Albums: *Songs To Remember* (1981), *Cupid And Psyche* (1985), *Provision* (1988).

Secret Affair

Led by Ian Page (b. Ian Paine, 1960, England; vocals/trumpet/piano/organ), and Dave Cairns (b. 1959, England; guitar/vocals), Secret Affair, one of the most creative neo-mod groups of the late 70s, emerged out of the lightweight UK new wave band New Hearts who folded in 1978. New Hearts released two lacklustre singles. The Secret Affair line-up was completed by Dennis Smith (bass/vocals, ex-Advertising), and Chris Bennett (drums, ex-Alternative TV). Bennett did not work out and was replaced by Seb Shelton (ex-Young Bucks). They debuted supporting the Jam (as the New Hearts had once done), but made their name at the Bridge House Tavern in Canning Town, London, centre of the mod revival. They appeared on the *Mods Mayday* live compilation but then set up their own I-Spy label through Arista Records. Subsequently they toured with Purple Hearts and Back To Zero under the banner 'March Of The Mods'. Their first single, 'Time For Action', was an immediate success for both band and label, featuring Chris Gent (of the

Autographs) on saxophone. They also signed Squire to the I-Spy label. Further singles in differing styles charted and the debut album was well received, particularly the epic title track which referred to their fan following. However, Shelton left late in 1980 to join the Up-Set, then Dexy's Midnight Runners and was replaced by Paul Bultitude. After two singles from the final Secret Affair album failed commercially, they disbanded. Dave Cairns went on to form the duo Flag, with Archie Brown, his former colleague from the Young Bucks. He subsequently formed another band called Walk On Fire with Dennis Smith. Page, who now writes fantasy books, formed Ian Page and Bop whose single 'Unity Street' created some interest. Bultitude joined the Mari Wilson's Wilsations and later founded the Dance Network label. Smith threw in his lot with Nik Kershaw's Krew, and Seb Shelton went on to manage, amongst others, the Woodentops.

Albums: *Glory Boys* (1979), *Behind Closed Doors* (1980), *Business As Usual* (1982).

Section 25

The nucleus of this Blackpool, Lancashire, England group started in November 1979 with brothers Vin Cassidy (electronics/drum machine) and Larry Cassidy (guitar/vocals). In April 1978, a guitarist called Phil joined and Section 25 performed their first gig on 1 June. November of that year saw Phil replaced by Paul. The group then introduced a second drummer, John and, since they were unable to find a suitable keyboard player, the appropriate passages were recorded on a tape machine, having first been constructed at SSRU, the group's rehearsal studio. The sound engineer, John Hurst, played a decisive role in the group's live sound. Their first single, 'Girls Don't Count' came out in early 1980. Over the next two years they toured Europe extensively and frequently supported Joy Division. After the release of their first album, Paul left after a gig in Helsinki. Lee Shallcross (drums) joined in February 1982 and toured with them in the USA. After their second album emerged on the Factory Benelux label, in February 1983, the Cassidys decided to cancel further live shows, drop all their old material and re-think their approach. By August 1983 they returned as a five piece with Angela Flowers (vocals/keyboards) and Jenny Ross (vocals/keyboards), with a first gig in December 1983. *From The Hip* was released in May 1984 on Factory Records.

Albums: *Always Now* (1981), *The Key Of Dreams* (1982), *From The Hip* (1984).

Selecter

When Coventry's Specials needed a b-side for their own debut 'Gangsters', they approached fellow local musician Noel Davies. With the assistance of John Bradbury aka Prince Rimshot (drums), and Barry Jones (trombone), Davies concocted the instrumental track 'The Selecter'. Released on the Specials own 2-Tone label, the single took off with both sides receiving airplay. This meant that a band had to be formed to tour. Bradbury was busy drumming for the Specials and Jones had returned to his newsagent business so Davies assembled the Selecter Mk II. This consisted of Pauline Black (vocals), Noel Davis (guitar), Crompton Amanor (drums/vocals), Charles H. Bainbridge (drums), Gappa Hendricks, Desmond Brown (keyboards) and Charlie Anderson (bass). Anderson claims the original ska superstar, Prince Buster, amongst his ancestors. The first album featured the renowned ska trombonist Rico Rodriques. Like many of the bands who first found fame on 2-Tone, the Selecter departed for pastures new - in this case 2-Tone's distributors Chrysalis. They managed a string of successful singles such as 'On My Radio', 'Three Minute Hero', and 'Missing Words'. Black left in 1981 and recorded the single 'Pirates Of The Airwaves' with Sunday Best before concentrating on acting. She reappeared to the general public as hostess of the children's pop/games show *Hold Tight*. Black rejoined Selector on tour in 1991 as signs of ska revival in London gained ground.

Albums: *Too Much Pressure* (1980), *Celebrate The Bullet* (1981), *Out On The Streets* (1992).

Senseless Things

Formed in west London, England, in 1987 by Mark Keds, Morgan Nicholls, Cass Browne and Ben Harding, Senseless Things soon set themselves up to be the teenage andidote to sythesized somnambulance. Taking their musical lead from the Ramones and the Dickies, and their spiritual lead from fellow guitar outfit Mega City Four, the foursome embarked upon a hectic tour-riddled schedule which always seemed to involve copious amounts of alcohol. Half cheeky charm, half frightening potential, their youthful zest initially outshone their musical achievements, simply because they persisted in playing so fast. Eventually, however, they began to redress this imbalance. After journeying through the independent wasteland - including a short stay on the American What Goes On? label, which folded under mysterious circumstances - and a series of enthusiastic singles, the Senseless Things were snapped up by Epic Records at the start of 1991. The subsequent *The First Of Too Many*, introduced acoustic guitars and gentler moods to the punky blitzes of yore, and with 'Got It At The Delmar' scuttling into the Top 60 of the UK singles chart, it would appear that a large-scale breakthrough is imminent.

Senseless Things

Albums: *Postcard CV* (1989), *The First Of Too Many* (1991).

Serious Drinking

Formed after attendance at the University Of East Anglia, Norwich, England in February 1981, this motley assortment of ex-students carved a niche for themselves in the independent charts of the early 80s by injecting their songs with comedic candour. Jem (bass) was an outspoken member of the Socialist Workers Party, although Lance (the only one not to attend UEA, drums), Martin Simon (ex-Higsons) and Eugene (the two singers) and Andy (ex-Farmers Boys; guitar) were more concerned with football and alcoholic beverages. The explanation for the presence of two singers was typically straightforward: 'Eugene is in the band because Martin wanted a lift to a practice and Eugene had a car and he's just stayed ever since'. They took their name from a headline announcing an interview with the Cockney Rejects in *Sounds*. Pigeonholed as leaders of some mythical 'herbert' movement, they did nevertheless have a penchant for traditional British leisure pursuits. The singles 'Love On The Terraces' and 'Hangover' both fared well in the independent charts, the former produced by Mark Bedford of Madness. The latter included the impressive 'Baby I'm Dying A Death' as its b-side, culled from the band's popular John Peel

radio session. 1983's *The Revolution Begins at Closing Time* and *They May Be Drinkers Robin, But They're Still Human Beings* fully displayed their eccentricity. The band's philosophy was still crystal clear, 'Basically what we're saying is go out, get drunk and enjoy yourself, and don't be nasty to other people.' Unfortunately, after 'Country Girl Became Drugs And Sex Punk' (another borrowed headline), both Gem and Lance departed. Karen Yarnell (ex-Gymslips) joined on drums and they released *Love On The Terraces*, a collection of favourite tracks and new recordings to coincide with the World Cup in 1990. *Stranger Than Tannadice* followed and was accompanied by sporadic live appearances.
Albums: *The Revolution Begins At Closing Time* (1983), *They May Be Drinkers Robin, But They're Still Human Beings* (1984), *Love On The Terraces* (1990), *Stranger Than Tannadice - The Hits, Misses and Own Goals Of Serious Drinking* (1991).

Servants

David Westlake's carefully crafted guitar pop tunes were the central attraction of west London's Servants. Accompanied by John Mahon (guitar), Philip King (bass - later with Felt, Biff Bang Pow!, the Apple Boutique and See See Rider), and John Wills (drums), the band featured on the *New Musical Express C86* cassette ('Transparent'). Their first single, 'She's Always Hiding' (1986), surfaced around the same time on the label Head, followed by a four-track EP, *The Sun, A Small Star*. But Westlake left soon after, joining Creation Records, forming Westlake and releasing a self-titled mini-album in 1987. The Servants later reformed in 1989, but the results were restricted to a one-off single, 'It's My Turn'.

Sex Gang Children

This London based post punk/gothic band were briefly in vogue in the early 80s. They were built around vocalist Andi Sex Gang, who talked himself into support slots for which he needed to quickly assemble a new band. He eventually settled on Dave Roberts (bass), Terry McLeay (guitar) and Rob Stroud (drums), who played their first gig under the name Panic Button. The name Sex Gang Children was lifted from a William Burroughs poem and was actually on a list of names that fellow King's Road fashion victim Boy George was toying with. It later transpired that Boy George had in turn taken it from Malcolm McLaren's original suggestion for a moniker for the band which would become Bow Wow Wow. By 1982 a number of bands in the same mould began breaking through in the capital. Their first vinyl release was a 12-inch titled 'Beasts', produced by Nicky Garrett (ex-UK Subs), after which Tony James (Generation X, future Sigue Sigue Sputnik) began to take an interest in the band. Their most fondly remembered release, 'Into The Abyss' closed 1982 with their debut long player arriving early the next year. The single lifted from it, 'Sebastiane', featured Jinni Hewes from Marc And The Mambas on violin. Andi then performed a debut with Marc Almond ('The Hungry Years') for the compilation *The Whip*, which also included a contribution from Roberts' other band Car Crash International. Stroud left to join Pink And Black (featuring future All About Eve bass player Andy Cousins), and was replaced by Nigel Preston (ex-Theatre Of Hate). He stayed long enough to record the single 'Mauritia Mayer', before he took part in a bizarre 'drummers' swop with Ray Mondo of Death Cult. Events took a further strange turn when the latter was deported back to Sierra Leonne for passport irregularities after a USA tour. Roberts also departed, leaving Andi and McLeay to recruit Cam Campbell (bass), and Kevin Matthews (drums). However, only one single, 'Deiche', was released before the band disintegrated and Andi set out on a solo career.

Albums: *Song And Legend* (1983), *Beasts* (1983), *Live* (1984), *Re-enter The Abyss* (1986).

Sex Pistols; Sid Vicious

Sex Pistols

This incandescent UK punk group came together under the aegis of entrepreneur Malcolm McLaren during the summer of 1975. Periodically known as the Swankers, with lead vocalist Wally Nightingale, they soon metamorphosed into the Sex Pistols with a line up comprising: Steve Jones (b. 3 September 1955, London, England; guitar), Paul Cook (b. 20 July 1956, London, England; drums), Glen Matlock (b. London, England; bass) and Johnny Rotten (b. John Lydon, 30 January 1956, London, England; vocals). By 1976, the group was playing irregularly around London and boasted a small following of teenagers, whose spiked hair, torn clothes and safety pins echoed the new fashion that McLaren was transforming into commodity. The group's gigs became synonymous with violence, which reached a peak during the 100 Club's Punk Rock Festival when

a girl was blinded in a glass-smashing incident involving the group's most fearful follower, Sid Vicious. The adverse publicity did not prevent the group from signing to EMI Records later that year when they also released their first single, 'Anarchy In The UK'. From Rotten's sneering laugh at the opening of the song to the final seconds of feedback, the single was a riveting debut. The Pistols promoted the work on London Weekend Television's *Today* programme, which ended in a stream of four-letter abuse that brought the group banner headlines in the following morning's tabloid press. More controversy ensued when the group's 'Anarchy' tour was decimated and the single suffered distribution problems and bans from shops. Eventually, it peaked at number 38 in the UK charts. Soon after, the group was dropped from EMI in a blaze of publicity. By February 1977, Matlock was replaced by that punk caricature Sid Vicious (b. John Simon Ritchie, 10 May 1957, London, England, d. 2 February 1979). The following month, the group was signed to A&M Records outside the gates of Buckingham Palace. One week later, A&M cancelled the contract, with McLaren picking up another parting cheque of £40,000. After reluctantly signing to the small label Virgin, the group issued 'God Save The Queen'. The single tore into the heart of British Nationalism at a time when the populace was celebrating the Queen' Jubilee. Despite a daytime radio ban the single rose to number 1 in the *NME* chart. The Pistols suffered for their art as outraged royalists attacked them whenever they appeared on the streets. A third single, the melodic 'Pretty Vacant' (largely the work of the departed Matlock) proved their most accessible single to date and restored them to the Top 10.

By the winter the group hit again with 'Holidays In The Sun' and issued their controversially-titled album, *Never Mind The Bollocks - Here's The Sex Pistols*. The work rocketed to number 1 in the UK album charts amid partisan claims that it was a milestone in rock. In truth, it was a more patchy affair, containing a preponderance of previously released material which merely underlined that the group was running short of ideas. An ill-fated attempt to capture the group's story on film wasted much time and revenue, while a poorly received tour of America fractured the Pistols' already strained relationship. In early 1978, Rotten announced that he was leaving the group after a gig in San Francisco. According to the manager Malcolm McLaren he was fired. McLaren, meanwhile, was intent on taking the group to Brazil in order that they could be filmed playing with the train robber Ronnie Biggs. Vicious, incapacitated by heroin addiction, could not make the trip, but Jones and Cook were happy to indulge in the publicity stunt. McLaren mischievously promoted Biggs as the group's new lead singer and

another controversial single emerged: 'God Save The Pistols'. It was later retitled 'No One Is Innocent (A Punk Prayer)' and issued as a double a-side with Vicious's tuneless rendition of the Frank Sinatra standard 'My Way'. McLaren's movie was finally completed by director Julien Temple under the title *The Great Rock 'n' Roll Swindle*. A self-conscious rewriting of history, it callously wrote Matlock out of the script and saw the unavailable Rotten relegated to old footage. While the film was being completed, the Pistols' disintegration was completed. Vicious, now the centre of the group, recorded a lame version of Eddie Cochran's 'C'mon Everybody' before returning to New York. On 12 October 1978, his girlfriend Nancy Spungen was found stabbed in his hotel room and Vicious was charged with murder. While released on bail, he suffered a fatal overdose of heroin and died peacefully in his sleep on the morning of 2 February 1979. Virgin Records continued to issue the desultory fragments of Pistols work that they had on catalogue, including the appropriately titled compilation, *Flogging A Dead Horse*. The group's impact as the grand symbol of UK punk rock has ensured their longevity. The unholy saga appropriately ended in the High Court a decade on in 1986 when Rotten and his fellow ex-Pistols won substantial damages against their former manager.
Albums: *Never Mind The Bollocks - Here's The Sex Pistols* (1977). Compilations: *The Great Rock 'N' Roll Swindle* (1979), *Some Product - Carri On Sex Pistols* (1979), *Flogging A Dead Horse* (1980).

Shack

Formed in 1986 by brothers Mick (b. 28 November 1961, Liverpool, England) and John Head (b. 4 October 1965), Shack emerged from the ashes of the Pale Fountains. Having had their fingers burnt by the major music industry - the Pale Fountains reached number 46 in the UK charts with 'Thank You', but were generally misunderstood by their employers - Shack joined up with independent label the Ghetto Recording Company. Experts at the cleverly understated melodic guitar pop song, 1988 saw the release of their acclaimed debut album, *Zilch*. Yet instead of persevering with their commercial instincts, Shack laid low until reappearing with a single in 1991 and a planned second album for the year after.
Albums: *Zilch* (1988).

Shakespear's Sister

Formed by Siobhan Marie Deidre Fahey-Stewart (b. 10 September 1958, Dublin, Eire) who was better known simply as Siobhan Fahey, and Marcella Detroit (b. 21 June 1959, Detroit, Michigan, USA) with producer and writer Richard Feldman keeping a low profile as third member. Siobhan, who had left

Ireland for the UK to become a press officer at Decca, was a member of the top 80s girl group Bananarama. She left in early 1988, though Detroit , too , had previously released some unsuccessful solo material. Taking their name from a Smiths' song and keeping the spelling mistake made by a designer, one of their first gigs took place in Leningrad, USSR, in January 1989. Their debut 'Break My Heart (You Really)' was not a hit. However, 'You're History', the second single and significantly different from the first, made the UK Top 10. The debut album made number 9, though the extracted single 'Run Silent' failed to reach the Top 50 in the UK. 1991 finally saw the unveiling of a follow-up with *Hormonally Yours*, much of it recorded while both participants were pregnant: 'It's self-deprecating but yet its very female without being militant or apologetic. Its just...what we are.' The group presently record in Los Angeles where Siobhan lives with husband Dave Stewart of the Eurythmics. In February 1992, Shakespear's Sister achieved their first UK number 1 with 'Stay With Me'.
Albums: *Sacred Heart* (1989), *Hormonally Yours* (1991).

Sham 69

Originally formed in London, England in 1976, this five-piece skinhead/punk-influenced group comprised Jimmy Pursey (vocals), Albie Slider (bass), Neil Harris (lead guitar), Johnny Goodfornothing (rhythm guitar) and Billy Bostik (drums). Pursey was a fierce, working-class idealist, an avenging angel of the unemployed, who sacked most of the above line-up within a year due to their lack of commitment. A streamlined aggregation featuring Dave Parsons (guitar), Dave Treganna (bass) and Mark Cain (drums) helped Pursey reach the UK charts with a series of anthemic hits including 'Angels With Dirty Faces', 'If The Kids Are United', 'Hurry Up Harry' and 'Hersham Boys'. Although Pursey championed proletarian solidarity, his rabble-rousing all too often brought violence and disruption from a small right-wing faction causing wary promoters to shun the group. After a troubled couple of years attempting to reconcile his ideals and their results, Pursey elected to go solo, but his time had passed. The group reformed in the early 90s and performed at punk nostalgia/revival concerts.
Albums: *Tell Us The Truth* (1978), *That's Life* (1978), *Adventures Of The Hersham Boys* (1979).

Shamen

From the ashes of the moderately successful Alone Again Or (named after the track from Love's *Forever Changes*) in 1986, the Shamen had a profound effect upon contemporary pop music over the next half decade. Formed in Aberdeen by Colin Angus (b. 24 August 1961, Aberdeen, Scotland; bass), Peter

Stephenson (b. 1 March 1962, Ayrshire, Scotland), Keith McKenzie (b. 30 August 1961, Aberdeen, Scotland) and Derek McKenzie (b. 27 February 1964, Scotland; guitar), the Shamen's formative stage relied heavily on crushing, psychedelic rock played by a relatively orthodox line-up. Their debut album, *Drop*, captured the sense of the colourful live shows and sealed the first chapter of the band's career. Soon after, Colin Angus became fascinated by the nascent underground hip-hop movement. Derek McKenzie was rather less enamoured with the hardcore dance explosion and departed, allowing William Sinnott (b. 23 December 1960, Glasgow, Scotland, d. 23 May 1991; bass) to join the ranks and further encourage the Shamen's move towards the dancefloor. In 1988, their hard-edged blend of rhythms, guitars, samples, sexually explicit slideshows and furious rhetoric drew anger from feminists, politicians and - after the scathing 'Jesus Loves Amerika' single - religious groups. That same year the band relocated to London, slimmed down to the duo of Angus and Sinnott and concentrated on exploring the areas of altered states with mind-expanding psychedelics. By 1990 the Shamen's influence - albeit unwitting - was vividly realised as the much-touted indie-dance crossover saw bands fuse musical cultures with great commercial success and the likes of Jesus Jones openly confessed to the Shamen's groundbreaking significance. By this time the Shamen themselves had taken to touring with a Synergy show, a unique four hour extravaganza featuring rappers and designed to take the band even further away from their rock roots. By the same token, their 'Pro Gen' single saw the Shamen welcomed into the very dance scene they had embraced so wholeheartedly long ago. After four years of such imaginative adventures into sound, 1991 promised a huge breakthrough for the Shamen and their fluctuating creative entourage. Unfortunately, just as the group inexorably toppled towards commercial riches, Will Sinnott drowned off the coast of Gomera, one of the Canary Islands, on 23 May. With the support of Sinnott's family, the Shamen persevered with a remix of 'Move Any Mountain (Pro Gen '91)' which climbed into the Top 10 of the UK chart, a fitting tribute to the tragic death of such a creative force.
Albums: *Drop* (1987), *In Gorbachev We Trust* (1989), *Phorward* (1989), *En-Tact* (1990), *Progeny* (1991).

Sharkey, Feargal

b. 13 August 1958, Derry, Northern Ireland. Sharkey first found fame as the lead singer of the Irish pop-punk group, the Undertones, whose sparkling singles provided some of the best pop of the late 70s. The group's reign lasted from 1976-83 after which Sharkey teamed up with Vince Clarke in the short-lived Assembly. The plaintive 'Never Never' was a

Top 10 hit for the group and highlighted the power of Sharkey's distinctive, quavering vocal style. In 1984, Sharkey recorded the underrated 'Listen To Your Heart' for Madness' label Zarjazz and this was followed by his biggest success, 'A Good Heart'. This insistent tune established him as a potential major act by reaching number 1 in the UK charts. The Top 10 follow-up 'You Little Thief' was almost equally distinctive and Sharkey's debut album, produced by the Eurythmics' David A. Stewart was very well received. Sharkey subsequently moved to America, where he recorded *Wish*. A long-delayed third album, *Songs From The Mardi Gras*, continued Sharkey's slow drift away from the mainstream, although it did spawn a surprise Top 20 hit, 'I've Got News For You'.
Albums: *Feargal Sharkey* (1985), *Wish* (1987), *Songs From The Mardi Gras* (1991).

Shear, Jules

b. 7 March 1952, Pittsburgh, Pennsylvania, USA. singer-songwriter Jules Shear recorded numerous albums both solo and with groups beginning in the late 70s, and wrote for such artists as Cyndi Lauper, the Bangles, Art Garfunkel and Olivia Newton-John. Shear moved from Pittsburgh to Los Angeles in the 70s. His first recorded work was with the band Funky Kings in 1976, also featuring singer-songwriter Jack Tempchin, who had written previously with the Eagles. Two years later Shear fronted Jules And The Polar Bears, a pop group that critics lumped in with the emerging new wave movement. The group debuted with the excellent *Got No Breeding*, which featured some of Shear's finest work, most notably 'Lovers By Rote'. After one more album, however, they disbanded in 1980. Shear next surfaced with the solo *Watch Dog* in 1983 and released three further albums under his own name. He briefly fronted the band Reckless Sleepers in 1988, which released one album, but Shear has yet to make a major commercial impact. In 1988, Iain Matthews recorded an entire album of Shear compositions, *Walking A Changing Line*, for Windham Hill Records.
Albums: *Funky Kings* (1976), *Got No Breeding* (1978), *Fenetiks* (1979), *Watch Dog* (1983), *The Eternal Return* (1985), *Demo-itis* (1986), *Big Boss Sounds* (1988), *The Third Party* (1989).

Shelley, Pete

b. Peter McNeish, 17 April 1955, Leigh, Lancashire, England. When the Buzzcocks disbanded in 1981, Shelley soon embarked on a variety of solo projects. In fact, his solo history extended before, and during, the Buzzcocks career. As one of the Invisible Girls, he helped out on John Cooper Clarke albums while the Buzzcocks were still active. Around the same time he also launched his own independent label, Groovy.

On this he released *Free Agents* (subtitled *Three Pounds And Three Pounds Thirty Three R.R.P.*, which was also its original price). This consisted primarily of tape loops and feedback, and general free-for-all improvisation. Meanwhile on New Hormones (the Buzzcocks original label) came *The Tiller Boys* EP, another of Shelley's pet projects. The second release on Groovy was *Sky Yen*, a solo album originally recorded by Shelley in 1974 using electronic instruments. Much akin to work by Kraftwerk, it prefaced the electro dance feel of his later solo work. However, it was 1982's *Homosapien*, a weighty slice of electro-pop concerning bisexuality, which marked the high point in Shelley's solo career. It was produced by Martin Rushent as a launch for his Generic label, and caused much discussion of Shelley's sexuality, and a re-examination of his Buzzcocks lyrics. *XL1* in 1983 was more tame, although it did boast the novelty of including a Sinclair computer programme that reproduced the lyrics. One review compounded matters by mentioning no less than five Buzzcocks titles in comparison, which was perhaps a trifle unfair. Again, it was produced by Rushent, this time with a predominantly disco feel. After 1986's *Heaven And The Sea* Shelley sought the comfort of a band again, and attempted to retain anonymity in Zip.
Albums: *Free Agents* (1980), *Sky Yen* (1980), *Homosapien* (1982), *XL1* (1983), *Heaven And The Sea* (1986).

Shelleyan Orphan

It was in 1980 when Caroline Crawley (vocals/clarinet) and Jemaur Tayle (acoustic guitar/vocals) first got together in their hometown of Bournemouth, England and discovered they had a mutual appreciation of the poet Shelley, so they took their name from his poem 'Spirit Of Solitude'. Neither of them could read or write music, or play any of their chosen instruments so in 1982 Caroline quit her A-Level studies and they moved to London in search of a string section and oboist, with the intention of using these traditionally classical instruments along with the guitar and their two voices, in a pop context. Inspired by T-Rex, Nick Drake and Van Morrison, the self-taught duo found their musicians and touted themselves around London, until in June 1984 they won a Kid Jensen BBC radio session. Following a baffling support to the Jesus And Mary Chain at the ICA, where their classical ensemble shocked the assembled crowd, they were swiftly signed up by Rough Trade Records. Two sweet and mellow singles followed, 'Cavalry Of Cloud' and 'Anatomy Of Love', both to reviews of poetic ecstasy, and after a memorable appearance on *The Tube* television programme, their controversial debut *Helleborine* was released in May 1987. Its swirling romanticism was promptly dubbed 'pretentious' by the music press, gaining Shelleyan Orphan the title of 'Pre-Raphaelite Fruitcakes'. The next two years were spent writing, recording and maturing their sound, and with the addition of more traditional rock instruments to their string orientated line-up, the band produced the more immediate and accessible *Century Flower*. The album was a significant step forward, using unusual time signatures and baroque instrumentation to spectacular effect. The richly harmonic 'Shatter' and superb 'Timeblind' were among the highlights. Supporting the Cure across Europe and America, they showed another side to their gentle image and betrayed a new found energy and exuberance.
Albums: *Helleborine* (1987), *Century Flower* (1989).

Shillelagh Sisters

This UK north London all-woman rockabilly group was formed in 1983. The group found themselves mixed-up with the emerging 'country cow-punk' scene which included Yip Yip Coyote and the Boothill Foot-Tappers. The Sisters, who as legend has it, first decided to form while congregated in a gent's toilet-room at a party, comprised Trisha (b. Patricia O'Flynn; saxophone), Jacqui Sullivan (vocals), Mitzi (drums) and Lynder (double bass). Having completed one album for CBS in 1984, they disappeared from view soon afterwards, leaving some observers debating to the present day whether or not they ever managed to spell 'Shillelagh' correctly or not! Jacqui later joined Bananarama as the replacement for Siobhan Fahey, while O'Flynn played in the original line-up of Coming Up Roses.
Album: *The Shillelagh Sisters* (1984).

Shirts

This US pop-rock act were formed from the ashes of the Lackeys and Schemers, who played several low-key gigs in the early 70s. The line-up featured Annie Golden (b. c.1953; vocals), Ronnie Ardito (guitar), Artie La Monica (guitar), Robert Racioppo (bass), John Piccolo (keyboards), and John 'Zeeek' Criscioni (drums). All members provided songs either on their own or in partnership with other personnel. Golden also worked as an actor, having a leading role in the screen adaptation of *Hair* in 1979. Other names which were suggested for the assembly included the Pants and the Sleeves. Shirts was the eventual choice, with the proviso that it should be pronounced Shoits in a thick New York accent. Unsurprisingly this tradition has lapsed with time. They initially earned a crust as a Top 40 covers band playing in bars, before graduating to clubs like CBGB's in 1975. Their first single, 'Tell Me Your Plans', was a surprise hit in Europe. Their big break came with a Peter Gabriel tour, before further singles and albums including the single 'Laugh And Walk Away'. Golden released a solo single in 1984, but the band disappeared from the annals of rock taking their pronunciation with them.

Albums: *The Shirts* (1978), *Street Light Shine* (1979), *Inner Sleeve* (1980).

Shockabilly

Formed in 1982 by guitarist Eugene Chadbourne, bassist Kramer and drummer Dave Licht, Shockabilly produced music that sounded like an unholy combination of the Electric Prunes and Karlheinz Stockhausen. They specialized in outrageous covers - 'Psychotic Reaction', '19th Nervous Breakdown', 'Day Tripper', 'Purple Haze' - and also more obscure items by John Lee Hooker, John Fogerty and Syd Barrett. When the song appears familiar it gives the listener a thread on which to hang the power trio-chaos they liked to indulge in. Chadbourne's background was in rock, blues, late 60s free jazz and free improvisation - he put it all into Shockabilly with an energy and spleen that gained a response from the more adventurous post-punk audiences. After they folded in 1985 Chadbourne, an inspired songwriter, pursued a solo career while Kramer set up Shimmy Disk, one of the great radical rock labels of the 80s and 90s.

Albums: *The Dawn Of Shockabilly* (1982), *Earth Versus Shockabilly* (1983), *Colosseum* (1984), *Vietnam* (1984), *Heaven* (1985). Compilation: *Greatest Hits* (1983).

Shocked, Michelle

b. 1962, Dallas, Texas, USA. This roots singer/songwriter's music draws on frequently tough experiences of a nomadic lifestyle. Her childhood had been divided between a religiously inclined mother (Catholic then Mormon), and her estranged father, a some-time mandolin player. She originally came to prominence via a Walkman recorded gig, taped around a campfire, complete with crickets on backing vocals. *Short Sharp Shocked* highlightened more varied and less self-conscious stylings than the more mainstream Suzanne Vega/Tracy Chapman school. *Captain Swing* was her 'big band' record, where she was joined once more by Dwight Yoakam's producer/guitarist Pete Anderson, as well as a plethora of famous extras (Fats Domino, Bobby 'Blue' Bland, Randy Newman). Despite songs with titles like 'God Is A Real Estate Developer', its jazzy rhythms and swishing brass made it her most commercially accessible. The album's title was taken from the 19th Century leader of a farm labourer's revolt, the type of subject matter which put her in good company with touring companion Billy Bragg. The recording of *Arkansas Traveller* was completed by travelling across the US and further afield with a portable studio. Hence musicians like Taj Mahal, Doc

Michelle Shocked

Watson, Levon Helm (the Band), Clarence 'Gatemouth' Brown and Hothouse Flowers made their contributions in Ireland, Australia and elsewhere. Shocked had spent time researching the origins of American music and in particular the black-faced minstrel legacy, which she attacked with her own traditional songs. Shocked is one of the most interesting of the new generation of folk artists.

Albums: *The Texas Campfire Tapes* (1987), *Short Sharp Shocked* (1988), *Captain Swing* (1989), *Arkansas Traveller* (1992).

Shop Assistants

Formed in Edinburgh, Scotland during 1984, this pop band used guitar inflections enthusiastically borrowed from the Buzzcocks. They were originally titled Buba And The Shop Assistants and released a solitary single 'Something To Do' under that name. With only 500 pressings on the obscure Villa 21 independent, it has gained a reputation amongst record collectors for its monetary value as well as the spirited songwriting. Guitarist David Keegan was the only one to reveal his full name to the press, and was joined by Alex (vocals), Sarah (bass), Ann and Laura (drums). 'All Day Long', on the Subway Organisation label, was allegedly Morrissey's favourite single of 1985, but by this time they had garnered adequate plaudits from their exposure in fanzines and magazines. The

following year's release on the 53rd & 3rd label, 'Safety Net' reached number 1 on the UK independent chart. Signing to the major Chrysalis label saw the release of their debut album, which made a brief appearance in the Top 100 and then disappeared - as did the band. When Alex left in 1987 to form the Motorcycle Boy the critical acclaim dried up. Keegan also left, taking up a post as skiing instructor, while Sarah and Laura went back to college. They reformed in 1990, with Laura switching to bass and Margarita taking her place on drums. One of their most recent singles, 'The Big E', was, typically, a tribute to the guitar chord rather than the fashionable drug of the period. By this time they had signed to Andrew Tulley's Avalanche label, although their status in the independent scene has been somewhat eroded by the passing years.
Album: *Shop Assistants* (1986).

Shriekback

Shriekback

Shriekback originally evolved around a three-man nucleus of ex-Gang Of Four member Dave Allen, Carl Marsh (fresh from his own band, Out On Blue Six), plus Barry Andrews, previously with XTC, League Of Gentlemen and Restaurant For Dogs. The trio fused funk and rock with a unique and complex rhythmic approach, creating a distinctive and influential sound. The first fruits of this project came in 1982 with the EP *Tench* and then 'Sexthinkone' on the Y label, but it was the next two singles, 'My Spine Is the Bassline' (1982) and 'Lined Up' (1983) that established the band. Two further singles, 'Working On The Ground' and 'Accretions', were enough to secure a deal with Arista Records, releasing *Jam Science* in 1984. The album also spawned two excellent singles, 'Hand On My Heart' and 'Mercy Dash'. The following year saw the release of *Oil And Gold*, which included 'Nemesis' and 'Fish Below The Ice'. Although more commercially based, the band had lost that hard, infectious funk vein that was previously so predominant. A move to Island yielded *Big Night Music*, early in 1987, accompanied

by 'Gunning For Buddha' a month earlier. 'Get Down Tonight' followed in 1988, but this presaged the last Shriekback album proper, *Go Bang*. Those looking for an introduction to Shriekback might opt for *The Infinite*, a collection of the Y singles released on the Kaz label. Since then, there have been two further collections, summarising the band's time with Arista and Island respectively.
Albums: *Jam Science* (1984), *Oil And Gold* (1985), *Big Night Music* (1987), *Go Bang* (1988). Compilations: *The Infinite - The Best Of Shriekback* (1985), *The Best Of Shriekback, Volume 2* (1988), *The Best Of Shriekback* (1990).

Sigue Sigue Sputnik

These UK punk/glam revivalists engineered themselves a briefly prosperous niche in the mid-80s. The creation of Tony James (ex-Chelsea, Generation X), Sigue Sigue Sputnik artlessly copied the shock tactics of Sex Pistols manager Malcolm McLaren. Instead of taking on board the Pistols' nihilism, James poached from cyberpunk novels and films (particularly *Blade Runner*) for their image. This consisted of dyed hair piled high, bright colours and an abundance of eye-liner. James had recruited clothes designer Martin Degville, Neal X, Ray Mayhew and Chris Cavanagh., taking pride in their apparent lack of musical experience. Taking their name from a Moscow street gang, they set about a publicity campaign which resulted in EMI, understandably keen not to let the next Pistols slip through their hands again, signing them for a reported £4 million pounds. The figure was deliberately exaggerated in order to provoke publicity. Their first single was 'Love Missile F1-11' which soared to number 3 in the UK charts in February 1986. However, though 'Twenty-First Century Boy' also made the Top 20, and a debut album sold advertising space between tracks, James' money-making ruse soon ended. Despite an avalanche of intentionally lurid press, the band split, and Tony James subsequently, albeit briefly, joined the Sisters Of Mercy in 1991.
Albums: *Flaunt It* (1986), *Dress For Excess* (1988).

Silverfish

Instigated in 1988 by budding guitarist and regular London gig-goer Andrew 'Fuzz' Duprey (b. 14 June 1963, Kent, England), who thought of the band name and had a desperate urge to play 'noise you could dance to'. Stuart Watson (b. 10 November 1962, Northamptonshire, England; drums) and Chris Mowforth (b. 30 May 1964, Middlesex, England; bass) joined up to start - literally - 'bashing around ideas', until Chris realised he could not sing and play bass simultaneously. Thus Lesley Rankine (b. April 11 1965, Edinburgh, Scotland) was discovered b(r)awling at a hardcore gig and subsequently became the vocalist. The title for their first album was derived from an early live review which compared her singing to that of a 'fat Axl Rose' (of Guns N' Roses). Silverfish were confrontational, to say the least: names of two EPs were *Total Fucking Asshole*, and *Fuckin' Drivin' Or What*, and the expletives were aligned with a suitably ferocious splatterpunk sound which gouged a uniquely noisy niche for itself in the British scheme of things, despite a brief spell spent under the unwanted umbrella of 'Camden Lurch' - a 'scene' half-invented by the ever-imaginative UK music press in an attempt to catagorize the burgeoning state of alternative music in north London which had limited success. In 1991, Silverfish took a potentially major step up the ladder by switching record labels, to Creation Records, prior to causing havoc on their first tour of America.

Albums: *Fat Axl* (1990), *Organ Fan* (1992). Compilation: *Cockeye* (1990).

Simple Minds

This Scottish group was formed in 1978 by Jim Kerr (b. 9 July 1959, Glasgow, Scotland; vocals), Charlie Burchill (b. 27 November 1959, Glasgow, Scotland; guitar), Tony Donald (bass) and Brian McGee (drums), former members of Glasgow punk group Johnny And The Self-Abusers. A second guitarist, Duncan Barnwell, was recruited following a newspaper advertisement. The unit was augmented by keyboard player Mick McNeil (b. 20 July 1958) before Derek Forbes (b. 22 June 1956) replaced a disaffected Donald. The upheavals of this initial era were completed with Barnwell's departure. Having established themselves as one of Scotland's leading live attractions, Simple Minds were signed to Zoom, an Edinburgh-based independent label marketed by Arista Records. 'Life In A Day', the group's debut single, broached the UK Top 50 in March 1979 while the attendant album reached number 30. Critics were divided over its merits, although a consensus deemed the set derivative. Within weeks the quintet began decrying their creation and embarked on a more radical direction. *Real To Real Cacophony* unfolded within the recording studio in an attempt to regain an early spontaneity and while this largely experimental collection was a commercial flop, it reinstated the group's self-respect and won unanimous music press approbation.

Empires And Dance, was released in September 1980. The set fused the flair of its predecessor to a newly established love of dance music and reflected influences garnered during European tours. It included 'I Travel', a pulsating travelogue which became a firm favourite throughout the club circuit and helped engender a new sense of optimism in the group's career. Now free of Arista, Simple Minds were signed to Virgin Records in 1981, and paired with producer Steve Hillage. The resultant sessions spawned two albums, *Sons And Fascination* and *Sister Feelings Call*, which were initially released together. It became the group's first UK Top 20 entrant, spawning three minor hit singles with 'The American', 'Love Song' and 'Sweat In Bullet' and began Simple Minds' transformation from cult to popular favourites. This very success unnerved Brian McGee, who abhorred touring. In August 1981 he was replaced by former Slik and Skids drummer Kenny Hyslop (b. 14 February 1951, Helensburgh, Strathclyde, Scotland), although the newcomer's recorded contribution was confined to 'Promised You A Miracle'. This powerful song reached number 13 in Britain, and proved popular in Europe and Australia where the group enjoyed an almost fanatical following.

Although Mike Ogletree joined on Hyslop's departure, a former musician, Mel Gaynor (b. 29 May 1959), eventually became the quintet's permanent drummer. Both musicians were featured on *New Gold Dream*, Simple Minds' most successful album to date which peaked at number 3. Here the group was harnessing a more commercial sound, and they achieved a series of hits with its attendant singles, 'Glittering Prize' and 'Someone, Somewhere In Summertime'. A sixth collection, *Sparkle In The Rain*, united the quintet with producer Steve Lillywhite, inspiring comparisons with his other proteges, U2. 'Waterfront', a brash, pulsating grandiose performance, and 'Speed Your Love To Me', prefaced its release, and the album entered the UK chart at number 1. The set also featured 'Up On The Catwalk', a further Top 30 entrant, and a version of Lou Reed's 'Street Hassle', a long-established group favourite.

Jim Kerr married Pretenders' singer Chrissie Hynde in 1984, but their relationship did not survive the rigours of touring. The following year Simple Minds chose to record in America under the aegis of Jimmy Iovine and Bob Clearmountain. It was during this period that the group contributed 'Don't You (Forget About Me)' to the soundtrack of the film *The Breakfast Club*. The quintet remained ambivalent about the song, which was written by Keith Forsey and Steve Schiff, but it paradoxically became a US number 1 when issued as a single. Although the group initially vetoed a world-wide release, they reneged in the light of this achievement whereupon the record became a massive international hit and confirmed the group's world-beating status. However, the track did not appear on the ensuing *Once Upon A Time* which, despite international success, drew considerable criticism for its bombastic approach. Three tracks, 'Alive And Kicking', 'Sanctify Yourself' and 'All The Things She Said' nonetheless reached the UK Top 10 while a concurrent world tour, documented on *Live In The City Of Light*, was one of the year's major events. The proceeds of several dates were donated to Amnesty International, reflecting a growing politicization within the group. In 1988 they were a major inspiration behind the concert celebrating Nelson Mandela's 70th birthday, but although a new composition, 'Mandela Day', was recorded for the event, Simple Minds refused to release it as a single, fearful of seeming opportunistic. The song was later coupled to 'Belfast Child', a lengthy, haunting lament for Northern Ireland based on a traditional folk melody, 'She Moved Through The Fair'. This artistically ambitious work topped the UK chart in February 1989 and set the tone for the group's subsequent album, *Street Fighting Years*, their first studio set in four years. Although it achieved platinum status within five days, sales then dropped rather dramatically, reflecting the uncompromising nature of its content. Three further singles entered the UK Top 20, while *The Amsterdam EP*, which included a version of Prince's 'Sign 'O' The Times', reached number 18 at the end of the year. This contradictory period closed with the rancorous departure of Mick McNeil, replaced by Peter Vitesse, and the ending of the group's ten-year association with Schoolhouse Management. Simple Minds entered the 90s with an official line-up of Jim Kerr and Charlie Burchill and a development almost impossible to predict. *Real Life* saw the band re-introducing more personal themes to their songwriting after the political concerns of previous albums. The new material recaptured the grand, epic sound that is Simple Minds' trademark. Kerr married Patsy Kensit in January 1992.

Albums: *Life In A Day* (1979), *Real To Real Cacophony* (1979), *Empires And Dance* (1980), *Sons And Fascination/Sister Feelings Call* (1981), *New Gold Dream (81, 82, 83, 84)* (1982), *Sparkle In The Rain* (1984), *Once Upon A Time* (1985), *Live In The City Of Light* (1987), *Street Fighting Years* (1989), *Real Life* (1991). Compilations: *Celebration* (1982), *Themes For Great Cities* (1982).

Siouxsie And The Banshees

Siouxsie Sioux (b. Susan Dallion, 27 May 1957, London, England) was part of the notorious 'Bromley contingent', including Steve Severin (b. Steven Bailey, 25 September 1955), which followed the Sex Pistols in their early days. Siouxsie had also taken part in the 100 Club Punk Festival, singing an elongated version of 'The Lord's Prayer' with a group that included Sid Vicious on drums. The fledgling singer also achieved some minor fame after a verbal exchange with television presenter Bill Grundy which unwittingly prompted the Sex Pistols' infamous

Siouxsie And The Banshees

swearing match on the programme *Today*. Within months of that incident, Siouxsie put together her backing group the Banshees, featuring Pete Fenton (guitar), Steve Severin (bass) and Kenny Morris (drums). Siouxsie flirted with Nazi imagery, highlighted by black make-up and frequently exposed breasts. By mid-1977, Fenton was replaced by John McGeogh, and the group supported Johnny Thunders And The Heartbreakers as well as recording a session for the BBC disc jockey, John Peel. By 1978, the group had signed to Polydor and released their first single, the excellent 'Hong Kong Garden', which reached the UK Top 10. An album, *The Scream*, soon followed, produced by Steve Lillywhite. Less commercial offerings followed with 'The Staircase (Mystery)' and 'Playground Twist', which was soon succeeded by *Join Hands*. During a promotional tour, Morris and McKay abruptly left, to be replaced by former Slits drummer Budgie and temporary Banshee Robert Smith, on leave from the Cure. Siouxsie's Germanic influences were emphasized on the stark 'Mittageisen (Metal Postcard)', which barely scraped into the Top 50. Both 'Happy House' and 'Christine' were more melodic offerings, which brought greater commercial success.

After the success of *Kaleidoscope*, the group embarked on a world tour, including a concert behind the Iron Curtain. Another Top 10 album *Juju* was followed by some extra-curricular activities. Siouxie and Budgie formed an occasional offshoot group, the Creatures, who enjoyed Top 10 success in their own right, as well as recording an album. Smith and Severin also recorded successfully together as the Glove. After the string-accompanied *A Kiss In The Dreamhouse*, the group reconvened in the autumn of 1983 to play a concert for Italy's Communist Party. A highly commercial version of the Beatles' 'Dear Prudence' provided the group with their biggest UK hit, peaking at number 3. Early in 1984, the evocative 'Swimming Horses' maintained their hit profile,

while further personnel changes ensued with the enlistment of John Carruthers from Clock DVA. He, in turn, was replaced by John Klein. Regular albums during the mid-80s showed that the group had established a loyal cult following and could experiment freely in the studio without a significant loss of commercial appeal. Having already enjoyed success with a cover song, Siouxsie tackled Bob Dylan's 'This Wheel's On Fire', which reached the UK Top 20. An entire album of cover versions followed with the interesting *Through The Looking Glass*. A change of musical direction with *Peep Show* revealed the group as uncompromising as ever. 1991 saw them back in the charts with the dance-oriented 'Kiss Them For Me' and *Superstition*. They continue to play adventurous music, occasionally tinged with forays into more commercial territory.
Albums: *The Scream* (1978), *Join Hands* (1979), *Kaleidoscope* (1980), *Juju* (1981), *A Kiss In The Dreamhouse* (1982), *Nocturne* (1983), *Hyaena* (1984), *Tinderbox* (1986), *Through The Looking Glass* (1987), *Peep Show* (1988), *Superstition* (1991). Compilation: *Once Upon A Time - The Singles* (1981).

Sisters Of Mercy

A post-punk rock outfit whose flirtations with gothic imagery would dog the public and media perception of them throughout an eclectic career. They formed in Leeds, Yorkshire, England in 1980, when Leeds and Oxford University drop-out Andrew Eldritch (b. Andrew Taylor, 15 May 1959, East Anglia, England; vocals) teamed up with Gary Marx (guitar) and a drum machine. After releasing 'The Damage Done' (on which Eldritch plays drums and guitar) on their own Merciful Release label, the band expanded to include Ben Gunn (guitar) and Craig Adams (bass) for supports with Clash, Psychedelic Furs and the Birthday Party. A cult reputation in the North of England was augmented by excellent press, and further enhanced by the release of 'Alice'. A magnificent gothic dance saga, together with the subsequent 'Temple Of Love', it hallmarked the band's early musical character. Inbetween these two landmark 45s Gunn left to be replaced by Wayne Hussey (ex-Pauline Murray, Dead Or Alive). WEA picked up the distribution for Merciful Release as the band's reputation continued to grow throughout 1983 and 1984. However, despite the release of their debut album, the following year brought a creative watershed. Continuing rivalries between Marx and Eldritch forced the former to depart. This was only a stop-gap treaty with the band announcing a final split in April 1985 after a concert at the Royal Albert Hall. The rest of the year witnessed extraordinary legal wrangles between Eldritch on one hand and Adams and Hussey on the other, each claiming use of the name Sisters Of Mercy. Eldritch went as far as releasing a record under the title Sisterhood simply to prevent Adams and Hussey from adopting this halfway-house title. The duo eventually settled on the Mission as their new home, while Eldritch moved to Berlin, West Germany. Still operating under the Sisters Of Mercy title, Eldritch recruited Patricia Morrison (b. 14 January 1962, ex-Gun Club) for hit singles 'This Corrosion' and 'Dominion', and the album *Floodland*. A two year spell of inactivity was broken in 1990 with 'More', showcasing another new line-up; Tony James (ex-Generation X, Sigue Sigue Sputnik; bass), Tim Bricheno (b. 6 July 1963, Huddersfield, Yorkshire, England; guitar - ex-All About Eve) and Andreas Bruhn (guitar). The *Vision Thing* indulged Eldritch's penchant for deep rooted, esoteric metaphor, which occasionally makes his lyrics futile and impenetrable. 1991 saw a loss-making, aborted tour with Public Enemy, though this has done little to erase the confidence of the self-confessed 'world's greatest lyricist'.
Albums: *First And Last And Always* (1985), *Floodland* (1988), *Vision Thing* (1990), *Some Girls Wander By Mistake* (1992).

Skeletal Family

No doubt influenced by the emergence of gothic punk in the early 80s, the Skeletal Family emerged from Bingley in Yorkshire towards the end of 1982. Early demos recorded in September and December comprised Anne Marie (lead vocals), Trotwood (bass), Stan Greenwood (guitar), Steve Crane (drums) and Karl Heinz (synthesizer). But after a debut single, 'Just A Friend' on the Luggage label, in March 1983, the band signed to Yorkshire's established indie label Red Rhino, by which time Howard Daniels had taken over on drums and .... 'The Night' shared the same influences championed by the band's 'goth' counterparts - the Cramps, Bauhaus and the Birthday Party. 'Alone She Cries' in January 1984, featured the new drummer Martin, and 'So Sure' in June, alongside *Recollect*, an EP comprising early demos. By the time of *Burning Oil* in August, the Skeletal Family had attracted a sizeable following, supporting the Sisters Of Mercy. This ascent continued with 'Promised Land' in February 1985, where they were aided by Graham Pleeth on synthesizer, backed by a cover of Ben E. King's 'Stand By Me'. *Futile* Combat fared well in the UK independent charts, securing a deal with Chrysalis, but singer Anne Marie had left to join Ghost Dance. Recruiting drummer Kevin Phillips and Katrina on vocals, it was a new, more commercial Skeletal Family that issued 'Restless' in March 1986 and 'Just A Minute' in August, but neither made significant headway and the band were soon dropped, a fate that Ghost Dance would ironically share later. Albums: *Burning Oil* (1984), *Futile Combat* (1985), *Ghosts* (1986).

Skids

A Scottish new wave band founded in Dunfermline in 1977 by Stuart Adamson (guitar/vocals, b. 11 April 1958, Manchester, UK), Richard Jobson (vocals) Tom Kellichan (drums) and Willie Simpson (bass). After issuing 'Reasons' on their own No Bad label, the group were signed by Virgin. David Batchelor produced 'Sweet Suburbia' and 'The Saints Are Coming' before both 'Into The Valley' reached the UK Top 10 in 1979. Despite criticism of Jobson's lyrics as pretentious, the Skids enjoyed a further year of chart success as 'Masquerade' and 'Working For The Yankee Dollar' reached the Top 20. Both came from the second album, which was produced by Bill Nelson of Be-Bop Deluxe. Soon afterwards the band was hit by personnel changes. Russell Webb and Mike Baillie replaced Simpson and Kellichan and more crucially, the Skids' songwriting team was split when Adamson left after the release of the third album, which proved to be the group's most commercial, reaching the Top 10 and containing the minor hit 'Circus Games'. Without Adamson, *Joy*, an exploration of Celtic culture, was more or less a Jobson solo effort. The Skids dissolved in 1982, with Fanfare issued by Virgin as a mixture of greatest hits and unreleased tracks. In 1983, Stuart Adamson launched the career of his new band, Big Country. Richard Jobson recorded one album with a new band, the Armoury Show before pursuing a solo career as poet, songwriter and broadcaster. He released albums on Belgian label Disques Crepuscules and on Parlophone.

Albums: *Scared To Dance* (1979), *Days In Europa* (1979), *Absolute Game* (1980), *Joy* (1981), *Fanfare* (1982), with Armoury Show *Waiting For The Floods* (1985), with Richard Jobson *The Ballad Of Etiquette* (1985), *The Other Man* (1986), *16 Years Of Alcohol* (1987), *Bad Man* (1988).

Slaughter And The Dogs

Formed in Manchester, England in 1976, this punk quartet comprise Wayne Barrett (vocals); Howard Bates (bass); Mike Rossi (guitar) and Mad Muffet (drums). One of the first groups to sign to Manchester's independent Rabid Records, the group won a contract with Decca Records on which they released the glam/punk *Do it Dog Style*. A dispute with their record company combined with the departure of Barrett, saw them marooned back in Manchester. Adding Billy Duffy on guitar, they auditioned Morrissey as their new vocalist, before deciding to stay as a four-piece with Rossi singing. An unsuccessful relaunch as Slaughter convinced them to change their name to the Studio Sweethearts, but they fell apart in the summer of 1979. For a time they soldiered on with Barrett briefly returning as vocalist. He was later replaced by Ed Banger (Eddie

Garrity) but soon after the unit folded.Duffy went on to form the Theatre of Hate and later joined the Cult.

Albums: *Do It Dog Style* (1978), *Live At The Belle Vue* (1979), *Bite Back* (1980), *The Way We Were* (1983).

Slits

Slits

This UK, feminist punk group formed in 1976 with a line-up featuring, Ari-Up (vocals), Kate Korus (guitar), Palmolive (drums) and Suzi Gutsy (bass). Korus soon left to form the Mo-dettes and Gutsy quit to team up with the Flicks. They were soon replaced by guitarist Viv Albertine and Tessa Pollitt and it was this line-up that supported the Clash during the spring of 1977. The group were known for their uncompromising attitude and professed lack of technique, but their music was as aggressive and confrontational as the best of the punk fraternity. Their failure to secure a record contract during the first wave of the punk explosion was surprising. By the time, they made their recording debut, Palmolive had been ousted and replaced by Big In Japan percussionist, Budgie. Signed to Island Records, they worked with reggae producer Dennis Bovell on the dub-influenced *Cut*. The album attracted considerable press interest for its sleeve, which featured the group naked, after rolling in the mud. The departure of Budgie to Siouxsie And The Banshees (replaced by the Pop Group's Bruce Smith), coincided with the arrival of reggae musician Prince Hammer and trumpeter Don Cherry (father of Neneh Cherry). A series of singles followed, including a memorable version of John Holt's 'Man Next Door'. By 1981, the Slits had lost much of their original cutting edge and it came as little surprise when they disbanded at the end of the year. Their unorthodox, tribal-influenced rhythms single them out as one of the more underrated units of the late 70s.

Albums: *Cut* (1979), *Bootleg Retrospective* (1980), *Return Of The Giant Slits* (1981), *The Peel Sessions* (1988).

Slowdive

Slowdive

Formed in 1989 by Rachel Goswell (b. 16 May 1971,
Hampshire, England; vocals/guitar), Neil Halstead (b.
7 October 1970, Luton, Bedfordshire, England;
vocals/guitar), Brook Christian Savill (b. 6 December
1970, Bury, Lancashire, England; guitar), Nicholas
Chaplin (b. 23 December 1970, Slough, Berkshire,
England; bass) and Adrian Sell (drums), who departed
after six months to go to University. His replacement
was Neil Carter, who also played with local Reading
band the Colour Mary, until eventually Simon Scott
(b. 3 March 1971, Cambridge, England) joined
permanently, having drummed for the Charlottes.
While this was happening, Slowdive were creating a
dreamy sound which frequently defied literary
analysis, but the main ingredients were floating
harmonies and ripples of guitar effects within a
traditional three-minute song framework. Snapped up
by a revitalised Creation Records on the basis of one
demotape, Slowdive made a surprising number of
friends with what seemed to be a blatantly esoteric
sound; indeed, by the summer of 1991 they had
reached number 52 in the UK chart with the *Holding
Our Breath* EP, promising a significant breakthrough
in the near future.
Album: *Just For A Day* (1991).

Smashing Orange

This promising band from Wilmington, Delaware,
USA, specialized in loud garage group material
flavoured with hardcore. Vocalists Rob Montejo and
Sara Montejo were sibling college dropouts, though
guitarist Rick Hodgson actually graduated in
marketing. They all worked at a record store in
Delaware, establishing their permanent line-up only
five days before their live debut. The other members
were Tim Supplee (drums) and Steve Wagner (bass).
Their first single was the critically lauded 'My
Deranged Heart' on Native, while they made a deep
impression on domestic audiences supporting Lush at
the Marquee Club in New York. Their debut album
arrived in the summer of 1991, and confirmed the
band's potential.
Album: *Smashing Orange* (1991).

Smith, Patti

b. 31 December 1946, Chicago, Illinois, USA. Smith
was raised in New Jersey and became infatuated by
music, principally the Rolling Stones, the Velvet
Underground, Jimi Hendrix and James Brown, Patti
Smith's initial talent focussed on poetry and art. Her
early writing, captured on three anthologies, *Seventh
Heaven* (1971), *Kodak* (1972) and *Witt* (1973), was

Patti Smith Group

Smithereens

inspired by Arthur Rimbaud and William Burroughs, but as the 70s progressed she was increasingly drawn towards fusing such work with rock. In 1971, Smith was accompanied by guitarist Lenny Kaye for a reading in St Mark's Church, and this informal liaison continued for three years until the duo was joined by Richard Sohl (piano) in the first Patti Smith Group. Their first recording, 'Hey Joe'/'Piss Factory', was in part financed by photographer Robert Mappelthorpe, later responsible for many of the artist's striking album portraits. By 1974 the unit had become one of the most popular acts at New York's pivotal CBGB's club. Ivan Kral (bass) and J.D. Daugherty (drums) were then added to the line-up featured on *Horses*. This highly-lauded set, produced by John Cale, skilfully invoked Patti's 60s' mentors but in a celebratory manner rather than that of pastiche. By simultaneously capturing the fire of punk, Smith completed a collection welcomed by both old and new audiences. However, *Radio Ethiopia* was perceived as self-indulgent and the artist's career was further undermined when she incurred a broken neck upon falling offstage early in 1977. A lengthy recuperation ensued but Smith re-emerged in July with a series of excellent concerts and the following year scored considerable commercial success with *Easter*. This powerful set included 'Because The Night', co-written with Bruce Springsteen, which deservedly reached the UK Top 5, but *Wave*, failed to sustain such acclaim. Patti then married former MC5 guitarist Fred 'Sonic' Smith, and retired from active performing for much of the 80s. She resumed recording in 1988 with *Dream Of Life*, which contained the artist's customary call-to-arms idealism ('People Have The Power') and respect for rock and poetic tradition.

Albums: *Horses* (1975), *Radio Ethiopia* (1976), *Easter* (1978), *Wave* (1979), *Dream Of Life* (1988).

Smithereens

Influenced by the 60s pop of the Beatles, Beach Boys and the Byrds, the Smithereens formed in New Jersey in 1980. Members Jim Babjak (guitar) and Dennis Diken (drums) had played together since 1971; Mike Mesaros (bass) was recruited in 1976 and finally Pat DiNizio (vocals). After recording two EPs, they backed songwriter Otis Blackwell ('Great Balls Of Fire') on two obscure albums. In 1986 the group signed to Enigma Records and released their first full album, *Especially For You*, which fared well among both college radio and mainstream rock listeners, as did the single 'Blood And Roses'. After a lengthy tour, the Smithereens recorded their second album, *Green Thoughts*, in 1988, this time distributed by Capitol Records. *Smithereens 11*, was their biggest selling album to date . The group's music has also been featured in several movie soundtracks including the teen-horror film, '*Class Of Nuke 'Em High*'. Their career faltered in 1991 with the poorly received *Blow Up* leaving critics to ponder if the band have run out of ideas.

Albums: *Especially For You* (1986), *Green Thoughts* (1988), *Smithereens 11* (1990), *Blow Up* (1991).

Smiths

Acclaimed by many as the most important UK group of the 80s, the Smiths were formed in Manchester during the spring of 1982. Morrissey (b. Steven Patrick Morrissey, 22 May 1959, Davyhulme, Manchester, England) and Johnny Marr (b. John Maher, 31 October 1963, Ardwick, Manchester, England) originally combined as a songwriting partnership, and only their names appeared on any contract bearing the title 'Smiths'. Morrissey had previously played for a couple of months in the Nosebleeds and also rehearsed and auditioned with a late version of Slaughter And The Dogs. After that he wrote reviews for *Record Mirror* and penned a couple of booklets on the New York Dolls and James Dean. Marr, meanwhile, had played in several Wythenshawe groups including the Paris Valentinos, White Dice, Sister Ray and Freaky Party. By the summer of 1982, the duo decided to form a group and recorded some demos with drummer Simon Wolstencroft and a recording engineer named Dale. Wolstencroft subsequently declined an offer to join the Smiths and in later years became a member of the Fall. Eventually, Mike Joyce (b. 1 June 1963, Fallowfield, Manchester, England) was recruited as drummer, having previously played with the punk-inspired Hoax and Victim. During their debut gig at the Ritz in Manchester, the group was augmented by go-go dancer James Maker, who went on to join Raymonde and later RPLA. By the end of 1982, the group appointed a permanent bassist. Andy Rourke (b. 1963, Manchester, England), was an alumnus of various past groups with Marr.

After being taken under the wing of local entrepreneur Joe Moss, the group strenuously rehearsed and after a series of gigs, signed to Rough Trade Records in the spring of 1983. By that time, they had issued their first single on the label, 'Hand In Glove', which failed to reach the Top 50. During the summer of 1983, the group became entwined in the first of several tabloid press controversies when it was alleged that their lyrics contained references to child molesting. The eloquent Morrissey, who was already emerging as a media spokesperson of considerable power, sternly refuted the rumours. During the same period the group commenced work on their debut album with producer Troy Tate, but the sessions were curtailed, and a new set of recordings undertaken with John Porter. In November 1983, the group issued their second single, 'This Charming Man', a striking pop record that infiltrated the UK Top 30. Following an ill-fated trip to the USA at the end of the year, the quartet began 1984 with a new single, the notably rockier 'What Difference Does It Make?', which took them to number 12.

The Smiths ably displayed the potential of the group, with Morrissey's oblique genderless lyrics coalescing with Marr's spirited guitar work. The closing track of the album was the haunting 'Suffer Little Children', a requiem to the child victims of the 60s Moors Murderers. The song later provoked a short-lived controversy in the tabloid press, which was resolved when the mother of one of the victims came out on Morrissey's side. A series of college gigs throughout Britain established the group as a cult favourite, with Morrissey displaying a distinctive image, complete with National Health spectacles, a hearing aid and bunches of gladioli. A collaboration with Sandie Shaw saw 'Hand In Glove' transformed into a belated hit, while Morrissey dominated music press interviews. His celibate stance provoked reams of speculation about his sexuality and his ability to provide good copy on subjects as various as animal rights, royalty, Oscar Wilde and 60s films, made him

a journalist's dream interviewee. The singer's celebrated miserabilism was reinforced by the release of the autobiographical 'Heaven Knows I'm Miserable Now', which reached number 19 in the UK. Another Top 20 hit followed with 'William, It Was Really Nothing'. While the Smiths commenced work on their next album, Rough Trade issued the interim *Hatful Of Hollow*, a bargain-priced set that included various flip sides and radio sessions. It was a surprisingly effective work, that captured the inchoate charm of the group.

By 1984, the Smiths found themselves feted as Britain's best group by various factions in the music press. The release of the sublime 'How Soon Is Now?' justified much of the hyperbole and this was reinforced by the power of their next album, *Meat Is Murder*. The work displayed Morrissey's increasingly tendency towards social commentary, which had been indicated in his controversial comments on Band Aid and the IRA bombings. The album chronicled violence at schools ('The Headmaster Ritual'), adolescent thuggery ('Rusholme Ruffians'), child abuse ('Barbarism Begins At Home') and animal slaughter ('Meat Is Murder'). The proseletyzing tone was brilliantly complemented by the musicianship of Marr, Rourke and Joyce. Marr's work on such songs as 'The Headmaster Ritual' and 'That Joke Isn't Funny Anymore' effectively propelled him to the position of one of Britain's most respected rock guitarists. Despite releasing a milestone album, the group's fortunes in the singles charts were relatively disappointing. 'Shakespeare's Sister' received a lukewarm response and stalled at number 26, amid ever growing rumours that the group were dissatisfied with their record label.

Another major UK tour in 1985 coincided with various management upheavals, which dissipated the group's energies. A successful trek across the USA was followed by the release of the plaintive summer single, 'The Boy With The Thorn In His Side' which, despite its commerciality, only reached number 23. A dispute with Rough Trade delayed the release of the next Smiths album, which was preceded by the superb 'Big Mouth Strikes Again', another example of Marr at his best. During the same period, Rourke was briefly ousted from the group due to his flirtation with heroin. He was soon reinstated, however, along with a second guitarist Craig Gannon, who had previously played with Aztec Camera, the Bluebells and Colourfield.

In June 1986, *The Queen Is Dead* was issued and won immediate critical acclaim for its diversity and unadulterated power. The range of mood and emotion offered on the album was startling to behold, ranging from the epic grandeur of the title track to the overt romanticism of 'There Is A Light That Never Goes Out' and the irreverent comedy of

Smiths

'Frankly Mr Shankly' and 'Some Girls Are Bigger Than Others'. A superb display of Morrissey/Marr at their apotheosis, the album was rightly placed alongside *Meat Is Murder* as one of the finest achievements of the decade. A debilitating stadium tour of the USA followed and during the group's absence they enjoyed a formidable Top 20 hit with the disco-denouncing 'Panic'. The sentiments of the song, coupled with Morrissey's negative comments on certain aspects of black music, provoked further adverse comments in the press. That controversy was soon replaced by the news that the Smiths were to record only one more album for Rough Trade and intended to transfer their operation to the major label EMI. Meanwhile, the light pop of 'Ask' contrasted with riotous scenes during the group's 1986 UK tour. At the height of the drama, the group almost suffered a fatality when Johnny Marr was involved in a car crash. While he recuperated, guitarist Craig Gannon was fired, a decision that prompted legal action. The group ended the year with a concert at the Brixton Academy supported by fellow Mancunians, the Fall. It was to prove their final UK appearance. After another hit with 'Shoplifters Of The World Unite' the group completed what would prove their final album. The glam rock inspired 'Sheila Take A Bow'

returned them to the Top 10 and their profile was maintained with the release of another sampler album *The World Won't Listen*. Marr was growing increasingly disenchanted with the group's musical direction, however, and privately announced that he required a break.

With the group's future still in doubt, press speculation proved so intense that an official announcement of a split occurred in August 1987. *Strangeways, Here We Come*, an intriguing transitional album, was issued posthumously. The work indicated the different directions that the major protagonists were progressing towards during their final phase. A prestigious television documentary of the group's career followed on *The South Bank Show* and a belated live album *"Rank"* was issued the following year. The junior members Rourke and Joyce initially appeared with Brix Smith's Adult Net, then backed Sinead O'Connor. Joyce finally found a permanent post playing with the Buzzcocks. Morrissey pursued a solo career, while Marr moved from the Pretenders to The The and Electronic, as well as appearing on a variety of sessions for artists as diverse as Bryan Ferry, Talking Heads, Billy Bragg, Kirsty MacColl, the Pet Shop Boys, Stex and Banderas.

Albums: *The Smiths* (1984), *Meat Is Murder* (1985),

The Queen Is Dead (1986), *Strangeways, Here We Come* (1987), *"Rank"* (1988). Compilations: *Hatful Of Hollow* (1984), *The World Won't Listen* (1987), *Louder Than Bombs* (1987), *The Peel Sessions* (1988). Further reading: *Morrissey & Marr: The Severed Alliance,* Johnny Rogan.

Snakes Of Shake

This 80s Scottish group comprised of Seori Burnette (guitar/lead vocals/harmonica), Tzen Vermillion (guitar), Sandy Brown (piano/accordion/vocals), Robert Renfrew (bass/slide guitar/vocals) and Rhod 'Lefty' Burnett (drums). Their debut album's highlight was the title-track 'Southern Cross' a slice of cajun-influenced folk pop which was persistently promoted to break the band, without success. Seori Burnette's songwriting talent was often over-shadowed by his excessively dramatic singing style. By the time a second album was released, the line-up comprised Burnette, Brown, Renfrew, Neil Scott (guitar) and Iain Shedden (drums), the last-named previously of pop/punk act, the Jolt. *Gracelands And The Natural Wood* highlighted prefectly the group's blend of folk and rock styles. However, any progress was irretrievably undermined when the group's outlet, Making Waves went into receivership, and they subsequently split up. Burnett and Shedden quickly resurfaced in a new act, Summerhill.
Albums: *Southern Cross* (1985), *Gracelands And The Natural Wood* (1986).

Snapper

This New Zealand band specialise in 60s garage punk rock were formed in Dunedin, a college town at the bottom of South Island, in 1988. Veteran singer/guitarist Peter Gutteridge was a founder member of both the Chills and the Clean, the island's two most inspired outfits of the late 70s and early 80s. Their debut album emerged on the tiny Avalanche label, based in Edinburgh, Scotland, a country which has long harboured a predilection for Antipodean pop. Songs like 'Death And Weirdness In The Surfing Zone' are typical fuzz guitar workouts with Christine Voice's organ augmenting. Gutteridge's love of the Velvet Underground and Stooges shines through much of their work.
Album: *Shotgun Blossom* (1991).

Snuff

Formed in London in 1988 by Andy (b. 4 July 1963, London England), Duncan (b. 22 August 1964, Louth, England) and Simon (b. 11 December 1966, London, England), Snuff started off as 'a joke' with a hectic mixture of implausibly fast guitars and exquisite melodies, the threesome soon created their own niche in a British music scene sorely lacking the hardcore hardware to rival the host of angry American bands. Next to their own creations such as 'Not Listening' Snuff added a litany of thrashed-up cover versions, ranging from Tiffany to Simon And Garfunkel and numerous British television commercial jingles in between. Such was the band's sense of economy, they once managed to squeeze over 30 tracks onto one 12-inch single! Had the band's ambition matched their liberal taste for cover versions, Snuff's potential would have been huge. However, by conscientiously adhering to a post-punk manifesto Snuff managed to stay resolutely independent in the face of large financial offers from the corporates. Somewhat fittingly given their stance, when Snuff tired of the demands of the band and the threat of a 'cabaret punk' tag, they immediately called it a day. Their farewell gig was at London's Kilburn National Ballroom in 1991, a great highpoint for any band to depart on. Simon and Duncan started working together on a new project, while bassist Andy joined fellow hardcore band Leatherface.
Album: *SnuffSaidButGorBlimeyGuvIfHeDidn'tThrowA-WobblerChaChaChaChaChaChaChaChaChaChaChaY ou'reGoingHomeInACosmicAmbience* (1989).

Soft Boys

When Syd Barrett gave up music for art, another Cambridge musician emerged to take on his mantle. Robyn Hitchcock started out as a solo performer and busker before becoming a member of B.B. Blackberry And The Swelterettes, then the Chosen Few, the Worst Fears, and Maureen And The Meatpackers. It was with the last named that Hitchcock first recorded (in 1976), although the results were not released until much later. His next group, Dennis And The Experts became the Soft Boys in 1976. The Soft Boys first recording session was in March 1977 by which point the line-up was Hitchcock (vocals/guitar/bass), Alan Davies (guitar), Andy Metcalfe (bass), and Morris Windsor aka Otis Fagg (drums). The original sessions remain unreleased but the same line-up also recorded a three track single – known as the *Give It To The Soft Boys* EP - for the local Cambridge label Raw. This was released in the autumn of 1977 after which Davies left and Kimberley Rew was installed on guitar, harmonica, and vocals. The Soft Boys now signed to Radar and released the single '(I Wanna Be An) Anglepoise Lamp', but it was not considered representative of their innovative live work. Forming their own Two Crabs label they released *Can Of Bees* in 1979 after which they replaced Metcalfe with Matthew Seligman. Jim Melton, who had been playing harmonica for a while, also left. Their remaining releases came on the Armageddon label and included *Underwater Moonlight*, which is considered amongst their finest moments. They split in early 1981 and Hitchcock went on to have an erratic solo career, recruiting along the way Metcalfe and Windsor the form the Egyptians. Rew joined Katrina And The Waves and wrote the classic 'Going Down To Liverpool', while Seligman joined Local Heroes SW9 and continued to contribute to Hitchcock's solo efforts.

Albums: *A Can Of Bees* (1979), *Underwater Moonlight* (1980), *Two Halves For The Price Of One* (1981), *Invisible Hits* (1983), *Live At The Portland Arms* (1987).

Soft Cell

Formed in Leeds, England, in 1980 this duo featured vocalist Marc Almond (b. Peter Marc Almond, 9 July 1957, Southport, Lancashire, England) and synthesizer player David Ball (b. 3 May 1950, Blackpool, Lancashire, England). The artschool twosome came to the attention of the Some Bizzare label entrepreneur Stevo following the release of their self-financed EP *Mutant Moments*. He duly included their 'Girl With The Patent Leather Face' on the compilation *Some Bizzare Album* and negotiated a licensing deal with Phonogram Records in Europe and Sire in the USA. Their debut single, 'Memorabilia', produced by Mute Records boss Daniel Miller, was an underground hit paving the way for the celebrated 'Tainted Love'. Composed by the Four Preps' Ed Cobb and already well known as a northern soul club favourite by Gloria Jones, 'Tainted Love' topped the UK charts, became the best selling British single of the year and remained in the US charts for an astonishing 43 weeks. Produced by the former producer of Wire, Mike Thorne, the single highlighted Almond's strong potential as a torch singer, a role which was developed on subsequent hit singles including 'Bedsitter, 'Say Hello Wave Goodbye', 'Torch' and 'What'. Almond's brand of erotic electronic sleaze could only partially be realized in the Soft Cell format and was more fully developed in the offshoot Marc And The Mambas. Implicit in Soft Cell's rise was a determined self-destructive streak, which meant that the group was never happy with the pop machinery of which it had inevitably became a part. The title of *The Art Of Falling Apart*, indicated how close they were to ending their hit collaboration. At the end of 1983 the duo announced their proposed dissolution and undertook a final tour early the following year followed by a farewell album, *This Last Night In Sodom*.

Albums: *Non-Stop Erotic Cabaret* (1981), *Non-Stop Ecstatic Dancing* (1982), *The Art Of Falling Apart* (1983), *The Last Night In Sodom* (1984). Compilations: *The Singles 1981-85* (1986), *Their Greatest Hits* (1988), *Memorabilia* (1991, also contains Marc Almond solo material).

Some Bizzare Records

Founded by the eccentric teenage entrepreneur, Stevo, the UK-based Some Bizzare Records was one of the most challenging and enterprising labels of the 80s. The pioneering *Some Bizzare Album* brought together an array of fringe groups including Throbbing Gristle, Classix Nouveaux, Clock DVA, Cabaret Voltaire, Blancmange, Depeche Mode, Soft Cell and The The. It was the last two acts that were to continue with the label and enable Stevo to continue mining for arcane talent. Cabaret Voltaire also returned for a spell, as did Genesis P. Orridge's Throbbing Gristle offshoot, Psychic TV. Stevo's interest in industrial music saw the signing of the first foreign group to the label, Einsturzende Neubauten. They were soon followed by London's Test Department. Mischievously subversive, sleazy and often controversial, Some Bizzare was a welcome haven for Jim Thilwell and his various releases under the banner Foetus. By the end of the 80s Stevo had lost a major signing, The The, and, not for the first time, the label's financial future was a matter of conjecture. The power of Some Bizzare lay in its wilful obscurity aligned with Stevo's remarkable capacity to bring unlikely acts to critical and occasionally acclaim. Whether new signings such as Stex, Tim Hutton and Kandis King will re-invigorate the label's catalogue is part of the test for the 90s.

Sonic Boom

b. Peter Kember, 19 November 1965. UK-based Sonic Boom's solo project was originally planned as an aside for his main love, the Spacemen 3. Signing to the Silvertone label, Sonic issued 'Angel' (a drug-related tale not dissimilar both lyrically and musically to the Velvet Underground's 'Heroin') in 1989. This was followed by *Spectrum* for which Sonic was helped by fellow Spacemen Jason and Will Carruthers, plus the Jazz Butcher and the Perfect Disaster's Phil Parfitt. Spectrum's hypnotic blend of repetitive guitar riffs and keyboard runs betrayed his love of New York duo Suicide, but nevertheless possessed a definite if quiet charm. It even sported a psychedelic, gatefold revolving sleeve. Early buyers could send away for an orange vinyl 10-inch, 'Octaves'/'Tremeloes', which featured two elongated, synthesized notes! Unfortunately, the Spacemen 3 split in his wake to form Spiritualized, although their swan-song appeared later, ironically charting. Sonic re-emerged in the summer of 1991 with a low-key instrumental demo single, '(I Love You) To The Moon And Back', distributed free at gigs.

Album: *Spectrum* (1990).

Sonic Youth

A product of New York's experimental, 'No-Wave' scene, Sonic Youth first recorded under the auspices of *avant garde* guitarist Glenn Branca. Thurston

Sonic Youth

Moore (guitar), Lee Ranaldo (guitar) and Kim Gordon (bass) performed together on Branca's *Symphony No. 3*, while the group debuted in its own right on his Neutral label. *Sonic Youth*, was recorded live at New York's Radio City Music Hall in December 1981 and featured original drummer Richard Edson. Three further collections, *Confusion Is Sex*, *Sonic Death* and a mini-album, *Kill Yr Idols*, completed the quartet's formative period which was marked by their pulsating blend of discordant guitars, impassioned vocals and ferocious, compulsive drum patterns, courtesy of newcomer Jim Sclavunos, or his replacement, Bob Bert. *Bad Moon Rising* was the first Sonic Youth album to secure a widespread release in both the USA and Britain. This acclaimed set included the compulsive 'I'm Insane' and the eerie 'Death Valley '69', a collaboration with Lydia Lunch which invoked the horror of the infamous Charles Manson murders. Bob Bert was then replaced by Steve Shelley, who has remained with the line-up to date. In 1986 the group unleashed *Evol* which continued their ability to mix melody with menace particularly on the outstanding 'Shadow Of A Doubt'. The album also introduced the Youth's tongue-in-cheek fascination with Madonna. 'Expressway To Yr Skull' was given two alternative titles, 'Madonna, Sean And Me' and 'The Cruxifiction Of Sean Penn', while later in the year the band were joined by Mike Watt from Firehose in a spin-off project, Ciccone Youth, which resulted in a mutated version of 'Into The Groove(y)'. (In 1989 this *alter ego* culminated in *Ciccone Youth*, which combined dance tracks with experimental sounds redolent of German groups Faust and Neu.) Sonic Youth's career continued with the highly-impressive *Sister*. This album contained 'Schizophrenia', '(I Got A) Catholic Block' and 'Pacific Coast Highway', three songs which joined a growing lexicon of strong performances. The quartet had eschewed the multi-track studios of their past two albums, and the resultant less cluttered,

immediate sound proved ideal for this particular collection. It was followed in 1988 by *Daydream Nation*, a double set which allowed the group to expand themes when required. Once again the result was momentous. The instrumentation was powerful, recalling the intensity of the Velvet Underground or Can while the songs themselves were highly memorable.

In 1990, Sonic Youth left the independent circuit by signing with the Geffen label. The resultant *Goo*, employed state-of-the-art high technology, yet the band's sense of purpose remained intact. The opening track, 'Dirty Boots', offered their customary power, while 'Kool Thing' acknowledged contemporary black music by showcasing rapper Chuck D. However, the highlight was, undoubtedly, 'Tunic (Song For Karen)', an icy homage to the late Karen Carpenter (see Carpenters). *Goo* indicates that Sonic Youth's talent is undiminished and augurs well for the future of one the most innovative and influential contemporary acts.

Albums: *Sonic Youth* (1982), *Confusion Is Sex* (1983), *Kill Yr Idols* (1983), *Sonic Death* (1984), *Bad Moon Rising* (1985), *Evol* (1986), *Sister* (1987), *Daydream Nation* (1988), *Ciccone Youth* (1989), *Goo* (1990), *Dirty Boots* (1991).

Sound

Adrian Borland (vocals/guitar) had already released *Calling On Youth* and *Close Up*, and the *One To Infinity* EP as leader of UK's Outsiders from 1977-78. Towards the end of 1978 Graham Green joined the band, replacing the original bass player Bob Lawrence, and Michael Dudley (drums) was recruited to play alongside Jan (percussion). The new line-up recorded three tracks, which emerged on the Tortch label as the *Physical World* EP in December 1979, credited not as the Outsiders but as the Sound. They had progressed musically from their punk roots and were anxious to leave behind a name that still conjured up the atmosphere of 1977. After the critical acclaim of the debut EP, they signed to Korova, releasing a string of singles, 'Heyday', 'Sense Of Purpose', 'Hothouse' and two albums *Jeopardy* and *From The Lions Mouth*. These stirred a great deal of interest from both critics and public alike, establishing Borland as one of the most creative and mature writers of the post-punk scene. During 1979, Borland and Green created Second Layer, a harder, more experimental project that ran parallel with the Sound, releasing two EPs and an album. Sporadic releases continued throughout the 80s for several different labels with varying degrees of quality and success, but never managing to equal those from 1980-81. In addition to the singles 'Counting The Days', 'One Thousand Reasons', Temperature Drop', 'Hand Of Love' and 'Iron Years', they also collaborated with singer Kevin Hewick on *This Cover Keeps* EP in 1984. The band finally fragmented in late 1987 but Borland continued to record for Play It Again Sam as Adrian Borland And The Citizens, as well as resurrecting Second Layer for a two albums.

Albums: *Jeopardy* (1980), *From The Lions Mouth* (1981), *All Fall Down* (1982), *Shock Of Daylight* (1984), *Heads And Hearts* (1985), *In The Hothouse* (1985), *Thunder* (1987).

Soup Dragons; Sean Dickson

Soup Dragons

The Soup Dragons emerged from Glasgow, Scotland, as one of a clutch of bands championed by the *New Musical Express* via their *C86* project. The group evolved around the enigmatic Sean Dickson (lead vocals/guitar/songwriter). In early 1985, he met up with Jim McCulloch (guitar), Ross A. Sinclair (drums) and Sushil K. Dade (bass), the collective taking their name from characters in the cult children's television programme, *The Clangers*. A flexi-disc, 'If You Were The Only Girl In The World', emerged at the end of the year, by which time the band were circulating a demonstration tape, *You Have Some Too*. The fledgling Subway Organisation label issued the Soup Dragons' first single 'Whole Wide World' (1986), a tight, exciting slab of Buzzcocks-styled pop, performed at breakneck pace.

This attracted ex-Wham! manager Jazz Summers, who set up a new label for them, Raw TV Products, in time for 'Hang-Ten!' (1986), which shared all the energy of 'Whole Wide World'. In the meantime, Sean and later Jim had left another group they were serving time with, the BMX Bandits. 'Head Gone Astray' (1987), revealed a marked change away from new wave, towards 60s rock. The Soup Dragons confirmed this with the storming 'Can't Take No More', which proved to be a minor UK hit. 'Soft As Your Face' also fared well commercially but its gentle, serene sound was at odds with the band's overall direction. Far better was 'The Majestic Head' (1988). Another minor hit, this finally lured Sire Records into a deal, but their next single, 'Kingdom Chairs' flopped. The debut *This Is Our Art* emerged without fanfare.

The Stooges'-influenced 'Backwards Dog' and 'Crotch Deep Trash' (both 1989), introduced a rockier feel and this was followed by the dance-orientated 'Mother Universe' (1990). Hinging around a Marc Bolan riff, the single was typical of the tracks on *Lovegod*, the band's second album. By this time, Sinclair had been replaced by new drummer Paul Quinn. After discovering an obscure Rolling Stones track from their 1965 *Out Of Our Heads*, the Soup Dragons teamed up with reggae singer Junior Reid and disc jockey remixer Terry Farley to create a formidable crossover between white 'indie' rock and dance music. The single was a massive hit, something that had eluded the band for so long. *Lovegod* was re-promoted and a remixed 'Mother Universe' was reissued, giving them further chart success.

Albums: *This Is Our Art* (1988), *Lovegod* (1990), *Hotwired* (1992).

Spacemen 3

Instigated in Rugby, Warwickshire, England, in 1982 by Sonic Boom (b. Pete Kember, 19 November 1965) and regional soulmate Jason Pierce (also, strangely enough, b. 19 November 1965). Augmented by the rhythm section of Rosco And Pete Baines, it took Spacemen 3 fully four years to blossom onto record. Initially crying shy of sounding too much like the Cramps, the band carefully evolved into one-chord wonders; masters of the hypnotic, blissed-out groove. Such was their languid approach to working, and so dream-inspiring was their music, Spacemen 3 made a habit of sitting down for the entirety of their gigs. 1989's *Playing With Fire* included the intensely repetitive blast of 'Revolutions'. By this time Baines and Rosco had formed what was tantamount to a Spacemen 3 spin-off in the Darkside, allowing Will Carruthers and John Mattock to step into their places, and although this was the peak of the band's career, fundamental problems were still inherence: Sonic Boom made no secret of his drug dependency, having replaced heroin with methadone, and he and Jason Pierce were gradually growing apart to the point where they were chasing different goals. The relationship became so strained that *Recurring,* although still a Spaceman 3 effort, saw the two forces working separately, Boom being attributed with side one and Pierce with side two. By this stage Boom had embarked upon a solo career and Pierce was working with Mattock and Carruthers in another band Spiritualized, a situation which further fanned the flames. When *Recurring* finally saw the light of day Spaceman 3's creative forces refused to even be interviewed together. A petty demise to what was, for some time, a creatively intense band.

Albums: *Sound Of Confusion* (1986), *The Perfect Prescription* (1987), *Performance* (1988), *Playing With Fire* (1989), *Recurring* (1991).

Spear Of Destiny

Formed from the ashes of Theatre Of Hate in early 1983, Spear Of Destiny took their name from the mythological weapon which pierced the body of Christ, and was supposedly acquired over the years by Attila The Hun, Napoleon and Hitler. This helped the band to attract quite a volume of destructive commentary in the press. The original line-up featured mainstay Kirk Brandon (b. 3 August 1956, Westminster, London, England; vocals/guitar), Chris Bell (drums), Lasettes Ames (saxophone) and Stan Stammers (ex-Theatre Of Hate; bass). They signed to CBS, but maintained their own label design, 'Burning Rome', which had appeared on previous Theatre Of Hate releases. The first single 'Flying Scotsman' arrived in 1983, and was featured on *The Grapes Of Wrath* alongside the relentless single 'The Wheel'. Critical response to the group was divided. By July, Bell and Ames had left, for reasons described by Bell as personal and religious. Brandon and Stammers brought in former Theatre Of Hate saxophonist John Lennard (b. Canada, ex-Diodes) and Nigel Preston (ex Theatre Of Hate, Sex Gang Children). A third line-up added Alan St Clair (guitar) and Neil Pyzor (ex-Case; keyboards, saxophone), Dolphin Taylor (ex-Tom Robinson Band and Stiff Little Fingers; drums) and Nicky Donnelly (ex-Case; saxophone). It was this formation which recorded *One Eyed Jacks*, arguably the band's best album, and the singles 'Rainmaker', 'Liberator' and 'Prisoner Of Love', the latter signalling a change in direction which would be more fully realized on the follow-up album. When *World Service* arrived, there was considerable disappointment from fans and critics alike. Having built an enviable reputation as a lyricist of considerable vigour, tracks like 'Mickey' seemed grotesque and clumsy. Further personnel changes became commonplace, and by 1987 and *Outlands* the line-up comprised Pete Barnacle (drums), Volker Janssen (keyboards) and Chris Bostock (bass) alongside Brandon. The summer of that year saw Brandon incapacitated for six months with an ankle injury that left him unable to walk, an affliction from which he still carries a limp. However, the band were soon back in the charts with 'Never Take Me Alive', and a support tour with U2. Their 1988 singles 'So In Love With You' and 'Radio Radio' saw them switch from Epic to Virgin. By December 1990, old colleague Stan Stammers returned on bass, alongside new drummer and guitarist Bobby Rae Mayhem and Mark Thwaite. 1991 opened with Brandon touring once more under the joint Theatre Of Hate/Spear Of Destiny banner.

Albums: *The Grapes Of Wrath* (1983), *One Eyed Jacks* (1984), *World Service* (1985) *Outlands* (1987), *The Price You Pay* (1988).

Specials

This Coventry, UK ska-influenced group was formed in the summer of 1977 as the Special AKA, with a line-up comprising Jerry Dammers (b. Gerald Dankin, 22 May 1954, India; keyboards), Terry Hall (b. 19 March 1959, Coventry, England; vocals), Neville Staples (vocals/percussion), Lynval Golding (b. 24 July 1951, Coventy, England; guitar), Roddy Radiation (b. Rodney Byers; guitar), Sir Horace Gentleman (b. Horace Panter; bass) and John Bradbury (drums). After touring with the Clash, they set up their own multi-racial 2-Tone label and issued the Prince Buster-inspired 'Gangsters', which reached the UK Top 10. After signing their label to Chrysalis, the group abbreviated their name to the Specials. Their Elvis Costello produced debut album was a refreshing, exuberant effort which included the Top 10 single 'A Message To You, Rudi'. The group spearheaded what became a 2-Tone movement and their label enjoyed an array of sparkling hits from Madness, the Beat and the Selecter. In January 1980, the Specials were at their peak following the release of their live EP *The Special AKA Live.* The pro-contraceptive title track 'Too Much Too Young' propelled them to number 1 in the UK charts. Further Top 10 hits with 'Rat Race' and 'Stereotype' and 'Do Nothing' followed. The Specials ability to 'capture the moment' in pop was most persuasively felt with 'Ghost Town' which topped the charts during the summer of 1981 while Britain was suffering inner-city riots. At this new peak of success, the group fragmented. Staples, Hall and Golding went on to form the intriguing Fun Boy Three, leaving Dammers to continue with a new line-up, which reverted to the old name, the Special AKA. After the minor success of 'Racist Friend' and the anthemic Top 10 hit 'Nelson Mandela', Dammers became more politically active with Artists Against Apartheid. He was also a major force behind the

Nelson Mandela 70th Birthday Party concert at London's Wembley Stadium on 11 June 1988. The retitled 'Free Nelson Mandela (70th Birthday Remake)' was issued to coincide with the show.

Albums: as the Specials *The Specials* (1979), *More Specials* (1980), as the Special AKA *In The Studio* (1984). Compilation: *Singles* (1991).

Spirea X

Spirea X

In 1988, tired of touring incessantly, Jim Beattie (vocals/guitar) left Primal Scream and moved back to Glasgow. Recharged, he formed Spirea X in the summer of 1990, their name taken from a Primal Scream b-side. He had been instrumental in Primal Scream's 'jangly' period, writing the classic 'Velocity Crescent', and he would continue to share Gillespie's nonchalant arrogance: 'We're going to do it. . . by having better songs, better melodies, better arrangements, better everything. By sheer force of ideas'. After a demo in July 1990, which attracted interest almost across the board, they played their first live gig in September at Queen Margaret Student Union. Despite heated competition to get Beattie's signature he eventually settled for the independent label 4AD. The band quickly lost their original bass player and guitarist, and by May 1991 featured Andy Kerr (drums), Judith Boyle (Beattie's girlfriend, vocals/guitar), Jamie O'Donnell (bass) and Thomas McGurk (rhythm guitar). Two well received EPs

followed, *Chlorine Dream* and *Speed Reaction*, before a debut album titled after a collection of Rimbaud's poetry.

Album: *Fireblade Skies* (1991).

Spiritualized

This dark, neo-psychedelic band were formed by Jason Pierce (b. 19 November, 1965; vocals, guitar) after his messy split from former writing partner and Spacemen 3 cohort Pete 'Sonic Boom' Kember. Based in Rugby, England, they were inaugurated while Spacemen 3 were still officially active. Pierce took the remnants of that band with him (Will; bass and Jon Mattock; drums) and added his girlfriend Kate Radley (organ) and Mark Retoy (guitar). Their first release was a cover of the Troggs' 'Anyway That You Want Me', then 'Feel So Sad', a sonic opera lasting over 13 minutes. Headliners at ICA's 'Irn Bru' Rock week, their familiar Velvet Underground guitar noise/barrage found favour with old Spacemen 3 bands as well as new converts. Singles like 'Why Don't You Smile' were something of a departure from Pierce's morbid and moribund legacy. Notoriously shy and reticent in interviews, he had a preference for sitting down while playing gigs, which an impressionable audience eagerly imitated. Their efforts thus far, whilst somewhat predictable, have surpassed those of a quiescent Kember.

Album: *Lazer Guided Melodies* (1992).

Spitfire

Formed in 1990, this post-My Bloody Valentine UK guitar pop group made rapid progress. The band consisted of Jeff Pitcher (vocals), younger brother Nick (bass), Simon Walker (guitar), Matt Wise (guitar) and Justin Welch (drums). Original drummer Scott Kenny decided to join his other group Ever, while guitarist Steve White also left because he did not want to tour. They leapt into the fray with two EPs, *Translucent* and *Superbaby*. Their debut included a daring cover of the *Six Million Dollar Man* theme, and 'Superbaby' was produced by That Petrol Emotion's Steve Mack. A tour with Blur helped bring them to national prominence, but more newsworthy were their infamous 'Back Stage' passes. Designed specifically to cater for groupies, their tongues were firmly in cheek, but the press latched on to them as misogynists.

Splodgenessabounds

The origins of this UK group are heavily tinged with apochrypha. Max (then a drummer) replaced Gerry Healy in Alien Sex Fiend in 1978 and stayed for a few months before forming a duo called the Faber Brothers with guitarist Pat Thetic. They performed at Butlins Holiday Camp in Bognor, Sussex, but were sacked and returned to London to start a band. As

Splodgenessabounds, the group started gigging in March 1979 and though various members came and went the line-up briefly comprised Max Splodge (vocals), his girlfriend Baby Greensleeves (vocals), Miles Flat (guitar), Donkey Gut (b. Winston Forbe; keyboards), Whiffy Archer (paper and comb), Desert Island Joe Lurch Slythe and a dog. Robert Rodent joined on bass in early 1980 and Miles Flat left. They came to the public's attention when, to the eternal annoyance of publicans everywhere, they had a freak hit with 'Two Pints Of Lager And A Packet Of Crisps Please' in 1980. Other memorable songs in their repertoire included 'I've Got Lots Of Famous People Living Under The Floorboards Of My Humble Abode', 'Simon Templar', and a savage re-working of Rolf Harris' 'Two Little Boys'. Max was also reputed to be working on a rock opera called *Malcolm*, and appeared in the play *Camberwell Beauty*. His stage performances were somewhat spoiled due to wolf-whistles from his girly fan club (numbering three) throughout the evening. After falling out with Deram in 1982, the band signed to Razor under the shortened title Splodge, where they released *In Search Of The Seven Golden Gussets*, a tribute to mythical items of ladies' underwear. By this time the line-up included the following miscreants; Ronnie Plonker (guitar), Smacked Arse O'Reardon (bass), Poodle (drums) and Tone Tone The Garden Gnome (guitar). Max later recorded solo on Neat releasing the Tony James (Sigue Sigue Sputnik) single 'Phut Phut Splodgenik'.

Albums: *Splodgenessabounds* (1981), *In Search Of The Seven Golden Gussets* (1982).

Squeeze

Formed in the south east London area of Deptford in 1974, Squeeze came to prominence in the late 70s riding on the new wave created by the punk movement. Original members Chris Difford (b. 4 November 1954, London, England; guitar/lead vocals), Glenn Tilbrook (b. 31 August 1957, London, England; guitar/vocals) and Julian 'Jools' Holland (b. 24 January 1958; keyboards) named the group after a disreputable Velvet Underground album. With the addition of Harry Kakoulli (bass), and original drummer Paul Gunn replaced by sessions drummer Gilson Lavis (b. 27 June 1951, Bedford, England), Squeeze released an EP *Packet Of Three* in 1977 on the Deptford Fun City label and produced by former Velvets member John Cale. The EP's title in itself reflected the group's main songwriters, Chris Difford and Glenn Tilbrook's pre-occupation for the underside side of life. The EP led to a major contract with A&M Records and a UK Top 20 hit in 1978 with 'Take Me I'm Yours'. Minor success with 'Bang Bang' and 'Goodbye Girl' that same year was followed in 1979 by two number 2 hits with 'Cool

Squeeze; Chris Difford

For Cats' and 'Up The Junction'. Difford's lyrics were by now beginning to show an acute talent in capturing the flavour of contemporary south London life with a sense of the tragi-comic. This began to fully flower with the release of 1980's *Argy Bargy* which spawned the singles 'Another Nail In My Heart' (UK Top 20) and 'Pulling Mussels (From A Shell)'. The set was Squeeze's most cohesive album to date, having finally thrown off any remaining traces of a punk influence they now displayed one of the finest 'kitchen sink' lyrics since Ray Davies' finest work. The album also featured the group's new bass player, John Bentley (b. 16 April 1951).

In 1980, Holland left for a solo career that included performing and recording with his own band Jools Holland And The Millionaires (which displayed his talent for the 'boogie-woogie' piano style) and, to a larger extent, hosting the UK television show *The Tube*. His replacement was singer/pianist Paul Carrack, formerly with pub-rock band Ace. He appeared on *East Side Story* which was co-produced by Elvis Costello. Carrack stamped his mark on the album with his performance on 'Tempted' and with the success of 'Labelled With Love' a UK Top 5 hit, the album became the band's most successful to date. Carrack departed soon after to join Carlene Carter's group and was replaced by Don Snow (b. 13 January 1957, Kenya, ex-Sinceros). The follow-up *Sweets*

From A Stranger was an uneven affair, although it did spawn the superb 'Black Coffee In Bed'.

At the height of the group's success, amid intense world tours, including selling out New York's Madison Square Garden, Difford And Tilbrook dissolved the group. However, the duo continued to compose together releasing an album in 1984. The following year they re-formed the band with Lavis, the returning Holland and a new bass player, Keith Wilkinson. *Cosi Fan Tutti Frutti* was hailed as a return to form, and although not supplying any hit singles, the tracks 'King George Street', 'I Learnt How To Pray' and Difford/Holland's 'Heartbreaking World' stood out well. In 1987, Squeeze achieved their highest position in the UK singles chart for almost six years when 'Hourglass' reached number 16 and subsequently gave the group their first US Top 40 hit, reaching number 15. '853-5937' also earned them a US Top 40 hit. The accompanying album *Babylon And On* featured contributions from former Soft Boy and one of Robyn Hitchcock's Egyptians, Andy Metcalfe (horns/keyboards/moog). After the release of 1989's *Frank*, which contained one of the most sensitive lyrics ever written by a man about menstruation ('She Doesn't Have To Shave'), Holland departed once again to concentrate on television work. With Matt Irving joining as a second keyboards player, Squeeze released a live album, *A Round And A Bout*, on their old Deptford Fun City label in 1990 before signing a new record deal with Warner Brothers. The release of Play confirmed, and continued, Chris Difford and Glenn Tilbrook's reputation as one of the UK's finest songwriting teams.

Albums: *Squeeze* (1978), *Cool For Cats* (1979), *Argy Bargy* (1980), *East Side Story* (1981), *Sweets From A Stranger* (1982), *Cosi Fan Tutti Frutti* (1985), *Babylon And On* (1987), *Frank* (1989), *A Round And About* (1990), *Play* (1991). Compilation: *Singles 45 And Under* (1982).

Stamey, Chris

b. Chapel Hill, North Carolina, USA. Singer/guitarist Stamey first rose to prominence as a member of the Sneakers, a short-lived pop/rock act which split up in 1976. Having become domiciled in New York, he was briefly associated with a group fronted by erstwhile Box Tops member, Alex Chilton, who in turn produced Stamey's solo debut single, 'The Summer Sun'. The artist subsequently formed the dBs, who completed a series of excellent, melodic albums. However, despite critical approbation, the group was not a commercial success and Stamey left to resume his solo career during the 80s. A period involved with the Golden Palominos, an informal attraction loosely-based on available, like-minded musicians, punctuated his albums, but although

unprolific, Stamey has continued to enjoy cult popularity. In 1991 he undertook live appearances in London, accompanied by former dBs partner Peter Holsapple.

Albums: *In The Winter Of Love* (1984), *It's Alright* (1987), with Peter Holsapple *Mavericks* (1991).

Martin Stephenson

Stephenson, Martin, And The Daintees

b. c.1965, Durham, England. This singer/songwriter's reputation has been bolstered by virtue of searing live performances throughout the UK. His early love of literature and music led to the formation of the first Daintees line-up in his early teens. With a regular turnover of staff and lack of proper gigs the band nevertheless became something of a busking sensation, on the evidence of which Newcastle record label Kitchenware sent them into the studio. After two singles, notable amongst which was the intoxicating 'Roll On Summertime', a debut album was embarked upon. The Daintees line-up at this time comprised Stephenson (guitar/vocals), Anthony Dunn (bass/acoustic guitar/vocals), John Steel (keyboards/harmonica/bass/vocals) and Paul Smith (drums/percussion). *Boat To Bolivia* was praised by the *New Musical Express* because it 'builds bridges between love and hate, between cradle and grave, between folk and pop, between the past and present'. An example of the candidness and honesty of Stephenson's lyrics is best portrayed on 'Caroline' and

'Crocodile Cryer'. He also revealed his appreciation of the folk/blues rag guitar style with 'Tribute To The Late Rev. Gary Davis' as well as regular live performances of Van Dyke Parks' 'High Coin'. However, a lengthy hiatus delayed the arrival of the follow-up until 1988. *Gladsome, Humour & Blue* contained the superb 'Wholly Humble Heart'. Once again reviews were excellent, and Stephenson already held an impressive reputation for hearty live shows. *Salutation Road* became the songwriter's most politicized work in 1990, prefaced by the single 'Left Us To Burn' which directly attacked Margaret Thatcher. He continues to be a consistent live draw, often appearing solo, or with the Daintees, who comprise any musician who fits the bill. Not yet considered a major songwriter, his elevation to that status may only be a matter of time.
Albums: *Boat To Bolivia* (1985), *Gladsome, Humour & Blue* (1988), *Salutation Road* (1990).

Stevo
b. Steven Pearse, 26 December 1962, Dagenham, Essex, England. One of the most outspoken, adventurous and original discoverers of arcane talent, Stevo came to the fore of the British music scene during the early 80s. A misfit and underachiever at school, he was virtually illiterate and underwent a self-improving course which coincided with his rise to prominence in the music industry. Originally a disc jockey, he compiled an 'electronic music' and 'futurist' chart for the music press which led to him being bombarded with roughly-hewn demos from unknown artists. During 1980, Stevo packaged the best of this material as the *Some Bizzare Album* (its misspelling was unintentional but apposite). Among the artists included were Throbbing Gristle, Classix Noveaux, Clock DVA, Cabaret Voltaire, Blancmange, Depeche Mode, Soft Cell and The The. The latter two artists came under Stevo's management and joined his innovative Some Bizzare record label. Stevo received instant recognition for his brusque behaviour and eccentric business dealings. After the chart-topping success of Soft Cell, major record companies anxious to license his acts were forced to endure the teenage entrepreneur's strange whims, which included signing a contract in the pouring rain while sitting on one of the lions in Trafalgar Square. With similar eccentricity, the contract for the hand of Psychic TV included a clause demanding a year's supply of baby food. It said much for Stevo's power and persuasion that he managed to license so many wilfully uncommercial acts to the major labels. His strength lay in an ability to capture innovative acts at an early stage when they were merely regarded as weird. In the case of Soft Cell and later The The, Stevo showed that he had the ear to nurture potentially major artists. Many other acts

were a testament to his love of the unusual. Berlin's Einsturzende Neubauten decried conventional rock instruments in favour of industrial sounds, and the scream of clanging metal as percussion could also be heard via Test Department. The unremitting aural depravity of Foetus threatened to complete Stevo's journey into the darker areas of the soul, and with commercial acts on the wane the future of his label was perpetually in doubt. In the early 90s, however, Stevo is still stalking the musical boundaries with a stream of new signings including Stex, Tim Hutton, Kandis King and Vicious Circle.
Further reading: *Starmakers And Svengalis: The History Of British Pop Management*, Johnny Rogan.

Stewart, David A.
b. 9 September 1952, Sunderland, Tyne & Wear, England. At the age of 15, the fledgeling guitarist Stewart introduced himself to the world of rock music by stowing-away in the back of Amazing Blondel's tour van, after the group had given a performance in Stewart's home town of Newcastle. He later teamed up with guitarist Brian Harrison to form a duo, who after releasing *Deep December*, went on to form Longdancer, on Elton John's Rocket label in 1973. During this time, Stewart had met ex-Royal Academy of Music student Annie Lennox in London where the couple co-habited. In 1977, together with friend Peter Coombes, they first recorded as a trio, the Catch, which developed into the Tourists. After establishing a following on the European continent, the Tourists achieved fame in the UK with minor hit singles, culminating in the number 4 hit cover version of Dusty Springfield's 1979 'I Only Want To Be With You' and 'So Good To Be Back Home Again'. This popularity with the public, however, was at odds with the particularly virulent and antagonistic attitude of the popular music press who viewed the band as 'old wave' cashing in on the 'new wave'. When the band split in late 1980, Stewart and Lennox, who had now ended their romantic relationship, continued working together and formed the Eurythmics. After a spell spent shaking off their reputation left over from the Tourists, the duo gradually won favourable reviews, to eventually emerge as one of the world's major pop acts of the 80s. They were awarded the Ivor Norvello award for Songwriter Of The Year in 1984 and Stewart received the Best British Producer award at the BRIT ceremony in 1986. He increased his role and reputation as a producer by working with, amongst others, Bob Dylan, Feargal Sharkey and Mick Jagger. A flurry of awards followed the next year for songwriting and production and in August, Stewart's married Siobhan Fahey of Bananarama. In 1989, Boris Grebenshikov, the first Russian rock artist to record and perform in the west, travelled to the US

and UK to record *Radio Silence* with Stewart. After the recording of the Eurythmics' *We To Are One*, the group's activities were put on hold while the duo allowed themselves time to rest and indulge in other projects. For Stewart, this included forming his own record label, Anxious; working with saxophonist Candy Dulfer on the UK Top 10 hit 'Lily Was Here' (1990); and the formation of his new group, the Spiritual Cowboys who achieved a minor UK chart placing for 'Jack Talking' (1990). Comprising Martin Chambers (drums, ex-Pretenders), John Turbull (guitar) and Chris James (bass), the group tour and record as a full time project, and their debut album reached the UK Top 40. Stewart is now regarded as one of the major figures of the pop establishment, and despite the attacks of a personal and artistic nature from the more radical quarters of the British press, it can be said that he has been responsible for some of the finest pop music produced throughout the 80s.

Albums: *Lily Was Here* (1990, film soundtrack), with the Spiritual Cowboys *Dave Stewart And The Spiritual Cowboys* (1990), with the Spiritual Cowboys *Honest* (1991).

Stiff Little Fingers

This Irish punk band formed from the ashes of rock cover group Highway Star. Stiff Little Fingers soon attracted most fervent fan based. Present at the Clash's Belfast gig in 1977, Jake Burns (vocals/lead guitar) led Henry Cluney (rhythm guitar), Ali McMordie (bass) and Brian Falloon (drums) as Ireland's first new wave cover band. The original drummer, Gordon Blair, had gone on to play with the group, Rudi. When journalist Gordon Ogilvie saw the band live he urged them to concentrate on their own material, quickly becoming their manager and co-lyricist. They recorded their first two original songs, 'Suspect Device'/'Wasted Life' soon after, on their own Rigid Digits label. The first pressing of 350 copies sold out almost as soon as BBC disc jockey John Peel enthusiastically played the singles. Rough Trade quickly picked up the distribution, and released the band's second single, 'Alternative Ulster', in conjunction with Rigid Digits. After a major tour supporting the Tom Robinson Band, the band were almost signed to Island, but remained on Rough Trade for their debut *Inflammable Material*. With songs concentrating on personal experiences in the politically charged climate of Northern Ireland, the album still managed to surprise many with its inclusion of diverse rock patterns and a flawed love song. The album marked the departure of Falloon who was replaced by Jim Reilly. The follow-up *Nobodys Heroes* revealed great strides in technique and sophistication, the band branching out into dub, reggae and pop. The dialogue with the audience was still direct, however, urging tolerance, self-respect and unity, and rejecting the trappings of rock stardom. They would still come in for criticism, however, for Ogilvie's patronage. After a disappointing live album, the impressive *Go For It!* saw the band at the peak of their abilities and popularity. Reilly left for the USA shortly afterwards, with Dolphin Taylor (ex-Tom Robinson Band) drafted in as his replacement. 1982's *Now Then* embraced songs of a more pop-rock nature, though in many ways the compromise was an unhappy one. Burns left at the beginning of the following year, forming Jake Burns And The Big Wheel. However, live and on record he was unable to shakie off comparisons to SLF, and he opted instead for a career as trainee producer at BBC Radio 1. McMordie formed Fiction Groove and contributed to Sinead O'Conner's *The Lion And The Cobra*, while Cluney taught guitar back in Ireland. Taylor returned for a brief stint of drumming with Tom Robinson Band, but the spectre of Stiff Little Fingers remained. One reunion gig gave birth to further events, until 1990 when they re-formed on a permanent basis. McMordie had grown tired of the rock circuit, however, and his replacement was the group's old friend Bruce Foxton (ex-Jam). In the autumn of 1991, they embarked on another major tour and recorded the respectable *Flags And Emblems*.

Albums: *Inflammable Material* (1979), *Nobody's Heroes* (1980), *Hanx!* (1980), *Go For It!* (1981), *Now Then* (1982), *Flags And Emblems* (1991). Compilation: *All The Best* (1983).

Stiff Records

Britain's premier 'new wave' label of the 70s was founded in 1976 by pub-rock producer and promoter Dave Robinson and Andrew Jakeman, tour manager of Dr Feelgood. The first release, 'Heart Of The City' by Nick Lowe, was financed by a £400 loan from Dr Feelgood's singer Lee Brilleaux. From 1976-77, the label released material by a range of London-based pub and punk rock bands such as Roogalator, Lew Lewis, the Adverts and the Damned. Stiff also signed Elvis Costello whose fourth single 'Watching The Detectives' was the label's first hit. Costello had achieved prominence as a member of Stiff's first package tour of numerous British cities. Like its 1978 successor, the tour served to publicise and popularise the label and its artists. During the early days it was extremely hip to be seen wearing a Stiff Tee-shirt bearing its uncompromising slogan, 'If it isn't Stiff it ain't worth a fuck'. Towards the end of 1977, Stiff suffered a setback when Jakeman, Costello and Nick Lowe left to join the Radar label. However, Stiff's fortunes were transformed by the success of Ian Dury whose anthem 'Sex And Drugs And Rock 'n' Roll' had made little impact when first issued in 1977. A year later, however, 'What A Waste' inaugurated a run of four hit singles. Lene Lovich, Jona Lewie and Madness also provided Top 20 records for the label in 1978-80, when Robinson switched distribution from EMI to CBS. In the early 80s, Stiff flirted with reggae (Desmond Dekker) and soul (various productions by Eddy Grant) but the bulk of its releases came from artists on the eccentric fringe of the new wave such as Tenpole Tudor and Wreckless Eric. The company also issued one album from Graham Parker before he moved to the larger RCA label. There were also hits from the Belle Stars and Dave Stewart with Barbara Gaskin. From the outset, Robinson had been interested in new wave developments in America and over the years Stiff licensed material by such artists as Rachel Sweet, Devo, the Plasmatics and Jane Aire. In 1984, Stiff was merged with Island Records and Robinson became managing director of both companies. This coincided with the departure of Madness to start their own label (Zarjazz), although Stiff's new signing, the Pogues provided hits throughout the mid-80s. The merger was not a success, however, and in 1986 Robinson resumed control of an independent Stiff, only to see it suffer an immediate cash-crisis. The assets of the company, which had a turnover of £4m at its peak, were sold to ZTT Records for a reputed £300,000. Under the new ownership there were initial releases from the Pogues, hard bop drummer Tommy Chase and female vocal group the Mint Juleps. But by the 90s, the pioneering Stiff had become simply a reissue label.

Stiv Bators

b. Stivin Bator, 22 October 1949, Cleveland, Ohio, USA, d. June 1990. Bators formed his first bands Mother Goose and Frankenstein, who were transmuted into a seminal US 'no wave' band the Dead Boys. They moved to New York in 1976. Although they officially split in 1978 there would be frequent reunions, as Bators moved to Los Angeles where he recorded demos with friend Jeff Jones (ex-Blue Ash). He also gigged with Akron band Rubber City Rebels. The first release from the demos was a version of the Choir's (later the Raspberries) 60s single 'It's Cold Outside', which was released on Greg Shaw's Bomp label. A second guitarist and debut album (USA only) followed in 1980 on which the duo was augmented by guitarist Eddy Best and drummer David Quinton (formerly in Toronto's the Mods). After appearing in John Walter's cult movie Polyester, Bators formed a touring band with Rick Bremner replacing Quinton. By 1981, Bators had become a permanent member of the Wanderers. The Stiv Bators Band played a final American tour in February 1981 with Brian James of the Damned guesting on guitar, after which Bators would concentrate on the Wanderers until September 1981.

After the impressive Only Lovers Left Alive (1981), Bators took Dave Treganna (ex-Sham 69) with him to join James and Nicky Turner (ex-Barracudas) in Lords Of The New Church. Following the Lords' demise, Bators resurfaced in London in 1989 for a 'Return Of The Living Boys' gig. This time his cohorts were drawn from a variety of local personnel, and it was not until he returned to Paris that he entered a recording studio once more. A new line-up included Dee Dee Ramone (Ramones), who had to be replaced by Neil X (Sigue Sigue Sputnik) before the sessions began, Kris Dollimore (ex-Godfathers) and guest appearances from Johnny Thunders. With six songs completed, Bators was hit by car in June 1990, and died the day after. There are hopes that his sessions will receive a posthumous release.
Album: Where The Action Is (1980).

Stone Roses

A classic case of an overnight success stretched over half a decade, the UK band Stone Roses, evolved through a motley collection of Manchester-based non-starters such as the Mill, the Patrol and English Rose before settling down as Stone Roses in 1985. They were acclaimed for their early warehouse gigs, at this time the line-up consisted of Ian Brown (b. Ian George Brown, 20 February 1963, Ancoats, Gt. Manchester, England; vocals), John Squire (b. 24 November 1962, Broadheath, Gt. Manchester, England; guitar), Reni (b. Alan John Wren, 10 April 1964, Manchester, England; drums), Andy Couzens (guitar) and Pete Garner (bass). In their hometown, at least, the band had little trouble in working up a following, in spite of their predilection for juxtaposing leather trousers with elegant melodies. In 1987, guitarist Andy Couzens left, later to form the High, and Pete Garner followed soon after, allowing Gary 'Mani' Mounfield (b. 16 November 1962, Crumpsall, Gt. Manchester, England), to take over bass guitar, but while the foursome were packing out venues in Manchester they were finding it difficult to get noticed in the rest of the country. A deal with the Silvertone label in 1988 produced the 'Elephant Stone' single and showed its' makers to be grasping the essence of classic 60s pop. A year later, they had carried it over the threshold of the independent scene and into the nation's front rooms. When the follow-up, 'Made Of Stone', attracted media attention the Stone Roses' ball started rolling at a phenomenal pace. Their debut album was hailed in all four quarters as a guitar/pop classic, and as the Manchester 'baggy' scene infiltrated Britain's consciousness, Stone Roses - alongside the funkier, grubbier Happy Mondays - were perceived to be leaders of the flare-wearing pack.

By the close of 1989, the Roses had moved from half-filling London's dingiest clubs to playing to

Stone Roses

7,500 people at Alexandra Palace. Having achieved such incredible success so quickly, when the band vanished to work on new material the rumour mongers inevitably came out in force. In 1990, the 'One Love' single reached the UK Top 10 UK charts, but aside from this singular vinyl artefact, the media was mainly concerned with the Roses' rows with a previous record company, who had reissued old material accompanied by a video made without the band's permission. This resulted in the group vandalising the company's property, which in turn led to a much-publicised court case. As if this was not enough, Stone Roses were back in court when they tried to leave Silvertone, who took an injunction out against their valuable proteges. This prevented any further Stone Roses material from being released, even though the band eventually won their case and signed to Geffen for a reported $4 million. At the end of 1991, their eagerly awaited new product was still stuck somewhere in the pipeline while, in true Stone Roses fashion after their live extravaganzas at Spike Island, Glasgow, London and Blackpool, plans were afoot for a massive open air comeback gig for the following Spring.

Album: *The Stone Roses* (1989).

Stranglers

One of the longest-surviving groups from the British new wave explosion of the late 70s, the Stranglers first rehearsed in Guildford as early as 1974. Two years later, the first full line-up emerged comprising: Hugh Cornwell (b. 28 August 1949, London, England; vocals/guitar), Jean Jacques Burnel (b. 21 February 1952, London, England; vocals/bass), Jet Black (b. Brian Duffy, 26 August 1943; drums) and Dave Greenfield. Following a tour supporting Patti Smith during 1976 and some favourable press reports (with comparisons with the Doors), the group were signed by United Artists Records. Courting controversy from the outset, the group caused a sensation and saw their date at London's Roundhouse cut short when Cornwell wore an allegedly obscene T-shirt. In February 1977, the Stranglers' debut single, '(Get A) Grip (On Yourself)' reached number 44 in the UK charts and inexplicably dropped out after only one week. According to the chart compilers, the sales were inadvertently assigned to another record, but it was too late to rectify the damage. 'Grip' saw the group at their early best. Bathed in swirling organ and backed by a throbbing beat, the single displayed Cornwell's gruff vocal to strong effect. The b-side, 'London Lady', was taken at a faster pace and revealed the first signs of an overbearing misogynism that would later see them fall foul of the critics. Initially bracketed with punk, the Stranglers owed as much to their pub-rock background and it soon emerged that they were older and more knowing than their teenage contemporaries. Nevertheless their first album *IV Rattus Norvegicus* was greeted with enthusiasm by the rock press and sold extremely well. The near 'blasphemous' lyrics of 'Hanging Around' and the gruesome imagery of 'Down In The Sewer' seemingly proved less acceptable than the women-baiting subject matter of their next single, 'Peaches'. Banned by BBC radio, the song still charted thanks to airplay offered the b-side 'Go Buddy Go'. Rather than bowing to the feminist criticisms levelled against them, the group subsequently compounded the felony by introducing strippers at a Battersea Park, London concert. Journalists were treated even more cavalierly and the group were renowned for their violent antics. Having initially alienated the press, their work was almost universally derided thereafter. The public kept faith, however, and ensured that the Stranglers enjoyed a formidable run of hits over the next few years. The lugubrious protest 'Something Better Change' and faster paced 'No More Heroes' both reached the UK Top 10, while 'Five Minutes' and 'Nice 'N Sleazy' each entered the Top 20. In the background there were the usual slices of bad publicity. Burnel and Black were arrested for being drunk and disorderly before charges were dropped. Cornwell was not so fortunate and found himself sentenced to three months' imprisonment on drugs charges in January 1980. Within two months of his release, the group found themselves under arrest in Nice, France, after allegedly inciting a riot. Later that year they received a heavy fine in a French court.

The group's uncompromising outlaw image tended to distract from subtle changes that had been occurring in their musical repertoire. Their brave cover of the Burt Bacharach/Hal David standard 'Walk On By' (with an identical arrangement to the Doors' 'Light My Fire') reached number 21 in spite of the fact that 100,000 copies of the record had already been issued gratis with the album *Black And White*. Equally effective and contrasting was the melodic 'Duchess', which displayed the Stranglers' plaintive edge to surprising effect. Their albums also revealed a new diversity from *The Raven* (with its elaborate 3-D cover) to the genuinely strange *Themeninblack*. The latter was primarily Cornwell's concept, and introduced the idea of extra-terrestrial hit-men who silence individuals that have witnessed UFO landings. For their next album, *La Folie*, the group were accompanied on tour by a ballet company. The album spawned the group's biggest hit, the evocative 'Golden Brown', with its startling, classical-influenced harpsichord arrangement. This

Stranglers

paean to heroin reached the UK number 2 spot, resting just behind Buck Fizz's 'Land Of Make Believe'. Even at their most melodic the Stranglers ran into a minor furore when it was alleged that the song was concerned with heroin consumption. Fortunately, the theme was so lyrically obscure that the accusations failed to prove convincing enough to provoke a ban. Another single from *La Folie* was the sentimental 'Strange Little Girl', which also climbed into the UK Top 10. The melodic influence continued on 'European Female', but in spite of the hits, the group's subsequent albums failed to attract serious critical attention. As unremittingly ambitious as ever, the Stranglers' 1986 album *Dreamtime* was inspired by Aborigine culture and complemented their outsider image. Just as it seemed that their appeal was becoming merely cultish, they returned to their old style with a cover of the Kinks' 'All Day And All Of The Night'. It was enough to provide them with their first Top 10 hit for five years. Increasingly unpredictable, the group re-recorded their first single 'Grip' which ironically fared better than the original, reaching the Top 40 in January 1989.

Despite their small handful of solo ventures, it seemed unlikely that either Cornwell or Burnel would ever consider abandoning the group for solo careers. Perpetual derision by the press finally took its

cumulative toll on the lead singer, however, and in the summer of 1990 Cornwall announced that he was quitting the group. Initial reports indicated that he was considering an acting career. Burnel, Black and Greenfield were left with the unenviable problem of finding an experienced replacement and deciding whether to retain the name Stranglers. Their task was made no easier by the realization that they had achieved one of the most stable and consistent group line-ups in rock history. Fifteen years on, it seems remarkable that this most anarchic of mid-70s groups should have turned into something of an institution.
Albums: *IV Rattus Norvegicus* (1977), *No More Heroes* (1977), *Black And White* (1978), *Live (X Cert)* (1979), *The Raven* (1979), *The Meninblack* (1981), *La Folie* (1981), *Feline* (1983), *Aural Sculpture* (1984), *Dreamtime* (1986), *All Live And All Of The Night* (1988). Compilation: *The Singles* (1989), *Greatest Hits: 1977-1990* (1990).

Strawberry Switchblade
This colourful duo, comprising Jill Bryson (vocals/guitar) and Rose McDowell (vocals/guitar), emerged as a product of the late 70s Glasgow punk scene. Their appearance in colourful polka-dotted frocks with frills, ribbons, flowers and cheap jewellery unfortunately distracted attention from their songwriting. Despite sounding like a happy pop band, their lyrics expressed sadness. The debut single in 1983, 'Trees And Flowers', was written as a result of Jill's agrophobia. Signed to the independent Ninety-Two Happy Customers label (under the aegis of producers David Balfe and Bill Drummond), this melancholy song was given a pastoral feel by the oboe playing of former Ravishing Beauties member Kate St. John. With added studio assistance from Roddy Frame (guitar) of Aztec Camera and Madness's Mark Bedford (bass) the single reached number 4 in the UK Independent chart. The duo found national success in late 1984 with the chirpy 'Since Yesterday' and were feted by the music media. An over-produced debut album, far removed from the simplicity of 'Trees And Flowers', entered the UK Top 25 but failed to supply the duo with the expected run of hit singles. Their last hit, came in 1985 with a cover of Dolly Parton's classic, 'Jolene'. Following the break-up of the group, Rose attempted to revive her career without Jill in the late 80s for a time working under the name Candy Cane but met with little success.
Album: *Strawberry Switchblade* (1985).

Streetband
This British rock band of the late 70s, notable mainly for the membership of Paul Young (b. 17 January 1956, Luton, Bedfordshire, England). Having played in local group, Kat Kool And The Kool Kats, Young formed Streetband in 1977 with John Gifford (guitar/vocals), Mick Pearl (bass/vocals), Roger Kelly (guitar) and Vince Chaulk (drums, ex-Mr Big, whose biggest hit was 'Romeo' in 1977). The group's R&B-tinged music brought a recording deal with Logo Records. The debut album was produced by Chas Jankel, Ian Dury's songwriting partner. The first single, 'Hold On' had a novelty b-side, 'Toast' which gained airplay and became a Top 20 hit in 1978. Streetband returned to their hard-rocking approach for later singles and a second album which included Jools Holland playing keyboards. Lack of further commercial success precipitated the break-up of the group in 1979 when Young, Gifford and Pearl formed the soul group Q-Tips.
Albums: *London* (1979), *Dilemma* (1979).

Stump
Of all the quirky, Captain Beefheart-indebted groups to reside at Manchester's Ron Johnson label, Stump were not only the most distinctive but also the most endearing. Unlike their manic stablemates, mad-eyed Mick Lynch (vocals), Chris Salmon (guitar), Kev Hopper (bass) and Rob McKahey (drums) avoided an aggressive, staccato-guitar onslaught, opting instead for awkward chord and rhythm changes and a wacky, humorous lyrical content, first heard on the charming EP *Mud On A Colon* in March 1986. BBC disc jockey John Peel was an early admirer and while Stump's Peel session of that year would eventually surface on vinyl the following January, the band were caught up in the *C86* programme organized by the *New Musical Express* and turned up on *The Tube* television show with the wacky video for their contribution, 'Buffalo'. A debut album, *Quirk Out*, was issued on the Stuff label as Ron Johnson ran into financial problems, and it was not long before Ensign lured the band into major territory. 'Chaos' preceded a second album, *A Fierce Pancake*, revealing a Stump that had lost none of their individuality, but it was 'Charlton Heston' (1988), with its 'lights camel action' line and frog-dominated video, that attracted most attention. A full-scale single release for the excellent 'Buffalo' looked set to chart in November, but after it failed, the band all but disappeared.
Albums: *Quirk Out* (1987), *A Fierce Pancake* (1988).

Style Council
Founded in 1983 by Paul Weller (b. 25 May 1958, England) and Mick Talbot (b. 11 September 1958). Weller had been lead singer of the Jam while Talbot was the former keyboards player with the Merton Parkas and the Bureau. Another constant collaborator was singer D.C. Lee, whom Weller married. Weller's avowed aim with the group was to merge his twin interests of soul music and social comment. In this his most important model was Curtis Mayfield, who appeared on Style Council's 1987 album. The

continuing popularity of the Jam ensured that Style Council's first four releases, in 1983, were UK hits. They included the EP, *Paris*. 'Speak Like a Child' and 'Long Hot Summer'. Tracey Thorn from Everything But The Girl was a guest vocalist on the band's first album. Perhaps the most effective Style Council song was the evocative 'My Ever Changing Moods', the first of three Top 10 hits in 1984 and the band's only US hit. During the mid-80s, Weller's political activism was at its height as he recorded 'Soul Deep' as the Council Collective with Jimmy Ruffin and Junior (Giscombe) to raise funds for the families of striking coal miners and became a founder member of Red Wedge, an artists' support group for the Labour Party. Style Council appeared at Live Aid in 1985 and in 1986 made a short film, *JerUSAlem*, a satirical attack on the pop music industry. There were continuing British hits, notably 'The Walls Come Tumbling Down' (1985), 'Have You Ever Had It Blue' (featured in the 1986 film *Absolute Beginners*) and 'Wanted' (1987). With its eclectic mix of soul, classical and pop influences, the 1988 album was less of a commercial success and by 1990, Style Council was defunct. Weller re-emerged the next year with a new band, the Paul Weller Movement, recording for his own Freedom High label.

Albums: *Cafe Bleu* (1984), *Our Favourite Shop* (1985), *Home And abroad* (1986), *The Cost of loving* (1987), *Confessions of A Pop Group* (1988).

Sub Pop Records

Based in Seattle, Washington, USA, the Sub Pop label has served as the natural focus for local acts since the late 80s. It has become closely associated with several noise/guitar bands fusing heavy riffs to a sound influenced by the Stooges. Releases by Mudhoney and Tad helped establish its cult following, while the subsequent success of Nirvana focused attention on the group's tenure with the company. Sub Pop was also noted for 'one-off' recordings and Dinosaur Jr, Rapeman and Thin White Rope were among those taking advantage of this practice. The label also established the Sub Pop Singles Club, whereby an annual subscriber would receive an exclusive, limited edition release each month. The idea was later adopted by Rough Trade Records in 1991.

Album: *Sub Pop Grunge Years* (1990).

Sudden, Nikki

Following the dissolution of premier UK art punk band Swell Maps, former lead singer and driving force Sudden joined the Abstract label to release *Waiting On Egypt*. He had continued to make music erratically before this. Among these recordings were sessions with Another Pretty Face (later Mike Scott's Waterboys) in Christmas 1980. His first solo single

was 'Back To The Start' on Rather Records, before the release of 'Channel Steamer' which would form part of the debut album. He was pleased with the results: 'Nearly everyone I know thinks it's the best thing I've ever done and I must admit when I listen to it I get a pleasant surprise'. Also included were 'Forest Fire' and 'New York', both unreleased Swell Maps songs. Sudden also wrote for several music magazines including the later issues of *Zig Zag*. The nucleus of musicians that he employed included Scott (guitar), Steve Burgess (bass), Anthony Thistlethwaite (saxophone) and Empire (ex-TV Personalities) on drums. His most recent album, *The Jewel Thief*, saw him work with his long-time fans, R.E.M..

Albums: *Waiting On Egypt* (1982), *Johnny Smile Slowly* (1982), *The Bible Belt* (1983), *Jacobites* (1984), *Texas* (1986), with the Jacobites *Dead Men Tell No Tales* (1987), with Rowland S. Howard *Kiss You Kidnapped Charabanc* (1987), with the French Revolution *Groove* (1989), *The Jewel Thief* (1991).

Sugarcubes

Sugarcubes

This offbeat pop band was formed in Reykjavic, Iceland on 8 June 1986, the date, taken from the birth of Bjork's son, Sindri. The settled line-up featured Bjork Gundmundsdottir (b. 1966, Reykjavic, Iceland; vocals/keyboards), Bragi Olaffson (bass), Einar Orn Benediktsson (vocals/trumpet), Margret 'Magga' Ornolfsdottir (keyboards, replacing original keyboard player Einar Mellax) Sigtryggur 'Siggi' Balduresson (drums) and Thor Eldon (guitar). Bjork's step-father was in a rock showband, and after early stage appearances she completed her first album at the age of 11. She was also the singer for prototype groups Toppie Tikarras then Theyr, alongside Siggi Balduresson. The latter band shot to prominence when Jaz Coleman and Youth (Killing Joke) mysteriously appeared in Iceland in March 1982, paranoid about an impending apocalypse, and collaborated on several projects with Theyr. Bjork, Einar and Siggi then went on to form Kukl, who toured Europe and released two records on the Crass label, establishing a link with the UK anarcho-punk scene which would be cemented when the band joined UK independent label One Little Indian.

Their debut single 'Birthday' and album *Life's Too Good* saw the band championed in the UK press almost immediately. In particular, praise was heaped on Bjork's distinctive and emotive vocals. The Sugarcubes ran their own company in Iceland called Bad Taste, an organization which encompassed an art gallery, poetry bookshop, record label, radio station and publishing house. Bjork's ex-husband Thor, a graduate in Media Studies from London Polytechnic and the band's guitarist, sired her son Sindri under a government incentive scheme to boost the island's population, the financial rewards for this action allowing him to buy a pair of contact lenses. He then married Magga Ornolfsdottir (ex-the Giant Lizard), who joined the band in time for their second album. In addition, Siggi Balduresson and Bragi Olaffson, the band's rhythm section, were brother-in-laws, having married twin sisters. Most bizarre of all, however, was the subsequent marriage of Einar and Bragi in Denmark in 1989, the first openly gay marriage in pop history! *Here Today, Tomorrow, Next Week*, its title taken from a line in Kenneth Graeme's book *Wind In The Willows*, was a much more elaborate album, with a full brass section on 'Tidal Wave' and strings on the single, 'Planet'. However, compared with the rapturous reception granted their first album, *Here Today* took a critical pasting. Even label boss Derek Birkett conceded that it was far too deliberate. The press was also quick to seize on the fact that Einar's vocal interjections detracted from the band's performance. After much touring the group returned to Reykjavik, where they followed their own interests for a time. Bjork collaborated on the Bad Taste album *Gling Glo*; 'Just Icelandic pop songs from the 50s with jazz influences'. Balduresson also contributed drums. Members of the band spent time as an alternative jazz orchestra. More recently, the band played a concert for President Mitterand of France, in Reykjavik, and Bjork joined 808 State on their *Ex:El* album and single 'Oops'. The group's third album found them back in favour with the music press and back in the chart with 'Hit'.

Albums: *Life's Too Good* (1988), *Here Today, Tomorrow, Next Week* (1989), *Stick Around For Joy* (1992).

Suicide

This US band were an influence on Birthday Party, Soft Cell, Sigue Sigue Sputnik and the Sisters Of Mercy with a potent fusion of rockabilly and electronic music on cheap equipment. Singer Alan Vega (b. 1948) and multi-instrumentalist Martin Rev polarized audiences in Max's Kansas City and other New York clubs in the early 70s, remaining unheard on vinyl until the advent of the new wave when their arrangement of 'Rocket 88' was included on *Max's Kansas City* (1976) compilation. Ramones associates Craig Leon and Martin Thau oversaw the duo's early recording career (on Thau's Red Star label) until a support spot on a Cars tour brought them to the notice of vocalist Ric Ocasek who produced *Alan Vega And Martin Rev* for Ze Records. Ocasek was also involved in the pair's solo albums. Of these, Vega's vocal-dominated efforts elicited most public interest – particularly with 1981's *Vega* (containing the European hit 'Juke Box Baby') and *Sunset Strip* with its revival of Hot Chocolate's 'Everyone's A Winner'. Vega also mounted a sculpture exhibition in New York and, with David Bowie and Philip Glass, had a hand in David Van Teighem's collage for the ballet *Fair Accompli* before Suicide resumed corporate activities in 1986.

Albums: *Suicide* (1977), *24 Minutes Over Brussels* (1978), *Live* (1979), *Half Alive* (1981), *Alan Vega And Martin Rev* (1981), *A Way Of Life* (1989). Solo albums: Martin Rev *Martin Rev* (1979), *Clouds Of Glory* (1985); Alan Vega *Vega* (1981), *Sunset Strip* (1983), *Just A Million Dreams* (1985), *Deuce Avenue* (1990).

Summerhill

Arising from the ashes of the Snakes Of Shake, the UK band Summerhill looked to the early Byrds' sound for inspiration, their brand of folk-rock first heard on *I Want You* on the Rocket label in 1988. Their prolific live schedule, often as support act, made the team of Seori Burnett (vocals/guitar), Neil Scott (guitar/vocals), Keith Gilles (bass/vocals) and Ian Shedden (drums) a popular live act and a move to Demon's Diablo label came in time for a mini-album, *Lowdown*, later that year. Signed to Polydor Records, it was a year before the partnership was fruitful, during which time Michael Sturgis had replaced Shedden. 'Here I Am' was an obvious stab at the mainstream and it was March 1990 before *West Of Here*, was released. From it came 'Don't Let It Die' that same month and then a one-off single cover of the Rolling Stones' 'Wild Horses'. Despite some encouraging reviews Summerhill failed to make a sufficient impact on the charts and disbanded later that year. Keith Gilles later joined Sumishta Brahm's group, 13 Frightened Girls, appearing on the Jazz Butcher produced 'Lost At Sea' (1991).

Albums: *I Want You* (1988), *Lowdown* (1988), *West Of Here* (1990).

Sundays

Formed in London in the summer of 1987 by songwriters David Gavurin (b. 4 April 1963, England; guitar) and Harriet Wheeler (b. June 26 1963, England; vocals), who had already gained prior singing experience in a band called Jim Jiminee. Later joined by the rhythm section of Paul Brindley (b. 6 November 1963, England; bass) and Patrick Hannan (b. 4 March 1966, England; drums), The Sundays' first ever live performance at the seminal Falcon 'Vertigo Club' in Camden Town, London in August 1988 sparked off abnormally excessive interest from both media and record business circles. Playing what many perceived to be a delicate, flawless mix of the Smiths' guitars and the Cocteau Twins' vocal acrobatics, the band's high profile ensured a Top 50 place in the UK charts for their debut single, 'Can't Be Sure' in January 1989. Despite this dramatic arrival, the Sundays did not capitalize on their success until exactly a year later, when *Reading, Writing, Arithmetic* took everyone by surprise by entering the UK charts at number 4. Notorious for being slow songwriters - legend has it that their label, Rough Trade Records, wanted to release a single from the album but the band did not have any other material for the b-side! This was to be their last release for two years, as touring commitments took the quartet to Europe, Japan and the equally reverential America, where *Rolling Stone* magazine had voted the Sundays Best Foreign Newcomer. Financial difficulties at their label also held up proceedings while they sought a new record deal during 1991, eventually signing to Parlophone in January 1992.

Album: *Reading, Writing, Arithmetic* (1990).

Swans

Like many early 80s American bands determined to stretch the boundaries of musical cacophony, Swans were drawn to New York's thriving underground that has produced Jim Thirlwell, Lydia Lunch and Sonic Youth over the years. Although the band have endured numerous line-up changes, Swans always centred on Michael Gira and, later, Jarboe. After a raucous debut EP in 1982, *Speak*, came the influential album *Filth* on the German Zensor label, which attracted a strong European audience later that year. In 1984, the band released *Cop* on their own Kelvin 422 label, their first to appear in the UK. Although *Cop* was awash with harsh guitars and awkward, dirge-like sounds, it was definitely more accessible than *Filth*, as was the subsequent EP, *Raping A Slave*, in March 1985. 'Time Is Money (Bastard)' kicked off 1986 with a typically uncompromising title, preceding *Greed* in February. Themes of depravity, sex, death and the more sinister aspects of human nature prevailed, also to be heard on *Holy Money* and 'A Screw' later that year. 1987 saw Swans move to Product Inc. for a double album, *Children Of The God*, although another less official effort, *Public Castration Is A Good Idea*, also surfaced that year. But most of the 1987 was taken up with Jarboe's new project, Skin, although there was a limited German-

only Swans release *Real Love*.

A third double album, 1988's *Feel Good Now*, emerged on the Rough Trade-distributed Love label. Meanwhile, a sinister cover of Joy Division's 'Love Will Tear Us Apart' climbed the indie charts in June, resulting in a deal with MCA. 'Saved', Swans' first single for the major label in April 1989, revealed a definite shift towards mainstream rock, further evident on *The Burning World*: the sombre, Germanic approach was still there, but the ingredients were certainly more palatable. August's 'Can't Find My Way Home' was far more melodic than earlier singles and it seemed that Swans were on the brink of crossing to a much wider audience. But the next two years concentrated on reissues of early material on Gira's own Young God label. In May 1991, Swans issued a *White Light From The Mouth Of Infinity*, which was both commercial and innovative and showed that Gira and Co. would always command the attention of those willing to listen.

Albums: *Filth* (1982, reissued 1990), *Cop* (1984), *Greed* (1986, reissued 1989), *Holy Money* (1986, reissued 1989), *Public Castration Is A Good Idea* (1987), *Children Of The God* (1987), *Feel Good Now* (1988), *The Burning World* (1989), *White Light From The Mouth Of Infinity* (1991).

Sweet, Rachel

b. 1963, Akron, Ohio, USA. Rachel Sweet sang professionally at the age of five, working as a child model for television commercials in New York and as a support act to Mickey Rooney. At the age of 12 she recorded her first single, the country song 'Faded Rose', on the Derrick label which, along with her follow-up, 'We Live In Two Different Worlds' reached the lower regions of the *Billboard* Country charts. Under the tutelage of manager and songwriter Liam Sternberg, Rachel landed a contract with the pioneering independent UK label Stiff Records. The company had previously distributed a compilation album of Akron acts which included two tracks by the singer. For the Stiff 78 Tour with fellow labelmates Lene Lovich, Wreckless Eric, Jona Lewie and Mickey Jupp, Rachel's backing band were the Records. The single, a version of the Isaac Hayes/David Porter song 'B-A-B-Y', reached the UK Top 40. Sweet possessed a mature voice for someone still in her mid-teens. *Fool Around* saw her tackling Del Shannon's 'I Go To Pieces' and Elvis Costello's 'Stranger In The House' as well as several Sternberg originals. Rachel's obvious talents were dogged by persistent, but tenuous, accusations of her being marketed as 'jail-bait'. After parting with Sternberg in 1979, her second album presented Rachel with a harder image, complete with an advertising campaign bizarrely depicting her as a leather-jacketed, sullen, child abductor. Backed by

Fingerprintz, the songs on the album contained cover versions of Lou Reed's 'New Age', Graham Parker's 'Fool's Gold' and the Damned's 'New Rose' as well as the usual quota of country rock. As with the first album, *Protect The Innocent* was a commercial failure, although this time it did not enjoy critical approbation. Her departure from Stiff to CBS saw the release of *...And Then He Kissed Me* which included the UK and US Top 40 hit duet with Rex Smith, 'Everlasting Love' in 1981. Despite this encouraging start, the mismanaged talents of Rachel Sweet saw her fade from the scene.

Albums: *Fool Around* (1978), *Protect The Innocent* (1980), *...And Then He Kissed Me* (1981).

Swell Maps

Although associated with the immediate post-punk aftermath, British group Swell Maps was formed in 1972. Five years later Nikki Sudden (guitar/vocals), Epic Soundtracks (drums/vocals), Jowe Head (bass), Richard Earl (vocals) and David Barrington (vocals) founded their own Rather label which issued material in conjunction with Rough Trade. Although their debut single, 'Read About Seymour', became a cult favourite, the group steadfastly refused to become categorized. Despite the pop element of successive singles - 'Dresden Style', 'Real Shocks' and 'Let's Build A Car' - their albums offered a bewildering array of sounds ranging from garage-band simplicity to new-age styled piano instrumentals. Although Swell Maps broke up in 1980, a series of reissues, some of which include archive material, has kept their reputation alive.

Albums: *A Trip To Marineville* (1979), *Jane From Occupied Europe* (1980). Compilations: *Whatever Happens Next* (1981), *Collision Time* (1984), *Train Out Of It* (1987).

Swervedriver

Swervedriver

Previously known as Shake Appeal, Swervedriver came into being at the end of 1989 when Adam Franklin (b. 19 July 1968, Essex, England; vocals),

Jimmy Hartridge (b. 27 November 1967, Oxfordshire, England; guitar) and Adrian Vines (b. 25 January 1968, Yorkshire, England; bass) moved from the Home Counties to London and linked up with Graham Bonnar (b. 28 April 1967, Scotland) who had previously drummed for British hardcore group, Ut. The collective's sound changed accordingly from Stooges-style grunge-rock to a more contemporary American stylisation - a definition which was hardly weakened by the band's apparent lyrical obsession with highways, pick-up trucks and several other things mid-Western! In spite of the unfavourable comparisons, Swervedriver and their squalid guitars battled their way from beneath the shadow of their supposedly more credible transatlantic counterparts, reaching number 63 in the UK charts with their third EP, *Sandblasted*.

Album: *Raise* (1991).

Sylvain Sylvain

Although a founder member of the rock band Actress with Johnny Thunders and Billy Murcia, Sylvain only joined his colleagues in their next venture, the pivotal, glam-rock group, the New York Dolls, as a replacement for original guitarist Rick Rivets. He remained with the group until their break-up in 1977, following which the artist formed the Criminals with Bobby Blain (keyboards), Michael Page (bass) and Tony Machine (drums). This highly-respected quartet completed one single, 'The Kids Are Back', for their own Sing Sing label, but progress was hampered by Sylvain's concurrent commitment to former Dolls' vocalist David Johansen. Ties as a composer and backing musician were sundered in 1979 when Syl established a new act, Sylvain Sylvain And The Teenage News, with two further refugees from the Johansen band, Johnny Rao (guitar) and Buz Verno (bass). Both *Sylvain Sylvain* and it's follow-up, *And The Teardrops* confirmed the artist's gift for classic pop melody, but were not a commercial success and the artist was subsequently dropped by his label, RCA. He resurrected his independent Sing Sing label for 'Out With The Wrong Woman' (1983), but its creator has since failed to sustain the profile he enjoyed throughout the 70s.

Album: *Sylvain Sylvain* (1979), *And The Teardrops* (1980). Compilation: *'78 Criminals* (1985).

T

Tackhead

This techno dance outfit was formed in 1987 and released a remarkable first single, 'The Game', with a Brian Moore (football commentator) sample and backbeat which comprised metal guitar and electro 'hi-energi' attack, together with football chants. The band consisted of Keith Leblanc on percussion (previously behind the groundbreaking 'Malcolm X' single), plus Doug Wimbush (bass) and Skip MacDonald (guitar) and Gary Clail (vocals); however Bernard Fowler soon replaced Clail as vocalist. Together they had previously operated as the Sugarhill Gang house band, in their home town of Bristol, Connecticut, USA, performing on 'Rapper's Delight', 'The Message' and 'White Lines'. Migrating to London in 1984, they became a central component in Adrian Sherwood's On U Sound label. In various forms they continued to be prime movers in the UK dance sector for the rest of the 80s. In 1991 Leblanc joined with Tim Simenon (Bomb The Bass) in a new project titled Interference.
Albums: *Friendly As A Hand Grenade* (1987), *Strange Things* (1990), *End Of The Century Party* (1990).

Tad

This US, Seattle-based act - Tad Doyle (guitar/vocals), Gary Thorstensen (guitar), Kurt Danielson (bass/vocals) and Steve Wied (drums) - was one of several local acts signed to the Sub Pop label. *God's Balls* established Tad's uncompromising style, in which heavy riffs underpinned the obese Doyle's growling vocals. Gary Thorstensen (guitar) was added to the group for *Salt Lick*, a mini-album produced by former Big Black guitarist Steve Albini, who retained the power of the group's music while attempting to expand their limited range. *8-Way Santa* was closer in sound to Tad's debut album, although it did contain the impressive 'Jack Pepsi' in which Doyle's spoken monologues contrasted with its ferocious chorus. Despite a considerable head-start, Tad have latterly been eclipsed by former label-mates Nirvana.
Albums: *God's Balls* (1989), *Salt Lick* (1990), *8-Way Santa* (1991).

Talking Heads

One of the most critically acclaimed groups of the past two decades, Talking Heads pursued an idiosyncratic path of (often) uncompromising brilliance. After graduating from the Rhode Island School of Design, students David Byrne (b. 14 May

Talking Heads

1952, Dumbarton, Scotland; vocals/guitar), Chris Frantz (b. Charlton Christopher Frantz, 8 May 1951, Fort Campbell, Kentucky, USA; drums) and Tina Weymouth (b. Martina Weymouth, 22 November 1950, Coronado, California, USA; bass) relocated to New York. In 1975, they lived and rehearsed in Manhattan and named themselves Talking Heads. After appearing at the club CBGBs, they were approached by Seymour Stein of Sire Records, who would eventually sign the group. Early in 1976, the line-up was expanded to include pianist Jerry Harrison (b. Jeremiah Harrison, 21 February 1949, Milwaukee, Wisconsin, USA), a former member of Jonathan Richman's Modern Lovers. The group's art school background, witty invention and musical unorthodoxy was evident on their intriguingly titled debut, 'Love Goes To Building On Fire'. After touring extensively, they issued *Talking Heads '77*, an exhilarating first album, which was widely praised for its verve and intelligence. The highlight of the set was the insistent 'Psycho Killer', a *tour de force*, in which singer Byrne displayed his deranged vocal dramatics to the full. His wide-eyed stare, jerky movements and onstage cool reminded many commentators of Anthony Perkins, star of Hitchcock's movie *Psycho*.
For their second album, the group turned to Brian Eno as producer. *More Songs About Buildings And Food* was a remarkable work, its title echoing Talking Heads' anti-romantic subject matter. Byrne's eccentric vocal phrasing was brilliantly complemented by some startling rhythm work and the songs were uniformly excellent. The climactic 'The Big Country' a satiric commentary on consumerist America, featured the scathing aside: 'I wouldn't live there if you paid me'. The album also featured one cover version, an interesting reading of Al Green's 'Take Me To The River', which was a minor hit. Eno's services were retained for the more opaque *Fear Of Music*, which included the popular 'Life During Wartime'. Byrne next collaborated with Eno on *My Life In The Bush Of Ghosts*, before the group reunited

for *Remain In Light*. The latter boasted the superb 'Once In A Lifetime', complete with 'found voices' and African polyrhythms. An edited version of the song provided one of the best hit singles of 1981. During the early 80s, the group's extra-curricular activites increased and while Byrne explored ballet on *The Catherine Wheel*, Franz and Weymouth found success with their spin-off project, Tom Tom Club. The live double *The Name Of This Band Is Talking Heads* served as a stop-gap until *Speaking In Tongues* appeared in the summer of 1983. As ambitious as ever, the album spawned the group's UK Top 10 single, 'Burning Down The House'. While touring with additional guitarist Alex Weir (formerly of the Brothers Four), the group were captured on film in *Stop Making Sense*, the soundtrack of which sold well. The excellent *Little Creatures*, a more accessible offering than their more experimental work, featured three strong singles in the title track, 'And She Was' and 'Road To Nowhere'. The latter brought the group their biggest chart hit and was accompanied by an imaginative and highly entertaining video. In 1986, Byrne moved more forcibly into movies with *True Stories*, for which Talking Heads provided the soundtrack; it was two more years before the group reconvened for *Naked*. Produced by Steve Lillywhite, the work included musical contributions from Level 42 producer Wally Badarou and guitarists Yves N'Djock and Johnny Marr (from the Smiths). Since then Talking Heads have branched out into various offshoot ventures; there was an official announcement of their break-up at the end of 1991.
Albums: *Talking Heads '77* (1977), *More Songs About Buildings And Food* (1978), *Fear Of Music* (1979), *Remain In Light* (1980), *The Name Of This Band Is Talking Heads* (1982), *Speaking In Tongues* (1983), *Stop Making Sense* (1984), *Little Creatures* (1985), *True Stories* (1986, film soundtrack), *Naked* (1988).

Talulah Gosh

Formed in Oxford, England in February 1986, the much-maligned Talulah Gosh emerged in the aftermath of the *New Musical Express*'s influential *C86* promotion. Taking their name from an *NME* Clare Grogan interview headline, the group came to symbolize a movement that would come to be tagged as 'shambling'. Its hard-core followers indulged in the fashion of wearing asexual basin hair-cuts (boys) or straight short fringes (girls), plain anoraks, plus the affectation of a child-like innocence. The music borrowed a great deal from the Ramones, Velvet Underground and US 60s girl-groups while the lyrics dealt with boy/girl relationships but barely mentioned sex in obvious 'rock 'n' roll' terms and their un-elitist sense of fun endeared them to many. The five piece band consisted of Peter Momtchiloff (b. 10 March 1962, Weybridge, Surrey, England; guitar), Pebbles

(b. Elizabeth Price, 6 November 1966, Bradford, Yorkshire, England; vocals/tambourine), Robert Pursey, replaced early on by Chris Scott (b. 31 October 1961, Hemel Hempstead, Hertfordshire, England; bass), Marigold (b. Amelia Fletcher, 1 January 1966, London, England; vocals/guitar) and her brother Mathew Fletcher (b. 5 November 1970, London, England; drums).
One of the group's most popular early songs was 'The Day She Lost Her Pastels Badge'. They scored two UK Independent Top 5 singles with 'Steaming Train'/'Just A Dream' and 'Beatnik Boy'/'My Best Friend', both on the Edinburgh-based 53rd & 3rd label which were later compiled on the best-selling *Steaming Train* EP in 1987. Elizabeth Price, who left in December 1986 was replaced by Eithne Farry (b. 21 May 1965, Chelsea, London, England) as second vocalist. Price later created the Cosmic English Music label with Gregory Webster (formerly of the Razorcuts) and as a duo also formed the Carousel. One final UK Independent chart hit ensued for Talulah Gosh with 'Bringing Up Baby' the following year and a later album, *They've Scoffed The Lot*, released on Sarah Records, contained tracks from various BBC Radio 1 sessions from both line-ups. The group split in early 1988, due to university commitments and a consensus that the group had run its course. Eithne and Scott later appeared in Saturn 5, while Peter, who had briefly played in the final line-up of the Razorcuts, joined Amelia and Mathew in a successful revival of the 'Gosh formula as Heavenly in 1990.
Albums: *They've Scoffed The Lot* (1991). Compilation: *Rock Legends Volume 69* (1987, collects single releases).

Taylor, James, Quartet

When the Medway Valley's psychedelic-mod hopefuls the Prisoners disbanded in 1986, organist James Taylor vowed to move into the realms of jazz, and away from rock. Assembling a quartet from Kent, England, comprising fellow Prisoner bassist Allan Crockford and ex-Daggermen personnel Simon Howard (drums) and Taylor's brother David (guitar), the band recorded a BBC session for disc jockey John Peel, before Taylor retired to Sweden for a break. But the broadcast made such an impression that the group were signed to new 'mod' label Re-Elect The President. A mini-album of cover versions, *Mission Impossible*, featured 'organ groovy' 60s soundtrack instrumentals like the single 'Blow Up', with Jimmy Smith and Booker T. And The MGs providing the strongest influences. *The Money Spyder* took the theme a stage further; while the Damned had mocked the psychedelic soundtrack as Naz Nomad And The Nightmares, the TJQ reminisced on the beat and jazz age. But Taylor become frustrated with the band's limitations and by the time *Wait A Minute* appeared on Polydor's dance off-shoot, Urban, in September 1988, only his brother remained with him in the group. For a powerful remake of the 'Starsky And Hutch Theme', new jazz musicians and ex-James Brown horn-players were recruited, as the JTQ found themselves central to a new, London-based 'acid jazz' movement. Howard and Crockford, meanwhile, provided the rhythm section for ex-Prisoner Graham Day's new project, the Prime Movers. 1989 saw a further development for the JTQ with the recruitment of two rappers for May's 'Breakout'. The single hinted at a move away from jazz towards the dance charts, but *Do The Right Thing* combined both elements, alongside a continuing debt to the original fusion of jazz/dance and rare groove, not least on their rousing rendition of the 70s club favourite, 'Got To Get Your Own'. While ex-Style Council and Jazz Renegades drummer Steve White served in the JTQ for a time, Taylor himself has also made several guest performances, including appearances for the Wonder Stuff.

Albums: *Mission Impossible* (1987), *The Money Spyder* (1987), *Wait A Minute* (1988), *Get Organised* (1989), *Do The Right Thing* (1990), *Absolute* (1991).

Teardrop Explodes

This highly promising Liverpool group was assembled by vocalist Julian Cope (b. 21 October 1957, Bargoed, Wales), a former member of the Crucial Three, which had featured Ian McCulloch (later of Echo And The Bunnymen) and Pete Wylie (later of Wah!). The Teardrop Explodes took their name from a page in a Marvel comic and the original group came together in late 1978 with a line-up featuring Cope, Michael Finkler (guitar), Paul Simpson (keyboards) and Gary Dwyer (drums). After signing to Bill Drummond and Dave Balfe's Liverpool record label Zoo, they issued 'Sleeping Gas' in early 1979. It was soon followed by the eccentric but appealing 'Bouncing Babies'. By then, Simpson had left to be replaced by Balfe, who had previously appeared in the short-lived Lori And The Chameleons. The exuberant 'Treason (It's Just A Story)' was the Teardrop Explodes' most commercial and exciting offering to date, and was unlucky not to chart. The shaky line-up next lost Finkler, who was replaced by Alan Gill, formerly of Dalek I Love You. A distribution deal with Phonogram coincided with a higher press profile for Cope, which was rewarded with the minor hit 'When I Dream'. *Kilimanjaro* followed and displayed the group as one of the most inventive and intriguing of their era. A repromoted/remixed version of 'Treason' belatedly charted, as did the stirring 'Passionate Friend'. By late 1981, Cope was intent on restructuring the group; new members included Alfie Agius and Troy Tate.

Wilder further displayed the wayward talents of Cope and revealed a group bristling with ideas, unusual melodies and strong arrangements influenced by late 60s psychedelia. When the sessions for a third album broke down, Cope curtailed the group's activities and in 1984 embarked on an erratic yet often inspired solo career. The irreverently-titled *Everybody Wants To Shag The Teardrop Explodes* was posthumously exhumed for release in 1990.

Albums: *Kilimanjaro* (1980), *Wilder* (1981), *Everybody Wants To Shag The Teardrop Explodes* (1990). Compilation: *Piano* (1990).

Teardrops

The Teardrops were an amalgamation of various stalwarts of the Manchester new wave scene. Buzzcocks bassist Steve Garvey was joined by original Fall bassist Tony Friel, who had played with Contact and the Passage, and drummer Karl Burns, also previously with the Fall and the Passage, plus Public Image Limted. The band's first outing, 'Seeing Double', on local label TJM was what might have been expected from the members involved: a fairly robust but murky brand of post-punk. After featuring on TJM's *Identity Parade* sampler ('Colours'), the Teardrops released a 12-inch EP, *Leave Me No Choice*, before calling it a day with the appropriately-titled *Final Vinyl* in 1981. Burns rejoined the Fall in time for their strong 'Lie, Dream Of Casino Soul'.

Album: *Final Vinyl* (1981).

Teenage Fanclub

Formerly the main bulk of the infamous Glaswegian band the Boy Hairdressers, Teenage Fanclub came into being after Norman Blake (b. 20 October 1965, Bellshill, Scotland; guitar/vocals), Raymond McGinley (b. 3 January 1964, Glasgow, Scotland; guitar/vocals) and Francis MacDonald (b. 21 November 1970, Bellshill, Scotland; drums) moved on from that particular pseudo-punk combo and linked up with Gerard Love (b. 31 August 1967, Motherwell, Scotland; bass/vocals). During 1989 the foursome recorded an entire album - completed a full three months before the band had even played live - until MacDonald (later to join the Pastels) made way for Brendan O'Hare (b. 16 January 1970, Bellshill, Scotland). As well as the historical connection with the Boy Hairdressers, members of Teenage Fanclub also had dealings with fellow Scots outfit, BMX Bandits. Thus brought up on a diet of fun, loud guitars and downright irreverence, Teenage Fanclub stamped their mark on 1990 with a series of drunken live shows and the erratic but highly promising Americanized rock with their *A Catholic Education*. In October the band paid tribute to John Lennon by covering his 'Ballad Of John & Yoko', releasing and deleting the record on the same day. A year on and,

Teenage Fanclub

supplemented by the voraciously impressed music press, Teenage Fanclub had slightly toned down their sound, allowing the melodies to come through even more forcefully than before and harking back to the 70s guitars of Big Star and Neil Young. Inevitably their 'Starsign' - with a cover of Madonna's 'Like A Virgin' on the b-side - threatened to barge into the top of the UK charts and suggested that both British and American success was just around the next corner. *Bandwagonesque* arrived at the tail end of 1991 and became one of the year's most memorable albums. Laced with chiming guitar and irresistible melody the album indicated a future major band.
Albums: *A Catholic Education* (1990), *The King* (1991), *Bandwagonesque* (1991).

Teenage Jesus And The Jerks
The 17-year-old Lydia Lunch formed Teenage Jesus And The Jerks in the UK during 1976 to channel her feelings of contempt towards a complacent music industry, but almost immediately clashed with founder member James Chance, who left soon after to form the Contortions. Lunch's distraught singing and atonal guitar cut against drummer Bradley Field and bassist Jim Sclavunos (later replaced by filmmaker Gordon Stevenson) to create an uncompromising, unholy noise labelled 'no wave', which was first heard on their single, 'Orphans', in 1978. 'Baby Doll' reared its ugly head nearly a year later, followed by two 12-inch EPs. *Pre*, on the Ze label which collected several early recordings, while *Pink* boasted seven excellent tracks. Teenage disbanded in 1980 when Lydia Lunch progressed to the less violent, murkier sound of Beirut Slump. However, the discordant, tortuous racket they exuded has influenced a variety of distinguished names since then, from the Birthday Party to Sonic Youth. It is no coincidence that Lunch has worked with them both.

Telescopes
Formed in 1988 by Stephen Lawrie (b. 28 March 1969, East Hartford, Northumberland, England; vocals), Joanna Doran (b. Wednesbury, West Midlands, England; guitar/vocals), David Fitzgerald (b. 30 August 1966, Wellingborough, Northamptonshire, England; bass), Robert Brooks (b. 11 April 1969, Burton-upon-Trent, Staffordshire, England) and Dominic Dillon (b. 26 September 1964, Bolton, Lancashire, England). The Telescopes started out peddling a fearsome noise which owed much to the path laid earlier in the decade by the Jesus And Mary Chain. Their first release was on a flexidisc shared with Loop and sold with the 'Sowing Seeds' fanzine, after which came two temperamental singles on Cheree records followed by a deal with the American What Goes On label. Unfortunately, after a

further brace of singles and one album in 1989 What Goes On succumbed to bankruptcy, leaving the Telescopes to battle for the rights to their own songs and sign to Creation Records. The change of label coincided with a change in musical style as the band added lighter shades and harmonies to their intense guitar-based sound, a development which paid dividends when their eighth single, 'Flying', reached number 79 in the UK charts in 1991.
Albums: *Taste* (1989), *Untitled* (1992).

Television

Television
Lead guitarist/vocalist Tom Verlaine (b. Thomas Miller, 13 December 1949, Mount Morris, New Jersey, USA) first worked with bassist Richard Hell (b. Richard Myers, 2 October 1949, Lexington, Kentucky, USA) and drummer Billy Ficca in the early 70s as the Neon Boys. By the end of 1973, with the addition of rhythm guitarist Richard Lloyd, they reunited as Television. Early the following year, they secured a residency at the Bowery club CBGB's and found themselves at the forefront of the New York new wave explosion. Conflicts between Verlaine and Hell led to the departure of the latter who would soon re-emerge with the Heartbreakers. Meanwhile, Television found a replacement bassist in Fred 'Sonic' Smith from Blondie. The new line-up recorded the raw but interesting 'Little Johnny Jewel' for their own label Ork Records. This led to their signing with Elektra Records for whom they recorded their debut album in 1977. *Marquee Moon* was largely ignored in their homeland, but elicited astonished, ecstatic reviews in the UK where it was applauded as one of rock's most accomplished debut albums. Verlaine's sneering, nasal vocal and searing, jagged twin guitar interplay with Lloyd were the hallmarks of Television's work, particularly on such stand-out tracks as 'Torn Curtain', 'Venus' and 'Prove It'. Although the group looked set for a long and distinguished career, the follow-up *Adventure* was a lesser work and the group split in 1978. Since then both Verlaine and Lloyd pursued solo careers with

mixed results. In November 1991, Verlaine, Lloyd, Smith and Ficca revived Television and spent the ensuing time rehearsing for a come back album for Capitol Records. They made an appearance at the 1992 Glastonbury Festival.

Albums: *Marquee Moon* (1978), *Adventure* (1979), *The Blow Up* (1990, rec. live 1978)

Television Personalities

A crass meeting of 60s pastiche and a tongue-in-cheek nod towards punk have characterised Dan Treacy's Television Personalities over their long, erratic career. Treacy teamed up with Edward Ball back in 1977, releasing the privately pressed '14th Floor' the following year. After Ball's solo single as O Level, the pair issued what was to be seen as a pivotal artefact of the time, the EP *Where's Bill Grundy Now?* (1978). BBC disc jockey John Peel latched onto one of the tracks, 'Part Time Punks' (a cruel send-up of a rapidly decaying London scene) and this exposure attracted the interest of the Rough Trade label. Ball spent some working on his solo projects in the early 80s, the Teenage Filmstars and the Times. The group's debut *And Don't The Kids Just Love It*, extended Treacy's exploration of 60s influences. From it came the whimsical 'I Know Where Syd Barrett Lives' as a single, their last for Rough Trade. Treacy then teamed up with Ed Ball to form the Whaam! label, for TVPs and Times products plus other signings, including the Marine Girls.

In 1982, the group's busiest recording year, saw *Mummy You're Not Watching Me* share the instant appeal of the the group's debut. 'Three Wishes' followed, and coincided with a minor psychedelic revival in London. *They Could Have Been Bigger Than The Beatles* was a surprisingly strong collection of demos and out-takes. The band were soon expanded by Mark Flunder (bass), Dave Musker (organ) and Joe Foster (12-string guitar) for a tour of Italy, with Flunder replaced by ex-Swell Maps Jowe Head for a similar tour of Germany. 1983's 'A Sense Of Belonging' saw a one-off return to Rough Trade and caused a minor scandal over its sleeve. But delays meant that *The Painted Word* (on Illuminated) was not issued until January 1985. Foster and Musker soon left to work at Creation Records. With a new drummer, Jeff Bloom, Treacy set up a new label, after Whaam! was folded due to pressure from the duo Wham!. In the meantime, the German album, *Chocolat-Art (A Tribute To James Last)*, captured one of their European live gigs. It was not until early 1990 that the next album emerged. *Privilege*, included the catchy 'Salvador Dali's Garden Party'. Then, the band laid low for a further two years. Planned future singles include 'Strangely Beautiful' and 'She's Never Read My Poems' but release dates are uncertain.

Albums: *And Don't The Kids Just Love It* (1981), *Mummy You're Not Watching Me* (1982), *They Could Have Been Bigger Than The Beatles* (1982), *The Painted Word* (1985), *Chocolat-Art (A Tribute To James Last)* (1985), *Privilege* (1990).

Temple Of The Dog

This one-off project involved members of the USA, Seattle-based bands Mother Love Bone and Soundgarden. The album was recorded as a tribute to the late Andrew Wood, former Mother Love Bone vocalist. The band comprised Chris Cornell (vocals), Matt Cameron (drums), Mike McCready (guitar), Stone Gossard (rhythm guitar) and Jeff Ament (bass). Signed to A&M Records, the album received widespread critical acclaim immediately upon release. The music fused the Doors/Joy Division/Stooges fixation of Mother Love Bone with the harder, dirtier and at times funkier rhythms of Soundgarden. A moving, powerful and genuine tribute to a great vocalist in every sense. Gossard and Ament later formed Pearl Jam.

Album: *Temple Of The Dog* (1991).

Tenpole Tudor

This theatrical UK punk-pop group was led by the inimitable Edward Tudor-Pole (b. 6 December 1955, London, England) who first took to the stage at the age of nine when he appeared in *A Christmas Carol*. After a course at Chiswick Polytechnic he went to train at the Royal Academy of Dramatic Arts. In 1977 he joined a band called the Visitors which also included future *Riverside* BBC televsion host Mike Andrews. Edward formed the band Tenpole Tudor with Visitors Gary Long (drums), Dick Crippen (bass) and Bob Kingston (guitar). Kingston came from a musical family and had previously been in the group Sta-Prest with his brother Ray, himself later in the Temper. His sister June would soon become a member of the Modettes. Tudor appeared in the film *The Great Rock 'N' Roll Swindle* (Malcolm McLaren had been a mentor to Eddie) and performed 'Who Killed Bambi' which appeared on the b-side of the Sex Pistols' 'Silly Thing'. Eddie also helped Paul Cook and Steve Jones write the title song to the film. Tenpole's first single under their own name was 'Real Fun' which came out on Korova. After signing to Stiff Records they released 'Three Bells In A Row'. Over the next few months they took part on the *Sons Of Stiff* tour, hit the charts three times starting with the raucous 'Swords Of A Thousand Men', recruited a second guitarist in the form of Munch Universe, and released two albums, before they suddenly went out of fashion again. In 1982 Eddie decided to split the band up. Crippen, Long, and Kingston became the Tudors and released 'Tied Up With Lou Cool' whilst Eddie formed a new cajun-style Tenpole Tudor and put out the 'Hayrick

Song'. He then left Stiff and moved in to jazz and swing style bands whilst also reviving his acting career. In 1985 he formed an old style Tenpole Tudor and toured the country dressed in armour but left the following year to concentrate on acting. He subsequently appeared on stage (in the critically acclaimed *Road* and *The Sinking Of The Belgrano*), film (*Straight To Hell*, *Absolute Beginners* and *Walker*) and television, most recently in the comedy *Roy's Raiders* (1991). Eddie also reformed Tenpole Tudor again in 1989 and it seems likely that he will continue to do so at regular intervals.

Albums: *Eddie, Old Bob, Dick and Gary* (1981), *Let The Four Winds Blow* (1981).

10,000 Maniacs

This American group emerged on the wave of popularity caused by the interest in world music. Lead vocalist Natalie Merchant is backed by Jerome Augustyniak (drums), Robert Buck (guitar), Dennis Drew (keyboards), Steven Gustafson (bass). The group started playing together in Jamestown, New York, in 1981. They specialized in cover versions of songs by such bands as Joy Division, and Gang Of Four. Their style encompassed reggae, country and bluegrass, folk and rock music. BBC disc jockey John Peel rated the group's 'My Mother The War', and it appeared in his Top 50 for 1983. Shortly afterwards, in 1984, the Maniacs toured the UK. The group were signed to Elektra Records in 1985, and after a UK tour, recorded *The Wishing Chair* with Joe Boyd as producer. Original member John Lombardo (guitar) left the group in 1986 following a great deal of touring. 1987 saw a change of producer for *In My Tribe*, with Peter Asher stepping in, as he did with the subsequent release *Blind Man's Zoo*. The production change obviously worked as the album went into the US Top 40 in 1987, going gold in 1988, and platinum the following year. 'Peace Train', taken from the former album, received a great deal of airplay, but following the alleged death threat declarations to American servicemen by Yusuf Islam, formerly Cat Stevens, the writer of the song, the group insisted that any re-pressing of the album should exclude the aforementioned track. *Blind Man's Zoo* went into the US Top 20 in 1989, achieving gold status the same year. Following the release of *Blind Man's Zoo*, the group were on the road from June to December of 1989. *Hope Chest* is a compilation, re-mixed, of the group's first two independently released albums.

Albums: *Human Conflict Number 5* (1982), *Secrets Of The I Ching* (1983), *The Wishing Chair* (1985), *In My Tribe* (1987), *Blind Man's Zoo* (1989). Compilation: *Hope Chest* (1990).

Test Department

This UK experimental/industrial band comprised Paul Jamrozy (b. 3 March 1959), Graham Cunnington (b. 23 August 1960), Alistair Adams (b. 5 October 1959), Tony Cudlip (b. 9 September 1959) and Gus Ferguson. Originally forming in 1982 as a loose collective in New Cross, London, England, they were all co-directors of Test Department's stable, Ministry of Power Records. However, they liaised with a variety of other artists and musicians in order to empower their large-scale projects. The most recent and impressive of these was the huge *The Second Coming* show for Glasgow's 1990 Year Of Culture, set in the abandoned St Rollox Railway Works. This served as the culmination of several years inaugurating spectacular musical events in unlikely settings. Others have included Cannon Street Station, Bishopsbridge Maintenance Depot, a sand quarry, a car factory in Wales and an ice rink in Friesland. 'From the beginning there was a realization that we wanted to make things pretty monumental'. Allied to their innovative use of spectacle was the employment of instruments from the natural and unnatural environment; scrap metal and industrial cast-offs beating a rhythm to film and slide shows. Powered by a four-piece anvil chorus, the music splendidly complemented visuals drawn from 20s and 30s industrial monochromes. Originally signed up to Stevo's Some Bizzare label, they came in the same wave as fellow travellers SPK and Einsturzende Neubaten. In early 1984 they published an open manifesto in a letter to the *New Musical Express*: '...we will continue a disciplined attack on the official wall of ignorance both in music and in politics'. This remains a constant objective, as witnessed by their latest album recorded with the help of the Scottish Chamber Orchestra and Choir as a critique of Thatcherism.

Albums: *Beating The Retreat* (1984), *Second Edition* (1984), *Shoulder To Shoulder With South Wales Striking Miners* (1985), *The Unacceptable Face Of Freedom* (1986), *A Good Night Out* (1988), *Terra Firma* (1988), with Brith Gof *The Gododdin* (1989), *Pax Britannica* (1991).

That Petrol Emotion

This critically lauded and highly skilled pop group's efforts to break in to the mainstream have been consistently thwarted despite a splendid arsenal of songs. The band was originally formed when the O'Neill brothers (Sean; guitar, Damian; bass) parted from the fragmenting Undertones. A new approach was immediate with Sean reverting to his Irish name (having always appeared as John in his former band), and Damian switching to bass instead of guitar. They added Ciaran McLaughlin (drums), Reamann O'Gormain (guitar; ex-Bam Bam And The Calling),

That Petrol Emotion

and, most importantly, dynamic American front man Steve Mack (vocals). They debuted with a single, 'Keen' on the small independent Pink. Both that and the subsequent 'V2' proved radical departures for those clamouring for a re-run of the Undertones, with frothing guitar and a fuller sound. There was now a political agenda too, ironic in view of the press' bombardment of the Undertones as to why they did not write songs about the troubles in Northern Ireland. The questioning of British imperialism, explored through factors like 'racist' jokes and the fate of political prisoners, would became a tenet of their music (and more particularly record sleeves). Both their pop-based debut and *Babble* were dominated by frantic guitar and Mack's wholehearted delivery. However, their one album deal with Polydor finished with *Babble* and they moved on to Virgin Records for the more diverse *End Of The Millenium Psychosis Blues*. This included the controversial but poignant ballad 'Cellophane', bone-shattering disco of 'Groove Check', and Sonic Youth-tainted 'Under The Sky'. Big Jimmy (trombone) and Geoff Barrett (saxophone), ex-Dexy's Midnight Runners, had been added to bolster the sound but finances could not stretch to take them on tour. McLaughlin was beginning to step out as a major songwriting force, as Sean O'Neill elected to give family matters more prominence and returned to Derry. His brother switched to guitar with John Marchini taking over on bass. *Chemicrazy* which followed was very strong, especially on singles like 'Hey Venus' and 'Sensitize'. Despite constant campaigning on their behalf by the press, 'Big Decision', a direct call to political activism which reached a paltry UK number 42, remains their biggest chart success.

Albums: *Manic Pop Thrill* (1986), *Babble* (1987), *End Of The Millenium Psychosis Blues* (1988), *Chemicrazy* (1990).

Theatre Of Hate

Formed in September 1981, this UK new wave group comprised Kirk Brandon (vocals), John Lennard (saxophone), Stan Stammers (bass), Billy Duffy (guitar) and Nigel Preston (drums). After establishing a strong live reputation for their hard, uncompromising lyrics, the group recorded their 1982 debut *Westworld*. Produced by Mick Jones of the Clash, the work proved commercial enough to infiltrate the UK Top 20. The attendant single, 'Do You Believe In The Westworld?' also gave the group their only Top 40 entry. Drummer Preston was replaced by Luke Rendle, while Duffy went on to form the Cult. Despite their promise and strong following, the group fell apart a year after their inception with Stammers and Brandon going on to form Spear Of Destiny.

Albums: *He Who Dares Wins Live At The Warehouse Leeds* (1981), *Live At The Lyceum* (1982), *Westworld* (1982), *He Who Dares Wins Live in Berlin* (1982).

The The

Formed in 1979, this UK group was centred on the activities of singer/songwriter Matt Johnson. Initially, the unit included Keith Laws and cartoonist Tom Johnston, but the line-up was continually changing and often featured Johnson alone. Following their debut at London's Africa Centre on 11 May 1979, The The's first single 'Controversial Subject' was issued by 4AD Records. Two years later, The The signed with Stevo's Some Bizzare label and released the excellent 'Cold Spell Ahead'. Since 4AD still had a one-record option, Johnson issued *Burning Blue Soul* for them under his own name. Manager Stevo found it difficult to license The The's material to a major label but eventually Phonogram invested £8,000 in 'Uncertain Smile' (a retitled version of 'Cold Spell Ahead'), produced in New York by Mike Thorne. It was an exceptionally impressive recording, but its impact was overshadowed by the managerial machinations which saw Johnson move to another label, CBS. A projected album, *The Pornography Of Despair*, took longer to complete than expected and was eventually vetoed by Johnson. It was eventually replaced by the superb *Soul Mining*, one of the most critically acclaimed albums of 1983. By now, Johnson was already known for his uncompromising attitude and lust for perfection. Three years passed before the release of *Infected*, but it was well worth the wait. The album served as a harrowing commentary on the sexual, spiritual, political and economic malaise of 80s Britain. The production was exemplary and emphasized Johnson's standing as one of the most important cult artists to emerge during the decade. In 1988, Johnson established a new version of The The featuring former Smiths guitarist Johnny Marr, bassist James Eller and drummer Dave Palmer. A worldwide tour coincided with the release of *Mind Bomb*, which garnered the least promising reviews of Johnson's career. The work was bombastic in tone and full of lyrical diatribes and anti-religious rants allied to distinctly unmelodic songs. Johnson retained the new group for another album, scheduled for release in 1992, at which point The The's contract with CBS will have expired.

Albums: *Soul Mining* (1983), *Infected* (1986), *Mind Bomb* (1989).

They Might Be Giants

They Might Be Giants

John Flansburgh and John Linnell formed this New York based duo in 1984 after an initial meeting in Massachusetts, USA. The group took their name from a 1972 George C. Scott movie. Their original intention to recruit a full band was abandoned, but Linnell learned the accordion and Flansburgh mastered the guitar. Following Linnell's broken wrist which decimated their early tour dates, they devised the 'Dial-A-Song Service' which still operates today, premiering their intelligent pop skills. A self-titled debut album collated many of these early songwriting ventures, gaining the band a considerable cult reputation. MTV picked up on their quirky visual appeal, and *Lincoln* became the biggest selling independent album of 1989 in the USA. With wry and perverse lyrics like 'I can't help but feel jealous each time she climbs on his knee' ('Santa's Beard')

they struck an immediate chord with college radio. The UK independent label One Little Indian released the album before the group tied up a major deal with Elektra. *Flood* showcased their obtuse lyrical approach, contrasting influences as diverse as the Ramones and Talking Heads. The UK hit single 'Birdhouse In Your Soul' was a beautifully crafted pop song highlighting the bands affection for the naive charm of the 60s ballad.

Albums: *They Might Be Giants* (1987), *Lincoln* (1989), *Don't Let's Start* (1989), *Flood* (1990), *Apollo 18* (1992).

This Mortal Coil

This Mortal Coil

This group was essentially the creation of Ivo Watts-Russell (b. circa 1955, England), the co-owner of 4AD Records, a highly successful Wandsworth, London-based independent label. This Mortal Coil was actually a collaboration of musicians recording in various permutations, overseen and directed by Ivo. The first single, an epic cover of Tim Buckley's 'Song To The Siren', was originally intended as a b-side. However, bolstered by the considerable talents of Robin Guthrie and Elizabeth Fraser (Cocteau Twins), it saw its own release and became a near permanent fixture in the independent charts as a result. The album which followed set the pattern for the occasional outings to come. Featuring a selection of artists from the 4AD roster plus various outsiders, the albums included several covers of Ivo's favourite songwriters (Buckley, Alex Chilton, Roy Harper, Gene Clark and Syd Barrett). At times shamefully indulgent, the series has nevertheless highlighted the occasional stunning performance and breathtaking arrangement. The most recent outing, which Ivo promises to be final, continues this tradition. In addition to label favourites Kim Deal (Pixies), Tanya Donelly (Throwing Muses/Breeders/Belly) and Heidi Berry, also recruited is Caroline Crawley (Shelleyan Orphan). Previous encumbents have included Howard Devoto and Gordon Sharp (Cindytalk).

Albums: *It'll End In Tears* (1984), *Filigree And Shadow*

(1986), *Blood* (1991).

Thomas, David, And The Pedestrians

After the original Pere Ubu broke up, the group's central figure, David Thomas, embarked on a fascinating body of work with the Pedestrians that was both musical and experimental. Alongside veteran female jazz pianist Lindsay Cooper, Thomas stayed at Rough Trade for a 45rpm album, *The Sound Of The Sand And Other Songs Of The Pedestrians*. A subsequent lull was broken by *Variations On A Theme* in 1984, continuing Thomas's avenue of *avant garde* rock. The release of *More Places Forever* and *The Monster Walks On Winter Lake* (with the Wooden Buds) allowed Thomas to interact with a plethora of diverse talent; he has worked with Chris Cutler, Mayo Thompson, Ralph Harney, Scott Kraus, Ian Green, Richard Thompson, Anton Fier, Philip Moxham (Young Marble Giants), Eddie Thornton and Allen Ravinstein. After the issuing *Winter Comes Home* on the experimental label Recommended, followed by *Blame The Messenger* on Rough Trade, the idiosyncratic Thomas later reformed Pere Ubu.

Albums: *The Sound Of Sand And Other Songs Of The Pedestrians* (1981), *Variations On A Theme* (1984), *More Places Forever* (1985), *The Monster Walks On Winter Lake* (1986), *Winter Comes Home* (1986), *Blame The Messenger* (1987).

Thompson Twins

The origins of this UK synthesizer pop act were much less conventional than their chart material might suggest. Their name derived from the *Tin Tin* cartoon books of Herge. Formed in 1977, the line-up featured Tom Bailey (b. 18 June 1957, Halifax, Yorkshire, England; vocals/keyboards/percussion), Peter Dodd and John Roog (guitar/vocals/percussion), who were friends living in Chesterfield when they decided to experiment with music. Several gigs later they relocated to London where they picked up drummer Chris Bell (later Spear Of Destiny and Gene Loves Jezebel). After sporadic gigs 1981 saw their line-up extended to include Joe Leeway (b.14 November 1949, Islington, London, England; percussion/vocals), Alannah Currie (b. 20 September, 1959, Auckland, New Zealand; percussion/saxophone), and Matthew Seligman (ex-Soft Boys; bass). This seven-piece became a cult attraction in the capital, where their favourite gimmick involved inviting their audience on stage to beat out a rhythmic backdrop to the songs. Their motivation was similar to that of the punk ethos: 'We were angry with the world in general - the deceit and the lies'. However, when *A Product Of...* was released it showed a band struggling to make the transition from stage to studio. Producer Steve Lillywhite took them in hand for *Set*, and the Bailey-penned 'In The

Name Of Love' saw them gain their first minor hit in the UK. It did much better in the US, staying at the top of the *Billboard* Disco charts for five weeks. Before this news filtered back, four of the band had been jettisoned, leaving just Bailey, Currie and Leeway. The cumbersome bohemian enterprise had evolved into a slick business machine, each member taking responsibility for either the music, visuals or production, in a manner not dissimilar to the original Public Image Limted concept. Reinventing their image as those of the Snap, Crackle and Pop characters of the Kelloggs' breakfast cereal, they set about a sustained assault on the upper regions of the UK charts. 1983's 'Love On Your Side' was their first major domestic hit, preceding *Quick Step And Side Kick*, their first album as a trio which rose to number 2 in 1983. Highly commercial singles 'Hold Me Now', 'Doctor Doctor' and 'You Take Me Up' put them firmly in the first division of UK pop acts. Further minor hits followed, most notably the anti-heroin 'Don't Mess With Doctor Dream'. However, when Leeway left at the end of 1986 the Thompson Twins became the duo their name had always implied. Bailey and Currie had been romantically involved since 1980, and had their first child eight years later. Unfortunately, success on the scale of their previous incarnation deserted them for the rest of the 80s although their songwriting talents earned Deborah Harry a UK Top 20 hit in 1989 with 'I Want That Man'.

Albums: *A Product Of...* (1981), *Set* (1982), *Quick Step And Side Kick* (1983), *Into The Gap* (1984), *Here's To The Future* (1986), *Close To The Bone* (1987), *Big Trash* (1989), *Queer* (1991). Compilations: *Greatest Mixes* (1988), *The Greatest Hits* (1990).

Three Johns

This Leeds, Yorkshire pop punk band, formed on the Royal Wedding Day in 1981, set themselves a characteristic precedent by being refused permission to play a 'Funk The Wedding' gig because they were drunk. The line-up featured John Brennan (ex-25 Rifles; bass), John Langford (ex-Mekons; guitar,), John Hyatt (ex-Sheeny And The Goys, Another Colour; vocals). They met in Leeds while they were at college, although individually they are from Wales, Belfast and Wolverhampton. A drum machine was used in preference to an extra member, although, ironically, all three musicians were competent drummers. They signed to CNT Records in 1982, and released two singles, one of which, 'English White Boy Engineer', was a re-working of an old Mekons number. The lyrical focus of the song attacked hypocritical attitudes towards South Africa and apartheid, and the group were quickly designated as left wing rockers, albeit heavy drinking ones: 'We all have socialist convictions and obviously that comes through . . . but we're not a socialist band. We're a group of socialists who are in a band. It's a fine distinction but an important one'. They quickly made their reputation via frenetic and comic live shows, even performing a version of Madonna's 'Like A Virgin'.

A legacy of fine singles populated the independents charts, including 'Pink Headed Bug', 'Men Like Monkeys' and 'Do The Square Thing'. 1985's 'Death Of A European' was the *New Musical Express'* single of the week, although by misfortune it emerged the week of the Heysel football tragedy and hence achieved no airplay. Unfortunately, there was insufficient success to allow the band to give up their day jobs. Langford earned his living as a part-time graphic designer for the Health Education Service, and Hyatt (who designed the band's covers) was a teacher of Fine Art at Leeds Polytechnic. The debut *Atom Drum Bop* , bore the legend 'Rock 'n' Roll versus Thaatchiism', and included contributions from schoolgirl Kate Morath on the oboe. They worked with Adrian Sherwood on 1987's *Never And Always*, while 1988's *The Death Of Everything And More* was summed up by one critic as 'messy, snappy, gutteral'. After that came a long break in their musical endeavours: 'We basically stopped working after our last gig in December 1988. We'd done a US tour which was a total disaster and we didn't speak to each other after that, we were all too busy having babies and things'. Hyatt had an art exhibition at Liverpool's Tate Gallery, and Langford continued to work with the Mekons. They returned with *Eat Your Sons* in 1990, a concept album dealing with, of all things, cannibalism.

Albums: *Atom Drum Bop* (1984), *The World By Storm* (1986), *Live In Chicago* (1986), *Crime Pays...Rock 'n' Roll In The Democracy* (1986), *Death Of Everything* (1988), *Eat Your Sons* (1990).

3 Mustaphas 3

This pseudo-Balkan group have often been included under the 'World Music' banner. Each group member has adopted 6 August as an official birthday in order to avoid confusion. Niaveti Mustapha III (flutes/German bagpipes), Hijaz Mustapha (violin/bouzouki), Houzam Mustapha (drums), Sabah Habas Mustapha (bass/percussion), Kemo "Kem Kem" Mustapha (accordion/piano), and Daoudi Mustapha (clarinet) made their UK debut in August 1982. They hail from Szegerley, and their major breakthrough was going from Balkan Beat Bastard Bad Boys to Godfathers Of World Music, without changing their direction. The Mustaphas are occasionally joined by Expensive Mustapha (trumpet). The humorous ensemble was first brought to public attention by John Peel. The group have attracted a degree of criticism for not taking their

music seriously, but the end product is still extremely popular with audiences both in Europe and the USA. As an indication of this, *Soup Of The Century* was number 1 in the *Billboard* World Music charts, and was voted the 'Best World Music/International' album for 1990 by NAIRD (National Association of Independent Record Distributors), in the USA. For *Heart Of Uncle*, on Globestyle Records, the group were joined by their sister Laura Tima Daviz Mustapha (vocals). They have backed a number of other artists, such as Ofra Haza where they sang 'Linda Linda' and managed to offend some people by singing half the lyrics in Hebrew and half in Arabic.

Albums: *Bam! Mustaphas Play Stereo* (1985), *From The Balkans To Your Heart-The Radio Years* (1985), *L'Orchestre Bam de Grand Mustapha International & Party Play "Local Music"* (1986), *Shopping* (1987), *Heart Of Uncle* (1989), *Soup Of The Century* (1990). Compilation: *Friends, Fiends & Fronds* (1991).

Three O'Clock

Of all the early 80s west coast outfits to profess a liking for psychedelia, the Three O'Clock were the most overtly pop-influenced. From Sun Valley, California, USA, Michael Quercio (lead vocals/bass), Louis Guttierez (guitar), Mike Mariano (keyboards) and Danny Benair (drums) had their debut, *Sixteen Tambourines*, released in Europe in 1984 by the French label Lolita. Riding on the crest of the so-called 'paisley underground' wave of publicity, the album created enough of a stir to clinch a deal with IRS, releasing *Arriving Without Travelling* (from which was drawn 'Hand In Hand'). But like their debut, this only hinted at psychedelia and owed more if anything to that other late 60s musical form, bubblegum. The release of *Ever After* in 1987 saw Guttierez replaced Steven Altenberg, and though melodically strong, suffered from its stylized production. There was even a hint of Prince in there somewhere, not least on the single 'Warm Aspirations', so it was no surprise when the band teamed up with his Paisley Park operation in 1988. But since *Vermillion*, issued soon after, the Three O'Clock have kept a low profile.

Albums: *Sixteen Tambourines* (1984), *Arriving Without Travelling* (1985), *Ever After* (1987), *Vermillion* (1988).

Throbbing Gristle

Formed in London in September 1975, the group comprised Genesis P-Orridge (vocals), Cosey Fanni Tutti (guitar), Peter Christopherson (electronics) and Chris Carter (synthesizers). Essentially a performance art ensemble whose work often bordered on the obscene, they achieved a vague cult status in the wake of punk. Although boasting their own record company, early releases were limited to a few hundred copies. Some of their best known compositions were characteristically tasteless with such titles as 'Hamburger Lady' and 'Five Knuckle Shuffle'. Their generally formless approach was sprinkled with arty in-jokes, such as speeding up a single to last a mere 16 seconds for inclusion on their second album. Other tricks involving misplaced grooves and misleading album titles were commonplace. Although derided or ignored by the music press they influenced a number of post-punk acts, not least Cabaret Voltaire. In May 1981 they split with the announcement: 'T.G. was a project not a life. . . we've exploited it completely - there's nothing else to say'. Except perhaps that their debut album *Second Annual Report* was reissued with the recording played backwards. Orridge and Christopherson soon resurfaced as Psychic TV while their erstwhile partners continued as Chris And Cosey.

Albums: *Second Annual Report* (1977), *D.O.A. The Third And Final Report* (1978), *20 Jazz Funk Greats* (1979), *Heathen Earth* (1980), *Second Annual Report* (1981), *Funeral In Berlin* (1981), *Music From The Death Factory* (1982), *Journey Through A Body* (1982), *Assume Power Focus* (1982), *Live At The Death Factory, May '79* (1982). Compilations: *Greatest Hits* (1984).

Throwing Muses

Throwing Muses

Formed in Boston, Massachusetts, USA, by Kirstin Hersh, Tanya Donelly, Leslie Langston and David Narcizo, Throwing Muses added an entirely new perspective to the pop model of the late 80s. Seemingly unaware of conventional constraints, the foursome peddled an off-kilter brand of guitar noise which demonstrated an earnest desire for female self-expression. Yet contrary to becoming too awkward for their own commercial good, the band were picked up by Britain's 4AD label and thrust into the European limelight alongside local contemporaries the Pixies. Over the next five years and five albums, the media made much of singer Kirstin Hersh's mild psychological disorders, drawing parallels between her state of mind and the music's unsettling idiosyncracies. Along the way, Leslie Langston departed to be replaced by bassist Fred Abong, and more problems were to manifest themselves by the end of the decade as Throwing Muses became embroiled in a series of legal disputes with their manager, the Musician's Union and over personal aspects of individual band members. During the recording of *The Real Ramona*, guitarist Tanya Donnelly - who had also moonlighted in the Breeders - announced her permanant departure from the Muses, although she stayed on for the subsequent tour. This left the Throwing Muses' picture in a decidedly muddled state by the close of 1991, although the group seemed certain to continue in some shape or form - no matter how bedraggled.

Albums: *Throwing Muses* (1986), *The Fat Skier* (1987, mini-album), *House Tornado* (1988), *Hunkpapa* (1989), *The Real Ramona* (1991).

Thunder, Johnny

b. Gil Hamilton, 15 August 1941, Leesburg, Florida, USA. Adopting the name Johnny Thunder, the singer first worked with street-corner groups in the late 50s. He worked briefly as a member of the Drifters in 1959 and recorded a few singles under his real name before meeting producer Teddy Vann. They co-wrote the dance song 'Loop De Loop', which was issued on the Diamond label and reached number 4 in the US pop charts in 1963. Finding himself typecast as a performer of novelty dance records, ('Ring Around The Rosey' and 'Everybody Do The Sloppy'), Thunder was unable to duplicate his initial success, although he continued recording for Diamond, Calla and United Artists. He was still performing into the late 80s.

Album: *Loop De Loop* (1963).

Timbuk 3

Formed in Madison, Wisconsin, USA in 1978, Timbuk 3 was a duo consisting of husband and wife, Pat MacDonald and Barbara Kooyman MacDonald. The pair met while attending the University of Madison and began writing and performing their songs. They went to New York City where they played on the street for tips before settling in Austin,

Johnny Thunders

Tardis' in the summer of 1988. Inspired by the television series *Dr Who*, the insistent tune incorporated the glam rock thud of Gary Glitter, who even joined the duo when they performed the song. The spoof was continued in *The Manual*, a book credited to the Timelords, in which Drummond espoused his theories of how to create a number 1 hit. The front cover of the tome enthused 'The Justified Ancients Of Mu Mu Reveal Their Zenarchistic Method Used In Making The Unthinkable Happen'. The Drummond/Cautry partnership soon enjoyed even greater success with the dance-orientated KLF, whose title also served as the Timelords' record label.

Further reading: *The Manual*, The Timelords.

Tom Tom Club

This US group was a spin-off of the Talking Heads featuring bassist Tina Weymouth (b. Martina Weymouth, 22 November 1950, Coronade, California, USA) and her husband, drummer Chris Frantz (b. Charlton Christopher Frantz, 8 May 1951, Fort Campbell, Kentucky, USA). The pair were on holiday in Nassau in the Bahamas (later buying a house there) when they met Stephen Stanley, the engineer at the studios and a keyboard player. They also met Monty Brown, the guitarist with T-Connection who were recording there. The four set about rehearsing and recording together and came up with 'Wordy Rappinghood' which was a UK hit in 1981 under the group name the Tom Tom Club, taken from the name of a hall where they practised. The quartet stayed together on and off as a studio project utilizing various other people when necessary. These included Tina's two sisters on vocals, plus Steve Scales (percussion), Alex Weir (guitar) and Tyron Downie (keyboards). 'Genius Of Love' topped the US disco charts, and was followed by a cover of 'Under The Boardwalk'. It seemed as though they were in danger of overstating their separateness from Talking Heads: 'We've deliberately embraced all the types of music that Talking Heads hasn't. We like the accessibility and fun of dance music, but that's not all we do'. Frantz and Weymouth had produced Ziggy Marley early in 1988, and September saw the band playing a three-week stint at CBGB's with Lou Reed and Debbie Harry as guests. They began a UK tour with guitarist Mark Roule and keyboard player Gary Posner as the latest semi-permanent personnel. After the release of their third album, which this time included a cover of the Velvet Underground's 'Femme Fatale', they rejoined Byrne for Talking Heads' first live appearance since 1984 at the Ritz, New York.

Albums: *Tom Tom Club* (1981), *Close To The Bone* (1983), *Boom Boom Chi Boom Boom* (1989).

Texas. While in Austin they became regulars at clubs such as the Hole in the Wall and the Austin Outhouse. They recorded a demo and made an appearance on MTV's *I.R.S. The Cutting Edge*, which led to a record deal with I.R.S. Records. Using a boombox for their rhythm section, the duo (playing acoustic and electric guitars) began making appearances on other television programmes and recorded their debut, *Greetings From Timbuk 3*, in 1986. It reached number 50 in the US, largely on the strength of the sparkling first single, 'The Future's So Bright, I Gotta Wear Shades', a danceable novelty song which climbed to number 19 (21 in the UK). The album was a mixture of similarly light fare and darker, more serious themes, as was the 1988 follow-up, *Eden Alley*. Following the release of *Edge Of Allegiance*, the couple was joined by drummer Wally Ingram, and by *Big Shot In The Dark* they had evolved into a full band with the addition of bassist Courtney Audain.

Albums: *Greetings From Timbuk 3* (1986), *Eden Alley* (1988), *Edge Of Allegiance* (1989), *Big Shot In The Dark* (1991).

Timelords

Conceived by the mischievous Bill Drummond and Jim Cautry, this fictitious group registered a surprise UK number 1 with the novelty 'Doctorin' The

Tones On Tail

This three-piece *avant garde* rock band's brief tenure stretched from the summer of 1983 to late 1985. The band was built around the remnants of the higher profile Northampton group Bauhaus. Both Kevin Haskins (drums) and Daniel Ash (vocals/guitar) had been an essential part of that band, and Glenn Campling (bass and keyboards) had previously been their roadie. 'We're doing things the other way round to what Bauhaus did. They started off as a live band, then went into the studio. We started off as a studio band and have to branch off into live to show ourselves'. However, when David J finished recording with the Jazz Butcher, he linked once more with his old Bauhaus colleagues and the more successful (and rock orientated) Love And Rockets signalled the death knell for Tones On Tail.
Album: *Pop* (1984).

Tourists

Tourists

A UK power-pop group of the late 70s, the Tourists were notable as the first setting in which the David A. Stewart-Annie Lennox partnership came into the spotlight. The band grew out of an earlier duo formed by ex-Longdancer guitarist Stewart (b. 9 September 1952, Sunderland, Tyne & Wear, England) with fellow Sunderland singer-songwriter Pete Coombes who had been a member of Peculiar Star. The pair played folk clubs and cabaret around Europe in 1974-76. Returning to London, they met Lennox (b 25 December 1954, Aberdeen, Scotland) a former Royal Academy of Music student who had toured with jazz-rock big band Red Brass. As Catch they made one single, 'Black Blood' (Logo 1977), before re-forming as the five-strong Tourists with Jim Toomey (drums) and Eddie Chin (bass). The first album appeared on Logo Records in 1979, recorded with German producer Conny Plank. All the songs, including two minor hit singles, were by Coombes, but the band's first real success came with a revival of the 1963 Dusty Springfield hit 'I Only Want To Be With You' and 'So Good To Be Back Home Again',

which both reached the Top 10. After a contractual dispute with Logo, the Tourists made *Luminous Basement* for RCA, produced by Tom Allom at George Martin's studio in Montserrat. It sold poorly and after a final UK tour The band split in 1980. Coombes and Chin formed Acid Drops while Lennox and Stewart re-emerged the next year as the Eurythmics.
Albums: *The Tourists* (1979), *Reality Effect* (1979), *Luminous Basement* (1980).

Tovey, Frank

Leaving behind his somewhat self-destructive *alter ego* Fad Gadget, Tovey continued to release an eclectic selection of recordings on the Mute label. After attending London's St. Martins School Of Art in 1974 he moved to Leeds Polytechnic, graduating in Fine Arts. Using the rising tide of techno pop as a flag of convenience, Gadget released five albums and 15 singles before he shed his skin and introduced himself as Tovey. Although the performance art was toned down, the melodrama of Tovey's soundscapes and lyrics was more familiar: 'So meet me by the old bridge when the sun is setting low, There's a new gambling game they call the Lemming Show, I've got two tickets front row seats for the river side, We can take a picnic and watch suicides' (from early single 'Bridge St. Shuffle', a testament to the madness of daily life in the UK's capital). By now Tovey had introduced many traditional rock elements to aid the electronic rhythms. This was much in evidence on Tovey's debut, *Snakes And Ladders* under his real name. Produced by Tovey and E.C. Radclife (ex-Assembly), who also featured as lead guitarist, its theme shifted to that of Spanish colonialism (British Imperialism had already been the subject of Gadget's 1982 *Under Two Flags*). A further shift came with 1989's *Tyranny And The Hired Hand*, whose songs were firmly rooted in the traditions of acoustic folk. Soon afterwards Tovey was joined by the Pyros, consisting of Irish musicians Paul Rodden (banjos), John Cutliffe (bass) and Charlie Llewelyn (drums).
Albums: with Boyd Rice *Easy Listening For The Hard Of Hearing* (1984), *Snakes And Ladders* (1986), *The Fad Gadget Singles* (1986), *Civilian* (1988), *Tyranny And The Hired Hand* (1989).

Toyah

One of the more talented individuals to have risen under the banner of punk, Toyah (b. Toyah Ann Wilcox, 18 May 1958, Kings Heath, Birmingham, England) roamed with the gangs of Birmingham before channelling her energy into Birmingham Old Rep Drama School. She later worked as a mime artist at the Ballet Rambert before getting her first professional acting role in the BBC television play *Glitter* with Noel Edmonds and Phil Daniels, in

which she sang with the band Bilbo Baggins. Her next major role was as Emma in *Tales From The Vienna Wood*. Actor Ian Charleston then took her to tea with film maker Derek Jarman who offered her the part of Mad in *Jubilee*. It was here she met Adam Ant and for a time the pair, plus Eve Goddard, formed a band called the Man Eaters. However, the clash of egos ensured that the band was shortlived. While acting in Vienna they formed their first group with Peter Bush (keyboards), Steve Bray (drums, ex-Boyfriends) and Mark Henry (bass). Toyah then appeared in the film *The Corn Is Green* with Katharine Kepburn, and played Monkey in *Quadrophenia*. The band was signed to Safari in 1979 and released 'Victims Of The Riddle'. In August, Charlie Francis (ex-Patrick Fitzgerald group) replaced Henry. Toyah's extravagant vocal style and arresting lyrical subject matter were particularly evident on the powerful 'Bird In Flight'. While she was appearing in *Quatermass* the band started recording the *Sheep Farming In Barnet* mini-album. 1979 was one of Toyah's busiest years as she also hosted the *Look! Hear!* television series for BBC Midland, had a bit part in *Shoestring*, and made several other acting appearances. She was considered for the leading role in *Breaking Glass*, but it was eventually offered to Hazel O'Connor. Further singles followed the release of *Blue Meaning*, before Toyah was rewarded with the success of the *Four From Toyah* EP in 1981. Of the offerings, the repetitive lisp of 'Its A Mystery' carved out her identity with both public and press. Her first UK Top 10 hit, 'I Want To Be Free' came across as a petulant nursery anthem, but was attractive enough to appeal to a nation's teenagers. 1981 ended with Toyah's biggest hit, the exuberant 'Thunder In The Mountains', which peaked at number 4. The following year, she also charted with the startling, hypnotic 'Ieya' and the raucous 'Be Loud Be Proud (Be Heard)'. Bogan remained by her side musically but subsequent albums were recorded using session musicians instead of the band. Further acting roles came with the movie *The Tempest* and the stage play *Trafford Tanzi*. She became a Buddhist, married guitarist Robert Fripp and later recorded with him. She stayed with Safari until *Minx*, after which she went to Epic and then EG. Her last major hit was with a cover of 'Echo Beach' in 1987. In Autumn 1991 she was appearing with Tim Piggott-Smith in Peter Shaffer's *Amadeus Of Bradford*.
Albums: *Sheep Farming In Barnet* (1980), *The Blue Meaning* (1980), *Toyah Toyah Toyah* (1981), *Anthem* (1981), *The Changeling* (1982), *Warrior Rock (Toyah On Tour)* (1982), *Love Is The Law* (1983), *Minx* (1985), *Mayhem* (1985), *Desire* (1987), *Prostitute* (1988), *Ophelia's Shadow* (1991).

T'Pau

Formed in 1986, this UK group began as a songwriting partnership between vocalist Carol Decker (b. 10 September 1957, London, England) and guitarist Ronnie Rogers (b. 13 March 1959, Shrewsbury, England). While recording a demonstration disc, they were joined by session musicians Michael Chetwood (b. 26 August 1954, Shrewsbury, England; keyboards), Paul Jackons (b. 8 August 1961; bass) and Tim Burgess (b. 6 October 1961, Shrewsbury, England; drums). The group then signed to Siren Records as T'Pau, the name being taken from a character in the science fiction television series *Star Trek*. Having acquired the services of producer Roy Thomas Baker, T'Pau recorded their first sessions in Los Angeles. The group's first two singles failed to make any impact in the UK market, until 'Heart And Soul' abruptly established them in the US charts, where it climbed to number 4 in 1987. The song was re-promoted in Britain and repeated that chart placing. In order to bolster the line-up, lead guitarist Dean Howard was recruited and a major UK tour followed. The flame-haired Decker's strong, expressive vocals were highlighted on 'China In Your Hand', which topped the UK charts, a feat repeated by *Bridge Of Spies*. Further Top 20 hits with 'Valentine', 'I Will Be With You' and 'Secret Garden' and two more albums consolidated their standing, without threatening a return to peak form.
Albums: *Bridge Of Spies* (1987), *Rage* (1988), *Promise* (1991).

Transvision Vamp

Transvision Vamp

Transvision Vamp was founded by the media-conscious Wendy James (b. 21 January 1966, London, England) and songwriter/guitarist Nick Christian Sayer (b. 1 August 1964). The group was completed by the arrival of Tex Axile (b. 30 July 1963; keyboards), Dave Parsons (b. 2 July 1962; bass) and Pol Burton (1 July 1964; drums). The band borrowed heavily, in terms of image and content, from a variety of sources such as T. Rex, the Clash

Triffids; David McComb

and most notably, Blondie. James was frequently compared, unusually favourably, to Blondie's former lead singer, the peroxide blonde Debbie Harry. Despite being an easy target for her detractors, James filled the space that had been long open for a British female teenage-rebel figure. On signing to MCA Records, Transvision Vamp made their initial foray on to the UK pop scene in 1987 with the single, 'Revolution Baby', but it was not until the cover of Holly And The Italians' 'Tell That Girl To Shut Up' that they made any impact on the UK chart, while the follow-up, 'I Want Your Love' reached the UK Top 5. Their first album, *Pop Art* reached the UK Top 5. In 1989 further single chart hits with 'Baby Don't Care' (number 3), 'The Only One' and 'Landslide Of Love' (both Top 20) paved the way for the number 1 album, *Velveteen*. This run of success halted in 1991, with the result that MCA refused to release *The Little Magnets Versus The Bubble Of Babble* in the UK. Transvision Vamp's low profile since has resulted in persistent rumours of a break-up. James's sense of self-publicity and cheap outrage has given the group's name a consistent high profile, making it increasingly likely that it will be her image and not the group's music that will have any lasting impression.

Albums: *Pop Art* (1988), *Velveteen* (1989), *The Little Magnets Versus The Bubble Of Babble* (1991).

Trettine, Caroline

b. Caroline Halcrow. Former Blue Aeroplanes member Trettine left the group in 1987 (where she appeared under her real name) and forged a solo career as an acoustic guitar playing singer/songwriter in the mould of Joni Mitchell and contemporary Tanita Tikaram. Her strength lay in the haunting and melancholic style of such songs as 'Sleep With Me' and 'Guilty, Imagination And Turning'. She signed to Billy Bragg's re-activated Utility label, recording one mini-album with assistance from Nick Jacobs (electric guitar), Ian Kearey (electric and acoustic guitar) and Tone Bank (drums). Her later live performances in London drew much critical praise upon which she has yet to capitalize.
Album: *Be A Devil* (1990).

Triffids

Hailing from the isolated Western Australian city of Perth, David McComb's group has, along with the Go-Betweens and Nick Cave, contributed greatly to increasing the northern hemisphere's respect for Antipodean rock, which for a long time was seldom taken seriously. The line-up was completed by McComb (b. 1962; lead vocals/guitar/keyboards), 'Evil' Graham Lee (pedal and lap steel guitar), Jill Birt (keyboards/vocals), Robert McComb (violin/guitar/vocals), Martyn Casey (bass) and Alsy MacDonald (drums/vocals). The group's biggest success, providing the great break-through into the European market was 1986's *Born Sandy Devotional* on the Australian independent Hot label. This atmospheric set boasted a brooding, almost Bruce Springsteen-like 'Wide Open Road' and the desolate 'Sea Birds'. The follow-up found the Triffids returning to a simpler recording technique - an outback sheep-shearing shed and an eight-track recorder, producing a collection of Australian C&W/folk-blues songs. Departing from Hot, the Triffids landed a major deal with Island Records. McComb's lyrics, which are starkly evocative of the rural Australian townships and psyche, reached new peaks on *The Black Swan*, their most mature set to date. *Stockholm* was a live set released on the MNW label

Albums: *Treeless Plain* (1983), *Raining Pleasure* (1984), *Born Sandy Devotional* (1986), *In The Pines* (1986), *Calenture* (1987), *The Black Swan* (1989), *Stockholm* (1990, a live set).

Truth

This UK Mod/R&B outfit unconnected to the 60s group of the same name were built around lead vocalist and guitarist Dennis Greaves (ex-Nine Below Zero). The line-up was completed by his co-writer Mick Lister (guitar/vocals), Brian Bethell (bass), Chris Skornia (Hammond organ) and Gary Wallis (drums). Greaves had grown tired of his former band's restrictive format, though it must be said that the Truth's brand of 60s soul was more energetic than original. Strategically they opted against joining the Jam's Respond label, strong comparisons to the former were already taking place in the media. Despite their obvious roots in mod fashion and music, the Truth would actually employ Spandau Ballet producers Tony Swain and Steve Jolley to craft a more modern pop sound. Their brief flirtation with chart success began with 'Confusion (Hits Us Every Time)', and followed through 'Step In The Right Direction', and 'No Stone Unturned'. These, their only chart hits, were all released on the Formation label, before they signed with IRS for one album. In 1987 they moved on to MCA, but returned to IRS the following year (as Dennis Greaves And The Truth). Under that moniker they recorded a version of Argent's 'God Gave Rock 'N' Roll To You' produced by Andy Piercy (ex-After The Fire), but this too failed to chart.

Albums: *Playground* (1985), *Weapons Of Love* (1987).

Tubes

Never short of personnel, the Tubes comprised Rick Anderson (b. 1 August 1947, Saint Paul, Minnesota, USA; bass), Michael Cotten (b. 25 January 1950, Kansas City, Missouri, USA; keyboards), Prairie Prince (b. 7 May 1950, Charlotte, North Carolina, USA; drums), Bill Spooner (b. 16 April 1949, Phoenix, Arizona, USA; guitar). Roger Steen (b. 13 November 1949, Pipestone, Minnesota, USA; guitar), Re Styles b. 3 March 1950, USA; vocals), Fee Waybill (b. John Waldo, 17 September 1950, Omaha, Nebraska, USA; vocals) and Vince Welnick (b. 21 February 1951, Phoenix, Arizona, USA; keyboards). Founder members Anderson, Spooner and Welmick got together in Phoenix in the late 60s, but it was in San Francisco in 1972 that the Tubes were born. Fronted by Waybill, the band's stage act became wilder and crazier, a manic mixture of loud rock music, outrageous theatrics and burlesque. The videos were risque with scantily-clad women, a 'drugged-out superstar' Quay Lude and 'a crippled Nazi' Dr. Strangekiss. The group were signed to A&M Records in 1975 and their debut album, produced by Al Kooper, included the bombastic UK Top 30 hit 'White Punks On Dope'. Their alleged sexism was tempered somewhat during the late 70s. Their fourth album, *Remote Control*, was produced by Todd Rundgren, after which they left A&M for Capitol Records. *Completion Backward Principle* was regarded as a compromise, despite its flashes of humour. The group's satirical thrust declined due to over-familiarity but prior to their demise, they enjoyed their greatest commercial success with the US Top 10 hit 'She's A Beauty' in 1983.

Albums: *The Tubes* (1975), *Young And Rich* (1976), *Now* (1977), *What Do You Want From Your Life* (1978), *Remote Control* (1979), *Completion Backward Principle* (1981), *Outside Inside* (1983). Compilation: *T.R.A.S.H./Best Of The Tubes* (1981).

Tucker, Maureen 'Mo'

b. 1945, New Jersey, USA. Maureen Tucker was a computer key-puncher who played drums part-time, when she was invited to join the nascent Velvet Underground in 1965. She remained an integral part of this highly-influencial attraction until its protracted disintegration seven years later. Tucker then retired from music, married and raised a family, but rekindled her career in 1980 with a single which coupled Chuck Berry's 'Around And Around' with the Shirelles' 'Will You Still Love Me Tomorrow'. The record was successfully distributed from the artist's home, and ensuing interest inspired the subsequent *Playin' Possum*. Recorded in piecemeal fashion over a year, the album offered a charmingly naive, post-punk style and included several of Tucker's favourite songs, notably Bob Dylan's 'I'll Be

Your Baby Tonight' and the Velvet Underground's 'Heroin'. Maureen then formed a short-lived group, Paris 1942, but did not record again until 1986 when she teamed with Jad Fair from Half Japanese for the *MoeJadKateBarry* EP. Fair also appeared on *Life In Exile After Abdication*, which was recorded in New York. Ex-colleague Lou Reed joined members of Sonic Youth in contributing to a highly-acclaimed set, and her rekindled relationship with the former helped inspire a brief Velvet Underground reunion in Paris in 1990. The entire group, albeit mostly separately, was featured on *I Spent A Week There The Other Night* on which Tucker continued her idiosyncratic, but fascinating, musical path.

Albums: *Playin' Possum* (1981), *Life In Exile After Abdication* (1989), *I Spent A Week There The Other Night* (1991).

TV Smith's Explorers

Formed from the punk debris of the Adverts, the Explorers saw TV Smith (vocals) and Tim Cross (guitar) combine with Erik Russell (guitar), Colin Stoner (bass) and John Towe (drums). After only one gig at the Marquee in March 1980, Cross quit and, three performances later, Towe followed suit. With Mel Wesson and Dave Sinclair, respectively, stopping the musical gap, the new line-up signed to Chiswick Records. The musically aggressive 'Tomahawk Cruise' was voted single of the week in the music paper *Sounds*, but failed to chart. Over the next two years, the group recorded several singles and an album for the Epic subsidiary Kaleidoscope, until Smith moved on to a short-lived solo career. After recording 'War Fever' and *Channel Five* (1983), he formed a new group Cheap, though he remains best known for his work with the Adverts.

Album: *Last Words Of The Great Explorer* (1981), *Channel Five* (1983).

20/20

This US group was formed in Los Angeles, California, in 1978 by Steve Allen (guitar/vocals) and Ron Flynt (bass/vocals), two ex-patriot musicians from Tulsa, Oklahoma. Drummer Mike Gallo completed the line-up featured on the group's early work for Bomp!, a leading independent label, which in turn inspired a major deal with Columbia Records' subsidiary Portrait. *20/20* was produced by former Sparks' vocalist Earl Mankey and featured newcomer Chris Silagyi (keyboards). Despite commercial indifference, its superior brand of power-pop was a critical success, and drew favourable comparisons with the Dwight Twilley Band. Gallo was later replaced by Joel Turrisi (ex-Gary Valentine And The Know), but when successive, meritorious albums failed to further the group's career, 20/20 was disbanded.

Albums: *20/20* (1979), *Look Out* (1981), *Sex Trap* (1983).

Twinkeyz

The Twinkeyz were one of the originators of a small, but thriving new wave scene in Sacramento, California, USA. Donnie Jupiter (guitar/bass/vocals), Honey (guitar/bass/vocals), Tom Darling (guitar/bass) and Keith McKee (drums) began performing together in 1976 and secured their early reputation with a series of excellent singles, notably 'Aliens In Our Midst'. This quirky composition inspired a cult following for the group when copies were imported to Europe and the Twinkeyz' lone album, *Alpha Jerk*, was released on the Dutch-based Plurex label. The quartet split up soon afterwards, following which Darling joined another Sacramento attraction, the Veil, before switching to Game Theory, the city's prime pop/rock attraction.

Album: *Alpha Jerk* (1979).

2 Live Crew

Formed in 1985 in Miami, Florida, USA, the rap group 2 Live Crew were to prove highly controversial. In 1990 they became the focus of the anti-censorship movement in the USA after a judge in Broward County, Florida ruled that their *As Nasty As They Wanna Be*, was obscene. It was the first record to be deemed so legally in the country. The group consists of Luther Campbell, also the founder of Luke Skywalker Records (shortened to Luke Records when film-maker George Lucas, who created the Luke Skywalker character in the film *Star Wars*, filed suit), rappers Trinidad-born Chris Wong Won, New Yorker Mark Ross and California DJ David Hobbs. Their frequently offensive lyrics to songs with titles such as 'We Want Some Pussy', 'Me So Horny' and 'Head, Booty And Cock', became a quick target for local law enforcement agencies. Advocates of record stickering such as the Parents Music Resource Center (PMRC) and Florida attorney/evangelist Jack Thompson, argued strongly that the group's records should not be available for sale to minors. The controversy escalated until even Florida Governor, Bob Martinez stated that he felt the group's records were obscene. A retail record store owner was subsequently arrested for selling a copy of their *Move Somethin'* - albeit to an adult. The salesman was later acquitted. The group itself was then arrested for performing music from the *Nasty* album in an adults-only club, sparking charges by anti-censorship groups that the law enforcement officials were over-zealous. Meanwhile, the controversy and attendant press coverage boosted sales of their album into the US Top 40. In the summer of 1990, 2 Live Crew recorded a 'clean' single about the controversy, 'Banned In The USA',

using music from Bruce Springsteen's 'Born In The USA' with the latter's permission.
Albums: *The 2 Live Crew Is What We Are* (1986), *Move Somethin'* (1988), *As Nasty As They Wanna Be* (US) *As Clean As They Wanna Be* (UK) (1990).

Two Nice Girls

Two Nice Girls from Austin, Texas, USA, emerged as a trio in 1989 and by the following year had expanded to a quartet. Gretchen Phillips, Kathy Korniloff and Laurie Freelove were the nucleus that sang and played guitars on the group's debut *2 Nice Girls*. An enticing work, filled with entwining vocal arrangements, the album showed the girls capable of writing songs of great sensitivity and humour. Phillips' songs, ranging from the sensuous 'The Sweet Postcard' (co-composed by Barbara Hofrenning) to the feminist Nashville pastiche 'I Spent My Last $10.00 (On Birth Control And Beer)' and the tenderly penetrating narrative of jealousy 'My Heart Crawls Off' announced the arrival of a considerable talent. Both Freelove and Korniloff also offered strong arrangements and well-scripted lyrics on such songs as 'Money' and 'The Holland Song'. A mini-album of covers, including a second airing of their fusion of the Velvet Underground's 'Sweet Jane' and Joan Armatrading's 'Love And Affection', followed. Line-up fluctuations in 1990 saw the apparent departure of Freelove and the arrival of Pam Barger and Meg Hentges.
Albums: *2 Nice Girls* (1989), *Like A Version* (1990).
Solo album: Laurie Freelove *Smells Like Truth* (1991).

Tyla, Sean

b. 3 August 1947, Barlow, Yorkshire, England. Guitarist/vocalist Tyla established his reputation with Geno Washington (And The Ram Jam Band) and pianist Freddie 'Fingers' Lee. Between 1972-75 he led Ducks Deluxe, a tough R&B band which was at the fore front of the UK pre-punk, pub rock scene, and highly popular in France. However, the lack of commercial success doomed the group to a premature demise, following which Tyla formed the Tyla Gang: Bruce Irvine (guitar), Mike Desmarais (drums) and Ken Whaley (bass, ex-Ducks and Help Yourself). The group were one of the first acts signed to Stiff Records releasing the lone single 'Styrofoam' in 1976 before completing *Yachtless* and *Moonshot* for the US-based Beserkley label. However, once again Tyla's ambitions proved uncommercial and the group broke up at the end of the 70s.
Albums: with the Tyla Gang *Yachtless* (1977), *Moonshot* (1978).

UB40

Named after the card issued to unemployed people in Britain to receive benefit, UB40 were the most long-lasting proponents of crossover reggae in the UK. The multi-racial band was formed around the brothers Robin (b. 25 December 1954, Birmingham, England; lead guitar) and Ali Campbell (b. 15 February 1959, Birmingham, England; lead vocals/guitar), the sons of Birmingham folk club singers Lorna and Ian Campbell. Other founder members included Earl Falconer (b. 23 January 1957, Birmingham, England; bass), Mickey Virtue (b. 19 January 1957, Birmingham, England; keyboards), Brian Travers (b. 7 February 1959; saxophone), Jim Brown (b. 21 November 1957; drums), and Norman Hassan (b. 26 January 1958, Birmingham, England; percussion). Reggae toaster Astro (b. Terence Wilson, 24 June 1957) joined UB40 to record 'Food For Thought' with local producer Bob Lamb (former drummer with Locomotive and the Steve Gibbons band). 'King' (coupled with 'Food For Thought') was a tribute to Martin Luther King. The debut *Signing Off*, boasted an album sleeve with a 12-inch square replica of the notorious, bright yellow unemployment card. This image attracted a large contingent of disaffected youth as well as proving popular with followers of the Two-Tone/ska scene. The following year the group formed their own label DEP International on which they released 'One In Ten', an impassioned protest about unemployment. *Labour Of Love*, a collection of cover versions, signalled a return to the reggae mainstream and it brought UB40's first number 1 in 'Red Red Wine' (1983). Originally written by Neil Diamond, it had been a big reggae hit for Tony Tribe in 1969. The album contained further hit singles in Jimmy Cliff's 'Many Rivers To Cross' (1983) and Eric Donaldson's 'Cherry Oh Baby' (1984). The follow-up, *Geoffrey Morgan*, a UK number 3 album, supplied the group with the Top 10 hit 'If It Happens Again'. 'I Got You Babe' (1986) was a different kind of cover version as Ali Campbell and Chrissie Hynde of the Pretenders duetted on the Sonny And Cher hit.
The same team had a further hit in 1988 with a revival of Lorna Bennett's 1969 reggae song 'Breakfast In Bed'. *Rat In Mi Kitchen* included the African liberation anthem 'Sing Our Own Song' with Herb Alpert on trumpet. After performing 'Red Red Wine' at the 1988 Nelson Mandela, Wembley concert, re-promotion in the USA resulted in the single reaching the number 1 spot. The group had

further single success with the Chi-lites' 'Homely Girl' (1989) and 'Kingston Town' (1990), both of which would appear on a second volume of cover versions, *Labour Of Love II*. In 1990, the group had separate Top 10 hits in the UK and USA as a Campbell/Robert Palmer duet on Bob Dylan's 'I'll Be You Baby Tonight' charted in Britain and a revival of the Temptations' 'The Way You Do The Things You Do' was a hit in America. Throughout the 80s, the group toured frequently in Europe and North America and played in Russia in 1986, filming the tour for video release. They have loyally stuck to their chosen musical path for which they now receive considerable success.

Albums: *Signing Off* (1980), *Present Arms* (1981), *Present Arms In Dub* (1981), *UB44* (1982), *UB40 Live* (1983), *Labour Of Love* (1983), *Geffrey Morgan* (1984), *Baggaraddim* (1985), *Rat In Mi Kitchen* (1986), *UB40* (1988), *Labour Of Love II* (1989). Compilations: *The Singles Album* (1982), *The Best Of UB40, Volume I* (1987).

UK Decay

Starting life as the Resistors, they formed in Luton, Bedfordshire, England, in the summer of 1978, a period when many of the original 1977 punk bands were already splitting up. After a few line-up changes, the band stabilized with Abbo (b. John Abbott; vocals/guitar), Segovia (b. Martyn Smith; bass) and Steve Harle (drums). During 1979, Adam And The Ants appeared to be their principle influence, both musically and visually. The Resistors' atmospheric live shows included 'Necrophilia', 'Middle Of The Road Man', 'Rising From The Dread', 'Disco Romance' and 'Christian Disguise'. In May they left behind the name and image of just another anonymous punk band and transformed into UK Decay, the title of one of their songs. 'UK Decay' and 'Carcrash' emerged on the Plastic label in August as part of a joint EP release with Pneu-Mania, another Luton punk band. It was pressed in a very limited edition which quickly sold out and demonstrated an early example of developing gothic punk. The band became a four-piece with the addition of Steve Spon, the guitarist from Pneu-Mania, and in early 1980 they released *The Black Cat* EP, which continued in the same vein as their debut, but with wider distribution. The early 80s saw an huge increase in the popularity of gothic punk and, riding on this crest, UK Decay achieved a great deal of independent chart success with their subsequent releases: 'For My Country', 'Unexpected Guest', 'Sexual', the re-release of *The Black Cat* EP and 'Rising From The Dead'. After Segovia's departure and a brief experimentation with Lol from the disbanded Twiggy, the bass position was finally filled by Eddie Branch. It was almost a year before the

Rising From The Dread EP was released. A few months later the band recorded their farewell concert at 'The Klub Foot' Clarendon Ballroom, Hammersmith, London on the 30 December for the tape-only release *A Night For Celebration*. Albums: *For Madmen Only* (1981), *A Night For Celebration* (1983).

UK Subs

UK Subs

This London band was formed in 1976, by veteran R&B singer Charlie Harper. Recruiting Nicky Garratt (guitar), Paul Slack (bass) and Pete Davies (drums), they specialized in shambolic sub-three minute bursts of alcohol-driven rock 'n' roll. They lacked the image and songs of their peers such as the Damned, Clash and Sex Pistols. The UK Subs released a string of minor classics during the late 70s, including 'I Live In A Car', 'Stranglehold' and 'Tomorrow's Girls'. The latter two dented the lower reaches of the UK Top 40 singles chart. The definitive Subs album was *Crash Course*, which captured the band in all its chaotic glory in front of a live audience. The band's line-up has rarely been stable, with only Harper surviving each new incarnation. The arrival of Alvin Gibbs (bass) and Steve Roberts (drums) marked a change in emphasis, with the band including metal elements in their songs for the first time. Harper also had a side-line project between 1983-85, Urban Dogs who were a Stooges/MC5 influenced garage outfit. The UK Subs are still active today, but their audience continues to diminish. *Mad Cow Fever* released in 1991 is a sad testimony to the band's longevity. It features an even mixture of rock 'n' roll standards and originals, but lacks the drive and spontaneity of old. The current line-up features Harper plus Darrell Barth (guitar), Matthew McCoy (drums) and Flea (bass).

Albums: *Another Kind Of Blues* (1979), *Brand New Age* (1980), *Crash Course* (1980), *Diminished Responsibility* (1981), *Endangered Species* (1982), *Flood Of Lies* (1983), *Demonstration Tapes* (1984), *Gross Out USA* (1984), *Huntington Beach* (1985), *Raw Material* (1986), *Killing Time* (1987), *Left For Dead* (1988), *Recorded 1979-81* (1989), *Japan Today* (1990), *In Action* (1990), *Mad Cow Fever* (1991). Compilation: *Subs Standards* (1989).

Ultravox

The initial premise of Ultravox came from the 70s school of electro-rock from pioneers Kraftwerk and the glam rock of Brian Eno/Roxy Music. Formed in 1974, the early line-up comprised John Foxx (b. Dennis Leigh, Chorley, Lancashire, England; vocals), Steve Shears (guitar), Warren Cann (b. 20 May 1952, Victoria, Canada; drums), Chris Cross (b. Christopher Allen, 14 July 1952; bass) and Billy Currie (b. 1 April 1952; keyboards/synthesizer/violin). Their rise coincided with the ascendancy of the new wave although they were for the most part ignored by a rock press more concerned with the activities of the burgeoning punk scene and consequently live gigs were frequently met with indifference. Signed to Island Records in 1976, their albums made little impact on the record buying public, despite the endorsement of Brian Eno who produced their first album. However, Ultravox's influence on a growing movement of British synthesizer music, in particular Gary Numan, was later acknowledged. Shears was replaced by Robin Simon in 1978, but after *Systems Of Romance* had garnered disappointing sales, Island dropped the act, with both Simon and Foxx (who many felt was the main creative force behind the group) leaving to pursue solo careers.

Ultravox were disbanded while the remaining members took stock. On a sojourn with Visage, Currie met Midge Ure (b. James Ure, 10 October 1953, Cambuslang, Strathclyde, Scotland; lead vocals/guitar) former member of Slik and the Rich Kids. The duo found a compatibility of ideas and decided to revive Ultravox as a quartet with Cross and Currie. Having departed from Island, the group signed to Chrysalis Records. Their new direction brought minor chart success with 'Sleepwalk' and 'Passing Strangers'. It was not until the magnificent 'Vienna' was released that Ultravox found the success that had eluded them for so long. Held at the UK number 2 spot in January and February of 1981 by Joe Dolce's inane 'Shaddap You Face' and hits from the recently murdered John Lennon, the song's moody and eerie atmosphere was enhanced by an enigmatic video. A string of Top 20 hits followed for the next three years, including 'All Stood Still' (1981), 'Reap The Wild Wind' (1982) and 'Dancing With Tears In My Eyes' (1984). Ure's anguished, melodramatic style blended well with the high-energy pop of their contemporaries, Duran Duran and Spandau Ballet, the UK's 'new romantics', finding success elsewhere in Europe, but never quite achieving the same level in the USA. While Ure's simultaneous solo career proved for a short time, successful, group projects became less cohesive. Their last album *U-Vox* was released in 1986, Billy Currie had assumed control of the group, before the unit disintegrated.

Albums: *Ultravox!* (1976), *Ha! Ha! Ha!* (1977), *Systems Of Romance* (1978), *Vienna* (1980), *Rage In Eden* (1981), *Quartet* (1982), *Monument - The Soundtrack* (1983), *Lament* (1984), *U-Vox* (1986). Compilations: *Three Into One* (1980, Island recordings), *The Collection* (1984). Solo album: Billy Currie *Stand Up And Walk* (1990).

Uncle Sam

Formed in 1987, Uncle Sam were the brainchild of guitarist Larry Millar. With the recruitment of fellow New Yorkers David Gentner (vocals), Bill Purol (bass) and Jeff Mann (drums), the band signed with the independent Razor Records. Influenced by both the punk and thrash movements, their songs were short, frantic and often devoid of melody. Gentner's vocals were monotonous, while the back beat lacked depth and colour. At best they came across as an updated, but pale version of the Stooges or MC5.

Albums: *Heaven Or Hollywood* (1988), *Letters From London* (1990).

Undertones

Formed in Londonderry, Northern Ireland, this much-loved punk/pop quintet comprised Feargal Sharkey (b. 13 August 1958, Londonderry, Northern Ireland; vocals), John O'Neill (guitar), Damian O'Neill (guitar), Michael Bradley (bass) and Billy Doherty (drums). By 1978, the group were signed to the Belfast label Good Vibrations. Their debut single, 'Teenage Kicks', was heavily promoted by the influential BBC disc jockey John Peel, who later nominated the track as his all-time favourite recording, saying that he cried when he first heard it. By the spring of 1979, the group had entered the Top 20 with the infectious 'Jimmy Jimmy' and gained considerable acclaim for their debut album, which was one of the most refreshing pop records of its time. The group's genuinely felt songs of teenage angst and small romance struck a chord with young

Undertones

listeners and ingratiated them to an older public weaned on the great tradition of early/mid-60s pop. *Hypnotised* was a more accomplished work, which featured strongly melodic hit singles in 'My Perfect Cousin' and 'Wednesday Week'. The former was particularly notable for its acerbic humour, including the sardonic lines: 'His mother bought him a synthesizer/she got the Human League in to advise her'.

Following a major tour of the USA, the group completed *Postive Touch* in 1981. The insistent 'It's Going To Happen' was a deserved success, but the romantic 'Julie Ocean' was not rewarded in chart terms. The Undertones' maturity did not always work in their favour as some critics longed for the innocence and naïvety of their initial recordings. With *The Sin Of Pride* and attendant 'The Love Parade' the group displayed a willingness to extend their appeal, both musically with the introduction of brass, and thematically with less obvious lyrics. With a growing need to explore new areas outside the restrictive Undertones banner, the group ended their association in June 1983. Sharkey went on to team up with Vince Clarke in the short-lived Assembly, before finding considerable success as a soloist. The O'Neill brothers subsequently formed the critically-acclaimed That Petrol Emotion.

Albums: *The Undertones* (1979), *Hypnotised* (1980), *Positive Touch* (1981), *The Sin Of Pride* (1983). Compilation: *All Wrapped Up* (1983), *Cher O'Bowlies: Pick Of Undertones* (1986).

Ure, Midge

b. James Ure, 10 October 1953, Cambuslang, Strathclyde, Scotland. Midge Ure began his professional career as guitarist/vocalist with Salvation, a popular Glasgow-based act which evolved into Slik in 1974. Although accomplished musicians, Slik's recording contract bound them to ill-fitting, 'teenybop' material, reminiscent of fellow-Scots the Bay City Rollers. Frustrated at this artistic impasse, Ure opted to join the Rich Kids, a punk/pop act, centred on former Sex Pistols' bassist Glen Matlock. However, despite strong support from EMI Records, the group's chemistry did not gel and they disbanded in November 1978, barely a year after inception. Midge subsequently joined the short-lived Misfits before founding Visage with Steve Strange (vocals) and Rusty Egan (drums). Ure's involvement with this informal 'new romantic' act ended when he replaced Gary Moore in Thin Lizzy midway through an extensive US tour. His position, however, was purely temporary as the artist had already agreed to join Ultravox, who rose from cult status to become one of the most popular acts of the early 80s. The ever-industrious Ure also produced sessions for Steve Harley and Modern Man, and in 1982 enjoyed a UK Top 10 solo hit with his version of 'No Regrets', penned by Tom Rush and previously a hit for the Walker Brothers. Two years later he formed Band Aid with Bob Geldof. Their joint composition, the multi-million selling 'Do They Know It's Christmas?', was inspired by harrowing film footage of famine conditions in Ethiopia and featured an all-star cast of pop contemporaries. This commitment completed, and with Ultravox in suspension, Ure resumed his solo career with *The Gift*. The album spawned a number 1 single, 'If I Was', since which the singer has enjoyed further success with 'That Certain Smile' (1985) and 'Call Of The Wild' (1986). However a second set, *Answers To Nothing* proved less successful. This effort was followed up until three years later when the singer, now signed to Arista Records, produced a new album in autumn 1991. He resurfaced with little fanfare in 1991 and immediately went back into the UK Top 20 charts with 'Cold, Cold Heart' which was closely followed by *Pure*. This clearly demonstrated that Ure had not lost his touch and that he still retained a considerable following for his blend of quality pop music.

Albums: *The Gift* (1985), *Answers To Nothing* (1988), *Pure* (1991).

U2

Indisputably, the most popular group of the 80s in

Britain, Irish unit U2 began their musical career at school in Dublin back in 1977. Bono (b. Paul Hewson, 10 May 1960, Dublin, Eire; vocals), The Edge (b. David Evans, 8 August 1961, Barking, Essex; guitar), Adam Clayton (b. 13 March 1960, Chinnor, Oxfordshire, England; bass) and Larry Mullen (b. Laurence Mullen, 1 October 1960, Dublin, Eire; drums) initially played Rolling Stones and Beach Boys cover versions in a group named Feedback. They then changed their name to the Hype before finally settling on U2 in 1978. After winning a talent contest in Limerick that year, they came under the wing of manager Paul McGuinness and were subsequently signed to CBS Ireland. Their debut EP *U2:3* featured 'Out Of Control' (1979), which propelled them to number 1 in the Irish charts. They repeated that feat with 'Another Day' (1980), but having been passed by CBS UK, they were free to sign a deal outside of Ireland with Island Records. Their UK debut '11 O'Clock Tick Tock', produced by Martin Hannett, was well received but failed to chart. Two further singles, 'A Day Without Me' and 'I Will Follow', passed with little sales while the group prepared their first album, produced by Steve Lillywhite.

Boy, a moving and inspired document of adolescence, received critical approbation, which was reinforced by the live shows that U2 were undertaking throughout the country. Bono's impassioned vocals and the group's rhythmic tightness revealed them as the most promising live unit of 1981. After touring America, the group returned to Britain where 'Fire' was bubbling under the Top 30. Another minor hit with the impassioned 'Gloria' was followed by the strident *October*. The album had an anthemic thrust reinforced by a religious verve that was almost evangelical in its force. In February 1983 the group reached the UK Top 10 with 'New Year's Day', a song of hope inspired by the Polish Solidarity Movement. *War* followed soon after to critical plaudits. The album's theme covered both religious and political conflicts, especially in the key track 'Sunday Bloody Sunday', which had already emerged as one of the group's most startling and moving live songs. Given their power in concert, it was inevitable that U2 would attempt to capture their essence on a live album. *Under A Blood Red Sky* did not disappoint and as well as climbing to number 2 in the UK brought them their first significant chart placing in the US at number 28.

By the summer of 1984, U2 were about to enter the vanguard of the rock elite. Bono duetted with Bob Dylan at the latter's concert at Slane Castle and U2 established their own company Mother Records, with the intention of unearthing fresh musical talent in Eire. *The Unforgettable Fire*, produced by Brian Eno and Daniel Lanois, revealed a new maturity and improved their commercial and critical standing in the US charts. The attendant single, 'Pride (In The Name Of Love)', displayed the passion and humanity that were by now familiar ingredients in U2's music and lyrics. The group's commitment to their ideals was further underlined by their appearances at Live Aid, Ireland's Self Aid, and their involvment with Amnesty International and guest spot on Little Steven's anti-Apartheid single, 'Sun City'. During this same period, U2 embarked on a world tour and completed work on their next album. *The Joshua Tree* emerged in March 1987 and confirmed U2's standing, now as one of the most popular groups in the world. The album topped both the US and UK charts and revealed a new, more expansive sound, which complemented their soul-searching lyrics. The familiar themes of spiritual salvation permeated the work and the quest motif was particularly evident on both 'With Or Without You' and 'I Still Haven't Found What I'm Looking For', which both reached number 1 in the US charts. After such a milestone album, 1988 proved a relatively quiet year for the group. Bono and the Edge appeared on Roy Orbison's *Mystery Girl* and the year ended with the double-live album and film, *Rattle And Hum*. The group also belatedly scored their first UK number 1 single with the R&B-influenced 'Desire'. The challenge to complete a suitable follow-up to *The Joshua Tree* took considerable time, with sessions completed in Germany with Lanois and Eno. Meanwhile, the group appeared on the Cole Porter tribute album *Red Hot + Blue*, performing a radical reading of 'Night And Day'. In late 1991, 'The Fly' entered the UK charts at number 1, emulating the success of 'Desire'. *Achtung Baby* was an impressive work, which captured the majesty of its predecessor yet also stripped down the sound to provide a greater sense of spontaneity. The work emphasized U2's standing as an international group, whose achievements since the late 70s have been extraordinarily cohesive and consistent.

Albums: *Boy* (1980), *October* (1981), *War* (1983), *Under A Blood Red Sky* (1983), *The Unforgettable Fire* (1984), *Wide Awake In America* (1985), *The Joshua Tree* (1987), *Rattle And Hum* (1988), *Achtung Baby* (1991).

Further reading: *Unforgettable Fire: The Story Of U2*, Eamon Dunphy. *The U2 File: A Hot Press U2 History*, ed. Niall Stokes. *U2: Three Chords And The Truth*, ed. Niall Stokes. *Rattle And Hum*, Peter Williams and Steve Turner.

V

Valley Of The Dolls

This UK group was formed in 1987 by ex-Geisha Girl Jill Myhill (vocals/keyboards) and ex-Fischer Z member Mandy Monkham (vocals), with a flux of transient personnel. Breaking away from the confines of their native Berkshire, they were to prove popular on the London club circuit as well as in northern Europe, with Myhill's street -urchin charm a potent ingredient for their success. Monkham and Myhill also became much in demand as session musicians for Dave Berry, Red Lorry Yellow Lorry and Alan Clayson. However, with no product in their own right issued, Monkham elected to front a new group while Myhill moved centre stage in a Valley Of The Dolls with Leila Liran (guitar), Beverley de Schoolmeester (bass) and Vas Antoniadou (drums) as permanent members, and a self-composed repertoire flavoured with a quirkiness that made songs like 'Where Were You', 'Driver' and 'Hello (Your World Is Next To Me)' distinctive. Produced by That Petrol Emotion's Steve Mac, the latter was the single attending *Cloud Cuckoo*.
Album: *Cloud Cuckoo* (1992).

Vapors

This UK power pop quartet, based in Guildford, Surrey, England, came together officially in April 1979, although an earlier incarnation had existed a year earlier. The common thread was Dave Fenton, a graduate who dabbled in the legal profession before turning to music. His first band, the Little Jimmies, was formed while he studied at Nottingham University. To his rhythm guitar and vocals were added the lead guitar of Ed Bazalgette and the drums of Howard Smith, both former members of the Ellery Bops. The line-up was completed by former Absolute drummer Steve Smith, who switched over to bass guitar. An early Vapors gig was watched by the Jam's Bruce Foxton who was impressed by their gutsy pop, not unlike the Jam's own style, and invited them to appear on the *Setting Sons* tour. Foxton also became the band's manager in partnership with John Weller. After a promising but unsuccessful debut single, 'Prisoners' for United Artists, the follow-up 'Turning Japanese' catapulted them to number 3 in the UK charts. By May 1980 *New Clear Days* was released. The most notable track was the single 'News At Ten', which underlined teenage insecurity with a power pop beat that recalled the Kinks. *Magnets* was more adventurous, with the lyrical focus moving from the Oriental to Americana. Unfortunately the band were receiving few plaudits for their ambitious efforts, with most critics unable to move away from the earlier Jam comparisons, which were no longer valid. The band disappeared from the scene quickly; the most recent sighting of Dave Fenton was as the landlord of a public house in Woking, Surrey.
Albums: *New Clear Days* (1980), *Magnets* (1981).

Vega, Suzanne

b. 12 August 1959, New York City, New York, USA. Vega is a highly literate singer-songwriter who found international success in the late 80s. She studied dance at the High School For the Performing Arts (as featured in the *Fame* television series) and at Barnard College, singing her own material in New York folk clubs. Signed by A&M Records in 1984, she recorded her first album with Lenny Kaye, former guitarist with Patti Smith. From this, 'Marlene On The Wall', a tale of bedsitter angst, became a hit. In 1987 'Luka' grabbed even more attention with its evocation of the pain of child abuse told from the victim's point of view. Vega's 'Left Of Center' appeared on the soundtrack of the film *Pretty In Pink* and she also contributed lyrics for two tracks on *Songs From Liquid Days* by Philip Glass. On her third album, Vega collaborated with keyboards player and co-producer Anton Sanko, who brought a new tightness to the sound. Meanwhile, Vega's lyrics took on a more surreal and precise character, notably on 'Book Of Dreams' and 'Men In A War', which dealt with the plight of amputees. In 1990 the serendipitous 'Tom's Diner' from *Solitude Standing* became a hit in Britain after it had been sampled by the group DNA. The track was remixed by Alan Coulthard for Vega's label A&M; its success led to the release of an album, *Tom's Album* (1991), devoted entirely to reworkings of the song by such artists as R.E.M. and rapper Nikki D. Vega was presumably bemused by the whole series of events.
Albums: *Suzanne Vega* (1985), *Solitude Standing* (1987), *Days Of Open Hand* (1990).

Verlaine, Tom

b. Thomas Miller, 13 December 1949, Mount Morris, New Jersey, USA. Trained as a classical pianist, guitarist/vocalist Verlaine became interested in rock music upon hearing the Rolling Stones' '19th Nervous Breakdown'. In 1968 he gravitated to New York's lower east side , and formed the Neon Boys with bassist Richard Hell and drummer Billy Ficca. Although collapsing within weeks, the band inspired the founding of Television, which made its debut in March 1974. Verlaine's desire for a regular venue transformed CBGB's from a struggling bar into New York's premier punk haven. Although his own group did not secure a major deal until 1976, his flourishing guitar work appeared on early releases by the Patti

Smith Group. Television's debut, *Marquee Moon*, was acclaimed a classic, although a lukewarm reception for the ensuing *Adventure* exacerbated inner tensions. The group was disbanded in 1978, and Verlaine began a solo career. *Tom Verlaine* and *Dreamtime* continued the themes of the artist's former outlet, but failed to reap due commercial reward. *Words From The Front*, which featured the lengthy 'Days On The Mountain', attracted considerable UK interest and when *Cover* was issued to fulsome reviews, Verlaine took up temporary residence in London. *Flash Light* and *Kaleidscopin'* revealed a undiminished talent with the latter, his most consistent release to date. Verlaine's gifted lyricism and brittle, yet shimmering, guitar work has ensured a reputation as one of rock's innovative and respected talents. In 1991 a decision was made to reform the original Television line-up and the following year was spent in rehearsals and recording. Meanwhile, Verlaine continued with his solo career, releasing the instrumental set *Warm And Cool* early in 1992.
Albums: *Tom Verlaine* (1979), *Dreamtime* (1981), *Words From The Front* (1983), *Cover* (1985), *Flash Light* (1987), *Kaleidsocopin'* (1990), *Warm And Cool* (1992).

Very Things

The Very Things were one of various outfits launched under the umbrella organization of the Dada Cravats Laboratory (DcL), based in Redditch, Worcestershire, England. This group operated a number of musical projects under Dada principals: 'Using that banner was a lot simpler than delivering lengthy manifestos'. The key personnel involved were The Shend (vocals) and Robin R. Dallaway (aka Robin Raymond; guitar), plus Gordon 'DisneyTime' (drums), and Fudger O'Mad aka Budge (ex-And Also The Trees; bass). Other groups operating out of the same stable included the Cravats, Babymen, and DcL Locomotive. Their first single, 'The Gong Man' explored responsibility and the work ethic. Although they were coming from a less strident political standpoint, they found allies in anarcho-punk band Crass, with this being the second of two singles coming out on their label (the previous one under the Cravats logo being 'Rub Me Out'). On the back of this, and a very successful radio session for BBC disc jockey John Peel, they were signed to Reflex Records for the release of *The Bushes Scream While My Daddy Prunes'*. An early appearance on television music programme *The Tube* helped bolster their fortunes, while the follow-up single 'Mummy You're A Wreck' was an equally entertaining offbeat production. After a series of personnel changes, they folded in 1988, leaving behind the Motown-influenced *Motortown* (produced by Ray Shulman ex-Gentle Giant and Derek Birkett

ex-Flux Of Pink Indians). The Shend turned to an acting career appearing in television series such as *The Bill* and *Eastenders* playing, somewhat predictably, intimidating characters. The two 'Robs' departed to form their own band under the title Hit The Roof.
Albums: *The Bushes Scream While My Daddy Prunes* (1984), *Motortown* (1988).

Vice Squad

Formed in Bristol, England, in 1978, the Vice Squad emerged from two local bands, the Contingent and TV Brakes. The Vice Squad's line-up comprised Beki Bondage (b. Rebecca Louise Bond, 3 June 1963, Bristol, England; vocals) Dave Bateman (guitar) Mark Hambly (bass) and Shane Baldwin (drums). Their first single, 'Last Rockers' was released on their own Riot City Records in 1980, and brought them some press in the weekly music press paper, *Sounds*. Their EPs *Resurrection* and *Out Of Reach* were distinctively melodic. However, the debut album was disappointing. After signing a deal licensing the Riot City label to EMI, for which they would come in for a fair amount of criticism from politically-minded punk artists, they were rushed into the studio. Taking only three days, the finished product was barely listenable. Much more polish went in to the superior *Stand Strong Stand Proud*, only six months later. Despite Beki's increasingly high profile and naïve exploitation of her sex (she was voted 'Punk's Prime Minister' in an absurd contest in *Punk Lives!* magazine), EMI wanted their success to transfer from the independent to national chart. Bondage left amid some degree of acrimony, commenting: 'It was very hard. I'd wanted to go for about a year. I realised that I wasn't doing anything. Looking back, it seems a funny situation. I joined when I was 15, the others were 17 and 18, and everyone was really nasty from the start. I never liked them and they never liked me.' The singer formed the short-lived Ligotage and then Beki And The Bombshells, while the band continued for a short time, recruiting a new female singer called Lia and guitarist Sooty. They released three excellent singles and an album, *Shot Away*.
Albums: *No Cause For Concern* (1981), *Stand Strong Stand Proud* (1982), *Shot Away* (1985).

Violent Femmes

Coming from Milwaukee, Wisconsin, USA, Gordon Gano (b. 7 June 1963, New York, USA; vocals/guitar), Brian Ritchie (b. 21 November 1960, Milwaukee, Wisconsin, USA; bass) and Victor De Lorenzo (b. 25 October 1954, Racine, Wisconsin, USA; drums) first brought the Violent Femmes to the UK with a 12-inch single release for Rough Trade, 'Ugly'. It was a time of flourishing US talent, and the band's debut self-titled offering, issued on the Slash label via London Records, had the unmistakable imprint of aspiring talent. A rough, acoustic style failed to hide the Femmes' intriguing variety of songs and lyrics; although they have since mellowed, this formed the basis of what was to follow. Two acclaimed singles, 'Gone Daddy Gone' and 'It's Gonna Rain' (both 1984) were drawn from *Violent Femmes* before *Hallowed Ground* followed a year later, a more full-bodied work that lacked the shambolic nature of their debut. *Hallowed Ground* contained, what is for many, the classic Violent Femmes composition, the macabre 'Country Death Song'. *The Blind Leading The Naked* nearly gave the group a hit single in their cover of T.Rex's 'Children Of The Revolution' early in 1986. There was then a long pause in the Femme's activities while Gordon Gano appeared with his side-project, the gospel-influenced Mercy Seat, while Ritchie recorded his eclectic solo album for the SST label. The release of the the succinctly-titled *3* introduced a more sophisticated Violent Femmes, although the grisly subject matter continued. 1991's *Why Do Birds Sing?* included a version of the Culture Club hit, 'Do You Really Want To Hurt Me?'

Albums: *Violent Femmes* (1984), *Hallowed Ground* (1985), *The Blind Leading The Naked* (1986), *3* (1989), *Why Do Birds Sing?* (1991). Solo albums: Gordon Gano in Mercy Seat *The Mercy Seat* (1988); Brian Ritchie *Sonic Temple And The Court Of Babylon* (1989).

Virgin Prunes

This Irish performance-art/*avant garde* musical ensemble was originally formed in 1976. Fionan Hanvey, better known under his pseudonym Gavin Friday, was invited by Paul Hewson (later Bono of U2) to join a group of Dublin youths with artistic leanings who were inspired by the new wave explosion in the UK. A rough community had been formed under the title of the Village, a social club bound in secrecy. The Virgin Prunes became an official band, and an extension of the Village, by the end of 1977. Friday was joined by Guggi (Derek Rowen) and Dave-id (b. David Watson; vocals), Strongman (b. Trevor Rowen; bass), Dik Evans (brother of U2's The Edge; guitar) and Pod (b. Anthony Murphy; drums). Early gigs were very much performance events, with audiences bemused by the expectations placed on them. However, by the turn of the decade they had attracted strong cult support, and on the strength of the self-financed 'Twenty Tens', were signed to Rough Trade. Pod was the band's first casualty, opting out of their new disaffected religious stance.

As a manifestation of their unconventional approach their first album was initially released as a set of 7, 10 and 12-inch singles, with component parts making up *New Forms Of Beauty*. After the brief tenure of Haa

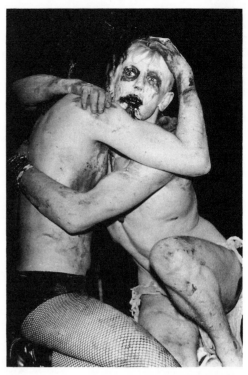

Virgin Prunes

Lacka Binttii, Mary O'Nellon took over on drums. His installment was in time for the band's second, and first complete album, *If I Die...I Die*. Less experimental and perverse than its predecessor, it continued nevertheless to explore the tenets of purity and beauty. At the same time a mixed studio/live album *Heresie* was released, which emphasized that the performance-art aspect of the group had not been totally neglected. By 1984 Guggi had become disenchanted with the music industry and departed. When Dik Evans defected for similar reasons, O'Nellon switched to guitar and Pod re-joined as drummer. 1986's *The Moon Looked Down And Laughed* witnessed another change in direction. Produced by Soft Cell's Dave Ball, it consisted largely of ballads and melodic pop, with little hint of the band's usual confrontational approach. However, following the continued lack of response from the record-buying public, Friday called a halt to his involvement with the band. Subsequent solo endeavours from former members failed to sustain the Virgin Prunes original spirit of adventure, although Gavin Friday's *Adam And Eve* set attracted music press acclaim.

Albums: *New Forms Of Beauty* (1981), *If I Die...I Die* (1982), *Heresie* (1982), *The Moon Looked Down And Laughed* (1986). Solo albums: Gavin Friday with Maurice Seezer *Each Man Kills The Things He Loves*

(1987), Gavin Friday *Adam And Eve* (1992).

Visage

A synthesizer 'jamming' band fronted by Steve Strange (b. Steve Harrington, 28 May 1959, Wales). Other members of the band included Midge Ure (b. James Ure, 10 October 1953, Cambuslang, Scotland; guitar), Rusty Egan (b. 19 September 1957), Billy Currie (b. 1 April 1952; violin), Dave Formula (keyboards), John McGeogh (guitar) and Barry Adamson (bass). The last three named were all members of Magazine. Ure rose to fame with teenybopper stars Slik before joining the Rich Kids with whom Egan played drums. Both Egan and Ure also played in the short lived Misfits during 1979 before Egan briefly joined the Skids and Ure linked with Thin Lizzy, then replaced John Foxx in Ultravox. Billy Currie was also in both Ultravox and Visage, not to mention Gary Numan's band at more or less the same time. The roots of Visage came about in late 1978 when Ure and Strange recorded a version of the old Zager And Evans' hit 'In The Year 2525' as a demo for EMI Records but had it turned down. The duo started recruiting instead, picking up the above-named musicians for rehearsals. The demo was hawked to Radar Records who signed them and released their first single, 'Tar', which concerned the joys of smoking. It was produced by Martin Rushent. Any hopes of releasing a follow-up on the label were dashed when Radar's parent company pulled the purse-strings tight and wound the label up. Polydor picked up on the band and were rewarded with a massive hit in 'Fade To Grey', which fitted in with the burgeoning synthesizer pop scene of the early 80s (New Romanticism). Although all of the band had other commitments, Visage made a brief effort to continue their existence. The third single, 'Mind Of A Toy', with its memorable Godley And Creme-produced video (their first), was a Top 20 hit but subsequent singles were released at greater and greater intervals and did increasingly less well. The band fizzled out in the mid-80s, with Strange forming Strange Cruise with Wendy Wu (ex-Photos), and his collaborators returning to their main bands.
Albums: *Visage* (1980), *The Anvil* (1982). Compilation: *The Singles Collection* (1983).

Voice Of The Beehive

Formed by sisters Tracey Bryn (b. 17 May 1962, Encino, California, USA) and Melissa Brooke Belland (b. 6 February 1966, Los Angeles, California, USA), this pop group had a strong pedigree. The girls' father was Brian Belland, a former member of the hit group, the Four Preps. Following a showbusiness childhood, in which they acted in various television commercials, the female duo decided to move to England and start a group. They soon infiltrated rock circles and were frequently seen in the company of Zodiac Mindwarp. After appearing on Bill Drummond's solo album, they formed Voice Of The Beehive, the title borrowed from a Bette Davis movie. With guitarist Mick Jones, the group began recording various demos. Their line-up was soon expanded following the recruitment of Daniel Woodgate (b. 19 October 1960, London, England; drums) and Mark Bedford (b. 24 August 1961, London, England; bass), who had previously played in Madness. After signing with David Balfe's Food label, they appeared on an EMI compilation album and subsequently recorded for London Records. Their early singles 'Just A City', 'I Say Nothing' and 'I Walk The Earth' encouraged comparisons with the Bangles and Blondie. Bedford, meanwhile, had left to form Butterfield 8 and was replaced by Martin Brett, who arrived in time to assist with the group's debut album. *Let It Bee* was a pleasant, witty pop confectionary, which included the UK Top 20 single, 'Don't Call Me Baby'. Further success followed with the Top 10, 'The Man In The Moon'. The appealing pop of Voice Of The Beehive continued on the punningly-titled *Honey Lingers* which climaxed in the heat of the summer of 91 with a series of live appearances in London which, tongue in cheek, were entitled Orgy Under The Underworld.
Albums: *Let It Bee* (1988), *Honey Lingers* (1991).

W

Waitresses

Formed in 1978 in Akron, Ohio, USA, the Waitresses were a new wave/pop band which achieved moderate popularity after relocating to the New York area in the early 80s. The group was led by Chris Butler (guitar, formerly of Tin Huey, an Akron, Ohio-based *avant garde* rock band), Patty Donahue (vocals), Dan Klayman (keyboards), Mars Williams (saxophone), Tracy Warmworth (bass), and Billy Ficca (drums, formerly of Television). After releasing an independent single on the Clone label in 1978, the Waitresses signed to the PolyGram subsidiary Ze Records in 1982. Their single 'I Know What Boys Like', which cast Donahue as a tease who delighted in *not* giving boys what they liked, was a popular dance hit in clubs and received substantial college radio airplay, reaching number 62 in the USA. The debut, *Wasn't Tomorrow Wonderful?*, on

Polydor, received critical acclaim and was their highest-charting record at number 41. The group's 1982 mini-album was issued in the USA under the title *I Could Rule The World If I Could Only Get The Parts*, and in the UK as *Make The Weather*; the USA version featured 'Christmas Wrapping', which became a popular rap hit in clubs.

Albums: *Wasn't Tomorrow Wonderful?* (1982), *I Could Rule The World If I Could Only Get The Parts* (1982), *Bruiseology* (1983).

Walking Seeds

Liverpool's premier psychedelic 'grunge' specialists arose early in 1986 out of the ashes of the Mel-O-Tones. In between, John Neesam (drums), Frank Martin (vocals) and Bob Parker (bass/guitar) formed the Corinthians for three months, recording a seven-track demo that formed the basis of the Walking Seeds set. The group's first EP, *Know Too Much* (1986), set the pace, fronted by the strong 'Tantric Wipeout'. By the time of the follow-up, 'Mark Chapman' (1987), Neesam had been replaced by two former members of Marshmallow Overcoat, Tony Mogan (drums) and Baz Sutton (guitar). This was followed by the extreme but patchy *Skullfuck* (the title influenced by a Grateful Dead album cover) later that year. After lying low, the band signed to Glass Records, issuing *Upwind Of Disaster, Downwind Of Atonement* in 1989. Recorded in New York, the presence of Bongwater's Mark Kramer as producer helped create a more defined, but nevertheless uncompromising aura to the proceedings. Sutton left to join the La's and was briefly replaced by Andy Rowan for 1989's *Shaved Beatnik* EP (wherein the band admirably slaughtered Cream's 'Sunshine Of Your Love'). The mini-album, *Sensory Deprivation Chamber Quartet Dwarf*, was assisted by psychedelic wizard Nick 'Bevis Frond' Saloman and new bassist Lee Webster. When Glass folded, the Walking Seeds recorded 'Gates Of Freedom' (1990) which included a b-side cover of Pink Floyd's 'Astronomy Domine'. This coincided with *Bad Orb...Whirling Ball*, a more considered but still aggressively garage-like effort. The Seeds tore through Bevis Frond's 'Reflections In A Tall Mirror' (1990), backed by Bevis's interpretation of the band's 'Sexorcist'. But at this point, the band 'self-destructed', despondent about their lack of success, despite recruiting ex-Dinosaur Jr. guitarist Don Fleming. A swan-song was offered in *Earth Is Hell* on the Snakeskin label, housing live material recorded in Germany earlier that year. Tony and Bob then set up the Del-Bloods, issuing 'Black Rabbit' (1991). The pair also surfaced in White Bitch for 'Animal Woman' and teamed up with Frank for Batloaf's 'Meat Out Of Hell' soon afterwards. Webster, meanwhile, had joined Baz in Froth that same year.

Albums: *Skullfuck* (1987), *Upwind Of Disaster, Downwind Of Atonement* (1989), *Sensory Deprivation Chamber Quartet Dwarf* (1989), *Bad Orb...Whirling Ball* (1990), *Earth Is Hell* (1990).

Wall

Formed in Sunderland, England, in early 1978, they settled on their first permanent line-up: Andzy, (bass/vocals), Lowery (vocals), Rab Fae Beith (drums) and Nick Ward (guitar, ex-Urban Gorillas). The band released their debut 'Exchange' for the Small Wonder label, shortly after which Lowery quit to be replaced by Keely, ex-Ruefrex. This line-up lasted from September 1979 to June 1980, and during this time they took on a fifth member, Heed, who had been with the Straps. The band had just released their *Ghetto* EP and *Personal Troubles And Public Issues* for Fresh Records. As 1980 closed Ward and Kelly both left, and the band continued as a three-piece. 'Ghetto' was reissued on Polydor, along with the single 'Remembrance', and the Wall set about a national tour in support of Stiff Little Fingers. An album followed but by now they were in dispute with their label over career direction. The next release was back on an independent, and featured a frenetic cover of the Beatles' 'Day Tripper'. Lowery later joined Ski Patrol and the Folk Devils.

Albums: *Personal Troubles And Public Issues* (1981), *Dirges And Anthems* (1982).

Wall Of Voodoo

Formed in Los Angeles, California, USA, in the immediate punk aftermath, Wall Of Voodoo was initially comprised Stan Ridgway (vocals/keyboards), Bill Noland (guitar/vocals), Charles Gray (bass/keyboards/synthesizer) and Joe Nanini (drums). However, by the release of *Dark Continent*, Noland had been replaced by Marc Moreland while Bruce Moreland had been added on bass. The latter was then dropped for *Call Of The West*, arguably the unit's finest album, on which their sense of rhythm and wash of synthesizer lines underscored Ridgway's droning, offhand vocals. Any potential this offered was sadly sundered with the singer's departure in 1985. While Ridgway enjoyed a UK Top 5 single with 'Camouflage', Wall Of Voodoo pursued a less successful career led by new vocalist Andy Prieboy. Further personnel changes undermined the group's progress and subsequent albums, although of intermittent interest, lacked the adventure of their second set.

Albums: *Dark Continent* (1981), *Call Of The West* (1982), *Seven Days In Sammy's Town* (1985), *Happy Planet* (1987), *The Ugly Americans In Australia* (1988). Compilation: *Grandma's House* (1984).

Walters, John

b. 16 May, 1938, Chesterfield, Derbyshire, England. Walters played trumpet with the Alan Price Set from the group's formation in 1965 until it was disbanded in 1968 (having scored five UK Top 20 hits along the way. From there Walters joined the BBC, eventually becoming the producer of BBC disc jockey John Peel's *Top Gear*. Together, Peel and Walters created a programme that remains in the musical vanguard and which featured the radio debuts of Cream and King Crimson among many notable firsts and played a significant role in the choice of music played for the next, influential 20 years. Walters voluntarily retired from this role as producer in the early 90s. During the late 70s, he had contributed a column in the rock magazine, *Zigzag* which revealed his comic personality. During this period had also presented his own Radio One arts programme, *Walters' Weekly* which introduced artists like Laurie Anderson, Native Hipsters and the Frank Chickens to British audiences. This show was later truncated and slotted in, as *Walter's Week*, to the mid-week evening radio shows of, successively, David 'Kid' Jensen, Richard Skinner and Janice Long. As well as discoursing on fringe arts events, it gave Walters the chance to indulge in his highly comic diary monologues. This led to appearances on BBC regional television presenting arts programmes (*Northern Lights*) and to Walters contributing to a wide range of radio talk programmes and periodicals.

Albums: with the Alan Price Set *The Price To Play* (1966), *A Price On His Head* (1967), *The Amazing* (1967), *Price Is Right* (1968), *The World Of Alan Price* (1970).

Warrior Soul

This psychotic art-rock quartet from New York was the brainchild of one-time video disc jockey, Kory Clarke. With the help of of Pete McClanahan (bass), John Ricco (guitar) and Paul Ferguson (drums), *Last Decade, Dead Century* was released in 1988. Influences as diverse as the Doors, Metallica, the Stooges and Joy Division were combined to produce a dark, intense, angst-ridden album. Lyrically, it criticised the establishment's inability to solve contemporary social problems, with references to political and police corruption, the homeless and narcotics. Mark Evans took over as drummer on *Drugs, God And The New Republic*, which built on previous themes, but increased the musical intensity of their delivery. Both works have received considerable critical acclaim, but this has yet to be converted into album sales.

Albums: *Last Decade, Dead Century* (1990), *Drugs, God And The New Republic* (1991).

Was (Not Was)

An unlikely US recording and production duo, childhood friends David Weiss and Don Fagenson used a variety of singers to front their records, including Sweat Pea Atkinson, Harry Bowens and Donny Ray Mitchell. 1983's *Born To Laugh At Tornadoes* included, bizarrely, Ozzy Osbourne rapping, and a snatch of Frank Sinatra. Geffen Records rewarded their eclecticism by dropping them. They moved on to Phonogram, managing to focus more clearly on their prospective dance market in the process. Their biggest hit was the anthemic 'Walk The Dinosaur', which topped the US singles chart for six weeks, while 'Spy In The House Of Love' had similar crossover appeal. However, the music industry knew them better for their numerous production credits. These included the B-52's, Iggy Pop, Bonnie Raitt and Bob Dylan. The latter fulfilled an ambition for Weiss, who had long held Dylan as his personal idol. 1990's *Are You Okay?* was critically lauded, and they remain an enigmatic attraction on the periphery of the dance scene.

Albums: *Was (Not Was)* (1981), *Born To Laugh At Tornadoes* (1983), *What Up, Dog?* (1988), *Are You Okay?* (1990).

Waterboys

Formed by vocalist Mike Scott (b. 14 December 1958, Edinburgh, Scotland), a former fanzine writer, the Waterboys evolved from Another Pretty Face, which included John Caldwell (guitar) and a frequently changing line-up from 1979-81. A series of failed singles followed until Scott elected to form a new group. Borrowing the name Waterboys from a line in 'The Kids' from Lou Reed's *Berlin*, Scott began advertising in the music press for suitable personnel. Anthony Thistlethwaite (b. 31 August 1955, Leicester, England; saxophone) and Karl Wallinger (b. 19 October 1957, Prestatyn, Clwyd, Wales; keyboards/percussion/vocals) were recruited and work was completed on 'A Girl Called Johnny', a sterling tribute to Patti Smith that narrowly failed to become a big hit. The group's self-titled debut was also a solid work, emphasizing Scott's ability as a singer/songwriter. 'December', with its religious connotations, was an excellent Christmas single that again narrowly failed to chart. Augmented by musicians Kevin Wilkinson (drums), Roddy Lorimar (trumpet) and Tim Blanthorn (violin), the Waterboys completed *A Pagan Place*, which confirmed their early promise. The key track for many was 'The Big Music', which became a handy simile for Scott's soul-searching mini-epics. For the following year's *This Is The Sea*, Scott brought in a new drummer Chris Whitten and added a folk flavour to the proceedings, courtesy of fiddler Steve Wickham. The attendant 'The Whole Of The Moon' only reached number 28 in the UK but later proved a spectacular Top 10 hit when reissued in 1990. It was a masterwork from a group seemingly at the height of its powers. Despite their promise, the Waterboys remained a vehicle for Scott's ideas and writing, a view reinforced when Karl Wallinger quit to form World Party. At this point Wickham, who had previously played with In Tua Nua, U2 and Sinead O'Connor, took on a more prominent role. He took Scott to Eire and a long sojourn in Galway followed. Three years passed before the Waterboys released their next album, the distinctively folk-flavoured *Fisherman's Blues*. Scott's assimilation of traditional Irish music, mingled with his own spiritual questing and rock background coalesced to produce a work of considerable charm and power.

Back in the ascendant, the group completed work on *Room To Roam*, which retained the folk sound, though to a lesser extent than its predecessor. Within days of the album's release, Wickham left the group, forcing Scott to reconstruct the Waterboys' sound once more. A revised line-up featuring Thistlethwaite, Hutchinson and new drummer Ken Blevins toured the UK playing a rocking set, minus the folk music that had permeated their recent work. After signing a US/Canadian deal with Geffen Records, the Waterboys line-up underwent further changes when, in February 1992, long-serving member Anthony Thistlethwaite left the group. During the rebuilding of the group, former Wendy And Lisa drummer Carla Azar took over the spot vacated by Ken Blevins, and Scott Thunes was recruited as the new bassist. Mercurial and uncompromising, Scott has continually steered the Waterboys through radically different musical phases, which have proven consistently fascinating.
Albums: *The Waterboys* (1983), *A Pagan Place* (1984), *This Is The Sea* (1985), *Fisherman's Blues* (1988), *Road To Roam* (1990). Compilation: *The Best Of 1981-90* (1991.)

Watt, Ben (see Everything But The Girl)

We Are Going To Eat You

This UK band was formed in 1986 by Julie Sorrell (b. London, England; vocals), Paul Harding (b. London, England; guitar), Paul 'Veg' Venables (b. London, England; bass) and Chris Knowles (b. London, England; drums), the cumbersomely-named group peddled a hybrid of pop and rock infused with a punk spirit. After several years of intense gigging and low-key releases, an appearance on BBC television's alternative *Snub TV* show, at the start of 1989, attracted copious amounts of interest from music business circles, resulting in a burst of media activity and much talk of a major record label deal. Unfortunately, the band's independent backers refused to allow the band to sign unless the price was right. In the ensuing legal mess the band lost the all-

important momentum and therefore by the time they were free of their old constraints, the quartet struggled to rekindle outside interest, in spite of a prestigious American deal. Eventually these frustrations came to a head in 1990 when the band vanished into the studio and reappeared with a new, more fashionable sound and the infinitely more sociable moniker of Melt.
Album: *Everywhen* (1990).

Weddings, Parties, Anything

Formed Melbourne 1985 and based around Mike Thomas (guitar/bass/vocals) and David Steel (guitar/vocals). The closest comparison to their sound is that of the Pogues, and the Sydney-based, Roaring Jack, both punk-influenced bands who also derived their inspiration from traditional Irish folk music. The line-up also comprised Mark Wallace (piano accordian), David Adams (drums, replaced in 1986 by Marcus Schintler) and Paul Clark (guitar). Their songs are concerned with Australian social issues, whilst the music, featuring Wallace's accordian complements the biting lyrics that depict the life of the down-and-out. The departure of song writer Steel (who later recorded his own well received solo album), in 1988, did no harm to the band. After their mini-album *No Show Without Punch*, was released on Billy Bragg's Utility label, the band attracted some favourable reviews in the UK, but have since failed to capitalize on this success.
Albums: *Scorn Of The Women* (1987), *Roaring Days* (1988), *The Big Don't Argue* (1989).

Wedding Present

Formed in Leeds, Yorkshire, England, in 1985 from the ashes of the Lost Pandas by David Gedge (b. 23 April 1960, Leeds, Yorkshire, England; guitar/vocals) with Keith Gregory (b. 2 January 1963, Co. Durham, England; bass), Peter Salowka (b. Middleton, Gt. Manchester, England; guitar) and Shaun Charman (b. Brighton, East Sussex, England; drums). The Wedding Present embodied the independent spirit of the mid-80s with a passion that few contemporaries could match. Furthermore, they staked their musical claim with a ferocious blend of implausibly fast guitars and lovelorn lyrics over a series of much-lauded singles on their own Reception Records label. As some cynics criticized the band's lack of imagination, the Wedding Present's debut *George Best*, showed the merits of the flamboyant but flawed football star and reached number 47 in the UK chart. Similarly, as those same critics suggested the band were 'one-trick phonies', Pete Salowka's East European upbringing was brought to bear on the Wedding Present sound, resulting in the frenzied Ukrainian folk songs on *Ukrainski Vistupi V Johna Peel*, so called because it was a compilation of tracks from sessions they had made

for John Peel's influential BBC Radio One show. Shaun Charman left the band as their debut was released, to join the Pop Guns, and was replaced by Simon Smith (b. 3 May 1965, Lincolnshire, England). Capitalizing on a still-burgeoning following, 'Kennedy' saw the band break into the Top 40 of the UK singles chart for the first time and revealed that, far from compromising on a major label, the Wedding Present were actually becoming more extreme. By their third album, *Seamonsters*, the band had forged a bizarre relationship with hardcore exponent Steve Albini (former member of the influential US outfit Big Black), whose harsh economic production technique encouraged the Wedding Present to juggle with broody lyrical mumblings and extraordinary slabs of guitar, killing the ghost of their 'jangly' beginnings. Before *Seamonsters* was released in 1991, Pete Salowka made way for Paul Dorrington, although he remained in the set-up, on the business side of the band. In 1992, the Wedding Present undertook an ambitious project of releasing one single, every month, throughout the year. Each single has, to date, briefly charted with 'Blue Eyes', 'Go Go Dancer', 'Three', 'Falling' and 'Come Play With Me' all peaking around the Top 20/30 regions.
Albums: *George Best* (1987), *Bizarro* (1989), *Seamonsters* (1991), *The Hit Parade Part One* (1992). Compilations: *Tommy* (1988), *Ukrainski Vistupi V Johna Peel* (1989).

Weekend

After the demise of the Young Marble Giants in 1980, Alison Statton (b. March 1958, Cardiff, Wales; vocals/bass) and fellow Cardiffian, Spike (guitarist/viola), moved to London. After teaming up the following year with Simon Booth (b. 12 March 1956), who worked at Mole Jazz record shop, they formed Weekend. Their debut single on Rough Trade Records, 'The View From Her Room', produced by Simon Jeffes of the Penguin Cafe Orchestra, presented a breezy jazz-shuffle driven by Statton's excellent bass-line. Amongst the studio support were two veterans of the British jazz scene, Harry Beckett (trumpet/flugelhorn) and former Centipede member Larry Stabbins (b. 9 September 1949; tenor sax). Mixed with Statton's introspective lyrics, the band's image of an 'anti-rock' outfit drawing on multi-cultural jazz influences, from the bossa nova of Gilberto Gill and Astrud Gilberto to the light African guitar style of King Sunny Ade, was quickly picked up by the then fashionable youthful London 'jazz-club' scene. Later singles 'Past Meets Present' and 'Drumbeat For Baby' gave Weekend further independent chart hits. Their debut *La Variété* perfectly captured the group's light summery feel. While live performances were few and far between,

London was blessed one memorable weekend in 1983 with two concerts, one at the Africa Centre, Covent Garden and another at the legendary Ronnie Scott's Club in Soho, where they were joined onstage by Keith Tippett. This set was recorded and later released on a posthumous mini-album. Statton's unease with live performances and Booth's desire to lead the group down a harder jazz-dance direction led to the group splitting, with Stabbins and Booth carrying on the bloodline with the formation of Working Week. Statton returned to Cardiff and her college studies, re-emerging in the late 80s with the duo Devine And Statton.
Albums: *La Verité* (1982), *Live At Ronnie Scott's* (1983). Compilation: with the Young Marble Giants and the Gist *Nipped In The Bud* (1984).

Weirdos

One of the strongest bands to emerge from the Los Angeles, California, USA punk explosion, the Weirdos were formed in 1976 following a short spell known as the Barbies and Luxurious Adults. Comprising John Denny (vocals), Dix Denny (guitar), Cliff Roman (guitar), David Trout (bass) and Nickey Beat (drums), the Weirdos recorded several excellent singles, notably 'Destroy All Music' (1977) and 'We Got The Neutron Bomb' (1978), but the group were plagued by internal problems. The mini-album, *Who, What, When, Where, Why?*, showed some of the Weirdos' early fire but further changes in the rhythm simply undermined their progress. They broke up in 1981, but reformed in 1990.
Album: *The Weirdos* (1980).

We've Got A Fuzzbox And We're Gonna Use It

Formed in Birmingham, England, in 1985, this all-female quartet comprised Maggie Dunne (b. 5 June 1964, Solihull, West Midlands, England; vocals/keyboards/guitar), Jo Dunne (b. 12 November 1968, Birmingham, England; bass/piano), Vickie Perks (b. 9 October 1968, Birmingham, England; vocals) and Tina O'Neill (b. 20 January 1969, Solihull, West Midlands, England; drums/percussion/saxophone). Their unusual name was coined after they had purchased a fuzzbox for their guitars and Maggie casually announced: 'We've Got A Fuzzbox And We're Gonna Use It!' The fuzzbox drone dominated their early work, particularly on such songs as 'XX Sex' and 'Rules And Regulations', which displayed a raw, intense sound overladen with strong harmonies and barbed sloganeering lyrics. The delightfully unselfconscious amateurish style of their work was reflected in their bizarre technicolour cartoon image, with multi-coloured, geometric hairstyles and garish clothes. Their schoolgirl playfulness and frequently-voiced disregard for

We've Got A Fuzzbox And We're Gonna Use It

musical precision extracted a condescending chauvinism from the music press of the period. This patronizing attitude was undeserved for Fuzzbox were considerably more interesting, technically and otherwise, than many of their male contemporaries. They played a variety of instruments, showed no reluctance to undertake major tours and wrote and arranged their own material.

An appearance on their record label's *Vindaloo Summer Special*, spawned a minor hit EP *Rockin' With Rita*, produced by Stuart Colman. A contract with WEA Records followed and in 1986 they scored another small UK hit with the glorious 'Love Is The Slug', with its distinctive wall of sound, embellished by piercing yet barely coherent vocals. Their debut album, *Bostin' Steve Austin*, included several old singles, plus the stage favourite 'What's The Point?'. After further touring, the group re-emerged without their bizarre hairstyles for the 1989 UK Top 20 hit 'International Rescue'. Another high-powered production, the single saw Fuzzbox dressed as *Thunderbirds* puppets with Vickie playing the role of Jane Fonda's *Barbarella*, complete with bacon-foil space garb, in the accompanying video. Having virtually abandoned their 'fuzzbox sound', they also reluctantly accepted the advice of their record company and abbreviated their name to 'Fuzzbox'. Thereafter, they moved increasingly towards the

mainstream. The next hit 'Pink Sunshine' was catchy enough, but lacked the distinction and originality of their earlier work. The accompanying *Big Bang!* was another largely self-penned effort, but included a surprise hit reading of Yoko Ono's 'Walking On Thin Ice'. A highly accomplished closing track 'Beauty' displayed their oft-neglected vocal and arranging talents to the full. In July 1990, after some months of speculation, Vickie Perks announced her intention to pursue a solo career. The remaining members agreed to end the Fuzzbox saga at that point and start afresh.
Albums: *Bostin' Steve Austin* (1987), *Big Bang!* (1989).

Wiedlin, Jane

b. 20 May 1958, Oconomowoc, Wisconsin, USA. Wiedlin was originally the guitarist of the top US female band, the Go-Go's. When the split came in 1984, all five members embarked on solo careers. Wiedlin released a self-titled album which contained a minor hit 'Blue Kiss'. However, her heart was also set on pursing an acting career and she made cameo appearances in *Clue* and *Star Trek 4: The Voyage Home*. A successful return to recording came in 1988 with the superb transatlantic hit, 'Rush Hour'. Much of Wiedlin's chart success however has largely been confined to the US charts. Her energies in the early 90s have been directed towards her involvement in the anti-fur trade movement. This resulted in the Go-Go's reforming briefly in 1990 at a benefit for PETA (People for the Ethical Treatment of Animals).
Albums: *Jane Wiedlin* (1986), *Fur* (1988), *Tangled* (1990).

Wilde, Kim

b. Kim Smith, 18 November 1960, Chiswick, London, England. The daughter of 50s pop idol Marty Wilde and Vernons Girls' vocalist Joyce Smith (née Baker), Kim was signed to Mickie Most's Rak Records in 1980 after the producer heard a demo Kim recorded with her brother Ricky. Her first single, the exuberant 'Kids In America', composed by Ricky and co-produced by Marty, climbed to number 2 in the UK charts. A further Top 10 hit followed with 'Chequered Love', while her debut *Kim Wilde* fared extremely well in the album charts. A more adventurous sound with 'Cambodia' indicated an exciting talent. By 1982, she had already sold more records than her father had done in his entire career. While 'View From A Bridge' maintained her standing at home, 'Kids In America' became a Top 30 hit in the USA. A relatively quiet period followed, although she continued to enjoy minor hits with 'Love Blonde', 'The Second Time' and a more significant success with the Dave Edmunds-produced 'Rage To Love'. An energetic reworking of the Supremes' classic 'You Keep Me

Hangin' On' took her back to UK number 2 at a time when her career seemed flagging. After appearing on the Ferry Aid charity single, 'Let It Be', Wilde was back in the Top 10 with 'Another Step (Closer To You)', a surprise duet with soul singer Junior Giscombe. Weary of her image as the girl-next-door, Wilde subsequently sought a sexier profile, which was used in the video to promote 'Say You Really Want Me'. Her more likely standing as an 'all- round entertainer' was underlined by the Christmas novelty hit 'Rockin' Around The Christmas Tree' in the company of comedian Mel Smith. In 1988, the dance-orientated 'You Came' reaffirmed her promise, and further Top 10 hits continued with 'Never Trust A Stranger' and 'Four Letter Word'. Her recent singles have gained only lowly positions in the charts and the subsequent *Love Is* was a pale shadow of *Close*.

Albums: *Kim Wilde* (1981), *Select* (1982), *Catch As Catch Can* (1983), *Teases And Dares* (1984), *Another Step* (1986), *Close* (1988), *Love Moves* (1990), *Love Is* (1992). Compilation: *The Very Best Of Kim Wilde* (1985).

Wild Flowers

Like Del Amitri, Wolverhampton's Wild Flowers became tired of a disinterested UK pop scene and looked to America for inspiration and appreciation. After two singles, 'Melt Like Ice' and 'Things Have Changed' and an album, *The Joy Of It All*, on Reflex in 1984, the fledgling outfit were dealt a blow when original guitarist Dave Newton left to form the Mighty Lemon Drops. The remaining members, Neal Cook (guitar/vocals), Mark Alexander (bass) and Dave Fisher (drums) eventually found a replacement in Dave Atherton, and the band duly signed to aspiring local label Chapter 22. They broke their two-year silence in 1986 with 'It Ain't So Easy' and was followed later that year by 'A Kind Of Kingdom'. Both singles were then coupled on a mini-album, *Dust*, primarily aimed at introducing the Wild Flowers to the US market which was more sympathetic to their New York-influenced rock sound. The band became the first British act to sign with Slash in the USA, releasing *Sometime Soon* in 1988, preceded by 'Broken Chains' and 'Take Me For A Ride' in the UK. The band's *Tales Like These* was recorded in the inspirational surroundings of California, by which time a new drummer, Simon Atkins, had been found. The album made little headway in the UK (where Slash is handled by London Records) and since then, the group have concentrated more on performing in the USA.

Albums: *The Joy Of It All* (1984), *Dust* (1987), *Sometime Soon* (1988), *Tales Like These* (1990).

Wild Swans

'Revolutionary Spirit', the last single for Liverpool's influential Zoo label, created quite a stir for the Wild Swans back in early 1982. A moving slice of uplifting pop set against guitar and synthesizer, the song looked set to elevate the band alongside those other Zoo graduates Echo And The Bunnymen and the Teardrop Explodes. However, the song's over-loud production did result in a loss of sound quality, and it could be argued that this prevented healthier sales. But instead, Paul Simpson (vocals, ex-Teardrop Explodes), Jerry Kelly (guitar, ex-Systems), Ged Quinn (keyboards), Alan Mills (drums) and Modernaires bassist Alan disbanded soon after, forming the Lotus Eaters. But 'Revolutionary Spirit' became a cult favourite and after the recording of a John Peel BBC session was warmly received in September 1986, the band decided to re-form. *Bringing Home The Ashes* was issued in 1988. Like its single offspring 'Young Manhood' and 'Bible Dreams', the album hinted at the Wild Swans' originality without really leaving a lasting impression.

Album: *Bringing Home The Ashes* (1988).

Wilson, Mari

b. Mari MacMillan Ramsey Wilson. 29 September 1957, London, England. In the mid-80s, Mari Wilson single-handedly led a revival of the world of 50s/early 60s English kitsch. Sporting a bee-hive hairdo, wearing a pencil skirt and fake mink stole, her publicity photos depicted a world of long-lost suburban curtain and furniture styles, tupperware, garish colours (often pink) and graphic designs from the period. The songs were treated in the same way, only affectionately and with genuine feeling. The whole image was the idea of Tot Taylor who, composing under the name of Teddy Johns and gifted with the ability to write pastiche songs from almost any era of popular music, also ran the Compact Organisation label. The label's sense of hype excelled itself as they immediately released a box-set of Compact Organisation artists, all of which, with the exception of Mari, failed to attract the public's attention. (Although 'model agent' Virna Lindt was a music press favourite.) Mari was quickly adopted by press, television and radio as a curiosity, all aiding her early 1982 singles 'Beat The Beat' and 'Baby It's True' to have a minor effect on the chart. 'Just What I Always Wanted' a Top 10 hit, fully encapsulated the Wilson style. However, it was the following year's cover of the Julie London torch-song number, 'Cry Me A River' which, despite only reaching number 27, most people have come to associate with Mari. The song also generated a revival of interest in London's recordings, resulting in many long-lost (and forgotten) albums to be re-released. After touring the world with her backing vocal group, the Wilsations -

which included within the line-up Julia Fordham - the return home saw a slowing-down in activity. Although for the most part Mari was out of the lime-light, she provided the vocals to the soundtrack to the Ruth Ellis bio-pic *Dance With A Stranger*. In 1985, she started playing small clubs with her jazz quartet performing standards, as well as writing her own material which led to her appear with Stan Getz at a London's Royal Festival Hall. Although still affectionately remembered for her beehive, she has been able to put that period behind her and is now taken more seriously as a jazz/pop singer and is able to fill Ronnie Scott's club for a season.

Albums: *Show People* (1983), *Dance With A Stranger* (1987, film soundtrack), *The Rhythm Romance* (1992).

Win

After the Fire Engines folded on New Year's Eve 1981, Davey Henderson formed Heartbeat with former Flower singer Hilary Morrison, releasing just one track, on a *New Musical Express* cassette. By mid-1984 he was working with former Dirty Reds and Fire Engines member Russel Burn (drums) once more, linking with Ian Stoddart from Everest The Hard Way to form Win in his native Edinburgh. Straight away they won single of the week awards with their debut for London Records 'You've Got The Power'. Live, they played advertising jingles between songs, and appropriately 'You've Got The Power' was used in a television advertising campaign by McEwans lager. With obvious irony the band's lyrics discussed mass media communication, paranoia and conspiracy. As Postcard Records boss Alan Horne noted: 'Win are the most exciting thing I've come across since Orange Juice were starting out'. However, just as the Fire Engines before them, Win proved too subtle to procure a mainstream audience. The *NME* was one of many papers that mourned their passing: '(they) ... must be both proud and guilty in the knowledge that they made some of the greatest pop never heard'. Henderson was last sighted recording demos under the name Nectorine No. 9.

Albums: *Uh! Tears Baby* (1987), *Freaky Trigger* (1989).

Wire

This inventive UK group were formed in October 1976, by Colin Newman (b. 16 September 1954, Salisbury, Wilshire, England; vocals/guitar), Bruce Gilbert (b. 18 May 1946, Watford, Hertfordshire, England; guitar), Graham Lewis (b. 22 February 1953, Grantham, Lincolnshire, England; bass/vocals) and Robert Gotobed (b. Mark Field, 1951, Leicester, England; drums) along with lead guitarist George Gill the latter member had previously been a member of the Snakes, releasing a single on the Skydog label, while the the rest of Wire all had art school backgrounds. Their early work was clearly influenced by punk and this incipient era was captured on a various artists' live selection, *The Roxy, London, WC2*, their first recording as a four-piece following Gill's dismissal. Although not out of place among equally virulent company, the group was clearly more ambitious than many contemporaries. Wire was signed to the Harvest label in September 1977. Their impressive debut *Pink Flag*, comprised of 21 tracks, and ranged from the furious assault of 'Field Day For The Sundays' and 'Mr Suit' to the more brittle, almost melodic, interlude provided by 'Mannequin' which became the group's first single. Producer Mike Thorne, who acted as an unofficial fifth member, enhanced the set's sense of tension with a raw, stripped-to-basics sound. *Chairs Missing* offered elements found in its predecessor, but couched them in a newfound maturity. Gilbert's buzzsaw guitar became more measured, allowing space for Thorne's keyboards and synthesizers to provide an implicit anger.

A spirit of adventure also marked *154* which contained several exceptional individual moments, including 'A Touching Display', a lengthy excursion into wall-of-sound feedback, and the haunting 'A Mutual Friend', scored for a delicate *cor anglais* passage and a striking contrast to the former's unfettered power. However, the album marked the end of Wire's Harvest contract and the divergent aims of the musicians became impossible to hold under one banner. The quartet was disbanded in the summer of 1980, leaving Newman free to pursue a solo career, while Gilbert and Lewis completed a myriad of projects under various identities including Dome, Duet Emmo and P'o plus a number of solo works. Gotobed meanwhile concentrated on session work for Colin Newman, Fad Gadget and later organic farming. A posthumous release, *Document And Eyewitness*, chronicled Wire's final concert at London's Electric Ballroom in February 1980, but it was viewed as a disappointment in the wake of the preceding studio collections. It was not until 1985 that the group was resurrected and it was a further two years before they began recording again. *The Ideal Copy* revealed a continued desire to challenge, albeit in a less impulsive manner, and the set quickly topped the independent chart. *A Bell Is A Cup (Until It's Struck)* maintained the newfound balance between art and commercial pop, including the impressive 'Kidney Bingos'. In 1990 the group abandoned the 'beat combo' concept adopted in 1985 and took on board the advantages and uses of computer and sequencer technology. The resulting *Manscape* showed that the group's sound had changed dramatically, but not altogether with satisfactory results. Following the album's release Gotobed announced his departure. The remaining trio ironically changed their name to Wir, but not until

The Drill had been released. It contained a collection of variations of 'Drill', a track that had appeared on the EP *Snakedrill* in 1987. The new group's first release 'The First Letter', showed a harder edge than their more recent work. It amusingly contained some reworked samples of *Pink Flag*.

Albums: *Pink Flag* (1977), *Chairs Missing* (1978), *154* (1979), *Document And Eyewitness* (1981), *The Ideal Copy* (1987), *A Bell Is A Cup Until It Is Struck* (1988), *It's Beginning To And Back Again* (1989), *Manscape* (1990), *The Peel Sessions* (1990), *The Drill* (1991). As Wir *The First Letter* (1991). Compilations: *Wire Play Pop* (1986), *In The Pink* (1986), *On Returning* (1989).

Further reading: *Wire ... Everybody Loves A History*, Kevin S. Eden.

Wobble, Jah

b. John Wardle, London, England. An innovative bass player, Wobble began his career with Public Image Limited. Previously he had been known as one of the 'four Johns' who hung around Malcolm McLaren's 'Sex' boutique. Heavily influenced by the experimental rhythms of bands like Can, his input to PiL's *Metal Box* collection inspired in turn many novice post-punk bass players. By August 1980 he had become one of the many instrumentalists to fall foul of Lydon in PiL's turbulent career, and set about going solo. 1983 saw him joining with his hero Holger Czukay and U2's The Edge for *Snake Charmer*, before he put together the Human Condition, a combo specializing in free-form jazz and dub improvisation. However, when they disbanded, the mid-80s quickly became wilderness years for Wobble: 'The biggest kickback I have had was from sweeping the platform at Tower Hill station. It was a scream. You felt like getting on the intercom and saying "The next train is the Upminster train, calling at all stations to Upminster and by the way, I USED TO BE SOMEONE!".'. However, when he began listening to North African, Arabic and Romany music, he was inspired to pick up his instrument once more. It was 1987 when he met guitarist Justin Adams, who had spent much of his early life in Arab countries. Their bonding resulted in Wobble putting together Invaders Of The Heart, with producer Mark Ferda on keyboards. After tentative live shows they released *Without Judgement* in the Netherlands, where Wobble had maintained cult popularity. As the late 80s saw a surge in the fortunes of dance and rhythmic expression, Invaders Of The Heart and Wobble suddenly achieved a surprise return to the mainstream. This was spearheaded by 1990's 'Bomba', remixed by Andy Weatherall on the fashionable Boys Own label. Wobble was in demand again, notably as collaborator on Sinead O'Connor's *I Do Not Want What I Haven't Got* and Primal Scream's 'Higher Than The Sun'. This was quickly followed by Invaders Of The Heart's *Rising Above Bedlam*, in turn featuring contributions from O'Connor (the dance hit, 'Visions Of You') and Natacha Atlas.

Albums: *Steel Leg Vs The Electric Dread* (1980), *The Legend Lives On...Jah Wobble In 'Betrayal'* (1980), *Jah Wobble's Bedroom Album* (1983), with Holger Czukay and The Edge *Snake Charmer* (1983), *The Human Condition* (1982), with Ollie Morland *Neon Moon* (1985), with Invaders Of The Heart *Without Judgement* (1990), with Invaders Of The Heart *Rising Above Bedlam* (1991).

Wolfhounds

Formed in Essex, England in 1985, the Wolfhounds' first recording line-up was Dave Callahan, Andrew Bolton, Paul Clark, Andrew Golding and Frank Stebbing. Having spent their formative months supporting dubious pub/punk rock bands around London, the Wolfhounds became fortuitously involved in the *New Musical Express*'s 'C86' venture. Toying with a gritty, angular guitar framework over which Callahan's vocals wandered, the Wolfhounds were famed for having as many labels as album releases; they bounced from Pink Records to Idea and on through September and Midnight Music Records, fittingly experiencing an alarming number of personnel changes. In spite of - or perhaps because of - their stubborn outlook, the band never achieved the respect they truly warranted, and finally ground to a halt at the end of the 80s. After their demise, Dave Callahan initiated a new band called Moonshake.

Albums: *Unseen Ripples From A Pebble* (1987), *Blown Away* (1989). Compilation: *Essential Wolfhounds* (1988).

Wonder Stuff

Wonder Stuff

Formed in Stourbridge, West Midlands, England, in 1986, this pop group featured Miles Hunt (lead vocals/guitar), Malcolm Treece (guitar), Rob Jones (bass) and former Mighty Lemon Drops drummer Martin Gilks. After amassing a sizeable local

following, and releasing an EP, *It's A Wonderful Day* (1987), they received favourable press coverage. Along with other Midland hopefuls Pop Will Eat Itself, Crazyhead and Gaye Bykers On Acid, the Wonder Stuff were lumped in under the banner of 'grebo rock' by the music press. But the Wonder Stuff's strength lay in their melodic pop songs, against an urgent, power pop backdrop. After an ill-fated involvement with EMI's *ICA Rock Week*, a second single, 'Unbearable', was strong enough to secure a deal with Polydor, at the end of 1987. 'Give Give Give Me More More More' (1988) proved a minor hit, followed by perhaps the group's finest moment to date. Full of soaring harmonies, 'A Wish Away' was the perfect precursor to the Wonder Stuff's vital, *The Eight Legged Groove Machine*, which followed later that year. The album established them in the UK charts. 'It's Yer Money I'm After Baby', also from the album, continued Miles' seemingly cynical attitude (further evident on the confrontational b-side, 'Astley In The Noose' - referring to contemporary chart star, Rick Astley) and started a string of UK Top 40 hits. 'Who Wants To Be The Disco King?' and the more relaxed 'Don't Let Me Down Gently' (both 1989) hinted at the diversity of the group's second album, *Hup*. Aided by fiddle and banjo player and keyboardist Martin Bell, the album contrasted a harder, hi-tech sound at times with a rootsy, folk feel on tracks like the hit 'Golden Green' (1989), a double a-side with a cover of the Youngbloods' 'Get Together'. But the band's well-documented internal wrangles came to a head with the departure of Rob Jones at the end of the decade. 'Circlesquare' (1990) introduced new bassist Paul Clifford and allowed for the band's first venture into 12-inch remix territory. A subsequent low profile was broken in April 1991 with 'Size Of A Cow'. A Top 10 hit, this was quickly followed by 'Caught In My Shadow' and *Never Loved Elvis*. Once again, the work revealed the Wonder Stuff's remarkable progression. Gone were the brash, punk-inspired three-minute classics, replaced by a richer musical content, both in Miles' songwriting and as performers. The extent of the group's popularity was emphasized in late 1991 when, in conjunction with comedian Vic Reeves, they topped the UK charts with a revival of Tommy Roe's 'Dizzy'. The group made a swift return to the Top 10 in February 1992 with the *Welcome To The Cheap Seats* EP.
Albums: *The Eight Legged Groove Machine* (1988), *Hup* (1989), *Never Loved Elvis* (1991).

Woodentops

At one point, it seemed likely that the Woodentops from Northampton, England, would be commercially successful. After the offbeat 'Plenty', a one-off single for the Food label in 1984, songwriter Rolo McGinty

Woodentops

(guitar/vocals), Simon Mawby (guitar), Alice Thompson (keyboards), Frank de Freitas (bass) and Benny Staples (drums) joined Geoff Travis's Rough Trade label and issued a string of catchy singles that fared increasingly well commercially. 1985's jolly 'Move Me' was followed by the menacing pace of 'Well Well Well' while 'It Will Come' seemed a likely hit. The band's critically acclaimed debut album, *Giant* was an enticing mixture of frantic acoustic guitars and a warm yet offbeat clutch of songs. After 'Love Affair With Everyday Living' (1986), McGinty decided upon a change in direction, hardening up the Woodentops sound and incorporating new technology within their live repertoire. The results were heard the following year on *Live Hypnobeat Live*, which relied on material from *Giant*, albeit performed live in a drastically revitalized way. *Wooden Foot Cops On The Highway* and the accompanying single 'You Make Me Feel'/'Stop This Car' showed how far the Woodentops had progressed by early 1988. Although less uncompromising than their live project, the sound was more mature with an emphasis on detail previously lacking. What the band failed to achieve in commercial terms was more than compensated for by the level of critical and public respect they earned. Much of the 1991/2 period was spent touring overseas, particularly in Japan where the group are immensely popular.
Albums: *Giant* (1986), *Live Hypnobeat Live* (1987), *Wooden Foot Cops On the Highway* (1988).

Wreckless Eric

b. Eric Goulden, Newhaven, Sussex, England. Launched by Stiff Records in the heyday of punk, Wreckless Eric, as his moniker suggested, specialized in chaotic, pub rock and roots-influenced rock. His often tuneless vocals belied some excellent musical backing, most notably by producer Nick Lowe. Wreckless' eccentric single, 'Whole Wide World'/'Semaphore Signals' has often been acclaimed as one of the minor classics of the punk era. During

1977-78, he was promoted via the famous Stiff live revues where he gained notoriety off-stage for his drinking. For his second album, *The Wonderful World Of Wreckless Eric*, the artist provided a more engaging work, but increasingly suffered from comparison with the other stars on his fashionable record label. Wreckless' commercial standing saw little improvement despite an attempt to produce a more commercial work, the ironically-titled *Big Smash*. Effectively retiring from recording for the first half of the 80s, Wreckless returned with *A Roomful Of Monkeys*, credited to Eric Goulden, and featuring members of Ian Dury's Blockheads. He then formed the Len Bright Combo with ex-Milkshakes members Russ Wilkins (bass) and Bruce Brand (drums), who released two albums and found nothing more than a small cult-following on the pub/club circuit. The eventual dissolution of that group led to the formation of Le Beat Group Electrique with Catfish Truton (drums) and André Barreau (bass). Now a resident in France, and a more sober personality, Eric has found an appreciative audience.

Albums: *Wreckless Eric* (1978), *The Wonderful World Of Wreckless Eric* (1979), *The Whole Wide World* (1979), *Big Smash* (1980), as Eric Goulden *A Roomful Of Monkeys* (1985), *The Len Bright Combo Present The Len Bright Combo* (1986), *Le Beat Group Electrique* (1989), *At The Shop* (1990), *The Donovan Of Trash* (1991).

Wynn, Steve

Guitarist/vocalist Wynn is one of the pivotal figures in the Los Angeles 'paisley underground' rock scene of the early 80s. A former member of the Suspects, which included Gavin Blair and Russ Tolman, later of True West, he briefly joined the Long Ryders, before founding the Dream Syndicate in 1981. Starved of a suitable record label, Wynn established Down There Records, which issued important early sets by Green On Red and Naked Prey in addition to his own group's debut. Dream Syndicate have since pursued an erratic career, blighted by commercial indifference. During a hiatus in its progress Wynn joined Dan Stuart from Green On Red in a ragged, bar-room influenced collection, *The Lost Weekend* (1985). Billed as by Danny And Dusty, the album featured support from friends and contemporaries and paradoxically outsold the musicians' more serious endeavours.

Albums: *The Lost Weekend* (1985), *Kerosene Man* (1990).

X

X

Formed in Los Angeles, California, USA in 1977, X originally comprised of Exene Cervenka (vocals), Billy Zoom (guitar), John Doe (bass) and Mick Basher (drums), although the last-named was quickly replaced by D.J. (Don) Bonebrake. The quartet made its debut with 'Adult Books'/'We're Desperate' (1978), and achieved a considerable live reputation for their imaginative blend of punk, rockabilly and blues. Major labels were initially wary of the group, but Slash, a leading independent, signed them in 1979. Former Doors' organist, Ray Manzarek, produced *Los Angeles* and *Wild Gift*, the latter of which established X as a major talent. Both the *New York Times* and the *Los Angeles Times* voted it Album Of The Year and such acclaim inspired a recording deal with Elektra. *Under The Big Black Sun* was another fine selection, although reception for *More Fun In The New World* was more muted, with several commentators deeming it 'over-commercial'. In the meantime X members were pursuing outside projects. *Adulterers Anonymous*, a poetry collection by Cervenka and Lydia Lunch, was published in 1982, while the singer joined Doe, Henry Rollins (Black Flag), Dave Alvin (the Blasters) and Jonny Ray Bartel in a part-time country outfit, the Knitters, releasing *Poor Little Critter On The Road* in 1985. Alvin replaced Billy Zoom following the release of *Ain't Love Grand* and X was subsequently augmented by ex-Lone Justice guitarist Tony Gilkyson. However, Alvin left for a solo career on the completion of *See How We Are*. Despite the release of *Live At The Whiskey A Go-Go*, X was clearly losing momentum and the group was latterly dissolved. Doe has since recorded as a solo act.

Albums: *Los Angeles* (1980), *Wild Gift* (1981), *Under*

The Big Black Sun (1982), *More Fun In The New World* (1983), *Ain't Love Grand* (1985), *See How We Are* (1987), *Live At The Whiskey A Go-Go On The Fabulous Sunset Strip* (1988).

XL Capris

Formed in Sydney, Australia at the end of 1978, the XL Capris soon acquired a healthy following on the punk/alternative circuit when they formed their own Axle Records and released two singles and an album in 1980. The songs on the album were mainly written by guitarist Tim Gooding, featuring simple instrumentation, sparse production and the plaintive vocals of Johanna Pigott (bass), singing lyrics that were very Sydney-orientated. Joining Julie Anderson aka Nancy Serapax (drums), former Dragon guitarist Todd Hunter boosted the line-up and a second album was recorded. *Weeds* featured many Pigott-Hunter compositions, obtaining a fuller, more polished sound. The band employed a second drummer, Michael Farmer - an unusual move which did not enhance the material and the band broke up shortly afterwards at the end of 1981. XL Capris were certainly one of the most original and interesting bands to emerge out of the punk era, but they did not achieve mainstream success. Hunter returned to the reformed Dragon and Piggott recorded three albums under the name Scribble before finding acclaim as a songwriter for Dragon. Original drummer Julie Anderson married the vocalist from UK band the Vapours and guitarist Kimble Rendall was a founder member of the Hoodoo Gurus.
Albums: *Where Is Hank* (1980), *Weeds* (1981).

Xmal Deutschland

This experimental and atmospheric band formed in the autumn of 1980 and were based in Hamburg, Germany. With no previous musical experience, the essential components were Anja Huwe (vocals), Manuela Rickers (guitar) and Fiona Sangster (keyboards). Original members Rita Simon and Caro May were replaced by Wolfgang Ellerbrock (bass) and Manuela Zwingmann (drums). Insisting on singing in their mother tongue and refusing to be visually promoted as a 'female' band (Ellerbrock is the 'token' male), they have continued to plough a singular and largely lonely furrow since their inception. They first came to England in 1982 to support the Cocteau Twins, joining 4AD Records soon afterwards. The debut *Fetisch* highlighted a sound which tied them firmly to both their Germanic ancestry and the hallmark spectral musicianship of their new label. Huwe's voice in particular, was used as a fifth instrument which made the cultural barrier redundant. After the release of two well-received singles, 'Qual' and 'Incubus Succubus II', they lost drummer Zwingmann who wished to remain in

England. Her replacement was Peter Bellendir who joined in time for rehearsals for the second album.
Albums: *Festisch* (1982), *Tocsin* (1984).

X-Ray Spex

X-Ray Spex

One of the most inventive, original and genuinely exciting groups to appear during the punk era, X-Ray Spex were the brainchild of the colourful Poly Styrene (Marion Elliot), whose exotic clothes and tooth brace established her as an instant punk icon. With a line-up completed by Lora Logic, later replaced by Glyn Johns (saxophone), Jak Stafford (guitar), Paul Dean (bass) and B.P. Hurding (drums), the group began performing in 1977 and part of their second gig was captured for posterity on the seminal *Live At The Roxy WC2*. A series of extraordinary singles including 'Germ Free Adolescence', 'Oh Bondage Up Yours', 'The Day The World Turned Dayglo' and 'Identity' were not only rivetting examples of high energy punk, but contained provocative, thoughtful lyrics berating the urban synthetic fashions of the 70s and urging individual expression. Always ambivalent about her pop-star status, Poly dismantled the group in 1979 and joined the Krishna Consciousness Movement. X-Ray Spex's final single, 'Highly Inflammable' was coupled with the pulsating 'Warrior In Woolworths', a parting reminder of Poly's early days as a shop assistant. Although she reactivated her recording career with the album *Translucence* (1980) and a 1986 EP *Gods And Goddesses*, no further commercial success was forthcoming.
Album: *Germ Free Adolescents* (1978).

XTC

Formed during the punk boom of 1977 and originally known as the Helium Kidz, the band adopted the name XTC (ecstasy) and signed to Virgin Records. Except for Andrews, all members hailed from the Wiltshire town of Swindon; the band then comprised of Andy Partridge (b. 11 December 1953; guitar/vocals), Barry Andrews (b. 12 September,

XTC

West Norwood, London, England), Colin Moulding (b. 17 August 1955) and Terry Chambers (b. 18 July 1955). The band's debut *White Music* lent more to pop than the energetic new wave sound; notwithstanding, the album was a hit and critics marked their name for further attention. Shortly after the release of *Go2*, Barry Andrews departed, eventually to resurface in Shriekback. With Andrews replaced by Dave Gregory, both *Go2* and the following *Drums And Wires* were commercial successes and the quirky hit single 'Making Plans For Nigel' exposed them to an eagerly awaiting audience. Singles were regularly taken from their subsequent albums and they continued making the charts with quality pop songs including 'Sgt Rock (Is Going To Help Me)' and the magnificently constructed 'Senses Working Overtime', which reached the UK Top 10. The main songwriter, Partridge, was able to put his sharp observations to paper in a humorous and childish way that was totally palatable. The double set *English Settlement* was a triumph; this critically applauded work made the UK Top 5 and was their most ambitious work to date. Partridge became ill through exhaustion and a stomach ulcer, and announced that XTC would continue only as recording artists (including promotional videos). Both *Mummer* and *The Big Express* failed to sell in the quantities their record company (and reviewers) had

envisaged. Their subsequent albums have found only limited success, although their *alter ego* Dukes Of Stratosphear's albums have reputedly sold more copies.

Their finest work, *Oranges And Lemons*, perceptively captured the feeling of the late 60s; this faultless album remains a perplexing commercial mystery. While it sold moderately well in the USA, it barely made the UK Top 30. The highly commercial 'Mayor Of Simpleton' found similar fate, at a desultory number 46. In 1992 the credible *Nonsuch* entered the UK album charts and two weeks later promptly disappeared. Quite what Andy Partridge, his colleagues in the band and Virgin Records feel they have to do remains uncertain. Partridge once joked that Virgin Records retain them only as a tax loss! XTC remain one of the most original pop bands of the era and Partridge's lyrics put him alongside Ray Davies as one of the UK's cleverest and most brilliantly eccentric writers.

Albums: *White Music* (1978), *Go2* (1978), *Drums And Wires* (1979), *Black Sea* (1980), *English Settlement* (1982), *Mummer* (1983), *The Big Express* (1984), *Skylarking* (1986), *Oranges And Lemons* (1989), *Nonsuch* (1992). Compilations: *Waxworks: Some Singles 1977-1982* (1982 - originally released with free compilation, *Beeswax*, a collection of b-sides), *The Compact XTC* (1986).

Yachts

Another UK new wave act to emerge from the Liverpool art school student pool of the late 70s, the Yachts started life as the seven-piece Albert And The Cod Fish Warriors. Reduced to a five-piece of Henry Priestman (vocals/keyboards), J.J. Campbell (vocals), Martin Watson (guitar), Martin Dempsey (bass), and Bob Ellis (drums), they played their debut gig at Eric's in Liverpool supporting Elvis Costello. This led Stiff to sign them in October 1977 and they released one Will Birch-produced single before they departed (with Costello and Nick Lowe) for the newly formed Radar. Campbell left at this point but with Priestman in control they released several singles including the minor new wave classic 'Love To Love You'. They recorded their debut album in New York with Richard Gottehrer at the helm. Dempsey left in January 1980 to join Pink Military and when Radar was liquidated they switched to Demon for a further single. Inevitably they disintegrated and Priestman spent some time with It's Immaterial before forming the Christians. The Yachts' popularity was fleeting but they left behind several great three-minute slices of pop, including a cover of R. Dean Taylor's 'There's A Ghost In My House'.

Albums: *The Yachts* (1979), *Yachts Without Radar* (1980).

Yazoo

This promising UK pop group was formed at the beginning of 1982 by former Depeche Mode keyboardist Vince Clarke (b. 3 July 1961) and vocalist Alison Moyet (b. 18 June 1961, Billericay, Essex, England). Their debut single 'Only You' climbed to number 2 in the UK charts in May and its appeal was further indicated by the success of the Flying Pickets' *a cappella* cover which topped the UK chart the following year. Yazoo enjoyed an almost equally successful follow-up with 'Don't Go', which climbed to number 3. A tour of the USA saw the group change their name to Yaz in order not to conflict with an American record company of the same name. Meanwhile, their album *Upstairs At Eric's* was widely acclaimed for its strong melodies and Moyet's expressive vocals. Yazoo enjoyed further hits with 'The Other Side Of Love' and 'Nobody's Diary' before completing one more album, *You And Me Both*. Despite their continuing success, the duo parted in 1983. Moyet enjoyed success as a solo singer, while Clarke maintained his high profile with the Assembly and particularly Erasure.

Albums: *Upstairs At Eric's* (1982), *You And Me Both* (1983).

Yeah Jazz

Hailing from Uttoxeter, Staffordshire, England and formed in 1986 by Kevin Head (vocals) and Chat (guitar), Yeah Jazz were completed by Stu (bass) and Tucker (drums). Their attempt to fuse pop and folk while chronicling the sagas of everyday life in a west Midlands rural town gained an Independent Top 30 hit in 1986 with 'This Is Not Love'. The addition of former Higsons' saxophonist and guitarist Terry Edwards to the line-up and the transferring to the Cherry Red label strengthened the group's sound. Edwards also lent his producing talents to Yeah Jazz's only album. Despite encouraging reviews and positive audience reaction Yeah Jazz's fortunes took a downward turn. Freeing themselves from their Cherry Red contract, the band re-surfaced in 1991 working on the west Midlands circuit with the promise of recording again in the near future.

Album: *Six Lane Ends* (1988).

Yello

This Swiss techno dance duo was led by Dieter Meier, a millionaire businessman, professional

gambler, and member of the Swiss national golf team. Meier provided the concepts while his partner Boris Blank wrote the music. Previously Meier had released two solo singles and was a former member of Periphery Perfume band, Fresh Colour. Yello's first recording contract was with Ralph Records in San Francisco, a label supported by the enigmatic Residents. Yello opened with 'Bimbo' and *Solid Pleasure*. In the UK they signed to the Do It label, launching their career with 'Bostisch', previously their second single for Ralph. They quickly proved popular with the Futurist and New Romantic crowds. Chart success started after a move to Stiff in 1983 where they released two singles and an album. A brief sojourn with Elektra preceded a move to Mercury where they saw major success with 'The Race'. Accompanied by a stunning video - Meier saw visual entertainment as crucial to their work - 'The Race' easily transgressed the pop and dance markets in the wake of the Acid House phenomenon. On *One Second*, they worked closely with Shirley Bassey and Billy McKenzie, and have recently become more and more embroiled in cinema. Recent soundtracks include *Nuns On The Run*, and the Polish-filmed *Snowball*, a fairytale whose creative impetus is entirely down to Yello.

Albums: *Solid Pleasure* (1980), *Claro Que Si* (1981), *You Gotta Say Yes To Another Excess* (1983), *Stella* (1985), *Yello* (1986), *1980-1985 The New Mix In One Go* (1986), *One Second* (1987), *Flag* (1988), *Baby* (1991).

Young Fresh Fellows

Young Fresh Fellows

Operating out of Seattle, USA since the early 80s, the Young Fresh Fellows have released a body of rough hewn, understated pop gems. Their debut album was recorded in 1983 and released a year later. The band comprises Scott McCaughey (vocals), Chuck Carroll (guitar) and Tad Hutchinson (drums). *The Fabulous Sounds Of The North Pacific* picked up immediate plaudits, *Rolling Stone Record* going so far as to describe it as 'perfect'. Joined by Jimbo (bass), they become a fully fledged off-beat new wave act, the dry humour and acute observations of their lyrics attracting a large college following. Their stylistic fraternity with the higher profile Replacements was confirmed by their joint tours, both bands sharing what *Billboard* magazine described as 'a certain deliberate crudity of execution'. After the mini-album *Refreshments* they moved to Frontier Records for 1988's *Totally Lost*. Despite being dogged by a 'joke band' reputation, brought about by an aptitude for satirizing high school traumas, the band's critical reaction was once more highly favourable. However, Carroll played his last gig for the band in winter 1989 in Washington. He was replaced by ex-Fastbacks guitarist Kurt Bloch. Their most polished album yet, *This One's For The Ladies*, highlighted McCaughey's successful adaptation of the spirit of the Kinks while Bloch's guitar melodies fitted in seamlessly. Elsewhere, McCaughey released his first solo album.

Albums: *The Fabulous Sounds Of The Pacific Northwest* (1984), *Topsy Turvy* (1986), *The Men Who Loved Music* (1987), *Refreshments* (1987), *Totally Lost* (1988), *Beans And Intolerance* (1989), *This One's For The Ladies* (1989), *Electric Bird Digest* (1991).

Young Gods

This heavily experimental trio originated from Geneva, Switzerland and specialized in hard electronic rock and rhythm. The main artistic engine was Franz Treichler (vocals), alongside original collaborators Cesare Pizzi (samples) and Frank Bagnoud (drums). Although singing mainly in French, they found an audience throughout Europe via the premier outlet for 'difficult' music, Play It Again Sam Records. Notable among their releases were 'L' Armourir', a version of Gary Glitter's 'Hello Hello I'm Back Again', and *Young Gods Play Kurt Weill*, which stemmed from a commission to provide a tribute performance of the composer's works. They had already been awarded a French Government Arts grant to tour the USA in 1987, where they maintain cult popularity.

Albums: *The Young Gods* (1987), *L' Eau Rouge* (1989), *Play Kurt Weill* (1991), *TV Sky* (1991).

Young Marble Giants

Formed in 1978, this seminal, yet short-lived trio, from Cardiff, Wales, comprised the group's main songwriter Stuart Moxham (guitar/organ), his brother Philip Moxham (bass) and Alison Statton (b. March 1958, Cardiff, Wales; vocals). Playing within minimalist musical landscapes the group utilized the superb lyrical bass playing of Philip Moxham. The combination of Stuart's twangy/scratchy guitar and reedy organ with Alison's clear diction was evident on tracks such as 'Searching For Mr Right', 'Credit In The Straight World' and 'Wurlitzer Jukebox' from

Colossal Youth released on Rough Trade. This highly acclaimed album was followed the next year by the impressive EP *Testcard*, which reached number 3 in the UK independent charts, by which time the group had amicably split. Statton formed Weekend, while Stuart established the Gist, recording *Embrace The Herd* (1982) which included the gorgeous, 'Love At First Sight' which reached the UK independent Top 20. Stuart's producing talents where called upon to oversee the recording of the Marine Girls second album, *Lazy Ways*. In later years Stuart's other profession as an animation painter gave him a credit on the film *Who Killed Roger Rabbit?* Phil Moxham found work sessioning for both Weekend and the Gist. In 1987, the Young Marble Giants reformed briefly to record a French release, 'It Took You'.

Album: *Colossal Youth* (1980). Compilation: with Weekend and the Gist *Nipped In The Bud* (1984).

Z

ZTT Records

Formed in 1983 by producer Trevor Horn, a former member of the Buggles and Yes, and his wife Jill Sinclair, ZTT was one of the most innovative UK labels of the early 80s. Horn employed the sharp marketing skills of former *New Musical Express* journalist Paul Morley, whose obtuse style and interest in unearthing obscure talent was allied to a love of ephemeral pop. ZTT was an abbreviation of Zang Tumb Tuum, a phrase used by the Italian futurist Russulo to describe the sound of machine-gun fire. The artistic notions of the label were emphasized through elaborate artwork and a release policy that encouraged the use of multi-format pressings. The label was distributed by Island Records until 1986, after which it pursued the independent route. Among the early signings to the label were the Art Of Noise and Propaganda, both of whom enjoyed chart success and enhanced the label's *avant garde* reputation. The key act, however, was undoubtedly Frankie Goes To Hollywood, which conjured a trilogy of spectacular UK number 1 hits in 1984 with 'Relax', 'Two Tribes' and 'The Power Of Love'. Their double album, *Welcome To The Pleasure Dome* was quintessentially ZTT with arresting artwork, political slogans, and mock merchandising ideas included on the sleeve. The Frankie flame burned brightly until the second album, *Liverpool*, which proved expensive and time consuming and sold far fewer copies than expected. The label continued its search for original talent, but all too often signed notably obscure acts who failed to find success in the mainstream. Among the artists who joined ZTT were Act, Anne Pigalle, Insignificance, Nasty Rox Inc. and Das Psych-Oh Rangers. Roy Orbison was also signed for a brief period and Grace Jones provided a formidable hit with 'Slave To The Rhythm'. ZTT suffered its most serious setback at the hands of former Frankie Goes To Hollywood singer Holly Johnson, who successfully took the label to the High Court in 1988 and won substantial damages after the group's contract was declared void, unenforceable and an unreasonable restraint of trade.